organizational
behavior
key concepts, skills & best practices

organizational behavior

key concepts, skills & best practices

Angelo Kinicki   **Robert Kreitner**
Both of Arizona   State University

McGraw-Hill
Irwin

Boston   Burr Ridge, IL   Dubuque, IA   Madison, WI   New York   San Francisco   St. Louis
Bangkok   Bogotá   Caracas   Kuala Lumpur   Lisbon   London   Madrid   Mexico City
Milan   Montreal   New Delhi   Santiago   Seoul   Singapore   Sydney   Taipei   Toronto

McGraw-Hill Higher Education ஜ

*A Division of The **McGraw-Hill** Companies*

ORGANIZATIONAL BEHAVIOR: KEY CONCEPTS, SKILLS AND BEST PRACTICES
Published by McGraw-Hill/Irwin, a business unit of The McGraw-Hill Companies, Inc.
1221 Avenue of the Americas, New York, NY, 10020. Copyright © 2003 by The
McGraw-Hill Companies, Inc. All rights reserved. No part of this publication may be
reproduced or distributed in any form or by any means, or stored in a database or retrieval
system, without the prior written consent of The McGraw-Hill Companies, Inc.,
including, but not limited to, in any network or other electronic storage or transmission,
or broadcast for distance learning.
Some ancillaries, including electronic and print components, may not be available
to customers outside the United States.

This book is printed on acid-free paper.

domestic   2 3 4 5 6 7 8 9 0 DOW/DOW 0 9 8 7 6 5 4 3 2
international 1 2 3 4 5 6 7 8 9 0 DOW/DOW 0 9 8 7 6 5 4 3 2

ISBN 0-07-251492-2

Publisher: *John E. Biernat*
Senior editor: *John Weimeister*
Senior developmental editor: *Christine Scheid*
Marketing manager: *Lisa Nicks*
Associate project manager: *Catherine R. Schultz*
Senior production supervisor: *Michael R. McCormick*
Director of design: *Keith J. McPherson*
Producer, media technology: *Mark Molsky*
Lead supplement producer: *Becky Szura*
Photo research coordinator: *Judy Kausal*
Cover design: *Maureen McCutcheon*
Interior design: *Maureen McCutcheon*
Cover images: *Upper Left: © Getty One; Upper Right: © Photonica;*
Lower Left: © Photonica; Lower Right: © Getty One
Typeface: *10.5/12 Times Roman*
Compositor: *GTS Graphics Inc.*
Printer: *R. R. Donnelley & Sons Company*

Library of Congress Control Number: 2002100737

INTERNATIONAL EDITION ISBN 0-07-115101-X
Copyright © 2003. Exclusive rights by The McGraw-Hill Companies, Inc., for
manufacture and export. This book cannot be re-exported from the country to which it is
sold by McGraw-Hill.
The International Edition is not available in North America.
www.mhhe.com

To my brothers and sisters: Robert Kinicki, Henry Kinicki, Jr.,
Madeline Campobenedetto, and Jacqueline Hackley

—A.K.

This book is dedicated to Calvin and Aaron Russell, with love and
best wishes from Uncle Bob

—B.K.

Angelo Kinicki is a Professor and Dean's Council of 100 Distinguished Scholar at Arizona State University. He joined the faculty in 1982, the year he received his doctorate in business administration from Kent State University. His specialty is Organizational Behavior.

Angelo is recognized for both his research and teaching. He has published over 60 articles in a variety of leading academic and professional jour-

Academy of Management Journal, Journal of Vocational Behavior, and the *Journal of Management.* He also received the All Time Best Reviewer Award from the *Academy of Management Journal* for the period 1996–99. Angelo's outstanding teaching performance resulted in his selection as the Graduate Teacher of the Year and the Undergraduate Teacher of the Year in the College of Business at Arizona State University. He also was acknowledged as the

One of Angelo's strengths is his ability to teach students at all levels within a university. He uses an interactive environment to enhance undergraduates' understanding about organizational behavior and management. He focuses MBAs on applying organizational behavior theories to solve complex problems. The PhD students learn the art and science of conducting scholarly research.

Angelo also is a busy consultant and speaker with companies around the world. His clients are many of the Fortune 500 companies as well as a variety of entrepreneurial firms. Much of his consulting work focuses on creating organizational change aimed at increasing organizational effectiveness and profitability. One of Angelo's most important and enjoyable pursuits is the practical application of his knowledge about organizational behavior.

Angelo and his wife Joyce have enjoyed living in the beautiful Arizona desert for 18 years, but are natives of Cleveland, Ohio. They enjoy traveling, hiking, and golfing.

nals devoted to organizational behavior. Angelo's success as a researcher also resulted in his selection to serve on the editorial review boards for the

Instructor of the Year for Executive Education from the Center for Executive Development at Arizona State University.

Robert Kreitner, PhD is an Emeritus Professor of Management at Arizona State University. Prior to joining ASU in 1975, Bob taught at Western Illinois University. He also has taught organizational behavior at the American Graduate School of International Management (Thunderbird). Bob is a popular speaker who has addressed a diverse array of audiences worldwide on management topics. Bob has authored articles for respected journals such as *Organizational Dynamics, Business Horizons,* and *Journal of Business Ethics.* He also is the co-author (with Fred Luthans) of the award-winning book *Organizational Behavior Modification and Beyond: An Operant and Social Learning Approach,* and the author of *Management,* 8th edition, a best-selling introductory management text.

Among his consulting and executive development clients have been American Express, SABRE Computer Services, Honeywell, Motorola, Amdahl, the Hopi Indian Tribe, State Farm Insurance, Goodyear Aerospace, Doubletree Hotels, Bank One-Arizona, Nazarene School of Large Church Management, US Steel, and Allied-Signal. In 1981–82 he served as Chairman of the Academy of Management's Management Education and Development Division.

On the personal side, Bob is a native of Buffalo, New York. After a four-year tour of duty in the US Coast Guard, including service on the icebreaker EASTWIND in Antarctica, Bob attended the University of Nebraska–Omaha on a football scholarship. Bob also holds an MBA from the University of Nebraska–Omaha and a PhD from the University of Nebraska–Lincoln. While working on his PhD in Business at Nebraska, he spent six months teaching management courses for the University in Micronesia. In 1996, Bob taught two courses in Albania's first-ever MBA program (funded by the US Agency for International Development and administered by the University of Nebraska–Lincoln). He taught a summer leadership program in Switzerland from 1995 to 1998. Bob and his wife, Margaret, live in Phoenix with their cats and an orphaned wild bird, and they enjoy travel, hiking, woodcarving, and fishing.

Angelo Kinicki and Robert Kreitner's

First Edition of Organizational Behavior: Key Concepts, Skills & Best Practices

—A better way to actively learn Organizational Behavior.

The **1st Edition** of **Organizational Behavior: Key Concepts, Skills & Best Practices** was developed to facilitate active learning by using such tools as hands-on exercises, chapter-opening cases, best practices boxes, and many real-world examples—all of which help readers actually experience organizational behavior concepts rather than just read about them.

If you are looking for a different way to teach Organizational Behavior, this new text may be just what you need. If you are looking for a better way to interest students in Organizational Behavior, Kinicki and Kreitner have developed a better way to learn organizational behavior.

Please take a moment to page through some of the highlights of this new edition and this new approach to organizational behavior education.

Active Learning

Angelo Kinicki and Robert Kreitner have developed this text to provide lean and efficient coverage of topics such as diversity in organizations, ethics, and globalization, which are recommended by AACSB International—the Association to Advance Collegiate Schools of Business. Timely chapter-opening cases, interactive exercises integrated into each chapter, four-color presentation, lively writing style, and real-world in-text examples are all used to enhance this overall educational package.

This successful author team has designed this new text to facilitate active learning by relying on the following:

HANDS-ON EXERCISE

Who Comes First? Employees, Customers, or Stockholders?

INSTRUCTIONS

1. Drawing from your own value system and business philosophy, rank the three groups in the title of this exercise first, second, and third in terms of managerial priority. What is the rationale for your ranking?
2. Read the two brief quotes below.
3. Based on the opinions of these two respected business leaders, would you change your initial priority ranking? Why? With whom do you agree more, Iacocca or Kelleher? Why?

Consult our website for an interpretation of this exercise: www.mhhe.com/kinickiob.

Lee Iacocca, former president of Ford and retired CEO of Chrysler:

Just be sure to take care of your customers. You have to go eyeball to eyeball with them and say, "Do I have a deal for you!" And then stand behind your product or service. Don't worry about stockholders or employees. If you take care of your customers, everything else will fall into place.

Herb Kelleher, cofounder and chairman of Southwest Airlines:

*In the old days, my mother told me that in business school they'd say, "This is a real conundrum: Who comes first, your employees, your shareholders, or your customers?" My mother taught me that your employees come first. If you treat them well, then they treat the customers well, and that means your customers come back and your shareholders are happy.***

SOURCES: *As quoted in L McCauley and C Canabou, eds., "Unit of One: The Voice of Experience," *Fast Company*, May 2001, p 82. **As quoted in J Huey, "Outlaw Flyboy CEOs," *Fortune*, November 13, 2000, p 246.

Hands-On Exercises—

These exercises (one per chapter) are included to help readers personalize and expand upon key concepts as they are presented in the text. These exercises encourage active and thoughtful interaction rather than passive reading.

Brief Chapter Opening Cases—

For some real-world context, these cases use topics that are timely and relevant to actual life situations. The text's website also features interpretations for each case.

SURPRISE: CHRYSLER LOVES ITS GERMAN BOSS

The man in charge of saving Chrysler might as well be Don Quixote.

Like that storied, righteous righter of wrongs, Chrysler CEO Dieter Zetsche faces the seemingly insurmountable. Sent by German parent company DaimlerChrysler . . . [in late 2000] to take over the U.S. automaker, Zetsche waded into a mess.

Sales of key models were off despite a blistering market, and trying to ignite them was costing a fortune. Chrysler lost $3 billion . . . [just prior to his arrival].

Zetsche (ZET-shuh), a German, is the third Chrysler boss in 14 months, and the first non-American CEO. He arrived when Chrysler employees still were mad about the Daimler-Benz takeover of their company, upset with German authority and anxious over the inevitable layoffs.

Zetsche was handed responsibility for the success of important models designed well before he arrived. And, as a German, he was seen as likely to manage with a heavy hand, not by consensus or empowerment.

It is almost magic, then, that Zetsche . . . has gone from loathed interloper to beloved insider. Despite some bumpy patches . . . , he's an emerging hero in Detroit.

"I think people were expecting Adolph Hitler, and who they got was Martin Luther. He wasn't coming to conquer the world, but to save it," offers David Cole, director of the Center for Automotive Research in Ann Arbor, Mich.

"The people I know at Chrysler say, 'We like him. We understand the task he has,' " says [consultant] Ron Harbour. . . .

Zetsche, who had been running DaimlerChrysler's US heavy-truck business, no doubt has an ego. It takes a big one to gamble billions of dollars and thousands of jobs on what is—after all the consumer clinics and planning sessions—gut instinct about what people will buy. But more than any car boss in memory, he keeps it pocketed. Chrysler people find that refreshing after years of bigger-than-life, domineering executives such as Lee Iacocca and Robert Lutz.

Zetsche has scored points by:

- **Being devoted.** He acts like a lifelong loyalist, despite being there less than 6 months. "Why does the world need Chrysler? Because without it, the world would be a boring, sad place," he says. He's working to revive market-rattling concept cars of the sort that defined Chrysler the last decade, but which Chrysler had pushed into the closet in fiscal fear. . . .
- **Being tactful.** It's close to impossible to get him to dispense a discouraging

Active Learning

SKILLS & BEST PRACTICES

The Effective Manager's Skill Profile

1. *Clarifies goals and objectives* for everyone involved.

2. *Encourages participation*, upward communication, and suggestions.

3. *Plans and organizes* for an orderly work flow.

4. Has *technical and administrative expertise* to answer organization-related questions.

5. *Facilitates work* through team building, training, coaching, and support.

6. *Provides feedback* honestly and constructively.

7. *Keeps things moving* by relying on schedules, deadlines, and helpful reminders.

8. *Controls details* without being overbearing.

9. Applies reasonable *pressure for goal accomplishment.*

10. *Empowers and delegates* key duties to others while maintaining goal clarity and commitment.

11. *Recognizes good performance* with rewards and positive reinforcement.

SOURCE: Adapted from material in C Wilson, "Identify Needs with Costs in Mind," *Training and Development Journal*, July 1980, pp 58–62; and F Shipper, "A Study of the Psychometric Properties of the Managerial Skill Scales of the Survey of Management Practices," *Educational and Psychological Measurement*, June 1995, pp 468–79.

Skills & Best Practices Boxes—

These additional readings and practice items (one to two per chapter) are designed to sharpen users' skills by either recommending how to apply a concept, theory, or model, or by giving an exemplary corporate application. Students will benefit from real-world experiences and direct skill-building opportunities.

Look at Juniper Networks Inc. In just three years, it came out of nowhere to capture 35% of the market for high-end Internet routers. Juniper outsources 100% of its production to contract manufacturers. Juniper's customers, mainly big telecom service providers, order their equipment on Juniper's Web portal—but the orders go straight to the contract manufacturers. . . . Thanks to the Net, Juniper has $726,000 in annual revenues per employee, versus $320,600 for older rival Nortel Networks, which handles considerably less of its sales online.[52]

Up-to-Date Real-World Examples—

Nothing brings material to life better than in-text examples featuring real companies, people, and situations. These examples permeate the text.

features

Active Learning

chapter summary

- *Identify at least four of Pfeffer's people-centered practices, and define the term management.* Pfeffer's seven people-centered practices are job security, careful hiring, power to the people, generous pay for performance, lots of training, less emphasis on status, and trust building. *Management* is the process of working with and through others to achieve organizational objectives in an efficient and ethical manner.

- *Profile the 21st-century manager.* They will be team players who will get things done cooperatively by relying on joint decision making, their knowledge instead of formal authority, and their multicultural skills. They will engage in life-long learning and be compensated on the basis of their skills and results. They will facilitate rather than resist change, share rather than hoard power and key information, and be multidirectional communicators. Ethics will be a forethought instead of an afterthought. They will be generalists with multiple specialties.

- *Contrast McGregor's Theory X and Theory Y assumptions about employees.* Theory X employees, according to traditional thinking, dislike work, require close supervision, and are primarily interested in security. According to the modern Theory Y view, employees are capable of self-direction, of seeking responsibility, and of being creative.

- *Explain the managerial significance of Deming's 85–15 rule, and identify the four principles of total quality management (TQM).* Deming claimed that about 85% of organizational failures are due to system breakdowns involving factors such as management, machinery, or work rules. He believed the workers themselves are responsible for

failures only about 15% of the time. Consequently, Deming criticized the standard practice of blaming and punishing individuals for what are typically *system* failures beyond their immediate control. The four principles of TQM are (a) do it right the first time to eliminate costly rework; (b) listen to and learn from customers and employees; (c) make continuous improvement an everyday matter; and (d) build teamwork, trust, and mutual respect.

- *Define the term E-business, and specify five ways the Internet is affecting the management of people at work.* E-business involves using the Internet to more effectively and efficiently manage *every* aspect of a business. The Internet is reshaping the management of people in the following areas: E-management (networking), E-communication (E-mail and telecommuting), goal setting and feedback, organizational structure (virtual teams and organizations), job design (desire for more challenge), decision making (greater speed and employee empowerment), knowledge management (E-learning), conflict and stress triggered by increased speed, rapid change and inevitable conflict and resistance, and ethical problems such as overwork and privacy issues.

- *Describe the sources of organizational behavior research evidence.* Five sources of OB research evidence are meta-analyses (statistically pooled evidence from several studies), field studies (evidence from real-life situations), laboratory studies (evidence from contrived situations), sample surveys (questionnaire data), and case studies (observation of a single person, group, or organization).

Chapter Summaries—
This section includes responses to the learning objectives in each chapter making it a handy review tool for all users.

internet exercise

www.hp.com

The purpose of this exercise is to focus on one well-known company with a good general reputation (Hewlett-Packard) and look for evidence of the seven people-centered practices discussed at the beginning of this chapter (go back and review them to refresh your memory). On the Internet, go to Hewlett-Packard's home page (**www.hp.com**) and select the heading "company information." Next, in the section "about hp," select "history & facts." Be sure to read the section titled "corporate objectives," especially the parts titled "our people" and "management."

QUESTIONS
1. On a scale of 1 = low to 10 = high, how people-centered is HP?
2. What *specific* evidence of each of the seven people-centered practices did you find?
3. Which of the seven practices appears to be HP's strongest suit?
4. Do HP's culture and values give it a strategic competitive advantage? Explain.
5. Would you like to work for HP? Why or why not?

Internet Exercises—
Detailed and challenging, these exercises are found at the end of each chapter. This resource helps students understand how to use the Internet as a powerful resource in business practice.

Instructor supplements

This incredible new book also uses some exciting and useful supplements for instructors and students.

Instructor's Resource Guide
ISBN 0072515295

The Instructor's Manual is a creative guide to understanding organizational behavior. It combines traditional elements of Instructor's Manuals with newer features such as questions posed throughout the chapter outline to guide the discussion/dialogue in class, a thought for the week represented by a relevant quote from a famous person, end of the chapter current events, experiential exercise, and much more. Each element will assist the instructor and students in maximizing the ideas, issues, concepts, and important management approaches included in each chapter.

Test Bank
ISBN 0072515317

Computerized Test Bank
ISBN 0072515341

The Test Bank contains approximately 1,200 questions, with a mix of true/false, multiple-choice, and essay questions. Multiple-choice questions are ranked (easy, medium, or hard) to help the instructor provide the proper mix of questions.

Instructor's Presentation CD-ROM
ISBN 0072515368

This CD-ROM allows professors to easily create their own custom presentation. They can pull from resources on the CD, like the Instructor's Manual, the Test Bank and PowerPoint, or from their own PowerPoint slides or Web screen shots.

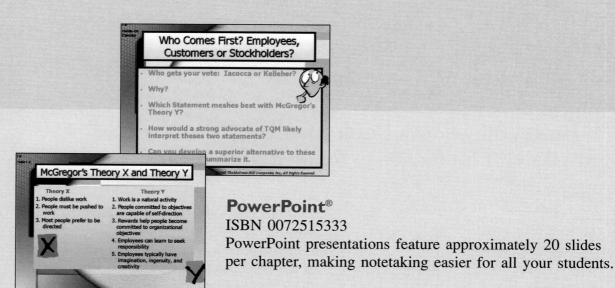

PowerPoint®
ISBN 0072515333

PowerPoint presentations feature approximately 20 slides per chapter, making notetaking easier for all your students.

Videos
ISBN 0072515325

A combination of NBC file footage, along with our newly developed Skills videos, offers instructors the opportunity to highlight such topics as Negotiating, Conflict Management, Self-Management/ Etiquette-Diversity, Listening, and Teamwork—all for situational analysis in the classroom.

Online Learning Center
ISBN 007251535X

www.mhhe.com/kinickiob

The Online Learning Center (OLC) is a website that follows the text chapter-by-chapter, with additional materials and quizzing that enhances the text and/or classroom experience. As students read the book, they can go online to take self-grading quizzes, review material, or work through interactive exercises. OLCs can be delivered multiple ways—professors and students can access them directly through the textbook website, through PageOut, or within a course management system (e.g. WebCT, Blackboard, TopClass, or eCollege).

Instructor

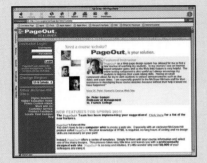

PageOut

McGraw-Hill's unique point-and click course website tool, enables users to create a full-featured, professional quality course website without knowing HTML coding. With PageOut you can post your syllabus online, assign McGraw-Hill Online Learning Center or eBook content, add links to important off-site resources, and maintain student results in the online grade book. You can send class announcements, copy your course site to share with colleagues, and upload original files. PageOut is free for every McGraw-Hill/Irwin user and, if you're short on time, we even have a team ready to help you create your site!

Primis Online

You can customize this text by using McGraw-Hill's Primis Online digital database. This feature offers you the flexibility to customize your course to include material from the largest online collection of textbooks, readings, and cases. Primis leads the way in customized eBooks with hundreds of titles available at prices that save your students over 20% off bookstore prices. Additional information is available at 800-228-0634.

Student supplements

Student CD-ROM

ISBN 0072515376

All NEW copies of this text are packaged with a
special Student CD-ROM. This added-value
feature includes:

- Interactive modules that encourage hands-on
  learning about such topics as Motivation, Leader-
  ship, and Organizational Communication
- Chapter outlines
- Interactive chapter quizzes
- Videos of real-world companies
- Exercises and quizzes to enhance videos
- A special link to Kinicki/Kreitner's
  Online Learning Center

McGraw-Hill's PowerWeb

Harness the assets of the Web by keeping current with PowerWeb! This
online resource provides high quality, peer-reviewed content including up-
to-date articles from leading periodicals and journals, current news, weekly
updates, interactive exercises, Web research guide, study tips, and much
more! http://www.dushkin.com/powerweb

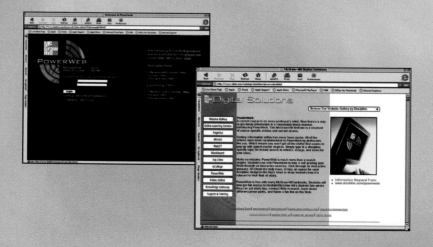

preface

In our many years of teaching organizational behavior and management to undergraduate and graduate students in various countries, we *never* had a student say, "I want a longer, more expensive textbook with more chapters." We got the message! Indeed, there is a desire for shorter and less expensive textbooks in today's fast-paced world where overload and tight budgets are a way of life. Within the field of organizational behavior, so-called "essentials" texts have attempted to satisfy this need. Too often, however, brevity has been achieved at the expense of up-to-date examples, artful layout, and learning enhancements. We believe "brief" does not have to mean outdated and boring.

A New Standard

Kinicki and Kreitner's *Organizational Behavior: Key Concepts, Skills & Best Practices* represents a new standard in OB essentials textbooks. The following guiding philosophy inspired our quest for this new standard: "Create a short, up-to-date, practical, user-friendly, interesting, and engaging introduction to the field

of organizational behavior." Thus, in this book, you will find lean and efficient coverage of topics recommended by AACSB International conveyed with pedagogical features found in full-length OB textbooks. Among those pedagogical enhancements are timely chapter-opening cases, a rich array of contemporary in-text examples, a strong skills emphasis including Skills & Best Practices boxes in every chapter, an interactive exercise integrated into each chapter, an appealing four-color presentation, interesting captioned photos, poignant cartoons, instructive chapter summaries, and chapter-closing Internet exercises.

Efficient and Flexible Structure

The 16 chapters in this text are readily adaptable to traditional 15-week semesters, 10-week terms, summer and intersessions, management development seminars, and distance learning programs via the Internet. Following up-front coverage of important topics—including ethics, international OB, and managing

diversity—the topical flow of this text goes from micro (individuals) to macro (groups, teams, and organizations). Mixing and matching chapters (and topics within each chapter) in various combinations is not only possible but strongly encouraged to create optimum teaching/learning experiences.

Engaging Pedagogy

We have a love and a passion for teaching organizational behavior in the classroom and via textbooks because it deals with the intriguing realities of working in modern organizations. Puzzling questions, insights, and surprises hide around every corner. Seeking useful insights about how and why people behave as they do in the workplace is a provocative, interesting, and oftentimes fun activity. After all, to know more about organizational behavior is to know more about both ourselves and life in general. We have designed this text to facilitate *active* learning by relying on the following learning enhancements:

- 6 to 7 learning objectives at the start of each chapter to focus attention on key topics and themes.
- brief chapter-opening cases to provide a real-world context for the topics at hand. Interpretations for each case may be found at our Web site: www.mhhe.com/kinickiob.
- an efficient get-right-down-to-business writing style.
- many real-world up-to-date examples from the real world weaved into textual discussions to bring them to life for the reader.
- Hands-On Exercises (one per chapter) to help the reader personalize and expand upon key concepts. These exercises call for *thoughtful interaction* rather than passive reading. Consult our Web site for interpretations.
- 1 to 2 Skills & Best Practices boxes per chapter to sharpen skills and to demonstrate possibilities.
- chapter summaries for each learning objective for handy review.
- a detailed and challenging Internet Exercise following each chapter to tap the immense potential of the Internet.
- a complimentary copy of McGraw-Hill's Interactive Exercises on Student CD with every new copy of the text.

Complete Teaching/Learning Package

For the Instructor:

- **Instructor's Resource Guide** (007-251529-5)—The Instructor's Manual is a creative guide to understanding organizational behavior. It has the traditional elements of chapter outline, learning

objectives, opening case introduction, website analysis, and a hands-on exercise guide with suggested answers to the questions. It also includes questions posed throughout the chapter outline to guide the discussion/dialogue in class, a thought for the week represented by a relevant quote from a famous person, a critical thinking exercise about the future, a behaviors-in-class section to help tie concepts to actual classroom interactions, a summary of the chapter with a bridge to the next chapter, and an end-of-the-chapter current events experiential exercise. Each element will assist the instructor and students in maximizing the ideas, issues, concepts and important management approaches included in each chapter.

- **Test Bank** (007-251531-7)—consists of 20 true/false, 40–50 multiple choice, and 5 essay questions per chapter.
- **Computerized Testing** (007-251534-1)—a hybrid version to work on both Windows and Mac platforms.
- **PowerPoint Slide Presentation**—(007-251533-3)—approximately 20 slides per chapter.
- **Videos**—(007-251532-5)—contains a variety of footage, including brand new situational analysis segments for students on topics such as Negotiating, Conflict Management, Self-Management/Etiquette-Diversity, Listening, and Teamwork.
- **Instructor's Presentation CD-ROM**—(007-251536-8)—This CD-ROM collects all of the text's visually oriented supplement items in one presentation management system. By collecting many features of the Instruc-

tor's Manual, videos, PowerPoint slides, and lecture material in an electronic format, this CD offers a comprehensive and convenient tool that allows you to customize your lectures and presentations.

- **Online Learning Center** (*www.mhhe.com/kinickiob*)

  - **Instructor Resource Center**— A secured Instructor Resource Center stores your essential course materials and saves you prep time before class. This area also stores the Instructor's Manual, presentation materials, video cases, and additional readings and exercises.

  - **Student Resource Center**— This is your perfect solution for Internet-based content. This website follows the textbook chapter by chapter and contains text pedagogy and supplementary material. As students read through their book, they can refer to the OLC for learning objectives, chapter summaries, video cases, interactive glossary, and more.

Grateful Appreciation

Our sincere thanks and gratitude go to our Editor, John Weimeister, and his first-rate team at McGraw-Hill/Irwin who encouraged and facilitated our pursuit of "something better." Key contributors include Christine Scheid, Senior Development Editor; Lisa Nicks, Marketing Manager; and Jean Hamilton/Cathy Schultz, Project Managers. We would also like to thank Mandy Goretcki for her wonderful work on the PowerPoint presentation, Anne Cowden of Sacramento State University for her fantastic work on the Instructor's

Resource Guide, Amit Shah of Frostburg State University for his work on the Test Bank and Online Student Quizzes, and Tom Lloyd of Westmoreland County Community College for his assistance with the Quizzes and Outlines on the Student CD-ROM.

Finally, we would like to thank our wives, Joyce and Margaret. Their love and support were instrumental throughout the writing of this textbook. They lifted our tired spirits when needed and encouraged us at every stage.

This project has been a joy from start to finish. Not only did we enjoy reading and learning more about the latest developments within the field of organizational behavior, but completion of this book has deepened a friendship between us that has spanned 20 years. We hope you enjoy this textbook. Best wishes for success and happiness!

brief contents

ontents

Part One
Managing People in a Global Economy 1

Part Two
Managing Individuals   63

Part Three
Making Decisions and Managing Social Processes   175

Part Four
Managing Organizational
Processes   237

Part Five
Managing Evolving Organizations   299

organizational behavior

behavior

key concepts, skills & best practices

Strategic Results: The 4-P Cycle of Continuous Improvement   **FIGURE 1–1**

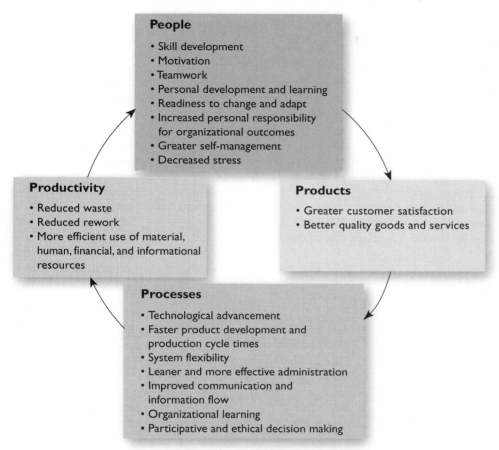

People
- Skill development
- Motivation
- Teamwork
- Personal development and learning
- Readiness to change and adapt
- Increased personal responsibility for organizational outcomes
- Greater self-management
- Decreased stress

Productivity
- Reduced waste
- Reduced rework
- More efficient use of material, human, financial, and informational resources

Products
- Greater customer satisfaction
- Better quality goods and services

Processes
- Technological advancement
- Faster product development and production cycle times
- System flexibility
- Leaner and more effective administration
- Improved communication and information flow
- Organizational learning
- Participative and ethical decision making

Managers Get Results with and through Others

For better or for worse, managers touch our lives in many ways. Schools, hospitals, government agencies, and large and small businesses all require systematic management. Formally defined, **management** is the process of working with and through others to achieve organizational objectives in an efficient and ethical manner. From the standpoint of organizational behavior, the central feature of this definition is "working with and through others." Managers play a constantly evolving role. Today's successful managers are no longer the I've-got-everything-under-control order givers of yesteryear. Rather, they need to creatively envision and actively sell bold new directions in an ethical and sensitive manner. Effective managers are team players empowered by the willing and active support of others who are driven by conflicting self-interests. Each of us has a huge stake in how well managers carry out their evolving role. Henry Mintzberg, a respected management scholar, observed: "No job is more vital to our society than that of the manager. It is the manager who determines whether our social institutions serve us well or whether they squander our talents and resources."[8]

Management

Process of working with and through others to achieve organizational objectives efficiently and ethically.

Extending our managerial thrust, let us take a closer look at the skills managers need to perform, the evolving relationship between employer and employee, and the future direction of management.

A Skills Profile for Managers

Observational studies by Mintzberg and others have found the typical manager's day to be a fragmented collection of brief episodes.[9] Interruptions are commonplace, while large blocks of time for planning and reflective thinking are not. In one particular study, four top-level managers spent 63% of their time on activities lasting less than nine minutes each. Only 5% of the managers' time was devoted to activities lasting more than a hour.[10] But what specific skills do effective managers perform during their hectic and fragmented workdays?

Many attempts have been made over the years to paint a realistic picture of what managers do.[11] Diverse and confusing lists of managerial functions and roles have been suggested. Fortunately, a stream of research over the past 20 years by Clark Wilson and others has given us a practical and statistically validated profile of managerial *skills*[12] (see Skills & Best Practices). Wilson's managerial skills profile focuses on 11 observable categories of managerial behavior. This is very much in tune with today's emphasis on managerial competency.[13] Wilson's unique skills-assessment technique goes beyond the usual self-report approach with its natural bias. In addition to surveying a given manager about his or her 11 skills, the Wilson approach also asks those who report directly to the manager to answer questions about their boss's skills. According to Wilson and his colleagues, the result is an assessment of skill *mastery,* not simply skill awareness.[14] The logic behind Wilson's approach is both simple and compelling. Who better to assess a manager's skills than the people who experience those behaviors on a day-to-day basis—those who report directly to the manager?

The Wilson managerial skills research yields three useful lessons:

1. Dealing effectively with *people* is what management is all about. The 11 skills constitute a goal creation/commitment/feedback/reward/accomplishment cycle with human interaction at every turn.

2. Managers with high skills mastery tend to have better subunit performance and employee morale than managers with low skills mastery.[15]

3. *Effective* female and male managers *do not* have significantly different skill profiles,[16] contrary to claims in the popular business press in recent years.[17]

SKILLS & BEST PRACTICES

The Effective Manager's Skill Profile

1. *Clarifies goals and objectives* for everyone involved.

2. *Encourages participation,* upward communication, and suggestions.

3. *Plans and organizes* for an orderly work flow.

4. Has *technical and administrative expertise* to answer organization-related questions.

5. *Facilitates work* through team building, training, coaching, and support.

6. *Provides feedback* honestly and constructively.

7. *Keeps things moving* by relying on schedules, deadlines, and helpful reminders.

8. *Controls details* without being overbearing.

9. Applies reasonable *pressure for goal accomplishment.*

10. *Empowers and delegates* key duties to others while maintaining goal clarity and commitment.

11. *Recognizes good performance* with rewards and positive reinforcement.

SOURCE: Adapted from material in C Wilson, "Identify Needs with Costs in Mind," *Training and Development Journal,* July 1980, pp 58–62; and F Shipper, "A Study of the Psychometric Properties of the Managerial Skill Scales of the Survey of Management Practices," *Educational and Psychological Measurement,* June 1995, pp 468–79.

Evolution of the 21st-Century Manager   **TABLE 1–1**

	Past Managers	Future Managers
Primary role	Order giver, privileged elite, manipulator, controller	Facilitator, team member, teacher, advocate, sponsor, coach
Learning and knowledge	Periodic learning, narrow specialist	Continuous life-long learning, generalist with multiple specialties
Compensation criteria	Time, effort, rank	Skills, results
Cultural orientation	Monocultural, monolingual	Multicultural, multilingual
Primary source of influence	Formal authority	Knowledge (technical and interpersonal)
View of people	Potential problem	Primary resource
Primary communication pattern	Vertical	Multidirectional
Decision-making style	Limited input for individual decisions	Broad-based input for joint decisions
Ethical considerations	Afterthought	Forethought
Nature of interpersonal relationships	Competitive (win–lose)	Cooperative (win–win)
Handling of power and key information	Hoard and restrict access	Share and broaden access
Approach to change	Resist	Facilitate

21st-Century Managers

Today's workplace is indeed undergoing immense and permanent changes.[18] Organizations are being "reengineered" for greater speed, efficiency, and flexibility.[19] Teams are pushing aside the individual as the primary building block of organizations.[20] Command-and-control management is giving way to participative management and empowerment.[21] Ego-centered leaders are being replaced by customer-centered leaders. Employees increasingly are being viewed as internal customers. All this creates a mandate for a new kind of manager in the 21st century. Table 1–1 contrasts the characteristics of past and future managers. As the balance of this book will demonstrate, the managerial shift in Table 1–1 is not just a good idea, it is an absolute necessity in the new workplace.

The Field of Organizational Behavior: Past and Present

Organizational behavior, commonly referred to as OB, is an interdisciplinary field dedicated to better understanding and managing people at work. By definition, organizational behavior is both research and application oriented. Three basic levels of analysis in OB are individual, group, and organizational. OB draws upon a diverse array of disciplines, including psychology, management, sociology, organization theory, social psychology, statistics, anthropology, general systems theory, economics, information technology, political science, vocational counseling, human stress management,

Organizational behavior

Interdisciplinary field dedicated to better understanding and managing people at work.

psychometrics, ergonomics, decision theory, and ethics. This rich heritage has spawned many competing perspectives and theories about human work behavior. By the mid-1980s, one researcher had identified 110 distinct theories about behavior within the field of OB.[22]

Organizational behavior is an academic designation. With the exception of teaching/research positions, OB is not an everyday job category such as accounting, marketing, or finance. Students of OB typically do not get jobs in organizational behavior, per se. This reality in no way demeans OB or lessens its importance in effective organizational management. OB is a *horizontal* discipline that cuts across virtually every job category, business function, and professional specialty. Anyone who plans to make a living in a large or small, public or private, organization needs to study organizational behavior.

A historical perspective of the study of people at work helps in studying organizational behavior. According to a management history expert, this is important because

> Historical perspective is the study of a subject in light of its earliest phases and subsequent evolution. Historical perspective differs from history in that the object of historical perspective is to sharpen one's vision of the present, not the past.[23]

In other words, we can better understand where the field of OB is today and where it appears to be headed by appreciating where it has been. Let us examine three significant landmarks in the evolution of understanding and managing people:

1. The human relations movement.
2. The total quality management movement.
3. The Internet revolution.

The Human Relations Movement

A unique combination of factors during the 1930s fostered the human relations movement. First, following legalization of union–management collective bargaining in the United States in 1935, management began looking for new ways of handling employees. Second, behavioral scientists conducting on-the-job research started calling for more attention to the "human" factor. Managers who had lost the battle to keep unions out of their factories heeded the call for better human relations and improved working conditions. One such study, conducted at Western Electric's Chicago-area Hawthorne plant, was a prime stimulus for the human relations movement. Ironically, many of the Hawthorne findings have turned out to be more myth than fact.

The Hawthorne Legacy   Interviews conducted decades later with three subjects of the Hawthorne studies and reanalysis of the original data with modern statistical techniques do not support initial conclusions about the positive effect of supportive supervision. Specifically, money, fear of unemployment during the Great Depression, managerial discipline, and high-quality raw materials—not supportive supervision—turned out to be responsible for high output in the relay assembly test room experiments.[24] Nonetheless, the human relations movement gathered momentum through the 1950s, as academics and managers alike made stirring claims about the powerful effect that individual needs, supportive supervision, and group dynamics apparently had on job performance.

McGregor's Theory X and Theory Y | **TABLE 1–2**

Outdated (Theory X) Assumptions about People at Work	Modern (Theory Y) Assumptions about People at Work
1. Most people dislike work; they avoid it when they can.	1. Work is a natural activity, like play or rest.
2. Most people must be coerced and threatened with punishment before they will work. People require close direction when they are working.	2. People are capable of self-direction and self-control if they are committed to objectives.
3. Most people actually prefer to be directed. They tend to avoid responsibility and exhibit little ambition. They are interested only in security.	3. People generally become committed to organizational objectives if they are rewarded for doing so.
	4. The typical employee can learn to accept and seek responsibility.
	5. The typical member of the general population has imagination, ingenuity, and creativity.

SOURCE: Adapted from D McGregor, *The Human Side of Enterprise* (New York: McGraw-Hill, 1960), Ch 4.

The Writings of Mayo and Follett   Essential to the human relations movement were the writings of Elton Mayo and Mary Parker Follett. Australian-born Mayo, who headed the Harvard researchers at Hawthorne, advised managers to attend to employees' emotional needs in his 1933 classic, *The Human Problems of an Industrial Civilization.* Follett was a true pioneer, not only as a woman management consultant in the male-dominated industrial world of the 1920s, but also as a writer who saw employees as complex combinations of attitudes, beliefs, and needs. Mary Parker Follett was way ahead of her time in telling managers to motivate job performance instead of merely demanding it, a "pull" rather than "push" strategy. She also built a logical bridge between political democracy and a cooperative spirit in the workplace.[25]

McGregor's Theory Y   In 1960, Douglas McGregor wrote a book entitled *The Human Side of Enterprise,* which has become an important philosophical base for the modern view of people at work.[26] Drawing upon his experience as a management consultant, McGregor formulated two sharply contrasting sets of assumptions about human nature (see Table 1–2). His Theory X assumptions were pessimistic and negative and, according to McGregor's interpretation, typical of how managers traditionally perceived employees. To help managers break with this negative tradition, McGregor formulated his **Theory Y,** a modern and positive set of assumptions about people. McGregor believed managers could accomplish more through others by viewing them as self-energized, committed, responsible, and creative beings.

Theory Y

McGregor's modern and positive assumptions about employees being responsible and creative.

A mid-1990s survey of 10,227 employees from many industries across the United States challenges managers to do a better job of acting on McGregor's Theory Y assumptions. From the employees' perspective, Theory X management practices are the major barrier to productivity improvement and employee well being. The researcher concluded:

The most noteworthy finding from our survey is that an overwhelming number of American workers—some 97%—desire work conditions known to facilitate high productivity. Workers uniformly reported—regardless of the type of organization, age, gender, pay schedule, or level in the organizational hierarchy—that they needed and wanted in their own workplaces the conditions for collaboration, commitment, and creativity research has demonstrated as necessary for both productivity and health. Just as noteworthy, however, is the finding that the actual conditions of work supplied by management are those conditions that research has identified as *competence suppressors*—procedures, policies, and practices that prevent or punish expressions of competence and most characterize unproductive organizations.[27]

New Assumptions about Human Nature   Unfortunately, unsophisticated behavioral research methods caused the human relationists to embrace some naive and misleading conclusions. For example, human relationists believed in the axiom, "A satisfied employee is a hardworking employee." Subsequent research, as discussed later in this book, shows the satisfaction–performance linkage to be more complex than originally thought.

Despite its shortcomings, the human relations movement opened the door to more progressive thinking about human nature. Rather than continuing to view employees as passive economic beings, managers began to see them as active social beings and took steps to create more humane work environments.

The Total Quality Management Movement

In 1980, NBC aired a television documentary titled "If Japan Can . . . Why Can't We?" It was a wake up call for North American companies to dramatically improve product quality or continue losing market share to Japanese electronics and automobile companies. A full-fledged movement ensued during the 1980s and 1990s. Much was written, said, and done about improving the quality of both goods and services.[28] Thanks to the concept of *total quality management* (TQM), the quality of much of what we buy today is significantly better than in the past. The underlying principles of TQM are more important than ever given the growth of both E-business on the Internet[29] and the overall service economy. According to one business writer:

> A company stuck in the industrial-age mentality is very likely to get squashed because "zero-defect" quality has become an ante to compete, not a differentiator. Even "zero-time" operations that address customers' expectations for immediate response and gratification are becoming common in today's digital age.[30]

In a recent survey of 1,797 managers from 36 countries by the American Management Association, "customer service" and "quality" ranked as the corporate world's top two concerns.[31] TQM principles have profound practical implications for managing people today.[32]

Total quality management

An organizational culture dedicated to training, continuous improvement, and customer satisfaction.

What Is TQM?   Experts on the subject offered this definition of **total quality management:**

> TQM means that the organization's culture is defined by and supports the constant attainment of customer satisfaction through an integrated system of tools, techniques, and training. This involves the continuous improvement of organizational processes, resulting in high-quality products and services.[33]

Quality consultant Richard J Schonberger sums up TQM as "continuous, customer-centered, employee-driven improvement."[34] TQM is necessarily employee driven because product/service quality cannot be continuously improved without the active learning and participation of *every* employee. Thus, in successful quality improvement programs, TQM principles are embedded in the organization's culture.[35]

The Deming Legacy   TQM is firmly established today thanks in large part to the pioneering work of W Edwards Deming.[36] Ironically, the mathematician credited with Japan's post–World War II quality revolution rarely talked in terms of quality. He instead preferred to discuss "good management" during the hard-hitting seminars he delivered right up until his death at age 93 in 1993.[37] Although Deming's passion was the statistical measurement and reduction of variations in industrial processes, he had much to say about how employees should be treated. Regarding the human side of quality improvement, Deming called for the following:

- Formal training in statistical process control techniques and teamwork.
- Helpful leadership, rather than order giving and punishment.
- Elimination of fear so employees will feel free to ask questions.
- Emphasis on continuous process improvements rather than on numerical quotas.
- Teamwork.
- Elimination of barriers to good workmanship.[38]

One of Deming's most enduring lessons for managers is his 85–15 rule.[39] Specifically, when things go wrong, there is roughly an 85% chance the *system* (including management, machinery, and rules) is at fault. Only about 15% of the time is the individual employee at fault. Unfortunately, as Deming observed, the typical manager spends most of his or her time wrongly blaming and punishing individuals for system failures. Statistical analysis is required to uncover system failures.

Principles of TQM   Despite variations in the language and scope of TQM programs, it is possible to identify four common TQM principles:

1. Do it right the first time to eliminate costly rework.
2. Listen to and learn from customers and employees (see Hands-On Exercise).
3. Make continuous improvement an everyday matter.
4. Build teamwork, trust, and mutual respect.[40]

Deming's influence is clearly evident in this list.[41] Once again, as with the human relations movement, we see people as the key factor in organizational success.

In summary, TQM advocates have made a valuable contribution to the field of OB by providing a *practical* context for managing people. When people are managed according to TQM principles, everyone is more likely to get the employment opportunities and high-quality goods and services they demand.[42] As you will see many times in later chapters, this book is anchored to Deming's philosophy and TQM principles.

The Internet Revolution

We can be forgiven if the Internet revolution has left us a bit dizzy. In just a few short years, dot-coms exploded onto the scene, with promises of *everything* for sale *cheap* on the Internet. Then, just as suddenly, many dot-coms truly did explode, leaving their overworked employees jobless and their founders telling bizarre riches-to-rags stories.[43] Strange and unforeseen things happened. For example, Pets.com, with a popular and expensive advertising campaign, went broke trying to sell $10 bags of dog food. Meanwhile, General Electric, that old-line stalwart, had great success selling $65,000 medical software packages over the Internet.[44]

As we continue to sift through the wreckage of the 2000–2001 dot-com crash looking for winning formulas, one thing is very clear. The **Internet**—the global network of computers, software, cables, servers, switches, and routers—is here to stay as a business tool.[45] In fact, while dot-coms were going out of business in droves in 2000, the overall Internet economy mushroomed 58% from the year before to $830 billion.[46]

Internet

The global system of networked computers.

The purpose of this section is to define *E-business* and identify significant OB implications in the ongoing Internet revolution (as signs of what lies ahead).

E-Business Is Much More than E-Commerce Experts on the subject draw an important distinction between *E-commerce* (buying and selling goods and services over the Internet) and **E-business,** using the Internet to facilitate *every* aspect of running a business.[47] *Business Week* recently offered this helpful perspective: "Strip away the highfalutin talk, and at bottom, the Internet is a tool that dramatically lowers the cost of communication. That means it can radically alter any industry or activity that depends heavily on the flow of information."[48] Relevant information includes everything from customer needs and

E-business

Running the *entire* business via the Internet.

product design specifications to prices, schedules, finances, employee performance appraisals, and corporate strategy. Intel, as a case in point, has taken the challenge of this broad view to heart. The computer-chip giant is striving to become an E-corporation, one that relies primarily on the Internet to not only buy and sell things, but to facilitate all business functions, exchange knowledge among its employees, and build partnerships with outsiders as well. Why? Consider this recent survey finding: "firms that embraced the Internet averaged a 13.4% jump in productivity . . . [in 2000], compared with 4.9% for those that did not."[49] E-business has significant implications for managing people at work because it eventually will seep into every corner of life both on and off the job.

E-Business Implications for OB The following list is intended to open doors and explore possibilities, not serve as a final analysis. It also is a preview of later discussions in this book (chapter linkages in parentheses):

Who doesn't remember the goofy, but endearing "mascot" of the now defunct website Pets.com? Pets.com spent a huge amount of advertising dollars on the concept, not to mention the ads, only to fall victim of the dot-com crash.

- *E-management*. 21st-century managers, profiled earlier in Table 1–1, are needed in the fast-paced Internet age. They are able to create, motivate, and lead teams of far-flung specialists linked by Internet E-mail and project management software and by fax and phone. Networking skills, applied both inside and outside the organization, are essential today (see Chapters 1, 6, 7, 13, and 14).

- *E-communication*. E-mail has become one of the most used and abused forms of organizational communication. Today's managers need to be masters of concise, powerful E-mail and voice-mail messages. Communicating via the Internet's World Wide Web is fast and efficient for those who know how to fully exploit it. Consider the recent experience of Pietro Senna, a buyer for Nestlé Switzerland:

  The time savings are immense. Each country's hazelnut buyer, for example, used to visit processing plants in Italy and Turkey. Hazelnuts, a key ingredient in chocolate bars, are prone to wild price swings and uneven quality. But after Senna stopped by some Turkish plants, he posted his report on the Web—and within a week, 73 other Nestlé buyers from around the globe had read it, saving them the trouble of a trip to Turkey. "For the first time, I get to take advantage of Nestlé's size," he says.[50]

  Additionally, employees who "telecommute" from home via the Internet present their managers with unique motivational and performance measurement problems. For their part, telecommuters must strike a productive balance between independence and feelings of isolation (see Chapter 12).

- *Goal setting and feedback*. Abundant research evidence supports the coupling of clear and challenging goals with timely and constructive feedback for keeping employees headed in the right direction. Thanks to Web-based software programs such as *eWorkbench,* managers can efficiently create, align, and track their employee's goals[51] (see Chapters 7 and 8).

- *Organizational structure*. The Internet and modern telecommunications technology have given rise to "virtual teams" and "virtual organizations." Time zones, facilities, and location no longer are hard constraints on getting things accomplished. Got a great product idea but don't have the time to build a factory? No problem, just connect with someone via the Internet who can get the job done.

Telecommuters need to strike a productive balance between independence and feelings of isolation.

Look at Juniper Networks Inc. In just three years, it came out of nowhere to capture 35% of the market for high-end Internet routers. Juniper outsources 100% of its production to contract manufacturers. Juniper's customers, mainly big telecom service providers, order their equipment on Juniper's Web portal—but the orders go straight to the contract manufacturers. . . . Thanks to the Net, Juniper has $726,000 in annual revenues per employee, versus $320,600 for older rival Nortel Networks, which handles considerably less of its sales online.[52]

This virtual workplace, with less face-to-face interaction, requires managers and employees who are flexible and adaptable and not bound by slow and rigid bureaucratic communication and methods. (See Chapters 10 and 15.)

- *Job design.* The *work itself* is a powerful motivator for many employees today, especially those in information technology. A recent New Economy study by Harvard's Rosabeth Moss Kanter led to this conclusion:

  [They] are attracted by the chance to take on big responsibility and stretch their skills even further. The "stickiest" work settings (the ones people leave less frequently and more reluctantly) involve opportunity and empowerment. Cutting-edge work with the best tools for the best customers is important in the present because it promises even greater responsibility and rewards in the future.[53]

Boring and unchallenging and/or dead-end jobs will repel rather than attract top talent in the Internet age (see Chapter 6).

- *Decision making.* Things indeed are moving faster and faster in the Internet age. Just ask the typical overloaded manager. A recent survey asking 479 managers about their last three years uncovered these findings: 77% reported making more decisions while 43% said they had less time to make decisions.[54] Adding to the pressure, databases linked to the Internet give today's decision makers unprecedented amounts of both relevant and irrelevant data. The trick is to be energized and selective, not overwhelmed. A clear sense of purpose is necessary when sifting for useful information. Moreover, decision makers cannot ignore the trend away from command-and-control tactics and toward employee empowerment and participation. In short, there is more "we" than "me" for Internet-age decision makers (see Chapters 9, 13, and 14).

- *Knowledge management.* Of growing importance today are E-training, E-learning, and distance learning. Management writer Kathryn Tyler offers this primer:

> E-learning is instruction that is delivered electronically. Almost anything that teaches a skill or conveys information in an organized fashion online can be considered E-learning. E-learning programs are administered through what are called learning management systems (LMSs).
>
> E-learning includes asynchronous—meaning it is not delivered to every user at the same time—text-based courses, job aids, educational games and video and audio segments, as well as synchronous media like videoconferencing and chat rooms.[55]

(See Chapter 16 and Skills & Best Practices.)

- *Speed, conflict, and stress.* The name of the popular Internet-age magazine, *Fast Company,* says it all. Unfortunately, conflict and stress are unavoidable by-products of strategic and operational speed. The good news is that conflict and stress can be managed. (See Chapter 11.)

- *Change and resistance to change.* As "old economy" companies race to become E-corporations, employees are being asked to digest huge doses of change in every aspect of their worklives. For example, imagine the changes in store for the 198,000 employees of Boeing, the world's largest aircraft maker. As *Fortune* recently observed: " . . . talk to Boeing execs and you'll find that everything at the company is being reexamined, from how it interacts with its customers and 15,000 suppliers right down to whether plane-making should be its core business. The goal is to change the entire fabric of the company."[56] Inevitable conflict and resistance to change will need to be skillfully managed at Boeing if it is to prosper. (See Chapters 11 and 16.)

- *Ethics.* Internet-centered organizations are littered with ethical landmines needing to be addressed humanely and responsibly. Among them are around-the-clock work binges, exaggerated promises about rewards, electronic monitoring, questionable anti-union tactics, repetitive-motion injuries from excessive keyboarding, unfair treatment of part-timers, and privacy issues[57]. (See Chapter 2.)

Overall, it is easy to see why the Internet revolution represents a significant new era for understanding and managing people at work. The problems, challenges, and opportunities are immense. Hang on tight; it promises to be an exciting ride!

Although Boeing moved its headquarters to Chicago in 2001, the attack of Sept. 11 is taking a toll on the company. Losing a lucrative defense contract to Lockheed Martin only compounded the effects. Change and its effects will necessitate Boeing taking a good look at itself and how it does business.

The Contingency Approach: Applying Lessons from Research and Practice

Contingency approach

Using management tools and techniques in a situationally appropriate manner; avoiding the one-best-way mentality.

Scholars have wrestled for many years with the problem of how best to apply the diverse and growing collection of management tools and techniques. Their answer is the contingency approach. The **contingency approach** calls for using management concepts and techniques in a situationally appropriate manner, instead of trying to rely on "one best way."

The contingency approach encourages managers to view organizational behavior within a situational context. According to this modern perspective, evolving situations, not hard-and-fast rules, determine when and where various management techniques are appropriate. For example, as discussed in Chapter 14, contingency researchers have determined that there is no single best style of leadership. Organizational behavior specialists embrace the contingency approach because it helps them realistically interrelate individuals, groups, and organizations. Moreover, the contingency approach sends a clear message to managers in today's global economy: Carefully read the situation and then apply lessons from published research studies and from personal experience in a situationally appropriate manner.

Learning from Research

Because of unfamiliar jargon and complicated statistical procedures, many current and future managers are put off by behavioral research.[58] This is unfortunate because practical lessons can be learned as OB researchers steadily push back the frontier of knowledge. Let us examine the various sources and uses of OB research evidence.

Five Sources of OB Research Insights   To enhance the instructional value of our coverage of major topics, we systematically cite "hard" evidence from five different categories. Worthwhile evidence was obtained by drawing upon the following *priority* of research methodologies:

- *Meta-analyses.* A **meta-analysis** is a statistical pooling technique that permits behavioral scientists to draw general conclusions about certain variables from many different studies.[59] It typically encompasses a vast number of subjects, often reaching the thousands. Meta-analyses are instructive because they focus on general patterns of research evidence, not fragmented bits and pieces or isolated studies.[60]

- *Field studies.* In OB, a **field study** probes individual or group processes in an organizational setting. Because field studies involve real-life situations, their results often have immediate and practical relevance for managers.

- *Laboratory studies.* In a **laboratory study,** variables are manipulated and measured in contrived situations. College students are commonly used as subjects. The highly controlled nature of laboratory studies enhances research precision. But generalizing the results to organizational management requires caution.[61]

- *Sample surveys.* In a **sample survey,** samples of people from specified populations respond to questionnaires. The researchers then draw conclusions about the relevant population. Generalizability of the results depends on the quality of the sampling and questioning techniques.

- *Case studies.* A **case study** is an in-depth analysis of a single individual, group, or organization. Because of their limited scope, case studies yield realistic but not very generalizable results.[62]

Meta-analysis

Pools the results of many studies through statistical procedure.

Field study

Examination of variables in real-life settings.

Laboratory study

Manipulation and measurement of variables in contrived situations.

Sample survey

Questionnaire responses from a sample of people.

Case study

In-depth study of a single person, group, or organization.

Three Uses of OB Research Findings   Organizational scholars point out that managers can put relevant research findings to use in three different ways:[63]

1. *Instrumental use.* This involves directly applying research findings to practical problems. For example, a manager experiencing high stress tries a relaxation technique after reading a research report about its effectiveness.

2. *Conceptual use.* Research is put to conceptual use when managers derive general enlightenment from its findings. The effect here is less specific and more indirect than with instrumental use. For example, after reading a meta-analysis showing a negative correlation between absenteeism and age,[64] a manager might develop a more positive attitude toward hiring older people.

3. *Symbolic use.* Symbolic use occurs when research results are relied on to verify or legitimize already held positions. Negative forms of symbolic use involve self-serving bias, prejudice, selective perception, and distortion. For example, tobacco industry spokespersons routinely deny any link between smoking and lung cancer because researchers are largely, but not 100%, in agreement about the negative effects of smoking. A positive example would be managers maintaining their confidence in setting performance goals after reading a research report about the favorable impact of goal setting on job performance.

By systematically reviewing and interpreting research relevant to key topics, this book provides instructive insights about OB.

Learning from Practice

Learning to manage people is like learning to ride a bicycle. You watch others do it. Sooner or later, you get up the courage to try it yourself. You fall off and skin your knee. You climb back on the bike a bit smarter, and so on, until wobbly first attempts turn into a smooth ride. Your chances of becoming a successful manager can be enhanced by studying the theory, research, and practical examples in this textbook. Figuratively speaking, however, you eventually must climb aboard the "managerial bicycle" and learn by doing.[65]

chapter summary

- *Identify at least four of Pfeffer's people-centered practices, and define the term* management. Pfeffer's seven people-centered practices are job security, careful hiring, power to the people, generous pay for performance, lots of training, less emphasis on status, and trust building. *Management* is the process of working with and through others to achieve organizational objectives in an efficient and ethical manner.

- *Profile the 21st-century manager.* They will be team players who will get things done cooperatively by relying on joint decision making, their knowledge instead of formal authority, and their multicultural skills. They will engage in life-long learning and be compensated on the basis of their skills and results. They will facilitate rather than resist change, share rather than hoard power and key information, and be multidirectional communicators. Ethics will be a forethought instead of an afterthought. They will be generalists with multiple specialties.

- *Contrast McGregor's Theory X and Theory Y assumptions about employees.* Theory X employees, according to traditional thinking, dislike work, require close supervision, and are primarily interested in security. According to the modern Theory Y view, employees are capable of self-direction, of seeking responsibility, and of being creative.

- *Explain the managerial significance of Deming's 85–15 rule, and identify the four principles of total quality management (TQM).* Deming claimed that about 85% of organizational failures are due to system breakdowns involving factors such as management, machinery, or work rules. He believed the workers themselves are responsible for

failures only about 15% of the time. Consequently, Deming criticized the standard practice of blaming and punishing individuals for what are typically *system* failures beyond their immediate control. The four principles of TQM are (a) do it right the first time to eliminate costly rework; (b) listen to and learn from customers and employees; (c) make continuous improvement an everyday matter; and (d) build teamwork, trust, and mutual respect.

- *Define the term* E-business, *and specify five ways the Internet is affecting the management of people at work.* *E-business* involves using the Internet to more effectively and efficiently manage *every* aspect of a business. The Internet is reshaping the management of people in the following areas: E-management (networking), E-communication (E-mail and telecommuting), goal setting and feedback, organizational structure (virtual teams and organizations), job design (desire for more challenge), decision making (greater speed and employee empowerment), knowledge management (E-learning), conflict and stress triggered by increased speed, rapid change and inevitable conflict and resistance, and ethical problems such as overwork and privacy issues.

- *Describe the sources of organizational behavior research evidence.* Five sources of OB research evidence are meta-analyses (statistically pooled evidence from several studies), field studies (evidence from real-life situations), laboratory studies (evidence from contrived situations), sample surveys (questionnaire data), and case studies (observation of a single person, group, or organization).

internet exercise

www.hp.com

The purpose of this exercise is to focus on one well-known company with a good general reputation (Hewlett-Packard) and look for evidence of the seven people-centered practices discussed at the beginning of this chapter (go back and review them to refresh your memory). On the Internet, go to Hewlett-Packard's home page (**www.hp.com**) and select the heading "company information." Next, in the section "about hp," select "history & facts." Be sure to read the section titled "corporate objectives," especially the parts titled "our people" and "management."

QUESTIONS

1. On a scale of 1 = low to 10 = high, how people-centered is HP?
2. What *specific* evidence of each of the seven people-centered practices did you find?
3. Which of the seven practices appears to be HP's strongest suit?
4. Do HP's culture and values give it a strategic competitive advantage? Explain.
5. Would you like to work for HP? Why or why not?

Cultivating Organizational Culture and Ethical Behavior

chapter Two

After reading the material in this chapter, you should be able to:

- Discuss the layers and functions of organizational culture.

- Describe the three general types of organizational culture and their associated normative beliefs.

- Summarize the methods used by organizations to embed their cultures.

- Describe the three phases in Feldman's model of organizational socialization.

- Explain the four types of development networks derived from a developmental network model of mentoring.

- Specify at least four actions managers can take to improve an organization's ethical climate.

FROM BOOM TO BUST AT YAHOO

They were the most successful sextet of the Internet boom. . . . Their company, Yahoo! Inc., rocketed to a market value of $134 billion, and the young leaders became legends, defining Silicon Valley start-up life. . . . On Wednesday [March 7, 2001] the game abruptly ended. With its stock down 92% from its peak and advertising sales plunging, Yahoo said it would launch a search for a new chief executive from outside the company. . . . The unexpected move amounted to a humbling acknowledgment of something people close to Yahoo have increasingly been saying: that the tight-knit, us-against-the-world management style that fueled Yahoo's astronomical rise may also have exacerbated its decline.

"Their culture helped them build a superb site and a really edgy brand, but it also held them back from making forward looking business decisions," says Holly Becker, an analyst at Lehman Brothers. "The culture that served them so incredibly well until the middle of last year is now letting them down."

Business partners and former executives say the small group's intense closeness made it hard for Yahoo to retain or attract experienced managers. Over a long acquisition spree, Yahoo spent billions to buy GeoCities Inc., Broadcast.com, and numerous smaller companies—yet many of the targets' top executives wound up leaving Yahoo, unable to penetrate its inner sanctum. Yahoo's top European and Asian executives and a slew of middle managers also left, amid complaints that the top team wouldn't delegate authority.

"They're very insular," says Stephen Hansen, former chief financial officer at GeoCities, a company acquired by Yahoo in 1999. "They see the world through the Yahoo lens."[1]

FOR DISCUSSION

How would you describe the organizational culture at Yahoo and how did it get embedded? For an interpretation of this case and additional comments, visit our website:

www.mhhe.com/kinickiob

Foundation of Organizational Culture

Organizational culture

Shared values and beliefs that underlie a company's identity.

Values

Enduring belief in a mode of conduct or end-state.

Espoused values

The stated values and norms that are preferred by an organization.

Organizational culture is "the set of shared, taken-for-granted implicit assumptions that a group holds and that determines how it perceives, thinks about, and reacts to its various environments."[2] This definition highlights three important characteristics of organizational culture. First, organizational culture is passed on to new employees through the process of socialization, a topic discussed later in this chapter. Second, organizational culture influences our behavior at work. Finally, organizational culture operates at different levels.

To gain a better understanding of how organizational culture is formed and used by employees, this section begins by discussing the layers of organizational culture. We then review the four functions of organizational culture, types of organizational culture, outcomes associated with organizational culture, and how cultures are embedded within organizations.

Layers of Organizational Culture

Figure 2–1 shows the three fundamental layers of organizational culture. Each level varies in terms of outward visibility and resistance to change, and each level influences another level.[3]

Observable Artifacts   At the more visible level, culture represents observable artifacts. Artifacts consist of the physical manifestation of an organization's culture. Organizational examples include acronyms, manner of dress, awards, myths and stories told about the organization, published lists of values, observable rituals and ceremonies, special parking spaces, decorations, and so on. This level also includes visible behaviors exhibited by people and groups. Artifacts are easier to change than the less visible aspects of organizational culture.

Espoused Values   Values possess five key components. "**Values** (1) are concepts or beliefs, (2) pertain to desirable end-states or behaviors, (3) transcend situations, (4) guide selection or evaluation of behavior and events, and (5) are ordered by relative importance."[4] It is important to distinguish between values that are espoused versus those that are enacted.

Espoused values represent the explicitly stated values and norms that are preferred by an organization. They are generally established by the founder of a new or small company and by the top management team in a larger organization. Gerald Levin, chairman of Time Warner Inc., for instance, is "putting groups of its most promising executives through an intensive two-day program designed to define and disseminate what the company calls its 'core values and guiding principles'—among them 'diversity,' 'respect,' and 'integrity.' "[5] Time Warner is sending 1,000 executives to these sessions. Because espoused values constitute aspirations that are explicitly communicated to employees, managers such as Levin hope that espoused values will directly influence employee behavior. Unfortunately, aspirations do not automatically produce the desired behaviors because people do not always "walk the talk."

Enacted values, on the other hand, represent the values and norms that actually are exhibited or converted into employee behavior. Let us consider the difference between these two types of values. Home Depot, for instance, has espoused that it values customer service and safety. If the organization displays customer service and safety through its store layouts and behavior of employees, then the espoused value is enacted and individual behavior is being influenced by the values of customer service and safety. Unfortunately, Home Depot appears to have a discrepancy between its espoused and enacted values:

> **Enacted values**
> The values and norms that are exhibited by employees.

> "Home Depot advertises having the best customer service, but it seems like everybody is so busy," says Priscilla High, a customer shopping in Atlanta recently for a rug and kitchen sink. "Lowe's [a Home Depot rival] has more customer service." . . . as sales volumes soared and product lines expanded in recent years, that busy warehouse action became a liability. Shoppers complained that pallets of merchandise cluttered the aisles. Injuries from falling merchandise grabbed headlines. And the company says many employees became more concerned with stocking socket wrenches than helping customers. . . . On a recent morning at a Home Depot near Stone Mountain, [Georgia], assistant manager Jill Roberts found three pallets of space heaters clogging an aisle of kitchen sinks and plumbing supplies. . . . Another priority for Home Depot is improved store safety in the wake of three deaths last year [2000] and other injuries caused by falling merchandise.[6]

It is important to reduce gaps between espoused and enacted values because they can significantly influence employee attitudes and organizational performance. For example, a study of 312 British rail drivers revealed that employees were more cynical about safety when they believed that senior managers' behaviors were inconsistent with the stated values regarding safety.[7] Home Depot is aware of this important issue and has instituted a program labeled Service Performance Improvement, or SPI, to reduce the gap between espoused and enacted values regarding customer service and safety. Preliminary results from six test stores indicated increases in store sales and the amount of time store employees spent helping customers.[8]

Basic Assumptions   Basic underlying assumptions are unobservable and represent the core of organizational culture. They constitute organizational values that have become so taken for granted over time that they become assumptions that guide organizational behavior. They thus are highly resistant to change. When basic assumptions are widely held among employees, people will find behavior based on an inconsistent value inconceivable. Southwest Airlines, for example, is noted for operating according to basic assumptions that value employees' welfare and providing high-quality service. Employees at Southwest Airlines would be shocked to see management act in ways that did not value employees' and customers' needs.[9]

Four Functions of Organizational Culture

As illustrated in Figure 2–2, an organization's culture fulfills four functions.[10] To help bring these four functions to life, let us consider how each of them has taken shape at 3M. 3M is a particularly instructive example because it has a long history of being

FIGURE 2–1
The Layers of Organizational Culture

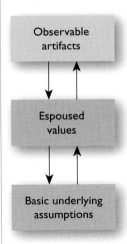

SOURCE: Adapted from E H Schein, *Organizational Culture and Leadership,* 2nd ed (San Francisco: Jossey-Bass, 1992), p 17.

FIGURE 2–2
Four Functions
of
Organizational
Culture

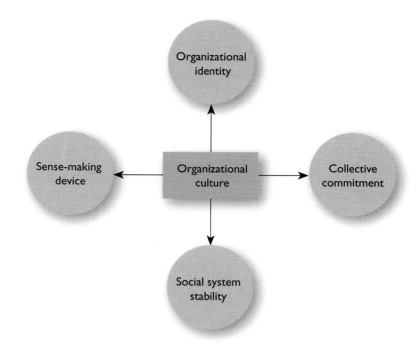

SOURCE: Adapted from discussion in L Smircich, "Concepts of Culture and Organizational Analysis," *Administrative Science Quarterly,* September 1983, pp 339–58. Reproduced by permission of John Wiley & Sons, Ltd.

an innovative company—the company was founded in 1902—and it was ranked as the 94th most admired company in the United States by *Fortune* in 1998, partly due to its strong and distinctive culture.[11]

1. *Give members an organizational identity.* 3M is known as being an innovative company that relentlessly pursues new-product development. One way of promoting innovation is to encourage the research and development of new products and services. For example, 3M regularly sets future sales targets based on the percentage of sales that must come from new products. In one year, the senior management decreed that 30% of its sales must come from products introduced within the past four years. The old standard was 25% in five years. This identity is reinforced by creating rewards that reinforce innovation. For example, "The 3M Corporation has its version of a Nobel Prize for innovative employees. The prize is the Golden Step award, whose trophy is a winged foot. Several Golden Steps are given out each year to employees whose new products have reached significant revenue and profit levels."[12]

2. *Facilitate collective commitment.* One of 3M's corporate values is to be "a company that employees are proud to be a part of." People who like 3M's culture tend to stay employed there for long periods of time. Approximately 24,000 of its employees have more than 15 years of tenure with the company while 19,600 have stayed more than 20 years. Consider the commitment and pride expressed by Kathleen Stanislawski, a staffing manager. "I'm a 27-year 3Mer because, quite frankly, there's no reason to leave. I've had great opportunities to do different jobs and to grow a career. It's just a great company."[13]

3. *Promote social system stability.* Social system stability reflects the extent to which the work environment is perceived as positive and reinforcing, and conflict and change are managed effectively. Consider how 3M dealt with its financial problems in 1998. "Even in tough times, which have now arrived because of the upheavals in Asia, 3M hasn't become a mean, miserly, or miserable place to work. It's shedding about 4,500 jobs, but slowly, and mostly by attrition."[14] This strategy helped to maintain a positive work environment in the face of adversity. The company also attempts to promote stability through a promote-from-within culture, a strategic hiring policy that ensures that capable college graduates are hired in a timely manner, and a layoff policy that provides displaced workers six months to find another job at 3M before being terminated.

4. *Shape behavior by helping members make sense of their surroundings.* This function of culture helps employees understand why the organization does what it does and how it intends to accomplish its long-term goals. 3M sets expectations for innovation in a variety of ways. For example, the company employs an internship and co-op program. 3M also shapes expectations and behavior by providing detailed career feedback to its employees. New hires are measured and evaluated against a career growth standard during their first six months to three years of employment.

Types of Organizational Culture

Researchers have attempted to identify and measure various types of organizational culture in order to study the relationship between types of culture and organizational effectiveness. This pursuit was motivated by the possibility that certain cultures were more effective than others. Unfortunately, research has not uncovered a universal typology of cultural styles that everyone accepts.[15] Just the same, there is value in providing an example of various types of organizational culture. Table 2–1 is thus presented as an illustration rather than a definitive conclusion about the types of organizational culture that exist. Awareness of these types provides you with greater understanding about the manifestations of culture.

Table 2–1 shows that there are three general types of organizational culture—constructive, passive–defensive, and aggressive–defensive—and that each type is associated with a different set of normative beliefs.[16] **Normative beliefs** represent an individual's thoughts and beliefs about how members of a particular group or organization are expected to approach their work and interact with others. A *constructive culture* is one in which employees are encouraged to interact with others and to work

> **Normative beliefs**
>
> Thoughts and beliefs about expected behavior and modes of conduct.

on tasks and projects in ways that will assist them in satisfying their need to grow and develop. This type of culture endorses normative beliefs associated with achievement, self-actualizing, humanistic-encouraging, and affiliative. In contrast, a *passive–defensive culture* is characterized by an overriding belief that employees must interact with others in ways that do not threaten their own job security. This culture reinforces the normative beliefs associated with approval, conventional, dependent, and avoidance (see Table 2–1). Finally, companies with an *aggressive–defensive culture* encourage employees to approach tasks in forceful ways in order to protect their status and job security. This type of culture is more characteristic of normative beliefs reflecting oppositional, power, competitive, and perfectionistic.

TABLE 2-1   Types of Organizational Culture

General Types of Culture	Normative Beliefs	Organizational Characteristics
Constructive	Achievement	Organizations that do things well and value members who set and accomplish their own goals. Members are expected to set challenging but realistic goals, establish plans to reach these goals, and pursue them with enthusiasm. (Pursuing a standard of excellence)
Constructive	Self-actualizing	Organizations that value creativity, quality over quantity, and both task accomplishment and individual growth. Members are encouraged to gain enjoyment from their work, develop themselves, and take on new and interesting activities. (Thinking in unique and independent ways)
Constructive	Humanistic-encouraging	Organizations that are managed in a participative and person-centered way. Members are expected to be supportive, constructive, and open to influence in their dealings with one another. (Helping others to grow and develop)
Constructive	Affiliative	Organizations that place a high priority on constructive interpersonal relationships. Members are expected to be friendly, open, and sensitive to the satisfaction of their work group. (Dealing with others in a friendly way)

Although an organization may predominately represent one cultural type, it still can manifest normative beliefs and characteristics from the others. Research demonstrates that organizations can have functional subcultures, hierarchical subcultures based on one's level in the organization, geographical subcultures, occupational subcultures based on one's title or position, social subcultures derived from social activities such as a bowling or golf league and a reading club, and counter-cultures.[17] It is important for managers to be aware of the possibility that conflict between subgroups that form subcultures can undermine an organization's overall performance.

Outcomes Associated with Organizational Culture

Both managers and academic researchers believe that organizational culture can be a driver of employee attitudes and organizational effectiveness and performance. To test this possibility, various measures of organizational culture have been correlated with a variety of individual and organizational outcomes. So what have we learned? First, several studies demonstrated that organizational culture was significantly correlated with employee behavior and attitudes. For example, a constructive culture was positively related with job satisfaction, intentions to stay at the company, and innovation and was negatively associated with work avoidance. In contrast, passive–defensive and aggressive–defensive cultures were negatively correlated with job satisfaction and intentions to stay at the company.[18] These results suggest that employees seem to prefer organizations that encourage people to interact and work with others in ways that assist them in satisfying their needs to grow and develop. Second, results from several studies revealed that the congruence between an individual's values and the organization's values was significantly associated with organizational commitment, job satisfaction, intention to quit, and turnover.[19]

(Continued) **TABLE 2–1**

General Types of Culture	Normative Beliefs	Organizational Characteristics
Passive–defensive	Approval	Organizations in which conflicts are avoided and interpersonal relationships are pleasant—at least superficially. Members feel that they should agree with, gain the approval of, and be liked by others. ("Going along" with others)
Passive–defensive	Conventional	Organizations that are conservative, traditional, and bureaucratically controlled. Members are expected to conform, follow the rules, and make a good impression. (Always following policies and practices)
Passive–defensive	Dependent	Organizations that are hierarchically controlled and nonparticipative. Centralized decision making in such organizations leads members to do only what they are told and to clear all decisions with superiors. (Pleasing those in positions of authority)
Passive–defensive	Avoidance	Organizations that fail to reward success but nevertheless punish mistakes. This negative reward system leads members to shift responsibilities to others and avoid any possibility of being blamed for a mistake. (Waiting for others to act first)
Aggressive–defensive	Oppositional	Organizations in which confrontation and negativism are rewarded. Members gain status and influence by being critical and thus are reinforced to oppose the ideas of others. (Pointing out flaws)
Aggressive–defensive	Power	Nonparticipative organizations structured on the basis of the authority inherent in members' positions. Members believe they will be rewarded for taking charge, controlling subordinates and, at the same time, being responsive to the demands of superiors. (Building up one's power base)
Aggressive–defensive	Competitive	Winning is valued and members are rewarded for outperforming one another. Members operate in a "win-lose" framework and believe they must work against (rather than with) their peers to be noticed. (Turning the job into a contest)
Aggressive–defensive	Perfectionistic	Organizations in which perfectionism, persistence, and hard work are valued. Members feel they must avoid any mistake, keep track of everything, and work long hours to attain narrowly defined objectives. (Doing things perfectly)

SOURCE: Reproduced with permission of authors and publisher from R A Cooke and J L Szumal, "Measuring Normative Beliefs and Shared Behavioral Expectations in Organizations: The Reliability and Validity of the Organizational Culture Inventory," *Psychological Reports*, 1993, pp. 72, 1299–1330. © *Psychological Reports*, 1993.

Third, a summary of 10 quantitative studies showed that organizational culture did not predict an organization's financial performance.[20] This means that there is not one type of organizational culture that fuels financial performance. That said, however, a study of 207 companies from 22 industries for an 11-year period demonstrated that financial performance was higher among companies that had adaptive and flexible cultures.[21] Finally, studies of mergers indicated that they frequently failed due to incompatible cultures. Due to the increasing number of corporate mergers around the world, and the conclusion that 7 out of 10 mergers and acquisitions failed to meet their financial promise, managers within merged companies would be well advised to

You wouldn't say "The Gap" and "Brooks Brothers" in the same breath when shopping for apparel. The Gap is able to differentiate not only the culture of its customers, but also its salespeople. In fact, this culture became famous (or infamous) as a skit on "Saturday Night Live."

consider the role of organizational culture in creating a new organization.[22]

These research results underscore the significance of organizational culture. They also reinforce the need to learn more about the process of cultivating and changing an organization's culture. An organization's culture is not determined by fate. It is formed and shaped by the combination and integration of everyone who works in the organization.

How Cultures Are Embedded in Organizations

An organization's initial culture is an outgrowth of the founder's philosophy. For example, an achievement culture is likely to develop if the founder is an achievement-oriented individual driven by success. Over time, the original culture is either embedded as is or modified to fit the current environmental situation. Edgar Schein, an OB scholar, notes that embedding a culture involves a teaching process. That is, organizational members teach each other about the organization's preferred values, beliefs, expectations, and behaviors. This is accomplished by using one or more of the following mechanisms:[23]

1. *Formal statements of organizational philosophy, mission, vision, values, and materials used for recruiting, selection, and socialization.* Texas Instruments, for example, published a list of corporate values that includes integrity, innovation, and commitment.[24]

2. *The design of physical space, work environments, and buildings.*

3. *Slogans, language, acronyms, and sayings.* For example, Bank One promoted its desire to provide excellent client service through the slogan "whatever it takes." Employees are encouraged to do whatever it takes to exceed customer expectations.

4. *Deliberate role modeling, training programs, teaching, and coaching by managers and supervisors.* General Semiconductor implemented the "People Plus" program. It is an in-house leadership development and problem-solving training program that uses the company's mission and values as the springboard for creating individual development plans.[25]

5. *Explicit rewards, status symbols (e.g., titles), and promotion criteria.* Consider how Jack Welch, former CEO of General Electric, describes the reward system at General Electric: "The top 20% should be rewarded in the soul and wallet because they are the ones who make magic happen. Losing one of these people must be held up as a leadership sin," Welch says. The middle 70% should be energized to improve; the rest should be shown the door. Not getting rid of the 10% early "is not only a management failure, but false kindness as well—a form of cruelty," Welch says. They will wind up being fired eventually and "stranded" in midcareer.[26]

6. *Stories, legends, and myths about key people and events.*

7. *The organizational activities, processes, or outcomes that leaders pay attention to, measure, and control.* Dick Brown, CEO at Electronic Data Systems, believes that leaders get the behavior they tolerate. He instituted the "performance call" to change the organization's culture from one that promoted individualism and information hoarding to one that supported teamwork and information sharing (see Skills & Best Practices).

8. *Leader reactions to critical incidents and organizational crises.*

9. *The workflow and organizational structure.* Hierarchical structures are more likely to embed an orientation toward control and authority than a flatter organization.

10. *Organizational systems and procedures.* An organization can promote achievement and competition through the use of sales contests.

11. *Organizational goals and the associated criteria used for recruitment, selection, development, promotion, layoffs, and retirement of people.* PepsiCo reinforces a high-performance culture by setting challenging goals. Executives strive to achieve a 15% increase in revenue per year.[27]

> ## Electronic Data Systems (EDS) Uses a Performance Call to Embed Its Culture
>
> Once a month, the top 100 or so EDS executives worldwide take part in a conference call where the past month's numbers and critical activities are reviewed in detail. Transparency and simultaneous information are the rules; information hoarding is no longer possible. Everyone knows who is on target for the year, who is ahead of projections, and who is behind. Those who are behind must explain the shortfall—and how they plan to get back on track. It's not enough for a manager to say she's assessing, reviewing, or analyzing a problem. Those aren't the words of someone who is acting, Brown [CEO Dick Brown] says. . . .
>
> The performance calls are also a mechanism for airing and resolving the conflicts inevitable in a large organization, particularly when it comes to cross-selling in order to accelerate revenue growth.
>
> SOURCE: R Charan, "Conquering a Culture of Indecision," *Harvard Business Review*, April 2001, p 79.

SKILLS & BEST PRACTICES

Embedding Organizational Culture through Socialization Processes and Mentoring

Organizational socialization is defined as "the process by which a person learns the values, norms, and required behaviors which permit him to participate as a member of the organization."[28] As previously discussed, organization socialization is a key mechanism used by organizations to embed their organizational cultures. In short, organizational socialization turns outsiders into fully functioning insiders by promoting and reinforcing the organization's core values and beliefs.

Organizational socialization

Process by which employees learn an organization's values, norms, and required behaviors.

The modern word *mentor* derives from "Mentor," the name of a wise and trusted counselor in Greek mythology. Terms typically used in connection with mentoring are teacher, coach, sponsor, and peer. **Mentoring** is defined as the process of forming and maintaining intensive and lasting developmental relationships between a variety of developers (i.e., people who provide career and psychosocial support) and a junior person (the protégé, if male; or protégée, if female).[29] Mentoring can serve to embed an organization's culture when developers and the protégé/protégée work in the same organization for two reasons. First, mentoring contributes to creating a sense of oneness by promoting the acceptance of the organization's core values throughout the organization. Second, the socialization aspect of mentoring also promotes a sense of membership.

Mentoring

Process of forming and maintaining developmental relationships between a mentor and a junior person.

This section enhances your understanding of socialization and mentoring by introducing a three-phase model of organizational socialization, examining the practical application of socialization research, and discussing how you can use the mentoring process to your advantage.

A Three-Phase Model of Organizational Socialization

One's first year in a complex organization can be confusing. There is a constant swirl of new faces, strange jargon, conflicting expectations, and apparently unrelated events. Some organizations treat new members in a rather haphazard, sink-or-swim manner. More typically, though, the socialization process is characterized by a sequence of identifiable steps.[30]

Organizational behavior researcher Daniel Feldman has proposed a three-phase model of organizational socialization that promotes deeper understanding of this important process. As illustrated in Figure 2–3, the three phases are (1) anticipatory socialization, (2) encounter, and (3) change and acquisition. Each phase has its associated perceptual and social processes. Feldman's model also specifies behavioral and affective outcomes that can be used to judge how well an individual has been socialized. The entire three-phase sequence may take from a few weeks to a year to complete, depending on individual differences and the complexity of the situation.

Phase 1: Anticipatory Socialization   Organizational socialization begins *before* the individual actually joins the organization. Anticipatory socialization information comes from many sources. US Marine recruiting ads, for example, prepare future recruits for a rough-and-tumble experience. All of this information—whether formal or informal, accurate or inaccurate—helps the individual anticipate organiza-

The second, or "Encounter" phase of Organizational Socialization begins when the employment contract is signed. Many companies use a combination of orientation and training programs so that employees can get to know not only the company, but each other as well, much like the corporate instruction track at Trilogy University.

A Model of Organizational Socialization FIGURE 2-3

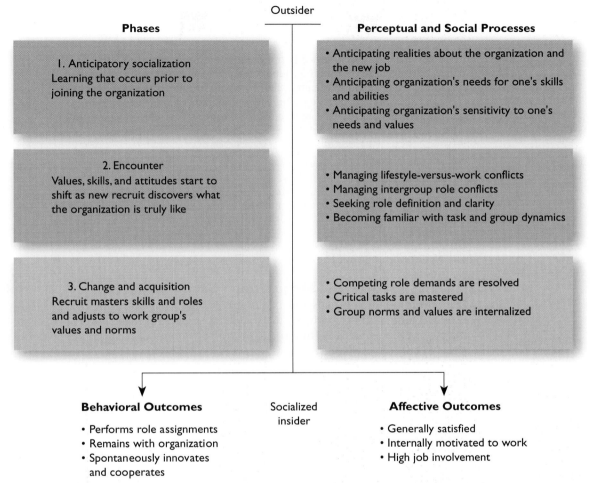

Outsider

Phases

I. Anticipatory socialization
Learning that occurs prior to joining the organization

2. Encounter
Values, skills, and attitudes start to shift as new recruit discovers what the organization is truly like

3. Change and acquisition
Recruit masters skills and roles and adjusts to work group's values and norms

Perceptual and Social Processes

- Anticipating realities about the organization and the new job
- Anticipating organization's needs for one's skills and abilities
- Anticipating organization's sensitivity to one's needs and values

- Managing lifestyle-versus-work conflicts
- Managing intergroup role conflicts
- Seeking role definition and clarity
- Becoming familiar with task and group dynamics

- Competing role demands are resolved
- Critical tasks are mastered
- Group norms and values are internalized

Socialized insider

Behavioral Outcomes

- Performs role assignments
- Remains with organization
- Spontaneously innovates and cooperates

Affective Outcomes

- Generally satisfied
- Internally motivated to work
- High job involvement

SOURCE: Adapted from material in D C Feldman, "The Multiple Socialization of Organization Members," *Academy of Management Review*, April 1981, pp 309–18.

tional realities. Unrealistic expectations about the nature of the work, pay, and promotions are often formulated during phase 1.

Phase 2: Encounter   This second phase begins when the employment contract has been signed. It is a time for surprise and making sense as the newcomer enters unfamiliar territory. Many companies use a combination of orientation and training programs to socialize employees during the encounter phase. Consider the socialization tactics used in Trilogy's renowned orientation program. The three-month orientation program takes place at the organization's corporate university, called Trilogy University (TU):

Month One. When you arrive at Trilogy University, you are assigned to a section and to an instruction track. Your section, a group of about 20, is your social group for the duration of TU. . . . Tracks are designed to be microcosms of future work life at Trilogy. . . . The technical challenges in such exercises closely mimic real customer engagements, but the time frames are dramatically compressed. The assignments pile up week after week for the first month, each one successively more challenging than the last. During that time, you're being constantly measured and evaluated, as assignment grades and comments are entered into a database monitoring your progress. . . .

Month Two. Month two is TU project month. . . . In teams of three to five people, they have to come up with an idea, create a business model for it, build the product, and develop the marketing plan. In trying to launch bold new ideas in a hyper-accelerated time frame, they gain a deep appreciation of the need to set priorities, evaluate probabilities, and measure results. Mind you, these projects are not hypothetical—they're the real thing. . . .

Month Three. Month three at Trilogy University is all about finding your place and having a broader impact in the larger organization. A few students continue with their TU projects, but most move on to "graduation projects," which generally are assignments within various Trilogy business units. People leave TU on a rolling basis as they find sponsors out in the company who are willing to take them on.[31]

The encounter phase at Trilogy is stressful, exhilarating, and critical for finding one's place within the organization. How would you like to work there?

Phase 3: Change and Acquisition   Mastery of important tasks and resolution of role conflict signals the beginning of this final phase of the socialization process. Those who do not make the transition to phase 3 leave voluntarily or involuntarily or become isolated from social networks within the organization. Senior executives frequently play a direct role in the change and acquisition phase.

Practical Application of Socialization Research

Past research suggests four practical guidelines for managing organizational socialization:

1. Managers should avoid a haphazard, sink-or-swim approach to organizational socialization because formalized socialization tactics positively affect new hires. A formalized orientation program positively influenced 116 new employees in a variety of occupations.[32]

2. Managers play a key role during the encounter phase. Studies of newly hired accountants demonstrated that the frequency and type of information obtained during their first six months of employment significantly affected their job performance, their role clarity, and the extent to which they were socially integrated.[33] Managers need to help new hires integrate within the organizational culture. Take a moment now to complete the Hands-On Exercise. It measures the extent to which you have been socialized into your current work organization. Have you been adequately socialized?

3. The organization can benefit by training new employees to use proactive socialization behaviors. A study of 154 entry-level professionals showed that effectively using proactive socialization behaviors influenced the newcomers' general anxiety and stress during the first month of employment and their motivation and anxiety six months later.[34]

4. Managers should pay attention to the socialization of diverse employees. Research demonstrated that diverse employees, particularly those with

Have You Been Adequately Socialized?

INSTRUCTIONS: Complete the following survey items by considering either your current job or one you held in the past. If you have never worked, identify a friend who is working and ask that individual to complete the questionnaire for his or her organization. Read each item and circle your response by using the rating scale shown below. Compute your total score by adding up your responses and compare it to the scoring norms.

	Strongly Disagree	Disagree	Neutral	Agree	Strongly Agree
1. I have been through a set of training experiences that are specifically designed to give newcomers a thorough knowledge of job-related skills.	1	2	3	4	5
2. This organization puts all newcomers through the same set of learning experiences.	1	2	3	4	5
3. I did not perform any of my normal job responsibilities until I was thoroughly familiar with departmental procedures and work methods.	1	2	3	4	5
4. There is a clear pattern in the way one role leads to another, or one job assignment leads to another, in this organization.	1	2	3	4	5
5. I can predict my future career path in this organization by observing other people's experiences.	1	2	3	4	5
6. Almost all of my colleagues have been supportive of me personally.	1	2	3	4	5
7. My colleagues have gone out of their way to help me adjust to this organization.	1	2	3	4	5
8. I received much guidance from experienced organizational members as to how I should perform my job.	1	2	3	4	5
Total Score	_____	_____ _____	_____	_____

SCORING NORMS
8–18 = Low socialization   19–29 = Moderate socialization   30–40 = High socialization

SOURCE: Adapted from survey items excerpted from D Cable and C Parsons, "Socialization Tactics and Person-Organization Fit," *Personnel Psychology*, Spring 2001, pp 1–23.

disabilities, experienced different socialization activities than other newcomers. In turn, these different experiences affected their long-term success and job satisfaction.[35]

Using Mentoring to Your Advantage

Research demonstrates that mentored employees perform better on the job and experience more rapid career advancement. Mentored employees also report higher job and career satisfaction and working on more challenging job assignments.[36] To use mentoring to your advantage, you first need to understand the various functions mentors can provide. With this information in hand, you are ready to use the various developmental networks that underlie the mentoring process. Let us now consider the functions of mentoring and the developmental networks associated with mentoring.

Bill Wear, a program manager for security at Hewlett-Packard, started out hacking into phone lines at the age of 10. At 14, he hacked into his school computer using a password he'd stolen from his guidance counselor. The counselor knew Wear had stolen the password, so he left this message for him: "I know that you're using my account. I also know about your father. I know he abuses you. I also know that we can do something. Call me. Let me help." The counselor helped get him into a private school, and through two engineering degrees. Wear today is a mentor. He even wrote a handbook for the company's Email-mentoring program.

Functions of Mentoring   Kathy Kram, a Boston University researcher, conducted in-depth interviews with both members of 18 pairs of senior and junior managers. As a by-product of this study, Kram identified two general functions—career and psychosocial—of the mentoring process. Five *career functions* that enhanced career development were sponsorship, exposure-and-visibility, coaching, protection, and challenging assignments. Four *psychosocial functions* were role modeling, acceptance-and-confirmation, counseling, and friendship. The psychosocial functions clarified the participants' identities and enhanced their feelings of competence.[37]

Developmental Networks Underlying Mentoring   Historically, it was thought that mentoring was primarily provided by one person who was called a mentor. Today, however, the changing nature of technology, organizational structures, and marketplace dynamics require us to seek career information and support from many sources. Mentoring is currently viewed as a process in which protégés and protégées seek developmental guidance from a network of people, who are referred to as developers. This implies that the diversity and strength of your network of relationships is instrumental in obtaining the type of career assistance you need to manage your career. Figure 2–4 presents a developmental network typology based on integrating the diversity and strength of developmental relationships.[38]

The diversity of your developmental relationships reflects the variety of people within your network that are used for developmental assistance. There are two subcomponents associated with network diversity: (1) the number of different people you are networked with and (2) the various social systems from which the networked relationships stem (e.g., employer, school, family, community, professional associations, and religious affiliations). As shown in Figure 2–4, developmental relationship diversity ranges from low (few people or social systems) to high (multiple people or social systems). Relationship strength reflects the quality of relationships among you and those involved in your development network. For example, strong ties are

Developmental Networks Associated with Mentoring

FIGURE 2–4

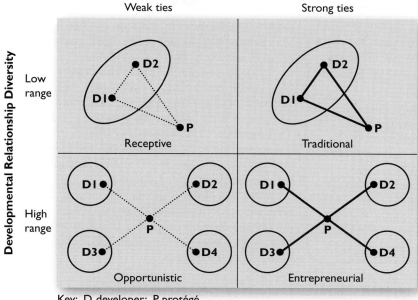

Key: D, developer; P, protégé

SOURCE: M Higgins and K Kram, "Reconceptualizing Mentoring at Work: A Developmental Network Perspective," *Academy of Management Review,* April 2001, p 270.

reflective of relationships based on frequent interactions, reciprocity, and positive affect. Weak ties, in contrast, are based more on superficial relationships. Together, the diversity and strength of your developmental relationships result in four types of developmental networks (see Figure 2–4): receptive, traditional, opportunistic, and entrepreneurial.

A receptive developmental network is composed of a few weak ties from one social system such as your employer or a professional association: The single oval around D1 and D2 in Figure 2–4 is indicative of two developers who come from one social system. In contrast, a traditional network contains a few strong ties between an employee and developers that all come from one social system. An entrepreneurial network, which is the strongest type of developmental network, is made up of strong ties among several developers (D1–D4) who come from four different social systems. Finally, an opportunistic network is associated with having weak ties with multiple developers from different social systems.

Personal and Organizational Implications   There are two key personal implications to consider. First, your job and career satisfaction are likely to be influenced by the consistency between your career goals and the type of developmental network at your disposal. For example, people with an entrepreneurial developmental network are more likely to experience change in their careers and to benefit from personal learning than people with receptive, traditional, and opportunistic networks. If this sounds attractive to you, you should try to increase the

Getting the Most Out of Mentoring

1. Train mentors and protégés/protégées on how to best use career and psychosocial mentoring.

2. Use both formal and informal mentoring, but do not dictate mentoring relationships.

3. Diverse employees should be informed about the benefits and drawbacks associated with establishing mentoring relationships with individuals of similar and different gender and race.

4. Women should be encouraged to mentor others. Perceived barriers need to be addressed and eliminated for this to occur.

5. Increase the number of diverse mentors in high-ranking positions.

diversity and strength of your developmental relationships. In contrast, lower levels of job satisfaction are expected when employees have receptive developmental networks and they desire to experience career advancement in multiple organizations. Receptive developmental networks, however, can be satisfying to someone who does not desire to be promoted up the career ladder.[39] First, a developer's willingness to provide career and psychosocial assistance is a function of the protégé/protégée's ability, potential, and the quality of the interpersonal relationship.[40] This implies that people must take ownership for enhancing their skills, abilities, and developmental networks if they desire to experience career advancement throughout their lives.

Organizationally, it is important to consider whether mentoring should be formal or informal and to implement training programs aimed at helping people to foster high-quality developmental relationships (see Skills & Best Practices).

Fostering Ethical Organizational Behavior

The issue of ethics and ethical behavior is receiving greater attention today. This interest is partly due to reported cases of questionable or potentially unethical behavior and the associated costs. For instance, US industries lose about $400 billion a year from unethical and criminal behavior. Another nationwide survey revealed that 20% of the respondents were asked to do something that violated their ethical standards: 41% complied.[41]

Ethics

Study of moral issues and choices.

Ethics involves the study of moral issues and choices. It is concerned with right versus wrong, good versus bad, and the many shades of gray in supposedly black-and-white issues. Moral implications spring from virtually every decision, both on and off the job. Managers are challenged to have more imagination and the courage to do the right thing. Consider the following managerial decision:

> The parent company of a California utility [Pacific Gas and Electric Co. (PG&E)] awarded about 6,000 bonuses and raises to midlevel managers and other employees hours before the utility filed for bankruptcy.[42]

Do you think that this was a fair and ethical thing to do to the utility's creditors? If you worked at PG&E, would you be happy with this decision? Clearly, any discussion of ethics entails a consideration of the motives and goals of those involved. To enhance your understanding about the causes of ethical and unethical behavior, we present a conceptual framework for making ethical decisions.

A Model of Ethical Behavior

Ethical and unethical conduct is the product of a complex combination of influences (see Figure 2–5). At the center of the model in Figure 2–5 is the individual decision maker. He or she has a unique combination of personality characteristics, values, and

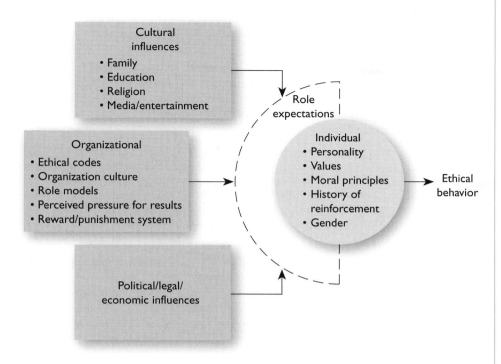

FIGURE 2–5
A Model of
Ethical Behavior
in the
Workplace

moral principles, leaning toward or away from ethical behavior. Personal experience with being rewarded or reinforced for certain behaviors and punished for others also shapes the individual's tendency to act ethically or unethically. Finally, gender plays an important role in explaining ethical behavior. Men and women have significantly different moral orientations toward organizational behavior.[43] This issue is discussed later in this section.

Next, Figure 2–5 illustrates three major sources of influence on one's role expectations. People play many roles in life, including those of employee or manager. One's expectations for how those roles should be played are shaped by cultural, organizational, and general environmental factors.

Focusing on one troublesome source of organizational influence, many studies have found a tendency among middle- and lower-level managers to act unethically in the face of perceived pressure for results. By fostering a pressure-cooker atmosphere for results, managers can unwittingly set the stage for unethical shortcuts by employees who seek to please and be loyal to the company. In contrast, consider how the organizational culture at Timberland reinforces and encourages employees to engage in socially responsible behaviors:

> Everyone gets paid for 40 hours a year of volunteer work. On Timberland's 25th anniversary, the whole place shut down so that employees could work on community projects. One employee described the event as a "religious experience."[44]

This example also highlights that an organization's reward system can influence ethical behavior. Individuals are more likely to behave ethically/unethically when they are given incentives to do so.[45] Managers are encouraged to examine their reward systems to ensure that the preferred types of behavior are being reinforced.

Because ethical or unethical behavior is the result of person–situation interactions, we need to discuss both the decision maker's moral principles and the organization's ethical climate.

Do Moral Principles Vary by Gender?

Yes, men and women view moral problems and situations differently. Carol Gilligan, a psychologist, proposed one underlying cause of these gender differences. Her research suggested that men and women differed in terms of how they conceived moral problems. Males perceived moral problems in terms of a **justice perspective** while women relied on a **care perspective.** The two perspectives are described as follows:

Justice perspective

Based on the ideal of reciprocal rights and driven by rules and regulations.

Care perspective

Involves compassion and an ideal of attention and response to need.

A justice perspective draws attention to problems of inequality and oppression and holds up an ideal of reciprocal rights and equal respect for individuals. A care perspective draws attention to problems of detachment or abandonment and holds up an ideal of attention and response to need. Two moral injunctions, not to treat others unfairly and not to turn away from someone in need, capture these different concerns.[46]

This description underscores the point that men are expected to view moral problems in terms of rights, whereas women are predicted to conceptualize moral problems as an issue of care involving empathy and compassion.

A recent meta-analysis of 113 studies tested these ideas by examining whether or not the justice and care orientations varied by gender. Results did not support Carol Gilligan's expectation that the care perspective was used predominantly by females and the justice orientation predominantly by males.[47] The authors concluded that "although distinct moral orientations may exist, these orientations are not strongly associated with gender."[48] This conclusion suggests that future research is needed to identify the source of moral reasoning differences between men and women.

How to Improve the Organization's Ethical Climate

A team of management researchers recommended the following actions for improving on-the-job ethics.[49]

- *Behave ethically yourself.* Managers are potent role models whose habits and actual behavior send clear signals about the importance of ethical conduct. Ethical behavior is a top-to-bottom proposition.

- *Screen potential employees.* Surprisingly, employers are generally lax when it comes to checking references, credentials, transcripts, and other information on applicant résumés. More diligent action in this area can screen out those given to fraud and misrepresentation. Integrity testing is fairly valid but is no panacea.[50]

- *Develop a meaningful code of ethics.* Codes of ethics can have a positive effect if they satisfy these four criteria:

  1. They are *distributed* to every employee.
  2. They are firmly *supported* by top management.
  3. They refer to *specific* practices and ethical dilemmas likely to be encountered by target employees (e.g., salespersons paying kickbacks, purchasing agents receiving payoffs, laboratory scientists doctoring data, or accountants "cooking the books").

4. They are evenly *enforced* with rewards for compliance and strict penalties for noncompliance.

- *Provide ethics training.* Employees can be trained to identify and deal with ethical issues during orientation and through seminar and video training sessions.

- *Reinforce ethical behavior.* Behavior that is reinforced tends to be repeated, whereas behavior that is not reinforced tends to disappear. Ethical conduct too often is punished while unethical behavior is rewarded.

- *Create positions, units, and other structural mechanisms to deal with ethics.* Ethics needs to be an everyday affair, not a one-time announcement of a new ethical code that gets filed away and forgotten. The Raytheon Company, for example, uses an "Ethics Quick Test" that asks employees to answer a series of questions when faced with ethical dilemmas. The answers help employees determine the best course of action.[51]

chapter summary

- *Discuss the layers and functions of organizational culture.* The three layers of organizational culture are observable artifacts, espoused values, and basic underlying assumptions. Each layer varies in terms of outward visibility and resistance to change. Four functions of organization culture are organizational identity, collective commitment, social system stability, and sense-making device.

- *Discuss the three general types of organizational culture and their associated normative beliefs.* The three general types of organizational culture are constructive, passive–defensive, and aggressive–defensive. Each type is grounded in different normative beliefs. Normative beliefs represent an individual's thoughts and beliefs about how members of a particular group or organization are expected to approach their work and interact with others. A constructive culture is associated with the beliefs of achievement, self-actualizing, humanistic-encouraging, and affiliative. Passive–defensive organizations tend to endorse the beliefs of approval, conventional, dependent, and avoidance. Aggressive–defensive cultures tend to endorse the beliefs of oppositional, power, competitive, and perfectionistic.

- *Summarize the methods used by organizations to embed their cultures.* Embedding a culture amounts to teaching employees about the organization's preferred values, beliefs, expectations, and behaviors. This is accomplished by using one or more of the following 11 mechanisms: (a) formal statements of organizational philosophy, mission, vision, values, and materials used for recruiting, selection, and socialization; (b) the design of physical space, work environments, and buildings; (c) slogans, language, acronyms, and sayings; (d) deliberate role modeling, training programs; teaching, and coaching by managers and supervisors; (e) explicit rewards, status symbols, and promotion criteria; (f) stories, legends, and myths about key people and events; (g) the organizational activities, processes, or outcomes that leaders pay attention to, measure, and control; (h) leader reactions to critical incidents and organizational crises; (i) the workflow and organizational structure; (j) organizational systems and procedures; and (k) organizational goals and associated criteria used for recruitment, selection, development, promotion, layoffs, and retirement of people.

- *Describe the three phases in Feldman's model of organizational socialization.* The three phases of Feldman's model are anticipatory socialization, encounter, and change and acquisition. Anticipatory socialization begins before an individual actually joins the organization. The encounter phase begins when the employment contract has been signed. Phase 3 involves the period in which employees master important tasks and resolve any role conflicts.

- *Explain the four types of development networks derived from a developmental network model of mentoring.* The four development networks are receptive, traditional, entrepreneurial, and opportunistic. A receptive network is composed of a few weak ties from one social system.

A traditional network contains a few strong ties between an employee and developers that all come from one social system. An entrepreneurial network is made up of strong ties among developers from several social systems, and an opportunistic network is associated with having weak ties with multiple developers from different social systems.

- *Specify at least four actions managers can take to improve an organization's ethical climate.* They can do so by (a) behaving ethically themselves, (b) screening potential employees, (c) developing a code of ethics, (d) providing ethics training, (e) reinforcing and rewarding ethical behavior, and (f) creating positions and structural mechanisms dealing with ethics.

internet exercise

This chapter focused on the role of values and beliefs in forming an organization's culture. We also discussed how cultures are embedded and reinforced through socialization and mentoring. The topic of organizational culture is big business on the Internet. Many companies use their Web pages to describe their mission, vision, and corporate values and beliefs. There also are many consulting companies that advertise how they help organizations to change their cultures. The purpose of this exercise is for you to obtain information pertaining to the organizational culture for two different companies. You can go about this task by very simply searching on the key words "organizational culture" or "corporate vision and val-

ues." This search will identify numerous companies for you to use in answering the following questions. You may want to select a company for this exercise that you would like to work for in the future.

QUESTIONS

1. What are the organization's espoused values and beliefs?
2. Using Table 2–1 as a guide, how would you classify the organization's culture? Be sure to provide supporting evidence.

Developing Global Managers

Three

chapter

LEARNING OBJECTIVES

After reading the material in this chapter, you should be able to:

- Explain how to strike a balance between cultural relativism and cultural imperialism and why ethnocentrism can hamper this effort.

- Discuss what Hofstede concluded about the applicability of American management theories in other countries.

- Draw a distinction between individualistic cultures and collectivist cultures.

- Demonstrate your knowledge of these two distinctions: high-context versus low-context cultures and monochronic versus polychronic cultures.

- Explain what cross-cultural studies have found about leadership styles.

- Explain why US managers have a comparatively high failure rate in foreign assignments, and identify an OB trouble spot for each stage of the foreign assignment cycle.

BATTLE LINES BEING DRAWN OVER SAUDI ARABIAN DRESS CODE

WASHINGTON—The US military directive requiring women deployed to Saudi Arabia to wear a head-to-toe robe conflicts with the official guidance that the Saudi government gives to foreigners and also with the State Department's policy for its employees.

The military policy provoked controversy . . . [in 2001] when an outspoken US Air Force female pilot complained that the dress code discriminates against women. Military officials defended the policy. They said it was implemented years ago out of respect for Islamic law and Saudi customs and to protect its women from harassment by the *mutawa,* or religious police, and from potential terrorists.

However, the Saudi government does not require non-Muslim women to wear a dark robe known as an *abaya,* according to the US Embassy in Riyadh, the Saudi capital. The official guidance, issued by the Saudi Embassy in Washington, says that foreigners should dress conservatively but they are not

required to wear the robe, US officials said.

The State Department bases its dress policy on the Saudi guidance. Its employees are not expected to wear an *abaya* when on official duty. When off-duty, women use their own judgment

about wearing the garment.

Military commanders in Saudi Arabia require women to wear an *abaya* and a headscarf when they leave their installations. Maj Martha McSally, the senior female fighter pilot in the Air Force, challenged that policy in an interview with USA TODAY. . . .

McSally, who has been serving in Saudi Arabia since

November [2000], called the dress code "ridiculous and unnecessary." She urged the US command responsible for troops in Saudi Arabia to modify the policy. She argued that women should be able to wear their uniforms on official business and dress in long pants and long-sleeve shirts when off-duty. . . .

Home to the holiest of Islamic sites, Mecca and Medina, Saudi Arabia is a religious state where freedom of worship is not allowed and where freedom of speech, press, and assembly are restricted. Women's rights also are restricted: They can't drive, and they must cover up head-to-foot.

The dress code for foreign women varies in Muslim countries. In general, foreign women are encouraged to dress modestly, but only Iran and Afghanistan require all foreign women to cover their bodies and their hair with a shapeless garment when in public.[1]

> How should US military officials respond to this issue? For an interpretation of this case and additional comments, visit our website:
>
> www.mhhe.com/kinickiob

FOR DISCUSSION

WE HEAR A LOT about the global economy these days. On one level, it all seems so grand, so vague, and so distant. But, on another level, it is here, it is now, and it is *very* personal. For example, consider this scenario:

> Liz awakens to a new workday in her Oregon home as her made-in-China alarm clock buzzes. She flips on a Japanese lamp with a bulb made by Philips, a Dutch company. After showering and applying French makeup, she puts on an outfit sewn in Singapore and slips into her favorite hand-crafted Italian shoes. A quick check of the weather on her assembled-in-Mexico television accompanies a hurried breakfast of juice from Brazilian oranges, an apple from New Zealand, a chunk of Danish cheese, and toast smeared with British marmalade. As she stops her German Mercedes SUV (made in Alabama) to fill up on gasoline refined from Venezuelan crude oil, her cell phone made by Finland's Nokia rings and she chats with her best friend thanks to equipment from Canada's Nortel Networks. Down the road, Liz parks outside the offices of her employer, Intel (the computer chip maker with factories in the United States, Ireland, China, Costa Rica, Malaysia, and Israel that earns most of its money outside the United States).

Yes, welcome to the global economy! And *you* are a big part of it—just check the labels on the products you buy and the clothes on your back. Goods, money, and talent are crossing international borders at an accelerating pace. For better or for worse, even more economic globalization lies ahead. During a protest-marred 2001 summit in Quebec, leaders from 34 Western Hemisphere countries focused on forming, by 2005, "the Free Trade Area of the Americas. Stretching from the Bering Strait to Cape Horn, with a population of 800 million and a combined gross domestic product of more than \$11 trillion, the FTAA would be the largest free-trade zone on the planet."[2] From an OB standpoint, all this means an exponential increase in both cross-cultural interactions and the demand for managers who are comfortable and effective working with people from other countries and cultures.

How ready are you to manage in the burgeoning global economy? Michelango (Mike) Volpi, chief strategist at Cisco Systems, the Internet equipment giant, is an inspiring measuring stick. *Business Week* recently offered this profile:

> With workers from all its acquisitions roaming the halls, Cisco sometimes resembles a mini United Nations. It's the perfect environment for Volpi's multicultural upbringing. Born in Milan to Italian parents, he still holds his Italian citizenship. He spent 12 years in Japan—from age 5 to 17—and speaks three languages: English, Italian, and Japanese. His father, Vittorio Volpi, the head of the Japanese subsidiary of Swiss UBS Bank, says his son has learned flexibility from the Italians, subtlety from the Japanese, and pragmatism and fairness from American business culture. "He is an interesting cocktail of cultures," the elder Volpi says.[3]

Mike Volpi of Cisco Systems.

Indeed, competition for both business and top jobs in the global economy promises to be very tough. The purpose of this chapter is to help you move toward meeting the challenge.

Developing a Global Mind-Set

Managing in a global economy is as much about patterns of thinking and behavior as it is about trade agreements, goods and services, and currency exchange rates. Extended periods in a single dominant culture ingrain assumptions about how things are and should be. Today's managers, whether they work at home for a foreign-owned company or actually work in a foreign country, need to develop a global mind-set (involving open-mindedness, adaptability, and a strong desire to learn).

This section encourages a global mind-set by defining societal culture and contrasting it with organizational culture, discussing differing cultural viewpoints, exploring ways to become a global manager, and examining the applicability of American management theories in other cultures.

A Model of Societal and Organizational Cultures

Societal culture involves "shared meanings" that generally remain below the threshold of conscious awareness because they involve *taken-for-granted assumptions* about how one should perceive, think, act, and feel.[4] Cultural anthropologist Edward T Hall put it this way:

> **Societal culture**
> Socially derived, taken-for-granted assumptions about how to think and act.

> Since much of culture operates outside our awareness, frequently we don't even know what we know. We pick . . . [expectations and assumptions] up in the cradle. We unconsciously learn what to notice and what not to notice, how to divide time and space, how to walk and talk and use our bodies, how to behave as men or women, how to relate to other people, how to handle responsibility, whether experience is seen as whole or fragmented. This applies to all people. The Chinese or the Japanese or the Arabs are as unaware of their assumptions as we are of our own. We each assume that they're part of human nature. What we think of as "mind" is really internalized culture.[5]

Peeling the Cultural Onion   Culture is difficult to grasp because it is multilayered. International management experts Fons Trompenaars (from the Netherlands) and Charles Hampden-Turner (from Britain) offer this instructive analogy in their landmark book, *Riding the Waves of Culture:*

> Culture comes in layers, like an onion. To understand it you have to unpeel it layer by layer.
>   On the outer layer are the products of culture, like the soaring skyscrapers of Manhattan, pillars of private power, with congested public streets between them. These are expressions of deeper values and norms in a society that are not directly visible (values such as upward mobility, "the more-the-better," status, material success). The layers of values and norms are deeper within the "onion," and are more difficult to identify.[6]

Merging Societal and Organizational Cultures   As illustrated in Figure 3–1, culture influences organizational behavior in two ways. Employees bring their societal culture to work with them in the form of customs and language. Organizational culture, a by-product of societal culture, in turn affects the individual's values/ethics, attitudes, assumptions, and expectations.[7] The term *societal* culture is used here instead of national culture because the boundaries of many modern nation-states were not drawn along cultural lines. The former Soviet Union, for example, included 15 republics and more than 100 ethnic nationalities, many with their own distinct

FIGURE 3–1 │ Cultural Influences on Organizational Behavior

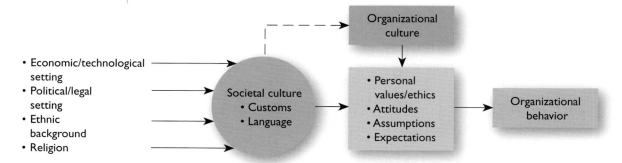

SOURCE: Adapted in part from B J Punnett and S Withane, "Hofstede's Value Survey Module: To Embrace or Abandon?" in *Advances in International Comparative Management*, vol 5, ed S B Prasad (Greenwich, CT: JAI Press, 1990), pp 69–89.

language.[8] Meanwhile, English-speaking Canadians in Vancouver are culturally closer to Americans in Seattle than to their French-speaking compatriots in Quebec. Societal culture is shaped by the various environmental factors listed in the left-hand side of Figure 3–1.

Once inside the organization's sphere of influence, the individual is further affected by the *organization's* culture. Mixing of societal and organizational cultures can produce interesting dynamics in multinational companies. For example, with French and American employees working side by side at General Electric's medical imaging production facility in Waukesha, Wisconsin, unit head Claude Benchimol has witnessed some culture shock:

> The French are surprised the American parking lots empty out as early as 5 PM; the Americans are surprised the French don't start work at 8 AM. Benchimol feels the French are more talkative and candid. Americans have more of a sense of hierarchy and are less likely to criticize. But they may be growing closer to the French. Says Benchimol: "It's taken a year to get across the idea that we are all entitled to say what we don't like to become more productive and work better."[9]

Same company, same company culture, yet GE's French and American co-workers have different attitudes about time, hierarchy, and communication. They are the products of different societal cultures.[10]

When managing people at work, the individual's societal culture, the organizational culture, and any interaction between the two need to be taken into consideration. For example, American workers' cultural orientation toward quality improvement differs significantly from the Japanese cultural pattern:

> Unlike Japanese workers, Americans aren't interested in making small step-by-step improvements to increase quality. They want to achieve the breakthrough, the impossible dream. The way to motivate them: Ask for the big leap, rather than for tiny steps.[11]

Cultural Relativism versus Cultural Imperialism: Balancing Ethical Extremes

When thinking about societal cultures, it is good to remember that nations and ethnic groups have fought countless bloody wars over cultural differences. Something this profound is bound to get in the way when judging the ethics of a cross-cultural

Guidelines for Behavior and Ethics in foreign Cultures: A Balancing Act TABLE 3–1

Cultural Relativism ("When in Rome, do as the Romans do")	Guiding Principles for a Middle Ground	Cultural Imperialism ("The sun never set on the British Empire")
Assumption: Each culture is right in its own way; there are no international or universal standards. **Problems:** • Morally inconsistent. • Fosters "anything is okay" attitude.	• Respect for core human values, which determine the absolute moral threshold for all business activities. • Respect for local traditions. • The belief that context matters when deciding what is right and what is wrong.	**Assumption:** People in all cultures should follow one set of behavioral and ethical standards. **Problems:** • Morally arrogant. • Insensitivity to local cultural traditions and tastes.

SOURCE: Three guidelines in center column quoted from (and other contents of table adapted from) discussion in T Donaldson, "Values in Tension: Ethics Away from Home," *Harvard Business Review*, September–October 1996, pp 48–62.

business deal. A good way to frame the ethical challenge in this area is to distinguish between *cultural relativism* and *cultural imperialism.* "According to cultural relativism, no culture's ethics are better than any other's; therefore there are no international rights and wrongs."[12] Sadly, this viewpoint has led to such unsavory practices as wealthy nations dumping hazardous wastes and selling unsafe products in less-developed countries with lax environmental and consumer protection laws. At the other extreme is cultural imperialism. It, too, has a bad reputation, such as when local populations in the former British Empire were forced to communicate in English and adopt English ways. Resentment against British cultural imperialism still simmers in India, Canada's Quebec Province, Northern Ireland, Scotland, and South Africa.

Global managers need to find a workable middle ground between these two cultural extremes. To facilitate a responsible ethical balance, international business ethics expert Thomas Donaldson suggests three guiding principles (see the middle column of Table 3–1). Ethical judgments in cross-cultural settings need to be made on a systematic decision-by-decision basis—with the guiding principles constantly in mind—and cultural relativism and imperialism pushed aside. But what are the "core human values"? According to respected management teacher and writer Stephen R Covey: "There is little disagreement in what the constitutional principles of a company should be when enough people get together. I find a universal belief in fairness, kindness, dignity, charity, integrity, honesty, quality, service, and patience."[13]

Curbing Ethnocentrism (the Driving force behind Cultural Imperialism)

Ethnocentrism, the belief that one's native country, culture, language, and modes of behavior are superior to all others, has its roots in the dawn of civilization. First identified as a behavioral science concept in 1906, involving the tendency of groups to reject outsiders,[14] the term *ethnocentrism* generally has a more encompassing (national or societal) meaning today. Worldwide evidence of ethnocentrism is plentiful. For example, consider this awkward international incident in a recent news item:

Ethnocentrism

Belief that one's native country, culture, language, and behavior are superior.

Hundreds of Ethnic
Albanians were
persecuted and killed
by ethnocentric Serbs
in Kosovo. Here
Albanians mourn over
relatives and friends
reportedly killed by
Serbian police.

Marine Corps Lt Gen Earl Hailston, the commander of the 26,000 US forces on the
Japanese island of Okinawa, has publicly apologized for calling his hosts "nuts and
a bunch of wimps." He won't be disciplined, the Pentagon said. The three-star general's remark was in an E-mail to officers in which he urged tighter discipline. A
corporal was arrested for lifting a high school girl's skirt to photograph her under-
wear.[15]

Ethnocentrism led to deadly "ethnic cleansing" in Bosnia and Kosovo and genocide
in the African nations of Rwanda and Burundi.

Less dramatic, but still troublesome, is ethnocentrism within managerial and organizational contexts. Experts on the subject framed the problem this way:

> [Ethnocentric managers have] a preference for putting home-country people in key
> positions everywhere in the world and rewarding them more handsomely for work,
> along with a tendency to feel that this group is more intelligent, more capable, or
> more reliable. . . . Ethnocentrism is often not attributable to prejudice as much as to
> inexperience or lack of knowledge about foreign persons and situations. This is not
> too surprising, since most executives know far more about employees in their home
> environments. As one executive put it, "At least I understand why our own man-
> agers make mistakes. With our foreigners, I never know. The foreign managers may
> be better. But if I can't trust a person, should I hire him or her just to prove we're
> multinational?"[16]

Research Insight   Research suggests ethnocentrism is bad for business. A survey of 918 companies with home offices in the United States (272 companies), Japan
(309), and Europe (337) found ethnocentric staffing and human resource policies to be
associated with increased personnel problems. Those problems included recruiting dif-
ficulties, high turnover rates, and lawsuits over personnel policies. Among the
three regional samples, Japanese companies had the most ethnocentric human
resource practices and the most international human resource problems.[17]

Dealing with Ethnocentrism in Ourselves and Others Current and future managers can effectively deal with ethnocentrism through education, greater cross-cultural awareness, international experience, and a conscious effort to value cultural diversity. (Take a moment to complete the Hands-On Exercise.) Results of the Hands-On Exercise need to be interpreted cautiously because this version has not been scientifically validated; thus, it is for instructional and discussion purposes only.

Becoming a Global Manager

On any given day in today's global economy, a manager can interact with colleagues from several different countries or cultures. For instance, at PolyGram, the British music company, the top 33 managers are from 15 different countries.[18] If they are to be effective, managers in such multicultural situations need to develop

Steps You Can Take <u>Now</u> to Become Global Manager Material

Skills	Action Steps
Global perspective	Broaden focus from one or two countries to a global business perspective.
Cultural responsiveness	Become familiar with many cultures.
Appreciate cultural synergies	Learn the dynamics of multicultural situations.
Cultural adaptability	Be able to live and work effectively in many different cultures.
Cross-cultural communication	Engage in cross-cultural interaction every day, whether at home or in a foreign country.
Cross-cultural collaboration	Work effectively in multicultural teams where everyone is equal.
Acquire broad foreign experience	Move up the career ladder by going from one foreign country to another, instead of taking frequent home-country assignments.

SOURCE: Adapted from N J Adler and S Bartholomew, "Managing Globally Competent People," *Academy of Management Executives*, August 1992, Table 1, pp 52–65.

global skills (see Skills & Best Practices). Developing skilled managers who move comfortably from culture to culture takes time. Consider, for example, this comment by the head of Gillette, who wants twice as many global managers on the payroll. "We could try to hire the best and the brightest, but it's the experience with Gillette that we need. About half of our [expatriates] are now on their fourth country—that kind of experience. It takes 10 years to make the kind of Gillette manager I'm talking about."[19]

Importantly, these global skills will help managers in culturally diverse countries such as the United States and Canada do a more effective job on a day-to-day basis.

How Well Do US Management Theories Apply in Other Countries?

The short answer to this important question: *not very well.* This answer derives from a landmark study conducted more than 25 years ago by Dutch researcher Geert Hofstede. His unique cross-cultural comparison of 116,000 IBM employees from 53 countries worldwide focused on four cultural dimensions:

- *Power distance.* How much inequality does someone expect in social situations?
- *Individualism-collectivism.* How loosely or closely is the person socially bonded?
- *Masculinity-femininity.* Does the person embrace stereotypically competitive, performance-oriented masculine traits or nurturing, relationship-oriented feminine traits?
- *Uncertainty avoidance.* How strongly does the person desire highly structured situations?

The US sample ranked relatively low on power distance, very high on individualism, moderately high on masculinity, and low on uncertainty avoidance.[20]

The high degree of variation among cultures led Hofstede to two major conclusions: (1) Management theories and practices need to be adapted to local cultures. This is particularly true for made-in-America management theories (e.g., Maslow's need hierarchy) and Japanese team management practices. *There is no one best way to manage across cultures.*[21] (2) Cultural arrogance is a luxury individuals, companies, and nations can no longer afford in a global economy.

Becoming Cross-Culturally Competent

Cultural anthropologists believe interesting and valuable lessons can be learned by comparing one culture with another. Many dimensions have been suggested over the years to help contrast and compare the world's rich variety of cultures. Four cultural dimensions, especially relevant to present and aspiring global managers, discussed in this section are individualism versus collectivism, high-context and low-context cultures, monochronic and polychronic time orientation, and cross-cultural leadership styles. This list is intended to be indicative rather than exhaustive. Separately or together these cultural distinctions can become huge stumbling blocks when doing business across cultures.

A qualification needs to be offered at this juncture. It is important to view all of the cultural differences in this chapter and elsewhere as *tendencies* and *patterns,* rather than as absolutes. As soon as one falls into the trap of assuming *all* Germans are this, *all* British are that, and so on, potentially instructive generalizations become mindless stereotypes.[22] Well-founded cultural generalizations are fundamental to successfully doing business in other cultures. But one needs to be constantly alert to *individuals* who are exceptions to the local cultural rule. For instance, it is possible to encounter talkative and aggressive Japanese and quiet and deferential Americans who simply do not fit their respective cultural molds. Also, tipping the scale against clear cultural differences are space age transportation; global telecommunications, television, and computer networks; tourism; global marketing; and music and entertainment. These areas are homogenizing the peoples of the world. The result, according to experts on the subject, is an emerging "world culture" in which, someday, people may be more alike than different.[23]

Individualism versus Collectivism

Have you ever been torn between what you personally wanted and what the group, organization, or society expected of you? If so, you have firsthand experience with a fundamental and important cultural distinction: individualism versus collectivism. Awareness of this distinction, as we will soon see, can spell the difference between success and failure in cross-cultural business dealings.

Individualistic cultures, characterized as "I" and "me" cultures, give priority to individual freedom and choice. **Collectivist cultures,** oppositely called "we" and "us" cultures, rank shared goals higher than individual desires and goals. People in collectivist cultures are expected to subordinate their own wishes and goals to those of the relevant social unit. A worldwide survey of 30,000 managers by Trompenaars and Hampden-Turner, who prefer the term *communitarianism* to collectivism, found the highest degree of individualism in Israel, Romania, Nigeria, Canada, and the United States. Countries ranking lowest in individualism—thus qualifying as collectivist cultures—were Egypt, Nepal, Mexico, India, and Japan. Brazil, China, and France also ended up toward the collectivist end of the scale.[24]

Individualistic culture

Primary emphasis on personal freedom and choice.

Collectivist culture

Personal goals less important than community goals and interests.

A Business Success Factor   Of course, one can expect to encounter both individualists and collectivists in culturally diverse countries such as the United States.[25] For example, imagine the frustration of Dave Murphy, a Boston-based mutual fund salesperson, when he recently tried to get Navajo Indians in Arizona interested in saving money for their retirement. After several fruitless meetings with groups of Navajo employees, he was given this cultural insight by a local official: "If you come to this environment, you have to understand that money is different. It's there to be spent. If you have some, you help your family."[26] To traditional Navajos, enculturated as collectivists, saving money is an unworthy act of selfishness. Subsequently, the sales pitch was tailored to emphasize the *family* benefits of individual retirement savings plans.

Allegiance to Whom?   The Navajo example brings up an important point about collectivist cultures. Specifically, which unit of society predominates? For the Navajos, family is the key reference group. But, as Trompenaars and Hampden-Turner observe, important differences exist among collectivist (or communitarian) cultures:

> For each single society, it is necessary to determine the group with which individuals have the closest identification. They could be keen to identify with their trade union, their family, their corporation, their religion, their profession, their nation, or the state apparatus. The French tend to identify with *la France, la famille, le cadre;* the Japanese with the corporation; the former eastern bloc with the Communist Party; and Ireland with the Roman Catholic Church. Communitarian goals may be good or bad for industry depending on the community concerned, its attitude and relevance to business development.[27]

High-Context and Low-Context Cultures

High-context cultures

Primary meaning derived from nonverbal situational cues.

People from **high-context cultures**—including China, Korea, Japan, Vietnam, Mexico, and Arab cultures—rely heavily on situational cues for meaning when perceiving and communicating with others.[28] Nonverbal cues such as one's official position, status, or family connections convey messages more powerfully than do spoken words. Thus, we come to better understand the ritual of exchanging *and reading* business cards in Japan. Japanese culture is relatively high context. One's business card, listing employer and official position, conveys vital silent messages about one's status to members of Japan's homogeneous society. Also, people from high-context cultures who are not especially talkative during a first encounter with a stranger are not necessarily being unfriendly; they are simply taking time to collect "contextual" information.

Low-context cultures

Primary meaning derived from written and spoken words.

Reading the Fine Print in Low-Context Cultures   In **low-context cultures,** written and spoken words carry the burden of shared meanings. Low-context cultures include those found in Germany, Switzerland, Scandinavia, North America, and Great Britain. True to form, Germany has precise written rules for even the smallest details of daily life. In *high*-context cultures, agreements tend to be made on the basis of someone's word or a handshake, after a rather prolonged get-acquainted and trust-building period. Low-context Americans and Canadians, who have cultural roots in Northern Europe, see the handshake as a signal to get a signature on a detailed, lawyer-approved, iron-clad contract.

Avoiding Cultural Collisions   Misunderstanding and miscommunication often are problems in international business dealings when the parties are from high- versus low-context cultures. A Mexican business professor recently made this instructive observation:

Over the years, I have noticed that across cultures there are different opinions on what is expected from a business report. US managers, for instance, take a pragmatic, get-to-the-point approach, and expect reports to be concise and action-oriented. They don't have time to read long explanations: "Just the facts, ma'am."

Latin American managers will usually provide long explanations that go beyond the simple facts. . . .

I have a friend who is the Latin America representative for a United States firm and has been asked by his boss to provide regular reports on sales activities. His reports are long, including detailed explanations on the context in which the events he is reporting on occur and the possible interpretations that they might have. His boss regularly answers these reports with very brief messages, telling him to "cut the crap and get to the point!"[29]

Awkward situations such as this can be avoided when those on both sides of the context divide make good-faith attempts to understand and accommodate their counterparts (see Skills & Best Practices).

Cultural Perceptions of Time

In North American and Northern European cultures, time seems to be a simple matter. It is linear, relentlessly marching forward, never backward, in standardized chunks. To the American who received a watch for his or her third birthday, time is like money. It is spent, saved, or wasted.[30] Americans are taught to show up 10 minutes early for appointments. When working across cultures, however, time becomes a very complex matter.[31] Imagine a New Yorker's chagrin when left in a waiting room for 45 minutes, only to find a Latin American government official dealing with three other people at once. The North American resents the lack of prompt and undivided attention. The Latin American official resents the North American's impatience and apparent self-centeredness.[32] This vicious cycle of resentment can be explained by the distinction between **monochronic time** and **polychronic time**:

The former is revealed in the ordered, precise, schedule-driven use of public time that typifies and even caricatures efficient Northern Europeans and North Americans. The latter is seen in the multiple and cyclical activities and concurrent involvement with different people in Mediterranean, Latin American, and especially Arab cultures.[33]

A Matter of Degree Monochronic and polychronic are relative rather than absolute concepts. Generally, the more things a person tends to do at once, the more polychronic that person is.[34] Thanks to computers and advanced telecommunications systems, highly polychronic managers can engage in "multitasking."[35] For instance, it is possible to talk on the telephone, read and respond to computer E-mail messages, print a report, check a pager message, *and* eat a stale sandwich all at the same time. Unfortunately, this extreme polychronic behavior too often is not as efficient as hoped and can be very stressful. Monochronic people prefer to do one thing at a time. What is your attitude toward time?

SKILLS & BEST PRACTICES

Breaking through the Context Barrier in Culturally Diverse US Workplaces

- People on both sides of the context barrier must be trained to make adjustments.

- A new employee should be greeted by a group consisting of his or her boss, the secretary, several colleagues who have similar duties, and an individual located near the newcomer.

- Background information is essential when explaining anything. Include the history and personalities involved.

- Do not assume the newcomer is self-reliant. Give explicit instructions not only about objectives, but also about the process involved.

- High-context workers from abroad need to learn to ask questions outside their department and function.

- Foreign workers must make an effort to become more self-reliant.

SOURCE: Excerpted from R Drew, "Working with Foreigners," *Management Review*, September 1999, p 6.

Monochronic time

Preference for doing one thing at a time because time is limited, precisely segmented, and schedule driven.

Polychronic time

Preference for doing more than one thing at a time because time is flexible and multidimensional.

Practical Implications   Low-context cultures, such as that of the United States, tend to run on monochronic time while high-context cultures, such as that of Mexico, tend to run on polychronic time. People in polychronic cultures view time as flexible, fluid, and multidimensional. The Germans and Swiss have made an exact science of monochronic time. In fact, a new radio-controlled watch made by a German company, Junghans, is "guaranteed to lose no more than one second in 1 million years."[36] Many a visitor has been a minute late for a Swiss train, only to see its taillights leaving the station. Time is more elastic in polychronic cultures. During the Islamic holy month of Ramadan in Middle Eastern nations, for example, the faithful fast during daylight hours, and the general pace of things markedly slows. Managers need to reset their mental clocks when doing business across cultures.

A Contingency Model for Cross-Cultural Leadership

If a manager has a favorite leadership style in his or her own culture, will that style be equally appropriate in another culture? According to a model that built upon Hofstede's work, the answer is "not necessarily."[37] Four leadership styles—directive, supportive, participative, and achievement—were matched with variations of three of Hofstede's cultural dimensions. The dimensions used were power distance, individualism–collectivism, and uncertainty avoidance.

By combining this model with Hofstede's findings, we derived the useful contingency model for cross-cultural leadership in Table 3–2. Participative leadership turned

TABLE 3–2   A Contingency Model for Cross-Cultural Leadership

Country	_	Most Culturally Appropriate Leadership Behaviors		
Country	Directive	Supportive	Participative	Achievement
Australia		X	X	X
Brazil	X		X	
Canada		X	X	X
France	X		X	
Germany*		X	X	X
Great Britain		X	X	X
Hong Kong**	X	X	X	X
India	X		X	X
Italy	X	X	X	
Japan	X	X	X	
Korea	X	X	X	
Netherlands		X	X	X
New Zealand			X	X
Pakistan	X	X	X	
Philippines	X	X	X	X
Sweden			X	X
Taiwan	X	X	X	
United States		X	X	X

*Former West Germany.
**Reunited with China.
SOURCES: Adapted in part from C A Rodrigues, "The Situation and National Culture as Contingencies for Leadership Behavior: Two Conceptual Models," in *Advances in International Comparative Management*, vol. 5, ed S B Prasad (Greenwich, CT: JAI Press, 1990), pp 51–68; and G Hofstede and M H Bond, "The Confucius Connection: From Cultural Roots to Economic Growth," *Organizational Dynamics*, Spring 1988, pp 4–21.

out to be culturally appropriate for all 18 countries. Importantly, this does *not* mean that the participative style is necessarily the *best* style of leadership in cross-cultural management. It simply has broad applicability. One exception surfaced in a more recent study in Russia's largest textile mill. The researchers found that both rewarding good performance with American-made goods and motivating performance with feedback and positive reinforcement improved output. But an employee participation program actually made performance *worse*. This may have been due to the Russians' lack of faith in participative schemes, which were found to be untrustworthy in the past.[38]

Also of note, with the exception of France, the directive style appears to be culturally *inappropriate* in North America, Northern Europe, Australia, and New Zealand. Some locations, such as Hong Kong and the Philippines, require great leadership versatility. Leadership needs to be matched to the prevailing cultural climate. (We will discuss leadership further in Chapter 14.)

Preparing for a Foreign Assignment

As the reach of global companies continues to grow, many opportunities for living and working in foreign countries will arise. Imagine, for example, the opportunities for foreign duty and cross-cultural experiences at Gillette, the maker of razors and other personal-care products. According to company calculations, an estimated 1.2 billion members of the world's population use a Gillette product on any given day.[39] Foreign business accounts for 70% of Gillette's annual sales of nearly $10 billion.[40] As mentioned earlier, Gillette and other global players need a vibrant and growing cadre of employees who are willing and able to do business across cultures. Thus, the purpose of this final section is to help you prepare yourself and others to work successfully in foreign countries.

A Poor Track Record for American Expatriates

As we use the term here, **expatriate** refers to anyone living and/or working outside their home country. Hence, they are said to be *expatriated* when transferred to another country and *repatriated* when transferred back home. US expatriate managers usually are characterized as culturally inept and prone to failure on international assignments. Sadly, research supports this view. A pair of international management experts recently offered this assessment:

> **Expatriate**
>
> Anyone living or working in a foreign country.

> Over the past decade, we have studied the management of expatriates at about 750 US, European, and Japanese companies. We asked both the expatriates themselves and the executives who sent them abroad to evaluate their experiences. In addition, we looked at what happened after expatriates returned home. . . .
>
> Overall, the results of our research were alarming. We found that between 10% and 20% of all US managers sent abroad returned early because of job dissatisfaction or difficulties in adjusting to a foreign country. Of those who stayed for the duration, nearly one-third did not perform up to the expectations of their superiors. And perhaps most problematic, one-fourth of those who completed an assignment left their company, often to join a competitor, within one year after repatriation. That's a turnover rate double that of managers who did not go abroad.[41]

Because of the high cost of sending employees and their families to foreign countries for extended periods, significant improvement is needed.

Research has uncovered specific reasons for the failure of US expatriate managers. Listed in decreasing order of frequency, the seven most common reasons are as follows:

1. The manager's spouse cannot adjust to new physical or cultural surroundings.
2. The manager cannot adapt to new physical or cultural surroundings.
3. Family problems.
4. The manager is emotionally immature.
5. The manager cannot cope with foreign duties.
6. The manager is not technically competent.
7. The manager lacks the proper motivation for a foreign assignment.[42]

Collectively, *family and personal adjustment problems,* not technical competence, are the main stumbling block for American managers working in foreign countries.

This conclusion is reinforced by the results of a survey that asked 72 human resource managers at multinational corporations to identify the most important success factor in a foreign assignment. "Nearly 35% said cultural adaptability: patience, flexibility, and tolerance for others' beliefs. Only 22% of them listed technical and management skills."[43] A recent Australian study documented how preparing the *entire family* for a foreign assignment was a key success factor.[44] Clearly, US multinational companies need to do a better job of managing the foreign assignment cycle.

Some Good News: North American Women on Foreign Assignments

Historically, a woman from the United States or Canada on a foreign assignment was a rarity. Things are changing, albeit slowly. A review of research evidence and anecdotal accounts uncovered these insights:

Research shows that being an expatriate is a bigger hurdle to "fitting in" or socializing in a foreign business culture than being a woman.

- The proportion of corporate women from North America on foreign assignments grew from about 3% in the early 1980s to between 11% and 15% in the late 1990s.
- Self-disqualification and management's assumption that women would not be welcome in foreign cultures—not foreign prejudice, itself—are the primary barriers for potential female expatriates.
- Expatriate North American women are viewed first and foremost by their hosts as being foreigners, and only secondarily as being female.
- North American women have a very high success rate on foreign assignments.[45]

Considering the rapidly growing demand for global managers today, self-disqualification by women and management's prejudicial policies are counterproductive. Our advice to women who have their heart set on a foreign assignment: "Go for it!"

The Foreign Assignment Cycle (with OB Trouble Spots)   **FIGURE 3–2**

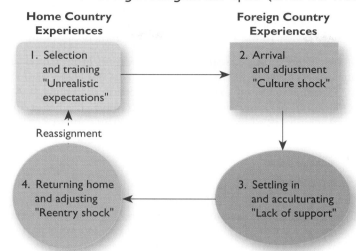

Avoiding OB Trouble Spots in the Foreign Assignment Cycle

Finding the right person (often along with a supportive and adventurous family) for a foreign position is a complex, time-consuming, and costly process.[46] For our purposes, it is sufficient to narrow the focus to common OB trouble spots in the foreign assignment cycle. As illustrated in Figure 3–2, the first and last stages of the cycle occur at home. The middle two stages occur in the foreign or host country. Each stage hides an OB-related trouble spot that needs to be anticipated and neutralized. Otherwise, the bill for another failed foreign assignment will grow.

Avoiding Unrealistic Expectations with Cross-Cultural Training

Realistic job previews (RJPs) have proven effective at bringing people's unrealistic expectations about a pending job assignment down to earth by providing a realistic balance of good and bad news. People with realistic expectations tend to quit less often and be more satisfied than those with unrealistic expectations. RJPs are a must for future expatriates. In addition, cross-cultural training is required.

Cross-cultural training is any type of structured experience designed to help departing employees adjust to a foreign culture. The trend is toward more such training. Although costly, companies believe cross-cultural training is less expensive than failed foreign assignments. Programs vary widely in type and also in rigor.[47] Of course, the greater the difficulty, the greater the time and expense:

> **Cross-cultural training**
>
> Structured experiences to help people adjust to a new culture/country.

* *Easiest.* Predeparture training is limited to informational materials, including books, lectures, films, videos, and Internet searches.
* *Moderately difficult.* Experiential training is conducted through case studies, role playing, assimilators (simulated intercultural incidents), and introductory language instruction.

• *Most difficult.* Departing employees are given some combination of the preceding methods plus comprehensive language instruction and field experience in the target culture. As an example of the latter, PepsiCo Inc. transfers "about 25 young foreign managers a year to the US for one-year assignments in bottling plants."[48]

Which approach is the best? Research to date does not offer a final answer. One study involving US employees in South Korea led the researcher to recommend a *combination* of informational and experiential predeparture training.[49] As a general rule of thumb, the more rigorous the cross-cultural training, the better. Our personal experience with teaching OB to foreign students both in the United States and abroad reminds us that there really is no substitute for an intimate knowledge of the local language and culture.[50]

Avoiding Culture Shock Have you ever been in a totally unfamiliar situation and felt disoriented and perhaps a bit frightened? If so, you already know something about culture shock. According to anthropologists, **culture shock** involves anxiety and doubt caused by an overload of unfamiliar expectations and social cues.[51] College freshmen often experience a variation of culture shock. An expatriate manager, or family member, may be thrown off balance by an avalanche of strange sights, sounds, and behaviors. Among them may be unreadable road signs, strange-tasting food, inability to use your left hand for social activities (in Islamic countries, the left hand is the toilet hand), or failure to get a laugh with your sure-fire joke. For the expatriate manager trying to concentrate on the fine details of a business negotiation, culture shock is more than an embarrassing inconvenience. It is a disaster! Like the confused college freshman who quits and goes home, culture-shocked employees often panic and go home early.

> **Culture shock**
>
> Anxiety and doubt caused by an overload of new expectations and cues.

The best defense against culture shock is comprehensive cross-cultural training, including intensive language study. Once again, the only way to pick up subtle—yet important—social cues is via the local language. Quantum, the Milpitas, California, maker of computer hard-disk drives has close ties to its manufacturing partner in Japan, Matsushita-Kotobuki Electronics (MKE):

> MKE is constantly proposing changes in design that make new disk drives easier to manufacture. When the product is ready for production, 8 to 10 Quantum engineers descend on MKE's plant in western Japan for at least a month. To smooth teamwork, Quantum is offering courses in Japanese language and culture, down to mastering etiquette at a tea ceremony.[52]

This type of program reduces culture shock by taking the anxiety-producing mystery out of an unfamiliar culture.[53]

Support During the Foreign Assignment Especially during the first six months, when everything is so new to the expatriate, a support system needs to be in place.[54] *Host-country sponsors,* assigned to individual managers or families, are recommended because they serve as "cultural seeing-eye dogs." In a foreign country, where even the smallest errand can turn into an utterly exhausting production, sponsors can get things done quickly because they know the cultural and geographical territory. Honda's Ohio employees, for example, enjoyed the help of family sponsors when training in Japan:

> Honda smoothed the way with Japanese wives who once lived in the US. They handled emergencies such as when Diana Jett's daughter Ashley needed stitches in her

chin. When Task Force Senior Manager Kim Smalley's daughter, desperate to fit in at elementary school, had to have a precisely shaped bag for her harmonica, a Japanese volunteer stayed up late to make it.[55]

Avoiding Reentry Shock   Strange as it may seem, many otherwise successful expatriate managers encounter their first major difficulty only after their foreign assignment is over. Why? Returning to one's native culture is taken for granted because it seems so routine and ordinary. But having adjusted to another country's way of doing things for an extended period of time can put one's own culture and surroundings in a strange new light. Three areas for potential reentry shock are work, social activities, and general environment (e.g., politics, climate, transportation, food). Ira Caplan's return to New York City exemplifies reentry shock:

> During the past 12 years, living mostly in Japan, he and his wife had spent their vacations cruising the Nile or trekking in Nepal. They hadn't seen much of the US. They are getting an eyeful now. . . .
> Prices astonish him. The obsession with crime unnerves him. What unsettles Mr Caplan more, though, is how much of himself he has left behind.
> In a syndrome of return no less stressful than that of departure, he feels displaced, disregarded, and diminished. . . .
> In an Italian restaurant, crowded at lunchtime, the waiter sets a bowl of linguine in front of him. Mr Caplan stares at it. "In Asia, we have smaller portions and smaller people," he says.
> Asia is on his mind. He has spent years cultivating an expertise in a region of huge importance. So what? This is New York.[56]

Work-related adjustments were found to be a major problem for samples of repatriated Finnish, Japanese, and American employees.[57] Upon being repatriated, a 12-year veteran of one US company said: "Our organizational culture was turned upside down. We now have a different strategic focus, different 'tools' to get the job done, and different buzzwords to make it happen. I had to learn a whole new corporate 'language.' "[58] Reentry shock can be reduced through employee career counseling and home-country sponsors. Simply being aware of the problem of reentry shock is a big step toward effectively dealing with it.[59]

Overall, the key to a successful foreign assignment is making it a well-integrated link in a career chain rather than treating it as an isolated adventure.

chapter summary

- *Explain how to strike a balance between cultural relativism and cultural imperialism and why ethnocentrism can hamper this effort.* Cultural relativism is the belief that each culture is correct in its own way and there are no international standards for conduct and ethics. Oppositely, cultural imperialism occurs when one nation's practices and ethics are forced on others as universal standards. Cultural imperialism thrives on ethnocentrism, a belief in the superiority of one's own culture, language, and ways. Donaldson's middle ground calls for three guiding principles: (a) respect for core

human values, (b) respect for local traditions, and (c) considering the context when distinguishing right from wrong.

- *Discuss what Hofstede concluded about the applicability of American management theories in other countries.* Due to the wide variations on key dimensions Hofstede found among cultures, he warned against directly applying American-made management theories to other cultures without adapting them first. He said there is no one best way to manage across cultures.

- *Draw a distinction between individualistic cultures and collectivist cultures.* People in individualistic cultures think primarily in terms of "I" and "me" and place a high value on freedom and personal choice. Collectivist cultures teach people to be "we" and "us" oriented and to subordinate personal wishes and goals to the interests of the relevant social unit (such as family, group, organization, or society).

- *Demonstrate your knowledge of these two distinctions: high-context versus low-context cultures and monochronic versus polychronic cultures.* People in high-context cultures (such as China, Japan, and Mexico) derive great meaning from situational cues, above and beyond written and spoken words. Low-context cultures (including Germany, the United States, and Canada) derive key information from precise and brief written and spoken messages. In monochronic cultures (e.g., the United States), time is precise and rigidly measured. Polychronic cultures, such as those found in Latin America and the Middle East, view time as multidimensional, fluid, and flexible. Monochronic people prefer to do one thing at a time, while polychronic people like to tackle multiple tasks at the same time.

- *Explain what cross-cultural studies have found about leadership styles.* One cross-cultural management study suggests the need to vary leadership styles from one culture to another. The participative style turned out to be the only leadership style applicable in all 18 countries studied. Still, the participative style has its limitations and is not universally effective.

- *Explain why US managers have a comparatively high failure rate in foreign assignments, and identify an OB trouble spot for each stage of the foreign assignment cycle.* American expatriates are troubled by family and personal adjustment problems; in other words, cultural problems, *not* technical competence problems. The four stages of the foreign assignment cycle (and OB trouble spots) are (a) selection and training (unrealistic expectations), (b) arrival and adjustment (culture shock), (c) settling in and acculturating (lack of support), and (d) returning home and adjusting (reentry shock).

internet exercise

www.lonelyplanet.com

Thanks to the power of the Internet you can take a trip to a far-flung corner of the world without ever leaving your chair. The purpose of this exercise is to enhance your cross-cultural awareness by using the Internet to learn about a foreign country of your choice. Our primary resource is the Internet site **www.lonelyplanet.com** based on the popular, highly readable, and somewhat off-beat Lonely Planet travel guides available in bookstores. (This is our favorite, but if you prefer another online travel guide, use it and tell others.) At the Lonely Planet Online home page, select "worldguide" from the main menu. Use the geographic menus on the Destinations page to *select a foreign country where your native language is not the primary language.* Explore the map of your selected country and then read the material in the "Facts for the Trav-eler," "History," and "Culture" sections. If you have the time and interest, read some of the other relevant sections such as "Money & Costs" and "Attractions."

QUESTIONS

1. How strong is your interest in taking a foreign assignment in your selected country? Explain.

2. Culturally, does your focus country seem to be high-context or low-context, individualistic or collectivist, and monochronic or polychronic? Cite specific clues from your Internet research.

3. What is the likelihood of experiencing "culture shock" in this country? How could you avoid or minimize it?

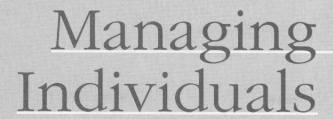

Managing Individuals

SOURCE: © PhotoDisc

Part Two

Understanding Social Perception and Managing Diversity

four
chapter

LEARNING OBJECTIVES

After reading the material in this chapter, you should be able to:

- Describe *perception* in terms of the social information processing model.

- Identify and briefly explain four managerial implications of social perception.

- Explain, according to Kelley's model, how external and internal causal attributions are formulated.

- Demonstrate your familiarity with the demographic trends that are creating an increasingly diverse workforce.

- Identify the barriers and challenges to managing diversity.

- Discuss the organizational practices used to manage diversity identified by Ann Morrison.

JOB OPPORTUNITIES INCREASE FOR HISPANICS

Corina Alvarez is the face of the new American workforce.

She's young, she's Hispanic, and she's very much in demand. Consider what happened when the 31-year-old Cuban-American went looking for a job. She wasn't too impressed by traditional job boards. But as soon as she posted her résumé on an online Hispanic job board, calls and contacts from companies came tumbling in.

"It was so exciting. I had zillions of calls from recruiters and companies," says Alvarez, now the public relations manager at a Miami-based Internet firm. "Companies are realizing that the more familiar they become with Hispanic culture and language, the more opportunities there will be for them. It's smart business sense."

It's a message more employers are heeding. As Hispanics continue to make up an ever-growing share of the American workforce, corporate America is responding with a simple message: *Bienvenidos,* or welcome. Businesses including PepsiCo, Chevron, Coors Brewing, and PricewaterhouseCoopers are stepping up recruitment and retention efforts. They're hir-

ing interpreters, translating employee handbooks into Spanish, and launching mentoring programs.

An unprecedented demographic shift is behind the emphasis.

The number of Hispanics in the country has surged nearly 60% since 1990—to 35.3 million—putting the population at a virtual tie with African-Americans as the nation's largest minority group, according to recently released census data. The increase is about 3 million more than had been projected. Meanwhile, the number of non-Hispanic whites increased by 5.3%.

As Hispanic workers make up an increasing number of clients, customers, and potential hires, employers are reaching out to this demographic group as a matter of business survival.[1]

What are the managerial opportunities and challenges associated with the changing demographics of the American workforce? For an interpretation on this case and additional comments, visit our Web site:

www.mhhe.com/kinickiob

FOR DISCUSSION

WHAT ARE YOUR PERCEPTIONS and feelings about the opening case? Do you think that different ethnic or racial groups are treated equally in the workplace? Your perceptions and feelings most likely are influenced by information you have received from newspapers, magazines, television, radio, family, and friends. You see, we all use information stored in our memories to interpret the world around us, and our interpretations, in turn, influence how we respond and interact with others. As human beings, we constantly strive to make sense of our surroundings. The resulting knowledge influences our behavior and helps us navigate our way through life. Think of the perceptual process that occurs when meeting someone for the first time. Your attention is drawn to the individual's physical appearance, mannerisms, actions, and reactions to what you say and do. You ultimately arrive at conclusions based on your perceptions of this social interaction. The brown-haired, green-eyed individual turns out to be friendly and fond of outdoor activities. You further conclude that you like this person and then ask him or her to go to a concert, calling the person by the name you stored in memory.

This reciprocal process of perception, interpretation, and behavioral response also applies at work. Consider the situation faced by Cornelius Cooper, an African-American lineman at Georgia Power Company:

> He says he was passed over for promotion, subjected to racial slurs, and repeatedly spray-painted in his genital area by white employees. Worse, co-workers made light of lynchings, tied hangman's nooses in his presence, and often left such knots displayed in company facilities. . . . In July, Mr Cooper and two others filed a lawsuit alleging that managers at Georgia Power Co. and its parent, Southern Co., unfairly denied promotions to African-American workers, gave lower pay to black employees than to similarly qualified whites, and were indifferent to overt harassment of blacks. Attached to the charges, which the companies vigorously deny, was an 8-by-10 color photograph of a noose hanging inside a company building in Cornelia, [Georgia]. Executives at Georgia Power and its parent company were taken aback. But their surprise wasn't at finding a noose on the premises; it was in discovering that African-Americans could be offended by one.[2]

Mr Cooper is suing because he perceives that his employer has a hostile work environment that is discriminatory. In contrast, David Ratcliffe, Georgia Power's president and chief executive, told a reporter from *The Wall Street Journal* that he did not perceive or think of nooses in a racial context until the lawsuit was filed. He now feels that displaying nooses is offensive.[3] This example illustrates the interplay between perceptual processes and managing diverse employees.

Managing diversity is a sensitive, potentially volatile, and sometimes uncomfortable issue. Yet managers are required to deal with it in the name of organizational survival. Accordingly, the purpose of this chapter is to enhance your understanding of the perceptual process and how it influences the manner in which managers manage diversity. We begin by focusing on a social information processing model of perception and then discuss the perceptual outcome of causal attributions. Next, we define diversity and describe the organizational practices used to manage diversity effectively.

A Social Information Processing Model of Perception

Perception is a cognitive process that enables us to interpret and understand our surroundings. Recognition of objects is one of this process's major functions. For example, both people and animals recognize familiar objects in their environments. You would recognize a picture of your best friend; dogs and cats can recognize their food dishes or a favorite toy. Reading involves recognition of visual patterns representing letters in the alphabet. People must recognize objects to meaningfully interact with their environment. But since OB's principal focus is on people, the following discussion emphasizes *social* perception rather than object perception.

> **Perception**
> Process of interpreting one's environment.

Social perception involves a four-stage information processing sequence (hence, the label "social information processing"). Figure 4–1 illustrates a basic social information processing model. Three of the stages in this model—selective attention/comprehension, encoding and simplification, and storage and retention—describe how specific social information is observed and stored in memory. The fourth and final stage, retrieval and response, involves turning mental representations into real-world judgments and decisions.

Keep the following everyday example in mind as we look at the four stages of social perception. Suppose you were thinking of taking a course in, say, personal finance. Three professors teach the same course, using different types of instruction and testing procedures. Through personal experience, you have come to prefer good professors who rely on the case method of instruction and essay tests. According to social perception theory, you would likely arrive at a decision regarding which professor to take following the steps outlined in the following sections.

Stage 1: Selective Attention/Comprehension

People are constantly bombarded by physical and social stimuli in the environment. Because they do not have the mental capacity to fully comprehend all this information, they selectively perceive subsets of environmental stimuli. This is where attention plays a role. **Attention** is the process of becoming consciously aware of something or someone. Attention can be focused on information either from the environment or from memory. Regarding the latter situation, if you sometimes find yourself thinking about

> **Attention**
> Being consciously aware of something or someone.

Social Perception: A Social Information Processing Model   **FIGURE 4–1**

SOURCE: *Organizational Behavior* (5th ed) (McGraw-Hill), p 173.

If you're reading this textbook late at night and having a munchies attack, this photo might have caught your attention before anything else on the page. It's an example of *salient* stimuli, or something that stands out from its context. The context for this example is the text on this page. One's needs or goals often affect what stimuli are salient. If you're having a munchie attack, a Big Mac would be *very* salient right now.

totally unrelated events or people while reading a textbook, your memory is the focus of your attention. Research has shown that people tend to pay attention to salient stimuli.

Salient Stimuli   Somethings is *salient* when it stands out from its context. For example, a 250-pound man would certainly be salient in a women's aerobics class but not at a meeting of the National Football League Players' Association. One's needs and goals often dictate which stimuli are salient. For a driver whose gas gauge is on empty, an Exxon or Shell sign is more salient than a McDonald's or Burger King sign. The reverse would be true for a hungry driver with a full gas tank. Moreover, research shows that people have a tendency to pay more attention to negative than positive information. This leads to a negativity bias.[4] This bias helps explain the gawking factor that slows traffic to a crawl following a car accident.

Back to Our Example   You begin your search for the "right" personal finance professor by asking friends who have taken classes from the three professors. You also may interview the various professors who teach the class to gather still more relevant information. Returning to Figure 4–1, all the information you obtain represents competing environmental stimuli labeled A through F. Because you are concerned about the method of instruction (e.g., line A in Figure 4–1), testing procedures (e.g., line C), and past grade distributions (e.g., line F), information in those areas is particularly salient to you. Figure 4–1 shows that these three salient pieces of information thus are perceived, and you then progress to the second stage of information processing. Meanwhile, competing stimuli represented by lines B, D, and E in Figure 4–1 fail to get your attention and are discarded from further consideration.

Stage 2: Encoding and Simplification

Observed information is not stored in memory in its original form. Encoding is required; raw information is interpreted or translated into mental representations. To accomplish this, perceivers assign pieces of information to **cognitive categories.** "By *category* we mean a number of objects that are considered equivalent. Categories are generally designated by names, e.g., *dog, animal*."[5] People, events, and objects are interpreted and evaluated by comparing their characteristics with information contained in schemata (or schema in singular form).

Cognitive categories

Mental depositories for storing information.

Schema   According to social information processing theory, a **schema** represents a person's mental picture or summary of a particular event or type of stimulus.[6] For example, picture your image of a sports car. Does it contain a smaller vehicle with two doors? Is it red? If you answered yes, you would tend to classify all small, two-door, fire-engine-red vehicles as sports cars because this type of car possesses characteristics that are consistent with your "sports car schema."

Schema

Mental picture of an event or object.

Stereotypes Are Used During Encoding   People use stereotypes during encoding in order to organize and simplify social information.[7] "A **stereotype** is an individual's set of beliefs about the characteristics or attributes of a group."[8] Stereotypes are not always negative. For example, the belief that engineers are good at math is certainly part of a stereotype. Stereotypes may or may not be accurate. Engineers may in fact be better at math than the general population. In general, stereotypic characteristics are used to differentiate a particular group of people from other groups.

> **Stereotype**
>
> Beliefs about the characteristics of a group.

Unfortunately, stereotypes can lead to poor decisions; can create barriers for women, older individuals, people of color, and people with disabilities; and can undermine loyalty and job satisfaction. For example, a recent study of 44 African-American managers and 80 white managers revealed that African-American managers experienced slower rates of promotion and less psychological support than white managers.[9] Another sample of 69 female executives and 69 male executives indicated women reported greater promotional barriers, fewer overseas assignments, and had more assignments with nonauthority relationships than men.[10]

Encoding Outcomes   We use the encoding process to interpret and evaluate our environment. Interestingly, this process can result in differing interpretations and evaluations of the same person or event. Table 4–1 describes five common

Commonly Found Perceptual Errors   TABLE 4–1

Perceptual Error	Description	Example
Halo	A rater forms an overall impression about an object and then uses that impression to bias ratings about the object.	Rating a professor high on the teaching dimensions of ability to motivate students, knowledge, and communication because we like him or her.
Leniency	A personal characteristic that leads an individual to consistently evaluate other people or objects in an extremely positive fashion.	Rating a professor high on all dimensions of performance regardless of his or her actual performance. The rater who hates to say negative things about others.
Central tendency	The tendency to avoid all extreme judgments and rate people and objects as average or neutral.	Rating a professor average on all dimensions of performance regardless of his or her actual performance.
Recency effects	The tendency to remember recent information. If the recent information is negative, the person or object is evaluated negatively.	Although a professor has given good lectures for 12 to 15 weeks, he or she is evaluated negatively because lectures over the last 3 weeks were done poorly.
Contrast effects	The tendency to evaluate people or objects by comparing them with characteristics of recently observed people or objects.	Rating a good professor as average because you compared his or her performance with three of the best professors you have ever had in college. You are currently taking courses from the three excellent professors.

This ad is a public service message that promotes the value of disabled people. It attempts to break down the *stereotypes* that often cause companies to overlook or simply not hire disabled workers.

perceptual errors that influence our judgments about others. Because these perceptual errors often distort the evaluation of job applicants and of employee performance, managers need to guard against them.

Back to Our Example Having collected relevant information about the three personal finance professors and their approaches, you compare this information with other details contained in schemata. This leads you to form an impression and evaluation of what it would be like to take a course from each professor. In turn, the relevant information contained on paths A, C, and F in Figure 4–1 are passed along to the third stage of information processing.

Stage 3: Storage and Retention

This phase involves storage of information in long-term memory. Long-term memory is like an apartment complex consisting of separate units connected to one another. Although different people live in each apartment, they sometimes interact. In addition, large apartment complexes have different wings (such as A, B, and C). Long-term memory similarly consists of separate but related categories. Like the individual apartments inhabited by unique residents, the connected categories contain different types of information. Information also passes among these categories. Finally, long-term memory is made up of three compartments (or wings) containing categories of information about events, semantic materials, and people.[11]

Event Memory This compartment is composed of categories containing information about both specific and general events. These memories describe appropriate sequences of events in well-known situations, such as going to a restaurant, going on a job interview, going to a food store, or going to a movie.[12]

Semantic Memory Semantic memory refers to general knowledge about the world. In so doing, it functions as a mental dictionary of concepts. Each concept contains a definition (e.g., a good leader) and associated traits (outgoing), emotional states (happy), physical characteristics (tall), and behaviors (works hard). Just as there are schemata for general events, concepts in semantic memory are stored as schemata. Given our previous discussion of international OB in Chapter 3, it should come as no surprise that there are cultural differences in the type of information stored in semantic memory.

Person Memory Categories within this compartment contain information about a single individual (your supervisor) or groups of people (managers).

Back to Our Example   As the time draws near for you to decide which personal finance professor to take, your schemata of them are stored in the three categories of long-term memory. These schemata are available for immediate comparison and/or retrieval.

Stage 4: Retrieval and Response

People retrieve information from memory when they make judgments and decisions. Our ultimate judgments and decisions are either based on the process of drawing on, interpreting, and integrating categorical information stored in long-term memory or on retrieving a summary judgment that was already made.[13]

Concluding our example, it is registration day and you have to choose which professor to take for personal finance. After retrieving from memory your schemata-based impressions of the three professors, you select a good one who uses the case method and gives essay tests (line C in Figure 4–1). In contrast, you may choose your preferred professor by simply recalling the decision you made two weeks ago.

Managerial Implications

Social cognition is the window through which we all observe, interpret, and prepare our responses to people and events. A wide variety of managerial activities, organizational processes, and quality-of-life issues are thus affected by perception. Consider, for example, the following implications.

Hiring   Interviewers make hiring decisions based on their impression of how an applicant fits the perceived requirements of a job. Inaccurate impressions in either direction produce poor hiring decisions. Moreover, interviewers with racist or sexist schemata can undermine the accuracy and legality of hiring decisions. Those invalid schemata need to be confronted and improved through coaching and training. Failure to do so can lead to poor hiring decisions. For example, a study of 46 male and 66 female financial institution managers revealed that their hiring decisions were biased by the physical attractiveness of applicants. More attractive men and women were hired over less attractive applicants with equal qualifications.[14] On the positive side, however, a recent study demonstrated that interviewer training can reduce the use of invalid schema. Training improved interviewers' ability to obtain high-quality, job-related information and to stay focused on the interview task. Trained interviewers provided more balanced judgments about applicants than did nontrained interviewers.[15]

Performance Appraisal   Faulty schemata about what constitutes good versus poor performance can lead to inaccurate performance appraisals, which erode work motivation, commitment, and loyalty. For example, a recent study of 166 production employees indicated that they had greater trust in management when they perceived that the performance appraisal process provided accurate evaluations of their performance.[16] Therefore, it is important for managers to accurately identify the behavioral characteristics and results indicative of good performance at the beginning of a performance review cycle. These characteristics then can serve as the benchmarks for evaluating employee performance. The importance of using objective rather than subjective measures of employee performance was highlighted in a meta-analysis involving 50 studies and 8,341 individuals. Results revealed that objective and subjective measures of employee performance were only moderately related. The researchers concluded that objective and subjective measures of performance are not inter-changeable.[17] Managers are thus advised to use more objectively based measures of performance as much as possible because subjective indicators are prone to bias and inaccuracy. In those cases where the job does not possess objective measures of per-formance, however, managers should still use subjective evaluations. Furthermore, because memory for specific instances of employee performance deteriorates over time, managers need a mechanism for accurately recalling employee behavior. Research reveals that individuals can be trained to be more accurate raters of performance.[18]

Leadership   Research demonstrates that employees' evaluations of leader effec-tiveness are influenced strongly by their schemata of good and poor leaders. A leader will have a difficult time influencing employees when he or she exhibits behaviors contained in employees' schemata of poor leaders. A team of researchers investigated the behaviors contained in our schemata of good and poor leaders. Good leaders were perceived as exhibiting the following behaviors: (1) assigning specific tasks to group members, (2) telling others that they had done well, (3) setting specific goals for the group, (4) letting other group members make decisions, (5) trying to get the group to work as a team, and (6) maintaining definite standards of performance. In contrast, poor leaders were perceived to exhibit these behaviors: (1) telling others that they had performed poorly, (2) insisting on having their own way, (3) doing things with-out explaining themselves, (4) expressing worry over the group members' sugges-tions, (5) frequently changing plans, and (6) letting the details of the task become overwhelming.[19]

Communication   Managers need to remember that social perception is a screen-ing process that can distort communication, both coming and going. Messages are interpreted and categorized according to schemata developed through past experiences and influenced by one's age, gender, and ethnic, geographic, and cultural orientations. Effective communicators try to tailor their messages to the receiver's perceptual schemata. This requires well-developed listening and observation skills and cross-cultural sensitivity.

Causal Attributions

Attribution theory is based on the premise that people attempt to infer causes for observed behavior. Rightly or wrongly, we constantly formulate cause-and-effect explanations for our own and others' behavior. Attributional state-ments such as the following are common: "Joe drinks too much because he has no willpower; but I need a couple of drinks after work because I'm under a lot of pres-sure." Formally defined, **causal attributions** are suspected or inferred causes of behavior. Even though our causal attributions tend to be self-serving and are often invalid, it is important to understand how people formulate attributions because they profoundly affect organizational behavior. For example, a supervisor who attributes an employee's poor perfor-mance to a lack of effort might reprimand that individual. However, training might be deemed necessary if the supervisor attributes the poor performance to a lack of ability.

> **Causal attributions**
>
> Suspected or inferred causes of behavior.

Generally speaking, people formulate causal attributions by considering the events preceding an observed behavior. This section introduces Harold Kelley's model of attribution and two important attributional tendencies.

Kelley's Model of Attribution

Current models of attribution, such as Kelley's, are based on the pioneering work of the late Fritz Heider. Heider, the founder of attribution theory, proposed that behavior can be attributed either to **internal factors** within a person (such as ability) or to **external factors** within the environment (such as a difficult task). Building on Heider's work, Kelley attempted to pinpoint major antecedents of internal and external attributions. Kelley hypothesized that people make causal attributions after gathering information about three dimensions of behavior: consensus, distinctiveness, and consistency.[20] These dimensions vary independently, thus forming various combinations and leading to differing attributions.

> **Internal factors**
> Personal characteristics that cause behavior.
>
> **External factors**
> Environmental characteristics that cause behavior.

Figure 4–2 presents performance charts showing low versus high consensus, distinctiveness, and consistency. These charts are now used to help develop a working knowledge of all three dimensions in Kelley's model.

- *Consensus* involves a comparison of an individual's behavior with that of his or her peers. There is high consensus when one acts like the rest of the group and low consensus when one acts differently. As shown in Figure 4–2, high consensus is indicated when persons A, B, C, D, and E obtain similar levels of individual performance. In contrast, person C's performance is low in consensus because it significantly varies from the performance of persons A, B, D, and E.

- *Distinctiveness* is determined by comparing a person's behavior on one task with his or her behavior on other tasks. High distinctiveness means the individual has performed the task in question in a significantly different manner than he or she has performed other tasks. Low distinctiveness means stable performance or quality from one task to another. Figure 4–2 reveals that the employee's performance on task 4 is highly distinctive because it significantly varies from his or her performance on tasks 1, 2, 3, and 5.

- *Consistency* is determined by judging if the individual's performance on a given task is consistent over time. High consistency implies that a person performs a certain task the same, time after time. Unstable performance of a given task over time would mean low consistency. The downward spike in performance depicted

Performance Charts Showing Low and High Consensus, Distinctiveness, and Consistency Information   **FIGURE 4–2**

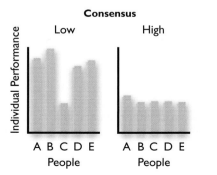
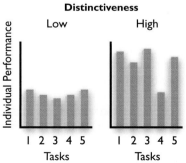
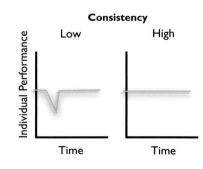

SOURCE: K A Brown, "Explaining Group Poor Performance: An Attributional Analysis." *Academy of Management Review,* January 1984, p 56. Used with permission.

in the consistency graph of Figure 4–2 represents low consistency. In this case, the employee's performance on a given task varied over time.

It is important to remember that consensus relates to other *people,* distinctiveness relates to other *tasks,* and consistency relates to *time.* The question now is: How does information about these three dimensions of behavior lead to internal or external attributions?

Kelley hypothesized that people attribute behavior to *external* causes (environmental factors) when they perceive high consensus, high distinctiveness, and low consistency. *Internal* attributions (personal factors) tend to be made when observed behavior is characterized by low consensus, low distinctiveness, and high consistency. So, for example, when all employees are performing poorly (high consensus), when the poor performance occurs on only one of several tasks (high distinctiveness), and the poor performance occurs during only one time period (low consistency), a supervisor will probably attribute an employee's poor performance to an external source such as peer pressure or an overly difficult task. In contrast, performance will be attributed to an employee's personal characteristics (an internal attribution) when only the individual in question is performing poorly (low consensus), when the inferior performance is found across several tasks (low distinctiveness), and when the low performance has persisted over time (high consistency). Many studies supported this predicted pattern of attributions.[21]

Attributional Tendencies

Researchers have uncovered two attributional tendencies that distort one's interpretation of observed behavior—*fundamental attribution bias* and *self-serving bias.*

> **Fundamental attribution bias**
>
> Ignoring environmental factors that affect behavior.

Fundamental Attribution Bias   The **fundamental attribution bias** reflects one's tendency to attribute another person's behavior to his or her personal characteristics, as opposed to situational factors. This bias causes perceivers to ignore important environmental forces that often significantly affect behavior. For example, a study of 1,420 employees of a large utility company demonstrated that supervisors tended to make more internal attributions about worker accidents than did the workers.[22]

> **Self-serving bias**
>
> Taking more personal responsibility for success than failure.

Self-Serving Bias   The **self-serving bias** represents one's tendency to take more personal responsibility for success than for failure. Referring again to Figure 4–2, employees tend to attribute their successes to internal factors (high ability and/or hard work) and their failures to uncontrollable external factors (tough job, bad luck, unproductive co-workers, or an unsympathetic boss).[23] This self-serving bias is evident in how students typically analyze their performance on exams. "A" students are likely to attribute their grade to high ability or hard work. "D" students, meanwhile, tend to pin the blame on factors like an unfair test, bad luck, or unclear lectures.

Managerial Application and Implications   Attribution models can be used to explain how managers handle poorly performing employees. One study revealed that managers gave employees more immediate, frequent, and negative feedback when they attributed their performance to low effort. This reaction was even more pronounced when the manager's success was dependent on an employee's performance. A second study indicated that managers tended to transfer employees whose poor performance was attributed to a lack of ability. These same managers also decided to take no immediate action when poor performance was attributed to external factors beyond an individual's control.[24]

The preceding situations have several important implications for managers. First, managers tend to disproportionately attribute behavior to *internal* causes.[25] This can result in inaccurate evaluations of performance, leading to reduced employee motivation. No one likes to be blamed because of factors they perceive to be beyond their control. Further, because managers' responses to employee performance vary according to their attributions, attributional biases may lead to inappropriate managerial actions, including promotions, transfers, layoffs, and so forth. This can dampen motivation and performance. Attributional training sessions for managers are in order. Basic attributional processes can be explained, and managers can be taught to detect and avoid attributional biases. Finally, an employee's attributions for his or her own performance have dramatic effects on subsequent motivation, performance, and personal attitudes such as self-esteem. For instance, people tend to give up, develop lower expectations for future success, and experience decreased self-esteem when they attribute failure to a lack of ability. Fortunately, attributional retraining can improve both motivation and performance. Research shows that employees can be taught to attribute their failures to a lack of effort rather than to a lack of ability.[26] This attributional realignment paves the way for improved motivation and performance.

Defining and Documenting Diversity

Diversity represents the multitude of individual differences and similarities that exist among people.[27] This definition underscores a key issue about managing diversity. There are many different dimensions or components of diversity. This implies that diversity pertains to everybody. It is not an issue of age, race, or gender. It is not an issue of being heterosexual, gay, or lesbian or of being Catholic, Jewish, Protestant, or Muslim. Diversity also does not pit white males against all other groups of people. Diversity pertains to the host of individual differences that make all of us unique and different from others.

> **Diversity**
>
> The host of individual differences that make people different from and similar to each other.

This section begins our journey into managing diversity by first reviewing the key dimensions of diversity. Because many people associate diversity with affirmative action, we then compare affirmative action with managing diversity. We conclude by reviewing the demographic trends that are creating an increasingly diverse workforce.

Layers of Diversity

Like seashells on a beach, people come in a variety of shapes, sizes, and colors. This variety represents the essence of diversity. Lee Gardenswartz and Anita Rowe, a team of diversity experts, identified four layers of diversity to help distinguish the important ways in which people differ (see Figure 4–3). Taken together, these layers define your personal identity and influence how each of us sees the world.[28]

Figure 4–3 shows that personality is at the center of the diversity wheel. Personality is at the center because it represents a stable set of characteristics that is responsible for a person's identity: The dimensions of personality are discussed later in Chapter 5. The next layer of diversity consists of a set of internal dimensions that are referred to as the primary dimensions of diversity.[29] These dimensions, for the most part, are not within our control, but strongly influence our attitudes and expectations and assumptions about others, which, in turn, influence our behavior. Take the

FIGURE 4-3   The Four Layers of Diversity

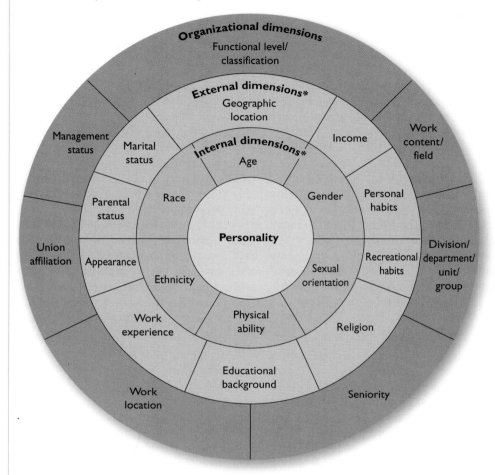

*Internal Dimensions and External Dimensions are adapted from Loden and Rosener, *Workforce America!* (Homewood, IL: Business One Irwin, 1991).

SOURCE: L Gardenswartz and A Rowe, *Diverse Teams at Work: Capitalizing on the Power of Diversity* (New York: McGraw-Hill, 1994), p 33. © 1994. Reproduced with permission of The McGraw-Hill Companies.

encounter experienced by an African-American woman in middle management while vacationing at a resort:

> While she was sitting by the pool, "a large 50-ish white male approached me and demanded that I get him extra towels. I said, 'Excuse me?' He then said, 'Oh, you don't work here,' with no shred of embarrassment or apology in his voice."[30]

Stereotypes regarding one or more of the primary dimensions of diversity most likely influenced this man's behavior toward the woman.

Figure 4–3 reveals that the next layer of diversity is composed of external influences, which are referred to as secondary dimensions of diversity. They represent individual differences that we have a greater ability to influence or control. Examples include where you grew up and live today, your religious affiliation, whether you are married and have children, and your work experiences. These dimensions also exert a significant influence on our perceptions, behavior, and attitudes.

Consider religion as an illustration. Given that Islam is expected to surpass Judaism as the second-most commonly practiced religion in the United States (Christianity is first), organizations need to consider both Muslim employees and customers when implementing their policies, procedures, and programs. Argenbright Security Inc. in Atlanta created problems for itself when management sent home seven Muslim women for wearing Islamic headscarves at their security jobs at Dulles International Airport. Because wearing headscarves in no way affected their job performance, the company had to reimburse the women for back pay and other relief in a settlement negotiated with the Equal Employment Opportunity Commission.[31] Similarly, a lack of sensitivity regarding the Muslim faith led Nike to recall a shoe line in 1997. The shoe was imprinted with a logo that looked like the Arabic script for Allah. Nike paid refunds for returned shoes, issued a public apology, sent employees to sensitivity training, and donated money to a Muslim elementary school in the United States.[32]

As you can see from these examples, a lack of awareness about the external layer of diversity can cause bad feelings among both employees and customers. The final layer of diversity includes organizational dimensions such as seniority, job title and function, and work location.

Affirmative Action and Managing Diversity

Effectively managing diversity requires organizations to adopt a new way of thinking about differences among people. Rather than pitting one group against another, managing diversity entails recognition of the unique contribution every employee can make. As found at The Container Store, a company that received the 2001 Optimas Award for excellence in people management, effectively managing diversity can create an infectiously positive work environment:

> In an industry where 100 percent turnover is common, The Container Store boasts a very low 15 to 20 percent. Forty-one percent of new hires come from employee referrals. But it's the enthusiasm among workers that's so palpable. . . . A stunning 97 percent of employees agree with the survey statement "People care about each other here." . . . Not long after creating the company, Boone and Tindell [the founders] created innovative parameters called foundation principles. They are a set of humanistic, spiritually based, do-unto-others philosophies. These principles are practiced internally among employees and are reflected in how they treat each other and how the company treats them.[33]

The management philosophies used at The Container Store are much different from that of affirmative action. This section highlights the differences between affirmative action and managing diversity.

Affirmative Action   Affirmative action focuses on achieving equality of opportunity in an organization and is legally mandated in the United States by Equal Opportunity laws. **Affirmative action** is an artificial intervention aimed at giving management a chance to correct an imbalance, an injustice, a mistake, and/or outright discrimination. Affirmative action does not legitimize quotas. Quotas are illegal. They can only be imposed by judges who conclude that a company has engaged in discriminatory practices. It also is important to note that under no circumstances does affirmative action require companies to hire unqualified people.

Affirmative action

Focuses on achieving equality of opportunity in an organization.

Although affirmative action created tremendous opportunities for women and minorities, it does not foster the type of thinking that is needed to effectively manage diversity.[34] For example, affirmative action is resisted more by white males than

Managing diversity

Creating organizational changes that enable all people to perform up to their maximum potential.

Although women seem to be making strides in overcoming the *glass ceiling* (see following page) as evidenced by such CEOs as Carly Fiorina of Hewlett-Packard (pictured here), or Andrea Jung of Avon, fewer than 1% of companies are headed by women. Add to this that many of them make far less in compensation than their male counterparts. For the 20 highest-paid male executives in the United States, total compensation averaged $138.5 million, while the 20 best-paid females barely eked out $11.2 million apiece. (Business Week Online, "For Female CEOs, It's Stingy at the Top," April 23, 2001.)

women and minorities because it is perceived as involving preferential hiring and treatment based on group membership. Affirmative action plans are more successful when employees view them as fair and equitable.[35]

Affirmative action programs also were found to negatively affect the women and minorities expected to benefit from them. Research demonstrated that women and minorities, supposedly hired on the basis of affirmative action, felt negatively stigmatized as unqualified or incompetent. They also experienced lower job satisfaction and more stress than employees supposedly selected on the basis of merit.[36]

Managing Diversity Managing diversity entails enabling people to perform up to their maximum potential. It focuses on changing an organization's culture and infrastructure such that people provide the highest productivity possible. Ann Morrison, a diversity expert, conducted a study of 16 organizations that successfully managed diversity. Her results uncovered three key strategies for success: education, enforcement, and exposure. She describes them as follows:

> The education component of the strategy has two thrusts: one is to prepare nontraditional managers for increasingly responsible posts, and the other is to help traditional managers overcome their prejudice in thinking about and interacting with people who are of a different sex or ethnicity. The second component of the strategy, enforcement, puts teeth in diversity goals and encourages behavior change. The third component, exposure to people with different backgrounds and characteristics, adds a more personal approach to diversity by helping managers get to know and respect others who are different.[37]

In summary, both consultants and academics believe that organizations should strive to manage diversity rather than only valuing it or simply using affirmative action.

Increasing Diversity in the Workforce

This section explores four demographic trends that are creating an increasingly diverse workforce: (1) women continue to enter the workforce in increasing numbers, (2) people of color (non-Caucasian) represent a growing share of the labor force, (3) there is a critical mismatch between workers' educational attainment and occupational requirements, and (4) the workforce is aging.

Women Entering the Workforce Table 4–2 shows that approximately 49.6% of the new entrants into the workforce between 1996 and 2006 are expected to be women. It also shows that women will account for 44.1% of the departures from the workforce. Men account for the largest share of retirement-bound employees.

In spite of the fact that women constituted 46% of the labor force in 1996 and are expected to represent 47% by 2006, they continue to encounter the **glass ceiling**.[38] The glass ceiling represents an invisible barrier that separates women and minorities

Projected Entrants and Departures in the US Workforce from 1996 to 2006 | **TABLE 4-2**

	ENTRANTS*		DEPARTURES*	
	1996–2006	Percent	1996–2006	Percent
Total**	39,670	100.0%	24,768	100.0%
Men	19,978	50.4	13,839	55.9
Women	19,692	49.6	10,929	44.1
White Non-Hispanic	24,214	61.0	16,963	68.5
Men	12,132	30.6	9,728	39.3
Women	12,082	30.5	7,236	29.2
African-American	6,191	15.6	5,003	20.2
Men	2,807	7.1	2,550	10.3
Women	3,384	8.5	2,453	9.9
Hispanic	5,920	14.9	1,293	5.2
Men	3,365	8.5	776	3.1
Women	2,555	6.4	516	2.1
Asian and Other Races	3,346	8.4	1,508	6.1
Men	1,674	4.2	785	3.2
Women	1,671	4.2	724	2.9

*Labor force entrants and departures, in thousands, 1996–2006.

**All groups add to total.

Note: Numbers may not add up due to rounding.

SOURCE: Data were taken from Table 6 in H Fullerton, Jr, "Employment Projections: Entrance to the Labor Force by Sex, Race, and Hispanic Origin," *Bureau of Labor Statistics Online*, January 1998 (http://stats.bls.gov/emptab3.htm).

from advancing into top management positions. It can be particularly demotivating because employees can look up and see coveted top management positions through the transparent ceiling but are unable to obtain them. A variety of statistics support the existence of a glass ceiling.

Glass ceiling

Invisible barrier blocking women and minorities from top management positions.

As of June 2000, women were still underpaid relative to men: Women received 76% of men's earnings.[39] Women also suffer in other areas of job opportunities. A study of 69 male and 69 female executives revealed that although there were no differences in base salary or bonus, the women received fewer stock options than males, even after controlling for level of education, performance, and job function.[40] Further, women still have not broken into the highest echelon of corporate America to any significant degree. As of November 2000 there were only two female CEOs in the nation's largest 500 companies: Carly Fiorina at Hewlett-Packard Co. and Andrea Jung at Avon.[41]

How can women overcome the glass ceiling? A team of researchers attempted to answer this question by surveying 461 executive women who held titles of vice president or higher in *Fortune* 1000 companies. Respondents were asked to evaluate the extent to which they used 13 different career strategies to break through the glass ceiling. The 13 strategies are shown in the Hands-On Exercise. Before discussing the results from this study, we would like you to complete the Hands-On Exercise.

What Are the Strategies for Breaking the Glass Ceiling?

INSTRUCTIONS: Read the 13 career strategies shown below that may be used to break the glass ceiling. Next, rank order each strategy in terms of its importance for contributing to the advancement of a woman to a senior management position. Rank the strategies from 1 (most important) to 13 (least important). Once this is completed, compute the gap between your rankings and those provided by the women executives who participated in this research. Their rankings are presented in Endnote 42 at the back of the book. In computing the gaps, use the absolute value of the gap. (Absolute values are always positive, so just ignore the sign of your gap.) Finally, compute your total gap score. The larger the gap, the greater the difference in opinion between you and the women executives. What does your total gap score indicate about your recommended strategies?

Strategy	My Rating	Survey Rating	Gap |Your Rating − Survey Rating|
1. Develop leadership outside office	——	——	——
2. Gain line management experience	——	——	——
3. Network with influential colleagues	——	——	——
4. Change companies	——	——	——
5. Be able to relocate	——	——	——
6. Seek difficult or high-visibility assignments	——	——	——
7. Upgrade educational credentials	——	——	——
8. Consistently exceed performance expectations	——	——	——
9. Move from one functional area to another	——	——	——
10. Initiate discussion regarding career aspirations	——	——	——
11. Have an influential mentor	——	——	——
12. Develop style that men are comfortable with	——	——	——
13. Gain international experience	——	——	——

SOURCE: Strategies and data were taken from B R Ragins, B Townsend, and M Mattis, "Gender Gap in the Executive Suite: CEOs and Female Executives Report on Breaking the Glass Ceiling," *The Academy of Management Executives*, February 1998, pp 28–42.

Findings indicated that the top nine strategies were central to the advancement of these female executives. Within this set, however, four strategies were identified as critical toward breaking the glass ceiling: consistently exceeding performance expectations, developing a style with which male managers are comfortable, seeking out difficult or challenging assignments, and having influential mentors.[43]

People of Color in the US Workforce   People of color in the United States are projected to add 38.9% of the new entrants in the workforce from 1996 to 2006 (see Table 4–2). African-Americans are predicted to account for the largest share of this increase (15.6%). Because fewer Hispanics will leave the workforce between 1996 and 2005 than any other racial group (5.2%), Hispanics will account for the greatest *net* percentage increase in new workers.

Unfortunately, two additional trends suggest that people of color are experiencing their own glass ceiling. First, people of color are advancing even less in the managerial and professional ranks than women. For example, African-Americans, Hispanics, and whites held 7%, 4.5%, and 88%, respectively, of all managerial and professional jobs in 1996.[44] Further, African-Americans and Hispanics together accounted for less than 2% of senior executive positions in the United States in 2000.[45] Second, people of color also tend to earn less than whites. Median household income in 1999 was $27,900, $30,700, and $44,400 for African-Americans, Hispanics, and whites, respectively. Interestingly, Asian and Pacific Islanders had the highest median income, $51,200[46]

Mismatch between Educational Attainment and Occupational Requirements   Approximately 26% of the labor force has a college degree.[47] Unfortunately, many of these people are working in jobs for which they are overqualified. This creates underemployment. **Underemployment** exists when a job requires less than a person's full potential as determined by his or her formal education, training, or skills. In 1995, approximately 40% of those individuals with some college and 10% of college graduates were underemployed.[48] Underemployment is negatively correlated with job satisfaction, work commitment, job involvement, internal work motivation, life satisfaction, and psychological well-being. Underemployment also is related to higher absenteeism and turnover.[49]

> **Underemployment**
>
> The result of taking a job that requires less education, training, or skills than possessed by a worker.

There is another important educational mismatch. The national high-school dropout rate is approximately 12%, and more than 20% of the adult US population read at or below a fifth-grade level, a level which is below that needed to earn a living wage. More than 40 million Americans age 16 and older also are illiterate.[50] Literacy is defined as "an individual's ability to read, write, and speak in English, compute and solve problems at levels of proficiency necessary to function on the job and in society, to achieve one's goals, and develop one's knowledge and potential."[51] These statistics are worrisome because 70% of on-the-job reading materials are written for ninth-grade to college levels.

The Aging Workforce   America's population and workforce are getting older. Between 1995 and 2020, the number of individuals in the United States over age 65 will increase by 60%, the 45- to 64-year-old population by 34%, and those between ages 18 and 44 by 4%.[52] Life expectancy is increasing as well. The number of people living into their 80s is increasing rapidly, and this group disproportionately suffers from chronic illness. The United States is not the only country with an aging population. Japan, Eastern Europe, and former Soviet republics, for example, are expected to encounter significant economic and political problems due to an aging population.

Managerial Implications of Increasing Diversity   Highly skilled women and people of color will be in high demand. To attract and retain the best workers, companies need to adopt policies and programs that meet the needs of women and people of color. Programs such as day care, elder care, flexible work schedules, and benefits such as paternal leaves, less rigid relocation policies, and mentoring programs are likely to become more popular. Before implementing such initiatives, however, companies should consider the recommendations derived from Deloitte & Touche's successful Women's Initiative program (see Skills & Best Practices). The company initiated this program after determining that it was having a problem retaining high-quality women in the firm.

SKILLS & BEST PRACTICES

Recommendations from Deloitte & Touche's Women's Initiative

Recommendations	Supportive Tactics
1. Make sure senior management is front and center.	The CEO actively led the Women's Initiative.
2. Make an airtight business case for cultural change.	The company documented the business imperative for change before it could justify the investment and effort required by the initiative.
3. Let the world watch you.	The company appointed an external advisory council and informed the press about its plans. The company did not the let the initiative become another "program of the year" that led nowhere.
4. Begin with dialogue as the platform for change.	Employees were required to attend intensive workshops to reveal and examine gender-based assumptions in mentoring and client assignments.
5. Use a flexible system of accountability.	Local offices measured their efforts with women professionals. Management worked with office heads to select their focus areas of change under the initiative.
6. Promote work-life balance for men and women.	The company implemented policies for flexible work arrangements and lighter travel schedules.

SOURCE: Excerpted and adapted from D M McCracken, "Winning the Talent War for Women: Sometimes It Takes a Revolution," *Harvard Business Review*, November–December 2000, p 166.

Given the projected increase in the number of Hispanics entering the workforce over the next 20 years, managers should consider progressive methods to recruit, retain, and integrate this segment of the population into their organizations. Consider the examples set by K-mart, the University of North Carolina Health Care System at Chapel Hill, PricewaterhouseCoopers, Chevron, and PepsiCo:

> K-mart recruits at colleges and universities that have large numbers of Hispanic students. The company also advertises in Hispanic publications and uses online Hispanic job boards. It also has translated employment and benefit information into Spanish. The University of North Carolina Health Care System at Chapel Hill, NC, has brought in Spanish interpreters at its new-employee orientations and printed part of its job application information in Spanish. . . . PricewaterhouseCoopers . . . set up employee support and socialization groups where Hispanic managers act as leaders to Hispanic employees, and the company provides scholarships for Hispanic accounting students. Chevron sponsors a Hispanic employee network . . . Pepsi works with national Hispanic organizations to help with recruiting and is planning a leadership forum for some Hispanic executives. The program will give the executives access to the CEO and other company leaders.[53]

Mismatches between the amount of education needed to perform current jobs and the amount of education possessed by members of the workforce are growing. Underemployment among college graduates threatens to erode job satisfaction and work motivation. As well-educated workers begin to look for jobs commensurate with their qualifications and expectations, absenteeism and turnover likely will increase. This problem underscores the need for job redesign (see the discussion in Chapter 7). On-the-job remedial skills and literacy training will be necessary to help the growing number of dropouts and illiterates cope with job demands. For example, a recent survey conducted by the Bureau of Labor Statistics revealed that almost 93% of those companies with 50 or more employees provide or finance formal training for their employees. These companies spent $7.7 billion on in-house training and another $5.5 billion on training conducted by outside vendors.[54]

Five managerial initiatives may help organizations effectively adapt to an aging workforce:[55]

1. Organizations might devise more flexible and creative retirement plans because many employees are delaying retirement. Some people want to work longer, and others have inadequate savings.

2. It will become critical to match individuals' skills and desires to job requirements as people age. An appropriate match is more likely to produce positive outcomes for individuals and organizations alike.

3. Organizations can conduct succession planning for older workers who will be retiring in the future.

4. Organizations can reengineer their production processes and capital equipment so as to operate with fewer employees.

5. Organizations need to be sensitive to issues associated with elder care. "More than 14 million US workers are estimated to be caring for older family members, and their efforts—which often take them away from the office—cost employers as much as $29 billion a year in lost productivity, according to a 1997 study for MetLife Inc."[56]

Organizational Practices Used to Effectively Manage Diversity

Many organizations throughout the United States are unsure of what it takes to effectively manage diversity. In addition, the sensitive and potentially volatile nature of managing diversity has led to significant barriers when trying to move forward with diversity initiatives. This section reviews the barriers to managing diversity and discusses a framework for categorizing organizational diversity initiatives developed by Ann Morrison.

Barriers and Challenges to Managing Diversity

Organizations encounter a variety of barriers when attempting to implement diversity initiatives. It thus is important for present and future managers to consider these barriers before rolling out a diversity program. The following is a list of the most common barriers to implementing successful diversity programs.[57]

1. *Inaccurate stereotypes and prejudice.* This barrier manifests itself in the belief that differences are viewed as weaknesses. In turn, this promotes the view that diversity hiring will mean sacrificing competence and quality.

2. *Ethnocentrism.* The ethnocentrism barrier represents the feeling that one's cultural rules and norms are superior or more appropriate than the rules and norms of another culture.

3. *Poor career planning.* This barrier is associated with the lack of opportunities for diverse employees to get the type of work assignments that qualify them for senior management positions.

4. *An unsupportive and hostile working environment for diverse employees.* Diverse employees are frequently excluded from social events and the friendly camaraderie that takes place in most offices.

5. *Lack of political savvy on the part of diverse employees.* Diverse employees may not get promoted because they do not know how to "play the game" of getting along and getting ahead in an organization. Research reveals that women and people of color are excluded from organizational networks.[58]

6. *Difficulty in balancing career and family issues.* Women still assume the majority of the responsibilities associated with raising children. This makes it harder for women to work evenings and weekends or to frequently travel once they have children. Even without children in the picture, household chores take more of a woman's time than a man's time.

7. *Fears of reverse discrimination.* Some employees believe that managing diversity is a smoke screen for reverse discrimination. This belief leads to very strong resistance because people feel that one person's gain is another's loss.

8. *Diversity is not seen as an organizational priority.* This leads to subtle resistance that shows up in the form of complaints and negative attitudes. Employees may complain about the time, energy, and resources devoted to diversity that could have been spent doing "real work."

9. *The need to revamp the organization's performance appraisal and reward system.* Performance appraisals and reward systems must reinforce the need to effectively manage diversity. This means that success will be based on a new set of criteria. Employees are likely to resist changes that adversely affect their promotions and financial rewards.

10. *Resistance to change.* Effectively managing diversity entails significant organizational and personal change. As discussed in Chapter 16, people resist change for many different reasons.

Ann Morrison Identifies Specific Diversity Initiatives

Ann Morrison conducted a landmark study of the diversity practices used by 16 organizations that successfully managed diversity. Her results uncovered 52 different practices, 20 of which were used by the majority of the companies sampled. She classified the 52 practices into three main types: accountability, development, and recruitment.[59] The top 10 practices associated with each type are shown in Table 4–3. They are discussed next in order of relative importance.

Accountability practices

Focus on treating diverse employees fairly.

Accountability Practices **Accountability practices** relate to managers' responsibility to treat diverse employees fairly. Table 4–3 reveals that companies predominantly accomplish this objective by creating administrative procedures aimed at integrating diverse employees into the management ranks (practice numbers 3, 4, 5, 6, 8, 9, and 10). In contrast, work and family policies, practice 7, focuses on creating an environment that fosters employee commitment and productivity. Moreover, organizations increasingly are attempting to build an accountability component into their diversity programs in order to motivate managers to effectively manage diversity. A recent survey of *Fortune* 500 companies indicated that 25% linked both compensation and performance to accomplishing diversity goals.[60]

Development practices

Focus on preparing diverse employees for greater responsibility and advancement.

Development Practices The use of development practices to manage diversity is relatively new compared with the historical use of accountability and recruitment practices. **Development practices** focus

Common Diversity Practices | **TABLE 4–3**

Accountability Practices	Development Practices	Recruitment Practices
1. Top management's personal intervention	1. Diversity training programs	1. Targeted recruitment of non-managers
2. Internal advocacy groups	2. Networks and support groups	2. Key outside hires
3. Emphasis on EEO statistics, profiles	3. Development programs for all high-potential managers	3. Extensive public exposure on diversity (AA)
4. Inclusion of diversity in performance evaluation goals, ratings	4. Informal networking activities	4. Corporate image as liberal, progressive, or benevolent
5. Inclusion of diversity in promotion decision, criteria	5. Job rotation	5. Partnerships with educational institutions
6. Inclusion of diversity in management succession planning	6. Formal mentoring program	6. Recruitment incentives such as cash supplements
7. Work and family policies	7. Informal mentoring program	7. Internships (such as INROADS)
8. Policies against racism, sexism	8. Entry development programs for all high-potential new hires	8. Publications or PR products that highlight diversity
9. Internal audit or attitude survey	9. Internal training (such as personal safety or language)	9. Targeted recruitment of managers
10. Active AA/EEO committee, office	10. Recognition events, awards	10. Partnership with nontraditional groups

SOURCE: Abstracted from Tables A.10, A.11, and A.12 in A M Morrison, *The New Leaders: Guidelines on Leadership Diversity in America* (San Francisco: Jossey-Bass, 1992).

on preparing diverse employees for greater responsibility and advancement. These activities are needed because most nontraditional employees have not been exposed to the type of activities and job assignments that develop effective leadership and social networks.[61] Table 4–3 indicates that diversity training programs, networks and support groups, and mentoring programs are among the most frequently used developmental practices. There is one particular developmental practice that more and more organizations are confronting: Teaching English to non–English-speaking workers. Successfully teaching English and learning to communicate in multiple languages will become increasingly important as employers continue to hire people for whom English is not their first language. Imagine the situation faced by Doubletree Hotels Corporation when it had to communicate about its revamped employee benefits to a workforce of 30,000 people who speak 20 different languages:

> Instead of being daunted by the prospect of explaining benefits in multiple languages and to many employees with limited educations, Doubletree launched an outreach program that spoke to virtually all employees in their own tongues, on their own terms. The main tools were audiocassette tapes, shipped to each work site and made available for employees to use with loaned tape players. The tapes explained changes in the benefits program, such as a greater selection of health maintenance organizations and the debut of flexible benefits.
>
> The tapes were recorded in 14 languages, including Spanish, Somali, Tongan, Creole, Mandarin, and Russian, and became very popular with employees, some of whom are illiterate and would not have understood written materials, said Lenny Sanicola, benefits manager of Phoenix-based Doubletree. The company decided to communicate in native languages with any group of at least 25 employees.[62]

| Recruitment practices | **Recruitment Practices**   **Recruitment practices** focus on attract-
| --- |
| Attempts to attract qualified, diverse employees at all levels. |

Recruitment Practices   **Recruitment practices** focus on attracting job applicants at all levels who are willing to accept challenging work assignments. This focus is critical because people learn the leadership skills needed for advancement by successfully accomplishing increasingly challenging and responsible work assignments. As shown in Table 4–3, targeted recruitment of nonmanagers (practice 1) and managers (practice 9) are commonly used to identify and recruit women and people of color.

chapter summary

- *Describe* perception *in terms of the social information processing model.* Perception is a mental and cognitive process that enables us to interpret and understand our surroundings. Social perception, also known as social cognition and social information processing, is a four-stage process. The four stages are selective attention/comprehension, encoding and simplification, storage and retention, and retrieval and response. During social cognition, salient stimuli are matched with schemata, assigned to cognitive categories, and stored in long-term memory for events, semantic materials, or people.

- *Identify and briefly explain four managerial implications of social perception.* Social perception affects hiring decisions, performance appraisals, leadership perceptions, and communication processes. Inaccurate schemata or racist and sexist schemata may be used to evaluate job applicants. Similarly, faulty schemata about what constitutes good versus poor performance can lead to inaccurate performance appraisals. Invalid schemata need to be identified and replaced with appropriate schemata through coaching and training. Further, managers are advised to use objective rather than subjective measures of performance. With respect to leadership, a leader will have a difficult time influencing employees when he or she exhibits behaviors contained in employees' schemata of poor leaders. Finally, communication is influenced by schemata used to interpret any message. Effective communicators try to tailor their messages to the receiver's perceptual schemata.

- *Explain, according to Kelley's model, how external and internal causal attributions are formulated.* Attribution theory attempts to describe how people infer causes for observed behavior. According to Kelley's model of causal attribution, external attributions tend to be made when consensus and distinctiveness are high and consistency is low. Internal (personal responsibility) attributions tend to be made when consensus and distinctiveness are low and consistency is high.

- *Demonstrate your familiarity with the demographic trends that are creating an increasingly diverse workforce.* There are four key demographic trends: (a) half of the new entrants into the workforce between 1990 and 2006 will be women, (b) people of color will account for more than a third of the new entrants into the workforce between 1990 and 2006, (c) a mismatch exists between worker's educational attainment and occupational requirements, and (d) the workforce is aging.

- *Identify the barriers and challenges to managing diversity.* There are 10 barriers to successfully implementing diversity initiatives: (a) inaccurate stereotypes and prejudice, (b) ethnocentrism, (c) poor career planning, (d) an unsupportive and hostile working environment for diverse employees, (e) lack of political savvy on the part of diverse employees, (f) difficulty in balancing career and family issues, (g) fears of reverse discrimination, (h) diversity is not seen as an organizational priority, (i) the need to revamp the organization's performance appraisal and reward system, and (j) resistance to change.

- *Discuss the organizational practices used to manage diversity identified by Ann Morrison.* Ann Morrison's study of diversity practices identified three main types or categories of activities. Accountability practices relate to a manager's responsibility to treat diverse employees fairly. Development practices focus on preparing diverse employees for greater responsibility and advancement. Recruitment practices emphasize attracting job applicants at all levels who are willing to accept challenging work assignments. Table 4–3 presents a list of activities that are used to accomplish each main type.

internet exercise

http://www.bls.gov/blshome.htm

This chapter discussed a variety of demographic statistics that underlie the changing nature of the US workforce. We discussed how a glass ceiling is affecting the promotional opportunities and pay for women and people of color. We also reviewed the mismatch between educational attainment and occupational requirements. We did not, however, discuss the employment opportunities within your chosen field of study. The purpose of this exercise is for you to conduct a more thorough examination of statistics related to the workforce as a whole and for statistics pertaining to your career goals. Visit the Web site for the Bureau of Labor Statistics at **http://www.bls.gov/blshome.htm**, and review information pertaining to the "Economy at a Glance" and "Other Statistics Sites." In particular, look at reports and tables pertaining to average hourly salaries and occupational employment statistics.

QUESTIONS

1. To what extent are income levels rising? Determine whether differences exist by race and gender.
2. What occupational categories are projected to experience the greatest growth in employment opportunities?
3. What are the employment prospects for your chosen field of study or targeted job? Be sure to identify job opportunities and projected wages. Are you happy with your career choice?

Appreciating Individual Differences: Self-Concept, Personality, Emotions

five

chapter

LEARNING OBJECTIVES

After reading the material in this chapter, you should be able to:

- Distinguish between self-esteem and self-efficacy.

- Contrast high and low self-monitoring individuals, and describe resulting problems each may have.

- Explain the social learning model of self-management.

- Identify and describe the Big Five personality dimensions, and specify which one is correlated most strongly with job performance.

- Explain the difference between an internal and external locus of control.

- Distinguish between positive and negative emotions, and describe a person with high emotional intelligence.

NO PLACE FOR THE OLD COMMAND-AND-CONTROL STYLE IN THE NEW ECONOMY

Boys, it seems, can't afford to be boys anymore. At least not if they want to succeed as managers in the New Economy, where the old-school style of command-and-control is about as effective as getting blitzed in front of your boss at the company cocktail party.

With more and more studies showing that qualities typically associated with women are what New Economy businesses need to thrive, a new

cottage industry is emerging that is taking the opposite view of Professor Henry Higgins in *My Fair Lady:* Why can't a man be more like a woman? "Men just don't have what it takes to be successful in the modern workplace,"

says London-based management guru James R Traeger. "They are deskilled."

Sure, the baby-faced Traeger has an ax to grind— he runs a for-men-only training program that helps guys understand the value of emotion in work relationships. Through a three-month seminar that involves intense personal scrutiny, coaching, networking, and public speaking, Traeger tries to get men to recognize and improve their abilities to communicate, build teams, and develop flexibility. "If you were to ask which of these qualities men had an upper hand at, the answer would be none," he says.

Indeed, in this vise-tight labor market, execs who are prone to scoff at such "soft skills" have found they need to listen to Traeger and his

cohorts. Managers everywhere are being forced to think more about creative leadership—the kind that can steer companies across the New Economy's bumpy terrain as well as hold on to valued workers who are constantly bombarded with new job offers. "The nature of modern business requires what's more typical to the female mold of building consensus as opposed to the top-down male military model," says Millington F McCoy, managing director at New York-based executive search firm Gould, McCoy & Chadick Inc.

After Traeger helps participants identify the gender issues, they work on communication skills, feelings, and emotional expression. "The program is about breaking down the stereo-type of an aggressive, controlling, and competitive man who always wants to be right, take charge, solve problems, and also has to have the last word," says David Bancroft-Turner, founder of 3D Training & Development, a UK-based consulting firm, who participated in the program. "It's about learning to listen and work in harmony."

Although the US hasn't yet seen this kind of men-only program, various coaching firms are similar to Traeger's. Hay Group, in Philadelphia, coaches execs to be "emotionally aware." Adapting theories from Daniel P Goleman's book *Emotional Intelligence,* Hay Group instructs managers "to recognize the emotional hot buttons" that are "not taught in business schools," says Annie McKee, Hay's director for management-development services.

One tip that all of the seminars advocate: If you're a man, follow the lead of your female co-worker. She probably has a lot to teach you.[1]

FOR DISCUSSION

Respond to a manager who made this statement: "Men will always be men." Do you believe women can teach men to be better managers? Explain. For an interpretation of this case and additional comments, see our website:

www.mhhe.com/kinickiob

THANKS TO A VAST array of individual differences, modern organizations have a rich and interesting human texture. On the other hand, individual differences make the manager's job endlessly challenging. In fact, according to research, "variability among workers is substantial at all levels but increases dramatically with job complexity. In life insurance sales, for example, variability in performance is around six times as great as in routine clerical jobs."[2]

Growing workforce diversity compels managers to view individual differences in a fresh new way. Rather than limiting diversity, as in the past, today's managers need to better understand and accommodate employee diversity and individual differences.[3]

This chapter explores the following important dimensions of individual differences: (1) self-concept and self-management, (2) personality traits, (3) attitudes, (4) mental abilities, and (5) emotions. Figure 5–1 is a conceptual model showing the relationship between self-concept (how you view yourself), personality (how you appear to others), and key forms of self-expression. Considered as an integrated package, these factors provide a foundation for better understanding yourself and others as unique and special individuals.

FIGURE 5–1   An OB Model for Studying Individual Differences

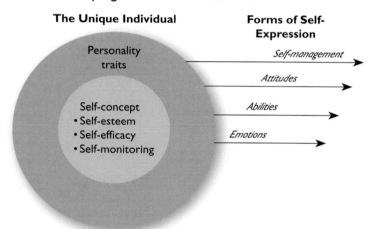

From Self-Concept to Self-Management

Self is the core of one's conscious existence. Awareness of self is referred to as one's self-concept. Individualistic North American cultures have been called self-centered. Not surprisingly, when people ages 16 to 70 were asked in a recent survey what they would do differently if they could live life over again, 48% chose the response category "Get in touch with self."[4] To know more about self-concept is to understand more about life in general. Sociologist Viktor Gecas defines **self-concept** as "the concept the individual has of himself as a physical, social, and spiritual or moral being."[5] In other words, because you have a self-concept, you recognize yourself as a distinct human being. A self-concept would be impossible without the capacity to think. This brings us to the role of cognitions. **Cognitions** represent "any knowledge, opinion, or belief about the environment, about oneself, or about one's behavior."[6] Among many differ-

Self-concept

Person's self-perception as a physical, social, spiritual being.

Cognitions

A person's knowledge, opinions, or beliefs.

ent types of cognitions, those involving anticipation, planning, goal setting, evaluating, and setting personal standards are particularly relevant to OB.[7] Cognitively based topics covered in this book include social perception, behavioral self-management, modern motivation theories, and decision-making styles.

Importantly, ideas of self and self-concept vary from one historical era to another, from one socioeconomic group to another, and from culture to culture.[8] How well one detects and adjusts to different cultural notions of self can spell the difference between success and failure in international dealings. For example, Japanese–US communication and understanding often are hindered by significantly different degrees of self-disclosure. With a comparatively large public self, Americans pride themselves in being open, honest, candid, and to the point. Meanwhile, Japanese, who culturally discourage self-disclosure, typically view Americans as blunt, prying, and insensitive to formalities. For their part, Americans tend to see Japanese as distant, cold, and evasive.[9] One culture is not right and the other wrong. They are just different, and a key difference involves culturally rooted conceptions of self and self-disclosure.

Keeping this cultural qualification in mind, let us explore three topics invariably mentioned when behavioral scientists discuss self-concept. They are self-esteem, self-efficacy, and self-monitoring. A social learning model of self-management is presented as a practical capstone for this section. Each of these areas deserves a closer look by those who want to better understand and effectively manage people at work.

Self-Esteem

Self-esteem is a belief about one's own self-worth based on an overall self-evaluation.[10] Self-esteem is measured by having survey respondents indicate their agreement or disagreement with both positive and negative statements. A positive statement on one general self-esteem survey is: "I feel I am a person of worth, the equal of other people."[11] Among the negative items is: "I feel I do not have much to be proud of."[12] Those who agree with the positive statements and disagree with the negative statements have high self-esteem. They see themselves as worthwhile, capable, and acceptable. People with low self-esteem view themselves in negative terms. They do not feel good about themselves and are hampered by self-doubts.[13]

> **Self-esteem**
>
> One's overall self-evaluation.

A Cross-Cultural Perspective   What are the cross-cultural implications for self-esteem, a concept that has been called uniquely Western? In a survey of 13,118 students from 31 countries worldwide, a moderate positive correlation was found between self-esteem and life satisfaction. But the relationship was stronger in individualistic cultures (e.g., United States, Canada, New Zealand, Netherlands) than in collectivist cultures (e.g., Korea, Kenya, Japan). The researchers concluded that individualistic cultures socialize people to focus more on themselves, while people in collectivist cultures "are socialized to fit into the community and to do their duty. Thus, how a collectivist feels about him- or herself is less relevant to . . . life satisfaction."[14] Global managers need to remember to deemphasize self-esteem when doing business in collectivist ("we") cultures, as opposed to emphasizing it in individualistic ("me") cultures.

Organization-Based Self-Esteem   The self-esteem just discussed is a global belief about oneself. But what about self-esteem in organizations, a more restricted context of greater importance to managers? A model of organization-based self-esteem was developed and validated with seven studies involving 2,444 teachers, students,

Organization-based self-esteem

An organization member's self-perceived value.

managers, and employees. The researchers defined **organization-based self-esteem (OBSE)** as the "self-perceived value that individuals have of themselves as organization members acting within an organizational context."[15] Those scoring high on OBSE tend to view themselves as important, worthwhile, effectual, and meaningful within the context of their employing organization.

OBSE tends to increase when employees believe their supervisors have a genuine concern for employees' welfare. Flexible, organic organization structures generate higher OBSE than do mechanistic (rigid bureaucratic) structures (the organic–mechanistic distinction is discussed in Chapter 15). Complex and challenging jobs foster higher OBSE than do simple, repetitive, and boring jobs. Significantly, these same factors also are associated with greater task motivation. Active enhancement of organization-based self-esteem promises to build a very important cognitive bridge to greater productivity and satisfaction[16] (see Skills & Best Practices).

Self-Efficacy ("I can do that.")

Have you noticed how those who are confident about their ability tend to succeed, while those who are preoccupied with failing tend to fail? Perhaps that explains the comparative golfing performance of your authors! One consistently stays in the fairways and hits the greens. The other spends the day thrashing through the underbrush, wading in water hazards, and blasting out of sand traps. At the heart of this performance mismatch is a specific dimension of self-esteem called self-efficacy.

Self-efficacy

Belief in one's ability to do a task.

Self-efficacy is a person's belief about his or her chances of successfully accomplishing a specific task. According to one OB writer, "Self-efficacy arises from the gradual acquisition of complex cognitive, social, linguistic, and/or physical skills through experience."[17]

Helpful nudges in the right direction from parents, role models, and mentors are central to the development of high self-efficacy. Consider, for example, this recent interview exchange with Nathan Lane, the successful Broadway and Hollywood actor:

> I asked Lane if he ever considered giving up during his early years of trying to succeed as an actor, when times were tough.
>
> He seemed startled by the question. "What else would I do?" he replied. "I have no other skills. I didn't for a moment think I *wasn't* going to make it. I just thought it may take a while. Certainly, at times you lose confidence, but I always believed there was a place for me. People believing in you is what gives you the confidence to go on. After that, it's a matter of perseverance, luck, and being ready when the opportunity does arrive."[18]

The relationship between self-efficacy and performance is a cyclical one. Efficacy → performance cycles can spiral upward toward success or downward toward failure.[19] Researchers have documented a strong linkage between high self-efficacy expectations and success in widely varied physical and mental tasks, anxiety reduction, addiction control, pain tolerance, illness

How to Build On-the-Job Self-Esteem

According to a study by the Society for Human Resource Management, managers can build employee self-esteem in four ways:

1. Be supportive by showing concern for personal problems, interests, status, and contributions.

2. Offer work involving variety, autonomy, and challenges that suit the individual's values, skills, and abilities.

3. Strive for management–employee cohesiveness and build trust. (Trust, an important teamwork element, is discussed in Chapter 10.)

4. Have faith in each employee's self-management ability. Reward successes.

SOURCE: Adapted from discussion in J K Matejka and R J Dunsing, "Great Expectations," *Management World*, January 1987, pp 16–17; and P Pascarella, "It All Begins with Self-Esteem," *Management Review*, February 1999, pp 60–61.

recovery, and avoidance of seasickness in naval cadets.[20] Oppositely, those with low self-efficacy expectations tend to have low success rates. Chronically low self-efficacy is associated with a condition called **learned helplessness,** the severely debilitating belief that one has no control over one's environment.[21] Although self-efficacy sounds like some sort of mental magic, it operates in a very straightforward manner, as a model will show.

> **Learned helplessness**
>
> Debilitating lack of faith in one's ability to control the situation.

Mechanisms of Self-Efficacy   A basic model of self-efficacy is displayed in Figure 5–2. It draws upon the work of Stanford psychologist Albert Bandura. Let us explore this model with a simple illustrative task. Imagine you have been told to prepare and

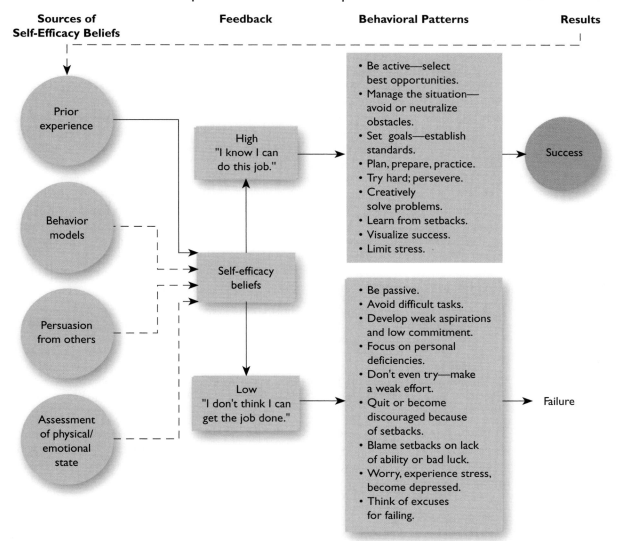

Self-Efficacy Beliefs Pave the Way for Success or Failure   **FIGURE 5–2**

SOURCES: Adapted from discussion in A Bandura, "Regulation of Cognitive Processes through Perceived Self-Efficacy," *Developmental Psychology,* September 1989, pp 729–35; and R Wood and A Bandura, "Social Cognitive Theory of Organizational Management," *Academy of Management Review,* July 1989, pp 361–84.

Self-efficacy expectations can come into play during public speaking sessions. Prior experience is the most potent source of these beliefs.

deliver a 10-minute talk to an OB class of 50 students on the workings of the self-efficacy model in Figure 5–2. Your self-efficacy calculation would involve cognitive appraisal of the interaction between your perceived capability and situational opportunities and obstacles.

As you begin to prepare for your presentation, the four sources of self-efficacy beliefs would come into play. Because prior experience is the most potent source, according to Bandura, it is listed first and connected to self-efficacy beliefs with a solid line.[22] Past success in public speaking would boost your self-efficacy. But bad experiences with delivering speeches would foster low self-efficacy. Regarding behavior models as a source of self-efficacy beliefs, you would be influenced by the success or failure of your classmates in delivering similar talks. Their successes would tend to bolster you (or perhaps their failure would if you were very competitive and had high self-esteem). Likewise, any supportive persuasion from your classmates that you will do a good job would enhance your self-efficacy. Physical and emotional factors also might affect your self-confidence. A sudden case of laryngitis or a bout of stage fright could cause your self-efficacy expectations to plunge. Your cognitive evaluation of the situation then would yield a self-efficacy belief—ranging from high to low expectations for success. Importantly, self-efficacy beliefs are not merely boastful statements based on bravado; they are deep convictions supported by experience.

Moving to the *behavioral patterns* portion of Figure 5–2, we see how self-efficacy beliefs are acted out. In short, if you have high self-efficacy about giving your 10-minute speech you will work harder, more creatively, and longer when preparing for your talk than will your low-self-efficacy classmates. The results would then take shape accordingly. People program themselves for success or failure by enacting their self-efficacy expectations. Positive or negative results subsequently become feedback for one's base of personal experience. Bob Schmonsees, a software entrepreneur, is an inspiring example of the success pathway through Figure 5–2:

> A contender in mixed-doubles tennis and a former football star, Mr Schmonsees was standing near a ski lift when an out-of-control skier rammed him. His legs were paralyzed. He would spend the rest of his life in a wheelchair.
>
> Fortunately, he discovered a formula for his different world: Figure out the new rules for any activity, then take as many small steps as necessary to master those rules. After learning the physics of a tennis swing on wheels and the geometry of playing a second bounce (standard rules), he became the world's top wheelchair player over age 40.[23]

Managerial Implications   On-the-job research evidence encourages managers to nurture self-efficacy, both in themselves and in others. In fact, a recent meta-analysis encompassing 21,616 subjects found a significant positive correlation between self-efficacy and job performance.[24] Self-efficacy requires constructive action in each of the following managerial areas:

1. *Recruiting/selection/job assignments.* Interview questions can be designed to probe job applicants' general self-efficacy as a basis for determining orientation and training needs. Pencil-and-paper tests for self-efficacy are not in an advanced stage of development and validation. Care needs to be taken

not to hire solely on the basis of self-efficacy because studies have detected below-average self-esteem and self-efficacy among women and protected minorities.[25]

2. *Job design.* Complex, challenging, and autonomous jobs tend to enhance perceived self-efficacy.[26] Boring, tedious jobs generally do the opposite.

3. *Training and development.* Employees' self-efficacy expectations for key tasks can be improved through guided experiences, mentoring, and role modeling.[27]

4. *Self-management.* Systematic self-management training involves enhancement of self-efficacy expectations.[28]

5. *Goal setting and quality improvement.* Goal difficulty needs to match the individual's perceived self-efficacy.[29] As self-efficacy and performance improve, goals and quality standards can be made more challenging.

6. *Coaching.* Those with low self-efficacy and employees victimized by learned helplessness need lots of constructive pointers and positive feedback.[30]

7. *Leadership.* Needed leadership talent surfaces when top management gives high self-efficacy managers a chance to prove themselves under pressure.

8. *Rewards.* Small successes need to be rewarded as stepping-stones to a stronger self-image and greater achievements.

Self-Monitoring

Consider these contrasting scenarios:

1. You are rushing to an important meeting when a co-worker pulls you aside and starts to discuss a personal problem. You want to break off the conversation, so you glance at your watch. He keeps talking. You say, "I'm late for a big meeting." He continues. You turn and start to walk away. The person keeps talking as if they never received any of your verbal and nonverbal signals that the conversation was over.

2. Same situation. Only this time, when you glance at your watch, the person immediately says, "I know, you've got to go. Sorry. We'll talk later."

In the first all-too-familiar scenario, you are talking to a "low self-monitor." The second scenario involves a "high self-monitor." But more is involved here than an irritating situation. A significant and measurable individual difference in self-expression behavior, called self-monitoring, is highlighted. **Self-monitoring** is the extent to which a person observes their own self-expressive behavior and adapts it to the demands of the situation.[31] Experts on the subject offer this explanation:

> **Self-monitoring**
>
> Observing one's own behavior and adapting it to the situation.

Individuals high in self-monitoring are thought to regulate their expressive self-presentation for the sake of desired public appearances, and thus be highly responsive to social and interpersonal cues of situationally appropriate performances. Individuals low in self-monitoring are thought to lack either the ability or the motivation to so regulate their expressive self-presentations. Their expressive behaviors, instead, are thought to functionally reflect their own enduring and momentary inner states, including their attitudes, traits, and feelings.[32]

In organizational life, both high and low monitors are subject to criticism. High self-monitors are sometimes called *chameleons,* who readily adapt their self-presentation to their surroundings. Low self-monitors, on the other hand, often are criticized

How Good Are You at Self-Monitoring?

INSTRUCTIONS: In an honest self-appraisal, mark each of the following statements as true (T) or false (F), and then consult the scoring key.

_____ **1.** I guess I put on a show to impress or entertain others.

_____ **2.** In a group of people I am rarely the center of attention.

_____ **3.** In different situations and with different people, I often act like very different persons.

_____ **4.** I would not change my opinions (or the way I do things) in order to please someone or win their favor.

_____ **5.** I have considered being an entertainer.

_____ **6.** I have trouble changing my behavior to suit different people and different situations.

_____ **7.** At a party I let others keep the jokes and stories going.

_____ **8.** I feel a bit awkward in public and do not show up quite as well as I should.

_____ **9.** I can look anyone in the eye and tell a lie with a straight face (if for a right end).

_____ **10.** I may deceive people by being friendly when I really dislike them.

SCORING KEY Score one point for each of the following answers:

1.T; 2. F; 3. T; 4. F; 5. T; 6. F; 7. F; 8. F; 9. T; 10. T

Score: _____

1–3 = Low self-monitoring

4–5 = Moderately low self-monitoring

6–7 = Moderately high self-monitoring

8–10 = High self-monitoring

SOURCE: Excerpted and adapted from M Snyder and S Gangestad, "On the Nature of Self-Monitoring: Matters of Assessment, Matters of Validity," *Journal of Personality and Social Psychology*, July 1986, p 137.

for being on their own planet and insensitive to others. Importantly, within an OB context, self-monitoring is like any other individual difference—not a matter of right or wrong or good versus bad, but rather a source of diversity that needs to be adequately understood by present and future managers.

A Matter of Degree   Self-monitoring is not an either-or proposition. It is a matter of degree; a matter of being relatively high or low in terms of related patterns of self-expression. The Hands-On Exercise is a self-assessment of your self-monitoring tendencies. It can help you better understand your*self*. Take a short break from your reading to complete the 10-item survey. Does your score surprise you in any way? Are you unhappy with the way you present yourself to others? What are the ethical implications of your score (particularly with regard to items 9 and 10)?

Research Insights and Practical Recommendations   According to field research, there is a positive relationship between high self-monitoring and career success. Among 139 MBA graduates who were tracked for five years, high self-monitors enjoyed more internal and external promotions than did their low self-monitoring classmates.[33] Another study of 147 managers and professionals found that high self-monitors had a better record of acquiring a mentor (someone to act as a personal career coach and professional sponsor).[34] These results mesh well with an earlier study that found managerial success (in terms of speed of promotions) tied to political savvy (knowing how to socialize, network, and engage in organizational politics).[35]

The foregoing evidence and practical experience lead us to make these practical recommendations:

For high, moderate, and low self-monitors: Become more consciously aware of your self-image and how it affects others (the Hands-On Exercise is a good start).

For high self-monitors: Don't overdo it by turning from a successful chameleon into someone who is widely perceived as insincere, dishonest, phoney, and untrustworthy. You cannot be everything to everyone.

For low self-monitors: You can bend without breaking, so try to be a bit more accommodating while being true to your basic beliefs. Don't wear out your welcome when communicating. Practice reading and adjusting to nonverbal cues in various public situations. If your conversation partner is bored or distracted, stop—because he or she is not really listening.

Self-Management: A Social Learning Model

Albert Bandura, the Stanford psychologist introduced earlier, extended his self-efficacy concept into a comprehensive model of human learning. According to Bandura's *social learning theory,* an individual acquires new behavior through the interplay of environmental cues and consequences and cognitive processes.[36] When you consciously control this learning process yourself, you are engaging in self-management. Bandura explains:

[A] distinguishing feature of social learning theory is the prominent role it assigns to self-regulatory capacities. By arranging environmental inducements, generating cognitive supports, and producing consequences for their own actions people are able to exercise some measure of control over their own behavior.[37]

In other words, to the extent that you can control your environment and your cognitive representations of your environment, you are the master of your own behavior. The practical model displayed in Figure 5–3 is derived from social learning theory. The two-headed arrows reflect dynamic interaction among all factors in the model. Each of the four major components of this self-management model requires a closer look. Since the focal point of this model is *behavior change,* let us begin by discussing the behavior component in the center of the triangle.[38]

An Agenda for Self-Improvement   In today's fast-paced Internet age, corporate hand-holding is pretty much a thing of the past when it comes to career management. Employees are told such things as "You own your own employability." They must make the best of themselves and any opportunities that may come along. A brochure at one large US company tells employees: "No one is more interested or qualified when it comes to evaluating your individual interests, values, skills, and goals than you are."[39] The new age of *career self-management* challenges you to do a better job of setting personal goals, having clear priorities, being well organized, skillfully managing your time, and developing a self-learning program.[40]

FIGURE 5–3   A Social Learning Model of Self-Management

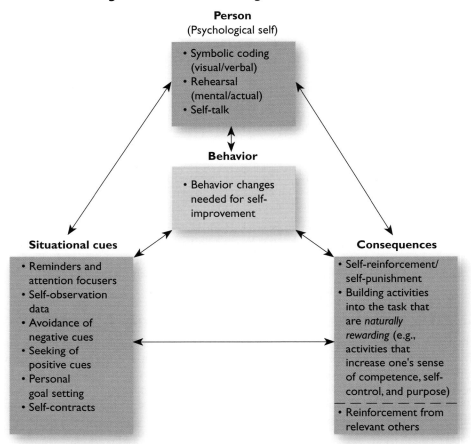

Fortunately, Stephen R Covey, in his best-selling book *The 7 Habits of Highly Effective People,* has given managers a helpful agenda for improving themselves (see Table 5–1). Covey refers to the seven habits, practiced by truly successful people, as "principle-centered, character-based."[41] The first step for putting the model in Figure 5–3 to work is to pick one or more of the seven habits that are personal trouble spots and translate them to specific behaviors. For example, "think win/win" might remind a conflict-prone manager to practice cooperative teamwork behaviors with co-workers. Habit number five might prompt another manager to stop interrupting others during conversations. Next, a supportive environment is needed for the target behavior.

Managing Situational Cues   When people try to give up a nagging habit such as smoking, the cards are stacked against them. Many people (friends who smoke) and situations (after dinner, when under stress at work, or when relaxing) serve as subtle yet powerful cues telling the individual to light up. If the behavior is to be changed, the cues need to be rearranged so as to trigger the alternative behavior. Six techniques for managing situational cues are listed in the left column of Figure 5–3.

Reminders and attention focusers do just that. For example, many students and managers cue themselves about deadlines and appointments with Post-it™ notes stuck all over their work areas, refrigerators, and dashboards. Self-observation data, when

Covey's Seven Habits: An Agenda for Managerial Self-Improvement   **TABLE 5–1**

1. *Be proactive.* Choose the right means and ends in life, and take personal responsibility for your actions. Make timely decisions and make positive progress.

2. *Begin with the end in mind.* When all is said and done, how do you want to be remembered? Be goal oriented.

3. *Put first things first.* Establish firm priorities that will help you accomplish your mission in life. Strike a balance between your daily work and your potential for future accomplishments.

4. *Think win/win.* Cooperatively seek creative and mutually beneficial solutions to problems and conflicts.

5. *Seek first to understand, then to be understood.* Strive hard to become a better listener.

6. *Synergize.* Because the whole is greater than the sum of its parts, you need to generate teamwork among individuals with unique abilities and potential. Value interpersonal differences.

7. *Sharpen the saw.* "This is the habit of self-renewal, which has four elements. The first is mental, which includes reading, visualizing, planning, and writing. The second is spiritual, which means value clarification and commitment, study, and meditation. Third is social/emotional, which involves service, empathy, synergy, and intrinsic security. Finally, the physical element includes exercise, nutrition, and stress management."

SOURCES: Adapted from discussion in S R Covey, *The 7 Habits of Highly Effective People* (New York: Simon & Schuster, 1989). Excerpt from "Q & A with Stephen Covey," *Training,* December 1992, p 38.

compared against a goal or standard, can be a potent cue for improvement. Those who keep a weight chart near their bathroom scale will attest to the value of this tactic. Successful self-management calls for avoiding negative cues while seeking positive cues. Managers in Northwestern Mutual Life Insurance Company's new business department appreciate the value of avoiding negative cues: "On Wednesdays, the department shuts off all incoming calls, allowing workers to speed processing of new policies. On those days, the unit averages 23% more policies than on other days."[42]

Goals, as repeatedly mentioned in this text, are the touchstone of good management. So it is with challenging yet attainable personal goals and effective self-management. Goals simultaneously provide a target and a measuring stick of progress. Finally, a self-contract is an "if-then" agreement with oneself. For example, if you can define all the key terms in this chapter, treat yourself to something special.

Arranging Cognitive Supports   Referring to the *person* portion of the self-management model in Figure 5–3, three cognitive supports for behavior change are symbolic coding, rehearsal, and self-talk. These amount to psychological, as opposed to environmental, cues. Yet, according to Bandura, they prompt appropriate behavior in the same manner. Each requires brief explanation:

• *Symbolic coding.* From a social learning theory perspective, the human brain stores information in visual and verbal codes. For example, a sales manager could use the visual picture of a man chopping down a huge tree to remember Woodman, the name of a promising new client. In contrast, people commonly rely on acronyms to recall names, rules for behavior, and other information. An acronym (or verbal code) that is often heard in managerial circles is the KISS principle, standing for "Keep It Simple, Stupid."

- *Rehearsal.* While it is true that practice often makes perfect, mental rehearsal of challenging tasks also can increase one's chances of success. Importantly, experts draw a clear distinction between systematic visualization of how one should proceed and daydreaming about success:

> The big difference between daydreaming and visualizing is that "visualizing is much more specific and detailed," says Philadelphia consultant Judith Schuster. "A daydream typically has gaps in it—we jump immediately to where we want to wind up. In visualization, we use building blocks and, step-by-step, construct the result we want."[43]

This sort of visualization has been recommended for use in managerial planning.[44]

Managers stand to learn a great deal about mental rehearsal and visualization from successful athletes. Kim Woodring, Wittenberg University's two-time All-American volleyball player, is a good example. She effectively combines visualization and self-talk:

> "I'm always positive," she says. "Even if I'm losing. I talk positively to myself. I go on with the next play and don't worry about the last one. When I visualize, I always see the perfect pass, perfect hit, perfect set, perfect kill, perfect result."[45]

Job-finding seminars are very popular on college campuses today because they typically involve mental and actual rehearsal of tough job interviews. This sort of manufactured experience can build the confidence and self-efficacy necessary for real-world success.[46]

Self-talk

Evaluating thoughts about oneself.

- *Self-talk.* According to an expert on the subject, "**self-talk** is the set of evaluating thoughts that you give yourself about facts and events that happen to you."[47] Personal experience tells us that self-talk tends to be a self-fulfilling prophecy. Negative self-talk tends to pave the way for failure, whereas positive self-talk often facilitates success. Replacing negative self-talk ("I'll never get a raise") with positive self-talk ("I deserve a raise and I'm going to get it") is fundamental to better self-management. One business writer, while urging salespeople to be their own cheerleaders, offered this advice for handling difficult situations:

> Tell yourself there's a positive side to everything and train yourself to focus on it. At first your new self-talk will seem forced and unnatural, but stick with it. Use mental imagery to help you concentrate on the benefits of what you think is a bad situation. If you don't like cold calling, for example, think of how good you'll feel when you're finished, knowing you have a whole list of new selling opportunities. Forming a new habit isn't easy, but the effort will pay off.[48]

Self-Reinforcement   The completion of self-contracts and other personal achievements calls for self-reinforcement. According to Bandura, three criteria must be satisfied before self-reinforcement can occur:

1. The individual must have *control over desired reinforcers.*
2. Reinforcers must be *self-administered on a conditional basis.* Failure to meet the performance requirement must lead to self-denial.
3. *Performance standards must be adopted* to establish the quantity and quality of target behavior required for self-reinforcement.[49]

In view of the following realities, self-reinforcement strategies need to be resourceful and creative:

> Self-granted rewards can lead to self-improvement. But as failed dieters and smokers can attest, there are short-run as well as long-run influences on self-reinforcement. For the overeater, the immediate gratification of eating has more influence than the promise of a new wardrobe. The same sort of dilemma plagues procrastinators. Consequently, one needs to weave a powerful web of cues, cognitive supports, and internal and external consequences to win the tug-of-war with status-quo payoffs. Primarily because it is so easy to avoid, self-punishment tends to be ineffectual. As with managing the behavior of others, positive instead of negative consequences are recommended for effective self-management.[50]

In addition, it helps to solicit positive reinforcement for self-improvement from supportive friends, co-workers, and relatives.

Personality Dynamics

Individuals have their own way of thinking and acting, their own unique style or *personality.* **Personality** is defined as the combination of stable physical and mental characteristics that give the individual his or her identity.[51] These characteristics or traits—including how one looks, thinks, acts, and feels—are the product of interacting genetic and environmental influences. In this section, we introduce the Big Five personality dimensions and discuss key personality dynamics including locus of control, attitudes, intelligence, and mental abilities.

> **Personality**
>
> Stable physical and mental characteristics responsible for a person's identity.

The Big Five Personality Dimensions

Long and confusing lists of personality dimensions have been distilled in recent years to the Big Five.[52] They are extraversion, agreeableness, conscientiousness, emotional stability, and openness to experience (see Table 5–2 for descriptions). Standardized personality tests determine how positively or negatively a person scores on each of the Big Five. For example, someone scoring negatively on extraversion would be an introverted person prone to shy and withdrawn behavior.[53] Someone scoring negatively on emotional stability would be nervous, tense, angry, and worried. A person's scores on the Big Five reveal a personality profile as unique as his or her fingerprints. Yet one important question lingers: Are personality models ethnocentric or unique to the culture in which they were developed? At least as far as the Big Five model goes,

The Big Five Personality Dimensions | **TABLE 5–2**

Personality Dimension	Characteristics of a Person Scoring Positively on the Dimension
1. Extraversion	Outgoing, talkative, sociable, assertive
2. Agreeableness	Trusting, good-natured, cooperative, softhearted
3. Conscientiousness	Dependable, responsible, achievement oriented, persistent
4. Emotional stability	Relaxed, secure, unworried
5. Openness to experience	Intellectual, imaginative, curious, broad-minded

SOURCE: Adapted from M R Barrick and M K Mount, "Autonomy as a Moderator of the Relationships between the Big Five Personality Dimensions and Job Performance," *Journal of Applied Psychology,* February 1993, pp 111–18.

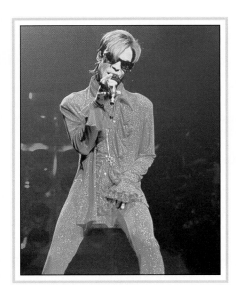

Successful movie and rock stars are often considered extraverts due to the fact that they have chosen a profession that places them "in the spotlight." But contrast the 2 performers pictured here. Jim Carrey would most probably be considered an extravert considering the way he acts both on screen and off. However, what about "stars" who tend to shy away from media attention, such as Prince? Can one be intraverted and still be a "star manager?"

recent cross-cultural research evidence points in the direction of "no." Specifically, the Big Five personality structure held up very well in a study of women and men from Russia, Canada, Hong Kong, Poland, Germany, and Finland.[54]

Personality and Job Performance   Those interested in OB want to know the connection between the Big Five and job performance. Ideally, Big Five personality dimensions that correlate positively and strongly with job performance would be helpful in the selection, training, and appraisal of employees. A meta-analysis of 117 studies involving 23,994 subjects from many professions offers guidance.[55] Among the Big Five, *conscientiousness* had the strongest positive correlation with job performance and training performance. According to the researchers, "those individuals who exhibit traits associated with a strong sense of purpose, obligation, and persistence generally perform better than those who do not."[56] Another expected finding: Extraversion (an outgoing personality) was associated with success for managers and salespeople. Also, extraversion was a stronger predictor of job performance than agreeableness, across all professions. The researchers concluded, "It appears that being courteous, trusting, straightforward, and softhearted has a smaller impact on job performance than being talkative, active, and assertive."[57]

Fruitless Search for the "Ideal Employee" Personality   Given the complexity of today's work environments, the diversity of today's workforce, and recent research evidence,[58] the quest for an ideal employee personality profile is sheer folly. Just as one shoe does not fit all people, one personality profile does not fit all job situations.

Locus of Control: Self or Environment?

Individuals vary in terms of how much personal responsibility they take for their behavior and its consequences. Julian Rotter, a personality researcher, identified a dimension of personality he labeled *locus of control* to explain these differences. He proposed that people tend to attribute the causes of their behavior primarily to either themselves or environmental factors.[59] This personality trait produces distinctly different behavior patterns.

SOURCE: *The Arizona Republic,* May 19, 2001, p D2.

People who believe they control the events and consequences that affect their lives are said to possess an **internal locus of control.** For example, such a person tends to attribute positive outcomes, such as getting a passing grade on an exam, to her or his own abilities. Similarly, an "internal" tends to blame negative events, such as failing an exam, on personal shortcomings—not studying hard enough, perhaps. Many entrepreneurs eventually succeed because their *internal* locus of control helps them overcome setbacks and disappointments. They see themselves as masters of their own fate and not simply lucky.[60]

On the other side of this personality dimension are those who believe their performance is the product of circumstances beyond their immediate control. These individuals are said to possess an **external locus of control** and tend to attribute outcomes to environmental causes, such as luck or fate. Unlike someone with an internal locus of control, an "external" would attribute a passing grade on an exam to something external (an easy test or a good day) and attribute a failing grade to an unfair test or problems at home.

> **Internal locus of control**
>
> Attributing outcomes to one's own actions.

> **External locus of control**
>
> Attributing outcomes to circumstances beyond one's control.

Research Lessons   Researchers have found important behavioral differences between internals and externals:

- Internals display greater work motivation.
- Internals have stronger expectations that effort leads to performance.
- Internals exhibit higher performance on tasks involving learning or problem solving, when performance leads to valued rewards.
- There is a stronger relationship between job satisfaction and performance for internals than for externals.
- Internals obtain higher salaries and greater salary increases than externals.
- Externals tend to be more anxious than internals.[61]

Managerial Implications   The preceding summary of research findings on locus of control has important implications for managing people at work. Let us examine two of them.

First, since internals have a tendency to believe they control the work environment through their behavior, they will attempt to exert control over the work setting. This can be done by trying to influence work procedures, working conditions, task assignments, or relationships with peers and supervisors. As these possibilities imply, internals may resist a manager's attempts to closely supervise their work. Therefore, management may want to place internals in jobs requiring high initiative and low compliance. Externals, on the other hand, might be more amenable to highly structured jobs requiring greater compliance. Direct participation also can bolster the attitudes and performance of externals. This conclusion comes from a field study of 85 computer system users in a wide variety of business and government organizations. Externals who had been significantly involved in designing their organization's computer information system had more favorable attitudes toward the system than their external-locus co-workers who had not participated.[62]

Second, locus of control has implications for reward systems. Given that internals have a greater belief that their effort leads to performance, internals likely would prefer and respond more productively to incentives such as merit pay or sales commissions.[63]

Attitudes

Hardly a day goes by without the popular media reporting the results of another attitude survey. The idea is to take the pulse of public opinion. What do we think about candidate X, the war on drugs, gun control, or abortion? In the workplace, meanwhile, managers conduct attitude surveys to monitor such things as job and pay satisfaction.[64] All this attention to attitudes is based on the assumption that attitudes somehow influence behavior such as voting for someone, working hard, or quitting one's job.

Attitude

Learned predisposition toward a given object.

Attitudes versus Values   An **attitude** is defined as "a learned predisposition to respond in a consistently favorable or unfavorable manner with respect to a given object."[65] Attitudes affect behavior at a different level than do values. While values represent global beliefs that influence behavior across *all* situations, attitudes relate only to behavior directed toward *specific* objects, persons, or situations.[66] Values and attitudes generally, but not always, are in harmony. A manager who strongly values helpful behavior may have a negative attitude toward helping an unethical co-worker.

How Stable Are Attitudes?   In one landmark study, researchers found the *job* attitudes of 5,000 middle-aged male employees to be very stable over a five-year period. Positive job attitudes remained positive; negative ones remained negative. Even those who changed jobs or occupations tended to maintain their prior job attitudes.[67] More recent research suggests the foregoing study may have overstated the stability of attitudes because it was restricted to a middle-aged sample. This time, researchers asked: What happens to attitudes over the entire span of adulthood? *General* attitudes were found to be more susceptible to change during early and late adulthood than during middle adulthood. Three factors accounted for middle-age attitude stability: (1) greater personal certainty, (2) perceived abundance of knowledge, and (3) a need for strong attitudes. Thus, the conventional notion that general attitudes become less likely to change as the person ages was rejected. Elderly people, along with young adults, can and do change their general attitudes because they are more open and less self-assured.[68]

Intelligence and Cognitive Abilities

Intelligence

Capacity for constructive thinking, reasoning, problem solving.

Although experts do not agree on a specific definition, **intelligence** represents an individual's capacity for constructive thinking, reasoning, and problem solving.[69] Historically, intelligence was believed to be an innate capacity, passed genetically from one generation to the next. Research since has shown, however, that intelligence (like personality) also is a function of environmental influences.[70] Organic factors have more recently been added to the formula as a result of mounting evidence of the connection between alcohol and drug abuse by pregnant women and intellectual development problems in their children.[71]

Researchers have produced some interesting findings about abilities and intelligence in recent years. A unique five-year study documented the tendency of people to "gravitate into jobs commensurate with their abilities."[72] This prompts the vision of the labor market acting as a giant sorting or sifting machine, with employees tumbling into various ability bins. Meanwhile, a steady and significant rise in average intelligence among those in developed countries has been observed over the last 70 years. Why? Experts at a recent American Psychological Association conference concluded, "Some combination of better schooling, improved socioeconomic status, healthier nutrition, and a more technologically complex society might account for the gains in IQ scores."[73] So if you think you're smarter than your parents and your teachers, you're probably right!

Two Types of Abilities   Human intelligence has been studied predominantly through the empirical approach. By examining the relationships between measures of mental abilities and behavior, researchers have statistically isolated major components of intelligence. Using this empirical procedure, pioneering psychologist Charles Spearman proposed in 1927 that all cognitive performance is determined by two types of abilities. The first can be characterized as a general mental ability needed for *all* cognitive tasks. The second is unique to the task at hand. For example, an individual's ability to complete crossword puzzles is a function of his or her broad mental abilities as well as the specific ability to perceive patterns in partially completed words.

Seven Major Mental Abilities   Through the years, much research has been devoted to developing and expanding Spearman's ideas on the relationship between cognitive abilities and intelligence. One research psychologist listed 120 distinct mental abilities. Table 5–3 contains definitions of the seven most frequently cited

Mental Abilities   **TABLE 5–3**

Ability	Description
1. Verbal comprehension	The ability to understand what words mean and to readily comprehend what is read.
2. Word fluency	The ability to produce isolated words that fulfill specific symbolic or structural requirements (such as all words that begin with the letter b and have two vowels).
3. Numerical	The ability to make quick and accurate arithmetic computations such as adding and subtracting.
4. Spatial	Being able to perceive spatial patterns and to visualize how geometric shapes would look if transformed in shape or position.
5. Memory	Having good rote memory for paired words, symbols, lists of numbers, or other associated items.
6. Perceptual speed	The ability to perceive figures, identify similarities and differences, and carry out tasks involving visual perception.
7. Inductive reasoning	The ability to reason from specifics to general conclusions.

SOURCE: Adapted from M D Dunnette, "Aptitudes, Abilities, and Skills," in *Handbook of Industrial and Organizational Psychology*, ed M D Dunnette (Skokie, IL: Rand McNally, 1976), pp 478–83.

mental abilities. Of the seven abilities, personnel selection researchers have found verbal ability, numerical ability, spatial ability, and inductive reasoning to be valid predictors of job performance for both minority and majority applicants.[74]

OB Gets Emotional

In the ideal world of management theory, employees pursue organizational goals in a logical and rational manner. Emotional behavior seldom is factored into the equation. Yet day-to-day organizational life shows us how prevalent and powerful emotions can be. Anger and jealousy, both potent emotions, often push aside logic and rationality in the workplace. Managers use fear and other emotions to both motivate and intimidate. For example, consider Selina Y Lo, the head of marketing at Alteon WebSystems in San Jose, California:

> A 15-year veteran of the networking business, she has honed her in-your-face style at three startups, earning a reputation as one of the smartest, toughest managers in the industry. Lo's temper and intensity are legendary: During a product meeting last fall, recalls Alteon software engineer John Taylor, she sprang up yelling from her chair, banged her fist on the table, and shoved a finger in his face after Taylor said he couldn't add a feature she had asked for. Taylor quickly relented. "I've left a few dead bodies behind me," Lo crows.[75]

Less noisy, but still emotion laden, is Intel Chairman Andy Grove's use of Grove's Law to keep a competitive edge in the global computer chip market. According to Grove's Law, "Only the paranoid survive."[76] A combination of curiosity and fear is said to drive Barry Diller, CEO of USA Networks, and one of the media world's legendary dealmakers. Says Diller: "I and my friends succeeded because we were scared to death of failing."[77] These admired corporate leaders would not have achieved what they have without the ability to be logical and rational decision makers *and* be emotionally charged. Too much emotion, however, could have spelled career and organizational disaster for any one of them.

In this final section, our examination of individual differences turns to defining emotions, reviewing a typology of 10 positive and negative emotions, and focusing on the topic of emotional intelligence.

Positive and Negative Emotions

Emotions

Complex human reactions to personal achievements and setbacks that may be felt and displayed.

Richard S Lazarus, a leading authority on the subject, defines **emotions** as "complex, patterned, organismic reactions to how we think we are doing in our lifelong efforts to survive and flourish and to achieve what we wish for ourselves."[78] The word *organismic* is appropriate because emotions involve the *whole* person—biological, psychological, and social. Importantly, psychologists draw a distinction between *felt* and *displayed* emotions.[79] For example, you might feel angry (felt emotion) at a rude co-worker but not make a nasty remark in return (displayed emotion). Emotions play roles in both causing and adapting to stress and its associated biological and psychological problems. The destructive effect of emotional behavior on social relationships is all too obvious in daily life.

Lazarus's definition of emotions centers on a person's goals. Accordingly, his distinction between positive and negative emotions is goal oriented. Some emotions are triggered by frustration and failure when pursuing one's goals. Lazarus calls these *negative* emotions. They are said to be goal incongruent. For example, which of the six negative emotions in Figure 5–4 are you likely to experience if you fail the final

Positive and Negative Emotions   **FIGURE 5–4**

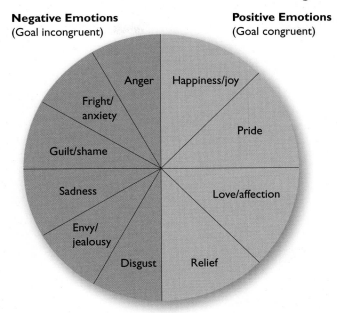

Negative Emotions
(Goal incongruent)

Positive Emotions
(Goal congruent)

SOURCE: Adapted from discussion in R S Lazarus, *Emotion and Adaptation* (New York: Oxford University Press, 1991), Chs 6, 7.

exam in a required course? Failing the exam would be incongruent with your goal of graduating on time. On the other hand, which of the four *positive* emotions in Figure 5–4 would you probably experience if you graduated on time and with honors? The emotions you would experience in this situation are positive because they are congruent (or consistent) with an important lifetime goal. The individual's goals, it is important to note, may or may not be socially acceptable. Thus, a positive emotion, such as love/affection, may be undesirable if associated with sexual harassment. Oppositely, slight pangs of guilt, anxiety, and envy can motivate extra effort. On balance, the constructive or destructive nature of a particular emotion must be judged in terms of both its intensity and the person's relevant goal.

More Attention Needed

The OB research literature is sparse regarding emotions. Emotional behavior typically is not covered as a central variable but rather as a subfactor in discussions of organizational politics, conflict, and stress. Here are some recent insights. According to a British organizational psychologist, we need to do a better job of dealing with emotions in career management programs.[80] Under the new employment contract, job-hunting skills are not enough. Emotional skills are needed to handle frequent and often difficult career transitions. A pair of laboratory studies with US college students as subjects found no gender difference in *felt* emotions. But the women were more emotionally *expressive* than the men.[81] Two field studies with nurses and accountants as subjects found a strong linkage between the work group's collective mood and the individual's mood.[82] The bad news: Foul moods are contagious. But so are good moods. Go spread the cheer!

We look forward to more comprehensive OB research on the causes and consequences of emotional behavior.

Emotional Intelligence

In 1995, Daniel Goleman, a psychologist turned journalist, created a stir in education and management circles with the publication of his book *Emotional Intelligence*. Hence, an obscure topic among psychologists became mainstream. According to Goleman, traditional models of intelligence (IQ) are too narrow. His approach to *emotional intelligence* includes

> . . . abilities such as being able to motivate oneself and persist in the face of frustrations; to control impulse and delay gratification; to regulate one's moods and keep distress from swamping the ability to think; to empathize and to hope. Unlike IQ, with its nearly one-hundred-year history of research with hundreds of thousands of people, emotional intelligence is a new concept. No one can yet say exactly how much of the variability from person to person in life's course it accounts for. But what data exist suggest it can be as powerful, and at times more powerful, than IQ.[83]

Self-assessment instruments supposedly measuring emotional intelligence have appeared in the popular management literature. Sample questions include: "I believe I can stay on top of tough situations,"[84] and "I am able to admit my own mistakes."[85] Recent research, however, casts serious doubt on the reliability and validity of such instruments.[86] Even Goleman concedes, "It's very tough to measure our own emotional intelligence, because most of us don't have a very clear sense of how we come across to other people. . . ."[87] Honest feedback from others is necessary. Still, the area of emotional intelligence is useful for teachers and organizational trainers because, unlike IQ, social problem solving and the ability to control one's emotions can be taught and learned (see Skills & Best Practices). Scores on emotional intelligence tests definitely should *not* be used for making hiring and promotion decisions until valid measuring tools are developed.

How to Manage Anger in Yourself and Others

SKILLS & BEST PRACTICES

Reducing Chronic Anger [in Yourself]

Guides for Action

- Appreciate the potentially valuable lessons from anger.
- Use mistakes and slights to learn.
- Recognize that you and others can do well enough without being perfect.
- Trust that most people want to be caring, helpful family members and colleagues.
- Forgive others and yourself.
- Confront unrealistic, blame-oriented assumptions.
- Adopt constructive, learning-oriented assumptions.

Pitfalls to Avoid

- Assume every slight is a painful wound.
- Equate not getting what you want with catastrophe.
- See every mistake and slip as a transgression that must be corrected immediately.
- Attack someone for your getting angry.
- Attack yourself for getting angry.
- Try to be and have things perfect.
- Suspect people's motives unless you have incontestable evidence that people can be trusted.
- Assume any attempt to change yourself is an admission of failure.
- Never forgive.

Responding to Angry Provocation

Guides for Action

- Expect angry people to exaggerate.
- Recognize the other's frustrations and pressures.
- Use the provocation to develop your abilities.
- Allow the other to let off steam.
- Begin to problem solve when the anger is at moderate levels.
- Congratulate yourself on turning an outburst into an opportunity to find solutions.
- Share successes with partners.

Pitfalls to Avoid

- Take every word literally.
- Denounce the most extreme statements and ignore more moderate ones.
- Doubt yourself because the other does.
- Attack because you have been attacked.
- Forget the experience without learning from it.

SOURCE: Reprinted with permission from D Tjosvold, *Learning to Manage Conflict: Getting People to Work Together Productively*, pp 127–29. Copyright © 1993 Dean Tjosvold. First published by Lexington Books.

chapter summary

- *Distinguish between self-esteem and self-efficacy.* Self-esteem is an overall evaluation of oneself, one's perceived self-worth. Self-efficacy is the belief in one's ability to successfully perform a task.

- *Contrast high and low self-monitoring individuals, and describe resulting problems each may have.* A high self-monitor strives to make a good public impression by closely monitoring his or her behavior and adapting it to the situation. Very high self-monitoring can create a "chameleon" who is seen as insincere and dishonest. Low self-monitors do the opposite by acting out their momentary feelings, regardless of their surroundings. Very low self-monitoring can lead to a one-way communicator who seems to ignore verbal and nonverbal cues from others.

- *Explain the social learning model of self-management.* Behavior results from interaction among four components: (a) situational cues, (b) the person's psychological self, (c) the person's behavior, and (d) consequences. Behavior, such as Covey's seven habits of highly effective people, can be developed by relying on supportive cognitive processes such as mental rehearsal and self-talk. Carefully arranged cues and consequences also help in the self-improvement process.

- *Identify and describe the Big Five personality dimensions, and specify which one is correlated most strongly with job performance.* The Big Five personality dimensions are extraversion (social and talkative), agreeableness (trusting and cooperative), conscientiousness (responsible and persistent), emotional stability (relaxed and unworried), and openness to experience (intellectual and curious). Conscientiousness is the best predictor of job performance.

- *Explain the difference between an internal and external locus of control.* People with an *internal* locus of control, such as entrepreneurs, believe they are masters of their own fate. Those with an *external* locus of control attribute their behavior and its results to situational forces.

- *Distinguish between positive and negative emotions, and describe a person with high emotional intelligence.* Positive emotions—happiness/joy, pride, love/affection, and relief—are personal reactions to circumstances congruent with one's goals. Negative emotions—anger, fright/anxiety, guilt/shame, sadness, envy/jealousy, and disgust—are personal reactions to circumstances incongruent with one's goals. Both types of emotions need to be judged in terms of intensity and the appropriateness of the person's relevant goal. According to Daniel Goleman, someone with high emotional intelligence has the ability to be self-motivating, is persistent in the face of adversity, willingly admits mistakes, and has his or her emotions under control. Unlike standard intelligence (IQ), emotional intelligence can be taught.

internet exercise

www.iqtest.com

Lots of interactive questionnaires can be found on the Internet to help you learn more about yourself. *Note: These self-tests are for instructional and entertainment purposes only.* They are not intended to replace rigorously validated and properly administered psychometric tests and should not be used to establish qualifications or make personnel decisions. Still, they can provide useful insights and stimulate discussion. The purpose of this exercise is to learn more about general intelligence (IQ).

A FREE ONLINE INTERACTIVE INTELLIGENCE (IQ) TEST

Go to Self Discovery Workshop's home page on the Internet, **www.iqtest.com**. For instructive background, select and read the first two menu items, "What is an IQ score?" and "History of this intelligence test." Then proceed to the third menu item, "Let me take this intelligence test now." Follow the prompts. You will be given some instructions, a sample three-item pretest, and then you will be asked to provide some personal data. *Note: As specified in the instructions, you do not have to fill out the name, address, etc. section to take the free IQ test.* Simply skip ahead to the test, making sure to read the instructions very carefully because you will be given only 13 minutes to complete the 38 true/false test items. Only one pass through the IQ test is appropriate if the results are to have any meaning at all. The test is scored automatically and you will be given both your IQ score and comparative norms. (Note: We recommend that you take this test when you are rested, refreshed, and have a clear mind. Also, people who do not respond well to time pressure may want to skip it to avoid unnecessary stress.)

QUESTIONS

1. What is your attitude toward this type of pencil-and-paper intelligence test? Explain.
2. Could self-serving bias, discussed in Chapter 4, influence the way people evaluate intelligence tests? Briefly, self-serving bias involves taking personal responsibility for your successes and blaming your failures on other factors.

For example, "I scored high, so I think it's a good test." "I scored low, so it's an unfair or invalid test." Explain.

3. Do you agree with psychologist Daniel Goleman that emotional intelligence (EQ) can be more important than IQ? Explain.

Motivation I: Needs, Job Design, and Satisfaction

Six

chapter

After reading the material in this chapter, you should be able to:

- Discuss the job performance model of motivation.

- Contrast Maslow's and McClelland's need theories.

- Describe the mechanistic, motivational, biological, and perceptual-motor approaches to job design.

- Explain the practical significance of Herzberg's distinction between motivators and hygiene factors.

- Discuss the causes and consequences of job satisfaction.

- Critique the four hypotheses that explain the nature of work-family relationships.

ROSENBLUTH INTERNATIONAL IS A PEOPLE-FOCUSED ORGANIZATION

There is a new breed of corporate leaders who have figured out that you can't barter for loyalty. Nor can you buy a person's heart, passion for work, or imagination or talent. These new leaders understand that those are things that people choose to give and that organizations must earn. Companies such as Rosenbluth International, Sears, and Norwest Corporation are trying to offer something less tangible and more

meaningful: an intellectual and emotional connection between people, their work, and the workplace. Firms are designing cultures in which people naturally want to do the work—not just for external rewards but also for the satisfaction that comes from doing challenging work that's of value to one's organization. And though those people strategies improve the bottom line, they also bring

about another benefit: People want to stay and give more.

Rosenbluth International: Service from the Heart
In his book, *The Customer Comes Second and Other Secrets of Exceptional Service,* Hal Rosenbluth, chairman and CEO of Rosenbluth International, a corporate travel company, says there's nothing he believes in more strongly than making people happy at work. His reasoning

is simple: If the highest achievable customer service comes from the heart, then reaching associates' (as Rosenbluth employees are called) hearts will lead to the best service....

Rosenbluth goes for the heart by asking people at all levels of the company for ideas, and he uses those ideas. Two-way rather than top-down communication is how business is done. Meet-

ing schedules and discussion topics are posted daily, and associates are encouraged to attend any meeting in which they have an interest or a concern....

He has also tried to eliminate the "superior-subordinate" language and behavior that often characterize manager-employee relationships, one reason employees are called associates. Team leaders are expected to know and care about each associate on their teams. Team leaders are also responsible for helping people understand the business strategy and how their work contributes. In fact, the bonuses of team leaders are tied to how well they help associates develop and contribute.[1]

FOR DISCUSSION

What lessons about motivating employees can we learn from Hal Rosenbluth? For an interpretation of this case and additional comments, visit our website:

www.mhhe.com/kinickiob

EFFECTIVE EMPLOYEE MOTIVATION has long been one of management's most difficult and important duties. Success in this endeavor is becoming more challenging in light of organizational trends to downsize and reengineer and the demands associated with managing a diverse workforce. As revealed in the opening case, companies such as Rosenbluth International consider employee motivation and satisfaction as critical for organizational success. The purpose of this chapter, as well as the next, is to provide you with a foundation for understanding the complexities of employee motivation.

After discussing the fundamentals of employee motivation, this chapter focuses on the motivational technique of job design and job satisfaction and work–family relationships. Coverage of employee motivation also extends to Chapter 7.

The Fundamentals of Employee Motivation

Motivation

Psychological processes that arouse and direct goal-directed behavior.

The term *motivation* derives from the Latin word *movere,* meaning "to move." In the present context, **motivation** represents "those psychological processes that cause the arousal, direction, and persistence of voluntary actions that are goal directed."[2] Managers need to understand these psychological processes if they are to successfully guide employees toward accomplishing organizational objectives. This section thus provides a conceptual framework for understanding motivation and examines need theories of motivation.

A Job Performance Model of Motivation

Terence Mitchell, a well-known OB researcher, proposed a broad conceptual model that explains how motivation influences job behaviors and performance. This model, which is shown in Figure 6–1, integrates elements from several of the theories we discuss in this book. It identifies the causes and consequences of motivation.[3]

Figure 6–1 shows that individual inputs and job context are the two key categories of factors that influence motivation. As discussed in Chapter 5, employees bring ability, job knowledge, dispositions and traits, emotions, moods, beliefs, and values to the work setting. The job context includes the physical environment, the tasks one completes, the organization's approach to recognition and rewards, the adequacy of supervisory support and coaching, and the organization's culture (recall our discussion in Chapter 2). These two categories of factors influence each other as well as the motivational processes of arousal, direction, and persistence. Consider the motivational implications associated with the job context at Great Plains Software in Fargo, ND:

> All employees get stock options. An expansive cafeteria offers a sweeping view of the 48-acre prairie campus. Casual dress is the standard. Daily extracurricular classes are offered in everything from aerobics and yoga to parenting and personal finance. And next year will bring an onsite day care facility.... What does make Great Plains such a great place to work is its commitment to the development of its people. Simply stroll down the hallways of Horizon, the company's main building, and you'll see that commitment evidenced in the posters promoting scores of training and educational opportunities available to team members.[4]

In support of the idea that job context influences employee motivation and commitment, Great Plains turnover rate is 5%, which is well below the information technology industry average of 18 to 25%.[5]

Figure 6–1 further reveals that *motivated behaviors* are directly affected by an individual's ability and job knowledge (skills), motivation, and a combination of enabling and limiting job context factors. For instance, it would be difficult to persist on a proj-

A Job Performance Model of Motivation   **FIGURE 6–1**

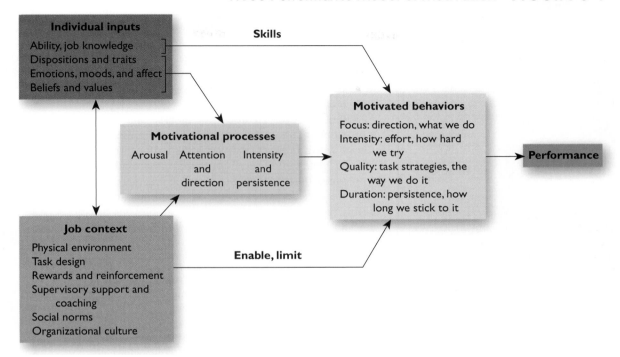

SOURCE: Adapted from T R Mitchell, "Matching Motivational Strategies with Organizational Contexts," in *Research in Organizational Behavior* (vol 19), eds L L Cummings and B M Staw (Greenwich, CT: JAI Press, 1997), p 63.

ect if you were working with defective raw materials or broken equipment. In contrast, motivated behaviors are likely to be enhanced when managers supply employees with adequate resources to get the job done and provide effective coaching. This coaching might entail furnishing employees with successful role models, showing employees how to complete complex tasks, and helping them maintain high self-efficacy and self-esteem (recall the discussion in Chapter 5). Performance is, in turn, influenced by motivated behavior.

Need Theories of Motivation

Need theories attempt to pinpoint internal factors that energize behavior. **Needs** are physiological or psychological deficiencies that arouse behavior. They can be strong or weak and are influenced by environmental factors. Thus, human needs vary over time and place. Two popular need theories are discussed in this section: Maslow's need hierarchy theory and McClelland's need theory.

> **Needs**
>
> Physiological or psychological deficiencies that arouse behavior.

Maslow's Need Hierarchy Theory   In 1943, psychologist Abraham Maslow published his now-famous need hierarchy theory of motivation. Although the theory was based on his clinical observation of a few neurotic individuals, it has subsequently been used to explain the entire spectrum of human behavior. Maslow proposed that motivation is a function of five basic needs—physiological, safety, love, esteem, and self-actualization.

Corporate honchos at Booz-Allen & Hamilton encourage employees to have a life outside of the office. Lloyd Howell, vice president, leaves the office around 5 PM on most Fridays to have a date night with his wife. CEO Ralph Shrader, pictured here, is known to make references to his own work/family conflicts in talks to his employees. Motivational opportunities can be organized and promoted by a company, but it can be doubly encouraging for employees to see the effort come from the very top.

Maslow said these five need categories are arranged in a pre-potent hierarchy. In other words, he believed human needs generally emerge in a predictable stair-step fashion. Accordingly, when one's physiological needs are relatively satisfied, one's safety needs emerge, and so on up the need hierarchy, one step at a time. Once a need is satisfied it activates the next higher need in the hierarchy. This process continues until the need for self-actualization is activated.[6]

Although research does not clearly support this theory of motivation, there is one key managerial implication of Maslow's theory worth noting. That is, a satisfied need may lose its motivational potential. Therefore, managers are advised to motivate employees by devising programs or practices aimed at satisfying emerging or unmet needs. Many companies have responded to this recommendation by offering employees flexible scheduling and benefit plans:

> At Accenture, the large consulting company based in Chicago, staffers can put in their 40 hours in four days instead of five, getting an extra day. Some companies also allow trading of benefits. For instance, workers might be able to forfeit their health insurance if they are covered by a spouse's plan and instead get an educational loan for the same amount. At Mellon Bank in Pittsburgh, employees get "credits" that can be used for a variety of benefits such as health, vision, and dental care—or extra days off.[7]

Other companies are beginning to offer "specialized" benefits aimed at satisfying the needs of unique employees. Consider the case of Tom Tyler:

> With two job offers in hand, mechanical engineer Tom Tyler knew he'd be moving from suburban Detroit to the San Francisco area. The only question was, which employer would get his services? "The only difference between what [his eventual employer] offered me and the other company was the housing assistance," Tyler says. "The other company even offered $5,000 more per year in salary. But, when all was said and done, the house buying and selling assistance was worth somewhere in the neighborhood of $30,000. . . ." The benefit that swayed Tyler's job decision was mortgage help through an employer-assisted housing (EAH) program.[8]

In conclusion, managers are more likely to fuel employee motivation by offering benefits and rewards that meet individual needs.

McClelland's Need Theory   David McClelland, a well-known psychologist, has been studying the relationship between needs and behavior since the late 1940s. Although he is most recognized for his research on the need for achievement, he also investigated the needs for affiliation and power. Let us consider each of these needs:

• The **need for achievement** is defined by the following desires:

Need for achievement

Desire to accomplish something difficult.

To accomplish something difficult. To master, manipulate, or organize physical objects, human beings, or ideas. To do this as rapidly and as independently as possible. To overcome obstacles and attain a high standard. To excel one's self. To rival and surpass others. To increase self-regard by the successful exercise of talent.[9]

Achievement-motivated people share three common characteristics: (1) a preference for working on tasks of moderate difficulty; (2) a preference for situations in which performance is due to their efforts rather than other factors, such as luck; and (3) they desire more feedback on their successes and failures than do low achievers. A review of research on the "entrepreneurial" personality showed that entrepreneurs were found to have a higher need for achievement than nonentrepreneurs.[10]

- People with a high **need for affiliation** prefer to spend more time maintaining social relationships, joining groups, and wanting to be loved. Individuals high in this need are not the most effective managers or leaders because they have a hard time making difficult decisions without worrying about being disliked.

> **Need for affiliation**
>
> Desire to spend time in social relationships and activities.

- The **need for power** reflects an individual's desire to influence, coach, teach, or encourage others to achieve. People with a high need for power like to work and are concerned with discipline and self-respect. There is a positive and negative side to this need. The negative face of power is characterized by an "if I win, you lose" mentality. In contrast, people with a positive orientation to power focus on accomplishing group goals and helping employees obtain the feeling of competence. More is said about the two faces of power in Chapter 13. Because effective managers must positively influence others, McClelland proposes that top managers should have a high need for power coupled with a low need for affiliation. He also believes that individuals with high achievement motivation are *not* best suited for top management positions. Several studies support these propositions.[11]

> **Need for power**
>
> Desire to influence, coach, teach, or encourage others to achieve.

There are three managerial implications associated with McClelland's need theory. First, given that adults can be trained to increase their achievement motivation, and achievement motivation is correlated with performance, organizations should consider the benefits of providing achievement training for employees.[12] Second, achievement, affiliation, and power needs can be considered during the selection process, for better placement. For example, a study revealed that people with a high need for achievement were more attracted to companies that had a pay-for-performance environment than were those with a low achievement motivation.[13] Finally, managers should create challenging task assignments or goals because the need for achievement is positively correlated with goal commitment, which, in turn, influences performance.[14]

Motivating Employees through Job Design

Job design, also referred to as job redesign, "refers to any set of activities that involve the alteration of specific jobs or interdependent systems of jobs with the intent of improving the quality of employee job experience and their on-the-job productivity."[15] A team of researchers examined the various methods for conducting job design and integrated them into an interdisciplinary framework that contains four major approaches: mechanistic, motivational, biological, and perceptual-motor.[16] As you will learn, each approach to job design emphasizes different outcomes.[17] This section discusses these four approaches to job design and focuses most heavily on the motivational methods.

> **Job design**
>
> Changing the content and/or process of a specific job to increase job satisfaction and performance.

The Mechanistic Approach

The mechanistic approach draws from research in industrial engineering and scientific management and is most heavily influenced by the work of Frederick Taylor. Taylor, a mechanical engineer, developed the principles of scientific management based on research and experimentation to determine the most efficient way to perform jobs. Because jobs are highly specialized and standardized when they are designed according to the principles of scientific management, this approach to job design targets efficiency, flexibility, and employee productivity.

Designing jobs according to the principles of scientific management has both positive and negative consequences. Positively, employee efficiency and productivity are increased. On the other hand, research reveals that simplified, repetitive jobs also lead to job dissatisfaction, poor mental health, higher levels of stress, and low sense of accomplishment and personal growth.[18] These negative consequences paved the way for the motivational approach to job design.

Motivational Approaches

The motivational approaches to job design attempt to improve employees' affective and attitudinal reactions such as job satisfaction and intrinsic motivation as well as a host of behavioral outcomes such as absenteeism, turnover, and performance.[19] We discuss three key motivational techniques: job enlargement, job enrichment, and a contingency approach called the job characteristics model.

Job Enlargement This technique was first used in the late 1940s in response to complaints about tedious and overspecialized jobs. **Job enlargement** involves putting more variety into a worker's job by combining specialized tasks of comparable difficulty. Some call this *horizontally loading* the job. Researchers recommend using job enlargement as part of a broader approach that uses multiple motivational methods because it does not have a significant and lasting positive effect on job performance by itself.[20]

Job enlargement

Putting more variety into a job.

Job Rotation As with job enlargement, job rotation's purpose is to give employees greater variety in their work. **Job rotation** calls for moving employees from one specialized job to another. Rather than performing only one job, workers are trained and given the opportunity to perform two or more separate jobs on a rotating basis. By rotating employees from job to job, managers believe they can stimulate interest and motivation while providing employees with a broader perspective of the organization. Other proposed advantages of job rotation include increased worker flexibility and easier scheduling because employees are cross trained to perform different jobs. Unfortunately, the promised benefits associated with job rotation programs have not been adequately researched.

Job rotation

Moving employees from one specialized job to another.

Job Enrichment Job enrichment is the practical application of Frederick Herzberg's motivator–hygiene theory of job satisfaction. Herzberg's theory is based on a landmark study in which he interviewed 203 accountants and engineers.[21] These interviews sought to determine the factors responsible for job satisfaction and dissatisfaction. Herzberg found separate and distinct clusters of factors associated with job satisfaction and dissatisfaction. Job satisfaction was more frequently associated with achievement, recognition, characteristics of the work, responsibility, and advancement. These factors were all related to outcomes associated with the *content* of the

Herzberg's Motivator–Hygiene Model   **FIGURE 6–2**

Motivators

No Satisfaction ⟶ Satisfaction
Jobs that do not   Jobs offering
offer achievement,   achievement,
recognition,   recognition,
stimulating work,   stimulating work,
responsibility,   responsibility,
and advancement.   and advancement.

Hygiene factors

Dissatisfaction ⟵ No Dissatisfaction
Jobs with poor   Jobs with good
company policies   company policies
and administration,   and administration,
technical supervision,   technical supervision,
salary, interpersonal   salary, interpersonal
relationships with   relationships with
supervisors, and   supervisors, and
working conditions.   working conditions.

SOURCE: Adapted in part from D A Whitsett and E K Winslow, "An Analysis of Studies Critical of the Motivator–Hygiene Theory," *Personnel Psychology,* Winter 1967, pp 391–415.

task being performed. Herzberg labeled these factors **motivators** because each was associated with strong effort and good performance. He hypothesized that motivators cause a person to move from a state of no satisfaction to satisfaction (see Figure 6–2). Therefore, Herzberg's theory predicts managers can motivate individuals by incorporating "motivators" into an individual's job.

> **Motivators**
>
> Job characteristics associated with job satisfaction.

Herzberg found job *dissatisfaction* to be associated primarily with factors in the work *context* or environment. Specifically, company policy and administration, technical supervision, salary, interpersonal relations with one's supervisor, and working conditions were most frequently mentioned by employees expressing job dissatisfaction. Herzberg labeled this second cluster of factors **hygiene factors.** He further proposed that they were not motivational. At best, according to Herzberg's interpretation, an individual will experience no job dissatisfaction when he or she has no grievances about hygiene factors (refer to Figure 6–2).

> **Hygiene factors**
>
> Job characteristics associated with job dissatisfaction.

The key to adequately understanding Herzberg's motivator–hygiene theory is recognizing that he believes that satisfaction is not the opposite of dissatisfaction. Herzberg concludes that "the opposite of job satisfaction is not job dissatisfaction, but rather no job satisfaction; and similarly, the opposite of job dissatisfaction is not job satisfaction, but no dissatisfaction."[22] Herzberg thus asserts that the dissatisfaction–satisfaction continuum contains a zero midpoint at which dissatisfaction and satisfaction are absent. Conceivably, an organization member who has good supervision, pay, and working conditions but a tedious and unchallenging task with little chance of advancement would be at the zero midpoint. That person would have no dissatisfaction (because of good hygiene factors) and no satisfaction (because of a lack of motivators).

Herzberg's theory generated a great deal of research and controversy. Although research does not support the two-factor aspect of his theory, it does support many of the theory's implications for job design.[23] Job enrichment is based on the application of Herzberg's ideas. Specifically, **job enrichment** entails modifying a job such that an employee has the opportunity to experience achievement, recognition, stimulating work, responsibility, and advancement. These characteristics are incorporated into a job through vertical loading. Rather than giving employees additional tasks of similar difficulty (horizontal loading), *vertical loading* consists of giving workers more responsibility. In other words, employees take on chores normally performed by their supervisors.

> **Job enrichment**
>
> Building achievement, recognition, stimulating work, responsibility, and advancement into a job.

The Job Characteristics Model Two OB researchers, J Richard Hackman and Greg Oldham, played a central role in developing the job characteristics approach. These researchers tried to determine how work can be structured so that employees are internally (or intrinsically) motivated. **Internal motivation** occurs when an individual is "turned on to one's work because of the positive internal feelings that are generated by doing well, rather than being dependent on external factors (such as incentive pay or compliments from the boss) for the motivation to work effectively."[24] These positive feelings power a self-perpetuating cycle of motivation. As shown in Figure 6–3, internal work motivation is determined by three psychological states. Consider the psychological state of experienced meaningfulness. A recent national survey of employees indicated that the primary contributor to workplace pride was that people felt they were doing work that mattered.[25] OB researcher Kenneth Thomas commented on this

> **Internal motivation**
>
> Motivation caused by positive internal feelings.

FIGURE 6–3   The Job Characteristics Model

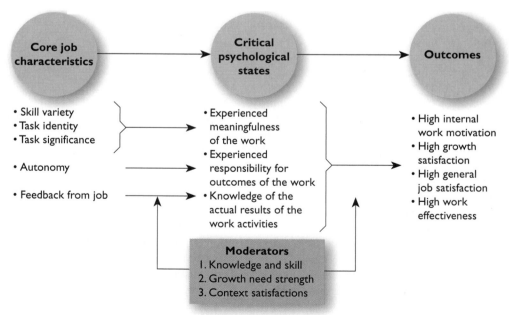

SOURCE: J R Hackman and G R Oldham, *Work Redesign,* © 1980, Addison-Wesley Publishing Co., Reading, MA, p 90. Reprinted with permission.

issue by noting, "It is not the task itself but the purpose of the task that provides much of the meaningfulness—the intrinsic motivation—of any job. When people say they are committed to their work, they usually mean they are committed to some worthy purpose served by their work."[26] Managers can foster the psychological states that drive intrinsic motivation by designing jobs that possess the five core job characteristics shown in Figure 6–3. Let us examine the core job dimensions.

In general terms, **core job dimensions** are common characteristics found to a varying degree in all jobs. Three of the job characteristics shown in Figure 6–3 combine to determine experienced meaningfulness of work:

> **Core job dimensions**
>
> Job characteristics found to various degrees in all jobs.

- *Skill variety.* The extent to which the job requires an individual to perform a variety of tasks that require him or her to use different skills and abilities.
- *Task identity.* The extent to which the job requires an individual to perform a whole or completely identifiable piece of work. In other words, task identity is high when a person works on a product or project from beginning to end and sees a tangible result.
- *Task significance.* The extent to which the job affects the lives of other people within or outside the organization.

Experienced responsibility is elicited by the job characteristic of autonomy, defined as follows:

- *Autonomy.* The extent to which the job enables an individual to experience freedom, independence, and discretion in both scheduling and determining the procedures used in completing the job.

Finally, knowledge of results is fostered by the job characteristic of feedback, defined as follows:

- *Feedback.* The extent to which an individual receives direct and clear information about how effectively he or she is performing the job.[27]

Hackman and Oldham recognized that everyone does not want a job containing high amounts of the five core job characteristics. They incorporated this conclusion into their model by identifying three attributes that affect how individuals respond to job enrichment. These attributes are concerned with the individual's knowledge and skill, growth need strength (representing the desire to grow and develop as an individual), and context satisfactions (see the box labeled Moderators in Figure 6–3). Context satisfactions represent the extent to which employees are satisfied with various aspects of their job, such as satisfaction with pay, coworkers, and supervision.

There are several practical implications associated with the using the job characteristics model to enhance intrinsic motivation: Steps for applying this model are shown in Skills & Best Practices. Managers may want to use this model to increase employee job satisfaction.

Steps for Applying the Job Characteristics Model

1. Diagnose the work environment to determine the level of employee motivation and job satisfaction. Job design should be used when employee motivation ranges from low to moderately high. The diagnosis can be made using employee surveys.

2. Determine whether job redesign is appropriate for a given group of employees. Job redesign is most likely to work in a participative environment in which employees have the necessary knowledge and skills to perform the enriched tasks and their job satisfaction is average to high.

3. Determine how to best redesign the job. The focus of this effort is to increase those core job characteristics that are low. Employee input is essential during this step to determine the details of a redesign initiative.

SKILLS & BEST PRACTICES

Lately, a boom in Training and Development has stemmed from the belief that a well-trained employee is a motivated and happy employee. According to a recent American Society for Training & Development (ASTD) study, employees tend to find training on the "basics" (courses on boosting sales and understanding their company's products) much more desirable than training in interpersonal communication, executive development, and customer relations. It also makes a difference if the employee is forced to attend the course, or chooses to do so on his own. The study found that employees are more likely to say that a course improved their performance if their attendance was voluntary.

Research overwhelmingly demonstrates a moderately strong relationship between job characteristics and satisfaction.[28] Sun Microsystems, for example, used drop-in centers to redesign the work environment of its employees in order to enhance employee satisfaction:

> Called alternative drop-in, hoteling, or telework locations, Sun's satellite work centers are comfortable but no-frills operations, little more than a series of cubicles, each quipped with a computer workstation and a telephone. . . . Sun opened its first three drop-in centers almost three years ago at the suggestion of a group of engineers who were tired of wasting so much time getting to and from work on the ever-more-congested Silicon Valley highway system. . . . Sun, which is very aware that its success depends on a happy workforce, has made giving its 40,000 employees worksite options a top priority, said Sun workspace architect Scott Ekman. "This initiative is part of our overall effort to keep Sun a competitive place to work. In today's tight labor market, employees are able to exert more control on where they live and work. . . ."[29]

Unfortunately, job redesign appears to reduce the quantity of output just as often as it has a positive effect. Caution and situational appropriateness are advised. For example, one study demonstrated that job redesign works better in less complex organizations (small plants or companies).[30] Nonetheless, managers are likely to find noticeable increases in the quality of performance after a job redesign program. Results from 21 experimental studies revealed that job redesign resulted in a median increase of 28% in the quality of performance.[31] Moreover, two separate meta-analyses support the practice of using the job characteristics model to help managers reduce absenteeism and turnover.[32] Athleta Corp., a sports apparel company in Petaluma, California, for instance, helped reduce employee turnover to less than 1% by using the job characteristic of autonomy to allow employees to set their own schedules and handle personal matters during the workday.[33]

Job characteristics research also underscores an additional implication for companies undergoing reengineering. Reengineering potentially leads to negative work outcomes because it increases job characteristics beyond reasonable levels. This occurs for two reasons: (1) reengineering requires employees to use a wider variety of skills to perform their jobs, and (2) reengineering typically results in downsizing and short-term periods of understaffing.[34] The unfortunate catch is that understaffing was found to produce lower levels of group performance, and jobs with either overly low or high levels of job characteristics were associated with higher stress.[35] Managers are advised to carefully consider the level of perceived job characteristics when implementing reengineering initiatives.

Biological and Perceptual-Motor Approaches

The biological approach to job design is based on research from biomechanics, work physiology, and ergonomics and focuses on designing the work environment to reduce employees' physical strain, effort, fatigue, and health complaints.[36] An attempt is made to redesign jobs so that they eliminate or reduce the amount of repetitive motions from a worker's job. The perceptual-motor approach is derived from human factors engineering, perceptual and cognitive skills, and information processing. This approach to job design emphasizes the reliability of work outcomes by examining error rates, accidents, and workers' feedback about facilities and equipment.[37]

The frequency of using both the biological and perceptual-motor approaches to job redesign is increasing in light of the 1.8 million workers who experience injuries each year related to overexertion or repetitive motion.[38] KeySpan Energy, for example, the nation's fourth-largest gas utility with 1.5 million customers, hired Ergonomic Technologies Corp. (ETC) to conduct job redesign using these methods to reduce repetitive stress back injuries:

> Using videos, site observations, and modeling, ETC produced a comprehensive workplace assessment of targeted jobs and responsibilities. Then, teaming with workers and staff, it developed cost-effective solutions. "About 80 percent of the recommendations were low cost—a combination of small fixes that would solve the problem like prescribing the right shovel for a task," Barracca [KeySpan's manager of electric research and development] says. "It was basic stuff, but it really paid off. The program cost $200,000 but, for every dollar spent, we saved four in reduced injuries."[39]

This example illustrates that job redesign can be an effective approach for reducing costs and increasing employees' well being and associated motivation.

Job Satisfaction and Work–Family Relationships

An individual's work motivation is related to his or her job satisfaction and work–family relationships. Motivation is not independent of an employee's work environment or personal life. For example, your desire to study for your next OB test is jointly affected by how much you like the course and the state of your health at the time you are studying. It is very hard to study when you have a bad cold or the flu. Consider Warren Buffett's feelings about this issue. Buffett is the founder and chairman and CEO of Berkshire Hathaway, an investment firm located in Omaha, Nebraska, and is one of the wealthiest individuals in the United States. This is what he said to a group of students at the University of Washington:

> I can certainly define happiness, because happy is what I am . . . I get to do what I like to do every single day of the year. I get to do it with people I like, and I don't have to associate with anybody who causes my stomach to churn. I tap-dance to work . . . I'd advise you that when you go to work, work for an organization of people you admire, because it will turn you on. I always worry about people who say, "I'm going to do this for 10 years; I really don't like it very well. And then I'll do this. . . ." That's a little like saving up sex for your old age. Not a very good idea. I have turned down business deals that were otherwise decent deals because I didn't like the people I would have to work with. I didn't see any sense in pretending.[40]

Buffett is clearly motivated by his job and work environment. Because of the dynamic relationships between motivation, job satisfaction, and work–family relationships, we conclude this chapter by discussing the causes and consequences of job satisfaction and work–family relationships. This information will increase your understanding about how to motivate others as well as yourself.

The Causes of Job Satisfaction

Job satisfaction is an affective or emotional response toward various facets of one's job. This definition means job satisfaction is not a unitary concept. Rather, a person can be relatively satisfied with one aspect of

Job satisfaction

An affective or emotional response to one's job.

How Satisfied Are You with Your Present Job?

		Very Dissatisfied				Very Satisfied
1.	The way I am noticed when I do a good job	1	2	3	4	5
2.	The recognition I get for the work I do	1	2	3	4	5
3.	The praise I get for doing a good job	1	2	3	4	5
4.	How my pay compares with that for similar jobs in other companies	1	2	3	4	5
5.	My pay and the amount of work I do	1	2	3	4	5
6.	How my pay compares with that of other workers	1	2	3	4	5
7.	The way my boss handles employees	1	2	3	4	5
8.	The way my boss takes care of complaints brought to him/her by employees	1	2	3	4	5
9.	The personal relationship between my boss and his/her employees	1	2	3	4	5

Total score for satisfaction with recognition (add questions 1–3), compensation (add questions 4–6), and supervision (add questions 7–9).

Comparative norms for each dimension of job satisfaction are: Total score of 3–6 = Low job satisfaction; 7–11 = Moderate satisfaction; 12 and above = High satisfaction.

SOURCE: Adapted from D J Weiss, R V Dawis, G W England, and L H Lofquist, *Manual for the Minnesota Satisfaction Questionnaire* (Minneapolis: Industrial Relations Center, University of Minnesota, 1967). Used with permission.

his or her job and dissatisfied with one or more other aspects. The Hands-On Exercise, for instance, assesses your satisfaction with recognition, compensation, and supervision. Please take a moment now to determine how satisfied you are with three aspects of your present or most recent job, and then use the norms to compare your score.[41] How do you feel about your job?

Research revealed that job satisfaction varied across countries. A recent study of 9,300 adults in 39 countries identified the percentage of workers who said they were "very satisfied with their jobs." The top five countries were Denmark (61%), India (urban middle- and upper-class only; 55%), Norway (54%), United States (50%), and Ireland (49%). Experts suggest that job satisfaction is highest in Denmark because labor and management have a great working relationship. The bottom five countries were Estonia (11%), China (11%), Czech Republic (10%), Ukraine (10%), and Hungary (9%). Why do Hungarian employees indicate the lowest job satisfaction? An average monthly salary of $302 and poor labor management relations are two possible causes.[42] OB researchers have identified other causes of job satisfaction and dissatisfaction.

Five predominant models of job satisfaction specify its causes. They are need fulfillment, discrepancy, value attainment, equity, and dispositional/genetic components. A brief review of these models will provide insight into the complexity of this seemingly simple concept.[43]

Need Fulfillment   These models propose that satisfaction is determined by the extent to which the characteristics of a job allow an individual to fulfill his or her needs. For example, a survey of 30 Massachusetts law firms revealed that 35% to 50% of law-firm associates left their employers within three years of starting because the firms did not accommodate family needs. This example illustrates that unmet needs can affect both satisfaction and turnover.[44] Although these models generated a great degree of controversy, it is generally accepted that need fulfillment is correlated with job satisfaction.[45]

Discrepancies   These models propose that satisfaction is a result of met expectations. **Met expectations** represent the difference between what an individual expects to receive from a job, such as good pay and promotional opportunities, and what he or she actually receives. When expectations are greater than what is received, a person will be dissatisfied. In contrast, this model predicts the individual will be satisfied when he or she attains outcomes above and beyond expectations. A meta-analysis of 31 studies that included 17,241 people demonstrated that met expectations were significantly related to job satisfaction.[46] Many companies use employee attitude or opinion surveys to assess employees' expectations and concerns (see Skills & Best Practices).

Value Attainment   The idea underlying **value attainment** is that satisfaction results from the perception that a job allows for fulfillment of an individual's important work values.[47] In general, research consistently supports the prediction that value fulfillment is positively related to job satisfaction.[48] Managers can thus enhance employee satisfaction by structuring the work environment and its associated rewards and recognition to reinforce employees' values.

Equity   In this model, satisfaction is a function of how "fairly" an individual is treated at work. Satisfaction results from one's perception that work outcomes, relative to inputs, compare favorably with a significant other's outcomes/inputs. A meta-analysis involving data from 30 different organizations and 12,979 people supported this model. Employees' perceived fairness of pay and promotions were significantly correlated with job satisfaction.[49] Chapter 7 explores this promising model in more detail.

Dispositional/Genetic Components   Have you ever noticed that some of your co-workers or friends appear to be satisfied across a variety of job circumstances, whereas others always seem dissatisfied? This model of satisfaction attempts to explain this pattern.[50] Specifically, the dispositional/genetic model is based on

Met expectations

The extent to which one receives what he or she expects from a job.

Value attainment

The extent to which a job allows fulfillment of one's work values.

Schwab Uses Surveys to Assess Employees' Job Satisfaction and Reduce Turnover

Four years ago the company started surveying its employees; now it quizzes the entire workforce annually. The questions ask about workloads, benefits, office culture, and career development. Schwab complements the survey with employee focus groups and online "town hall" meetings, where people can log on for live chats with executives.

Schwab uses the information it gathers to gauge concerns about companywide issues. More important (on the retention front, anyway), it narrows the replies to individual departments and holds front-line managers responsible for addressing any serious problems that surface. Managers meet individually with each subordinate and develop plans to address the concerns. Mentoring programs, specialized training tracks, flexible schedules, and a host of other changes have been initiated as a result.

Perhaps the most significant outcome of all this, however, is the coaching and training of department heads themselves. Dozens of managers have gone back to classrooms in response to critiques offered by the employees they oversee. If, for instance, a manager's interpersonal skills are criticized, Schwab may enroll him in a communications seminar or have him shadow a senior colleague.

SOURCE: Excerpted from K Dobbs, "Plagued by Turnover? Train Your Managers," *Training*, August 2000, p 64.

SKILLS & BEST PRACTICES

the belief that job satisfaction is partly a function of both personal traits and genetic factors. As such, this model implies that stable individual differences are just as important in explaining job satisfaction as are characteristics of the work environment. In support of this prediction, a recent meta-analysis demonstrated that job satisfaction was significantly related to the dispositional traits of self-esteem, generalized self-efficacy, internal locus of control, and emotional stability.[51] Other studies have shown that job satisfaction was significantly correlated with personal traits over time periods ranging from 2 to 50 years.[52] Genetic factors also were found to significantly predict life satisfaction, well-being, and general job satisfaction.[53] Additional research is needed to test this new model of job satisfaction.

The Consequences of Job Satisfaction

This area has significant managerial implications because thousands of studies have examined the relationship between job satisfaction and other organizational variables. Because it is impossible to examine them all, we will consider a subset of the more important variables from the standpoint of managerial relevance.

Table 6–1 summarizes the pattern of results. The relationship between job satisfaction and these other variables is either positive or negative. The strength of the relationship ranges from weak (very little relationship) to strong. Strong relationships imply that managers can significantly influence the variable of interest by increasing job satisfaction. Let us now consider several of the key correlates of job satisfaction.

Motivation   A recent meta-analysis of nine studies and 1,739 workers revealed a significant positive relationship between motivation and job satisfaction. Because satisfaction with supervision also was significantly correlated with motivation, managers are advised to consider how their behavior affects employee satisfaction.[54] Managers can potentially enhance employees' motivation through various attempts to increase job satisfaction.

TABLE 6–1   Correlates of Job Satisfaction

Variables Related with Satisfaction	Direction of Relationship	Strength of Relationship
Motivation	Positive	Moderate
Job involvement	Positive	Moderate
Organizational citizenship behavior	Positive	Moderate
Organizational commitment	Positive	Strong
Absenteeism	Negative	Weak
Tardiness	Negative	Weak
Turnover	Negative	Moderate
Heart disease	Negative	Moderate
Perceived stress	Negative	Strong
Pro-union voting	Negative	Moderate
Job performance	Positive	Weak
Life satisfaction	Positive	Moderate
Mental health	Positive	Moderate

Job Involvement   Job involvement represents the extent to which an individual is personally involved with his or her work role. A meta-analysis involving 27,925 individuals from 87 different studies demonstrated that job involvement was moderately related with job satisfaction.[55] Managers are thus encouraged to foster satisfying work environments in order to fuel employees' job involvement.

Organizational Citizenship Behavior   Organizational citizenship behaviors consist of employee behaviors that are beyond the call of duty. Examples include "such gestures as constructive statements about the department, expression of personal interest in the work of others, suggestions for improvement, training new people, respect for the spirit as well as the letter of housekeeping rules, care for organizational property, and punctuality and attendance well beyond standard or enforceable levels."[56] Managers certainly would like employees to exhibit these behaviors. A meta-analysis covering 6,746 people and 28 separate studies revealed a significant and moderately positive correlation between organizational citizenship behaviors and job satisfaction.[57] Moreover, additional research demonstrated that employees' citizenship behaviors were determined more by leadership and characteristics of the work environment than by an employee's personality.[58] It thus appears that managerial behavior significantly influences an employee's willingness to exhibit citizenship behaviors. This relationship is important to recognize because organizational citizenship behaviors were positively correlated with performance ratings and measures of organizational effectiveness.[59]

Organizational Commitment   Organizational commitment reflects the extent to which an individual identifies with an organization and is committed to its goals. A meta-analysis of 68 studies and 35,282 individuals uncovered a significant and strong relationship between organizational commitment and satisfaction.[60] Managers are advised to increase job satisfaction in order to elicit higher levels of commitment. In turn, higher commitment can facilitate higher productivity.

Absenteeism   Absenteeism is costly, and managers are constantly on the lookout for ways to reduce it. One recommendation has been to increase job satisfaction. If this is a valid recommendation, there should be a strong negative relationship (or negative correlation) between satisfaction and absenteeism. In other words, as satisfaction increases, absenteeism should decrease. A researcher tracked this prediction by synthesizing three separate meta-analyses containing a total of 74 studies. Results revealed a weak negative relationship between satisfaction and absenteeism.[61] It is unlikely, therefore, that managers will realize any significant decrease in absenteeism by increasing job satisfaction.

Turnover   Turnover is important to managers because it both disrupts organizational continuity and is very costly. A meta-analysis of 67 studies covering 24,566 people demonstrated a moderate negative relationship between satisfaction and turnover[62] (see Table 6−1). Given the strength of this relationship, managers would be well advised to try to reduce turnover by increasing employee job satisfaction.

Perceived Stress   Stress can have very negative effects on organizational behavior and an individual's health. Stress is positively related to absenteeism, turnover, coronary heart disease, and viral infections.[63] Based on a meta-analysis of seven studies covering 2,659 individuals, Table 6−1 reveals that perceived stress has a strong, negative relationship with job satisfaction.[64] It is hoped that managers would attempt to reduce the negative effects of stress by improving job satisfaction.

Job Performance   One of the biggest controversies within organizational research centers is the relationship between satisfaction and job performance. Some, such as Herzberg, argue that satisfaction leads to higher performance while others contend that high performance leads to satisfaction. In an attempt to resolve this controversy, a meta-analysis accumulated results from 74 studies. Overall, the relationship between job satisfaction and job performance was examined for 12,192 people. It was discovered that there was a small positive relationship between satisfaction and performance.[65] It thus appears that managers can positively affect performance by increasing employee job satisfaction.

Work–Family Relationships

Have you ever been stressed at home because of something that happened at work? Conversely, have you found it hard to focus at work because of problems occurring at home? If you answered yes, then you have experienced the dynamic interplay between work and family relationships. This relationship is becoming increasingly important in light of the increased number of women in the workforce (particularly those with children), the growth in dual-career couples, an aging population, and organizational pressures to accomplish more with constrained resources.

This section helps you to understand and manage your work–family relationships by examining four alternative hypotheses that explain the interaction between work and family and by discussing organizational responses to this issue.

Hypotheses Regarding Work–Family Relationships   OB researchers have proposed a variety of mechanisms linking work and family[66] We discuss four hypotheses that pertain to a subset of these mechanisms. The first hypothesis, called the *compensation effect,* suggests that job and life satisfaction are negatively related. That is, we compensate for low job or life satisfaction by seeking satisfying activities in the other domains. A meta-analysis of 34 studies covering 19,811 people failed to support this prediction. Results revealed a significant and positive correlation between job and life satisfaction.[67] The *segmentation hypothesis* proposes that job satisfaction and life satisfaction are independent—one supposedly does not influence the other. Research also did not confirm this model. Recent research supports the third hypothesis, which is called the *spillover model.*

> **Spillover model**
>
> Describes the reciprocal relationship between job and life satisfaction.

The **spillover model** hypothesizes that job satisfaction or dissatisfaction spills over into one's personal life and vice versa. In other words, each affects the other both positively and negatively on an ongoing basis. Consider the case of Erik Kopp:

Rising at 5 AM to get to his previous job, Erik Kopp, an engineer, was wiped out by 7 PM when he came home to his wife and three-year-old son. His peers, mostly older men with wives staying at home, had little empathy for his stress. He, in turn, found it hard to have empathy for his wife, who also worked and was tired when she got home. "I'd be thinking, 'Now I've got to do bath time and bedtime,' and she's thinking, 'I got him ready, I made him lunch, and I had to work, too.' A distance opens up between you. The really dangerous thing is you start blaming other people for your stress," he says. As pressures mounted, his wife confronted him: "You're not putting our family first," Mr Kopp says she told him.[68]

Erik resolved this situation by quitting his job and finding another that contained more flexibility. This example also illustrates the essence of the fourth hypothesis regarding work–family relationships. This hypothesis, labeled *work–family conflict,* is based on the idea that the roles we assume in our work and family domains are mutually incompatible. This means that the roles and associated expectations in one domain of our life (e.g., work) make it difficult to meet the demands in the other (e.g., family). In turn, these competing roles create a fundamental source of work–family conflict that influences our well being and happiness. Research clearly supports the existence of work–family conflict and its effect on important personal and organizational outcomes.[69]

Organizational Response to Work–Family Issues

Organizations are increasingly implementing a variety of "family friendly" programs and services aimed at helping employees to manage the interplay between their work and personal lives. They can include providing child-care services, flexible work schedules, cafeteria benefit plans, telecommuting, dry-cleaning services, concierge services, ATMs at work, and stress reduction programs.[70] Organizations hope that such programs will enhance employees' satisfaction and productivity. Ernst & Young's life-balance program, for example, saved $14 to $17 million in turnover costs. Here is how their program works:

> Employees and managers negotiate life-balance agreements every six months. These cover various issues, including how many days the employee will travel. To accommodate the travel requirements, solution teams redesigned the overall travel schedule to allow employees more time at home. Utilization committees meet regularly to oversee workloads and ensure that they're distributed evenly. The firm has a rule that no one is required to check e-mail or voice-mail on weekends or vacations.[71]

Although results from Ernst & Young's program are quite promising, researchers have only recently begun to conduct rigorous evaluations of family friendly programs.[72] Nonetheless, it seems reasonable to conclude that organizations will continue to search for ways to help employees cope with the potentially conflicting demands within their personal and work lives given the dynamics of modern-day life. We believe that this recommendation is a win-win solution that helps individuals and organizations alike.

Single working-parent families face a tough challenge in balancing work and home life. Single moms—divorced, widowed, or never married—account for some 9.8 million of single-parent households. For single parents, business travel and other routine demands of a corporate career—including overtime and interoffice transfers—can turn life upside down. Sometimes single parents decline promotions or high-profile assignments to preserve time with their children. In some organizations, experts say, it may be assumed single-mom staffers can't handle new duties because of the responsibilities they're shouldering at home.

chapter summary

- *Discuss the job performance model of motivation.* Individual inputs and job context variables are the two key categories of factors that influence motivation. In turn, motivation leads to motivated behaviors, which then affect performance.

- *Contrast Maslow's and McClelland's need theories.* Two well-known need theories of motivation are Maslow's need hierarchy and McClelland's need theory. Maslow's notion of a prepotent or stair-step hierarchy of five levels of needs has not stood up well under research. McClelland believes that motivation and performance vary according to the strength of an individual's need for achievement. High achievers prefer moderate risks and situations where they can control their own destiny. Top managers should have a high need for power coupled with a low need for affiliation.

- *Describe the mechanistic, motivational, biological, and perceptual-motor approaches to job design.* The mechanistic approach is based on industrial engineering and scientific management and focuses on increasing efficiency, flexibility, and employee productivity. Motivational approaches aim to improve employees' affective and attitudinal reactions and behavioral outcomes. Job enlargement, job enrichment, and a contingency approach called the job characteristics model are motivational approaches to job design. The biological approach focuses on designing the work environment to reduce employees' physical strain, effort, fatigue, and health complaints. The perceptual-motor approach emphasizes the reliability of work outcomes.

- *Explain the practical significance of Herzberg's distinction between motivators and hygiene factors.* Herzberg believes job satisfaction motivates better job performance. His *hygiene* factors, such as policies, supervision, and salary, erase sources of dissatisfaction. On the other hand, his *motivators,* such as achievement, responsibility, and recognition, foster job satisfaction. Although Herzberg's motivator—hygiene theory of job satisfaction has been criticized on methodological grounds, it has practical significance for job enrichment.

- *Discuss the causes and consequences of job satisfaction.* Job satisfaction is an affective or emotional response toward various facets of one's job. Five models of job satisfaction specify its causes. They are need fulfillment, discrepancy, value attainment, equity, and trait/genetic components. Job satisfaction has been correlated with hundreds of consequences. Table 6–1 summarizes the pattern of results found for a subset of the more important variables.

- *Critique the four hypotheses that explain the nature of work—family relationships.* The compensation effect predicts that job and life satisfaction are negatively related, and the segmentation hypothesis proposes that job satisfaction and life satisfaction are independent. Neither of these hypotheses are supported by research. The spillover hypothesis, which is confirmed by research, predicts that job satisfaction and life satisfaction affect each other both positively and negatively on an ongoing basis. The work—family conflict hypothesis is based on the idea that the roles we assume in our work and family life domains are mutually incompatible. This creates an inherent conflict between our work and family relationships.

internet exercise

www.fcd.org/library/index.html

This chapter discussed a variety of approaches for motivating employees. The purpose of this exercise is for you to identify motivational techniques or programs that are being used at different companies. Begin by visiting the website for the Foundation for Enterprise Development at **www.fcd.org/library/index.html**. The Foundation is a nonprofit organization that helps managers to implement equity-based compensation and broad-based participation programs aimed at improving corporate performance. To begin your search, select the resource library and follow up by choosing to view the library by subject. You will be given a variety of categories to choose from. Use the categories of "case studies of private companies" or "case studies of public companies," and then pick one company that you would like to analyze.

QUESTIONS

1. In what ways is this company using the theories and models discussed in this chapter?
2. To what extent is employee motivation related to this organization's culture?
3. What motivational methods is this company using that were not discussed in this chapter?

Motivation II: Equity, Expectancy, and Goal Setting

Seven

chapter

After reading the material in this chapter, you should be able to:

• Discuss the role of perceived inequity in employee motivation.

• Describe the practical lessons derived from equity theory.

• Explain Vroom's expectancy theory.

• Describe the practical implications of expectancy theory.

• Identify five practical lessons to be learned from goal-setting research.

• Specify issues that should be addressed before implementing a motivational program.

BONUSES ARE TIED TO PERFORMANCE AT TYCO INTERNATIONAL

L Dennis Kozlowski has been the chief executive officer at Tyco International since mid-1992. Under his strategic direction and leadership the company has grown from $3 billion in sales to one that will achieve $38.5 billion for the fiscal year ending September 30, 2001. Consider the motivational techniques he used to transform the company:

Kozlowski's ambitions stretch far beyond his audacious five-year plan of adding another $50 billion of acquisitions and reaching $100 billion in sales while maintaining 25%-plus annual earnings growth. He aspires to nothing less than guru status, the sort of peer recognition that would once and for all put behind him an army of short-sellers and other critics. He isn't modest in stating his goals. "Hopefully, we can become the next General Electric," Kozlowski muses in his Exeter (NH) office as his helicopter waits outside to whisk him to yet another dealmaking session. He wants to be remembered as "some combination of what Jack Welch put together at

GE . . . and Warren Buffett's very practical ideas on how you go about creating return for shareholders. . . ."

In Tyco's entrepreneurial culture, managers have enormous autonomy. Kozlowski relies on a computerized reporting system that gives him a detailed snapshot of how each business is performing. It's updated several times a week with information including sales, profit margins, and order backlog sliced by geography and product area. If he spots a problem, Kozlowski invariably uses the phone rather than E-mail. "If you're on forecast, there's no need to talk with me," he tells managers. "But if there is any bad news at all, find me wherever I am, so we can figure out what actions to take." He doesn't have a quick temper, but those who don't deliver don't last.

Kozlowski seeks out managers cast from the same mold as himself: someone who is "smart, poor, and wants to be rich." He keeps them motivated with a demanding compensation plan. Tyco executives don't receive bonuses unless they come close to meeting the aggressive earnings targets set by Kozlowski: typically about 15%. If they hit the target, they'll get a bonus at least equal to their salary. And if they blow past the target, the sky's the limit. Last year, Gromer received a base salary of $625,000. But after he nearly tripled Tyco Electronics' operating income on 62% higher sales, he pocketed a $13 million bonus. Kozlowski, with a $1.35 million salary, took home $125.3 million in total compensation—more than GE's Welch.[1]

> How would you describe Kozlowski's approach to motivating employees? For an interpretation on this case and additional comments, visit our website:
>
> www.mhhe.com/kinickiob

FOR DISCUSSION

The opening case illustrates how Tyco International uses goal setting and monetary rewards to motivate its employees. It also shows how Dennis Kozlowski's need for achievement, which was discussed in the last chapter, fuels his personal motivation. This chapter completes our discussion of motivation by exploring three cognitive theories of work motivation: equity, expectancy, and goal setting. Each theory is based on the premise that employees' cognitions are the key to understanding their motivation. To help you apply what you have learned about employee motivation, we conclude the chapter by highlighting the prerequisites of successful motivational programs.

Adams's Equity Theory of Motivation

Equity theory

Holds that motivation is a function of fairness in social exchanges.

Defined generally, **equity theory** is a model of motivation that explains how people strive for *fairness* and *justice* in social exchanges or give-and-take relationships. Equity theory is based on cognitive dissonance theory, developed by social psychologist Leon Festinger in the 1950s.[2]

According to Festinger's theory, people are motivated to maintain consistency between their cognitive beliefs and their behavior. Perceived inconsistencies create cognitive dissonance (or psychological discomfort), which, in turn, motivates corrective action. For example, a cigarette smoker who sees a heavy-smoking relative die of lung cancer probably would be motivated to quit smoking if he or she attributes the death to smoking. Accordingly, when victimized by unfair social exchanges, our resulting cognitive dissonance prompts us to correct the situation. Corrective action may range from a slight change in attitude or behavior to stealing to the extreme case of trying to harm someone. For example, researchers have demonstrated that people attempt to "get even" for perceived injustices by using either direct (e.g., theft or sabotage) or indirect (e.g., intentionally working slowly, giving a co-worker the silent treatment) retaliation, and the cost of this retaliation can be staggering. Experts estimate that the costs of employee theft, which is partly caused by feelings of inequity, is approximately $200 billion annually.[3]

Psychologist J Stacy Adams pioneered application of the equity principle to the workplace. Central to understanding Adams's equity theory of motivation is an awareness of key components of the individual–organization exchange relationship. This relationship is pivotal in the formation of employees' perceptions of equity and inequity.

The Individual–Organization Exchange Relationship

Adams points out that two primary components are involved in the employee–employer exchange, *inputs* and *outcomes*. An employee's inputs, for which he or she expects a just return, include education/training, skills, creativity, seniority, age, personality traits, effort expended, and personal appearance. On the outcome side of the exchange, the organization provides such things as pay/bonuses, fringe benefits, challenging assignments, job security, promotions, status symbols, recognition, and participation in important decisions.[4] These outcomes vary widely, depending on one's organization and rank.

Negative and Positive Inequity

On the job, feelings of inequity revolve around a person's evaluation of whether he or she receives adequate rewards to compensate for his or her contributive inputs. People perform these evaluations by comparing the perceived fairness of their employment exchange to that of relevant others. This comparative process, which is based on an equity norm, was found to generalize across countries.[5] People tend to compare themselves to other individuals with whom they have close interpersonal ties—such as friends—and/or to similar others—such as people performing the same job or individuals of the same gender or educational level—rather than dissimilar others.[6]

Three different equity relationships are illustrated in Figure 7–1: equity, negative inequity, and positive inequity. Assume the two people in each of the equity relationships in Figure 7–1 have equivalent backgrounds (equal education, seniority, and so forth) and perform identical tasks. Only their hourly pay rates differ. Equity exists for an individual when his or her ratio of perceived outcomes to inputs is equal to the ratio of outcomes to inputs for a relevant co-worker (see part A in Figure 7–1). Because equity is based on comparing *ratios* of outcomes to inputs, inequity will not necessarily be perceived just because someone else receives greater rewards. If the

Negative and Positive Inequity   **FIGURE 7–1**

A. An Equitable Situation   **B. Negative Inequity**

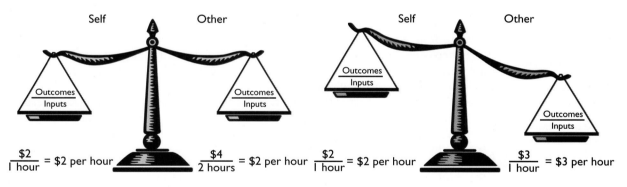

C. Positive inequity

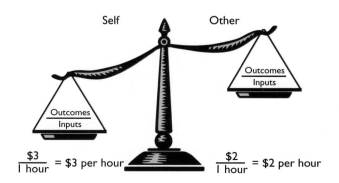

Perhaps one of the most readily identifiable inequities is Chief Executive Officer pay as compared to workers' pay. The average CEO earned a stupendous $13.1 million last year, according to the results of Business Week's 51st annual Executive Pay Scoreboard, compiled with Standard & Poor's Institutional Market Services. Steve Jobs, of Apple Computer Inc., landed the mother of all bonuses after three years of working for free: his own $90 million jet, a Gulfstream V.

Negative inequity

Comparison in which another person receives greater outcomes for similar inputs.

Positive inequity

Comparison in which another person receives lesser outcomes for similar inputs.

Equity sensitivity

An individual's tolerance for negative and positive equity.

other person's additional outcomes are due to his or her greater inputs, a sense of equity may still exist. However, if the comparison person enjoys greater outcomes for similar inputs, **negative inequity** will be perceived (see part B in Figure 7–1). On the other hand, a person will experience **positive inequity** when his or her outcome to input ratio is greater than that of a relevant co-worker (see part C in Figure 7–1).

Dynamics of Perceived Inequity

Managers can derive practical benefits from Adams's equity theory by recognizing that (1) people have varying sensitivities to perceived equity and inequity and (2) inequity can be reduced in a variety of ways.

Thresholds of Equity and Inequity   Have you ever noticed that some people become very upset over the slightest inequity whereas others are not bothered at all? Research has shown that people respond differently to the same level of inequity due to an individual difference called equity sensitivity. **Equity sensitivity** reflects an individual's "different preferences for, tolerances for, and reactions to the level of equity associated with any given situation."[7] Equity sensitivity spans a continuum ranging from benevolents to sensitives to entitled.

Benevolents are people who have a higher tolerance for negative inequity. They are altruistic in the sense that they prefer their outcome/input ratio to be lower than ratios from comparison others. In contrast, equity *sensitives* are described as individuals who adhere to a strict norm of reciprocity and are quickly motivated to resolve both negative and positive inequity. Finally, *entitleds* have no tolerance for negative inequity. They actually expect to obtain greater output/input ratios than comparison others and become upset when this is not the case.[8]

Reducing Inequity   Equity ratios can be changed by attempting to alter one's outcomes or adjusting one's inputs. For example, negative inequity might be resolved by asking for a raise or a promotion (i.e., raising outputs) or by reducing inputs (i.e., working fewer hours or exerting less effort). It also is important to note that equity can be restored by altering one's equity ratios behaviorally and/or cognitively. A cognitive strategy entails psychologically distorting perceptions of one's own or one's comparison person's outcomes and inputs (e.g., conclude that comparison other has more experience or works harder).

Expanding the Concept of Equity

Beginning in the 1980s, researchers began to expand the role of equity theory in explaining employee attitudes and behavior. This led to a domain of research called *organizational justice*. Organizational justice reflects the extent to which people perceive that they are treated fairly at work. This, in turn, led to the identification of three different components of organizational justice: distributive, procedural, and interactional. **Distributive justice** reflects the perceived fairness of how resources and rewards are distributed or allocated.

Procedural justice is defined as the perceived fairness of the process and procedures used to make allocation decisions. Research shows that positive perceptions of distributive and procedural justice are enhanced by giving employees a "voice" in decisions that affect them. Voice represents the extent to which employees who are affected by a decision can present relevant information about the decision to others. Voice is analogous to asking employees for their input into the decision-making process.[9]

The last justice component pertains to the interpersonal side of how employees are treated at work. Specifically, **interactional justice** "refers to the interpersonal side of decision making, specifically to the fairness of the decision maker's behavior in the process of decision making. Decision makers behave in an interactionally fair manner when they treat those affected by the decision properly and enact the decision policy or procedure properly."[10] Fair interpersonal treatment necessitates that managers communicate truthfully and treat people with courtesy and respect. Fair enactment of procedures further requires that managers suppress personal biases, consistently apply decision-making criteria, provide timely feedback, and justify decisions.

> **Distributive justice**
>
> The perceived fairness of how resources and rewards are distributed.
>
> **Procedural justice**
>
> The perceived fairness of the process and procedures used to make allocation decisions.
>
> **Interactional justice**
>
> The perceived fairness of the decision maker's behavior in the process of decision making.

Practical Lessons from Equity Theory

Equity theory has at least eight important practical implications. First, equity theory provides managers with yet another explanation of how beliefs and attitudes affect job performance. According to this line of thinking, the best way to manage job behavior is to adequately understand underlying cognitive processes. Indeed, we are motivated powerfully to correct the situation when our ideas of fairness and justice are offended.

Second, research on equity theory emphasizes the need for managers to pay attention to employees' perceptions of what is fair and equitable. No matter how fair management thinks the organization's policies, procedures, and reward system are, each employee's *perception* of the equity of those factors is what counts. People respond positively when they perceive organizational and interpersonal justice. For example, research demonstrates that employees perceptions of distributive, procedural, and interactional justice are positively associated with job satisfaction and organizational commitment and negatively with intentions to quit.[11] Managers thus are encouraged to make hiring and promotion decisions on merit-based, job-related information. Moreover, because justice perceptions are influenced by the extent to which managers explain their decisions, managers are encouraged to explain the rationale behind their decisions.[12]

Third, managers benefit by allowing employees to participate in making decisions about important work outcomes. For example, employees were more satisfied with their performance appraisals and resultant outcomes when they had a "voice" during the appraisal review.[13] Fourth, employees should be given the opportunity to appeal decisions that affect their welfare. Being able to appeal a decision promotes the belief that management treats employees fairly.

Fifth, employees are more likely to accept and support organizational change when they believe it is implemented fairly and when it produces equitable outcomes.[14]

HANDS-ON EXERCISE

Measuring Perceived Fair Interpersonal Treatment

INSTRUCTIONS Indicate the extent to which you agree or disagree with each of the following statements by considering what your organization is like most of the time. Then compare your overall score with the arbitrary norms that are presented.

	Strongly Disagree	Disagree	Neither	Agree	Strongly Agree
1. Employees are praised for good work.	1	2	3	4	5
2. Supervisors do not yell at employees.	1	2	3	4	5
3. Employees are trusted.	1	2	3	4	5
4. Employees' complaints are dealt with effectively.	1	2	3	4	5
5. Employees are treated with respect.	1	2	3	4	5
6. Employees' questions and problems are responded to quickly.	1	2	3	4	5
7. Employees are treated fairly.	1	2	3	4	5
8. Employees' hard work is appreciated.	1	2	3	4	5
9. Employees' suggestions are used.	1	2	3	4	5
10. Employees are told the truth.	1	2	3	4	5

Total score = —————

ARBITRARY NORMS
Very fair organization = 38–50
Moderately fair organization = 24–37
Unfair organization = 10–23

SOURCE: Adapted in part from M A Donovan, F Drasgow, and L J Munson, "The Perceptions of Fair Interpersonal Treatment Scale Development and Validation of a Measure of Interpersonal Treatment in the Workplace," *Journal of Applied Psychology*, October 1998, pp 683–92.

Sixth, managers can promote cooperation and teamwork among group members by treating them equitably. Research reveals that people are just as concerned with fairness in group settings as they are with their own personal interests.[15] Seventh, treating employees inequitably can lead to litigation and costly court settlements. Employees denied justice at work are more likely to turn to arbitration and the courts.[16] Finally, managers need to pay attention to the organization's climate for justice. For example, an organization's climate for justice was found to significantly influence employees' job satisfaction.[17] Researchers also believe that a climate of justice can significantly influence the type of customer service provided by employees. In turn, this level of service is likely to influence customers' perceptions of "fair service" and their subsequent loyalty and satisfaction.[18]

Managers can attempt to follow these practical implications by monitoring equity and justice perceptions through informal conversations, interviews, or attitude surveys. For example, researchers have developed and validated a host of surveys that can be used for this purpose. Please take a moment now to complete the Hands-On Exercise. It contains part of a survey that was developed to measure employees' perceptions of fair interpersonal treatment. If you perceive your work organization as interpersonally unfair, you are probably dissatisfied and have contemplated quitting. In contrast, your organizational loyalty and attachment are likely greater if you believe you are treated fairly at work.

Expectancy Theory of Motivation

Expectancy theory holds that people are motivated to behave in ways that produce desired combinations of expected outcomes. Perception plays a central role in expectancy theory because it emphasizes cognitive ability to anticipate likely consequences of behavior. Embedded in expectancy theory is the principle of hedonism. Hedonistic people strive to maximize their pleasure and minimize their pain. Generally, expectancy theory can be used to predict behavior in any situation in which a choice between two or more alternatives must be made. For example, it can be used to predict whether to quit or stay at a job; whether to exert substantial or minimal effort at a task; and whether to major in management, computer science, accounting, marketing, psychology, or communication.

> **Expectancy theory**
>
> Holds that people are motivated to behave in ways that produce valued outcomes.

This section explores Victor Vroom's version of expectancy theory. Understanding the cognitive processes underlying this theory can help managers develop organizational policies and practices that enhance employee motivation.

Vroom's Expectancy Theory

Victor Vroom formulated a mathematical model of expectancy theory in his 1964 book *Work and Motivation.* Vroom's theory has been summarized as follows:

> The strength of a tendency to act in a certain way depends on the strength of an expectancy that the act will be followed by a given consequence (or outcome) and on the value or attractiveness of that consequence (or outcome) to the actor.[19]

Motivation, according to Vroom, boils down to the decision of how much effort to exert in a specific task situation. This choice is based on a two-stage sequence of expectations (effort → performance and performance → outcome). First, motivation is affected by an individual's expectation that a certain level of effort will produce the intended performance goal. For example, if you do not believe increasing the amount of time you spend studying will significantly raise your grade on an exam, you probably will not study any harder than usual. Motivation also is influenced by the employee's perceived chances of getting various outcomes as a result of accomplishing his or her performance goal. Finally, individuals are motivated to the extent that they value the outcomes received.

Vroom used a mathematical equation to integrate these concepts into a predictive model of motivational force or strength. For our purposes, however, it is sufficient to define and explain the three key concepts within Vroom's model—*expectancy, instrumentality,* and *valence.*

Expectancy   An **expectancy,** according to Vroom's terminology, represents an individual's belief that a particular degree of effort will be followed by a particular level of performance. In other words, it is an effort → performance expectation. Expectancies take the form of subjective probabilities. As you may recall from a course in statistics, probabilities range from zero to one. An expectancy of zero indicates effort has no anticipated impact on performance.

> **Expectancy**
>
> Belief that effort leads to a specific level of performance.

For example, suppose you do not know how to type on a keyboard. No matter how much effort you exert, your perceived probability of typing 30 error-free words per minute likely would be zero. An expectancy of one suggests that performance is totally dependent on effort. If you decided to take a typing course as well as practice a couple of hours a day for a few weeks (high effort), you should be able to type 30 words per minute without any errors. In contrast, if you do not take a typing course and only practice an hour or two per week (low effort), there is a very low probability (say, a 20% chance) of being able to type 30 words per minute without any errors.

The following factors influence an employee's expectancy perceptions:

- Self-esteem.
- Self-efficacy.
- Previous success at the task.
- Help received from a supervisor and subordinates.
- Information necessary to complete the task.
- Good materials and equipment to work with.[20]

Instrumentality

A performance → outcome perception.

Instrumentality An **instrumentality** is a performance → outcome perception. It represents a person's belief that a particular outcome is contingent on accomplishing a specific level of performance. Performance is instrumental when it leads to something else. For example, passing exams is instrumental to graduating from college.

Instrumentalities range from −1.0 to 1.0. An instrumentality of 1.0 indicates attainment of a particular outcome is totally dependent on task performance. An instrumentality of zero indicates there is no relationship between performance and outcome. For example, most companies link the number of vacation days to seniority, not job performance. Finally, an instrumentality of −1.0 reveals that high performance reduces the chance of obtaining an outcome while low performance increases the chance. For example, the more time you spend studying to get an A on an exam (high performance), the less time you will have for enjoying leisure activities. Similarly, as you lower the amount of time spent studying (low performance), you increase the amount of time that may be devoted to leisure activities.

The concept of instrumentality can be seen in practice by considering the incentive program used by Don Clark, Chief Financial Officer at Net2000, a Herndon, VA, integrated communication provider:

> An employee who's been around for two years and met a designated performance rating can earn a three-year lease on a BMW, Dodge Durango, or Audi TT. Failure to maintain the necessary performance ranking sends the vehicle back to the dealer and the employee also has to pay any early lease termination penalties. But with nearly 70 cars awarded since the program began, Clark says, "We've never had to take one away."[21]

The incentive program clearly makes performance instrumental for receiving a leased vehicle.

Valence

The value of a reward or outcome.

Valence As Vroom used the term, **valence** refers to the positive or negative value people place on outcomes. Valence mirrors our personal preferences.[22] For example, most employees have a positive valence for receiving additional money or recognition. In contrast, job stress and being laid off would likely be negatively valent for most individuals. In Vroom's expectancy model, *outcomes* refer to different consequences that are contingent on performance, such as pay, promotions, or recognition. An outcome's valence depends on an individual's needs and can be measured for research purposes with scales ranging from a negative value to a positive value. For example, an individual's valence toward more recognition can be assessed on a scale ranging from -2 (very undesirable) to 0 (neutral) to $+2$ (very desirable).

Vroom's Expectancy Theory in Action

Vroom's expectancy model of motivation can be used to analyze a real-life motivation program. Consider the following performance problem described by Frederick W Smith, founder and chief executive officer of Federal Express Corporation:

> . . . we were having a helluva problem keeping things running on time. The airplanes would come in, and everything would get backed up. We tried every kind of control mechanism that you could think of, and none of them worked. Finally, it became obvious that the underlying problem was that it was in the interest of the employees at the cargo terminal—they were college kids, mostly—to run late, because it meant that they made more money. So what we did was give them all a minimum guarantee and say, "Look, if you get through before a certain time, just go home, and you will have beat the system." Well, it was unbelievable. I mean, in the space of about 45 days, the place was way ahead of schedule. And I don't even think it was a conscious thing on their part.[23]

How did Federal Express get its college-age cargo handlers to switch from low effort to high effort? According to Vroom's model, the student workers originally exerted low effort because they were paid on the basis of time, not output. It was in their best interest to work slowly and accumulate as many hours as possible. By offering to let the student workers *go home early if and when they completed their assigned duties,* Federal Express prompted high effort. This new arrangement created two positively valued outcomes: guaranteed pay plus the opportunity to leave early. The motivation to exert high effort became greater than the motivation to exert low effort.

Research on Expectancy Theory and Managerial Implications

Many researchers have tested expectancy theory. In support of the theory, a meta-analysis of 77 studies indicated that expectancy theory significantly predicted performance, effort, intentions, preferences, and choice.[24] Another summary of 16 studies revealed that expectancy theory correctly predicted occupational or organizational choice 63.4% of the time; this was significantly better than chance predictions.[25]

Nonetheless, expectancy theory has been criticized for a variety of reasons. For example, the theory is difficult to test, and the measures used to assess expectancy, instrumentality, and valence have questionable validity.[26] In the final analysis, however, expectancy theory has important practical implications for individual managers and organizations as a whole (see Table 7–1).

Oftentimes employees feel that "borrowing" a few office supplies from their company's supply compensates for any perceived inequities in pay or other benefits.

TABLE 7–1 Managerial and Organizational Implications of Expectancy Theory

Implications for Managers	Implications for Organizations
Determine the outcomes employees value.	Reward people for desired performance, and do not keep pay decisions secret.
Identify good performance so appropriate behaviors can be rewarded.	Design challenging jobs.
Make sure employees can achieve targeted performance levels.	Tie some rewards to group accomplishments to build teamwork and encourage cooperation.
Link desired outcomes to targeted levels of performance.	Reward managers for creating, monitoring, and maintaining expectancies, instrumentalities, and outcomes that lead to high effort and goal attainment.
Make sure changes in outcomes are large enough to motivate high effort.	Monitor employee motivation through interviews or anonymous questionnaires.
Monitor the reward system for inequities.	Accommodate individual differences by building flexibility into the motivation program.

Managers are advised to enhance effort → performance expectancies by helping employees accomplish their performance goals. Managers can do this by providing support and coaching and by increasing employees' self-efficacy. It also is important for managers to influence employees' instrumentalities and to monitor valences for various rewards. This raises the issue of whether organizations should use monetary rewards as the primary method to reinforce performance. Although money is certainly a positively valent reward for most people, there are three issues to consider when deciding on the relative balance between monetary and nonmonetary rewards.

First, research shows that some workers value interesting work and recognition more than money.[27] Second, extrinsic rewards can lose their motivating properties over time and may undermine intrinsic motivation.[28] This conclusion, however, must be balanced by the fact that performance is related to the receipt of financial incentives. A recent meta-analysis of 39 studies involving 2,773 people showed that financial incentives were positively related to performance quantity but not to performance quality.[29] Third, monetary rewards must be large enough to generate motivation. For example, Steven Kerr, chief learning officer at General Electric, estimates that monetary awards must be at least 12% to 15% above employees' base pay to truly motivate people.[30]

Although this percentage is well above the typical salary increase received by most employees, some organizations have designed their incentive systems with this recommendation in mind. For example, Egon Zehnder International, an executive search firm, pays its partners substantial monetary rewards based on a combination of overall corporate performance and tenure (see Skills & Best Practices). The company's annual turnover rate among partners of 2% suggests the incentive system is working: The industry average is 30%.[31] In summary, there is no one best type of reward. Individual differences and need theories tell us that people are motivated by different rewards. Managers should therefore focus on linking employee performance to valued rewards regardless of the type of reward used to enhance motivation.

There are four prerequisites to linking performance and rewards:

1. Managers need to develop and communicate performance standards to employees.

2. Managers need valid and accurate performance ratings with which to compare employees. Inaccurate ratings create perceptions of inequity and thereby erode motivation.

3. Managers need to determine the relative mix of individual versus team contribution to performance and then reward accordingly. For example, pharmaceutical giant Pharmacia designed its reward system around its belief in creating an organizational culture that reinforced collaboration, customer focus, and speed. "The company's reward system reinforced this collaborative model by explicitly linking compensation to the actions of the group. Every member's compensation would be based on the time to bring the drug to market, the time for the drug to reach peak profitable share, and total sales. The system gave group members a strong incentive to talk openly with one another and to share information freely."[32]

4. Managers should use the performance ratings to differentially allocate rewards among employees. That is, it is critical that managers allocate significantly different amounts of rewards for various levels of performance.

Egon Zehnder International (EZI) Rewards Employee Tenure

For partners, compensation comes in three ways: salary, equity stake in EZI, and profit shares. . . . To begin with, each partner has an equal number of shares in the firm's equity, whether he has been a partner for 30 years or one year. The shares rise in value each year, because we put 10% to 20% of our profits back into the firm. . . . The remaining 80% to 90% of the profit is distributed among the partners in two ways. Sixty percent is divided equally among all the partners, and the remaining 40% is allocated according to years of seniority. . . . So a 15-year partner gets 15 times more from this portion of the profit pool than a one-year partner.

SOURCE: E Zehnder, "A Simpler Way to Pay," *Harvard Business Review*, April 2001, pp 54, 56.

Motivation through Goal Setting

Regardless of the nature of their specific achievements, successful people tend to have one thing in common. Their lives are goal oriented. This is as true for politicians seeking votes as it is for world-class athletes. Within the context of employee motivation, this section explores the theory, research, and practice of goal setting.

Goals: Definition and Background

Edwin Locke, a leading authority on goal setting, and his colleagues define a **goal** as "what an individual is trying to accomplish; it is the object or aim of an action."[33] The motivational effect of performance goals and goal-based reward plans has been recognized for a long time. At the turn of the century, Frederick Taylor attempted to scientifically establish how much work of a specified quality an individual should be assigned each day. He proposed that bonuses be based on accomplishing those output standards. More recently, goal setting has been promoted through a widely used management technique called management by objectives (MBO).

> **Goal**
> What an individual is trying to accomplish.

Management by objectives

Management system incorporating participation in decision making, goal setting, and feedback.

Management by objectives is a management system that incorporates participation in decision making, goal setting, and objective feedback.[34] A meta-analysis of MBO programs showed productivity gains in 68 of 70 different organizations. Specifically, results uncovered an average gain in productivity of 56% when top management commitment was high. The average gain was only 6% when commitment was low. A second meta-analysis of 18 studies further demonstrated that employees' job satisfaction was significantly related to top management's commitment to an MBO implementation.[35] These impressive results highlight the positive benefits of implementing MBO and setting goals. To further understand how MBO programs can increase both productivity and satisfaction, let us examine the process by which goal setting works.

How Does Goal Setting Work?

Despite abundant goal-setting research and practice, goal-setting theories are surprisingly scarce. An instructive model was formulated by Locke and his associates. According to Locke's model, goal setting has four motivational mechanisms.

Goals Direct Attention   Goals that are personally meaningful tend to focus one's attention on what is relevant and important. If, for example, you have a term project due in a few days, your thoughts tend to revolve around completing that project. Similarly, the members of a home appliance salesforce who are told they can win a trip to Hawaii for selling the most refrigerators will tend to steer customers toward the refrigerator display.

Goals Regulate Effort   Not only do goals make us selectively perceptive, they also motivate us to act. The instructor's deadline for turning in your term project would prompt you to complete it, as opposed to going out with friends, watching television, or studying for another course. Generally, the level of effort expended is proportionate to the difficulty of the goal.

Goals Increase Persistence   Within the context of goal setting, persistence represents the effort expended on a task over an extended period of time: It takes effort to run 100 meters; it takes persistence to run a 26-mile marathon. Persistent people tend to see obstacles as challenges to be overcome rather than as reasons to fail. A difficult goal that is important to an individual is a constant reminder to keep exerting effort in the appropriate direction. Steven Spielberg is a great example of someone who persisted at his goal to be a filmmaker:

> As the most popular and successful filmmaker ever, the 52-year-old Spielberg has directed nine of the 50 top-grossing films of all time. All totaled, films he has directed have brought in more than $5 billion worldwide, and films he's produced have brought in another $4 billion. . . . Spielberg identified his dream early in life and tenaciously pursued it. He allowed himself to imagine and trusted his imagination in his art. . . . Spielberg started making movies at age 11 when he learned how to use his father's eight-millimeter windup camera. . . . Having defined his ambition to direct movies from a young age, Spielberg suffered a setback when the prestigious UCLA and USC film schools rejected him because of low high school grades. Instead, because it was near Hollywood, he enrolled as an English major at California State University at Long Beach.

The summer before college, Spielberg took the Universal Studios Tour, and when the tour guides weren't watching, he broke away from the group to wander the giant movie-making factory.

"I went back there every day for three months," says Spielberg in Frank Sanello's *Spielberg: The Man, the Movies, the Mythology.* "I walked past the guard every day, waved at him and he waved back. I always wore a suit and carried a briefcase, and he assumed I was some kid related to some mogul."

He took over an unused office and put his name in the building directory with plastic letters: Steven Spielberg, room 23C. He immersed himself in film production at the industry's epicenter, wandering the Universal property to watch directors at work, and once got to see one of his heroes, Alfred Hitchcock, direct scenes for *Torn Curtain.*

Hanging out with directors, writers, and editors, Spielberg learned that to get the attention of studio executives he had to demonstrate his directing ability on the professional film width of 35 millimeters. A friend who wished to become a producer fronted $15,000 for Spielberg to make the short film *Amblin,* which caught the eye of Universal executive Sid Sheinberg, who offered Spielberg a contract to direct television shows. Still several months short of graduating from college, Spielberg hesitated. In a now famous retort, Sheinberg shot back, "Kid, do you want to go to college or do you want to direct?" Spielberg dropped out and took the job.[36]

Goals Foster Strategies and Action Plans   If you are here and your goal is out there somewhere, you face the problem of getting from here to there. For example, the person who has resolved to lose 20 pounds must develop a plan for getting from "here" (his or her present weight) to "there" (20 pounds lighter). Goals can help because they encourage people to develop strategies and action plans that enable them to achieve their goals.[37] By virtue of setting a weight-reduction goal, the dieter may choose a strategy of exercising more, eating less, or some combination of the two. For a work-related example, consider the goals, strategies, and plans being used by Monica Luechtefeld, the executive vice president heading up Office Depot Inc.'s online business:

> Under her leadership, the Delray Beach (Fla.)-based company has quietly become the second-largest E-tailer in the world behind Amazon.com. . . . And this year [2001], online sales are expected to nearly double, to $1.5 billion, representing 20% of the company's overall sales. Now, she aims to push to 50% from 40% the number of Office Depot customers ordering online by year end. . . . To do that, she plans to offer them more than just office supplies. "I want us to serve them both as coach and trusted adviser," she says. To Luechtefeld that means expanding to include online services such as tax preparation and bookkeeping. Office Depot has no expertise in this area, so Luechtefeld is making alliances with those that do, including software giant Microsoft Corp.[38]

Insights from Goal-Setting Research

Research consistently has supported goal setting as a motivational technique. Setting performance goals increases individual, group, and organizational performance. Further, the positive effects of goal setting were found in six other countries or regions: Australia, Canada, the Caribbean, England, West Germany, and Japan. Goal setting works in different cultures. Reviews of the many goal-setting studies conducted over the past few decades have given managers five practical insights:

FIGURE 7–2 | Relationship between Goal Difficulty and Performance

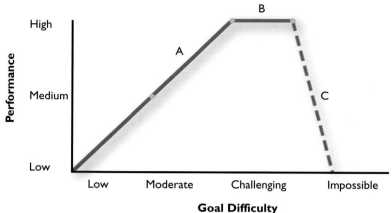

A Performance of committed individuals with adequate ability
B Performance of committed individuals who are working at capacity
C Performance of individuals who lack commitment to high goals

SOURCE: *A Theory of Goal Setting and Task Performance*, by Locke/Latham, © 1990. Adapted by permission of Prentice-Hall, Upper Saddle River, NJ Reprinted by permission of Prentice-Hall, Inc., Englewood Cliffs, NJ.

Goal difficulty

The amount of effort required to meet a goal.

1. *Difficult goals lead to higher performance.* **Goal difficulty** reflects the amount of effort required to meet a goal. It is more difficult to sell nine cars a month than it is to sell three cars a month. A meta-analysis spanning 4,000 people and 65 separate studies revealed that goal difficulty was positively related to performance.[39] As illustrated in Figure 7–2, however, the positive relationship between goal difficulty and performance breaks down when goals are perceived to be impossible. Figure 7–2 reveals that performance goes up when employees are given hard goals as opposed to easy or moderate goals (section A). Performance then plateaus (section B) and drops (section C) as the difficulty of a goal goes from challenging to impossible.[40]

Goal specificity

Quantifiability of a goal.

2. *Specific, difficult goals lead to higher performance for simple rather than complex tasks.* **Goal specificity** pertains to the quantifiability of a goal. For example, a goal of selling nine cars a month is more specific than telling a salesperson to do his or her best. In an early review of goal-setting research, 99 of 110 studies (90%) found that specific, hard goals led to better performance than did easy, medium, do-your-best, or no goals. This result was confirmed in a meta-analysis of 70 studies conducted between 1966 and 1984, involving 7,407 people.[41]

In contrast to these positive effects, several recent studies demonstrated that setting specific, difficult goals leads to poorer performance under certain circumstances. For example, a meta-analysis of 125 studies indicated that goal-setting effects were strongest for easy tasks and weakest for complex tasks.[42] There are two explanations for this finding. First, employees are not likely to put forth increased effort to achieve complex goals unless they "buy-in" or support them.[43] Thus, it is important for managers to obtain employee buy-in to the goal-setting process. Second, novel and complex tasks take employees longer to complete. This occurs because employees spend more time thinking about how to approach and solve these tasks. In contrast, employees do not have to spend much time thinking about solutions for easy tasks. Specific difficult goals thus impair performance on novel, complex tasks when employees do not have clear strategies for solving these types of problems. On a positive note, however, a study demonstrated that goal setting led to gradual improvements in performance on complex tasks when people were encouraged to explicitly solve the problem at hand.[44]

3. *Feedback enhances the effect of specific, difficult goals.* Feedback plays a key role in all of our lives. For example, consider the role of feedback in bowling. Imagine going to the bowling lanes only to find that someone had hung a sheet from the ceiling to the floor in front of the pins. How likely is it that you would reach your goal score or typical bowling average? Not likely, given your inability to see the pins. Regardless of your goal, you would have to guess where to throw your second ball if you did not get a strike on your first shot. The same principles apply at work.

   Feedback lets people know if they are headed toward their goals or if they are off course and need to redirect their efforts. Goals plus feedback is the recommended approach.[45] Goals inform people about performance standards and expectations so that they can channel their energies accordingly. In turn, feedback provides the information needed to adjust direction, effort, and strategies for goal accomplishment.

4. *Participative goals, assigned goals, and self-set goals are equally effective.* Both managers and researchers are interested in identifying the best way to set goals. Should goals be participatively set, assigned, or set by the employee him- or herself? A summary of goal-setting research indicated that no single approach was consistently more effective than others in increasing performance.[46]

   Managers are advised to use a contingency approach by picking a method that seems best suited for the individual and situation at hand. For example, employees' preferences for participation should be considered. Some employees desire to participate in the process of setting goals, whereas others do not. Employees are also more likely to respond positively to the opportunity to participate in goal setting when they have greater task information, higher levels of experience and training, and greater levels of task involvement. Finally, a participative approach helps reduce employees' resistance to goal setting.

5. *Goal commitment and monetary incentives affect goal-setting outcomes.* **Goal commitment** is the extent to which an individual is personally committed to achieving a goal. In general, an individual is expected to persist in attempts to accomplish a goal when he or she is committed to it. Researchers believe that goal commitment moderates the relationship between the difficulty of a goal and performance. That is, difficult goals lead to higher performance only when employees are committed to their goals. Conversely, difficult goals are hypothesized to lead to lower performance when people are not committed to their goals. A meta-analysis of 21 studies based on 2,360 people supported these predictions.[47] It also is important to note that people are more likely to commit to difficult goals when they have high self-efficacy about successfully

> **Goal commitment**
>
> Amount of commitment to achieving a goal.

accomplishing their goals.[48] Managers thus are encouraged to consider employees' self-efficacy when setting goals.

Like goal setting, the use of monetary incentives to motivate employees is seldom questioned. Unfortunately, recent research uncovered some negative consequences when goal achievement is linked to individual incentives. Case studies, for example, reveal that pay should not be linked to goal achievement unless (a) performance goals are under the employees' control; (b) goals are quantitative and measurable; and (c) frequent, relatively large payments are made for performance achievement.[49] Goal-based incentive systems are more likely to produce undesirable effects if these three conditions are not satisfied.

Moreover, empirical studies demonstrated that goal-based bonus incentives produced higher commitment to easy goals and lower commitment to difficult goals. People were reluctant to commit to difficult goals that were tied to monetary incentives. People with high goal commitment also offered less help to their co-workers when they received goal-based bonus incentives to accomplish difficult individual goals. Individuals neglected aspects of the job that were not covered in the performance goals.[50]

These findings underscore some of the dangers of using goal-based incentives, particularly for employees in complex, interdependent jobs requiring cooperation. Managers need to consider the advantages, disadvantages, and dilemmas of goal-based incentives prior to implementation.

Practical Application of Goal Setting

There are three general steps to follow when implementing a goal-setting program. Serious deficiencies in one step cannot make up for strength in the other two. The three steps need to be implemented in a systematic fashion.

Step I: Set Goals A number of sources can be used as input during this goal-setting stage. Time and motion studies are one source. Goals also may be based on the average past performance of job holders. Third, the employee and his or her manager may set the goal participatively, through give-and-take negotiation. Fourth, goals can be set by conducting external or internal benchmarking. Benchmarking is used when an organization wants to compare its performance or internal work processes to those of other organizations (external benchmarking) or to other internal units, branches, departments, or divisions within the organization (internal benchmarking). For example, a company might set a goal to surpass the customer service levels or profit of a benchmarked competitor. Finally, the overall strategy of a company (e.g., become the lowest-cost producer) may affect the goals set by employees at various levels in the organization.

In accordance with available research evidence, goals should be "SMART." SMART is an acronym that stands for specific, measurable, attainable, results oriented, and time bound. Table 7–2 contains a set of guidelines for writing SMART goals. There are two additional recommendations to consider when setting goals. First, for complex tasks, managers should train employees in problem-solving techniques and encourage them to develop a performance action plan. Action plans specify the strategies or tactics to be used in order to accomplish a goal.

Second, because of individual differences (recall our discussion in Chapter 5), it may be necessary to establish different goals for employees performing the same job. For example, a study of 103 undergraduate business students revealed that individu-

Guidelines for Writing SMART Goals | **TABLE 7–2**

Specific	Goals should be stated in precise rather than vague terms. For example, a goal that provides for 20 hours of technical training for each employee is more specific than stating that a manager should send as many people as possible to training classes. Goals should be quantified when possible.
Measurable	A measurement device is needed to assess the extent to which a goal is accomplished. Goals thus need to be measurable. It also is critical to consider the quality aspect of the goal when establishing measurement criteria. For example, if the goal is to complete a managerial study of methods to increase productivity, one must consider how to measure the quality of this effort. Goals should not be set without considering the interplay between quantity and quality of output.
Attainable	Goals should be realistic, challenging, and attainable. Impossible goals reduce motivation because people do not like to fail. Remember, people have different levels of ability and skill.
Results oriented	Corporate goals should focus on desired end-results that support the organization's vision. In turn, an individual's goals should directly support the accomplishment of corporate goals. Activities support the achievement of goals and are outlined in action plans. To focus goals on desired end-results, goals should start with the word "to," followed by verbs such as complete, acquire, produce, increase, and decrease. Verbs such as develop, conduct, implement, or monitor imply activities and should not be used in a goal statement.
Time bound	Goals specify target dates for completion.

SOURCE: A J Kinicki, *Performance Management Systems* (Superstition Mt., AZ: Kinicki and Associates Inc., 1992), pp 2–9. Reprinted with permission; all rights reserved.

als high in conscientiousness had higher motivation, had greater goal commitment, and obtained higher grades than students low in conscientiousness.[51] An individual's goal orientation is another important individual difference to consider when setting goals. There are two types of goal orientation: a learning goal orientation and a performance goal orientation. A team of researchers described the differences and implications for goal setting in the following way:

> Individuals with a learning goal orientation are primarily concerned with developing their skills and ability. Given this focus, a difficult goal should be of interest because it provides a challenging opportunity that can lead to personal growth. In contrast, individuals with a performance goal orientation are concerned with obtaining positive evaluations about their ability. Given this focus, a difficult goal should be of lower interest because it provides a greater potential for failure. As goal difficult increases, the probability of obtaining a positive evaluation through goal attainment decreases.[52]

Although some studies showed that people set higher goals, exerted more effort, and achieved higher performance when they possessed a learning orientation toward goal setting rather than a performance orientation, other research demonstrated a more complex series of relationships.[53] Specifically, performance was influenced by the interaction between an individual's goal orientation and the difficulty of the task being performed. A performance orientation had beneficial effects on performance for easy tasks, whereas a learning orientation facilitated higher performance on complex tasks.[54] In conclusion, managers should consider individual differences when setting goals.

Step 2: Promote Goal Commitment

Obtaining goal commitment is important because employees are more motivated to pursue goals they view as reasonable, obtainable, and fair. Goal commitment may be increased through a variety of methods. For example, managers are encouraged to conduct participative goal-setting sessions and to train employees in how to develop effective action plans. Goal commitment also can be enhanced by setting goals that are under employees control and providing them with the necessary resources.

Step 3: Provide Support and Feedback

Step 3 calls for providing employees with the necessary support elements or resources to get the job done. This includes ensuring that each employee has the necessary abilities and information to reach his or her goals. As a pair of goal-setting experts succinctly stated, "Motivation without knowledge is useless."[55] Training often is required to help employees achieve difficult goals. Moreover, managers should pay attention to employees' perceptions of effort → performance expectancies, self-efficacy, and valence of rewards. Finally, as we discuss in detail in Chapter 8 employees should be provided with timely, specific feedback (knowledge of results) on how they are doing.

Putting Motivational Theories to Work

Successfully designing and implementing motivational programs is not easy. Managers cannot simply take one of the theories discussed in this book and apply it word for word. Dynamics within organizations interfere with applying motivation theories in "pure" form. According to management scholar Terence Mitchell,

> There are situations and settings that make it exceptionally difficult for a motivational system to work. These circumstances may involve the kinds of jobs or people present, the technology, the presence of a union, and so on. The factors that hinder the application of motivational theory have not been articulated either frequently or systematically.[56]

With Mitchell's cautionary statement in mind, this section uses Figure 6–1 (see page 113 in Chapter 6) to raise issues that need to be addressed before implementing a motivational program. Our intent is not to discuss all relevant considerations but rather to highlight a few important ones.

Assuming a motivational program is being considered to improve productivity, quality, or customer satisfaction, the first issue revolves around the difference between motivation and performance. As shown in Figure 6–1, motivation and performance are not one and the same. Motivation is only one of several factors that influence performance. For example, poor performance may be more a function of outdated or inefficient materials and machinery, not having goals to direct one's attention, a monotonous job, feelings of inequity, a negative work environment characterized by political behavior and conflict, poor supervisory support and coaching, or poor work flow. Motivation cannot make up for a deficient job context (see Figure 6–1). Managers, therefore, need to carefully consider the causes of poor performance and employee misbehavior.

Importantly, managers should not ignore the individual inputs identified in Figure 6–1. As discussed in this chapter as well as Chapters 5 and 6, individual differences are an important input that influence motivation and motivated behavior. Managers are advised to develop employees so that they have the ability and job knowledge to effectively perform their jobs. In addition, attempts should be made to nurture positive employee characteristics, such as self-esteem, self-efficacy, positive emotions, a learning goal orientation, and need for achievement.

Because motivation is goal directed, the process of developing and setting goals should be consistent with our previous discussion. Moreover, the method used to evaluate performance also needs to be considered. Without a valid performance appraisal system, it is difficult, if not impossible, to accurately distinguish good and poor performers. Consider the motivational effect of using a performance rating system in which managers are required to rank employees against each other according to some specified distribution:

> At GE, which has used the system for several years, this means that 20% of salaried, managerial, and executive employees are rated outstanding each year, 70% "high-performance middle," and 10% in need of improvement. At Enron, where some have nicknamed the system "rank and yank," employees are put in one of five categories: 5% are identified as superior, 30% excellent, 30% strong, 20% satisfactory, and 15% "needs improvement." And Ford, which began using rating systems last year, dictates that 10% of the auto maker's 18,000 managers will get A grades, 85% Bs, and 5% Cs. (Initially, it asked for 10% Cs.) Those who receive a second consecutive C can be fired.[57]

The problem with ranking systems is that they are based on subjective judgments. Motivation thus is decreased to the extent these judgments are inaccurate. Managers need to keep in mind that both equity theory and expectancy theory suggest that employee motivation is squelched by inaccurate performance ratings. Not only can inaccurate performance rating systems negatively influence motivation, but they can lead to lawsuits. For example, employees and former employees with Microsoft, Ford, and Conoco have filed lawsuits claiming that ranking systems are biased toward some groups over others.[58]

Consistent with expectancy theory and the principles of behavior modification discussed in Chapter 8 managers should make rewards contingent on performance.[59] In doing so, it is important that managers consider the accuracy and fairness of the reward system. As discussed under expectancy theory, the promise of increased rewards will not prompt higher effort and good performance unless those rewards are clearly tied to performance and they are large enough to gain employees' interest or attention.

Consider the practices used by Hyde Manufacturing and Cigna Corporation:

> Hyde Manufacturing Co., Southbridge, Mass., maker of putty knives, wallpaper scrapers, and animal-hoof cleaners, last year began quarterly bonus payouts to workers when certain profit levels are reached, on top of other performance rewards the company says have produced record sales. . . . In a program begun in late 1997 by Cigna Corp.'s health-care unit in Bloomfield, Conn., about 35% of eligible employees, such as claims processors, are boosting pay, with monthly bonuses, as much as 50% over their base salary—and lifting productivity, too—by increasing the number of calls they handle, for example.[60]

Moreover, equity theory tells us that motivation is influenced by employee perceptions about the fairness of reward allocations. Motivation is decreased when employees believe rewards are inequitably allocated. Rewards also need to be integrated appropriately into the appraisal system. If performance is measured at the individual level, individual achievements need to be rewarded. On the other hand, when performance is the result of group effort, rewards should be allocated to the group.[61]

Feedback also should be linked with performance. Feedback provides the information and direction needed to keep employees focused on relevant tasks, activities, and goals. Managers should strive to provide specific, timely, and accurate feedback to employees.

Finally, we end this chapter by noting that an organization's culture significantly influences employee motivation and behavior. A positive self-enhancing culture such as that at Rhino Foods, for example, is more likely to engender higher motivation and commitment than a culture dominated by suspicion, fault finding, and blame.

chapter summary

- *Discuss the role of perceived inequity in employee motivation.* Equity theory is a model of motivation that explains how people strive for fairness and justice in social exchanges. On the job, feelings of inequity revolve around a person's evaluation of whether he or she receives adequate rewards to compensate for his or her contributive inputs. People perform these evaluations by comparing the perceived fairness of their employment exchange with that of relevant others. Perceived inequity creates motivation to restore equity.

- *Describe the practical lessons derived from equity theory.* Equity theory has at least eight practical implications. First, because people are motivated to resolve perceptions of inequity, managers should not discount employees' feelings and perceptions when trying to motivate workers. Second, managers should pay attention to employees' *perceptions* of what is fair and equitable. It is the employee's view of reality that counts when trying to motivate someone, according to equity theory. Third, employees should be given a voice in decisions that affect them. Fourth, employees should be given the opportunity to appeal decisions that affect their welfare. Fifth, employees are more likely to accept and support organizational change when they believe it is implemented fairly and when it produces equitable outcomes. Sixth, managers can promote cooperation and teamwork among group members by treating them equitably. Seventh, treating employees inequitably can lead to litigation and costly court settlements. Finally, managers need to pay attention to the organization's climate for justice because it influences employee attitudes and behavior.

- *Explain Vroom's expectancy theory.* Expectancy theory assumes motivation is determined by one's perceived

chances of achieving valued outcomes. Vroom's expectancy model of motivation reveals how effort → performance expectancies and performance → outcome instrumentalities influence the degree of effort expended to achieve desired (positively valent) outcomes.

- *Describe the practical implications of expectancy theory.* Managers are advised to enhance effort → performance expectancies by helping employees accomplish their performance goals. With respect to instrumentalities and valences, managers should attempt to link employee performance and valued rewards. There are four prerequisites to linking performance and rewards: (a) Managers need to develop and communicate performance standards to employees, (b) managers need valid and accurate performance ratings, (c) managers need to determine the relative mix of individual versus team contribution to performance and then reward accordingly, and (d) managers should use performance ratings to differentially allocate rewards among employees.

- *Identify five practical lessons to be learned from goal-setting research.* Difficult goals lead to higher performance than easy or moderate goals: goals should not be impossible to achieve. Specific, difficult goals lead to higher performance for simple rather than complex tasks. Third, feedback enhances the effect of specific, difficult goals. Fourth, participative goals, assigned goals, and self-set goals are equally effective. Fifth, goal commitment and monetary incentives affect goal-setting outcomes.

- *Specify issues that should be addressed before implementing a motivational program.* Managers need to consider the variety of causes of poor performance and employee misbehavior. Undesirable employee performance and behavior may be due to a host of deficient individual inputs (e.g., ability, dispositions, emotions, and beliefs) or job context factors (e.g., materials and machinery, job characteristics, reward systems, supervisory support and coaching, and social norms). The method used to evaluate performance as well as the link between performance and rewards must be examined. Performance must be accurately evaluated and rewards should be equitably distributed. Managers should also recognize that employee motivation and behavior are influenced by organizational culture.

internet exercise

www.ge.com

This chapter discussed how employee motivation is influenced by goal setting and the relationship between performance and rewards. We also reviewed the variety of issues that managers should consider when implementing motivational programs. The purpose of this exercise is for you to examine the motivational techniques used by General Electric (GE). GE is one of the most successful companies in the world. The company is well known for establishing clear corporate goals and then creating the infrastructure (e.g., rewards) to achieve them. Begin by visiting GE's home page at **www.ge.com**. Begin your search by locating GE's corporate values and corporate goals. Then expand your search by looking for information that discusses the different incentives GE uses to motivate its employees.

QUESTIONS
1. Based on GE's values and goals, what type of behavior is the organization trying to motivate?
2. What rewards does GE use to reinforce desired behavior and performance?
3. To what extent are GE's practices consistent with the material covered in this chapter?

Improving Performance with Feedback, Rewards, and Positive Reinforcement

Eight

chapter

LEARNING OBJECTIVES

After reading the material in this chapter, you should be able to:

- Specify the two basic functions of feedback and three sources of feedback.

- Define upward feedback and 360-degree feedback, and summarize the general tips for giving good feedback.

- Briefly explain the four different organizational reward norms.

- Summarize the reasons rewards often fail to motivate employees.

- State Thorndike's "law of effect" and explain Skinner's distinction between respondent and operant behavior.

- Demonstrate your knowledge of positive reinforcement, negative reinforcement, punishment, and extinction.

- Demonstrate your knowledge of behavior shaping.

AND THE WINNER IS . . . !

Imagine for a moment that your job worked like a game show. Maybe you'd have Pat Sajak for a boss. Or Alex Trebek. Now suppose the rules stated that every time you went above and beyond the call of duty, you could win a prize. Work over the weekend and take home a new five-iron. Make that impossible sales target, and, yes, you too could be basking in the tropical sun on a Caribbean beach. Think of it as Merv Griffin meets management.

That's exactly the idea that San Francisco–based Netcentives sold to Nortel, which now uses Netcentives' system for the majority of its 80,000 employees worldwide. Here's how it works: For a job well done, your boss rewards you with points (or a co-worker can nominate you). Trade those points for a cash bonus right now . . . or save them up and trade them for anything from a tool kit to a trip to the Super Bowl.

The whole thing sounds kind of corny, but there are advantages. First off, as Regis could tell you, the game

show dynamic has always grabbed people's attention. Everybody wants to be a winner. Once they buy into the prize mentality, employees soon realize that taking the goodies has a major benefit over taking the cash—namely, no taxes. In most cases Nortel pays all the taxes for the employees. So instead of losing up to 39.6% of that hard-earned cash bonus, your $1,000 worth of points gets you a prize worth pretty much that. Which leads to another benefit. Cash can quickly disappear in a pile of car payments and Visa bills. But that brand-spanking-new DVD player will serve as a permanent, tangible reminder of your company's appreciation. And

there are benefits for Nortel too. Since the entire program is online, it's faster and more efficient than older, offline alternatives.

Already 25,000 Nortel employees have received a points award, and 40% of those have redeemed them for prizes. After three years of exemplary work, one recipient, Kathy Gorley, an executive assistant, was able to remodel her bathroom—a prize she calls "a really nice pat on the back." Then there's Jessica Flynn, a Nortel senior financial analyst, who describes getting her all-expenses-paid trip to the Pro Bowl in Maui as "almost like Christmas." At just 26, Jessica believes that she's in for the long haul at Nortel. This year, Hawaii; next year, Door No. 2.[1]

From a management standpoint, do you approve or disapprove of this reward plan? Explain. As an employee, what do you think about it? Explain. For an interpretation of this case and additional comments, visit our website:

www.mhhe.com/kinickiob

FOR DISCUSSION

PRODUCTIVITY AND TOTAL QUALITY EXPERTS tell us we need to work smarter, not harder. While it is true that a sound education and appropriate skill training are needed if one is to work smarter, the process does not end there. Today's employees need instructive and supportive feedback and desired rewards if they are to translate their knowledge into improved productivity and superior quality. This point was reinforced by a recent survey of 612 employees in the United States. When asked about the changes top management needs to make to attract and keep good people, these two items headed the list: "improving salaries and benefits" (72%) and "recognizing and rewarding good employee performance" (69%).[2] Figure 8–1 illustrates a learning- and development-focused cycle in which feedback enhances ability, encourages effort, and acknowledges results. Rewards and reinforcement, in turn, motivate effort and compensate results.

This chapter concludes our coverage of individual behavior by discussing the effects of feedback, rewards, and positive reinforcement on behavior and by integrating those insights with what you have learned about perception, individual differences, and various motivational tools such as goal setting.

FIGURE 8–1   Bolstering the Job Performance Cycle with Feedback, Rewards, and Reinforcement

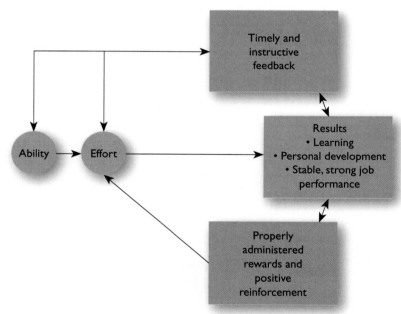

Providing Effective Feedback

Numerous surveys tell us employees have a hearty appetite for feedback.[3] So also do achievement-oriented students. Following a difficult exam, for instance, students want to know two things: how they did and how their peers did. By letting students know how their work measures up to grading and competitive standards, an instructor's feedback permits the students to adjust their study habits so they can reach their goals. Likewise, managers in well-run organizations follow up goal setting with a feedback program to provide a rational basis for adjustment and improvement. For example, notice the importance Fred Smith, the founder and head of Federal Express, places on feedback when outlining his philosophy of leadership:

> When people walk in the door, they want to know: What do you expect out of me? What's in this deal for me? What do I have to do to get ahead? Where do I go in this organization to get justice if I'm not treated appropriately? They want to know how they're doing. They want some feedback. And they want to know that what they are doing is important.
>
> If you take the basic principles of leadership and answer those questions over and over again, you can be successful dealing with people.[4]

Feedback too often gets shortchanged. In fact, "poor or insufficient feedback" was the leading cause of deficient performance in a survey of US and European companies.[5]

As the term is used here, **feedback** is objective information about individual or collective performance shared with those in a position to improve the situation. Subjective assessments such as, "You're doing a poor job," "You're too lazy," or "We really appreciate your hard work" do not qualify as objective feedback. But hard data such as units sold, days absent, dollars saved, projects completed, customers satisfied, and quality rejects are all candidates for objective feedback programs. Management consultants Chip Bell and Ron Zemke offered this helpful perspective of feedback:

Feedback

Objective information about performance.

> Feedback is, quite simply, any information that answers those "How am I doing?" questions. *Good* feedback answers them truthfully and productively. It's information people can use either to confirm or correct their performance.
>
> Feedback comes in many forms and from a variety of sources. Some is easy to get and requires hardly any effort to understand. The charts and graphs tracking group and individual performance that are fixtures in many workplaces are an example of this variety. Performance feedback—the numerical type at least—is at the heart of most approaches to total quality management.
>
> Some feedback is less accessible. It's tucked away in the heads of customers and managers. But no matter how well-hidden the feedback, if people need it to keep their performance on track, we need to get it to them—preferably while it's still fresh enough to make an impact.[6]

Two Functions of Feedback

Experts say feedback serves two functions for those who receive it; one is *instructional* and the other *motivational*. Feedback instructs when it clarifies roles or teaches new behavior. For example, an assistant accountant might be advised to handle a certain entry as a capital item rather than as an expense item. On the other hand, feedback motivates when it serves as a reward or promises a reward.[7] Having the boss tell you that a grueling project you worked on earlier has just been completed can be a rewarding piece of news. As documented in one study, the motivational function of feedback can be significantly enhanced by pairing *specific,* challenging goals with *specific* feedback about results.[8]

Three Sources of Feedback: Others, Task, and Self

It almost goes without saying that employees receive objective feedback from *others* such as peers, supervisors, lower-level employees, and outsiders. Perhaps less obvious is the fact that the *task* itself is a ready source of objective feedback.[9] Anyone who has spent hours on a "quick" Internet search can appreciate the power of task-provided feedback. Similarly, skilled tasks such as computer programming or landing a jet airplane provide a steady stream of feedback about how well or poorly one is doing. A third source of feedback is *oneself,* but self-serving bias and other perceptual problems can contaminate this source. Those high in self-confidence tend to rely on personal feedback more than those with low self-confidence. Although circumstances vary, an employee can be bombarded by feedback from all three sources simultaneously. This is where the gatekeeping functions of perception and cognitive evaluation are needed to help sort things out.

The Recipient's Perspective of Feedback

The need for feedback is variable, across both individuals and situations (see Hands-On Exercise). Feedback can be positive or negative. Generally, people tend to perceive and recall positive feedback more accurately than they do negative feedback.[10] But negative feedback (e.g., being told your performance is below average) can have a *positive* motivational effect. In fact, in one study, those who were told they were below average on a creativity test subsequently outperformed those who were led to believe their results were above average. The subjects apparently took the negative feedback as a challenge and set and pursued higher goals. Those receiving positive feedback apparently were less motivated to do better.[11] Nonetheless, feedback with a negative message or threatening content needs to be administered carefully to avoid creating insecurity and defensiveness.[12] Self-efficacy also can be damaged by negative feedback, as discovered in a pair of experiments with business students. The researchers concluded, "To facilitate the development of strong efficacy beliefs, managers should be careful about the provision of negative feedback. Destructive criticism by managers which attributes the cause of poor performance to internal factors reduces both the beliefs of self-efficacy and the self-set goals of recipients."[13]

Upon receiving feedback, people cognitively evaluate factors such as its accuracy, the credibility of the source, the fairness of the system (e.g., performance appraisal system), their performance-reward expectancies, and the reasonableness of the standards. Any feedback that fails to clear one or more of these cognitive hurdles will be rejected or downplayed. Personal experience largely dictates how these factors are weighed.

Behavioral Outcomes of Feedback

In Chapter 7, we discussed how goal setting gives behavior direction, increases expended effort, and fosters persistence. Because feedback is intimately related to the goal-setting process, it involves the same behavioral outcomes: direction, effort, and persistence. However, while the fourth outcome of goal setting involves formulating goal-attainment strategies, the fourth possible outcome of feedback is *resistance.* Feedback schemes that smack of manipulation or fail one or more of the perceptual and cognitive evaluation tests mentioned above breed resistance.[14]

Nontraditional Upward Feedback and 360-Degree Feedback

Traditional top-down feedback programs have given way to some interesting variations in recent years. Two newer approaches, discussed in this section, are upward feedback and so-called 360-degree feedback. Aside from breaking away from a strict superior-to-subordinate feedback loop, these newer approaches are different because they typically

Measuring Your Desire for Performance Feedback

INSTRUCTIONS Circle one number indicating the strength of your agreement or disagreement with each statement. Total your responses, and compare your score with our arbitrary norms.

	Disagree				Agree
1. As long as I think that I have done something well, I am not too concerned about how other people think I have done.	5	4	3	2	1
2. How other people view my work is not as important as how I view my own work.	5	4	3	2	1
3. It is usually better not to put much faith in what others say about your work, regardless of whether it is complimentary or not.	5	4	3	2	1
4. If I have done something well, I know it without other people telling me so.	5	4	3	2	1
5. I usually have a clear idea of what I am trying to do and how well I am proceeding toward my goal.	5	4	3	2	1
6. I find that I am usually a pretty good judge of my own performance.	5	4	3	2	1
7. It is very important to me to know what people think of my work.	1	2	3	4	5
8. It is a good idea to get someone to check on your work before it's too late to make changes.	1	2	3	4	5
9. Even though I may think I have done a good job, I feel a lot more confident of it after someone else tells me so.	1	2	3	4	5
10. Since one cannot be objective about their own performance, it is best to listen to the feedback provided by others.	1	2	3	4	5

Total score = _____

ARBITRARY NORMS   10–23 = Low desire for feedback
24–36 = Moderate desire for feedback
37–50 = High desire for feedback

SOURCE: Excerpted and adapted from D M Herold, C K Parsons, and R B Rensvold, "Individual Differences in the Generation and Processing of Performance Feedback," *Educational and Psychological Measurement*, February 1996, Table 1, p 9. Copyright © 1996 by Sage Publications. Reprinted by permission of Sage Publications, Inc.

involve *multiple sources* of feedback. Instead of getting feedback from one boss, often during an annual performance appraisal, more and more managers are getting structured feedback from superiors, lower-level employees, peers, and even outsiders such as customers. Nontraditional feedback is growing in popularity for at least six reasons:

1. Traditional performance appraisal systems have created widespread dissatisfaction.

2. Team-based organization structures are replacing traditional hierarchies. This trend requires managers to have good interpersonal skills that are best evaluated by team members.

3. Multiple-rater systems are said to make feedback more valid than single-source feedback.[15]

4. Advanced computer network technology (the Internet and company Intranets) greatly facilitates multiple-rater systems.[16]

5. Bottom-up feedback meshes nicely with the trend toward participative management and employee empowerment.

6. Co-workers and lower-level employees are said to know more about a manager's strengths and limitations than the boss.[17]

Together, these factors make a compelling case for looking at better ways to give and receive performance feedback.

Upward feedback

Employees evaluate their boss.

Upward Feedback Upward feedback stands the traditional approach on its head by having lower-level employees provide feedback on a manager's style and performance. This type of feedback is generally anonymous. Most students are familiar with upward feedback programs from years of filling out anonymous teacher evaluation surveys. Early adopters of upward evaluations include AT&T, General Mills, Motorola, and Procter & Gamble.[18]

Managers typically resist upward feedback programs because they believe it erodes their authority. Other critics say anonymous upward feedback can become little more than a personality contest or, worse, be manipulated by managers who make promises or threats. What does the research literature tell us about upward feedback? Studies with diverse samples have given us these useful insights:

- The question of whether upward feedback should be *anonymous* was addressed by a study at a large US insurance company. All told, 183 employees rated the skills and effectiveness of 38 managers. Managers who received anonymous upward feedback received *lower* ratings and liked the process *less* than did those receiving feedback from identifiable employees. This finding confirmed the criticism that employees will tend to go easier on their boss when not protected by confidentiality.[19]

- A large-scale study at the US Naval Academy, where student leaders and followers live together day and night, discovered a positive impact of upward feedback on leader behavior.[20]

- In a field study of 238 corporate managers, upward feedback had a positive impact on the performance of low-to-moderate performers.[21]

360-Degree Feedback Letting individuals compare their own perceived performance with behaviorally specific (and usually anonymous) performance information from their manager, subordinates, and peers is known as **360-degree feedback.**

360-degree feedback

Comparison of anonymous feedback from one's superior, subordinates, and peers with self-perceptions.

Even outsiders may be involved in what is sometimes called full-circle feedback. The idea is to let the individual know how their behavior affects others, with the goal of motivating change. In a 360-degree feedback program, a given manager will play different roles, including focal person, superior, subordinate, and peer. Of course, the focal person role is played only once. The other roles are played more than once for various other focal persons. As a barometer of popularity, the Society for Human Resource

Management found 32% of the companies it surveyed in 2000 using 360-degree feed-back.[22]

Because upward feedback is a part of 360-degree feedback programs, the evidence reviewed earlier applies here as well. As with upward feedback, peer- and self-evaluations, central to 360-degree feedback programs, also are a significant affront to tradition.[23] But advocates say co-workers and managers themselves are appropriate performance evaluators because they are closest to the action.[24] Generally, research builds a stronger case for peer appraisals than for self-appraisals.[25] Self-serving bias, discussed in Chapter 4, is a problem.

Rigorous research evidence of 360-degree feedback programs is scarce. A two-year study of 48 managers given 360-degree feedback in a large US public utility company led to these somewhat promising results. According to the researchers, "The group as a whole developed its skills, but there was substantial variability among individuals in how much change occurred."[26] Thus, as with any feedback, individuals vary in their response to 360-degree feedback.

Practical Recommendations   Research evidence on upward and 36-degree feedback leads us to *favor* anonymity and *discourage* use for pay and promotion decisions. Otherwise, managerial resistance and self-serving manipulation would prevail.[27] We enthusiastically endorse the use of upward and/or 360-degree feedback for management development and training purposes.

Why Feedback Often Fails

Experts on the subject cite the following six common trouble signs for organizational feedback systems:

1. Feedback is used to punish, embarrass, or put down employees.
2. Those receiving the feedback see it as irrelevant to their work.
3. Feedback information is provided too late to do any good.
4. People receiving feedback believe it relates to matters beyond their control.
5. Employees complain about wasting too much time collecting and recording feedback data.
6. Feedback recipients complain about feedback being too complex or difficult to understand.[28]

Managers can provide effective feedback by consciously avoiding these pitfalls and following the practical tips in Skills & Best Practices.

How to Make Sure Feedback Gets Results

- Relate feedback to existing performance *goals* and clear *expectations*.
- Give *specific* feedback tied to observable behavior or measurable results.
- Channel feedback toward *key result areas*.
- Give feedback as *soon* as possible.
- Give positive feedback for *improvement*, not just final results.
- Focus feedback on *performance*, not personalities.
- Base feedback on *accurate* and *credible* information.

SKILLS & BEST PRACTICES

Organizational Reward Systems

Rewards are an ever-present and always controversial feature of organizational life.[29] Some employees see their job as the source of a paycheck and little else. Others derive great pleasure from their job and association with co-workers. Even volunteers who donate their time to charitable organizations, such as the Red Cross, walk away with rewards in the form of social recognition and pride of having given unselfishly of their time. Hence, the subject of organizational rewards includes, but goes far beyond, monetary compensation.[30] This section examines key components of organizational reward systems.

Despite the fact that reward systems vary widely, it is possible to identify and interrelate some common components. The model in Figure 8–2 focuses on four important components: (1) types of rewards, (2) reward norms, (3) distribution criteria, and (4) desired outcomes. Let us examine these components.

Types of Rewards

Including the usual paycheck, the variety and magnitude of organizational rewards boggles the mind—from subsidized day care to college tuition reimbursement to stock options.[31] A US Bureau of Labor Statistics economist offered the following historical perspective of employee compensation:

> One of the more striking developments . . . over the past 75 years has been the growing complexity of employee compensation. Limited at the outbreak of World War I largely to straight-time pay for hours worked, compensation now includes a variety of employer-financed benefits, such as health and life insurance, retirement income, and paid time off. Although the details of each vary widely, these benefits are today standard components of the compensation package, and workers generally have come to expect them.[32]

Today, it is common for nonwage benefits to be 50% or more of total compensation.

FIGURE 8–2   Key Factors in Organizational Reward Systems

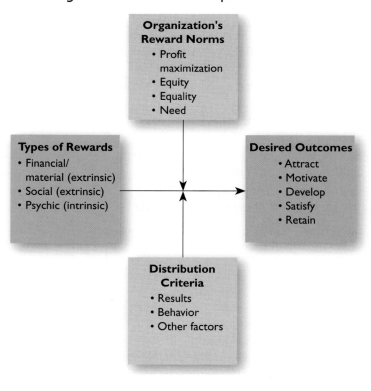

In addition to the obvious pay and benefits, there are less obvious social and psychic rewards. Social rewards include praise and recognition from others both inside and outside the organization. Psychic rewards come from personal feelings of self-esteem, self-satisfaction, and accomplishment.

An alternative typology for organizational rewards is the distinction between extrinsic and intrinsic rewards. Financial, material, and social rewards qualify as **extrinsic rewards** because they come from the environment. Psychic rewards, however, are **intrinsic rewards** because they are self-granted. An employee who works to obtain extrinsic rewards, such as money or praise, is said to be extrinsically motivated. One who derives pleasure from the task itself or experiences a sense of competence or self-determination is said to be intrinsically motivated.[33] The relative importance of extrinsic and intrinsic rewards is a matter of culture and personal tastes.

> **Extrinsic rewards**
> Financial, material, or social rewards from the environment.

> **Intrinsic rewards**
> Self-granted, psychic rewards.

Organizational Reward Norms

As discussed in Chapter 7 under the heading of equity theory, the employer–employee linkage can be viewed as an exchange relationship. Employees exchange their time and talent for rewards. Ideally, four alternative norms dictate the nature of this exchange. In pure form, each would lead to a significantly different reward distribution system. They are as follows:

- *Profit maximization.* The objective of each party is to maximize its net gain, regardless of how the other party fares. A profit-maximizing company would attempt to pay the least amount of wages for maximum effort. Conversely, a profit-maximizing employee would seek maximum rewards, regardless of the organization's financial well-being, and leave the organization for a better deal.

- *Equity.* According to the **reward equity norm,** rewards should be allocated proportionate to contributions. Those who contribute the most should be rewarded the most. A cross-cultural study of American, Japanese, and Korean college students led the researchers to the following conclusion: "Equity is probably a phenomenon common to most cultures, but its strength will vary."[34] Basic principles of fairness and justice, evident in most cultures, drive the equity norm. However, pay equity between women and men in the United States remains an unresolved issue.[35]

> **Reward equity norm**
> Rewards should be tied to contributions.

- *Equality.* The **reward equality norm** calls for rewarding all parties equally, regardless of their comparative contributions. Because absolute equality does not exist in today's hierarchical organizations, researchers recently explored the impact of pay *inequality.* They looked at *pay dispersion* (the pay gap between high-level and low-level employees). Result: The smaller the pay gap, the better the individual and organizational performance.[36] Thus, the outlandish compensation packages for many of today's top executives is not only a widely debated moral issue, it is a productivity issue as well.[37]

> **Reward equality norm**
> Everyone should get the same rewards.

- *Need.* This norm calls for distributing rewards according to employees' needs, rather than their contributions.[38]

A pair of researchers concluded that these contradictory norms are typically intertwined:

In 2001, Delta Air Lines Inc. raised its mechanics' pay to make them the highest paid in the industry, doing so amid an intense union drive to organize its 10,000 mechanics. The pay raises were in response to comparisons with industry peers, according to Delta spokesman Tom Donahue, but there was not "... a correlation between our compensation structure and any organizing efforts at Delta." Hmmm.

> We propose that employer–employee exchanges are governed by the contradictory norms of profit maximization, equity, equality, and need. These norms can coexist; what varies is the extent to which the rules for correct application of a norm are clear and the relative emphasis different managements will give to certain norms in particular allocations.[39]

Conflict and ethical debates often arise over the perceived fairness of reward allocations because of disagreement about reward norms. Stockholders might prefer a profit-maximization norm, while technical specialists would like an equity norm, and unionized hourly workers would argue for a pay system based on equality. A reward norm anchored to need might prevail in a family owned and operated business. Effective reward systems are based on clear and consensual exchange norms.

Distribution Criteria

According to one expert on organizational reward systems, three general criteria for the distribution of rewards are as follows:

- *Performance: results.* Tangible outcomes such as individual, group, or organization performance; quantity and quality of performance.
- *Performance: actions and behaviors.* Such as teamwork, cooperation, risk taking, creativity.
- *Nonperformance considerations.* Customary or contractual, where the type of job, nature of the work, equity, tenure, level in hierarchy, etc., are rewarded.[40]

As illustrated in the following example, the trend today is toward *performance* criteria and away from nonperformance criteria:

> Del Wallick wears his pride under his sleeve. A handshake reveals his prized wristwatch, given to mark his 25th anniversary with Timken Co. "I only take it off to shower and sleep," he says.
>
> The hallways of Mr. Wallick's home in Canton, Ohio, are filled with an array of certificates marking the milestones in his 31-year career as a Timken steel-mill worker. Down in his rec room, a mantel clock that he and his wife picked out from a Timken gift catalog rests atop the family television.
>
> But these days, once-paternal companies like Timken are trying to move away from rewarding employees for long service. Many are reducing service-award programs—and a few are eliminating them entirely. Besides wanting to save money, these companies hope to tilt recognition more toward performance and away from years of loyal service.[41]

Desired Outcomes

As listed in Figure 8–2, a good reward system should attract talented people and motivate and satisfy them once they have joined the organization.[42] Further, a good reward system should foster personal growth and development and keep talented people from leaving. A prime example is Herman Miller Inc., the profitable office-furniture maker. Not only does the firm maintain a much lower than average ratio between top management and shop-floor pay levels, Herman Miller shares generous productivity bonuses with its employees as well. The net results: low turnover, a strong supportive culture, and excellent employee–management working relationships.[43]

Why Rewards Often Fail to Motivate

Despite huge investments of time and money for organizational reward systems, the desired motivational effect often is not achieved. A management consultant/writer recently offered these eight reasons:

1. Too much emphasis on monetary rewards.
2. Rewards lack an "appreciation effect."
3. Extensive benefits become entitlements.
4. Counterproductive behavior is rewarded. (For example, "a pizza delivery company focused its rewards on the on-time performance of its drivers, only to discover that it was inadvertently rewarding reckless driving."[44])
5. Too long a delay between performance and rewards.
6. Too many one-size-fits-all rewards.
7. Use of one-shot rewards with a short-lived motivational impact.
8. Continued use of demotivating practices such as layoffs, across-the-board raises and cuts, and excessive executive compensation.[45]

These stubborn problems have fostered a growing interest in more effective reward and compensation practices.[46]

Positive Reinforcement

Feedback and reward programs all too often are ineffective because they are administered in haphazard ways. For example, consider these scenarios:

*   A young programmer stops E-mailing creative suggestions to his boss because she never responds.
*   The office politician gets a great promotion while her more skilled co-workers scratch their heads and gossip about the injustice.

In the first instance, a productive behavior faded away for lack of encouragement. In the second situation, unproductive behavior was unwittingly rewarded. Feedback and rewards need to be handled more precisely. Fortunately, the field of behavioral psychology can help. Thanks to the pioneering work of Edward L Thorndike, B F Skinner, and many others, a behavior modification technique called *positive reinforcement* helps managers achieve needed discipline and desired effect when providing feedback and granting rewards.[47]

Thorndike's Law of Effect

During the early 1900s, Edward L Thorndike observed in his psychology laboratory that a cat would behave randomly and wildly when placed in a small box with a secret trip lever that opened a door. However, once the cat accidentally tripped the lever and escaped, the animal would go straight to the lever when placed back in the box. Hence, Thorndike formulated his famous **law of effect,** which says *behavior with favorable consequences tends to be repeated, while behavior with unfavorable consequences tends to disappear.*[48] This was a dramatic departure from the prevailing notion a century ago that behavior was the product of inborn instincts.

> **Law of effect**
>
> Behavior with favorable consequences is repeated; behavior with unfavorable consequences disappears.

Skinner's Operant Conditioning Model

Skinner refined Thorndike's conclusion that behavior is controlled by its consequences. Skinner's work became known as *behaviorism* because he dealt strictly with observable behavior.[49] As a behaviorist, Skinner believed it was pointless to explain behavior in terms of unobservable inner states such as needs, drives, attitudes, or thought processes.[50] He similarly put little stock in the idea of self-determination.

In his 1938 classic, *The Behavior of Organisms,* Skinner drew an important distinction between two types of behavior: respondent and operant behavior.[51] He labeled unlearned reflexes or stimulus–response (S–R) connections **respondent behavior.** This category of behavior was said to describe a very small proportion of adult human behavior. Examples of respondent behavior would include shedding tears while peeling onions and reflexively withdrawing one's hand from a hot stove.[52] Skinner attached the label **operant behavior** to behavior that is learned when one "operates on" the environment to produce desired consequences. Some call this the response–stimulus (R–S) model. Years of controlled experiments with pigeons in "Skinner boxes" helped Skinner develop a sophisticated technology of behavior control, or operant conditioning. For example, he taught pigeons how to pace figure eights and how to bowl by reinforcing the underweight (and thus hungry) birds with food whenever they more closely approximated target behaviors. Skinner's work has significant implications for OB because the vast majority of organizational behavior falls into the operant category.[53]

> **Respondent behavior**
>
> Skinner's term for unlearned stimulus–response reflexes.
>
> **Operant behavior**
>
> Skinner's term for learned, consequence-shaped behavior.

Contingent Consequences

Contingent consequences, according to Skinner's operant theory, control behavior in four ways: positive reinforcement, negative reinforcement, punishment, and extinction.[54] The term *contingent* means there is a systematic if-then linkage between the target behavior and the consequence. Remember Mom (and Pink Floyd) saying something to this effect: "If you don't finish your dinner, you don't get dessert" (see Figure 8–3)? To avoid the all-too-common mislabeling of these consequences, let us review some formal definitions.

> **Positive reinforcement**
>
> Making behavior occur more often by contingently presenting something positive.

Positive Reinforcement Strengthens Behavior Positive **reinforcement** is the process of strengthening a behavior by contingently presenting something pleasing. (Importantly, a behavior is strengthened when it increases in frequency and weakened when it decreases in frequency.) A design engineer who works overtime because of praise and

Contingent Consequences in Operant Conditioning   FIGURE 8–3

Behavior-Consequence Relationship

Nature of Consequence

	Positive or Pleasing	Negative or Displeasing
Contingent Presentation	**Positive Reinforcement** *Behavioral outcome:* Target behavior occurs *more* often.	**Punishment** *Behavioral outcome:* Target behavior occurs *less* often.
Contingent Withdrawal	**Punishment (Response Cost)** *Behavioral outcome:* Target behavior occurs *less* often.	**Negative Reinforcement** *Behavioral outcome:* Target behavior occurs *more* often.

(no contingent consequence)
Extinction
Behavioral outcome:
Target behavior occurs *less* often.

recognition from the boss is responding to positive reinforcement.[55] Similarly, people tend to return to restaurants where they are positively reinforced with good food and friendly, high-quality service.[56]

Negative Reinforcement Also Strengthens Behavior

Negative reinforcement is the process of strengthening a behavior by contingently withdrawing something displeasing. For example, an army sergeant who stops yelling when a recruit jumps out of bed has negatively reinforced that particular behavior. Similarly, the behavior of clamping our hands over our ears when watching a jumbo jet take off is negatively reinforced by relief from the noise. Negative reinforcement is often confused with punishment. But the two strategies have opposite effects on behavior. Negative reinforcement, as the word *reinforcement* indicates, strengthens a behavior because it provides relief from an unpleasant situation.

Negative reinforcement

Making behavior occur more often by contingently withdrawing something negative.

Punishment Weakens Behavior

Punishment is the process of weakening behavior through either the contingent presentation of something displeasing or the contingent withdrawal of something positive. A manager assigning a tardy employee to a dirty job exemplifies the first type of punishment. Docking a tardy employee's pay is an example of the second type of punishment, called "response cost" punishment. Legal fines involve response cost punishment. Sales people who must make up any cash register shortages out of their own pockets are being managed through response cost punishment. Ethical questions can and should be raised about this type of on-the-job punishment.[57]

Punishment

Making behavior occur less often by contingently presenting something negative or withdrawing something positive.

Extinction Also Weakens Behavior

Extinction is the weakening of a behavior by ignoring it or making sure it is not reinforced. Getting rid of a former boyfriend or girlfriend by refusing to return their phone calls is an extinction strategy. A good analogy for extinction is to

Extinction

Making behavior occur less often by ignoring or not reinforcing it.

At Granite Construction in Watsonville, California, 20% of every manager's bonus depends on the person's "people skills." For most of its 80 years, a call from the boss's office meant bad news. "Employees were only contacted when something went wrong," says division manager Bruce McGowan, a 20-year veteran who oversees a staff of 700. Now the emphasis is on positive reinforcement.

imagine what would happen to your houseplants if you stopped watering them. Like a plant without water, a behavior without occasional reinforcement eventually dies. Although very different processes, both punishment and extinction have the same weakening effect on behavior.

Schedules of Reinforcement

As just discussed, contingent consequences are an important determinant of future behavior. The *timing* of behavioral consequences can be even more important. Based on years of tedious laboratory experiments with pigeons in highly controlled environments, Skinner and his colleagues discovered distinct patterns of responding for various schedules of reinforcement.[58] Although some of their conclusions can be generalized to negative reinforcement, punishment, and extinction, it is best to think only of positive reinforcement when discussing schedules.

Continuous Reinforcement   As indicated in Table 8–1, every instance of a target behavior is reinforced when a **continuous reinforcement** (CRF) schedule is in effect. For instance, when your television set is operating properly, you are reinforced with a picture every time you turn it on (a CRF schedule). But, as with any CRF schedule of reinforcement, the behavior of turning on the television will undergo rapid extinction if the set breaks.

Intermittent   Reinforcement   Unlike   CRF   schedules,   **intermittent reinforcement** involves reinforcement of some but not all instances of a target behavior. Four subcategories of intermittent schedules, described in Table 8–1, are fixed and variable ratio schedules and fixed and variable interval schedules. Reinforcement in *ratio* schedules is contingent on the number of responses emitted. *Interval* reinforcement is tied to the passage of time. Some common examples of the four types of intermittent reinforcement are as follows:

- *Fixed ratio*—piece-rate pay; bonuses tied to the sale of a fixed number of units.
- *Variable ratio*—slot machines that pay off after a variable number of lever pulls; lotteries that pay off after the purchase of a variable number of tickets.
- *Fixed interval*—hourly pay; annual salary paid on a regular basis.
- *Variable interval*—random supervisory praise and pats on the back for employees who have been doing a good job.

Proper Scheduling Is Important   The schedule of reinforcement can more powerfully influence behavior than the magnitude of reinforcement. Although this proposition grew out of experiments with pigeons, subsequent on-the-job research confirmed it. Consider, for example, a field study of 12 unionized beaver trappers employed by a lumber company to keep the large rodents from eating newly planted tree seedlings.[59]

The beaver trappers were randomly divided into two groups that alternated weekly between two different bonus plans. Under the first schedule, each trapper earned his

Schedules of Reinforcement | **TABLE 8–1**

Schedule	Description	Probable Effects on Responding
Continuous (CRF)	Reinforcer follows every response.	Steady high rate of performance as long as reinforcement continues to follow every response.
		High frequency of reinforcement may lead to early satiation.
		Behavior weakens rapidly (undergoes extinction) when reinforcers are withheld.
		Appropriate for newly emitted, unstable, or low-frequency responses.
Intermittent	Reinforcer does not follow every response.	Capable of producing high frequencies of responding.
		Low frequency of reinforcement precludes early satiation.
		Appropriate for stable or high-frequency responses.
Fixed ratio (FR)	A fixed number of responses must be emitted before reinforcement occurs.	A fixed ratio of 1:1 (reinforcement occurs after every response) is the same as a continuous schedule.
		Tends to produce a high rate of response, which is vigorous and steady.
Variable ratio (VR)	A varying or random number of responses must be emitted before reinforcement occurs.	Capable of producing a high rate of response, which is vigorous, steady, and resistant to extinction.
Fixed interval (FI)	The first response after a specific period of time has elapsed is reinforced.	Produces an uneven response pattern varying from a very slow, unenergetic response immediately following reinforcement to a very fast, vigorous response immediately preceding reinforcement.
Variable interval (VI)	The first response after varying or random periods of time have elapsed is reinforced.	Tends to produce a high rate of response, which is vigorous, steady, and resistant to extinction.

SOURCE: F Luthans and R Kreitner, *Organizational Behavior Modification and Beyond: An Operant and Social Learning Approach* (Glenview, IL: Scott, Foresman, 1985), p 58. Used with authors' permission.

regular $7 per hour wage plus $1 for each beaver caught. Technically, this bonus was paid on a CRF schedule. The second bonus plan involved the regular $7 per hour wage plus a one-in-four chance (as determined by rolling the dice) of receiving $4 for each beaver trapped. This second bonus plan qualified as a varable ratio (VR-4) schedule. In the long run, both incentive schemes averaged out to a $1-per-beaver bonus. Surprisingly, however, when the trappers were under the VR-4 schedule, they were 58% more productive than under the CRF schedule, despite the fact that the net amount of pay averaged out the same for the two groups during the 12-week trapping season.

Continuous reinforcement

Reinforcing every instance of a behavior.

Intermittent reinforcement

Reinforcing some but not all instances of behavior.

SKILLS & BEST PRACTICES

How to Effectively Shape Job Behavior

1. *Accommodate the process of behavioral change.* Behaviors change in gradual stages, not in broad, sweeping motions.

2. *Define new behavior patterns specifically.* State what you wish to accomplish in explicit terms and in small amounts that can be easily grasped.

3. *Give individuals feedback on their performance.* A once-a-year performance appraisal is not sufficient.

4. *Reinforce behavior as quickly as possible.*

5. *Use powerful reinforcement.* To be effective, rewards must be important to the employee—not to the manager.

6. *Use a continuous reinforcement schedule.* New behaviors should be reinforced every time they occur. This reinforcement should continue until these behaviors become habitual.

7. *Use a variable reinforcement schedule for maintenance.* Even after behavior has become habitual, it still needs to be rewarded, though not necessarily every time it occurs.

8. *Reward teamwork—not competition.* Group goals and group rewards are one way to encourage cooperation in situations in which jobs and performance are interdependent.

9. *Make all rewards contingent on performance.*

10. *Never take good performance for granted.* Even superior performance, if left unrewarded, will eventually deteriorate.

SOURCE: Adapted from A T Hollingsworth and D Tanquay Hoyer, "How Supervisors Can Shape Behavior," *Personnel Journal*, May 1985, pp 86, 88.

Work Organizations Typically Rely on the Weakest Schedule Generally, variable ratio and variable interval schedules of reinforcement produce the strongest behavior that is most resistant to extinction. As gamblers will attest, variable schedules hold the promise of reinforcement after the next target response. For example, the following drama at a Laughlin, Nevada, gambling casino is one more illustration of the potency of variable ratio reinforcement:

> An elderly woman with a walker had lost her grip on the slot [machine] handle and had collapsed on the floor.
> "Help," she cried weakly.
> The woman at the machine next to her interrupted her play for a few seconds to try to help her to her feet, but all around her the army of slot players continued feeding coins to the machines.
> A security man arrived to soothe the woman and take her away.
> "Thank you," she told him appreciatively.
> "But don't forget my winnings."[60]

Organizations without at least some variable reinforcement are less likely to prompt this type of dedication to task. Despite the trend toward pay-for-performance, time-based pay schemes such as hourly wages and yearly salaries that rely on the weakest schedule of reinforcement (fixed interval) are still the rule in today's workplaces.

Shaping Behavior with Positive Reinforcement

Have you ever wondered how trainers at aquarium parks manage to get bottle-nosed dolphins to do flips, killer whales to carry people on their backs, and seals to juggle balls? The results are seemingly magical. Actually, a mundane learning process called shaping is responsible for the animals' antics.

Two-ton killer whales, for example, have a big appetite, and they find buckets of fish very reinforcing. So if the trainer wants to ride a killer whale, he or she reinforces very basic behaviors that will eventually lead to the whale being ridden. The killer whale is contingently reinforced with a few fish for coming near the trainer, then for being touched, then for putting its nose in a harness, then for being straddled, and eventually for swimming with the trainer on its back. In effect, the trainer systematically raises the behavioral requirement for reinforcement. Thus, **shaping** is defined as the process of reinforcing closer and closer approximations to a target behavior.

Shaping works very well with people, too, especially in training and quality programs involving continuous improvement. Praise, recognition,

Shaping

Reinforcing closer and closer approximations to a target behavior.

and instructive and credible feedback cost managers little more than moments of their time.[61] Yet, when used in conjunction with a behavior-shaping program, these consequences can efficiently foster significant improvements in job performance.[62] The key to successful behavior shaping lies in reducing a complex target behavior to easily learned steps and then faithfully (and patiently) reinforcing any improvement. For example, Continental Airlines used a cash bonus program to improve its on-time arrival record from one of the worst in the industry to one of the best. Employees originally were promised a $65 bonus each month Continental earned a top-five ranking. Now it takes a second- or third-place ranking to earn the $65 bonus and a $100 bonus awaits employees when they achieve a No. 1 ranking.[63] (Skills & Best Practices lists practical tips on shaping.)

chapter summary

- *Specify the two basic functions of feedback and three sources of feedback.* Feedback, in the form of *objective* information about performance, both instructs and motivates. Individuals receive feedback from others, the task, and from themselves.

- *Define upward feedback and 360-degree feedback, and summarize the general tips for giving good feedback.* Lower-level employees provide upward feedback (usually anonymous) to their managers. A focal person receives 360-degree feedback from subordinates, the manager, peers, and selected others such as customers or suppliers. Good feedback is tied to performance *goals* and clear *expectations,* linked with *specific* behavior and/or results, reserved for *key result areas,* given as *soon* as possible, provided for *improvement* as well as for final results, focused on *performance* rather than on personalities, and based on *accurate* and *credible* information.

- *Briefly explain the four different organizational reward norms.* Maximizing individual gain is the object of the *profit maximization* reward norm. The *equity* norm calls for distributing rewards proportionate to contributions (those who contribute the most should earn the most). Everyone is rewarded equally when the *equality* reward norm is in force. The *need* reward norm involves distributing rewards based on employees' needs.

- *Summarize the reasons rewards often fail to motivate employees.* Reward systems can fail to motivate employees for these reasons: overemphasis on money, no appreciation effect, benefits become entitlements,

wrong behavior is rewarded, rewards are delayed too long, use of one-size-fits-all rewards, one-shot rewards with temporary effect, and demotivating practices such as layoffs.

- *State Thorndike's "law of effect," and explain Skinner's distinction between respondent and operant behavior.* According to Edward L Thorndike's law of effect, behavior with favorable consequences tends to be repeated, while behavior with unfavorable consequences tends to disappear. B F Skinner called unlearned stimulus–response reflexes *respondent behavior.* He applied the term *operant behavior* to all behavior learned through experience with environmental consequences.

- *Demonstrate your knowledge of positive reinforcement, negative reinforcement, punishment, and extinction.* Positive and negative reinforcement are consequence management strategies that strengthen behavior, whereas punishment and extinction weaken behavior. These strategies need to be defined objectively in terms of their actual impact on behavior frequency, not subjectively on the basis of intended impact.

- *Demonstrate your knowledge of behavior shaping.* Behavior shaping occurs when closer and closer approximations of a target behavior are reinforced. In effect, the standard for reinforcement is made more difficult as the individual learns. The process begins with continuous reinforcement, which gives way to intermittent reinforcement when the target behavior becomes strong and habitual.

internet exercise

www.panoramicfeedback.com

As discussed in this chapter, 360-degree feedback is getting a good deal of attention these days. Our purpose here is to introduce you to a sample 360-degree evaluation from an innovative Internet-based program marketed by Panoramic Feedback. (Note: Our use of this sample is for instructional purposes only and does not constitute an endorsement of the program, which may or may not suit your needs.)

Go to the Internet home page (**www.panoramicfeedback. com**), and select "Samples: Questionnaire" from the main menu. The sample evaluation is for a hypothetical supervisor named Terry Smith. For our purposes, substitute the name of *your manager* from your present or past job. The idea is to do an *upward* evaluation of someone you actually know. Read the brief background piece, and proceed to Part One of the Questionnaire. Read and follow the instructions for the eight performance dimensions. All responses you click and any comments you type into the two boxes in Part One will show up on your printed copy, if you choose to make one. Move to Part Two and type your personal evaluations of your manager in the box provided. These comments also will be on any printed copy you may make.

QUESTIONS

1. How would you rate the eight performance dimensions in this brief sample? Relevant? Important? Good basis for constructive feedback?
2. If you were to expand this evaluation, what other performance scales would you add?
3. Is this a *fair* evaluation, as far as it goes? Explain.
4. How comfortable would you be evaluating the following people with this type of *anonymous* 360-degree instrument: Boss? Peers? Self? People reporting directly to you?
5. Would you like to be the focal person in a 360-degree review? Under what circumstances? Explain.
6. Results of anonymous 360-degree reviews should be used for which of the following purposes: Promotions? Pay raises? Job assignments? Feedback for personal growth and development? Explain.

Making
Decisions
and Managing
Social Processes

SOURCE: © Comstock

Three

part

Making Decisions

Nine
chapter

After reading the material in this chapter, you should be able to:

- Compare and contrast the rational model of decision making and Simon's normative model.

- Discuss the contingency model for selecting a solution.

- Explain the model of decision-making styles and the stages of the creative process.

- Explain how participative management affects performance.

- Review Vroom and Jago's decision-making model.

- Contrast brainstorming, the nominal group technique, the Delphi technique, and computer-aided decision making.

ANDREA JUNG MAKES TOUGH DECISIONS AS AVON'S CEO

In her red floor-length ball gown with spaghetti straps and white shoes with sharp-pointed toes, [Andrea] Jung, at 41, looks more like a movie star than the CEO of a $5.3 billion company. As she strides onto the stage, she is met by an explosion of applause from some 13,000 mostly forty- and fifty-something Avon women reps....

Jung's vision for a new Avon is what she grandiosely calls the "ultimate relationship marketer of products and services for women." Her idea is to rebuild the organization from the ground up into a company that does much more than sell lipstick door-to-door. The Avon that Jung envisions will one day be the source for anything and everything a woman wants to buy. More than that, she wants to give busy women a choice in how they do their buying: through an Avon rep, in a store, or online....

It's the Web, however, that is Avon's best hope for the future, Jung says. Her biggest dilemma is figuring out just where all those Avon ladies fit in. One thing she's sure of: they will play a key role in Avon's reinvention. Jung knows independent sales reps

have been the backbone of the company ever since one Mrs. Albee of Winchester, NH, sold her neighbor a package of assorted perfumes in 1886. Today, reps still produce 98% of the company's revenue, though the top 20% of producers account for about 80% of sales. "If we

don't include them in everything we do, then we're just another retail brand, just another Internet site, and I don't see the world needing more of those," says Jung.

Late Start. Can Jung really move Avon forward into an E-tailing future while keeping her reps happy? It's a long shot, but she has an ambitious plan. Jung is promising to offer them more business on the Net and ways for

them to better manage the new reps that they recruit. She's earmarked $60 million to build a website focused around the reps and the Avon catalog....

To ensure the reps' concerns are considered, Avon has been polling them about the site, asking them what kind of technology could help them. Focus groups include both the Web-savvy and the technologically illiterate to create a site that everyone can use. The result: a website design that gives customers an option to shop with Avon directly but first asks them if they'd like an E-representative in their zip code....

More than anything, Jung proved she was decisive. She would approve a detailed, million-dollar ad campaign in as little as 15 minutes. Early on, she sacked Avon's ad agency and ordered a complete packaging redesign. She killed Avon's hodgepodge of regional brands and replaced them with global brands like Avon Color, a line of cosmetics. That cut out 35% to 40% of Avon catalog items.[1]

To what extent does Andrea Jung rely on participative decision making? For an interpretation on this case and additional comments, visit our website:

www.mhhe.com/kinickiob

FOR DISCUSSION

In Part Two, we studied individual and personal factors within organizational settings. Now, in Part Three, our attention turns to the collective or social dimensions of organizational behavior. We begin this new focus by examining individual and group decision making.

Decision making

Identifying and choosing solutions that lead to a desired end result.

Decision making is a means to an end. It entails identifying and choosing alternative solutions that lead to a desired state of affairs. The process begins with a problem and ends when a solution has been chosen. To gain an understanding of how managers can make better decisions, this chapter focuses on (1) models of decision making, (2) the dynamics of decision making, and (3) group decision making.

Models of Decision Making

There are two fundamental models of decision making: (1) the rational model and (2) Simon's normative model. Each is based on a different set of assumptions and offers unique insights into the decision-making process.

The Rational Model

Rational model

Logical four-step approach to decision making.

The **rational model** proposes that managers use a rational, four-step sequence when making decisions: (1) identifying the problem, (2) generating alternative solutions, (3) selecting a solution, and (4) implementing and evaluating the solution. According to this model, managers are completely objective and possess complete information to make a decision. Despite criticism for being unrealistic, the rational model is instructive because it analytically breaks down the decision-making process and serves as a conceptual anchor for newer models.[3] Let us now consider each of these four steps.

Problem

Gap between an actual and desired situation.

Identifying the Problem A **problem** exists when the actual situation and the desired situation differ. For example, a problem exists when you have to pay rent at the end of the month and don't have enough money. Your problem is not that you have to pay rent. Your problem is obtaining the needed funds. Consider the situation faced by General Motors Corporation as it attempts to slash more than $1 billion from its annual warranty repair expenses.

GM manufactures about 25,000 cars and trucks a day, which means little glitches can rapidly become epidemics. And behind every sick car is an unhappy customer. GM handles 22.5 million warranty claims a year, ranging from minor tweaks most customers barely notice to catastrophes such as engine failure. GM has made it a top priority for the entire company, from designers to dealers, to reduce warranty repairs with improved design and quality and early detection of problems. The goal is to eliminate some nine million claims and to save $1.6 billion in costs by 2001. Detecting problems early also is critical to avoiding costly recalls like the one of about a million trucks that GM announced last month, in which it will foot the bill to fix a switch miswired during manufacturing.[4]

General Motors' problem is the amount of warranty expenses the company is incurring: The company is spending far too much on repairing cars that are under warranty. Potential causes of the problem include poor design, defective parts, and manufacturing glitches.

Generating Solutions   After identifying a problem, the next logical step is generating alternative solutions. For repetitive and routine decisions such as deciding when to send customers a bill, alternatives are readily available through decision rules. For example, a company might routinely bill customers three days after shipping a product. This is not the case for novel and unstructured decisions. Because there are no cut-and-dried procedures for dealing with novel problems, managers must creatively generate alternative solutions. Managers can use a number of techniques to stimulate creativity.

Selecting a Solution   Optimally, decision makers want to choose the alternative with the greatest value. Decision theorists refer to this as maximizing the expected utility of an outcome. This is no easy task. First, assigning values to alternatives is complicated and prone to error. Not only are values subjective, but they also vary according to the preferences of the decision maker. Further, evaluating alternatives assumes they can be judged according to some standards or criteria. This further assumes that (1) valid criteria exist, (2) each alternative can be compared against these criteria, and (3) the decision maker actually uses the criteria. As you know from making your own key life decisions, people frequently violate these assumptions.

Implementing and Evaluating the Solution   Once a solution is chosen, it needs to be implemented. After the solution is implemented, the evaluation phase assesses its effectiveness. If the solution is effective, it should reduce the difference between the actual and desired states that created the problem. If the gap is not closed, the implementation was not successful, and one of the following is true: Either the problem was incorrectly identified, or the solution was inappropriate.

Summarizing the Rational Model   The rational model is based on the premise that managers optimize when they make decisions. **Optimizing** involves solving problems by producing the best possible solution. As noted by Herbert Simon, a decision theorist who in 1978 earned the Nobel Prize for his work on decision making, "The assumptions of perfect rationality are contrary to fact. It is not a question of approximation; they do not even remotely describe the processes that human beings use for making decisions in complex situations."[5] Thus, the rational model is at best an instructional tool. Since decision makers do not follow these rational procedures, Simon proposed a normative model of decision making.

> **Optimizing**
>
> Choosing the best possible solution.

Simon's Normative Model

This model attempts to identify the process that managers actually use when making decisions. The process is guided by a decision maker's bounded rationality. **Bounded rationality** represents the notion that decision makers are "bounded" or restricted by a variety of constraints when making decisions. These constraints include any personal or environmental characteristics that reduce rational decision making. Examples are the limited capacity of the human

> **Bounded rationality**
>
> Constraints that restrict decision making.

mind, problem complexity and uncertainty, amount and timeliness of information at hand, criticality of the decision, and time demands.[6]

As opposed to the rational model, Simon's normative model suggests that decision making is characterized by (1) limited information processing, (2) the use of judgmental heuristics, and (3) satisficing. Each of these characteristics is now explored.

Limited Information Processing   Managers are limited by how much information they process because of bounded rationality. This results in the tendency to acquire manageable rather than optimal amounts of information. In turn, this practice makes it difficult for managers to identify all possible alternative solutions. In the long run, the constraints of bounded rationality cause decision makers to fail to evaluate all potential alternatives.

Judgmental heuristics

Rules of thumb or shortcuts that people use to reduce information-processing demands.

Availability heuristic

Tendency to base decisions on information readily available in memory.

Representativeness heuristic

Tendency to assess the likelihood of an event occurring based on impressions about similar occurrences.

Judgmental Heuristics   **Judgmental heuristics** represent rules of thumb or shortcuts that people use to reduce information processing demands.[7] We automatically use them without conscious awareness. The use of heuristics helps decision makers to reduce the uncertainty inherent within the decision-making process. Because these shortcuts represent knowledge gained from past experience, they can help decision makers evaluate current problems. But they also can lead to systematic errors that erode the quality of decisions. There are two common categories of heuristics that are important to consider: the availability heuristic and the representativeness heuristic.

The **availability heuristic** represents a decision maker's tendency to base decisions on information that is readily available in memory.[8] Information is more accessible in memory when it involves an event that recently occurred, when it is salient (e.g., a plane crash), and when it evokes strong emotions (e.g., a high school student shooting other students). This heuristic is likely to cause people to overestimate the occurrence of unlikely events such as a plane crash or a high school shooting. This bias also is partially responsible for the recency effect discussed in Chapter 4. For example, a manager is more likely to give an employee a positive performance evaluation if the employee exhibited excellent performance over the last few months.

The **representativeness heuristic** is used when people estimate the probability of an event occurring. It reflects the tendency to assess the likelihood of an event occurring based on one's impressions about similar occurrences. A manager, for example, may hire a graduate from a particular university because the past three people hired from this university turned out to be good performers. In this case, the "school attended" criterion is used to facilitate complex information processing associated with employment interviews. Unfortunately, this shortcut can result in a biased decision. Similarly, an individual may believe that he or she can master a new software package in a short period of time because he or she was able to learn how to use a different type of software. This estimate may or may not be accurate. For example, it may take the individual a much longer period of time to learn the new software because it requires the person to learn a new programming language.

Satisficing

Choosing a solution that meets a minimum standard of acceptance.

Satisficing   People satisfice because they do not have the time, information, or ability to handle the complexity associated with following a rational process. This is not necessarily undesirable. **Satisficing** consists of choosing a solution that meets some minimum qualifications, one that is "good enough." Satisficing resolves problems by producing solutions that are satisfactory, as opposed to optimal. Finding a radio station to listen to in your car is a good example of satisficing. You cannot optimize because it is impossible to listen to all stations at the same time. You thus stop searching for a station when you find one playing a song you like or do not mind hearing.

I'm always horrified when I see a car with a small temporary spare tire *(satisficing)* driving 70 mph on the interstate, instead of driving slowly to the nearest tire repair shop.

Dynamics of Decision Making

Decision making is part science and part art. Accordingly, this section examines four dynamics of decision making—contingency considerations, decision-making styles, escalation of commitment, and creativity—that affect the "science" component. An understanding of these dynamics can help managers make better decisions.

Selecting Solutions: A Contingency Perspective

The previous discussion of decision-making models noted that managers typically satisfice when they select solutions. However, we did not probe how managers actually evaluate and select solutions. Let us explore the model in Figure 9–1 to better understand how individuals make decisions.

A Contingency Model for Selecting a Solution   **FIGURE 9–1**

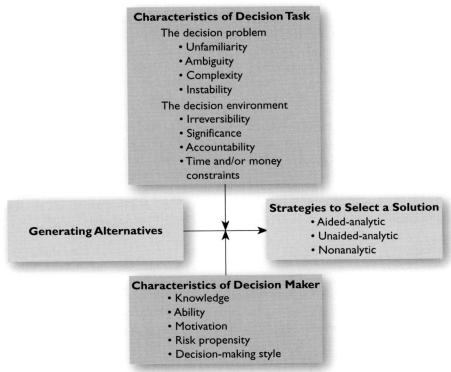

SOURCE: Based on L R Beach and T R Mitchell, "A Contingency Model for the Selection of Decision Strategies," *Academy of Management Review*, July 1978, pp 439–44.

Strategies for Selecting a Solution   What procedures do decision makers use to evaluate the costs and benefits of alternative solutions? According to management experts Lee Roy Beach and Terence Mitchell, one of three approaches is used: aided-analytic, unaided-analytic, and nonanalytic.[9] Decision makers systematically use tools such as mathematical equations, calculators, or computers to analyze and

> **Aided-analytic**
>
> Using tools to make decisions.

evaluate alternatives within an **aided-analytic** approach. Weather forecasters, astronomers, and insurance analysts are good examples of people who make their decisions by using an aided-analytic strategy. These types of professionals tend to make decisions by analyzing data with complex computer models.[10]

In contrast, decision makers rely on the confines of their minds when using an

> **Unaided-analytic**
>
> Analysis is limited to processing information in one's mind.
>
> **Nonanalytic**
>
> Using preformulated rules to make decisions.

unaided-analytic strategy. In other words, the decision maker systematically compares alternatives, but the analysis is limited to evaluating information that can be directly processed in his or her head. Decision-making tools such as a personal computer are not used. Chess masters and counselors use this strategy in the course of their work. Finally, a **nonanalytic** strategy consists of using a simple preformulated rule to make a decision. Examples are flipping a coin, habit, normal convention ("we've always done it that way"), using a conservative approach ("better safe than sorry"), or following procedures offered in instruction manuals. Both the cost and level of sophistication decrease as one moves from an aided-analytic to a nonanalytic strategy.

Determining which approach to use depends on two sets of contingency factors: characteristics of the decision task and characteristics of the decision maker (refer again to Figure 9–1).

Characteristics of the Decision Task   This set of contingency factors reflects the demands and constraints a decision maker faces. These characteristics are divided into two components: those pertaining to the specific problem and those related to the general decision environment. In general, the greater the demands and constraints encountered by a decision maker, the higher the probability that an aided-analytic approach will be used.[11]

Characteristics of the Decision Maker   Chapter 5 highlighted a variety of individual differences that affect employee behavior and performance. In the present context, knowledge, ability, motivation, risk propensity, and decision-making style affect the type of analytical procedure used by a decision maker. For example, a recent meta-analysis revealed that entrepreneurs took more risks when making decisions than managers in general.[12] Research supports the conclusion that aided-analytic strategies are more likely to be used by competent and motivated individuals.[13]

Contingency Relationships   There are many ways in which characteristics of the decision task and decision maker can interact to influence the strategy used to select a solution. In choosing a strategy, decision makers compromise between their desire to make correct decisions and the amount of time and effort they put into the decision-making process. Table 9–1 lists contingency relationships that help reconcile these competing demands. As shown in this table, analytic strategies are more likely to be used when the problem is unfamiliar and irreversible. In contrast, nonanalytic methods are employed on familiar problems or problems in which the decision can be reversed.

Contingency Relationships in Decision Making | **TABLE 9–1**

1. Analytic strategies are used when the decision problem is unfamiliar, ambiguous, complex, or unstable.
2. Nonanalytic methods are employed when the problem is familiar, straightforward, or stable.
3. Assuming there are no monetary or time constraints, analytic approaches are used when the solution is irreversible and significant and when the decision maker is accountable.
4. Nonanalytic strategies are used when the decision can be reversed and is not very significant or when the decision maker is not held accountable.
5. As the probability of making a correct decision goes down, analytic strategies are used.
6. As the probability of making a correct decision goes up, nonanalytic strategies are employed.
7. Time and money constraints automatically exclude some strategies from being used.
8. Analytic strategies are more frequently used by experienced and educated decision makers.
9. Nonanalytic approaches are used when the decision maker lacks knowledge, ability, or motivation to make a good decision.

SOURCE: Adapted from L R Beach and T R Mitchell, "A Contingency Model for the Selection of Decision Strategies," *Academy of Management Review*, July 1978, pp 439–44.

General Decision-Making Styles

The previous section highlighted that individual differences or characteristics of a decision maker influence the decision-making process. This section expands on this discussion by focusing on how an individual's decision-making style affects his or her approach to decision making.

A **decision-making style** reflects the combination of how an individual perceives and comprehends stimuli and the general manner in which he or she chooses to respond to such information.[14] A team of researchers developed a model of decision-making styles that is based on the idea that styles vary along two different dimensions: value orientation and tolerance for ambiguity.[15] *Value orientation* reflects the extent to which an individual focuses on either task and technical concerns or people and social concerns when making decisions. The second dimension pertains to a person's *tolerance for ambiguity*. This individual difference indicates the extent to which a person has a high need for structure or control in his or her life. When the dimensions of value orientation and tolerance for ambiguity are combined, they form four styles of decision making (see Figure 9–2): directive, analytical, conceptual, and behavioral.

> **Decision-making style**
>
> A combination of how individuals perceive and respond to information.

Directive People with a directive style have a low tolerance for ambiguity and are oriented toward task and technical concerns when making decisions. They are efficient, logical, practical, and systematic in their approach to solving problems. People with this style are action oriented and decisive and like to focus on facts. In their pursuit of speed and results, however, these individuals tend to be autocratic, exercise power and control, and focus on the short run.

FIGURE 9–2   Decision-Making Styles

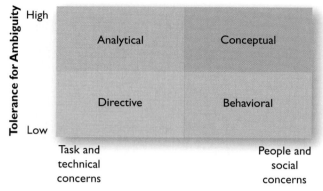

SOURCE: Based on discussion contained in A J Rowe and R O Mason, *Managing with Style: A Guide to Understanding, Assessing, and Improving Decision Making* (San Francisco: Jossey-Bass, 1987), pp 1–17.

Analytical   This style has a much higher tolerance for ambiguity and is characterized by the tendency to overanalyze a situation. People with this style like to consider more information and alternatives than do directives. Analytic individuals are careful decision makers who take longer to make decisions but who also respond well to new or uncertain situations. They can often be autocratic.

Conceptual   People with a conceptual style have a high tolerance for ambiguity and tend to focus on the people or social aspects of a work situation. They take a broad perspective to problem solving and like to consider many options and future possibilities. Conceptual types adopt a long-term perspective and rely on intuition and discussions with others to acquire information. They also are willing to take risks and are good at finding creative solutions to problems. On the downside, however, a conceptual style can foster an idealistic and indecisive approach to decision making.

Behavioral   People with this style work well with others and enjoy social interactions in which opinions are openly exchanged. Behavioral types are supportive, receptive to suggestions, show warmth, and prefer verbal to written information. Although they like to hold meetings, people with this style have a tendency to avoid conflict and to be too concerned about others. This can lead behavioral types to adopt a "wishy-washy" approach to decision making and to have a hard time saying no to others and to have difficulty making difficult decisions.

Research and Practical Implications   Please take a moment now to complete the Hands-On Exercise. It assesses your decision-making style. How do your scores compare with the following norms: directive (75), analytical (90), conceptual (80), and behavioral (55)?[16] What do the differences between your scores and the survey norms suggest about your decision-making style?

Research shows that very few people have only one dominant decision-making style. Rather, most managers have characteristics that fall into two or three styles. Studies also show that decision-making styles vary across occupations, job level, and countries.[17] You can use knowledge of decision-making styles in three ways. First, knowledge of styles helps you to understand yourself. Awareness of your style assists

What Is Your Decision-Making Style?

INSTRUCTIONS   This survey consists of 20 questions, each with four responses. You must consider each possible response for a question and then rank them according to how much you prefer each response. Because many of the questions are anchored to how individuals make decisions at work, you can feel free to use your student role as a frame of reference to answer the questions. For each question, use the space on the survey to rank the four responses with either a 1, 2, 4, or 8. Use the number 8 for the responses that are **most** like you, a 4 for those that are **moderately** like you, a 2 for those that are **slightly** like you, and a 1 for the responses that are **least** like you. For example, a question could be answered [8], [4], [2], [1]. Do not repeat any number when answering a question, and place the numbers in the boxes next to each of the answers. Once all of the responses for the 20 questions have been ranked, total the scores in each of the four columns. The total score for column one represents your directive style, column two your analytical style, column three your conceptual style, and column four your behavioral style.

1. My prime objective in life is to:	have a position with status	be the best in whatever I do	be recognized for my work	feel secure in my job
2. I enjoy work that:	is clear and well defined	is varied and challenging	lets me act independently	involves people
3. I expect people to be:	productive	capable	committed	responsive
4. My work lets me:	get things done	find workable approaches	apply new ideas	be truly satisfied
5. I communicate best by:	talking with others	putting things in writing	being open with others	having a group meeting
6. My planning focuses on:	current problems	how best to meet goals	future opportunities	needs of people in the organization
7. I prefer to solve problems by:	applying rules	using careful analysis	being creative	relying on my feelings
8. I prefer information:	that is simple and direct	that is complete	that is broad and informative	that is easily understood
9. When I'm not sure what to do:	I rely on my intuition	I search for alternatives	I try to find a compromise	I avoid making a decision
10. Whenever possible, I avoid:	long debates	incomplete work	technical problems	conflict with others
11. I am really good at:	remembering details	finding answers	seeing many options	working with people
12. When time is important, I:	decide and act quickly	apply proven approaches	look for what will work	refuse to be pressured
13. In social settings, I:	speak with many people	observe what others are doing	contribute to the conversation	want to be part of the discussion
14. I always remember:	people's names	places I have been	people's faces	people's personalities
15. I prefer jobs where I:	receive high rewards	have challenging assignments	can reach my personal goals	am accepted by the group
16. I work best with people who:	are energetic and ambitious	are very competent	are open minded	are polite and understanding
17. When I am under stress, I:	speak quickly	try to concentrate on the problem	become frustrated	worry about what I should do
18. Others consider me:	aggressive	disciplined	imaginative	supportive
19. My decisions are generally:	realistic and direct	systematic and logical	broad and flexible	sensitive to the other's needs
20. I dislike:	losing control	boring work	following rules	being rejected

Total score

SOURCE: © Alan J. Rowe, Professor Emeritus. Revised 12/18/98. Reprinted by permission.

you in identifying your strengths and weaknesses as a decision maker and facilitates the potential for self-improvement. Second, you can increase your ability to influence others by being aware of styles. For example, if you are dealing with an analytical person, you should provide as much information as possible to support your ideas. This same approach is more likely to frustrate a directive type. Finally, knowledge of styles gives you an awareness of how people can take the same information and yet arrive at different decisions by using a variety of decision-making strategies. It is important to conclude with the caveat that there is not a best decision-making style that applies in all situations.

Escalation of Commitment

Escalation situations involve circumstances in which things have gone wrong but where the situation can possibly be turned around by investing additional time, money, or effort.[18] **Escalation of commitment** refers to the tendency to stick to an ineffective course of action when it is unlikely that the bad situation can be reversed. Personal examples include investing more money into an old or broken car, waiting an extremely long time for a bus to take you somewhere that you could have walked just as easily, or trying to save a disruptive interpersonal relationship that has lasted 10 years. Case studies also indicate that escalation of commitment is partially responsible for some of the worst financial losses experienced by organizations. For example, from 1966 to 1989 the Long Island Lighting Company's investment in the Shoreham nuclear power plant escalated from $65 million to $5 billion, despite a steady flow of negative feedback. The plant was never opened.[19]

> **Escalation of commitment**
>
> Sticking to an ineffective course of action too long.

OB researchers Jerry Ross and Barry Staw identified four reasons for escalation of commitment. They involve psychological and social determinants, organizational determinants, project characteristics, and contextual determinants.[20]

Psychological and Social Determinants   Ego defense and individual motivations are the key psychological contributors to escalation of commitment. Individuals "throw good money after bad" because they tend to (1) bias facts so that they support previous decisions, (2) take more risks when a decision is stated in negative terms (to recover losses) rather than positive ones (to achieve gains), and (3) get too ego-involved with the project. Because failure threatens an individual's self-esteem or ego, people tend to ignore negative signs and push forward.

Social pressures can make it difficult for a manager to reverse a course of action. For instance, peer pressure makes it difficult for an individual to drop a course of action when he or she publicly supported it in the past. Further, managers may continue to support bad decisions because they don't want their mistakes exposed to others.

Organizational Determinants   Breakdowns in communication, workplace politics, and organizational inertia cause organizations to maintain bad courses of action.

Project Characteristics   Project characteristics involve the objective features of a project. They have the greatest impact on escalation decisions. For example, because most projects do not reap benefits until some delayed time period, decision makers are motivated to stay with the project until the end.[21] Thus, there is a tendency to attribute setbacks to temporary causes that are correctable with additional expenditures. Moreover, escalation is related to whether the project has clearly defined goals and whether people receive clear feedback about performance. One study, for instance, revealed that escalation was fueled by ambiguous performance feedback and the lack of performance standards.[22]

Contextual Determinants These causes of escalation are due to forces outside an organization's control. For instance, a recent study showed that a manager's national culture influenced the amount of escalation in decision making. Samples of decision makers in Mexico and the United States revealed that Mexican managers exhibited more escalation than US managers.[23] External political forces also represent a contextual determinant. The continuance of the previously discussed Shoreham nuclear power plant, for example, was partially influenced by pressures from other public utilities interested in nuclear power, representatives of the nuclear power industry, and people in the federal government pushing for the development of nuclear power.[24]

Reducing Escalation of Commitment It is important to reduce escalation of commitment because it leads to poor decision making for both individuals and groups. Barry Staw and Jerry Ross, the researchers who originally identified the phenomenon of escalation, recommended several ways to reduce it (see Skills & Best Practices).

Recommendations to Reduce Escalation of Commitment

- Set minimum targets for performance, and have decision makers compare their performance with these targets.
- Have different individuals make the initial and subsequent decisions about a project.
- Encourage decision makers to become less ego-involved with a project.
- Provide more frequent feedback about project completion and costs.
- Reduce the risk or penalties of failure.
- Make decision makers aware of the costs of persistence.

Creativity

In light of today's need for fast-paced decisions, an organization's ability to stimulate the creativity and innovation of its employees is becoming increasingly important. Although many definitions have been proposed, **creativity** is defined here as the process of using intelligence, imagination, and skill to develop a new or novel product, object, process, or thought.[25] It can be as simple as locating a new place to hang your car keys or as complex as developing a pocket-size microcomputer. This definition highlights three broad types of creativity. One can create something new (creation), one can combine or synthesize things (synthesis), or one can improve or change things (modification).

Creativity
Process of developing something new or unique.

Researchers are not absolutely certain how creativity takes place. Nonetheless, we do know that creativity involves "making remote associations" between unconnected events, ideas, information stored in memory (recall our discussion in Chapter 4), or physical objects. Consider how remote associations led to a creative idea that ultimately increased revenue for Japan Railways (JR) East, the largest rail carrier in the world:

> While JR East was building a new bullet-train line, water began to cause problems in the tunnel being dug through Mount Tanigawa. As engineers drew up plans to drain it away, some of the workers had found a use for the water—they were drinking it. A maintenance worker, whose job was to check the safety of the tunneling equipment, thought it tasted so good that he proposed that JR East should bottle and market it as premium mineral water. This past year, "Oshimizu" water generated some $60 million of sales for JR East.[26]

As these employees of Hallmark show, creativity is an active, not passive, process.

The maintenance worker obviously associated the tunnel water with bottled water, and this led to the idea of marketing the water as a commercial product. Researchers, however, have identified five stages underlying the creative process: preparation, concentration, incubation, illumination, and verification. Let us consider these stages.

The *preparation* stage reflects the notion that creativity starts from a base of knowledge. Experts suggest that creativity involves a convergence between tacit or implied knowledge and explicit knowledge. During the *concentration* stage, an individual focuses on the problem at hand. Interestingly, Japanese companies are noted for encouraging this stage as part of a quality improvement process more than American companies. For example, the average number of suggestions per employee for improving quality and productivity is significantly lower in the typical US company than in comparable Japanese firms.[27]

Incubation is done unconsciously. During this stage, people engage in daily activities while their minds simultaneously mull over information and make remote associations. These associations ultimately are generated in the *illumination* stage. Finally, *verification* entails going through the entire process to verify, modify, or try out the new idea.

In concluding this section it is important to point out that organizations can enhance creativity by effectively managing the five stages underlying the creativity process.[28] Hallmark does a good job of managing the creativity process:

> It takes 740 creative people to produce 18,000 new Hallmark greeting cards each year. To manage that creative energy, CEO Irv Hockaday says, "We have the largest creative staff in the world. If you mismanage, it's like a sack full of cats. You have to strike a balance between defining for them generally what you want and then giving them a lot of running room to try ways to respond to it. You don't overmanage, but you anchor them in well-articulated consumer needs. Then allow them exposure to all kinds of trends going on. We encourage them to travel and we support their traveling. They follow fashion trends, go to museums, look at what the automotive industry is doing in terms of design and color pallets. We have a wonderful pastoral environment, a retreat where they can go and reflect."[29]

Group Decision Making

This section explores issues associated with group decision making. Specifically, we discuss (1) advantages and disadvantages of group-aided decision making, (2) participative management, (3) when to use groups in decision making, and (4) group problem-solving techniques.

Advantages and Disadvantages of Group-Aided Decision Making

Including groups in the decision-making process has both pros and cons (see Table 9–2). On the positive side, groups contain a greater pool of knowledge, provide more varied perspectives, create more comprehension of decisions, increase decision acceptance, and create a training ground for inexperienced employees. These advan-

Advantages and Disadvantages of Group-Aided Decision Making **TABLE 9–2**

Advantages	Disadvantages
1. *Greater pool of knowledge.* A group can bring much more information and experience to bear on a decision or problem than can an individual acting alone.	1. *Social pressure.* Unwillingness to "rock the boat" and pressure to conform may combine to stifle the creativity of individual contributors.
2. *Different perspectives.* Individuals with varied experience and interests help the group see decision situations and problems from different angles.	2. *Domination by a vocal few.* Sometimes the quality of group action is reduced when the group gives in to those who talk the loudest and longest.
3. *Greater comprehension.* Those who personally experience the give-and-take of group discussion about alternative courses of action tend to understand the rationale behind the final decision.	3. *Logrolling.* Political wheeling and dealing can displace sound thinking when an individual's pet project or vested interest is at stake.
4. *Increased acceptance.* Those who play an active role in group decision making and problem solving tend to view the outcome as "ours" rather than "theirs."	4. *Goal displacement.* Sometimes secondary considerations such as winning an argument, making a point, or getting back at a rival displace the primary task of making a sound decision or solving a problem.
5. *Training ground.* Less experienced participants in group action learn how to cope with group dynamics by actually being involved.	5. *"Groupthink."* Sometimes cohesive "in groups" let the desire for unanimity override sound judgment when generating and evaluating alternative courses of action. (Groupthink is discussed in Chapter 10.)

SOURCE: R Kreitner, *Management,* 7th ed (Boston: Houghton Mifflin, 1998), p 234.

tages must be balanced, however, with the disadvantages listed in Table 9–2. In doing so, managers need to determine the extent to which the advantages and disadvantages apply to the decision situation. The following three guidelines may then be applied to help decide whether groups should be included in the decision-making process:

1. If additional information would increase the quality of the decision, managers should involve those people who can provide the needed information.

2. If acceptance is important, managers need to involve those individuals whose acceptance and commitment are important.

3. If people can be developed through their participation, managers may want to involve those whose development is most important.[30]

Group versus Individual Performance   Before recommending that managers involve groups in decision making, it is important to examine whether groups perform better or worse than individuals. After reviewing 61 years of relevant research, a decision-making expert concluded that "Group performance was generally qualitatively and quantitatively superior to the performance of the average individual."[31] Although subsequent research of small-group decision making generally supported this conclusion, additional research suggests that managers should use a contingency approach when determining whether to include others in the decision-making process. Let us now consider these contingency recommendations.

Practical Contingency Recommendations   If the decision occurs frequently, such as deciding on promotions or who qualifies for a loan, use groups because they tend to produce more consistent decisions than do individuals. Given time constraints, let the most competent individual, rather than a group, make the decision. In the face of environmental threats such as time pressure and the potentially serious effects of a decision, groups use less information and fewer communication channels. This increases the probability of a bad decision.[32] This conclusion underscores a general recommendation that managers should keep in mind: Because the quality of communication strongly affects a group's productivity, on complex tasks it is essential to devise mechanisms to enhance communication effectiveness.

Participative Management

An organization needs to maximize its workers' potential if it wants to successfully compete in the global economy. Participative management and employee empowerment, which is discussed in Chapter 13, are highly touted methods for meeting this productivity challenge. Interestingly, employees also seem to desire or recognize the need for participative management. A nationwide survey of 2,408 employees, for example, revealed that almost 66% desired more influence or decision-making power in their jobs.[33]

Confusion exists about the exact meaning of participative management (PM).[34]

> **Participative management**
> Involving employees in various forms of decision making.

One management expert clarified this situation by defining **participative management** as the process whereby employees play a direct role in (1) setting goals, (2) making decisions, (3) solving problems, and (4) making changes in the organization. Without question, participative management entails much more than simply asking employees for their ideas or opinions.

Advocates of PM claim employee participation increases employee satisfaction, commitment, and performance. To get a fuller understanding of how and when participative management works, we begin by discussing a model of participative management.

A Model of Participative Management   Consistent with both Maslow's need theory and the job characteristics model of job design (see Chapter 6), participative management is predicted to increase motivation because it helps employees fulfill three basic needs: (1) autonomy, (2) meaningfulness of work, and (3) interpersonal contact. Satisfaction of these needs enhances feelings of acceptance and commitment, security, challenge, and satisfaction. In turn, these positive feelings supposedly lead to increased innovation and performance.[35]

Participative management does not work in all situations. The design of work, the level of trust between management and employees, and the employees' competence and readiness to participate represent three factors that influence the effectiveness of PM. With respect to the design of work, individual participation is counterproductive when employees are highly interdependent on each other, as on an assembly line. The problem with individual participation in this case is that interdependent employees generally do not have a broad understanding of the entire production process. Participative management also is less likely to succeed when employees do not trust management. Finally, PM is more effective when employees are competent, prepared, and interested in participating.[36]

Research and Practical Suggestions for Managers   Participative management can significantly increase employee job involvement, organizational commitment, creativity, and perceptions of procedural justice and personal control.[37] Two additional meta-analyses provided additional support for the value of participative management. Results from a meta-analysis involving 27 studies and 6,732 individuals revealed that employee participation in the performance appraisal process was positively related to an employee's satisfaction with his or her performance review, perceived value of the appraisal, motivation to improve performance following a performance review, and perceived fairness of the appraisal process.[38] A second meta-analysis of 86 studies involving 18,872 people further demonstrated that participation had a small but significant effect on job performance and a moderate relationship with job satisfaction.[39] This later finding questions the widespread conclusion that participative management should be used to increase employee performance.

So what is a manager to do? We believe that PM is not a quick-fix solution for low productivity and motivation, as some enthusiastic supporters claim. Nonetheless, because participative management is effective in certain situations, managers can increase their chances of obtaining positive results by using once again a contingency approach. For example, the effectiveness of participation depends on the type of interactions between managers and employees as they jointly solve problems. Effective participation requires a constructive interaction that fosters cooperation and respect, as opposed to competition and defensiveness. Managers are advised not to use participative programs when they have destructive interpersonal interactions with their employees.

When to Have Groups Participate in Decision Making: The Vroom/Yetton/Jago Model

Victor Vroom and Philip Yetton developed a model in 1973 to help managers determine the degree of group involvement in the decision-making process. It was later expanded by Vroom and Arthur Jago.[40] The model is prescriptive in that it specifies decision-making styles that should be effective in different situations.

Vroom and Jago's model is represented as a decision tree. The manager's task is to move from left to right along the various branches of the tree. A specific decision-making style is prescribed at the end point of each branch. Before we apply the model, however, it is necessary to consider the different decision styles managers ultimately choose from and an approach for diagnosing the problem situation.

Five Decision-Making Styles Vroom and Yetton identified five distinct decision-making styles. In Table 9–3, each style is represented by a letter. The letter indicates the basic thrust of the style. For example, A stands for *autocratic,* C for *consultive,* and G for *group.* Style choice depends on the type of problem situation.

Matching the Situation to Decision-Making Style Vroom and Jago developed eight problem attributes that managers can use to diagnose a situation. They are shown at the top of the decision tree presented in Figure 9–3 and are expressed as questions. Answers to these questions lead managers along different branches, pointing the way to potentially effective decision-making styles.

Applying the Model Because Vroom and Jago developed four decision trees, the first step is to choose one of the trees. Each tree represents a generic type of problem that managers frequently encounter. They are (1) an individual-level problem with time constraints, (2) an individual-level problem in which the manager wants to develop an employee's decision-making abilities, (3) a group-level problem in which the manager wants to develop employees' decision-making abilities, and (4) a time-driven group problem[41] (illustrated in Figure 9–3).

TABLE 9–3   Management Decision Styles

AI	You solve the problem or make the decision yourself, using information available to you at that time.
AII	You obtain the necessary information from your subordinate(s), then decide on the solution to the problem yourself. You may or may not tell your subordinates what the problem is in getting the information from them. The role played by your subordinates in making the decision is clearly one of providing the necessary information to you rather than generating or evaluating solutions.
CI	You share the problem with relevant subordinates individually, getting their ideas and suggestions without bringing them together as a group. Then you make the decision that may or may not reflect your subordinates' influence.
CII	You share the problem with your subordinates as a group, collectively obtaining their ideas and suggestions. Then you make the decision that may or may not reflect your subordinates' influence.
GII	You share a problem with your subordinates as a group. Together you generate and evaluate alternatives and attempt to reach agreement (consensus) on a solution. Your role is much like that of a chairman. You do not try to influence the group to adopt "your" solution, and you are willing to accept and implement any solution that has the support of the entire group.

SOURCE: "A New Look at Managerial Decision Making" by V H Vroom. Reprinted from *Organizational Dynamics,* Spring 1973, p 67, © 1973 American Management Association International. Reprinted by permission of American Management Association International, New York, NY. All rights reserved. http://www.amanet.org.

To use the model in Figure 9–3, start at the left side and move toward the right by asking yourself the questions associated with each decision point (represented by a box in the figure) encountered. A decision-making style is prescribed at the end of each branch.

Let us track a simple example through Figure 9–3. Suppose you have to determine the work schedule for a group of part-time workers who report to you. The first question is "How important is the technical quality of this decision?" It seems rather low. This leads us to the second question: "How important is subordinate commitment to the decision?" Assuming acceptance is important, this takes us along the branch leading to the question about commitment probability (CP). If you were to make the decision by yourself, is it reasonably certain that your subordinate(s) would be committed to the decision? A yes answer suggests you should use an AI decision-making style (see Table 9–3) and a GII style if you answered no.

Managerial Implications   The model can help managers determine when, and to what extent, they should involve employees in decision making. By simply being aware of the eight diagnostic questions, managers can enhance their ability to structure ambiguous problems. This should ultimately enhance the quality of managerial decisions.

Group Problem-Solving Techniques

Consensus

Presenting opinions and gaining agreement to support a decision.

Using groups to make decisions generally requires that they reach a consensus. According to a decision-making expert, a **consensus** "is reached when all members can say they either agree with the decision or have had their 'day in court' and were unable to convince the others of their

Vroom and Jago's Decision-Making Model   **FIGURE 9–3**

QR	Quality Requirement	How important is the technical quality of this decision?
CR	Commitment Requirement	How important is subordinate commitment to the decision?
LI	Leader's Information	Do you have sufficient information to make a high-quality decision?
ST	Problem Structure	Is the problem well structured?
CP	Commitment Probability	If you were to make the decision by yourself, is it reasonably certain that your subordinate(s) would be committed to the decision?
GC	Goal Congruence	Do subordinates share the organizational goals to be attained in solving this problem?
CO	Subordinate Conflict	Is conflict among subordinates over preferred solutions likely?
SI	Subordinate Information	Do subordinates have sufficient information to make a high-quality decision?

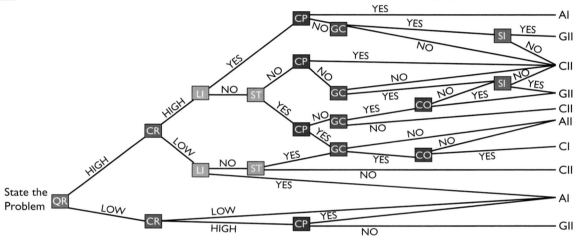

SOURCE: Reprinted from *The New Leadership: Managing Participation in Organizations* by Victor H Vroom and Arthur G Jago, 1988, Englewood Cliffs, NJ: Prentice Hall. © 1987 by V H Vroom and A G Jago. Used with permission of the authors.

viewpoint. In the final analysis, everyone agrees to support the outcome."[42] This definition indicates that consensus does not require unanimous agreement because group members may still disagree with the final decision but are willing to work toward its success.

Groups can experience roadblocks when trying to arrive at a consensus decision. For one, groups may not generate all relevant alternatives to a problem because an individual dominates or intimidates other group members. This is both overt and/or subtle. For instance, group members who possess power and authority, such as a CEO, can be intimidating, regardless of interpersonal style, simply by being present in the room. Moreover, shyness inhibits the generation of alternatives. Shy or socially anxious individuals may withhold their input for fear of embarrassment or lack of confidence. Satisficing is another hurdle to effective group decision making. As previously noted, groups satisfice due to limited time, information, or ability to handle large amounts of information.[43] A management expert offered the following "do's" and "don'ts" for successfully achieving consensus: Groups should use active listening skills, involve as many members as possible, seek out the reasons behind arguments, and dig for the facts. At the same time, groups should not horse trade (I'll support you on this decision because you supported me on the last one), vote, or agree just to avoid "rocking the boat."[44] Voting is not encouraged because it can split the group into winners and losers.

Decision-making experts have developed three group problem-solving techniques—brainstorming, the nominal group technique, and the Delphi technique—to reduce the above roadblocks. Knowledge of these techniques can help current and future managers to more effectively use group-aided decision making. Further, the advent of computer-aided decision making enables managers to use these techniques to solve complex problems with large groups of people.

Brainstorming   Brainstorming was developed by A F Osborn, an advertising executive, to increase creativity.[45] **Brainstorming** is used to help groups generate multiple ideas and alternatives for solving problems. This technique is effective because it helps reduce interference caused by critical and judgmental reactions to one's ideas from other group members.

Brainstorming

Process to generate a quantity of ideas.

When brainstorming, a group is convened, and the problem at hand is reviewed. Individual members then are asked to silently generate ideas/alternatives for solving the problem. Silent idea generation is recommended over the practice of having group members randomly shout out their ideas because it leads to a greater number of unique ideas. Next, these ideas/alternatives are solicited and written on a board or flip chart. A recent study suggests that managers or team leaders may want to collect the brainstormed ideas anonymously. Results demonstrated that more controversial ideas and more nonredundant ideas were generated by anonymous than nonanonymous brainstorming groups.[46] Finally, a second session is used to critique and evaluate the alternatives. Managers are advised to follow four rules for brainstorming:[47]

1. *Stress quantity over quality.* Managers should try to generate and write down as many ideas as possible. Encouraging quantity encourages people to think beyond their favorite ideas.

2. *Freewheeling should be encouraged; do not set limits.* Group members are advised to offer any and all ideas they have. The wilder and more outrageous, the better.

Successful brainstorming relies on nonjudgmental collection of as many ideas as possible to foster later discussion and evaluation.

3. *Suspend judgment.* Don't criticize during the initial stage of idea generation. Phrases such as "we've never done it that way," "it won't work," "it's too expensive," and "the boss will never agree" should not be used.

4. *Ignore seniority.* People are reluctant to freewheel when they are trying to impress the boss or when their ideas are politically motivated. The facilitator of a brainstorming session should emphasize that everyone has the same rank. No one is given "veto power" when brainstorming.

Brainstorming is an effective technique for generating new ideas/alternatives. It is not appropriate for evaluating alternatives or selecting solutions.

The Nominal Group Technique   The **nominal group technique** (NGT) helps groups generate ideas and evaluate and select solutions. NGT is a structured group meeting that follows this format:[48] A group is convened to discuss a particular problem or issue. After the problem is understood, individuals silently generate ideas in writing. Each individual, in round-robin fashion, then offers one idea from his or her list. Ideas are recorded on a black-board or flip chart; they are not discussed at this stage of the process. Once all ideas are elicited, the group discusses them. Anyone may criticize or defend any item. During this step, clarification is provided as well as general agreement or disagreement with the idea. The "30-second soap box" technique, which entails giving each participant a maximum of 30 seconds to argue for or against any of the ideas under consideration, can be used to facilitate this discussion. Finally, group members anonymously vote for their top choices with a weighted voting procedure (e.g., 1st choice = 3 points; 2nd choice = 2 points; 3rd choice = 1 point). The group leader then adds the votes to determine the group's choice. Prior to making a final decision, the group may decide to discuss the top ranked items and conduct a second round of voting.

> **Nominal group technique**
>
> Process to generate ideas and evaluate solutions.

The nominal group technique reduces the roadblocks to group decision making by (1) separating brainstorming from evaluation, (2) promoting balanced participation among group members, and (3) incorporating mathematical voting techniques in order to reach consensus. NGT has been successfully used in many different decision-making situations.

The Delphi Technique   This problem-solving method was originally developed by the Rand Corporation for technological forecasting.[49] It now is used as a multipurpose planning tool. The **Delphi technique** is a group process that anonymously generates ideas or judgments from physically dispersed experts. Unlike the NGT, experts' ideas are obtained from questionnaires or via the Internet as opposed to face-to-face group discussions.

> **Delphi technique**
>
> Process to generate ideas from physically dispersed experts.

A manager begins the Delphi process by identifying the issue(s) he or she wants to investigate. For example, a manager might want to inquire about customer demand, customers' future preferences, or the effect of locating a plant in a certain region of the country. Next, participants are identified and a questionnaire is developed. The questionnaire is sent to participants and returned to the manager. In today's computer-networked environments, this often means that the questionnaires are E-mailed to participants. The manager then summarizes the responses and sends feedback to the participants. At this stage, participants are asked to (1) review the feedback, (2) prioritize the issues being considered, and (3) return the survey within a specified time period. This cycle repeats until the manager obtains the necessary information.

The Delphi technique is useful when face-to-face discussions are impractical, when disagreements and conflict are likely to impair communication, when certain individuals might severely dominate group discussion, and when groupthink is a probable outcome of the group process.[50]

Computer-Aided Decision Making The purpose of computer-aided decision making is to reduce consensus roadblocks while collecting more information in a shorter period of time. There are two types of computer-aided decision making systems: chauffeur driven and group driven.[51] Chauffeur-driven systems ask participants to answer predetermined questions on electronic keypads or dials. Live television audiences on shows such as "Who Wants to Be a Millionaire" and "Whose Line Is It Anyway?" are frequently polled with this system. The computer system tabulates participants' responses in a matter of seconds.

Group-driven electronic meetings are conducted in one of two major ways. First, managers can use E-mail systems, which are discussed in Chapter 12, or the Internet to collect information or brainstorm about a decision that must be made. For example, MedPanel, a Cambridge, MA, medical consulting company, uses E-mail to obtain information and feedback from medical doctors around the country about new and existing drugs. Consider how MedPanel's system works:

> A client contracts with MedPanel for a research project—looking for, perhaps, advice on how to structure clinical trials for a cancer drug. MedPanel consults its database of participating physicians and E-mails invitations to the most appropriate doctors. The doctors who sign up (earning a fee for their time) log onto **www. medpanel.com**, type in a password, and call up a screen that looks a lot like a bulletin-board-style discussion group. Individual messages are listed in chronological order. A moderator poses questions and helps guide the discussion. Doctors drop in whenever they can, catch up on recent postings, and type their own messages. It's simple technology, but the results can be powerful.[52]

MedPanel has found that it can collect information faster and cheaper using its electronic system of data collection.

The second method of computer-aided, group-driven meetings are conducted in special facilities equipped with individual workstations that are networked to each other. Instead of talking, participants type their input, ideas, comments, reactions, or evaluations on their keyboards. The input simultaneously appears on a large projector screen at the front of the room, thereby enabling all participants to see all input. This computer-driven process reduces consensus roadblocks because input is anonymous, everyone gets a chance to contribute, and no one can dominate the process. Research demonstrated that computer-aided decision making produced greater quality and quantity of ideas than either traditional brainstorming or the nominal group technique for both small and large groups of people.[53]

chapter summary

- *Compare and contrast the rational model of decision making and Simon's normative model.* The rational decision-making model consists of identifying the problem, generating alternative solutions, evaluating and selecting a solution, and implementing and evaluating the solution. Research indicates that decision makers do not follow the series of steps outlined in the rational model.

Simon's normative model is guided by a decision maker's bounded rationality. Bounded rationality means that decision makers are bounded or restricted by a variety of constraints when making decisions. The normative model suggests that decision making is characterized by (a) limited information processing, (b) the use of judgmental heuristics, and (c) satisficing.

- *Discuss the contingency model for selecting a solution.* Decision makers use either an aided-analytic, unaided-analytic, or non-analytic strategy when selecting a solution. The choice of a strategy depends on the characteristics of the decision task and the characteristics of the decision maker. In general, the greater the demands and constraints faced by a decision maker, the higher the probability that an aided-analytic approach will be used. Aided-analytic strategies are more likely to be used by competent and motivated individuals. Ultimately, decision makers compromise between their desire to make correct decisions and the amount of time and effort they put into the decision-making process.

- *Explain the model of decision-making styles and the stages of the creative process.* The model of decision-making styles is based on the idea that styles vary along two different dimensions: value orientation and tolerance for ambiguity. When these two dimensions are combined, they form four styles of decision making: directive, analytical, conceptual, and behavioral. People with a directive style have a low tolerance for ambiguity and are oriented toward task and technical concerns. Analytics have a higher tolerance for ambiguity and are characterized by a tendency to overanalyze a situation. People with a conceptual style have a high threshold for ambiguity and tend to focus on people or social aspects of a work situation. This behavioral style is the most people oriented of the four styles.

  Creativity is defined as the process of using intelligence, imagination, and skill to develop a new or novel product, object, process, or thought. There are five stages of the creative process: preparation, concentration, incubation, illumination, and verification.

- *Explain how participative management affects performance.* Participative management reflects the extent to which employees participate in setting goals, making decisions, solving problems, and making changes in the organization. Participative management is expected to increase motivation because it helps employees fulfill three basic needs: (a) autonomy, (b) meaningfulness of work, and (c) interpersonal contact. Participative management does not work in all situations. The design of work and the level of trust between management and employees influence the effectiveness of participative management.

- *Review Vroom, Yetton, and Jago's decision-making model.* Vroom, Yetton, and Jago developed a model to help managers determine the extent to which they should include groups in the decision-making process. Through the use of decision trees, the model identifies appropriate decision-making styles for various types of managerial problems. The styles range from autocratic to highly participative.

- *Contrast brainstorming, the nominal group technique, the Delphi technique, and computer-aided decision making.* Group problem-solving techniques facilitate better decision making within groups. Brainstorming is used to help groups generate multiple ideas and alternatives for solving problems. The nominal group technique assists groups both to generate ideas and to evaluate and select solutions. The Delphi technique is a group process that anonymously generates ideas or judgments from physically dispersed experts. The purpose of computer-aided decision making is to reduce consensus roadblocks while collecting more information in a shorter period of time.

internet exercise

www.brainstorming.co.uk

There are countless brainstorming sessions conducted by individuals and groups within organizations on a daily basis. We do not expect this trend to stop. To help you successfully facilitate and participate in a brainstorming session, this chapter provided a set of guidelines for conducting a brainstorming session. We did not, however, discuss different techniques that can be used to enhance individual and group creativity while brainstorming. The purpose of this exercise is for you to learn two techniques that can be used to enhance creative idea generation and to complete two creativity puzzles.

Begin the exercise by going to the following Internet site: **www.brainstorming.co.uk**. Then select their home page. Once at the home page, click on the option for "training on creative techniques." After a brief discussion about creativity, you will be given the option to learn more about a variety of different techniques that can be used to enhance creativity. Choose any two techniques and then answer questions 1 and 2 below.

Now return to the home page, and select the option for creativity puzzles. Follow the instructions and attempt to complete two puzzles. Don't peek ahead to see the answers until you have tried to finish the activity. Based on your experience with these creativity puzzles, answer questions 3 and 4.

QUESTIONS

1. How might you use these techniques in a class project?
2. Should different techniques be used in different situations? Explain.
3. Why do these puzzles help people to think outside of the box?
4. How might these puzzles be used during a brainstorming session?

Effective Groups and Teamwork

Ten

chapter

After reading the material in this chapter, you should be able to:

- Describe the five stages of Tuckman's theory of group development.

- Contrast roles and norms, and specify four reasons norms are enforced in organizations.

- Explain how a work group becomes a team.

- List at least four things managers can do to build trust.

- Describe self-managed teams and virtual teams.

- Describe groupthink, and identify at least four of its symptoms.

TEAMING UP FOR BETTER HOSPITAL CARE

BETHESDA, Md.—Billie Joyce Sturey lies in an intensive care unit bed at Suburban Hospital here. Her 70-year-old heart is the concern today, but like so many ICU patients, she has other medical problems that complicate her care.

Outside her room, a team of specialists meets to debate the best treatments for her. Is the medicine that's keeping her heart going hurting her? Should she have an angiogram? Is she ready

to be moved out of the ICU?

Such face-to-face meetings are rare in most of the nation's community hospitals, where medical decisions

are often dictated by phone or scribbled into charts as doctors dash to and fro.

Yet in an ICU, poor communication can be deadly. . . .

Suburban, a 217-bed hospital just outside Washington, has used a team approach in its ICU since 1996. Members of the team include a specially trained intensivist (a doctor who specializes in intensive care medicine), a pharmacist, a social worker, a nutritionist, the chief ICU nurse, a respiratory therapist and a chaplain.

Each morning they go room-by-room, talking with every patient's bedside nurse

to discuss and debate among themselves the best course of treatment. The intensivists stay in the ICU during their shift, overseeing patients' care.

Suburban credits team care with reducing errors, shortening the amount of time patients spend in its 12-bed ICU and improving communication between families and medical staff.

Since it began its ICU team program in 1996, Suburban has cut the amount of time patients spend on ventilators by 23%. That's important because the longer patients are on ventilators, the greater the chance they'll develop pneumonia. Nationally, ventilator patients who develop pneumonia have a 50% greater chance of dying, and their hospitalization costs rise—sometimes by more than $20,000, says Dr. Tom Rainey, medical director for critical care services at Suburban.

"The cost of complications is avoided, in dollars, not to mention human misery," Rainey says.

While it costs money to hire intensivists and keep a team available in the ICU around the clock, a reduction in errors, complications, and the length of ICU stays ends up saving money, Rainey says. Plus, primary care doctors save time by not needing to run back and forth to the hospital as often. . . .

Suburban's medical staff is among a growing number in the country that are embracing the idea—borrowed from other industries—that a team approach trumps lone-wolf behavior. But while the concept has been discussed and debated within the medical community for decades, it has been slow to be adopted outside of academic medical centers.

"Teams like this are probably the best way to close the gap on errors. Yet only 10% of intensive care units have this level of care," Rainey says.

One reason for the delay is the very culture of medicine.

Doctors are used to being autonomous, for one thing. And some doctors could see their incomes fall when hospital-based intensivists take over many of their patients in the ICU. So launching a team requires a lot of diplomacy. In ICUs that have adopted the team approach, there's usually one major advocate who persuades primary care doctors and specialists to work with the intensivist-led team.

"We have to be clear that we are in this together," Rainey says. "We make a treatment plan that all the doctors agree on."[1]

From a hospital patient's perspective, what do you like about this team approach? How quickly do you think the team approach will spread to other hospitals? Explain. For an interpretation of this case and additional comments, visit our website:

www.mhhe.com/kinickiob

BOTH DAILY EXPERIENCE and research reveal the importance of social skills for individual and organizational success. An ongoing study by the Center for Creative Leadership (involving diverse samplings from Belgium, France, Germany, Italy, the United Kingdom, the United States, and Spain) found four stumbling blocks that tend to derail executives' careers. According to the researchers, "A derailed executive is one who, having reached the general manager level, finds that there is little chance of future advancement due to a misfit between job requirements and personal skills."[2] The four stumbling blocks, consistent across the cultures studied, are as follows:

1. Problems with interpersonal relationships.
2. Failure to meet business objectives.
3. Failure to build and lead a team.
4. Inability to change or adapt during a transition.[3]

Notice how both the first and third career stumbling blocks involve interpersonal skills—the ability to get along and work effectively with others. Managers with interpersonal problems typically were described as manipulative and insensitive. Interestingly, two-thirds of the derailed European managers studied had problems with interpersonal relationships. That same problem reportedly plagued one-third of the derailed US executives.[4] Management, as defined in Chapter 1, involves getting things done with and through others. The job is simply too big to do it alone.[5]

The purpose of this chapter is to shift the focus from individual behavior to collective behavior. We explore groups and teams, key features of modern life, and discuss how to make them effective while avoiding common pitfalls. Among the interesting variety of topics in this chapter are group development, trust, self-managed teams, virtual teams, and groupthink.

Fundamentals of Group Behavior

Group

Two or more freely interacting people with shared norms and goals and a common identity.

Drawing from the field of sociology, we define a **group** as two or more freely interacting individuals who share collective norms and goals and have a common identity.[6] Organizational psychologist Edgar Schein shed additional light on this concept by drawing instructive distinctions between a group, a crowd, and an organization:

> The size of a group is thus limited by the possibilities of mutual interaction and mutual awareness. Mere aggregates of people do not fit this definition because they do not interact and do not perceive themselves to be a group even if they are aware of each other as, for instance, a crowd on a street corner watching some event. A total department, a union, or a whole organization would not be a group in spite of thinking of themselves as "we," because they generally do not all interact and are not all aware of each other. However, work teams, committees, subparts of departments, cliques, and various other informal associations among organizational members would fit this definition of a group.[7]

Take a moment now to think of various groups of which you are a member. Does each of your "groups" satisfy the four criteria in our definition?

Formal and Informal Groups

Formal group

Formed by the organization.

Individuals join groups, or are assigned to groups, to accomplish various purposes. If the group is formed by a manager to help the organization accomplish its goals, then it qualifies as a **formal group.** Formal groups typically wear such labels as work group, team, committee, or task force. An **informal group** exists when the members' overriding purpose of getting together is friendship.[8] Although formal and informal groups often overlap, such as a team of corporate auditors heading for the tennis courts

Informal group

Formed by friends.

after work, some employees are not friends with their co-workers. The desirability of overlapping formal and informal groups is problematic. Some managers firmly believe personal friendship fosters productive teamwork on the job while others view workplace "bull sessions" as a serious threat to productivity. Both situations are common, and it is the manager's job to strike a workable balance, based on the maturity and goals of the people involved.

Functions of formal Groups

Researchers point out that formal groups fulfill two basic functions: *organizational* and *individual*.[9] The various functions are listed in Table 10–1. Complex combinations of these functions can be found in formal groups at any given time.

For example, consider what Mazda's new American employees experienced when they spent a month working in Japan before the opening of the firm's Flat Rock, Michigan, plant:

> After a month of training in Mazda's factory methods, whipping their new Japanese buddies at softball and sampling local watering holes, the Americans were fired up. . . . [A maintenance manager] even faintly praised the Japanese practice of holding group calisthenics at the start of each working day: "I didn't think I'd like doing exercises every morning, but I kind of like it."[10]

While Mazda pursued the organizational functions it wanted—interdependent teamwork, creativity, coordination, problem solving, and training—the American workers benefited from the individual functions of formal groups. Among those benefits were affiliation with new friends, enhanced self-esteem, exposure to the Japanese social reality, and reduction of anxieties about working for a foreign-owned company. In short, Mazda created a workable blend of organizational and individual group functions by training its newly hired American employees in Japan.

Formal Groups fulfill Organizational and Individual functions   **TABLE 10–1**

Organizational Functions	Individual Functions
1. Accomplish complex, interdependent tasks that are beyond the capabilities of individuals.	1. Satisfy the individual's need for affiliation.
2. Generate new or creative ideas and solutions.	2. Develop, enhance, and confirm the individual's self-esteem and sense of identity.
3. Coordinate interdepartmental efforts.	3. Give individuals an opportunity to test and share their perceptions of social reality.
4. Provide a problem-solving mechanism for complex problems requiring varied information and assessments.	4. Reduce the individual's anxieties and feelings of insecurity and powerlessness.
5. Implement complex decisions.	5. Provide a problem-solving mechanism for personal and interpersonal problems.
6. Socialize and train newcomers.	

SOURCE: Adapted from E H Schein, *Organizational Psychology*, 3rd ed (Englewood Cliffs. NJ: Prentice-Hall, 1980), pp 149–51.

The Group Development Process

Groups and teams in the workplace go through a maturation process, such as one would find in any life-cycle situation (e.g., humans, organizations, products). While there is general agreement among theorists that the group development process occurs in identifiable stages, they disagree about the exact number, sequence, length, and nature of those stages.[11] One oft-cited model is the one proposed in 1965 by educational psychologist Bruce W Tuckman. His original model involved only four stages (forming, storming, norming, and performing). The five-stage model in Figure 10–1 evolved when Tuckman and a doctoral student added "adjourning" in 1977.[12] A word of caution is in order. Somewhat akin to Maslow's need hierarchy theory, Tuckman's theory has been repeated and taught so often and for so long that many have come to view it as documented fact, not merely a theory. Even today, it is good to remember Tuckman's own caution that his group development model was derived more from group therapy sessions than from natural-life groups. Still, many in the OB field like Tuckman's five-stage model of group development because of its easy-to-remember labels and common-sense appeal.

Let us briefly examine each of the five stages in Tuckman's model. Notice in Figure 10–1 how individuals give up a measure of their independence when they join and participate in a group. Also, the various stages are not necessarily of the same duration or intensity. For instance, the storming stage may be practically non-

FIGURE 10–1   Tuckman's Five-Stage Theory of Group Development

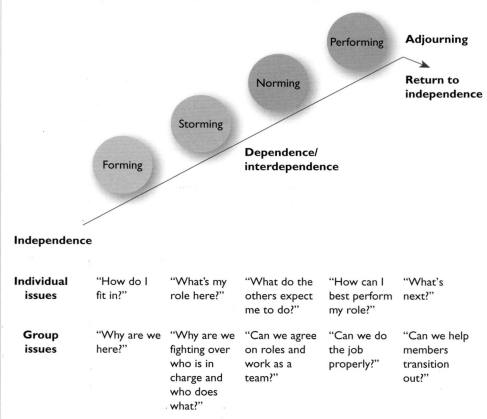

	Forming	Storming	Norming	Performing	Adjourning
Individual issues	"How do I fit in?"	"What's my role here?"	"What do the others expect me to do?"	"How can I best perform my role?"	"What's next?"
Group issues	"Why are we here?"	"Why are we fighting over who is in charge and who does what?"	"Can we agree on roles and work as a team?"	"Can we do the job properly?"	"Can we help members transition out?"

existent or painfully long, depending on the goal clarity and the commitment and maturity of the members. You can make this process come to life by relating the various stages to your own experiences with work groups, committees, athletic teams, social or religious groups, or class project teams. Some group happenings that surprised you when they occurred may now make sense or strike you as inevitable when seen as part of a natural development process.

Group cohesiveness or a "we feeling" can help groups develop through the norming stage like this group from Herman Miller who, when faced with a problem, pulled together to find a solution.

Stage 1: Forming   During this "ice-breaking" stage, group members tend to be uncertain and anxious about such things as their roles, who is in charge, and the group's goals. Mutual trust is low, and there is a good deal of holding back to see who takes charge and how. If the formal leader (e.g., a supervisor) does not assert his or her authority, an emergent leader will eventually step in to fulfill the group's need for leadership and direction. Leaders typically mistake this honeymoon period as a mandate for permanent control. But later problems may force a leadership change.

Stage 2: Storming   This is a time of testing. Individuals test the leader's policies and assumptions as they try to determine how they fit into the power structure.[13] Subgroups take shape, and subtle forms of rebellion, such as procrastination, occur. Many groups stall in stage 2 because power politics erupts into open rebellion.

Stage 3: Norming   Groups that make it through stage 2 generally do so because a respected member, other than the leader, challenges the group to resolve its power struggles so something can be accomplished. Questions about authority and power are resolved through unemotional, matter-of-fact group discussion. A feeling of team spirit is experienced because members believe they have found their proper roles. **Group cohesiveness,** defined as the "we feeling" that binds members of a group together, is the principal by-product of stage 3.[14]

Group cohesiveness

A "we feeling" binding group members together.

Stage 4: Performing   Activity during this vital stage is focused on solving task problems. As members of a mature group, contributors get their work done without hampering others. There is a climate of open communication, strong cooperation, and lots of helping behavior. Conflicts and job boundary disputes are handled constructively and efficiently. Cohesiveness and personal commitment to group goals help the group achieve more than could any one individual acting alone.

Stage 5: Adjourning   The work is done; it is time to move on to other things. Having worked so hard to get along and get something done, many members feel a compelling sense of loss. The return to independence can be eased by rituals celebrating "the end" and "new beginnings." Parties, award ceremonies, graduations, or mock funerals can provide the needed punctuation at the end of a significant group project. Leaders need to emphasize valuable lessons learned in group dynamics to prepare everyone for future group and team efforts.

Group Member Roles

Four centuries have passed since William Shakespeare had his character Jaques speak the following memorable lines in Act II of *As You Like It:* "All the world's a stage, And all the men and women merely players; They have their exits and their entrances; And one man in his time plays many parts. . . ." This intriguing notion of all people as actors in a universal play was not lost on 20th-century sociologists who developed a complex theory of human interaction based on roles. According to an OB scholar, "**roles** are sets of behaviors that persons expect of occupants of a position."[15] As described in Table 10–2, both task and maintenance roles need to be performed if a work group is to accomplish anything.[16]

Roles

Expected behaviors for a given position.

Task versus Maintenance Roles   **Task roles** enable the work group to define, clarify, and pursue a common purpose. Meanwhile, **maintenance roles** foster supportive and constructive interpersonal relationships. In short, task roles keep the group *on track* while maintenance roles keep the group *together.* A project team member is performing a task function when he or she says at an update meeting, "What is the real issue here? We don't seem to be getting anywhere." Another individual

Task roles

Task-oriented group behavior.

Maintenance roles

Relationship-building group behavior.

Task and Maintenance Roles   **TABLE 10–2**

Task Roles	Description
Initiator	Suggests new goals or ideas.
Information seeker/giver	Clarifies key issues.
Opinion seeker/giver	Clarifies pertinent values.
Elaborator	Promotes greater understanding through examples or exploration of implications.
Coordinator	Pulls together ideas and suggestions.
Orienter	Keeps group headed toward its stated goal(s).
Evaluator	Tests group's accomplishments with various criteria such as logic and practicality.
Energizer	Prods group to move along or to accomplish more.
Procedural technician	Performs routine duties (e.g., handing out materials or rearranging seats).
Recorder	Performs a "group memory" function by documenting discussion and outcomes.
Maintenance Roles	**Description**
Encourager	Fosters group solidarity by accepting and praising various points of view.
Harmonizer	Mediates conflict through reconciliation or humor.
Compromiser	Helps resolve conflict by meeting others "half way."
Gatekeeper	Encourages all group members to participate.
Standard setter	Evaluates the quality of group processes.
Commentator	Records and comments on group processes/dynamics.
Follower	Serves as a passive audience.

SOURCE: Adapted from discussion in K D Benne and P Sheats, "Functional Roles of Group Members," *Journal of Social Issues,* Spring 1948, pp 41–49.

who says, "Let's hear from those who oppose this plan," is performing a maintenance function. Importantly, each of the various task and maintenance roles may be played in varying combinations and sequences by either the group's leader or any of its members.

Checklist for Managers   The task and maintenance roles listed in Table 10–2 can serve as a handy checklist for managers and group leaders who wish to ensure proper group development. Roles that are not always performed when needed, such as those of coordinator, evaluator, and gatekeeper, can be performed in a timely manner by the formal leader or assigned to other members. The task roles of initiator, orienter, and energizer are especially important because they are *goal-directed* roles. Research studies on group goal setting confirm the motivational power of challenging goals. As with individual goal setting (in Chapter 7), difficult but achievable goals are associated with better group results.[17] Also in line with individual goal-setting theory and research, group goals are more effective if group members clearly understand them and are both individually and collectively committed to achieving them. Initiators, orienters, and energizers can be very helpful in this regard.

International managers need to be sensitive to cultural differences regarding the relative importance of task and maintenance roles. In Japan, for example, cultural tradition calls for more emphasis on maintenance roles, especially the roles of harmonizer and compromiser:

> Courtesy requires that members not be conspicuous or disputatious in a meeting or classroom. If two or more members discover that their views differ—a fact that is tactfully taken to be unfortunate—they adjourn to find more information and to work toward a stance that all can accept. They do not press their personal opinions through strong arguments, neat logic, or rewards and threats. And they do not hesitate to shift their beliefs if doing so will preserve smooth interpersonal relations. (To lose is to win.)[18]

Norms

Norms are more encompassing than roles. While roles involve behavioral expectations for specific positions, norms help organizational members determine right from wrong and good from bad. According to one respected team of management consultants: "A **norm** is an attitude, opinion, feeling, or action—shared by two or more people—that guides their behavior."[19] Although norms are typically unwritten and seldom discussed openly, they have a powerful influence on group and organizational behavior.[20] PepsiCo Inc., for instance, has evolved a norm that equates corporate competitiveness with physical fitness. According to observers,

Norm

Shared attitudes, opinions, feelings, or actions that guide social behavior.

> Leanness and nimbleness are qualities that pervade the company. When Pepsi's brash young managers take a few minutes away from the office, they often head straight for the company's physical fitness center or for a jog around the museum-quality sculptures outside of PepsiCo's Purchase, New York, headquarters.[21]

At PepsiCo and elsewhere, group members positively reinforce those who adhere to current norms with friendship and acceptance. On the other hand, nonconformists experience criticism and even **ostracism,** or rejection by group members. Anyone who has experienced the "silent treatment" from a group of friends knows what a potent social weapon ostracism can be. Norms can be put into proper perspective by understanding how they develop and why they are enforced.

Ostracism

Rejection by other group members.

How Norms Are Developed   Experts say norms evolve in an informal manner as the group or organization determines what it takes to be effective. Generally speaking, norms develop in various combinations of the following four ways:

1. *Explicit statements by supervisors or co-workers.* For instance, a group leader might explicitly set norms about not drinking alcohol at lunch.

2. *Critical events in the group's history.* At times there is a critical event in the group's history that establishes an important precedent. (For example, a key recruit may have decided to work elsewhere because a group member said too many negative things about the organization. Hence, a norm against such "sour grapes" behavior might evolve.)

3. *Primacy.* The first behavior pattern that emerges in a group often sets group expectations. If the first group meeting is marked by very formal interaction between supervisors and employees, then the group often expects future meetings to be conducted in the same way.

4. *Carryover behaviors from past situations.* Such carryover of individual behaviors from past situations can increase the predictability of group members' behaviors in new settings and facilitate task accomplishment. For instance, students and professors carry fairly constant sets of expectations from class to class.[22]

We would like you to take a few moments and think about the norms that are currently in effect in your classroom. List the norms on a sheet of paper. Do these norms help or hinder your ability to learn? Norms can affect performance either positively or negatively.

Why Norms Are Enforced   Norms tend to be enforced by group memebers when they

- Help the group or organization survive.
- Clarify or simplify behavioral expectations.
- Help individuals avoid embarrassing situations.
- Clarify the group's or organization's central values and/or unique identity.[23]

Teams, Trust, and Teamwork

The team approach to managing organizations is having diverse and substantial impacts on organizations and individuals. Teams promise to be a cornerstone of progressive management for the foreseeable future. According to management expert Peter Drucker, tomorrow's organizations will be flatter, information based, and organized around teams.[24] This means virtually all employees will need to polish their team skills. Southwest Airlines, a company that credits a strong team spirit for its success, puts team skills above all else. Case in point:

> **Team**
>
> Small group with complementary skills who hold themselves mutually accountable for common purpose, goals, and approach.

Southwest rejected a top pilot from another airline who did stunt work for movie studios because he was rude to a receptionist. Southwest believes that technical skills are easier to acquire than a teamwork and service attitude.[25]

Fortunately, the trend toward teams has a receptive audience today. Both women and younger employees, according to recent studies, thrive in team-oriented organizations.[26]

In this section, we define the term *team,* discuss trust as a key to real teamwork, and explore two evolving forms of teamwork—self-managed teams and virtual teams.

A Team Is More Than Just a Group

Jon R Katzenbach and Douglas K Smith, management consultants at McKinsey & Company, say it is a mistake to use the terms *group* and *team* interchangeably. After studying many different kinds of teams—from athletic to corporate to military—they concluded that successful teams tend to take on a life of their own. Katzenbach and Smith define a **team** as "a small number of people with complementary skills who are committed to a common purpose, performance goals, and approach for which they hold themselves mutually accountable."[27]

Thus, a group becomes a team when the following criteria are met:

1. *Leadership* becomes a shared activity.
2. *Accountability* shifts from strictly individual to both individual and collective.
3. The group develops its own *purpose* or mission.
4. *Problem solving* becomes a way of life, not a part-time activity.
5. *Effectiveness* is measured by the group's collective outcomes and products.[28]

Relative to Tuckman's theory of group development covered earlier—forming, storming, norming, performing, and adjourning—teams are task groups that have matured to the *performing* stage. Because of conflicts over power and authority and unstable interpersonal relations, many work groups never qualify as a real team.[29] Katzenbach and Smith clarified the distinction this way: "The essence of a team is common commitment. Without it, groups perform as individuals; with it, they become a powerful unit of collective performance"[30] (see Skills & Best Practices).

When Katzenbach and Smith refer to "a small number of people" in their definition, they mean between 2 and 25 team members. They found effective teams to typically have fewer than 10 members. This conclusion was echoed in a survey of 400 workplace team members in the United States and Canada: "The average North American team consists of 10 members. Eight is the most common size."[31]

Teaming Up to Learn at Germany's Siemens

A start-up company that needs entrepreneurial managers can go out and hire them as it builds its organization. By contrast, established companies like Siemens, a worldwide provider of everything from mobile phones to gas turbines, already have tens of thousands of managers around the world and have no choice but to find ways to make its old managers into new ones. So collaboration became the central goal of an in-house management development program at Siemens. The program was created for all managers in the late 1990s.

Many companies have established "active learning" curricula focused on the study of cases and other real-life problems. But we realized that changing people's behavior is less about intellectual learning than it is about blasting them loose from nearly impenetrable, self-imposed—and often company-rewarded—boundaries. We started our people off with some classroom teaching, but the bulk of the program put them in teams working on actual projects.

These "business impact projects" had to show measurable results and typically lasted about four months. It wasn't enough for a team to recommend a new marketing strategy or propose a new procedure for product development. We didn't want the end result to be a paper no one would read. Instead, we wanted people to get their hands dirty in the real work of organizational maneuvering and achievement.

Once a team settled on an opportunity to pursue, they had to recruit a "coach," usually a high-level executive in the business area that the team was focusing on. Executives were free to decline these requests; some teams had to try several times before landing their coaches. . . .

In each case, it helped that the teams consisted of people from different product areas, functions, and geographies. But diverse teammates and their existing contact networks weren't enough; the projects wouldn't work without each team figuring out how to win support from people who had little interest in—or who even felt threatened by—the team's efforts.

In interviews after the projects ended, nearly all the participants reported a new perspective on their organizational comfort zones.

At first, they said, they had felt liberated by their status in the program—as though they were immune from risk. But in retrospect, they came to understand that the program conferred no special status on them at all; their previous hesitation toward risk-taking had been largely self-imposed. The management program had given them the unique sense of "permission" to venture that they had actually had all along.

SOURCE: Excerpted from M Bellmann and R H Schaffer, "Freeing Managers to Innovate," *Harvard Business Review*, June 2001, pp 32–33.

Trust: A Key Ingredient of Teamwork

These have not been good times for trust in the corporate world. Years of mergers, downsizings, layoffs, bloated executive bonuses, and broken promises have left many employees justly cynical about trusting management. After conducting a series of annual workplace surveys, one management consultant recently concluded: "Trust in corporate America is at a low point."[32] While challenging readers of *Harvard Business Review* to do a better job of investing in what they call "social capital," experts recently offered this constructive advice:

> No one can manufacture trust or mandate it into existence. When someone says, "You can trust me," we usually don't, and rightly so. But leaders can make deliberate investments in trust. They can give people reasons to trust one another instead of reasons to watch their backs. They can refuse to reward successes that are built on untrusting behavior. And they can display trust and trustworthiness in their own actions, both personally and on behalf of the company.[33]

Trust

Reciprocal faith in others' intentions and behavior.

Three Dimensions of Trust   Trust is defined as reciprocal faith in others' intentions and behavior.[34] Experts on the subject explain the reciprocal (give-and-take) aspect of trust as follows:

> When we see others acting in ways that imply that they trust us, we become more disposed to reciprocate by trusting in them more. Conversely, we come to distrust those whose actions appear to violate our trust or to distrust us.[35]

In short, we tend to give what we get: trust begets trust; distrust begets distrust.

Trust is expressed in different ways. Three dimensions of trust are *overall trust* (expecting fair play, the truth, and empathy), *emotional trust* (faith that someone will not misrepresent you to others or betray a confidence), and *reliableness* (believe that promises and appointments will be kept and commitments met).[36] These different dimensions contribute to a wide and complex range of trust, from very low to very high.

How to Build Trust   Management professor/consultant Fernando Bartolomé offers the following six guidelines for building and maintaining trust:

1. *Communication.* Keep team members and employees informed by explaining policies and decisions and providing accurate feedback. Be candid about one's own problems and limitations. Tell the truth.[37]

2. *Support.* Be available and approachable. Provide help, advice, coaching, and support for team members' ideas.

3. *Respect.* Delegation, in the form of real decision-making authority, is the most important expression of managerial respect. Actively listening to the ideas of others is a close second. (Empowerment is not possible without trust.)[38]

4. *Fairness.* Be quick to give credit and recognition to those who deserve it. Make sure all performance appraisals and evaluations are objective and impartial.[39]

5. *Predictability.* Be consistent and predictable in your daily affairs. Keep both expressed and implied promises.

6. *Competence.* Enhance your credibility by demonstrating good business sense, technical ability, and professionalism.[40]

Trust needs to be earned; it cannot be demanded.

Self-Managed Teams

Have you ever thought you could do a better job than your boss? Well, if the trend toward self-managed work teams continues to grow as predicted, you just may get your chance. Entrepreneurs and artisans often boast of not having a supervisor. The same generally cannot be said for employees working in organizational offices and factories. But things are changing. In fact, an estimated half of the employees at *Fortune* 500 companies are working on teams.[41] A growing share of those teams are self-managing. For example, "At a General Mills cereal plant in Lodi, California, teams . . . schedule, operate, and maintain machinery so effectively that the factory runs with no managers present during the night shift."[42] More typically, managers are present to serve as trainers and facilitators. Self-managed teams come in every conceivable format today, some more autonomous than others (see Hands-On Exercise).

Self-managed teams are defined as groups of workers who are given administrative oversight for their task domains. Administrative oversight involves delegated activities such as planning, scheduling, monitoring, and staffing. These are chores normally performed by managers. In short, employees in these unique work groups act as their own supervisor.[43] Self-managed teams are variously referred to as semiautonomous work groups, autonomous work groups, and superteams.

> **Self-managed teams**
>
> Groups of employees granted administrative oversight for their work.

Something much more complex is involved than this apparently simple label suggests. The term *self-managed* does not mean simply turning workers loose to do their own thing. Indeed, an organization embracing self-managed teams should be prepared to undergo revolutionary changes in management philosophy, structure, staffing and training practices, and reward systems. Moreover, the traditional notions of managerial authority and control are turned on their heads. Not surprisingly, many managers strongly resist giving up the reins of power to people they view as subordinates. They see self-managed teams as a threat to their job security.[44]

How Autonomous Is Your Work Group?

INSTRUCTIONS Think of your current (or past) job and work group. Characterize the group's situation by circling one number on the following scale for each statement. Add your responses for a total score:

Strongly Disagree						Strongly Agree
1	2	3	4	5	6	7

Work Method Autonomy

1. My work group decides how to get the job done. _____

2. My work group determines what procedures to use. _____

3. My work group is free to choose its own methods when carrying out its work. _____

Work Scheduling Autonomy

4. My work group controls the scheduling of its work. _____

5. My work group determines how its work is sequenced. _____

6. My work group decides when to do certain activities. _____

Work Criteria Autonomy

7. My work group is allowed to modify the normal way it is evaluated so some of our activities are emphasized and some deemphasized. _____

8. My work group is able to modify its objectives (what it is supposed to accomplish). _____

9. My work group has some control over what it is supposed to accomplish. _____

Total score = _____

NORMS

9–26 = Low autonomy
27–45 = Moderate autonomy
46–63 = High autonomy

SOURCE: Adapted from an individual autonomy scale in J A Breaugh, "The Work Autonomy Scales: Additional Validity Evidence," *Human Relations*, November 1989, pp 1033–56.

Cross-Functionalism A common feature of self-managed teams, particularly among those above the shop-floor or clerical level, is **cross-functionalism**.[45] In other words, specialists from different areas are put on the same team. Amgen, a rapidly growing biotechnology company in Thousand Oaks, California, is literally run by cross-functional, self-managed teams:

> **Cross-functionalism**
>
> Team made up of technical specialists from different areas.

> There are two types: product development teams, known as PDTs, which are concerned with everything that relates to bringing a new product to market, and task forces, which do everything else. The members of both come from all areas of the company, including marketing and finance as well as the lab bench. The groups range from five or six employees up to 80 and usually report directly to senior management. In a reversal of the normal process, department heads called facilitators don't run teams; they work for them, making sure they have the equipment and money they need. Teams may meet weekly, monthly, or whenever the members see fit.[46]

Among companies with self-managed teams, the most commonly delegated tasks are work scheduling and dealing directly with outside customers. The least common team chores are hiring and firing.[47] Most of today's self-managed teams remain bunched at the shop-floor level in factory settings. Experts predict growth of the practice in the managerial ranks and in service operations.[48]

Are Self-Managed Teams Effective? The Research Evidence

Much of what we know about self-managed teams comes from testimonials and case studies. Fortunately, a body of higher quality field research is slowly developing. A review of three meta-analyses covering 70 individual studies concluded that self-managed teams had

- A positive effect on productivity.
- A positive effect on specific attitudes relating to self-management (e.g., responsibility and control).
- No significant effect on general attitudes (e.g., job satisfaction and organizational commitment).
- No significant effect on absenteeism or turnover.[49]

In today's "wired workplaces," it is possible to be a member of a virtual team while working alone.

Although encouraging, these results do not qualify as a sweeping endorsement of self-managed teams. Nonetheless, experts say the trend toward self-managed work teams will continue upward in North America because of a strong cultural bias in favor of direct participation. Managers need to be prepared for the resulting shift in organizational administration.

Virtual Teams

Virtual teams are a product of modern times. They take their name from *virtual reality* computer simulations, where "it's almost like the real thing." Thanks to evolving information technologies such as the Internet, E-mail, videoconferencing, groupware, and fax machines, you can be a member of a work team without really being there.[50] Traditional team meetings are location specific. Team members are either physically present or absent. Virtual teams, in contrast, convene electronically with members reporting in from different locations, different organizations, and even different time zones.

Because virtual teams are so new, there is no consensual definition. Our working definition of a **virtual team** is a physically dispersed task group that conducts its business through modern information technology.[51] Advocates say virtual teams are very flexible and efficient because they are driven by information and skills, not by time and location. People with needed information and/or skills can be team members, regardless of where or when they actually do their work. On the negative side, lack of face-to-face interaction can weaken trust, communication, and accountability.

Virtual team

Information technology allows group members in different locations to conduct business.

Research Insights   As one might expect with a new and ill-defined area, research evidence to date is a bit spotty. Here is what we have learned so far from recent studies of computer-mediated groups:

- Virtual groups formed over the Internet follow a group development process similar to that for face-to-face groups.[52]
- Internet chat rooms create more work and yield poorer decisions than face-to-face meetings and telephone conferences.[53]

- Successful use of groupware (software that facilitates interaction among virtual group members) requires training and hands-on experience.[54]
- Inspirational leadership has a positive impact on creativity in electronic brainstorming groups.[55]

Practical Considerations   Virtual teams may be in fashion, but they are not a cure-all. In fact, they may be a giant step backward for those not well versed in modern information technology. Managers who rely on virtual teams agree on one point: *Meaningful face-to-face contact, especially during early phases of the group development process, is absolutely essential.* Virtual group members need "faces" in their minds to go with names and electronic messages.[56] Additionally, virtual teams cannot succeed without some old-fashioned factors such as top-management support, hands-on training, a clear mission and specific objectives, effective leadership, and schedules and deadlines.[57]

Threats to Group and Team Effectiveness

No matter how carefully managers staff and organize task groups, group dynamics can still go haywire. Forehand knowledge of two major threats to group effectiveness—groupthink and social loafing—can help managers and team members alike take necessary preventive steps.

Groupthink

Systematic analysis of the decision-making processes underlying the war in Vietnam and other US foreign policy fiascoes prompted Yale University's Irving Janis to coin the term *groupthink*.[58] Modern managers can all too easily become victims of groupthink, just like professional politicians, if they passively ignore the danger.

Groupthink

Janis's term for a cohesive ingroup's unwillingness to realistically view alternatives.

Janis defines **groupthink** as "a mode of thinking that people engage in when they are deeply involved in a cohesive in-group, when members' strivings for unanimity override their motivation to realistically appraise alternative courses of action."[59] He adds, "Groupthink refers to a deterioration of mental efficiency, reality testing, and moral judgment that results from in-group pressures."[60] Members of groups victimized by groupthink tend to be friendly and tightly knit.

According to Janis's model, there are eight classic symptoms of groupthink. The greater the number of symptoms, the higher the probability of groupthink:

1. *Invulnerability:* An illusion that breeds excessive optimism and risk taking.
2. *Inherent morality:* A belief that encourages the group to ignore ethical implications.
3. *Rationalization:* Protects pet assumptions.
4. *Stereotyped views of opposition:* Cause group to underestimate opponents.
5. *Self-censorship:* Stifles critical debate.
6. *Illusion of unanimity:* Silence interpreted to mean consent.
7. *Peer pressure:* Loyalty of dissenters is questioned.
8. *Mindguards:* Self-appointed protectors against adverse information.[61]

These symptoms thrive in the sort of climate outlined in the following critique of corporate directors in the United States:

Many directors simply don't rock the boat. "No one likes to be the skunk at the garden party," says [management consultant] Victor H Palmieri. . . . "One does not make friends and influence people in the boardroom or elsewhere by raising hard questions that create embarrassment or discomfort for management."[62]

In short, policy- and decision-making groups can become so cohesive that strong-willed executives are able to gain unanimous support for poor decisions.[63]

Janis believes that prevention is better than cure when dealing with groupthink (see Skills & Best Practices for his preventive measures).

Social Loafing

Is group performance less than, equal to, or greater than the sum of its parts? Can three people, for example, working together accomplish less than, the same as, or more than they would working separately? An interesting study conducted more than a half century ago by a French agricultural engineer named Ringelmann found the answer to be "less than."[64] In a rope-pulling exercise, Ringelmann reportedly found that three people pulling together could achieve only two and a half times the average individual rate. Eight pullers achieved less than four times the individual rate. This tendency for individual effort to decline as group size increases has come to be called **social loafing**.[65] Let us briefly analyze this threat to group effectiveness and synergy with an eye toward avoiding it.

Social loafing

Decrease in individual effort as group size increases.

Social Loafing Theory and Research   Among the theoretical explanations for the social loafing effect are (1) equity of effort ("Everyone else is goofing off, so why shouldn't I?"), (2) loss of personal accountability ("I'm lost in the crowd, so who cares?"), (3) motivational loss due to the sharing of rewards ("Why should I work harder than the others when everyone gets the same reward?"), and (4) coordination loss as more people perform the task ("We're getting in each other's way.").

Laboratory studies refined these theories by identifying situational factors that moderated the social loafing effect. Social loafing occurred when

- The task was perceived to be unimportant, simple, or not interesting.[66]
- Group members thought their individual output was not identifiable.[67]
- Group members expected their co-workers to loaf.[68]

But social loafing did *not* occur when group members in two laboratory studies expected to be evaluated.[69] Also, recent research suggests that self-reliant "individualists" are more prone to social loafing than are group-oriented "collectivists." But individualists can be made more cooperative by keeping the group small and holding each member personally accountable for results.[70]

Practical Implications   These findings demonstrate that social loafing is not an inevitable part of group effort. Management can curb this threat to group effectiveness by making sure the task is challenging and perceived as important. Additionally, it is a good idea to hold group members personally accountable for identifiable portions of the group's task.[71] (Recall our discussion of the power of goal-setting in Chapter 7.)

chapter summary

- *Describe the five stages of Tuckman's theory of group development.* The five stages in Tuckman's theory are *forming* (the group comes together), *storming* (members test the limits and each other), *norming* (questions about authority and power are resolved as the group becomes more cohesive), *performing* (effective communication and cooperation help the group get things done), and *adjourning* (group members go their own way).

- *Contrast roles and norms, and specify four reasons norms are enforced in organizations.* While roles are specific to the person's position, norms are shared attitudes that differentiate appropriate from inappropriate behavior in a variety of situations. Norms evolve informally and are enforced because they help the group or organization survive, clarify behavioral expectations, help people avoid embarrassing situations, and clarify the group's or organization's central values.

- *Explain how a work group becomes a team.* A team is a mature group where leadership is shared, accountability is both individual and collective, the members have developed their own purpose, problem solving is a way of life, and effectiveness is measured by collective outcomes.

- *List at least four things managers can do to build trust.* Six recommended ways to build trust are through

communication, support, respect (especially delegation), fairness, predictability, and competence.

- *Describe self-managed teams and virtual teams.* Self-managed teams are groups of workers who are given administrative oversight for various chores normally performed by managers—such as planning, scheduling, monitoring, and staffing. They are typically cross functional, meaning they are staffed with a mix of specialists from different areas. Self-managed teams vary widely in the autonomy or freedom they enjoy. A virtual team is a physically dispersed task group that conducts its business through modern information technology such as the Internet. Periodic and meaningful face-to-face contact seems to be crucial for virtual team members, especially during the early stages of group development.

- *Describe groupthink, and identify at least four of its symptoms.* Groupthink plagues cohesive in-groups that shortchange moral judgment while putting too much emphasis on unanimity. Symptoms of groupthink include invulnerability, inherent morality, rationalization, stereotyped views of opposition, self-censorship, illusion of unanimity, peer pressure, and mindguards. Critical evaluators, outside expertise, and devil's advocates are among the preventive measures recommended by Irving Janis, who coined the term *groupthink*.

internet exercise

Free Self-Assessment Questionnaires for Social Skills

Managers, who are responsible for getting things accomplished with and through others, simply cannot be effective if they are unable to interact skillfully in social settings. As with any skill development program, you need to know *where you are* before constructing a learning agenda for *where you want to be*. Go to the Internet home page for Body-Mind Queen-Dom (**www.queendom.com**), and select the category "Tests & Profiles." (Note: Our use of this site is for instructional purposes only and does not constitute an endorsement of any products that may or may not suit your needs. There is no obligation to buy anything.) Next, choose "Relationships" and scroll down to the list of 19 relationships tests. Select the "Communication Skills Test," read the brief instructions, complete all 34 items, and click on the "score" button for automatic scoring. It is possible, if you choose, to print a personal copy of your completed questionnaire and results.

If you have time, some of the other relationships tests are interesting and fun. We recommend trying the following ones: Arguing Style Test; Assertiveness Test; Conflict Management Test; Leadership Test; and Self-Esteem Test.

QUESTIONS
1. How did you score? Are you pleasantly (or unpleasantly) surprised by your score?
2. What is your strongest social/communication skill?
3. Reviewing the questionnaire item by item, can you find obvious weak spots in your social/communication skills? For instance, are you a poor listener? Do you interrupt too often? Do you need to be more aware of others, both verbally and nonverbally? Do you have a hard time tuning into others' feelings or expressing your own feelings? How do you handle disagreement?
4. Based on the results of this questionnaire, what is your learning agenda for improving your social and communication skills?

Managing Conflict and Negotiating

Eleven

chapter

LEARNING OBJECTIVES

After reading the material in this chapter, you should be able to:

- Define the term *conflict,* distinguish between functional and dysfunctional conflict, and identify three desired outcomes of conflict.

- Define *personality conflicts,* and explain how they should be managed.

- Discuss the role of in-group thinking in intergroup conflict, and explain what can be done to avoid cross-cultural conflict.

- Explain *programmed conflict,* and identify the five conflict-handing styles.

- Identify and describe at least four alternative dispute resolution (ADR) techniques.

- Draw a distinction between distributive and integrative negotiation, and explain the concept of added-value negotiation.

WELCOME TO ORGANIZATIONAL BOOT CAMP

Margaret Boitano, *Fortune* Magazine:

It's Monday, 11 AM, and I'm in the boss's office thinking I'm finally going to get that long-awaited promotion. "I want to tell you that we think you have great potential," she says with a stern face. "But you really need to do something about your style." My mind races as I try to figure out what she could possibly mean. I make a mental note never to trust people who start

work looking like Erin Brockovich, and that's considered inappropriate for a manager. I don't know whether to laugh or scream, and I briefly toy with the idea of simply storming out of her office. This can't be happening.

It isn't.

My "boss" isn't really a boss at all. She designs exhibits for a science museum. Surrounding us in the lobby of the Marriott hotel in Cambridge, Mass., are 120 other people having similar

"Conflict is a growth industry," says Bruce Patton, an associate director of the Program on Negotiation who worked with the US and Iranian governments to end the hostage crisis in 1980. "Most companies aim to minimize it, but the best companies learn to harness it to spur creativity." In fact, difficult conversations are increasingly common these days, as companies move to flattened management structures and the economy grinds through a painful slowdown. If you run a small business, chances are you're on one end of just about every difficult conversation that takes place—plus all those that don't take place but should. . . .

The 120 attendees of this class are from small businesses and from giant corporations like Procter & Gamble, McDonald's, Pfizer, and Bayer. For Paige Ireland of Canal Bridge Consulting, a private company in Bethesda, Md., with 16 employees, just getting into the course elicited an uncomfortable exchange. She found a flier on her desk one morning with the word "Interested?" scribbled on it by

conversations with compliments. "Well . . . ah . . . it's nice to know that I'm appreciated," I stammer, stomach churning. "But I have to be honest. I don't know what you're talking about." She leans forward and says, "You need to dress more conservatively." Apparently I've been coming to

conversations. We're all here for a two-day seminar on Managing the Difficult Business Conversation, and if the subject sounds overly touchie-feelie, like a grown-up version of *Barney*, stop smirking. The seminar is run by Harvard Law School's Program on Negotiation, an applied-research center that studies dispute resolution around the world.

her boss. "Is there something you're trying to tell me?" she asked. Fortunately, he laughed it off. . . .

The second morning, for example, we covered Managing Your Feelings and Getting Straight on Purposes, or how to get what you want from employees without letting emotions overwhelm the discussion. However, we picked up some concrete guidance as well. One of the first rules: Erase the word "but" from your vocabulary and replace it with "and." (As in, "I understand how you could feel that way, and. . . .") According to the instructors, saying "but" creates an either/or situation, which can put subordinate employees on the defensive.

As elementary as instructions like these sound,

they're surprisingly difficult to put into practice, even in role-playing situations. Though I'd never met the woman playing my boss, I still somehow resented her for taking issue with my hypothetical attire. (For the record, I don't dress all that much like Erin Brockovich.) At the cocktail reception that evening, I learned I wasn't alone in my feelings. A number of people—mainly women, who made up about 40% of the attendees—were still stewing from the conversations they'd had that morning. . . .

The professors didn't have sure-fire solutions for any of these issues. They offered us some Zen-like advice—for example, learn to recognize the difference between "expressing emotions" and "being emotional"—and they listed the five things you should never say when someone is upset: " Calm down";

"What did you expect?"; "It's not so bad"; "What you need to understand is . . . "; and "I see your point, but . . ." (there's that "but" again). Then they showed us how to map out both our feelings and what we think the other person might be feeling. Don't assume the worst about things you don't know, they cautioned. If you feel you don't have enough information, try bouncing your thoughts off a co-worker.[1]

How would you rate yourself as a conflict manager? How many of the "rules" mentioned here do you typically break? What do you need to do to improve? For an interpretation of this case and additional comments, visit our website:

www.mhhe.com/kinickiob

MAKE NO MISTAKE about it. Conflict is an unavoidable aspect of modern life. These major trends conspire to make *organizational* conflict inevitable:

- Constant change.
- Greater employee diversity.
- More teams (virtual and self-managed).
- Less face-to-face communication (more electronic interaction).
- A global economy with increased cross-cultural dealings.

Dean Tjosvold, from Canada's Simon Fraser University, notes that "Change begets conflict, conflict begets change"[2] and challenges us to do better with this sobering global perspective:

> Learning to manage conflict is a critical investment in improving how we, our families, and our organizations adapt and take advantage of change. Managing conflicts well does not insulate us from change, nor does it mean that we will always come out on top or get all that we want. However, effective conflict management helps us keep in touch with new developments and create solutions appropriate for new threats and opportunities.
>
> Much evidence shows we have often failed to manage our conflicts and respond to change effectively. High divorce rates, disheartening examples of sexual and physical abuse of children, the expensive failures of international joint ventures, and bloody ethnic violence have convinced many people that we do not have the abilities to cope with our complex interpersonal, organizational, and global conflicts.[3]

But respond we must. As outlined in this chapter, tools and solutions are available, if only we develop the ability and will to use them persistently. The choice is ours: Be active managers of conflict, or be managed by conflict.

A Modern View of Conflict

Conflict

One party perceives its interests are being opposed or set back by another party.

A comprehensive review of the conflict literature yielded this consensus definition: "**conflict** is a process in which one party perceives that its interests are being opposed or negatively affected by another party."[4] The word *perceives* reminds us that sources of conflict and issues can be real or imagined. The resulting conflict is the same. Conflict can escalate (strengthen) or deescalate (weaken) over time. "The conflict process unfolds in a context, and whenever conflict, escalated or not, occurs the disputants or third parties can attempt to manage it in some manner."[5] Consequently, current and future managers need to understand the dynamics of conflict and know how to handle it effectively (both as disputants and as third parties).

A Conflict Continuum

Ideas about managing conflict underwent an interesting evolution during the 20th century. Initially, scientific management experts such as Frederick W Taylor believed all conflict ultimately threatened management's authority and thus had to be avoided or quickly resolved.[6] Later, human relationists recognized the inevitability of conflict and advised managers to learn to live with it. Emphasis remained on resolving conflict whenever possible, however. Beginning in the 1970s, OB specialists realized conflict had both positive and negative outcomes, depending on its nature and intensity.

This perspective introduced the revolutionary idea that organizations could suffer from *too little* conflict.

Work groups, departments, or organizations that experience too little conflict tend to be plagued by apathy, lack of creativity, indecision, and missed deadlines. Excessive conflict, on the other hand, can erode organizational performance because of political infighting, dissatisfaction, lack of teamwork, and turnover. Workplace aggression and violence can be manifestations of excessive conflict.[7] Appropriate types and levels of conflict energize people in constructive directions.[8]

Functional versus Dysfunctional Conflict

The distinction between **functional conflict** and **dysfunctional conflict** pivots on whether the organization's interests are served. According to one conflict expert,

> **Functional conflict**
> Serves organization's interests.
>
> **Dysfunctional conflict**
> Threatens organization's interests.

> Some [types of conflict] support the goals of the organization and improve performance; these are functional, constructive forms of conflict. They benefit or support the main purposes of the organization. Additionally, there are those types of conflict that hinder organizational performance; these are dysfunctional or destructive forms. They are undesirable and the manager should seek their eradication.[9]

Functional conflict is commonly referred to in management circles as constructive or cooperative conflict.[10]

Often, a simmering conflict can be defused in a functional manner or driven to dysfunctional proportions, depending on how it is handled. For example, consider these two very different outcomes at Southwest Airlines and Gateway, the computer maker with the familiar black-and-white cow shipping boxes:

> Recently tensions broke out between flight attendants and their schedulers (the ones with the sorry job of telling flight attendants they have to work on a day off). The flight attendants believed the schedulers were overworking them; the schedulers claimed the attendants were hostile and uncooperative. The solution was very, well, Southwest: Both sides had to switch jobs for a day and see how difficult the other side had it. For now, at least, the tactic has eased tensions.[11]

Meanwhile, trouble was brewing at Gateway, where sales were off sharply. Company founder Ted Waitt had retired one year earlier when his hand-picked successor, Jeff Weitzen, took over after being hired from AT&T. *Fortune* magazine followed the action:

> It all came to a head at Gateway's Jan. 17 [2001] board meeting. In a hostile and combative proceeding, insiders say, Waitt and the board interrogated Weitzen relentlessly. At one point, after Weitzen had finished talking about his plans to improve customer service, one board member snapped, "Why should we believe you?"
>
> After the meeting Weitzen was furious. Stewing all weekend, he confronted Waitt the following Monday. High-level insiders say they argued for hours behind locked doors over how and by whom Gateway should be run. Waitt told Weitzen that he wanted him to stay on as CEO while Waitt took a more active role as chairman. For Weitzen, this arrangement—effectively a demotion—was unacceptable. Weitzen delivered an ultimatum: Back off or he was quitting.
>
> Taking a day to think about it, Waitt decided he wasn't backing off.[12]

A few days later, Weitzen and most of his top-management team were gone and Waitt's brief retirement was over.

Antecedents of Conflict

Certain situations produce more conflict than others. By knowing the antecedents of conflict, managers are better able to anticipate conflict and take steps to resolve it if it becomes dysfunctional. Among the situations that tend to produce either functional or dysfunctional conflict are

Layoff survivors typically complain about being overworked, thus paving the way for stress and conflict.

- Incompatible personalities or value systems.
- Overlapping or unclear job boundaries.
- Competition for limited resources.
- Interdepartment/intergroup competition.
- Inadequate communication.
- Interdependent tasks (e.g., one person cannot complete his or her assignment until others have completed their work).
- Organizational complexity (conflict tends to increase as the number of hierarchical layers and specialized tasks increase).
- Unreasonable or unclear policies, standards, or rules.
- Unreasonable deadlines or extreme time pressure.
- Collective decision making (the greater the number of people participating in a decision, the greater the potential for conflict).
- Decision making by consensus.
- Unmet expectations (employees who have unrealistic expectations about job assignments, pay, or promotions are more prone to conflict).
- Unresolved or suppressed conflicts.[13]

Proactive managers carefully read these early warnings and take appropriate action. For example, group conflict sometimes can be reduced by making decisions on the basis of majority approval rather than striving for a consensus.

SOURCE: The Arizona Republic, June 15, 2001, p D2.

Desired Outcomes of Conflict

Within organizations, conflict management is more than simply a quest for agreement. If progress is to be made and dysfunctional conflict minimized, a broader agenda is in order. Tjosvold's cooperative conflict model calls for three desired outcomes:

1. *Agreement.* But at what cost? Equitable and fair agreements are best. An agreement that leaves one party feeling exploited or defeated will tend to breed resentment and subsequent conflict.

2. *Stronger relationships.* Good agreements enable conflicting parties to build bridges of goodwill and trust for future use. Moreover, conflicting parties who trust each other are more likely to keep their end of the bargain.

3. *Learning.* Functional conflict can promote greater self-awareness and creative problem solving. Like the practice of management itself, successful conflict handling is learned primarily by doing. Knowledge of the concepts and techniques in this chapter is a necessary first step, but there is no substitute for hands-on practice. In a contentious world, there are plenty of opportunities to practice conflict management.[14]

Major Forms of Conflict

Certain antecedents of conflict deserve a closer look. This section explores the nature and organizational implications of three common forms of conflict: personality conflict, intergroup conflict, and cross-cultural conflict. Our discussion of each type of conflict includes some practical tips.

Personality Conflicts

As discussed in Chapter 5, your *personality* is the package of stable traits and characteristics creating your unique identity. According to experts on the subject:

> Each of us has a unique way of interacting with others. Whether we are seen as charming, irritating, fascinating, nondescript, approachable, or intimidating depends in part on our personality, or what others might describe as our style.[15]

Given the many possible combinations of personality traits, it is clear why personality conflicts are inevitable. We define a **personality conflict** as interpersonal opposition based on personal dislike and/or disagreement.

Personality conflict

Interpersonal opposition driven by personal dislike or disagreement.

Workplace Incivility: The Seeds of Personality Conflict

Somewhat akin to physical pain, chronic personality conflicts often begin with seemingly insignificant irritations. For instance, a manager can grow to deeply dislike someone in the next cubicle who persistently whistles off-key while drumming his foot on the side of a filing cabinet. Sadly, grim little scenarios such as this are all too common today, given the steady erosion of civility in the workplace. Researchers recently noted how increased informality, pressure for results, and employee diversity have fostered an "anything goes" atmosphere in today's workplaces. They view incivility as a self-perpetuating vicious cycle that can end in violence.[16] A new study indicates the extent of workplace incivility: "71% of 1,100 workers surveyed said they'd experienced put-downs or condescending and outright rude behavior on the job."[17]

Vicious cycles of incivility need to be avoided (or broken early) with an organizational culture that places a high value on respect for co-workers. This requires managers and leaders to act as caring and courteous role models. A positive spirit of cooperation, as opposed to one based on negativism and aggression, also helps. Some organizations have resorted to workplace etiquette training. More specifically, constructive feedback and/or skillful behavior modification can keep a single irritating behavior from precipitating a full-blown personality conflict (or worse).

Dealing with Personality Conflicts   Personality conflicts are a potential minefield for managers. Let us frame the situation. Personality traits, by definition, are stable and resistant to change. Moreover, according to the American Psychiatric Association's *Diagnostic and Statistical Manual of Mental Disorders,* there are 410 psychological disorders that can and do show up in the workplace.[18] This brings up legal issues. Employees in the United States suffering from psychological disorders such as depression and mood-altering diseases such as alcoholism are protected from discrimination by the Americans with Disabilities Act.[19] (Other nations have similar laws.) Also, sexual harassment and other forms of discrimination can grow out of apparent personality conflicts.[20] Finally, personality conflicts can spawn workplace aggression and violence.[21]

Traditionally, managers dealt with personality conflicts by either ignoring them or transferring one party. In view of the legal implications, just discussed, both of these options may be open invitations to discrimination lawsuits. Skills & Best Practices presents practical tips for both nonmanagers and managers who are involved in or affected by personality conflicts. Our later discussions of handling dysfunctional conflict and alternative dispute resolution techniques also apply.

SKILLS & BEST PRACTICES

How to Deal with Personality Conflicts

Tips for Employees Having a Personality Conflict	Tips for Third-Party Observers of a Personality Conflict	Tips for Managers Whose Employees Are Having a Personality Conflict
• All employees need to be familiar with and *follow* company policies for diversity, antidiscrimination, and sexual harassment.		
• Communicate directly with the other person to resolve the perceived conflict (emphasize problem solving and common objectives, not personalities). • Avoid dragging co-workers into the conflict. • If dysfunctional conflict persists, seek help from direct supervisors or human resource specialists.	• Do not take sides in someone else's personality conflict. • Suggest the parties work things out themselves in a constructive and positive way. • If dysfunctional conflict persists, refer the problem to parties' direct supervisors.	• Investigate and document conflict. • If appropriate, take corrective action (e.g., feedback or behavior modification). • If necessary, attempt informal dispute resolution. • Refer difficult conflicts to human resource specialists or hired counselors for formal resolution attempts and other interventions.

Intergroup Conflict

Conflict among work groups, teams, and departments is a common threat to organizational competitiveness. For example, when Michael Volkema became CEO of Herman Miller in the mid-1990s, he found an inward-focused company with divisions fighting over budgets. He has since curbed intergroup conflict at the Michigan-based furniture maker by emphasizing collaboration and redirecting everyone's attention outward, to the customer.[22] Managers who understand the mechanics of intergroup conflict are better equipped to face this sort of challenge.

In-Group Thinking: The Seeds of Intergroup Conflict As we discussed in the previous chapter, *cohesiveness*—a "we feeling" binding group members together—can be a good or bad thing. A certain amount of cohesiveness can turn a group of individuals into a smooth-running team. Too much cohesiveness, however, can breed groupthink because a desire to get along pushes aside critical thinking. The study of in-groups by small group researchers has revealed a whole package of changes associated with increased group cohesiveness. Specifically,

- Members of in-groups view themselves as a collection of unique individuals, while they stereotype members of other groups as being "all alike."
- In-group members see themselves positively and as morally correct, while they view members of other groups negatively and as immoral.
- In-groups view outsiders as a threat.
- In-group members exaggerate the differences between their group and other groups. This typically involves a distorted perception of reality.[23]

Avid sports fans who simply can't imagine how someone would support the opposing team exemplify one form of in-group thinking. Also, this pattern of behavior is a form of ethnocentrism, discussed as a cross-cultural barrier in Chapter 3. Reflect for a moment on evidence of in-group behavior in your life. Does your circle of friends make fun of others because of their race, gender, nationality, sexual preference, or major in college?

In-group thinking is one more fact of organizational life that virtually guarantees conflict. Managers cannot eliminate in-group thinking, but they certainly should not ignore it when handling intergroup conflicts.

Research Lessons for Handling Intergroup Conflict Sociologists have long recommended the contact hypothesis for reducing intergroup conflict. According to the *contact hypothesis,* the more the members of different groups interact, the less intergroup conflict they will experience. Those interested in improving race, international, and union-management relations typically encourage cross-group interaction. The hope is that *any* type of interaction, short of actual conflict, will reduce stereotyping and combat in-group thinking. But research has shown this approach to be naive and limited. For example, one recent study of 83 health center employees (83% female) at a midwest US university probed the specific nature of intergroup relations and concluded:

> The number of *negative* relationships was significantly related to higher perceptions of intergroup conflict. Thus, it seems that negative relationships have a salience that overwhelms any possible positive effects from friendship links across groups.[24]

FIGURE 11–1 │ Minimizing Intergroup Conflict: An Updated Contact Model

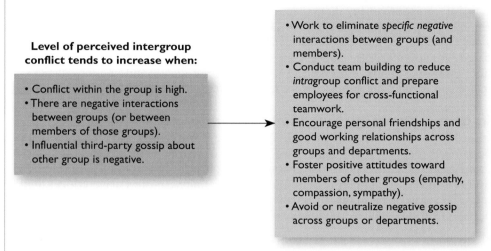

Level of perceived intergroup conflict tends to increase when:

- Conflict within the group is high.
- There are negative interactions between groups (or between members of those groups).
- Influential third-party gossip about other group is negative.

Recommended actions:

- Work to eliminate *specific negative* interactions between groups (and members).
- Conduct team building to reduce *intra*group conflict and prepare employees for cross-functional teamwork.
- Encourage personal friendships and good working relationships across groups and departments.
- Foster positive attitudes toward members of other groups (empathy, compassion, sympathy).
- Avoid or neutralize negative gossip across groups or departments.

SOURCE: Based on research evidence in G Labianca, D J Brass, and B Gray, "Social Networks and Perceptions of Intergroup Conflict: The Role of Negative Relationships and Third Parties," *Academy of Management Journal*, February 1998, pp 55–67; C D Batson et al., "Empathy and Attitudes: Can Feeling for a Member of a Stigmatized Group Improve Feelings toward the Group?" *Journal of Personality and Social Psychology*, January 1997, pp 105–18; and S C Wright et al., "The Extended Contact Effect: Knowledge of Cross-Group Friendships and Prejudice," *Journal of Personality and Social Psychology*, July 1997, pp 73–90.

Intergroup friendships are still desirable, as documented in many studies,[25] but they are readily overpowered by negative intergroup interactions. Thus, *priority number 1 for managers faced with intergroup conflict is to identify and root out specific negative linkages among groups.* A single personality conflict, for instance, may contaminate the entire intergroup experience. The same goes for an employee who voices negative opinions or spreads negative rumors about another group. Our updated contact model in Figure 11–1 is based on this and other recent research insights, such as the need to foster positive attitudes toward other groups.[26] Also, notice how conflict within the group and negative gossip from third parties are threats that need to be neutralized if intergroup conflict is to be minimized.

Cross-Cultural Conflict

Doing business with people from different cultures is commonplace in our global economy where cross-border mergers, joint ventures, and alliances are the order of the day.[27] Because of differing assumptions about how to think and act, the potential for cross-cultural conflict is both immediate and huge.[28] Success or failure, when conducting business across cultures, often hinges on avoiding and minimizing actual or perceived conflict. For example, consider this cultural mismatch:

> Mexicans place great importance on saving face, so they tend to expect any conflicts that occur during negotiations to be downplayed or kept private. The prevailing attitude in the [United States], however, is that conflict should be dealt with directly and publicly to prevent hard feelings from developing on a personal level.[29]

This is not a matter of who is right and who is wrong; rather it is a matter of accommodating cultural differences for a successful business transaction. Awareness of the cross-cultural differences we discussed in Chapter 3 is an important first step. Beyond that, cross-cultural conflict can be moderated by using international consultants and building cross-cultural relationships.

Using International Consultants

In response to broad demand, there is a growing army of management consultants specializing in cross-cultural relations. Competency and fees vary widely, of course. But a carefully selected cross-cultural consultant can be helpful, as this illustration shows:

> Last year, when electronics-maker Canon planned to set up a subsidiary in Dubai through its Netherlands division, it asked consultant Sahid Mirza of Glocom, based in Dubai, to find out how the two cultures would work together.

Mirza sent out the test questionnaires and got a sizable response. "The findings were somewhat surprising," he recalls. "We found that, at the bedrock level, there were relatively few differences. Many of the Arab businessmen came from former British colonies and viewed business in much the same way as the Dutch."

But at the level of behavior, there was a real conflict. "The Dutch are blunt and honest in expression, and such expression is very offensive to Arab sensibilities." Mirza offers the example of a Dutch executive who says something like, "We can't meet the deadline." Such a negative expression—true or not—would be gravely offensive to an Arab. As a result of Mirza's research, Canon did start the subsidiary in Dubai, but it trained both the Dutch and the Arab executives first.[30]

Consultants also can help untangle possible personality, value, and intergroup conflicts from conflicts rooted in differing national cultures. Note: Although we have discussed basic types of conflict separately, they typically are encountered in complex, messy bundles.

Building Relationships across Cultures

Rosalie L Tung's recent study of 409 expatriates from US and Canadian multinational firms, mentioned in Chapter 3, is very instructive.[31] Her survey sought to pinpoint success factors for the expatriates (14% female) who were working in 51 different countries worldwide. Nine specific ways to facilitate interaction with host-country nationals, as ranked from most useful to least useful by the respondents, are listed in Skills & Best Practices. Good listening skills topped the list, followed by sensitivity to others and cooperativeness rather than competitiveness.

How to Build Cross-Cultural Relationships

Behavior	Rank
Be a good listener	1
Be sensitive to needs of others	2 ⎱ Tie
Be cooperative, rather than overly competitive	2 ⎰
Advocate inclusive (participative) leadership	3
Compromise rather than dominate	4
Build rapport through conversations	5
Be compassionate and understanding	6
Avoid conflict by emphasizing harmony	7
Nurture others (develop and mentor)	8

SOURCE: Adapted from R L Tung, "American Expatriates Abroad: From Neophytes to Cosmopolitans," *Journal of World Business*, Summer 1998, Table 6, p 136.

Racial, ethnic, and religious differences can make cross-cultural conflict all the more challenging.

Interestingly, US managers are culturally characterized as just the opposite: poor listeners, blunt to the point of insensitivity, and excessively competitive. Some managers need to add self-management to the list of ways to minimize cross-cultural conflict.

Managing Conflict

As we have seen, conflict has many faces and is a constant challenge for managers who are responsible for reaching organizational goals. Our attention now turns to the active management of both functional and dysfunctional conflict. We discuss how to stimulate functional conflict, how to handle dysfunctional conflict, and how third parties can deal effectively with conflict.

Programming Functional Conflict

Sometimes committees and decision-making groups become so bogged down in details and procedures that nothing substantive is accomplished. Carefully monitored functional conflict can help get the creative juices flowing once again. Managers basically have two options. They can fan the fires of naturally occurring conflict—although this approach can be unreliable and slow. Alternatively, managers can resort to programmed

Programmed conflict

Encourages different opinions without protecting management's personal feelings.

conflict. Experts in the field define **programmed conflict** as "conflict that raises different opinions *regardless of the personal feelings of the managers*."[32] The trick is to get contributors to either defend or criticize ideas based on relevant facts rather than on the basis of personal preference or political interests. This requires disciplined role playing and effective leadership. For example, it is easy to detect the climate for programmed conflict in these recent statements by Joseph Tucci, the new CEO of EMC, a leading data storage equipment maker: "Good leaders always leave room for debate and different opinions. . . . The team has to be in harmony. But before you move out, there needs to be a debate."[33]

Alternative Styles for Handling Dysfunctional Conflict

People tend to handle negative conflict in patterned ways referred to as *styles*. Several conflict styles have been categorized over the years. According to conflict specialist Afzalur Rahim's model, five different conflict-handling styles can be plotted on a 2 × 2 grid. High to low concern for *self* is found on the horizontal axis of the grid while low to high concern for *others* forms the vertical axis (see Figure 11–2).

FIGURE 11–2   Five Conflict-Handling Styles

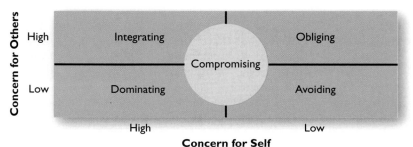

SOURCE: M A Rahim, "A Strategy for Managing Conflict in Complex Organizations, *Human Relations*, January 1985, p 84. Used with author's permission of Plenum Publishing.

Various combinations of these variables produce the five different conflict-handling styles: integrating, obliging, dominating, avoiding, and compromising.[34] There is no single best style; each has strengths and limitations and is subject to situational constraints.

Integrating (Problem Solving) In this style, interested parties confront the issue and cooperatively identify the problem, generate and weigh alternative solutions, and select a solution. Integrating is appropriate for complex issues plagued by misunderstanding. However, it is inappropriate for resolving conflicts rooted in opposing value systems. Its primary strength is its longer lasting impact because it deals with the underlying problem rather than merely with symptoms. The primary weakness of this style is that it is very time consuming.

Obliging (Smoothing) "An obliging person neglects his or her own concern to satisfy the concern of the other party."[35] This style, often called smoothing, involves playing down differences while emphasizing commonalities. Obliging may be an appropriate conflict-handling strategy when it is possible to eventually get something in return. But it is inappropriate for complex or worsening problems. Its primary strength is that it encourages cooperation. Its main weakness is that it's a temporary fix that fails to confront the underlying problem.

Dominating (Forcing) High concern for self and low concern for others encourages "I win, you lose" tactics. The other party's needs are largely ignored. This style is often called forcing because it relies on formal authority to force compliance. Dominating is appropriate when an unpopular solution must be implemented, the issue is minor, or a deadline is near. It is inappropriate in an open and participative climate. Speed is its primary strength. The primary weakness of this domineering style is that it often breeds resentment.

Avoiding This tactic may involve either passive withdrawal from the problem or active suppression of the issue. Avoidance is appropriate for trivial issues or when the costs of confrontation outweigh the benefits of resolving the conflict. It is inappropriate for difficult and worsening problems. The main strength of this style is that it buys time in unfolding or ambiguous situations. The primary weakness is that the tactic provides a temporary fix that sidesteps the underlying problem.

Compromising This is a give-and-take approach involving moderate concern for both self and others. Compromise is appropriate when parties have opposite goals or possess equal power. But compromise is inappropriate when overuse would lead to inconclusive action (e.g., failure to meet production deadlines). The primary strength of this tactic is that the democratic process has no losers, but it's a temporary fix that can stifle creative problem solving. (Take a short break from your reading and complete the Hands-On Exercise to determine your primary and backup conflict-handling styles.)

Third-Party Interventions: Alternative Dispute Resolution

Disputes between employees, between employees and their employer, and between companies too often end up in lengthy and costly court battles. A more constructive, less expensive approach called alternative dispute resolution has enjoyed enthusiastic

What Is Your Conflict-Handling Style?

INSTRUCTIONS   For each of the 15 items, indicate how often you rely on that tactic by circling the appropriate number.

Conflict-Handling Tactics	Rarely				Always

1. I argue my case with my co-workers to show the merits of my position.   1 2 3 4 5

2. I negotiate with my co-workers so that a compromise can be reached.   1 2 3 4 5

3. I try to satisfy the expectations of my co-workers.   1 2 3 4 5

4. I try to investigate an issue with my co-workers to find a solution acceptable to us.   1 2 3 4 5

5. I am firm in pursuing my side of the issue.   1 2 3 4 5

6. I attempt to avoid being "put on the spot" and try to keep my conflict with my co-workers to myself.   1 2 3 4 5

7. I hold on to my solution to a problem.   1 2 3 4 5

8. I use "give and take" so that a compromise can be made.   1 2 3 4 5

9. I exchange accurate information with my co-workers to solve a problem together.   1 2 3 4 5

10. I avoid open discussion of my differences with my co-workers.   1 2 3 4 5

11. I accommodate the wishes of my co-workers.   1 2 3 4 5

12. I try to bring all our concerns out in the open so that the issues can be resolved in the best possible way.   1 2 3 4 5

13. I propose a middle ground for breaking deadlocks.   1 2 3 4 5

14. I go along with the suggestions of my co-workers.   1 2 3 4 5

15. I try to keep my disagreements with my co-workers to myself in order to avoid hard feelings.   1 2 3 4 5

SCORING AND INTERPRETATION

Enter your responses, item by item, in the five categories below, and then add the three scores for each of the styles. Note: There are no right or wrong answers, because individual differences are involved.

Integrating		Obliging		Dominating	
Item	Score	Item	Score	Item	Score
4.	_____	3.	_____	1.	_____
9.	_____	11.	_____	5.	_____
12.	_____	14.	_____	7.	_____
Total =	_____	Total =	_____	Total =	_____

Avoiding		Compromising	
Item	Score	Item	Score
6.	_____	2.	_____
10.	_____	8.	_____
15.	_____	13.	_____
Total =	_____	Total =	_____

Your primary conflict-handling style is: _____
   (The category with the highest total.)

Your backup conflict-handling style is: _____
   (The category with the second highest total.)

SOURCE: Adapted from a longer instrument in M A Rahim, "A Measure of Styles of Handling Interpersonal Conflict," *Academy of Management Journal*, June 1983, pp 368–76. A validation of the original instrument can be found in E Van De Vliert and B Kabanoff, "Toward Theory-Based Measures of Conflict Management," *Academy of Management Journal*, March 1990, pp 199–209.

growth in recent years.[36] In fact, the widely imitated "People's Court"–type television shows operating outside the formal judicial system are part of this trend toward what one writer calls "do-it-yourself justice."[37] **Alternative dispute resolution (ADR),** according to a pair of Canadian labor lawyers, "uses faster, more user-friendly methods of dispute resolution, instead of traditional, adversarial approaches (such as unilateral decision making or litigation)."[38] The following ADR techniques represent a progression of steps third parties can take to resolve organizational conflicts.[39] They are ranked from easiest and least expensive to most difficult and costly. A growing number of organizations have formal ADR policies involving an established sequence of various combinations of these techniques:

> **Alternative dispute resolution**
>
> Avoiding costly lawsuits by resolving conflicts informally or through mediation or arbitration.

- *Facilitation.* A third party, usually a manager, informally urges disputing parties to deal directly with each other in a positive and constructive manner.

- *Conciliation.* A neutral third party informally acts as a communication conduit between disputing parties. This is appropriate when conflicting parties refuse to meet face to face. The immediate goal is to establish direct communication, with the broader aim of finding common ground and a constructive solution.

- *Peer review.* A panel of trustworthy co-workers, selected for their ability to remain objective, hears both sides of a dispute in an informal and confidential meeting. Any decision by the review panel may or may not be binding, depending on the company's ADR policy. Membership on the peer review panel often is rotated among employees.

- *Ombudsman.* Someone who works for the organization, and is widely respected and trusted by his or her co-workers, hears grievances on a confidential basis and attempts to arrange a solution. This approach, more common in Europe than North America, permits someone to get help from above without relying on the formal hierarchy chain.

- *Mediation.* "The mediator—a trained, third-party neutral—actively guides the disputing parties in exploring innovative solutions to the conflict. Although some companies have in-house mediators who have received ADR training, most also use external mediators who have no ties to the company."[40] Unlike an arbitrator, a mediator does *not* render a decision. It is up to the disputants to reach a mutually acceptable decision.

- *Arbitration.* Disputing parties agree ahead of time to accept the decision of a neutral arbitrator in a formal courtlike setting, often complete with evidence and witnesses. Statements are confidential. Decisions are based on legal merits. Trained arbitrators, typically from outside agencies such as the American Arbitration Association, are versed in relevant laws and case precedents. Historically, employee participation in arbitration was voluntary. A 2001 US Supreme Court decision changed things. As part of the employment contract with nonunion workers, employers in the United States now have the legal right to insist upon *mandatory* arbitration in lieu of a court battle. A vigorous debate now rages over the fairness and quality of mandatory arbitration.[41]

"People's Court"–type T.V. shows illustrates positive and negative aspects of ADR/binding arbitration outside the formal judicial system.

Negotiating

Negotiation

Give-and-take process between conflicting interdependent parties.

Formally defined, **negotiation** is a give-and-take decision-making process involving interdependent parties with different preferences.[42] Common examples include labor-management negotiations over wages, hours, and working conditions and negotiations between supply chain specialists and vendors involving price, delivery schedules, and credit terms. Self-managed work teams with overlapping task boundaries also need to rely on negotiated agreements. Negotiating skills are more important than ever today.[43]

Two Basic Types of Negotiation

Negotiation experts distinguish between two types of negotiation—*distributive* and *integrative*. Understanding the difference requires a change in traditional "fixed-pie" thinking:

> A *distributive* negotiation usually involves a single issue—a "fixed-pie"—in which one person gains at the expense of the other. For example, haggling over the price of a rug in a bazaar is a distributive negotiation. In most conflicts, however, more than one issue is at stake, and each party values the issues differently. The outcomes available are no longer a fixed-pie divided among all parties. An agreement can be found that is better for both parties than what they would have reached through distributive negotiation. This is an *integrative* negotiation.
>
> However, parties in a negotiation often don't find these beneficial trade-offs because each *assumes* its interests *directly* conflict with those of the other party. "What is good for the other side must be bad for us" is a common and unfortunate perspective that most people have. This is the mind-set we call the *mythical* "fixed-pie."[44]

Distributive negotiation involves traditional win-lose thinking. Integrative negotiation calls for a progressive win-win strategy.[45]

Added-Value Negotiation

One practical application of the integrative approach is **added-value negotiation** (AVN). During AVN, the negotiating parties cooperatively develop multiple deal packages while building a productive long-term relationship. AVN consists of these five steps:

Added-value negotiation

Cooperatively developing multiple-deal packages while building a long-term relationship.

1. *Clarify interests.* After each party identifies its tangible and intangible needs, the two parties meet to discuss their respective needs and find *common ground* for negotiation.
2. *Identify options.* A *marketplace of value* is created when the negotiating parties discuss desired elements of value (such as property, money, behavior, rights, and risk reduction).
3. *Design alternative deal packages.* While aiming for *multiple deals,* each party mixes and matches elements of value from both parties in workable combinations.
4. *Select a deal.* Each party analyzes deal packages proposed by the other party. Jointly, the parties discuss and select from feasible deal packages, with a spirit of *creative agreement.*
5. *Perfect the deal.* Together the parties discuss unresolved issues, develop a written agreement, and *build relationships* for future negotiations.[46]

chapter summary

- *Define the term* conflict, *distinguish between functional and dysfunctional conflict, and identify three desired outcomes of conflict.* Conflict is a process in which one party perceives that its interests are being opposed or negatively affected by another party. It is inevitable and not necessarily destructive. Too little conflict, as evidenced by apathy or lack of creativity, can be as great a problem as too much conflict. Functional conflict enhances organizational interests while dysfunctional conflict is counterproductive. Three desired conflict outcomes are agreement, stronger relationships, and learning.

- *Define* personality conflicts, *and explain how they should be managed.* Personality conflicts involve interpersonal opposition based on personal dislike and/or disagreement (or as an outgrowth of workplace incivility). Care needs to be taken with personality conflicts in the workplace because of the legal implications of diversity, discrimination, and sexual harassment. Managers should investigate and document personality conflicts, take corrective actions such as feedback or behavior modification if appropriate, or attempt informal dispute resolution. Difficult or persistent personality conflicts need to be referred to human resource specialists or counselors.

- *Discuss the role of in-group thinking in intergroup conflict, and explain what can be done to avoid cross-cultural conflict.* Members of in-groups tend to see themselves as unique individuals who are more moral than outsiders, whom they view as a threat and stereotypically as all alike.

In-group thinking is associated with ethnocentric behavior. International consultants can prepare people from different cultures to work effectively together. Cross-cultural conflict can be minimized by having expatriates build strong cross-cultural relationships with their hosts (primarily by being good listeners, being sensitive to others, and being more cooperative than competitive).

- *Explain* programmed conflict, *and identify the five conflict-handing styles.* Functional conflict can be programmed by leaders who encourage discussion and debate without letting personal feelings or politics get in the way. The five conflict-handling styles are integrating (problem solving), obliging (smoothing), dominating (forcing), avoiding, and compromising. There is no single best style.

- *Identify and describe at least four alternative dispute resolution (ADR) techniques.* Alternative dispute resolution (ADR) involves avoiding costly court battles with more informal and user-friendly techniques such as facilitation, conciliation, peer review, ombudsman, mediation, and arbitration.

- *Draw a distinction between distributive and integrative negotiation, and explain the concept of added-value negotiation.* Distributive negotiation involves fixed-pie and win-lose thinking. Integrative negotiation is a win-win approach to better results for both parties. The five steps in added value negotiation are as follows: Step 1, clarify interests; Step 2, identify options; Step 3, design alternative deal packages; Step 4, select a deal; and Step 5, perfect the deal. Elements of value, multiple deals, and creative agreement are central to this approach.

internet exercise

www.pon.harvard.edu

Research Updates on Negotiation

Harvard Law School, in cooperation with other leading universities, hosts the Internet site "Program on Negotiation" (**www.pon.harvard.edu**). Select the heading "Publications" from the main menu. Next, click on "Negotiation Journal," scroll down and click on the hyper-link *"Negotiation Journal* homepage," select "Browse through the Table of Contents," and survey the brief article summaries from recent issues of that quarterly journal. Focus on topics and findings related to managing organizational behavior.

QUESTIONS

1. What new insights did you pick up from the *Negotiation Journal* article summaries? Explain.

2. Do you now have a greater appreciation of the importance and complexity of the field of negotiation? Explain.

3. What do you need to do to become a better negotiator in important aspects of your life (such as relationships, family disagreements, pay raises and promotions, legal disputes, and academic assignments and grades)?

Managing
Organizational
Processes

SOURCE: © PhotoDisc

four
part

Communicating in the Internet Age

Twelve
chapter

After reading the material in this chapter, you should be able to:

- Describe the perceptual process model of communication.

- Demonstrate your familiarity with four antecedents of communication distortion between managers and employees.

- Contrast the communication styles of assertiveness, aggressiveness, and nonassertiveness.

- Discuss the primary sources of nonverbal communication and 10 keys to effective listening.

- Explain the information technology of Internet/Intranet/Extranet, E-mail, videoconferencing, and collaborative computing, and explain the related use of telecommuting.

- Describe the process, personal, physical, and semantic barriers to effective communication.

EFFECTIVE COMMUNICATION INVOLVES STRAIGHTFORWARD CONVERSATION

Organizations that like to start the work day with a horn blast's downbeat aren't unusual. At other workplaces, the official start time comes and goes without fanfare. Then there's PQ Systems.

At 7:55 AM each and every weekday, a simple message sounds off through employees' phone speakers: "Coffee's ready, coffee's ready." All 40 employees head to the company's training room,

Miles away, deep in the heart of Dallas, something similar goes on at Texas Nameplate. The company's biweekly DO-IT meetings—as in "daily operations innovation team"—bring together supervisors and team leaders from all areas of the operation. The sessions have your usual one-way reporting, but there's a level of sharing and helping across functional areas that most companies only

brave participants got people talking and listening like never before. Cy Wentworth is human resources director for the 500-employee agency, and he recalls that breakthrough conversation. "Today there is not the least reluctance to say anything to anyone," he says. "I'm not sure we would have done that prior to that meeting three years ago." . . .

It's hard to imagine anything getting done in an organization without honest-to-goodness conversation. And it's exciting to imagine how much more could get done, and how much better things would be, if genuine dialogue happened every work day. Yet so many "conversations" are more like one-way debates and static-filled discussions.[1]

taking the chairs that form a big circle. By 8 AM, it begins: a simple gathering, lasting anywhere from 10 to 30 minutes, in which people openly talk about everything from financials to new-product development to whose son or daughter just graduated from high school. "It gives us a sense of connectedness," says product manager Soren Gormley.

dream of. . . .

And at the South Carolina Forestry Commission, managers are still talking about their big conversation back in 1997. Fifteen key leaders got together to conduct a self-assessment using leadership excellence criteria. It seemed like a fairly straightforward proposition—until the assessment itself, some skillful facilitators, and a few

FOR DISCUSSION

How are PQ Systems, Texas Nameplate, and the South Carolina Forestry Commission encouraging meaningful communication among employees? For an interpretation on this case and additional comments, visit our website:

www.mhhe.com/kinickiob

MANAGEMENT IS COMMUNICATION. Every managerial function and activity involves some form of direct or indirect communication. Whether planning and organizing or directing and leading, managers find themselves communicating with and through others. Managerial decisions and organizational policies are ineffective unless they are understood by those responsible for enacting them. Consider, for example, the role of communication within Continental Airlines as management transformed the company from near bankruptcy in 1995 to revenue of $7.9 billion in 1997 and to being named as one of *Fortune's* 100 best places to work in 1999:

> The key to Continental's dramatic turnaround, she says [Michelle Meissner, the company's director of human resource development in Houston], has been the leadership of CEO Gordon Bethune and president/COO Greg Brenneman. Their visibility, involvement and commitment to the company's vision makes them credible leaders, Meissner says. Perhaps equally important, they have been able to clearly communicate that vision to their employees. Frequent communication now appears to be the norm at Continental. Says Meissner: "It's the most common thing in the world to see Gordon out at a breakroom in an airport talking about what's going on—and it's common to see Greg out talking with employees. I've run into them both at the airport on a Friday night where they're just stopping by to talk to employees."[2]

Effective communication clearly contributed to Continental's organizational turnaround.

Moreover, effective communication is critical for employee motivation and job satisfaction. For example, a study of 274 students revealed that student motivation was positively related to the quality of student-faculty communication in the instructor's office. Another study involving 65 savings and loan employees and 110 manufacturing employees revealed that employee satisfaction with organizational communication was positively and significantly correlated with job satisfaction and performance.[3]

This chapter will help you better understand how managers can both improve their communication skills and design more effective communication programs. We discuss (1) basic dimensions of the communication process, (2) interpersonal communication, (3) communication in the computerized age, and (4) communication barriers.

Basic Dimensions of the Communication Process

Communication

Interpersonal exchange of information and understanding.

Communication is defined as "the exchange of information between a sender and a receiver, and the inference (perception) of meaning between the individuals involved."[4] Analysis of this exchange reveals that communication is a two-way process consisting of consecutively linked elements (see Figure 12–1). Managers who understand this process can analyze their own communication patterns as well as design communication programs that fit organizational needs. This section reviews a perceptual process model of communication and discusses communication distortion.

A Perceptual Process Model of Communication

As we all know, communicating is not that simple or clear-cut. Communication is fraught with miscommunication. In recognition of this, researchers have begun to examine communication as a form of social information processing (recall the discussion in Chapter 4) in which receivers interpret messages by cognitively processing information.

A Perceptual Model of Communication   **FIGURE 12–1**

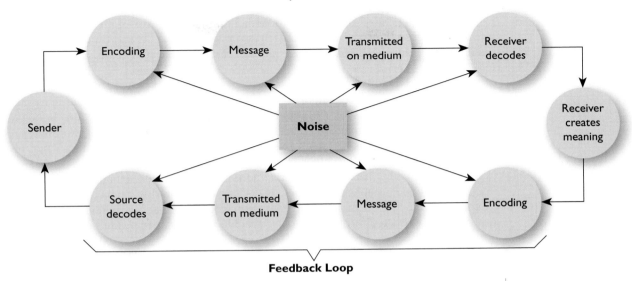

Feedback Loop

This view led to development of a perceptual model of communication that depicts communication as a process in which receivers create meaning in their own minds. Let us briefly examine the elements of the perceptual process model shown in Figure 12–1.

Sender   The sender is an individual, group, or organization that desires or attempts to communicate with a particular receiver. Receivers may be individuals, groups, or organizations.

Encoding   Communication begins when a sender encodes an idea or thought. Encoding translates mental thoughts into a code or language that can be understood by others. Managers typically encode using words, numbers, gestures, nonverbal cues such as facial expressions, or pictures. Moreover, different methods of encoding can be used to portray similar ideas.

The Message   The output of encoding is a message. There are two important points to keep in mind about messages. First, they contain more than meets the eye. Messages may contain hidden agendas as well as trigger affective or emotional reactions. Second, messages need to match the medium used to transmit them. How would you evaluate the match between the message of letting someone know they have been laid off and the communication medium used in the following examples?

> A man finds out he has been let go when a restaurant won't accept his company credit card. A woman manager gets the news via a note placed on her chair during lunch. Employees at a high-tech firm learn of their fate when their security codes no longer open the front door of their office building.[5]

These horrible mismatches reveal how thoughtless managers can be when they do not carefully consider the interplay between a message and the medium used to convey it.

Selecting a Medium   Managers can communicate through a variety of media. Potential media include face-to-face conversations, telephone calls, electronic mail, voice mail, videoconferencing, written memos or letters, photographs or drawings, meetings, bulletin boards, computer output, and charts or graphs. Choosing the appropriate media depends on many factors, including the nature of the message, its intended purpose, the type of audience, proximity to the audience, time horizon for disseminating the message, personal preferences, and the complexity of the problem/situation at hand.

All media have advantages and disadvantages and should be used in different situations. Face-to-face conversations, for example, are useful for communicating about sensitive or important issues that require feedback and intensive interaction. In contrast, telephones are convenient, fast, and private, but lack nonverbal information. Although writing memos or letters is time consuming, it is a good medium when it is difficult to meet with the other person, when formality and a written record are important, and when face-to-face interaction is not necessary to enhance understanding. Electronic communication, which is discussed later in this chapter, can be used to communicate with a large number of dispersed people and is potentially a very fast medium when recipients of messages regularly check their E-mail.[6]

Decoding   Decoding is the receiver's version of encoding. Decoding consists of translating verbal, oral, or visual aspects of a message into a form that can be interpreted. Receivers rely on social information processing to determine the meaning of a message during decoding. Decoding is a key contributor to misunderstanding in interracial and intercultural communication because decoding by the receiver is subject to social values and cultural values that may not be understood by the sender.

Creating Meaning   The perceptual model of communication is based on the belief that a receiver creates the meaning of a message in his or her head. A receiver's interpretation of a message can thus differ from that intended by the sender. In turn, receivers act according to their own interpretations, not the communicator's.

Feedback   The receiver's response to a message is the crux of the feedback loop. At this point in the communication process, the receiver becomes a sender. Specifically, the receiver encodes a response and then transmits it to the original sender. This new message is then decoded and interpreted. As you can see from this discussion, feedback is used as a comprehension check. It gives senders an idea of how accurately their message is understood.

Noise

Interference with the transmission and understanding of a message.

Noise   Noise represents anything that interferes with the transmission and understanding of a message. It affects all linkages of the communication process. Noise includes factors such as a speech impairment, poor telephone connections, illegible handwriting, inaccurate statistics in a memo or report, poor hearing and eyesight, and physical distance between sender and receiver. Managers can improve communication by reducing noise. For example, Chris Schneck, a Merrill Lynch financial consultant, reduces communication noise for hearing-impaired clients by discussing their investments through his typewriter or a sign interpreter.[7]

Communication Distortion between Managers and Employees

Communication distortion

Purposely modifying the content of a message.

Communication distortion occurs when an employee purposely modifies the content of a message, thereby reducing the accuracy of communication between managers and employees. Employees tend to engage in

Sources of Distortion in Upward Communication | **FIGURE 12–2**

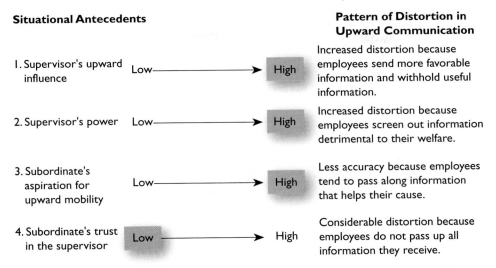

Situational Antecedents		Pattern of Distortion in Upward Communication
1. Supervisor's upward influence	Low ⟶ High	Increased distortion because employees send more favorable information and withhold useful information.
2. Supervisor's power	Low ⟶ High	Increased distortion because employees screen out information detrimental to their welfare.
3. Subordinate's aspiration for upward mobility	Low ⟶ High	Less accuracy because employees tend to pass along information that helps their cause.
4. Subordinate's trust in the supervisor	Low ⟶ High	Considerable distortion because employees do not pass up all information they receive.

SOURCE: Adapted in part from J Fulk and S Mani,"Distortion of Communication in Hierarchical Relationships," in *Communication Yearbook 9,* ed M L McLaughlin (Beverly Hills, CA: Sage Publications, 1986).

this practice because of workplace politics, a desire to manage impressions, or fear of how a manager might respond to a message.[8] Communication experts point out the organizational problems caused by distortion:

> Distortion is an important problem in organizations because modifications to messages cause misdirectives to be transmitted, nondirectives to be issued, incorrect information to be passed on, and a variety of other problems related to both the quantity and quality of information.[9]

Knowledge of the antecedents or causes of communication distortion can help managers avoid or limit these problems.

Studies have identified four situational antecedents of distortion in upward communication (see Figure 12–2). Distortion tends to increase when supervisors have high upward influence and/or power. Employees also tend to modify or distort information when they aspire to move upward and when they do not trust their supervisors.[10] Because managers generally do not want to reduce their upward influence or curb their direct reports' desire for upward mobility, they can reduce distortion in several ways:

1. Managers can deemphasize power differences between themselves and their direct reports.

2. They can enhance trust through a meaningful performance review process that rewards actual performance.

3. Managers can encourage staff feedback by conducting smaller, more informal meetings.

4. They can establish performance goals that encourage employees to focus on problems rather than personalities.

5. Distortion can be limited by encouraging dialogue between those with opposing viewpoints.

Interpersonal Communication

The quality of interpersonal communication within an organization is very important. People with good communication skills helped groups make better decisions and were promoted more frequently than individuals with less developed abilities.[11] With this in mind, the goal of this section is to provide information that can help you improve your interpersonal communication skills. We begin by discussing the communication styles of assertiveness, aggressiveness, and nonassertiveness and then review material pertaining to nonverbal communication and active listening. We conclude this section by highlighting gender differences in communication.

Assertiveness, Aggressiveness, and Nonassertiveness

Assertive style

Expressive and self-enhancing, but does not take advantage of others.

Aggressive style

Expressive and self-enhancing, but takes unfair advantage of others.

Nonassertive style

Timid and self-denying behaviour.

Nonverbal communication

Messages sent outside of the written or spoken word.

The saying, "You can attract more flies with honey than with vinegar," captures the difference between using an assertive communication style and an aggressive style. Research studies indicate that assertiveness is more effective than aggressiveness in both work-related and consumer contexts.[12] An **assertive style** is expressive and self-enhancing and is based on the "ethical notion that it is not right or good to violate our own or others' basic human rights, such as the right to self-expression or the right to be treated with dignity and respect."[13] In contrast, an **aggressive style** is expressive and self-enhancing and strives to take unfair advantage of others. A **nonassertive style** is characterized by timid and self-denying behavior. Nonassertiveness is ineffective because it gives the other person an unfair advantage.

Managers may improve their communication competence by trying to be more assertive and less aggressive or nonassertive. This can be achieved by using the appropriate nonverbal and verbal behaviors listed in Table 12–1. For instance, managers should attempt to use the nonverbal behaviors of good eye contact, a strong, steady, and audible voice, and selective interruptions. They should avoid nonverbal behaviors such as glaring or little eye contact, threatening gestures, slumped posture, and a weak or whiny voice. Appropriate verbal behaviors include direct and unambiguous language and the use of "I" messages instead of "you" statements. For example, when you say, "Mike, I was disappointed with your report because it contained typographical errors," rather than "Mike, your report was poorly done," you reduce defensiveness. "I" statements describe your feelings about someone's performance or behavior instead of laying blame on the person.

Managers with an assertive style tend to be better communicators with their colleagues. In this photo, which person do you think is the manager, and which one is the employee?

Sources of Nonverbal Communication

Nonverbal communication is "Any message, sent or received independent of the written or spoken word . . . [It] includes such factors as use of time and space, distance between persons when conversing, use of color, dress, walking behavior, standing, positioning, seating arrangement, office locations and furnishing."[14]

Communication Styles **TABLE 12–1**

Communication Style	Description	Nonverbal Behavior Pattern	Verbal Behavior Pattern
Assertive	Pushing hard without attacking; permits others to influence outcome; expressive and self-enhancing without intruding on others	Good eye contact Comfortable but firm posture Strong, steady, and audible voice Facial expressions matched to message Appropriately serious tone Selective interruptions to ensure understanding	Direct and unambiguous language No attributions or evaluations of other's behavior Use of "I" statements and cooperative "we" statements
Aggressive	Taking advantage of others; expressive and self-enhancing at other's expense	Glaring eye contact Moving or leaning too close Threatening gestures (pointed finger; clenched fist) Loud voice Frequent interruptions	Swear words and abusive language Attributions and evaluations of other's behavior Sexist or racist terms Explicit threats or put-downs
Nonassertive	Encouraging others to take advantage of us; inhibited; self-denying	Little eye contact Downward glances Slumped posture Constantly shifting weight Wringing hands Weak or whiny voice	Qualifiers ("maybe"; "kind of") Fillers ("uh," "you know," "well") Negaters ("It's not really that important"; "I'm not sure")

SOURCE: Adapted in part from J A Waters, "Managerial Assertiveness," *Business Horizons*, September–October 1982, pp 24–29.

Experts estimate that 65% to 90% of every conversation is partially interpreted through body language.[15] Because of the prevalence of nonverbal communication and its significant effect on organizational behavior (including, but not limited to, perceptions of others, hiring decisions, work attitudes, turnover, and the acceptance of one's ideas in a presentation),[16] it is important that managers become consciously aware of the sources of nonverbal communication.

Body Movements and Gestures Body movements, such as leaning forward or backward, and gestures, such as pointing, provide additional nonverbal information that can either enhance or detract from the communication process. Open body positions such as leaning backward, communicate *immediacy,* a term used to represent openness, warmth, closeness, and availability for communication. *Defensiveness* is communicated by gestures such as folding arms, crossing hands, and crossing one's legs. Although it is both easy and fun to interpret body movements and gestures, it is important to remember that body-language analysis is subjective, easily misinterpreted, and highly dependent on the context and cross-cultural differences.[17] Thus, managers need to be careful when trying to interpret body movements. Inaccurate interpretations can create additional "noise" in the communication process.

In your present employment as general manager, have you ever given someone the evil eye, hexed someone, or voodooed anyone?

SOURCE: Harvard Business Review, April 2001.

Touch   Touching is another powerful nonverbal cue. People tend to touch those they like. A meta-analysis of gender differences in touching indicated that women do more touching during conversations than men.[18] Touching conveys an impression of warmth and caring and can be used to create a personal bond between people. Be careful about touching people from diverse cultures, however, as norms for touching vary significantly around the world.[19]

Facial Expressions   Facial expressions convey a wealth of information. Smiling, for instance, typically represents warmth, happiness, or friendship, whereas frowning conveys dissatisfaction or anger. Do you think these interpretations apply to different cross-cultural groups? A recent summary of relevant research revealed that the association between facial expressions and emotions varies across cultures.[20] A smile, for example, does not convey the same emotion in different countries. Therefore, managers need to be careful in interpreting facial expressions among diverse groups of employees.

Eye Contact   Eye contact is a strong nonverbal cue that varies across cultures. Westerners are taught at an early age to look at their parents when spoken to. In contrast, Asians are taught to avoid eye contact with a parent or superior in order to show obedience and subservience.[21] Once again, managers should be sensitive to different orientations toward maintaining eye contact with diverse employees.

Practical Tips   It is important to have good nonverbal communication skills in light of the fact that they are related to the development of positive interpersonal relationships. Consider, for example, the problems noted by Anne Warfield, a management consultant, as she worked with a manager whose department had bad morale:

> He [the manager] asked his staff what they wanted from him. They requested that he drop by their offices once in a while and also schedule regular meetings with them. The manager did both, but the morale got worse. . . . I found that the man's body language was causing all of the problems. It was domineering. When he

dropped into people's offices, he'd take up the whole doorway or walk up to their desks and look them in the eye—even if they were on the phone! People found his behavior unnerving. It sent the message that their personal space belonged to him. At meetings, the manager would place his hands behind his head, cross his legs, lean back, and look at the ceiling. That body language said that he already had all of the answers.[22]

Ms Warfield helped this manager to improve his employees' morale by pointing out and correcting the messages being sent by his body language. The Skills & Best Practices box offers insights into improving your nonverbal communication skills.

Active Listening

Some communication experts contend that listening is the keystone communication skill for employees involved in sales, customer service, or management. In support of this conclusion, listening effectiveness was positively associated with success in sales and obtaining managerial promotions.[23]

Listening involves much more than hearing a message. Hearing is merely the physical component of listening. **Listening** is the process of *actively* decoding and interpreting verbal messages. Listening requires cognitive attention and information processing; hearing does not. With these distinctions in mind, we examine listening styles and offer some practical advice for becoming a more effective listener.

Listening Styles A pair of communication experts identified three different listening styles. Their research indicated that people prefer to hear information that is suited to their own listening style. People also tend to speak in a style that is consistent with their own listening style. Because inconsistent styles represent a barrier to effective listening, it is important for managers to understand and respond to the different listening styles. The three listening styles are called "results," "reasons," and "process." It is important to note that one style is not necessarily better than the others.[24]

Results-style listeners don't like beating around the bush. They are direct, action oriented, like to ask questions, and are interested in hearing the bottom line of the communication message first. They can be perceived as blunt or rude. **Reasons-style listeners** want to know the rationale for what someone is saying or proposing. They like to weigh and balance information and expect others to present information in a logical manner. In contrast, **process-style listeners** like to discuss issues in detail. They are more people than results oriented and have high concern for relationships, believing that people and relationships are the keys to long-term success. Process-style listeners also like to consider or receive a lot of information when making decisions, and they tend to use indirect language. The use of indirect language can frustrate results-style listeners who prefer direct communications.

Advice to Improve Nonverbal Communication Skills

Positive nonverbal actions include the following:

- Maintain eye contact.
- Nod your head to convey that you are listening or that you agree.
- Smile and show interest.
- Lean forward to show the speaker you are interested.
- Use a tone of voice that matches your message.

Negative nonverbal behaviors include the following:

- Avoiding eye contact and looking away from the speaker.
- Closing your eyes or tensing your facial muscles.
- Excessive yawning.
- Using body language that conveys indecisiveness or lack of confidence (e.g., slumped shoulders, head down, flat tones, inaudible voice).
- Speaking too fast or too slow.

Listening

Actively decoding and interpreting verbal messages.

Results-style listeners

Interested in hearing the bottom line or result of a message.

Reasons-style listeners

Interested in hearing the rationale behind a message.

Process-style listeners

Likes to discuss issues in detail.

Managers can gain greater acceptance of their ideas and proposals by adapting the form and content of a message to fit a receiver's listening style:

1. For a results-style listener, for instance, the sender should present the bottom line at the beginning of the discussion.
2. Explain your rationale to a reasons-style listener.
3. For a process-style listener, describe the process and the benefits.

Becoming a More Effective Listener The Hands-On Exercise contains a listening skills instrument to assess your listening skills. We would like you to complete this survey at this time. How do your listening skills stack up to the norms provided in the exercise? If you desire to enhance your listening skills, you can use the preceding recommendations along with those presented in Table 12–2. Try to avoid the 10 habits of bad listeners while cultivating the 10 good listening habits.

Women and Men Communicate Differently

Women and men have communicated differently since the dawn of time. Gender-based differences in communication are partly caused by linguistic styles commonly used by women and men. Deborah Tannen, a communication expert, defines **linguistic style** as follows:

Linguistic style

A person's typical speaking pattern.

> Linguistic style refers to a person's characteristic speaking pattern. It includes such features as directness or indirectness, pacing and pausing, word choice, and the use of such elements as jokes, figures of speech, stories, questions, and apologies. In other words, linguistic style is a set of culturally learned signals by which we not only communicate what we mean but also interpret others' meaning and evaluate one another as people.[25]

Linguistic style not only helps explain communication differences between women and men, but it also influences our perceptions of others' confidence, competence, and abilities. Increased awareness of linguistic styles can thus improve communication accuracy and your communication competence. This section strives to increase your understanding of interpersonal communication between women and men by discussing alternative explanations for differences in linguistic styles, various communication differences between women and men, and recommendations for improving communication between the sexes.

Communication styles vary by gender.

Why Linguistic Styles Vary between Women and Men Although researchers do not completely agree on the cause of communication differences between women and men, there are two competing explanations that involve the well-worn debate between *nature* and *nurture*. Some researchers believe that interpersonal differences between women and men are due to inherited biological differences between the sexes. More specifically, this perspective, which also is called the "Darwinian perspective" or "evolutionary psychology," attributes gender differences in communication to drives, needs, and conflicts associated with reproductive strategies used by women and men. For example, proponents would say that males

Assessing Your Listening Skills

INSTRUCTIONS   The following statements reflect various habits we use when listening to others. For each statement, indicate the extent to which you agree or disagree with it by selecting one number from the scale provided. Circle your response for each statement. Remember, there are no right or wrong answers. After completing the survey, add up your total score for the 17 items, and record it in the space provided.

Listening Skills Survey

1 = Strongly disagree
2 = Disagree
3 = Neither agree nor disagree
4 = Agree
5 = Strongly agree

1. I daydream or think about other things when listening to others.   1 2 3 4 5

2. I do not mentally summarize the ideas being communicated by a speaker.   1 2 3 4 5

3. I do not use a speaker's body language or tone of voice to help interpret what he or she is saying.   1 2 3 4 5

4. I listen more for facts than overall ideas during classroom lectures.   1 2 3 4 5

5. I tune out dry speakers.   1 2 3 4 5

6. I have a hard time paying attention to boring people.   1 2 3 4 5

7. I can tell whether someone has anything useful to say before he or she finishes communicating a message.   1 2 3 4 5

8. I quit listening to a speaker when I think he or she has nothing interesting to say.   1 2 3 4 5

9. I get emotional or upset when speakers make jokes about issues or things that are important to me.   1 2 3 4 5

10. I get angry or distracted when speakers use offensive words.   1 2 3 4 5

11. I do not expend a lot of energy when listening to others.   1 2 3 4 5

12. I pretend to pay attention to others even when I'm not really listening.   1 2 3 4 5

13. I get distracted when listening to others.   1 2 3 4 5

14. I deny or ignore information and comments that go against my thoughts and feelings.   1 2 3 4 5

15. I do not seek opportunities to challenge my listening skills.   1 2 3 4 5

16. I do not pay attention to the visual aids used during lectures.   1 2 3 4 5

17. I do not take notes on handouts when they are provided.   1 2 3 4 5

Total Score = _____

NORMS

Use the following norms to evaluate your listening skills:

17–34 = Good listening skills
35–53 = Moderately good listening skills
54–85 = Poor listening skills.

How would you evaluate your listening skills?

TABLE 12–2   The Keys to Effective Listening

Keys to Effective Listening	The Bad Listener	The Good Listener
1. Capitalize on thought speed	Tends to daydream	Stays with the speaker, mentally summarizes the speaker, weighs evidence, and listens between the lines
2. Listen for ideas	Listens for facts	Listens for central or overall ideas
3. Find and area of interest	Tunes out dry speakers or subjects	Listens for any useful information
4. Judge content, not delivery	Tunes out dry or monotone speakers	Assesses content by listening to entire message before making judgments
5. Hold your fire	Gets too emotional or worked up by something said by the speaker and enters into an argument	Withholds judgment until comprehension is complete
6. Work at listening	Does not expend energy on listening	Gives the speaker full attention
7. Resist distractions	Is easily distracted	Fights distractions and concentrates on the speaker
8. Hear what is said	Shuts out or denies unfavorable information	Listens to both favorable and unfavorable information
9. Challenge yourself	Resists listening to presentations of difficult subject matter	Treats complex presentations as exercise for the mind
10. Use handouts, overheads, or other visual aids	Does not take notes or pay attention to visual aids	Takes notes as required and uses visual aids to enhance understanding of the presentation

SOURCES: Derived from N Skinner, "Communication Skills," *Selling Power,* July/August 1999, pp 32–34; and G Manning, K Curtis, and S McMillen, *Building the Human Side of Work Community* (Cincinnati, OH: Thomson Executive Press, 1996), pp 127–54.

communicate more aggressively, interrupt others more than women, and hide their emotions because they have an inherent desire to possess features attractive to females in order to compete with other males for purposes of mate selection. Although males are certainly not competing for mate selection during a business meeting, evolutionary psychologists propose that men cannot turn off the biologically based determinants of their behavior.[26]

In contrast, social role theory is based on the idea that females and males learn ways of speaking as children growing up. Research shows that girls learn conversational skills and habits that focus on rapport and relationships, whereas boys learn skills and habits that focus on status and hierarchies. Accordingly, women come to view communication as a network of connections in which conversations are negotiations for closeness. This orientation leads women to seek and give confirmation and support more so than men. Men, on the other hand, see conversations as negotiations in which people try to achieve and maintain the upper hand. It thus is important for males to protect themselves from others' attempts to put them down or push them around. This perspective increases a male's need to maintain independence and avoid failure.[27]

Gender Differences in Communication   Research demonstrates that women and men communicate differently in a number of ways.[28] Women, for example, are more likely to share credit for success, to ask questions for clarification, to tactfully give feedback by mitigating criticism with praise, and to indirectly tell others what to do. In contrast, men are more likely to boast about themselves, to bluntly give feedback, to withhold compliments, and are less likely to ask questions and to admit fault or weaknesses.

There are two important issues to keep in mind about these trends. First, the trends identified cannot be generalized to include all women and men. Some men are less likely to boast about their achievements while some women are less likely to share the credit. The point is that there are always exceptions to the rule. Second, your linguistic style influences perceptions about your confidence, competence, and authority. These judgments may, in turn, affect your future job assignments and subsequent promotability.

Improving Communications between the Sexes Deborah Tannen recommends that everyone needs to become aware of how linguistic styles work and how they influence our perceptions and judgments. She believes that knowledge of linguistic styles helps to ensure that people with valuable insights or ideas get heard. Consider how gender-based linguistic differences affect who gets heard at a meeting:

> Those who are comfortable speaking up in groups, who need little or no silence before raising their hands, or who speak out easily without waiting to be recognized are far more likely to get heard at meetings. Those who refrain from talking until it's clear that the previous speaker is finished, who wait to be recognized, and who are inclined to link their comments to those of others will do fine at a meeting where everyone else is following the same rules but will have a hard time getting heard in a meeting with people whose styles are more like the first pattern. Given the socialization typical of boys and girls, men are more likely to have learned the first style and women the second, making meetings more congenial for men than for women.[29]

Knowledge of these linguistic differences can assist managers in devising methods to ensure that everyone's ideas are heard and given fair credit both in and out of meetings. Furthermore, it is useful to consider the organizational strengths and limitations of your linguistic style. You may want to consider modifying a linguistic characteristic that is a detriment to perceptions of your confidence, competence, and authority. In conclusion, communication between the sexes can be improved by remembering that women and men have different ways of saying the same thing.

Communication in the Computerized Information Age

Organizations are increasingly using information technology as a lever to improve productivity and customer and employee satisfaction. In turn, communication patterns at work are radically changing. Consider how Gregory Summe, chief executive officer at EG&G Inc., is using information technology to stay on top of his job:

> In between downhill runs [at Park City ski resort in Utah], Mr Summe pulled out his tiny cellular phone and his 1.4 ounce Franklin Rex electronic organizer with its 12,000-name contact list, and rang up his bankers at Goldman, Sachs & Co. about a planned purchase of an instruments business by his company, a maker of airport X rays and laboratory instruments based in Wellesley, Massachusetts. With his cell phone and organizer, he can work anywhere and contact anyone."I'm dangerous," he jokes. The 42-year-old Mr Summe exemplifies how the executive's role is changing in the information age. "There's an expectation for CEOs to be much more in

touch with customers, employees, and investors than in the past," he says. "A big part of the reason may be technology." Being more in touch, of course, also can mean being bombarded with more information—more reports, more memos, more data.[30]

The computerized information age is, of course, influencing all employees, not just CEOs such as Gregory Summe. For example, a recent Harris poll revealed that 63% of adults used computers, and 26% used them both at home and at work. Average weekly use of computers was 15 hours, and 6 of them were on the Internet. For people between the ages of 30 and 39, the age range of many supervisors and managers, computer use averaged 21 hours a week, with 9 of them on the Internet.[31] Interestingly, some people use the Internet with such frequency that they become dependent on it. For example, a recent study of 1,300 students at eight colleges revealed that nearly 10% were dependent on the Internet and that their Internet usage affected their academics, ability to meet new people, and sleep patterns.[32] This section explores five key components of information technology that influence communication patterns and management within a computerized workplace: Internet/Intranet/Extranet, electronic mail, videoconferencing, collaborative computing, and telecommuting.

Internet/Intranet/Extranet

The Internet, or more simply "the Net," is more than a computer network. It is a network of computer networks. The **Internet** is a global network of independently operating, but interconnected computers. It links more than 140,000 smaller networks in more than 200 countries. The Internet connects everything from supercomputers, to large mainframes contained in businesses, government, and universities, to the personal computers in our homes and offices. An **Intranet** is nothing more than an organization's private Internet. Intranets also have *firewalls* that block outside Internet users from accessing internal information. This is done to protect the privacy and confidentiality of company documents. More than half of companies with more than 500 employees have corporate Intranets according to Information Data Corporation.[33] In contrast to the internal focus of an Intranet, an **Extranet** is an extended Intranet in that it connects internal employees with selected customers, suppliers, and other strategic partners. Ford Motor Company, for instance, has an Extranet that connects its dealers worldwide. Ford's Extranet was set up to help support the sales and servicing of cars and to enhance customer satisfaction.

Internet

A global network of computer networks.

Intranet

An organization's private internet.

Extranet

Connects internal employees with selected customers, suppliers, and strategic partners.

The primary benefit of the Internet, Intranet, and Extranet is that they can enhance the ability of employees to find, create, manage, and distribute information. The effectiveness of these "nets," however, depends on how organizations set up and manage their Intranet/Extranet and how employees use the acquired information because information by itself cannot solve or do anything; information is knowledge or a thing.[34] For example, communication effectiveness actually can decrease if a corporate Intranet becomes a dumping ground of unorganized information. In this case, employees will find themselves flailing in a sea of information. Cisco Systems, an Internet-networking company located in San Jose, California, is aware of this problem and has instituted policies to manage its Intranet:

> The company has centralized most of its employee-relations functions and some corporate activities at its site—even sensitive information such as computer codes and details of its components and prices. There are about 300 people who are author-

ized to post whatever they want, whether it be departmental mission statements or photos of themselves and their co-workers at some after-work soiree. . . . To help keep overload to a minimum, Cisco spends a lot of time and money organizing the Intranet to make it as efficient and user-friendly as possible. The company has done a number of studies, watching how employees organize words on paper flash cards to help the company figure out how to arrange the data on the Internet. . . . But Cisco has decided to restrict access to some information to certain groups of employees, both for security reasons and to stave off information overload.[35]

To date, no rigorous research studies have been conducted that directly demonstrate productivity increases from using the Internet, Intranet, or Extranet. There are, however, case studies that reveal other organizational benefits. For example, Cisco systems uses the Internet to recruit potential employees: The company has hired 66% of its people and received 81% of its resumes from the Net. This translated into reduced costs because the company was able to employ fewer in-house recruiters as it grew from 2,000 to 8,000 people. Cisco's cost per hire in 1999 was $6,556 versus an industry average of $10,800.[36]

IBM also saved $1 million in costs in 2000 by asking 140,000 employees located in Armonk, New York, to enroll for employee benefits on the company's Intranet: 80% enrolled electronically.[37] General Mills similarly used the Internet to reduce costs:

> It used to be that General Mills Inc. had to send researchers across the country to conduct focus groups or hire marketing companies to poll consumers on a new kind of cereal or yet another variety of Hamburger Helper. Now the Minneapolis food company conducts 60% of its consumer research online, reducing costs by 50%. . . . The company also makes purchases from Transora, an electronic-marketplace consortium. And it shares trucking services through an online network—expecting to shave 7% off shippings costs.[38]

In contrast to these positive case studies, other reports detail stories of people spending hours surfing the Net only to find themselves overwhelmed with information. Using the Internet can be very time consuming because the Internet is an unstructured repository of information that is becoming increasingly slow to access. Only the future will tell whether the Internet is more useful as a marketing/sales tool, a device to conduct personal transactions such as banking or ordering movies, or a management vehicle that enhances employee motivation and productivity.

Electronic Mail

Electronic mail or E-mail uses the Internet/Intranet to send computer-generated text and documents between people. The use of E-mail is on the rise throughout the world. For example, recent surveys reveal that US employees receive somewhere between 20 to 30 E-mail messages per day.[39] Further, a another survey of executives by the administrative staffing firm Office Team showed that 73% of the respondents believed that E-mail would be the leading form of business communication for employees by 2005.[40] E-mail is becoming a major communication medium because of four key benefits:[41]

> **Electronic mail**
>
> Uses the Internet/Intranet to send computer-generated text and documents.

1. E-mail reduces the cost of distributing information to a large number of employees. Consider the cost savings obtained by Craig Aberle, president of MicroBiz, a software developer in Mahwah, New Jersey, after installing E-mail:

About 95% of MicroBiz's $5 million in sales come through resellers across the country. Aberle sent each a letter saying, "We require all dealers to get on E-mail, or we won't give you any leads." He threatened to stop doing business with those who refused to comply, figuring that "if only 50% of them agree to go on E-mail, those are the 50% that are going to be in business next year."

At first there were grumblings, but within a few months all were on-line, either using E-mail software with an Internet link or going through on-line services such as CompuServe and America Online. Since the mandate, MicroBiz's monthly phone bill has dropped from $35,000 to $16,000 because employees now E-mail the resellers instead of calling them with leads. And the dealers have begun E-mailing one another with ideas and referrals.[42]

2. E-mail is a tool for increasing teamwork. It enables employees to quickly send messages to colleagues on the next floor, in another building, or in another country. In support of this benefit, a study of 375 managers indicated they used E-mail for three dominant reasons: (a) to keep others informed, (b) to follow up an earlier communication, and (c) to communicate the same thing to many people.[43]

3. E-mail reduces the costs and time associated with print duplication and paper distribution. Keep in mind, however, that the benefits of cost reduction should not override the effectiveness of electronic publications. Experts recommend that electronic publications should be carefully written in order to maximize communication effectiveness (see Skills & Best Practices).

4. E-mail fosters flexibility. This is particularly true for employees with a portable computer because they can log onto E-mail whenever and wherever they want.

In spite of these positive benefits, there are three key drawbacks to consider. First, sending and receiving E-mail can lead to a lot of wasted time and effort, or it can distract employees from completing critical job duties. For example, a recent national survey of US workers indicated that between 33% and 50% of their E-mail messages were unimportant.[44] Bernard Ebbers, president and chief executive officer of MCI WorldCom Inc., also believes that employees waste a lot of time using E-mail instead of focusing on the important work at hand. "I love for people to use lots of E-mail, because that's good for the telecom business," says Mr Ebbers. "Except for our own employees. In my opinion, it is the biggest deterrent to employee productivity in the company."[45]

Information overload is the second problem associated with the increased use of E-mail. People tend to send more messages to others, and there is a lot of "spamming" going on: sending junk mail, bad jokes, or irrelevant memos (e.g., the "cc" of E-mail). Consider the situation faced by David Canham, vice president of sales and marketing for Pinacor:

"It used to be that the lack of information was a problem," Canham points out. "Today the reverse is true. The amount of information people are being blasted with these days is unbelievable. E-mail is just

SKILLS & BEST PRACTICES

Tips for Writing Electronic Publications

- Think of each article as a personal note to the employees.
- Address the readers as "you."
- Keep stories short and sweet. (*MacWeek* suggests 300 words or less for stories on a website.)
- Write in a concise, conversational tone.
- Use simple words, short sentences and active verbs.
- Break copy into short, readable segments.
- Divide stories with subheads.
- Use bullet points and lists whenever possible.

SOURCE: Excerpted from B Sosnin, "Digital Newsletters 'E-volutionize' Employee Communications," *HRMagazine*, May 2001, p 101.

one example. You come into the office in the morning, and you have 120 messages in your box. And maybe only 10 of them include worthwhile information, but you still have to sift through the whole 120 to get to those 10. . . . To help the company's salespeople with the sifting process, Pinacor developed a Web-based tool that allows reps to pick and choose the information they want to receive. According to Canham, the program was so successful that customers soon began clamoring for a similar tool to address their own struggle with the information glut.[46]

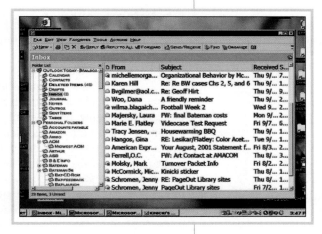

As you can see from this example, organizations should make a concerted effort to manage the problem of information overload associated with the use of E-mail.

Finally, preliminary evidence suggests that people are using electronic mail to communicate when they should be using other media. This practice can result in reduced communication effectiveness. A four-year study of communication patterns within a university demonstrated that the increased use of electronic mail was associated with decreased face-to-face interactions and with a drop in the overall amount of organizational communication. Employees also expressed a feeling of being less connected and less cohesive as a department as the amount of E-mails increased.[47] This interpersonal "disconnection" may be caused by the trend of replacing everyday face-to-face interactions with electronic messages. It is important to remember that employees' social needs are satisfied through the many different interpersonal interactions that occur at work.

There are three additional issues to consider when using E-mail: (1) E-mail only works when the party you desire to communicate with also uses it. E-mail may not be a viable communication medium in all cases. (2) The speed of getting a response to an E-mail message is dependent on how frequently the receiver examines his or her messages. It is important to consider this issue when picking a communication medium. (3) Many companies do not have policies for using E-mail, which can lead to misuse and potential legal liability. For instance, four female employees working at Chevron filed a suit claiming that they were sexually harassed through E-mail. The company settled for $2.2 million, plus legal fees and court costs. Do not assume that your E-mail messages are private and confidential. Organizations are advised to develop policies regarding the use of E-mail.[48]

Videoconferencing

Videoconferencing, also known as teleconferencing, uses video and audio links along with computers to enable people located at different locations to see, hear, and talk with one another. This enables people from many locations to conduct a meeting without having to travel. Videoconferencing thus can significantly reduce an organization's travel expenses. Many organizations set up special videoconferencing rooms or booths with specially equipped television cameras. More recent equipment enables people to attach small cameras and microphones to their desks or computer monitors. This enables employees to conduct long-distance meetings and training classes without leaving their office or cubicle.

Collaborative Computing

Collaborative computing entails using state-of-the-art computer software and hardware to help people work better together. Collaborative systems enable people to share information without the constraints of time and space. This is accomplished by utilizing computer networks to link people across a room or across the globe. Collaborative applications include messaging and E-mail systems, calendar management, videoconferencing, computer teleconferencing, electronic whiteboards, and the type of computer-aided decision-making systems discussed in Chapter 9.

Organizations that use full-fledged collaborative systems have the ability to create virtual teams or to operate as a virtual organization: Virtual organizations are discussed in Chapter 15. You may recall from Chapter 10 that a virtual team represents a physically dispersed task group that conducts its business by using the types of information technology currently being discussed. Specifically, virtual teams tend to use Internet/Intranet systems, collaborative software systems, and videoconferencing systems.[49] These real-time systems enable people to communicate with anyone at anytime.

It is important to keep in mind that modern-day information technology only enables people to interact virtually; it doesn't guarantee effective communications. Interestingly, there are a whole host of unique communication problems associated with using the information technology needed to operate virtually.[50]

Telecommuting

Telecommuting involves doing work that is generally performed in the office away from the office using a variety of information technologies. Employees typically receive and send work from home via phone and fax or by using a modem to link a home computer to an office computer. Telecommuting is more common for jobs that involve computer work, writing, and phone or brain work that requires concentration and limited interruptions. The US Department of Labor estimates that between 13 and 19 million full- and part-time workers telecommute in the United States, and experts predict that more than 137 million workers around the world will be involved in some type of remote work by 2003.[51] Proposed benefits of telecommuting include the following:

1. *Reduction of capital costs.* AT&T and IBM reported lower costs by letting employees work at home.

2. *Increased flexibility and autonomy for workers.*

3. *Competitive edge in recruitment.* Arthur Anderson, Merrill Lynch, and Cisco used telecommuting to increase their ability to keep and attract qualified personnel.

4. *Increased job satisfaction and lower turnover.* Employees like telecommuting because it helps resolve work-family conflicts. Merrill Lynch's turnover fell significantly after it implemented a telework program.

5. *Increased productivity.* Telecommuting resulted in productivity increases of 25% and 35% for FourGen Software and Continental Traffic Services, respectively.

6. *Tapping nontraditional labor pools* (such as prison inmates and homebound disabled persons).[52]

Although telecommuting represents an attempt to accommodate employee needs and desires, it requires adjustments and is not for everybody. Many people thoroughly enjoy the social camaraderie that exists within an office setting. These individuals probably would not like to telecommute. Others lack the self-motivation needed to work at home. Finally, organizations must be careful to implement telecommuting in a nondiscriminatory manner. Organizations can easily and unknowingly violate one of several antidiscrimination laws.[53]

Barriers to Effective Communication

Communication noise is a barrier to effective communication because it interferes with the accurate transmission and reception of a message. Management awareness of these barriers is a good starting point to improve the communication process. There are four key barriers to effective communication: (1) process barriers, (2) personal barriers, (3) physical barriers, and (4) semantic barriers.

Process Barriers

Every element of the perceptual model of communication shown in Figure 12–1 is a potential process barrier. Consider the following examples:

1. *Sender barrier.* A customer gets incorrect information from a customer service agent because he or she was recently hired and lacks experience.

2. *Encoding barrier.* An employee for whom English is a second language has difficulty explaining why a delivery was late.

3. *Message barrier.* An employee misses a meeting for which he or she never received a confirmation memo.

4. *Medium barrier.* A salesperson gives up trying to make a sales call when the potential customer fails to return three previous phone calls.

5. *Decoding barrier.* An employee does not know how to respond to a manager's request to stop exhibiting "passive aggressive" behavior.

6. *Receiver barrier.* A student who is talking to his or her friend during a lecture asks the professor the same question that was just answered.

7. *Feedback barrier.* The nonverbal head nodding of an interviewer leads an interviewee to think that he or she is doing a great job answering questions.

Barriers in any of these process elements can distort the transfer of meaning. Reducing these barriers is essential but difficult given the current diversity of the workforce.

Personal Barriers

There are many personal barriers to communication. We highlight eight of the more common ones. The first is our *ability to effectively communicate.* As highlighted throughout this chapter, people possess varying levels of communication skills. The *way people process and interpret information* is a second barrier. Chapter 4 highlighted the fact that people use different frames of reference and experiences to interpret the world around them. We also learned that people selectively attend to various stimuli. All told, these differences affect both what we say and what we think we hear. Third, the *level of interpersonal trust between people* can either be a barrier or enabler of effective communication. Communication is more likely to be distorted when people do not trust each other. *Stereotypes and prejudices* are a fourth barrier. They can powerfully distort what we perceive about others. Our *egos* are a fifth barrier. Egos can cause political battles, turf wars, and pursuit of power, credit, and resources. Egos influence how people treat each other as well as our receptiveness to being influenced by others. *Poor listening skills* are a sixth barrier.[54]

Carl Rogers, a renowned psychologist, identified the seventh and eighth barriers that interfere with interpersonal communication.[55] The seventh barrier is a *natural tendency to evaluate or judge a sender's message*. To highlight the natural tendency to evaluate, consider how you might respond to the statement "I like the book you are reading." What would you say? Your likely response is to approve or disapprove the statement. You may say, "I agree," or alternatively, "I disagree, the book is boring." The point is that we all tend to evaluate messages from our own point of view or frame of reference. The tendency to evaluate messages is greatest when one has strong feelings or emotions about the issue being discussed. An *inability to listen with understanding* is the eighth personal barrier to effective communication. Listening with understanding occurs when a receiver can "see the expressed idea and attitude from the other person's point of view, to sense how it feels to him, to achieve his frame of reference in regard to the thing he is talking about."[56] Listening with understanding reduces defensiveness and improves accuracy in perceiving a message.

Physical Barriers

The distance between employees can interfere with effective communication. It is hard to understand someone who is speaking to you from 20 yards away. Time zone differences between the East and West Coasts also represent physical barriers. Work and office noise are additional barriers. The quality of telephone lines or crashed computers represent physical barriers that impact our ability to communicate with information technology.

In spite of the general acceptance of physical barriers, they can be reduced. For example, employees on the East Coast can agree to call their West Coast peers prior to leaving for lunch. Distracting or inhibiting walls also can be torn down. It is important that managers attempt to manage this barrier by choosing a medium that optimally reduces the physical barrier at hand.

Semantic Barriers

Semantics is the study of words. Semantic barriers show up as encoding and decoding errors because these phases of communication involve transmitting and receiving words and symbols. These barriers occur very easily. Consider the following statement: Crime is ubiquitous.

Do you understand this message? Even if you do, would it not be simpler to say that "crime is all around us" or "crime is everywhere"? Choosing our words more carefully is the easiest way to reduce semantic barriers. This barrier can also be decreased by attentiveness to mixed messages and cultural diversity. Mixed messages occur when a person's words imply one message while his or her actions or nonverbal cues suggest something different. Obviously, understanding is enhanced when a person's actions and nonverbal cues match the verbal message.

chapter summary

- *Describe the perceptual process model of communication.* Communication is a process of consecutively linked elements. This model of communication depicts receivers as information processors who create the meaning of messages in their own mind. Because receivers' interpretations of messages often differ from those intended by senders, miscommunication is a common occurrence.

- *Demonstrate your familiarity with four antecedents of communication distortion between managers and employees.* Communication distortion is a common problem that consists of modifying the content of a message. Employees distort upward communication when their supervisor has high upward influence and/or power. Distortion also increases when employees aspire to move upward and when they do not trust their supervisor.

- *Contrast the communication styles of assertiveness, aggressiveness, and nonassertiveness.* An assertive style is expressive and self-enhancing but does not violate others' basic human rights. In contrast, an aggressive style is expressive and self-enhancing but takes unfair advantage of others. A nonassertive style is characterized by timid and self-denying behavior. An assertive communication style is more effective than either an aggressive or nonassertive style.

- *Discuss the primary sources of nonverbal communication and 10 keys to effective listening.* There are several identifiable sources of nonverbal communication effectiveness. Body movements and gestures, touch, facial expressions, and eye contact are important nonverbal cues. The interpretation of these nonverbal cues significantly varies across cultures. Good listeners use the following 10 listening habits: (a) capitalize on thought speed by staying with the speaker and listening between the lines, (b) listen for ideas rather than facts, (c) identify areas of interest between the speaker and listener, (d) judge content and not delivery, (e) do not judge until the speaker has completed his or her message, (f) put energy and effort into listening, (g) resist distractions, (h) listen to both favorable and unfavorable information, (i) read or listen to complex material to exercise the mind, and (j) take notes when necessary and use visual aids to enhance understanding.

- *Explain the information technology of Internet/Intranet/Extranet, E-mail, videoconferencing, and collaborative computing, and explain the related use of telecommuting.* The Internet is a global network of computer networks. An Intranet is an organization's private Internet. It contains a firewall that blocks outside Internet users from accessing private internal information. An Extranet connects an organization's internal employees with selected customers, suppliers, and strategic partners. The primary benefit of these "nets" is that they can enhance the ability of employees to find, create, manage, and distribute information. E-mail uses the Internet/Intranet/Extranet to send computer-generated text and documents between people. Videoconferencing uses video and audio links along with computers to enable people located at different locations to see, hear, and talk with one another. Collaborative computing entails using state-of-the-art computer software and hardware to help people work better together. Information is shared across time and space by linking people with computer networks. Telecommuting involves doing work that is generally performed in the office away from the office using a variety of information technologies.

- *Describe the process, personal, physical, and semantic barriers to effective communication.* Every element of the perceptual model of communication is a potential process barrier. There are eight personal barriers that commonly influence communication: (a) the ability to effectively communicate, (b) the way people process and interpret information, (c) the level of interpersonal trust between people, (d) the existence of stereotypes and prejudices, (e) the egos of the people communicating, (f) the ability to listen, (g) the natural tendency to evaluate or judge a sender's message, and (h) the inability to listen with understanding. Physical barriers pertain to distance, physical objects, time, and work and office noise. Semantic barriers show up as encoding and decoding errors because these phases of communication involve transmitting and receiving words and symbols. Cultural diversity is a key contributor to semantic barriers.

internet exercise

As covered in this chapter, communication styles vary from nonassertive to aggressive. We recommended that you strive to use an assertive style while avoiding the tendencies of being nonassertive or aggressive. In trying to be assertive, however, keep in mind that too much of a good thing is bad. That is, the use of an assertive style can transform to an aggressive one if it is taken too far.

A Free Self-Assessment Questionnaire for Assertiveness

The purpose of this exercise is to provide you with feedback on the extent to which you use an assertive communication style. Go to the Internet home page for Body-Mind Queen-Dom (**www.queendom.com**), and select the tests and profiles icon. (Note: Our use of this questionnaire is for instructional purposes only and does not constitute an endorsement of any products that may or may not suit your needs. There is no obligation to buy anything.) At the tests and profiles page, select the career icon. Now select the "Assertiveness Test," and then read the instructions, complete all 32 items, and click on the "score" button for automatic scoring. Read the interpretation of your results.

QUESTIONS

1. Possible scores on the self-assessment questionnaire range from 0 to 100. How did you score? Are you surprised by the results? Do you agree with the interpretation of your score?

2. Reviewing the questionnaire item by item, can you find aspects of communication in which you are either nonassertive or possibly too assertive? Do you think that your communication style can be improved by making adjustments within these areas of communication?

Influence, Power, and Politics: An Organizational Survival Kit

LEARNING OBJECTIVES

After reading the material in this chapter, you should be able to:

- Name five "soft" and four "hard" influence tactics, and summarize the practical lessons from influence research.

- Identify and briefly describe French and Raven's five bases of power.

- Define the term *empowerment,* and explain how to make it succeed.

- Define *organizational politics,* explain what triggers it, and specify the three levels of political action in organizations.

- Distinguish between favorable and unfavorable impression management tactics.

- Explain how to manage organizational politics.

JAMMED UP AT XEROX

One morning . . . [in 2000], G Richard Thoman arrived for work to find an urgent summons from Paul A Allaire, the man he had replaced as chief executive of Xerox Corp. just 13 months earlier. Allaire, who had remained as chairman, was waiting next door in his office at Xerox headquarters. A man of few words even on happy occasions, Allaire delivered the bad news without preamble. He said that Thoman's colleagues had lost confidence in him and that the next afternoon the board would announce his resignation. In other words, Thoman, who had left IBM in 1997 to join Xerox as heir apparent to Allaire, would be out of a job in about 30 hours.

Thoman was livid, but obligingly fell on the sword Allaire handed him. Late the next day, after the board had announced Allaire's reinstatement as CEO, Thoman sat alone in a Xerox conference room and fielded calls from the press. "The board and I agreed that it made more sense to implement our strategy with an internal team," he told one caller. Actually, he could only guess at what his fellow directors wanted. Thoman had not

been invited to the board meeting or even asked to defend himself by speakerphone. He had been fired in absentia, the bizarre but perhaps inevitable outcome of a CEO succession that had begun so promisingly yet ended in utter disaster for Allaire and Xerox no less than for

Rick Thoman. . . .

In the end, though, each would blame the other for screwing up the implementation of the strategic plan they developed together.

Thoman contends that he never had the authority he needed to be an effective leader because Xerox's board, dominated by Allaire, denied him the crucial prerogative of assembling a full management team of his own. . . . However, Allaire

insists that he did nothing to impair Thoman's authority. "There can only be one CEO, and I respected that," he says, adding that Thoman erred in forcing a pace of change on Xerox that it simply could not withstand. "The problem Rick had was he did not connect well enough with people to get a good feel of what was going on in the organization and what was and wasn't possible." . . .

The irony, no doubt a bitter one for all concerned, is that Allaire yearned to leave Xerox behind and take full retirement. But duty—and his board—would not let him. "Even before the transition, Paul thought he should step aside and be on his way," says Nicholas J Nicholas Jr, a former CEO of Time-Warner Inc. and a longtime Xerox director. "But a number of people on the board wanted him to stay [as chairman] because Rick was an outsider. The thinking was, 'We like what we see so far with Rick, but we'd like you to be here, just in case.' "[1]

Was Thoman "set up" to fail or did he make the wrong moves? Explain. For an interpretation of this case and additional comments, visit our website:

www.mhhe.com/kinickiob

FOR DISCUSSION

IN A PERFECT WORLD, individual and collective interests would be closely aligned and everyone would move forward as one. Instead, we typically find a rather messy situation in which self-interests often override the collective mission. Personal hidden agendas are pursued, political coalitions are formed, false impressions are made, and people end up working at cross purposes. Managers need to be able to guide diverse individuals, who are often powerfully motivated to put their own self-interests first, to pursue common objectives. At stake in this tug-of-war between individual and collective interests is no less than the ultimate survival of the organization.

The purpose of this chapter is to give you a survival kit for the rough-and-tumble side of organizational life. We do so by exploring the interrelated topics of organizational influence, social power, employee empowerment, organizational politics, and impression management.

Influencing Others

How do you get others to carry out your wishes? Do you simply tell them what to do? Or do you prefer a less direct approach, such as promising to return the favor? Whatever approach you use, the crux of the issue is *social influence*. A large measure of interpersonal interaction involves attempts to influence others, including parents, bosses, co-workers, spouses, teachers, friends, and children.

Let's start sharpening your influence skills with a familiarity of the following research insights.

Nine Generic Influence Tactics

A particularly fruitful stream of research, initiated by David Kipnis and his colleagues in 1980, reveals how people influence each other in organizations. The Kipnis methodology involved asking employees how they managed to get either their bosses, co-workers, or subordinates to do what they wanted them to do.[2] Statistical refinements and replications by other researchers over a 13-year period eventually yielded nine influence tactics. The nine tactics, ranked in diminishing order of use in the workplace are as follows:

1. *Rational persuasion.* Trying to convince someone with reason, logic, or facts.
2. *Inspirational appeals.* Trying to build enthusiasm by appealing to others' emotions, ideals, or values.
3. *Consultation.* Getting others to participate in planning, making decisions, and changes.
4. *Ingratiation.* Getting someone in a good mood prior to making a request; being friendly, helpful, and using praise or flattery.
5. *Personal appeals.* Referring to friendship and loyalty when making a request.
6. *Exchange.* Making express or implied promises and trading favors.
7. *Coalition tactics.* Getting others to support your effort to persuade someone.
8. *Pressure.* Demanding compliance or using intimidation or threats.
9. *Legitimating tactics.* Basing a request on one's authority or right, organizational rules or policies, or express or implied support from superiors.[3]

These approaches can be considered *generic* influence tactics because they characterize social influence in all directions. Researchers have found this ranking to be fairly consistent regardless of whether the direction of influence is downward, upward, or lateral.[4]

Some call the first five influence tactics—rational persuasion, inspirational appeals, consultation, ingratiation, and personal appeals—"soft" tactics because they are friendlier and not as coercive as the last four tactics. Exchange, coalition, pressure, and legitimating tactics accordingly are called "hard" tactics because they involve more overt pressure.

Three Influence Outcomes

Put yourself in this familiar situation. It's Wednesday and a big project you've been working on for your project team is due Friday. You're behind on the preparation of your computer graphics for your final report and presentation. You catch a friend who is great at computer graphics as they head out of the office at quitting time. You try this *exchange tactic* to get your friend to help you out: "I'm way behind. I need your help. If you could come back in for two to three hours tonight and help me with these graphics, I'll complete those spreadsheets you've been complaining about." According to researchers, your friend will engage in one of three possible influence outcomes:

1. *Commitment.* Your friend enthusiastically agrees and will demonstrate initiative and persistence while completing the assignment.
2. *Compliance.* Your friend grudgingly complies and will need prodding to satisfy minimum requirements.
3. *Resistance.* Your friend will say no, make excuses, stall, or put up an argument.[5]

The best outcome is commitment because the target person's intrinsic motivation will energize good performance. However, managers often have to settle for compliance in today's hectic workplace. Resistance means a failed influence attempt.

Practical Research Insights

Laboratory and field studies have taught us useful lessons about the relative effectiveness of influence tactics along with other instructive insights:

• Commitment is more likely when people rely on consultation, strong rational persuasion, and inspirational appeals and *do not* rely on pressure and coalition tactics.[6] Interestingly, in one study, managers were not very effective at *downward* influence. They relied most heavily on inspiration (an effective tactic), ingratiation (a moderately effective tactic), and pressure (an ineffective tactic).[7]

• A 1996 meta-analysis of 69 studies suggests ingratiation (making the boss feel good) can slightly improve your performance appraisal results and make your boss like you significantly more.[8]

• Commitment is more likely when the influence attempt involves something *important* and *enjoyable* and is based on a *friendly* relationship.[9]

• In a recent survey, 214 employed MBA students (55% female) tended to perceive their superiors' "soft" influence tactics as fair and "hard" influence tactics as unfair. *Unfair* influence tactics were associated with greater *resistance* among employees.[10]

How to Turn Your Co-Workers into Strategic Allies

1. *Mutual respect.* Assume they are competent and smart.

2. *Openness.* Talk straight to them. It isn't possible for any one person to know everything, so give them the information they need to know to help you better.

3. *Trust.* Assume that no one will take any action that is purposely intended to hurt another, so hold back no information that the other could use, even if it doesn't help your immediate position.

4. *Mutual benefit.* Plan every strategy so that both parties win. If that doesn't happen over time, the alliance will break up. When dissolving a partnership becomes necessary as a last resort, try to do it in a clean way that minimizes residual anger. Some day, you may want a new alliance with that person.

SOURCE: Excerpted from A R Cohen and D L Bradford, *Influence without Authority* (New York: John Wiley & Sons, 1990), pp 23–24.

Strategic Alliances and Reciprocity

In their book, *Influence without Authority,* Allan R Cohen and David L Bradford extended the concept of corporate strategic alliances to interpersonal influence.[11] Hardly a day goes by without another mention in the business press of a new strategic alliance between two global companies intent on staying competitive. These win-win relationships are based on complementary strengths. According to Cohen and Bradford, managers need to follow suit by forming some strategic alliances of their own with anyone who has a stake in their area. This is particularly true given today's rapid change, crossfunctional work teams, and diminished reliance on traditional authority structures.

While admitting the task is not an easy one, Cohen and Bradford recommend the tips in Skills & Best Practices for dealing with potential allies: True, these tactics involve taking some personal risks. But the effectiveness of interpersonal strategic alliances is anchored to the concept of reciprocity. "**Reciprocity** is the almost universal belief that people should be paid back for what they do—that one good (or bad) turn deserves another."[12] In short, people tend to get what they give when attempting to influence others.

By demonstrating the rich texture of social influence, the foregoing research evidence and practical advice whet our appetite for learning more about how today's managers can and do reconcile individual and organizational interests. Let us focus on social power.

Social Power and Empowerment

The term *power* evokes mixed and often passionate reactions. To skeptics, Lord Acton's time-honored declaration that "power corrupts and absolute power corrupts absolutely" is truer than ever. However, OB specialists remind us that, like it or not, power is a fact of life in modern organizations. According to one management writer:

> Power must be used because managers must influence those they depend on. Power also is crucial in the development of managers' self-confidence and willingness to support subordinates. From this perspective, power should be accepted as a natural part of any organization. Managers should recognize and develop their own power to coordinate and support the work of subordinates; it is powerlessness, not power, that undermines organizational effectiveness.[13]

Reciprocity

Widespread belief that people should be paid back for their positive and negative acts.

Social power

Ability to get things done with human, informational, and material resources.

Thus, power is a necessary and generally positive force in organizations.[14] As the term is used here, **social power** is defined as "the ability to marshal the human, informational, and material resources to get something done."[15]

Importantly, the exercise of social power in organizations is not necessarily a downward proposition. Employees can and do exercise power upward and laterally. An example of an upward power play occurred at Alberto-

Culver Company, the personal care products firm. Leonard Lavin, founder of the company, was under pressure to revitalize the firm because key employees were departing for more innovative competitors such as Procter & Gamble. Lavin's daughter Carol Bernick, and her husband Howard, both long-time employees, took things into their own hands. As *Business Week* reported:

> Even the Bernicks were thinking of jumping ship. Instead, in September 1994, they marched into Lavin's office and presented him with an ultimatum: Either hand over the reins as CEO or run the company without them. It was a huge blow for Lavin, forcing him to face selling his company to outsiders or ceding control to the younger generation. Unwilling to sell, he reluctantly stepped down, though he remains chairman.
>
> How does it feel to push aside your own father and wrest operating control of the company he created? "It isn't an easy thing to do with the founder of any company, whether he's your father or not," says Carol Bernick, 46, now vice-chairman and president of Alberto-Culver North America.[16]

How could this man (retired CEO of G.E. Jack Welch) of short stature with a high voice become one of the most powerful men in business? As this high-five from the boss indicates, Welch knows how to wield power for the greater good.

Howard Bernick became CEO, the firm's top-down management style was scrapped in favor of a more open culture, and Lavin reportedly is happy with how things have turned out.

Five Bases of Power

A popular classification scheme for social power traces back to the landmark work of John French and Bertram Raven. They proposed that power arises from five different bases: reward power, coercive power, legitimate power, expert power, and referent power.[17] Each involves a different approach to influencing others. Each has advantages and drawbacks.

Reward Power   Managers have **reward power** if they can obtain compliance by promising or granting rewards. Pay-for-performance plans and positive reinforcement programs attempt to exploit reward power.

Coercive Power   Threats of punishment and actual punishment give an individual **coercive power.** A marketing manager who threatens to fire any salesperson who uses a company car for recreational purposes is relying on coercive power.

Legitimate Power   This base of power is anchored to one's formal position or authority. Thus, managers who obtain compliance primarily because of their formal authority to make decisions have **legitimate power.** Legitimate power may be expressed either positively or negatively. Positive legitimate power focuses constructively on job performance. Negative legitimate power tends to be threatening and demeaning to those being influenced. Its main purpose is to build the power holder's ego.

Expert Power   Valued knowledge or information gives an individual **expert power** over those who need such knowledge or information. The power of supervisors is enhanced because they know about work assignments and schedules before

Reward power

Obtaining compliance with promised or actual rewards.

Coercive power

Obtaining compliance through threatened or actual punishment.

Legitimate power

Obtaining compliance through formal authority.

Expert power

Obtaining compliance through one's knowledge or information.

How Much Power Do You Have?

INSTRUCTIONS Score your various bases of power for your current (or former) job, using the following scale:

1 = Strongly disagree   4 = Agree
2 = Disagree   5 = Strongly agree
3 = Slightly agree

Reward Power Score = _____

1. I can reward persons at lower levels. _____

2. My review actions affect the rewards gained at lower levels. _____

3. Based on my decisions, lower level personnel may receive a bonus. _____

Coercive Power Score = _____

1. I can punish employees at lower levels. _____

2. My work is a check on lower level employees. _____

3. My diligence reduces error. _____

Legitimate Power Score = _____

1. My position gives me a great deal of authority. _____

2. The decisions made at my level are of critical importance. _____

3. Employees look to me for guidance. _____

Expert Power Score = _____

1. I am an expert in this job. _____

2. My ability gives me an advantage in this job. _____

3. Given some time, I could improve the methods used on this job. _____

Referent Power Score = _____

1. I attempt to set a good example for other employees. _____

2. My personality allows me to work well in this job. _____

3. My fellow employees look to me as their informal leader. _____

Arbitrary norms for each of the five bases of power are: 3–6 = Weak power base; 7–11 = Moderate power base; 12–15 = Strong power base.

SOURCE: Adapted and excerpted in part from D L Dieterly and B Schneider, "The Effect of Organizational Environment on Perceived Power and Climate: A Laboratory Study." *Organizational Behavior and Human Performance*, June, 1974, pp 316–37.

their employees do. Skillful use of expert power played a key role in the effectiveness of team leaders in a study of three physician medical diagnosis teams.[18] Knowledge *is* power in today's high-tech workplaces.

Referent Power Also called charisma, **referent power** comes into play when one's personality becomes the reason for compliance. Role models have referent power over those who identify closely with them.[19]

To further your understanding of these five bases of power, take a moment to complete the questionnaire in the Hands-On Exercise. What is your power profile? Where do you need improvement?

Referent power

Obtaining compliance through charisma or personal attraction.

Practical Lessons from Research

Researchers have identified the following relationships between power bases and work outcomes such as job performance, job satisfaction, and turnover:

- Expert and referent power had a generally positive effect.
- Reward and legitimate power had a slightly positive effect.
- Coercive power had a slightly negative effect.[20]

A follow-up study involving 251 employed business seniors looked at the relationship between influence styles and bases of power. This was a bottom-up study. In other words, employee perceptions of managerial influence and power were examined. Rational persuasion was found to be a highly acceptable managerial influence tactic. Why? Because employees perceived it to be associated with the three bases of power they viewed positively: legitimate, expert, and referent.[21]

In summary, expert and referent power appear to get the best *combination* of results and favorable reactions from lower-level employees.[22]

Employee Empowerment

An exciting trend in today's organizations centers on giving employees a greater say in the workplace. This trend wears various labels, including "participative management" and "open-book management."[23] Regardless of the label one prefers, it is all about empowerment. One management writer defines **empowerment** in terms of serving the customer:

> Empowerment quite simply means granting supervisors or workers permission to give the customer priority over other issues in the operation. In practical terms, it relates to the resources, skill, time and support to become leaders rather than controllers or mindless robots.[24]

Empowerment

Sharing varying degrees of power with lower-level employees to better serve the customer.

Cooking Up Empowerment at Campbell's Soup

When Ron Ferner first joined Campbell's Soup, in the 1960s, none of the company's executives believed in sharing any kind of information with anybody. By the time he retired, in 1996, Ferner and his colleagues had started sharing everything—goals, financials, product news—with employees.

"At first I was very skeptical about sharing information with employees, but now I'm a believer. I saw the power of the thing. But we always drew the line at salaries. And if we had a supersecret project that we were not sure we would actually launch, we may not have told. But everything else was fair game. Even with the hourly employees that ran the filling machines, putting soup in the cans, we shared the financials.

"At one point Campbell's had a philosophy of meeting with all employees every quarter. I had 1,800 people in my plant. It took three days to hold the meetings. It was quite a chore, but worth it. The employees got very comfortable. It was a real change from the old days, when we would stand behind a post and peek out to watch them work.

"That approach doesn't work overnight. If you don't talk to employees for 10 years and then show up and say that today we start talking, you'll be really disappointed. You have to pick where to draw the line very carefully. You're building trust and don't want to backtrack. It took us years to talk to employees and make them comfortable. Once they were, we started getting their ideas and finding out what the real problems were. A lot of things amazed us.

"One time a packaging team in Sacramento was having problems with boxes breaking. Some of us managers started talking to them about what the problems were and realized they really had a good handle on what was wrong. So we said 'Why don't you guys call the supplier?' Then we called the supplier to tell them they would be hearing from our crew, and they said, 'Why not have them talk directly to our hourly employees?'

"If the managers alone had tried to solve this problem, it would have gone on forever. Instead, we rented a van, sent our people over, and solved the whole thing. Afterward, we had a party. It gave the workers great confidence. That never would have happened in the days when Campbell's had a policy of not telling anybody anything that wasn't written down for them."

SOURCE: T Singer, "Share It All with Employees, Soup to Nuts," *Inc.*, Tech 1999, no. 1, p 48, www.campbellsoup.com.

Steve Kerr, the chief learning officer at General Electric, a pioneer in employee empowerment, explains: "We say empowerment is moving decision making down to the lowest level *where a competent decision can be made*."[25] Of course, it is naive and counterproductive to hand power over to unwilling and/or unprepared employees.

The concept of empowerment requires some adjustment in traditional thinking. First and foremost, power is *not* a zero-sum situation where one person's gain is another's loss. Social power is unlimited. This requires win-win thinking. Frances Hesselbein, the woman credited with modernizing the Girl Scouts of the USA, put it this way: "The more power you give away, the more you have."[26] Authoritarian managers who view employee empowerment as a threat to their personal power are missing the point because of their win-lose thinking.[27] Managers at Campbell's Soup, as illustrated in Skills & Best Practices, have learned to appreciate the wisdom of empowerment.

Making Empowerment Work

We believe empowerment has good promise if managers go about it properly. Empowerment is a sweeping concept with many different definitions. Consequently, researchers use inconsistent measurements, and cause-effect relationships are fuzzy. Managers committed to the idea of employee empowerment need to follow the path of continuous improvement, learning from their successes and failures. Eight years of research with 10 "empowered" companies led consultant W Alan Randolph to formulate the three-pronged empowerment plan in Figure 13–1. Notice how open-book management and active information sharing are needed to build the necessary foundation of trust. Beyond that, clear goals and lots of relevant training are needed. While noting that the empowerment process can take several years to unfold, Randolph offered this perspective:

> While the keys to empowerment may be easy to understand, they are hard to implement. It takes tremendous courage to start sharing sensitive information. It takes true strength to build more structure just at the point when people want more freedom of action. It takes real growth to allow teams to take over the management decision-making process. And above all, it takes perseverance to complete the empowerment process.[28]

Randolph's Empowerment Model   **FIGURE 13–1**

The Empowerment Plan

Share Information
- Share company performance information.
- Help people understand the business.
- Build trust through sharing sensitive information.
- Create self-monitoring possibilities.

Create Autonomy through Structure	**Let Teams Become the Hierarchy**
• Create a clear vision and clarify the little pictures. • Create new decision-making rules that support empowerment. • Clarify goals and roles collaboratively. • Establish new empowering performance management processes. • Use heavy doses of training.	• Provide direction and training for new skills. • Provide encouragement and support for change. • Gradually have managers let go of control. • Work through the leadership vacuum stage. • Acknowledge the fear factor.

Remember: Empowerment is not magic;
it consists of a few simple steps and a lot of persistence.

SOURCE: "Navigating the Journey to Empowerment," by W Alan Randolph. Reprinted from *Organizational Dynamics*, Spring 1995. © 1995 American Management Association International. Reprinted by permission of the American Management Association International, New York, NY. All rights reserved. http://www.amanet.org

Organizational Politics and Impression Management

Most students of OB find the study of organizational politics intriguing. Perhaps this topic owes its appeal to the antics of Hollywood's corporate villains who get their way by stepping on anyone and everyone. As we will see, however, organizational politics includes, but is not limited to, dirty dealing. Organizational politics is an ever-present and sometimes annoying feature of modern work life. "According to 150 executives from large US companies, office politics wastes an average of 20% of their time; that's 10 weeks a year."[29] On the other hand, organizational politics is often a positive force in modern work organizations. Skillful and well-timed politics can help you get your point across, neutralize resistance to a key project, or get a choice job assignment.[30]

We explore this important and interesting area by (1) defining the term *organizational politics*, (2) identifying three levels of political action, (3) discussing eight specific political tactics, (4) considering a related area called *impression management*, and (5) discussing how to curb organizational politics.

Definition and Domain of Organizational Politics

"**Organizational politics** involves intentional acts of influence to enhance or protect the self-interest of individuals or groups."[31] An emphasis on *self-interest* distinguishes this form of social influence. Managers are endlessly challenged to achieve a workable balance between employees' self-interests and organizational interests, as discussed at the beginning of

Organizational politics

Intentional enhancement of self-interest.

this chapter. When a proper balance exists, the pursuit of self-interest may serve the organization's interests. Political behavior becomes a negative force when self-interests erode or defeat organizational interests. For example, researchers have documented the political tactic of filtering and distorting information flowing up to the boss. This self-serving practice put the reporting employees in the best possible light.[32]

Political Behavior Triggered by Uncertainty Political maneuvering is triggered primarily by *uncertainty*. Five common sources of uncertainty within organizations are

1. Unclear objectives.
2. Vague performance measures.
3. Ill-defined decision processes.
4. Strong individual or group competition.[33]
5. Any type of change.

Regarding this last source of uncertainty, organization development specialist Anthony Raia noted, "Whatever we attempt to change, the political subsystem becomes active. Vested interests are almost always at stake and the distribution of power is challenged."[34]

Thus, we would expect a field sales representative, striving to achieve an assigned quota, to be less political than a management trainee working on a variety of projects. While some management trainees stake their career success on hard work, competence, and a bit of luck, many do not. These people attempt to gain a competitive edge through some combination of the political tactics discussed below. Meanwhile, the salesperson's performance is measured in actual sales, not in terms of being friends with the boss or taking credit for others' work. Thus, the management trainee would tend to be more political than the field salesperson because of greater uncertainty about management's expectations.

Because employees generally experience greater uncertainty during the earlier stages of their careers, are junior employees more political than more senior ones? The answer is yes, according to a survey of 243 employed adults in upstate New York. In fact, one senior employee nearing retirement told the researcher: "I used to play political games when I was younger. Now I just do my job."[35]

Three Levels of Political Action Although much political maneuvering occurs at the individual level, it also can involve group or collective action. Figure 13–2 illustrates three different levels of political action: the individual level, the coalition level, and the network level.[36] Each level has its distinguishing characteristics. At the individual level, personal self-interests are pursued by the individual. The political aspects of coalitions and networks are not so obvious, however.

People with a common interest can become a political coalition by fitting the following definition. In an organizational context, a **coalition** is an informal group bound together by the *active* pursuit of a *single* issue. Coalitions may or may not coincide with formal group membership. When the target issue is resolved (a sexually harassing supervisor is fired, for example), the coalition disbands. Experts note that political coalitions have "fuzzy boundaries," meaning they are fluid in membership, flexible in structure, and temporary in duration.[37]

Coalition

Temporary groupings of people who actively pursue a single issue.

Levels of Political Action in Organizations   **FIGURE 13–2**

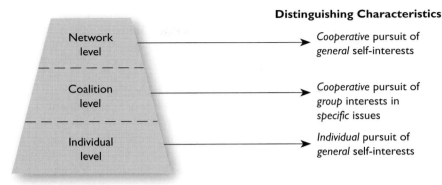

Distinguishing Characteristics

Cooperative pursuit of *general* self-interests

Cooperative pursuit of *group* interests in *specific* issues

Individual pursuit of *general* self-interests

Network level

Coalition level

Individual level

Coalitions are a potent political force in organizations. During the 1990s, coalitions on the corporate boards of American Express, IBM, and General Motors ousted the heads of those giant companies.

A third level of political action involves networks.[38] Unlike coalitions, which pivot on specific issues, networks are loose associations of individuals seeking social support for their general self-interests. Politically, networks are people oriented, while coalitions are issue oriented. Networks have broader and longer term agendas than do coalitions. For instance, Avon's Hispanic employees have built a network to enhance the members' career opportunities.

Eight Political Tactics   Anyone who has worked in an organization has first-hand knowledge of blatant politicking. Blaming someone else for your mistake is an obvious political ploy. But other political tactics are more subtle. Researchers have identified a range of political behavior.

One landmark study, involving in-depth interviews with 87 managers from 30 electronics companies in Southern California, identified eight political tactics. Top-, middle-, and low-level managers were represented about equally in the sample. According to the researchers: "Respondents were asked to describe organizational political tactics and personal characteristics of effective political actors based upon their accumulated experience in *all* organizations in which they had worked."[39] Listed in descending order of occurrence, the eight political tactics that emerged were

1. Attacking or blaming others.
2. Using information as a political tool.
3. Creating a favorable image. (Also known as *impression management*.)[40]
4. Developing a base of support.
5. Praising others (ingratiation).
6. Forming power coalitions with strong allies.
7. Associating with influential people.
8. Creating obligations (reciprocity).

The researchers distinguished between reactive and proactive political tactics. Some of the tactics, such as scapegoating, were *reactive* because the intent was to *defend* one's self-interest. Other tactics, such as developing a base of support, were *proactive* because they sought to *promote* the individual's self-interest.

Impression Management

Impression management

Getting others to see us in a certain manner.

Impression management is defined as "the process by which people attempt to control or manipulate the reactions of others to images of themselves or their ideas."[41] This encompasses how one talks, behaves, and looks. Most impression management attempts are directed at making a *good* impression on relevant others. But, as we will see, some employees strive to make a *bad* impression. For purposes of conceptual clarity, we will focus on *upward* impression management (trying to impress one's immediate supervisor) because it is most relevant for managers. Still, it is good to remember that *anyone* can be the intended target of impression management. Parents, teachers, peers, employees, and customers are all fair game when it comes to managing the impressions of others.

Making a good first impression varies from culture to culture. North Americans prefer neat dress, a positive attitude, a firm handshake, and an attentive gaze.

Good Impressions If you "dress for success," project an upbeat attitude at all times, and avoid offending others, you are engaging in favorable impression management—particularly so if your motive is to improve your chances of getting what you want in life.[42] There are questionable ways to create a good impression, as well. For instance, Stewart Friedman, director of the University of Pennsylvania's Leadership Program, recently offered this gem:

Last year, I was doing some work with a large bank. The people there told me a story that astounded me: After 7 PM, people would open the door to their office, drape a spare jacket on the back of their chair, lay a set of glasses down on some reading material on their desk—and then go home for the night. The point of this elaborate gesture was to create the illusion that they were just out grabbing dinner and would be returning to burn the midnight oil.[43]

Impression management often strays into unethical territory.

A statistical factor analysis of the influence attempts reported by a sample of 84 bank employees (including 74 women) identified three categories of favorable upward impression management tactics.[44] Favorable upward impression management tactics can be *job-focused* (manipulating information about one's job performance), *supervisor-focused* (praising and doing favors for one's supervisor), and *self-focused* (presenting oneself as a polite and nice person). A moderate amount of upward impression management is a necessity for the average employee today. Too little, and busy managers are liable to overlook some of your valuable contributions when they make job assignment, pay, and promotion decisions. Too much, and you run the risk of being branded a "schmoozer," a "phony," and other unflattering things by your co-workers.[45] Excessive flattery and ingratiation can backfire by embarrassing the target person and damaging one's credibility. Also, the risk of unintended insult is very high when impression management tactics cross gender, racial, ethnic, and cultural lines.[46] International management experts warn:

The impression management tactic is only as effective as its correlation to accepted norms about behavioral presentation. In other words, slapping a Japanese subordinate on the back with a rousing "Good work, Hiro!" will not create the desired impression in Hiro's mind that the expatriate intended. In fact, the behavior will likely create the opposite impression.[47]

Bad Impressions   At first glance, the idea of consciously trying to make a bad impression in the workplace seems absurd.[48] But an interesting new line of impression management research has uncovered both motives and tactics for making oneself look *bad*. In a survey of the work experiences of business students at a large northwestern US university, more than half "reported witnessing a case of someone intentionally looking bad at work."[49] Why? Four motives came out of the study:

(1) *Avoidance:* Employee seeks to avoid additional work, stress, burnout, or an unwanted transfer or promotion. (2) *Obtain concrete rewards:* Employee seeks to obtain a pay raise or a desired transfer, promotion, or demotion. (3) *Exit:* Employee seeks to get laid off, fired, or suspended, and perhaps also to collect unemployment or workers' compensation. (4) *Power:* Employee seeks to control, manipulate, or intimidate others, get revenge, or make someone else look bad.[50]

Within the context of these motives, *unfavorable* upward impression management makes sense.

Five unfavorable upward impression management tactics identified by the researchers are as follows:

- *Decreasing performance*—restricting productivity, making more mistakes than usual, lowering quality, neglecting tasks.
- *Not working to potential*—pretending ignorance, having unused capabilities.
- *Withdrawing*—being tardy, taking excessive breaks, faking illness.
- *Displaying a bad attitude*—complaining, getting upset and angry, acting strangely, not getting along with co-workers.
- *Broadcasting limitations*—letting co-workers know about one's physical problems and mistakes (both verbally and nonverbally).[51]

Recommended ways to manage employees who try to make a bad impression can be found throughout this book. They include more challenging work, greater autonomy, better feedback, supportive leadership, clear and reasonable goals, and a less stressful work setting.[52]

Keeping Organizational Politics in Check

Organizational politics cannot be eliminated. A manager would be naive to expect such an outcome. But political maneuvering can and should be managed to keep it constructive and within reasonable bounds. Harvard's Abraham Zaleznik put the issue this way: "People can focus their attention on only so many things. The more it lands on politics, the less energy—emotional and intellectual—is available to attend to the problems that fall under the heading of real work."[53]

An individual's degree of politicalness is a matter of personal values, ethics, and temperament. People who are either strictly nonpolitical or highly political generally pay a price for their behavior. The former may experience slow promotions and feel

TABLE 13–1 | Practical Tips for Managing Organizational Politics

To Reduce System Uncertainty

Make clear what are the bases and processes for evaluation.

Differentiate rewards among high and low performers.

Make sure the rewards are as immediately and directly related to performance as possible.

To Reduce Competition

Try to minimize resource competition among managers.

Replace resource competition with externally oriented goals and objectives.

To Break Existing Political Fiefdoms

Where highly cohesive political empires exist, break them apart by removing or splitting the most dysfunctional subgroups.

If you are an executive, be keenly sensitive to managers whose mode of operation is the personalization of political patronage. First, approach these persons with a directive to "stop the political maneuvering." If it continues, remove them from the positions and, preferably, the company.

To Prevent Future Fiefdoms

Make one of the most important criteria for promotion an apolitical attitude that puts organizational ends ahead of personal power ends.

SOURCE: D R Beeman and T W Sharkey, "The Use and Abuse of Corporate Politics." Reprinted with permission of *Business Horizons,* March–April 1987, p 30. Copyright © 1987 by the Board of Trustees at Indiana University, Kelley School of Business.

left out, while the latter may run the risk of being called self-serving and lose their credibility. People at both ends of the political spectrum may be considered poor team players. A moderate amount of prudent political behavior generally is considered a survival tool in complex organizations. Experts remind us that

> . . . political behavior has earned a bad name only because of its association with politicians. On its own, the use of power and other resources to obtain your objectives is not inherently unethical. It all depends on what the preferred objectives are.[54]

With this perspective in mind, the practical steps in Table 13–1 are recommended. Notice the importance of reducing uncertainty through standardized performance evaluations and clear performance-reward linkages. Measurable objectives are management's first line of defense against negative expressions of organizational politics.[55]

chapter summary

- *Name five "soft" and four "hard" influence tactics, and summarize the practical lessons from influence research.* Five soft influence tactics are rational persuasion, inspirational appeals, consultation, ingratiation, and personal appeals. They are more friendly and less coercive than the four hard influence tactics: exchange, coalition tactics, pressure, and legitimating tactics. According to research, soft tactics are better for generating commitment and are perceived as more fair than hard tactics.

- *Identify and briefly describe French and Raven's five bases of power.* French and Raven's five bases of power are reward power (rewarding compliance), coercive power (punishing noncompliance), legitimate power (relying on formal authority), expert power (providing needed information), and referent power (relying on personal attraction).

- *Define the term* empowerment, *and explain how to make it succeed.* Empowerment involves sharing varying degrees of power and decision-making authority with lower-level employees to better serve the customer. According to Randolph's model, empowerment requires active sharing of key information, structure that encourages autonomy, transfer of control from managers to teams, and persistence. Trust and training also are very important.

- *Define organizational politics, explain what triggers it, and specify the three levels of political action in organizations.* Organizational politics is defined as intentional acts of influence to enhance or protect the self-interests of individuals or groups. Uncertainty triggers most politicking in organizations. Political action occurs at individual, coalition, and network levels. Coalitions are informal, temporary, and single-issue alliances.

- *Distinguish between favorable and unfavorable impression management tactics.* Favorable upward impression management can be job-focused (manipulating information about one's job performance), supervisor-focused (praising or doing favors for the boss), or self-focused (being polite and nice). Unfavorable upward impression management tactics include decreasing performance, not working to potential, withdrawing, displaying a bad attitude, and broadcasting one's limitations.

- *Explain how to manage organizational politics.* Because organizational politics cannot be eliminated, managers need to learn to deal with it. Uncertainty can be reduced by evaluating performance and linking rewards to performance. Measurable objectives are key. Participative management also helps.

internet exercise

www.influenceatwork.com

A Free Tutorial on Social Influence

Do you get the feeling advertisers, the media, politicians, salespeople, parents and teachers, and friends sometimes are trying to "trick" you by manipulating words and images in self-serving ways? According to Professor Robert B Cialdini and his colleague. consultant Kelton Rhoads. you are right to feel a bit put upon. After all, as their research has documented, each of us is the recipient (or victim) of countless social influence attempts during every waking hour. Their fascinating Internet site (**www.influenceatwork.com**) provides an inside look at social influence so we will not be unfairly or unwittingly manipulated.

At the home page, select the "Academic" path. We recommend you start by clicking on the "What's Your Influence Quotient?" icon. The short quiz will get you thinking about the power and pervasiveness of social influence. Back at the main menu, you might want to select the heading "The Authors" for relevant background. Returning once again to the Academic page, select "Introduction to Influence" from the main menu. All of the tutorial pieces are worth exploration, but we especially recommend the first six categories, including the two on ethics. The "6 Principles" and collection of readings on "Framing" are very interesting and instructive.

QUESTIONS

1. Having read selections from the social influence tutorial, are you more aware of day-to-day influence processes and tactics? Explain.

2. What were the most valuable insights you picked up from the social influence tutorial? Generally, do you see social influence as a constructive or sinister force in society? Explain.

3. Is it possible that employees are becoming more difficult to influence because they have become hardened or numbed as a result of excessive exposure to influence attempts?

4. How can managers use social influence *ethically*?

Leadership

fourteen
chapter

After reading the material in this chapter, you should be able to:

- Review trait theory research, and discuss the idea of one best style of leadership, using the Ohio State studies and the Leadership Grid® as points of reference.

- Explain, according to Fiedler's contingency model, how leadership style interacts with situational control.

- Discuss House's path–goal theory and Hersey and Blanchard's situational leadership theory.

- Describe how charismatic leadership transforms followers and work groups.

- Explain the leader–member exchange (LMX) model of leadership and the substitutes for leadership.

- Review the principles of servant-leadership and superleadership.

DID FORD'S FORMER CEO TRY TO CHANGE TOO MUCH TOO FAST?

With the Firestone tire fiasco and other woes on Jacques A Nasser's desk, the last thing the Ford Motor Co. CEO needed were doubts about his authority. Yet that's what he faced last week as rumors swirled that the board might revamp management and pull Ford's European chief back to Detroit for a key operating role. And although no one suggested Nasser might soon be out of a job, Nasser made a point of telling a Bloomberg reporter that Ford's directors, led by Chairman William C Ford Jr, were "extremely supportive" of him. Still, that hardly means things are hunky-dory on the executive floor. It has become obvious lately that the aggressive and often controversial CEO has gotten himself into deep trouble, and he is going to need a hand or two to help pull Ford out of the muck.

SHAKE UP. Even before the Bridgestone/Firestone Inc. tire mess, Nasser had stretched himself too thin. Since taking over as CEO in January, 1999, he has pushed Ford in a host of ambitious new directions, piling on one initiative after another. He urged employees to get closer to customers. He overhauled management pay and performance practices. He hired a slew of outsiders to shake up Ford's culture. He adopted General Electric Co.'s approach to improving quality. He expanded Ford's luxury-car portfolio through

acquisitions. He bought repair shops and auto junkyards. He even set up John F Welch's transformation of GE as a model for his company, and for himself as CEO.

In short, Nasser wanted Ford to be not only the world's top carmaker, but also among the top companies, period. But now he is learning the downside of aiming so high. The problem is, while Nasser has been leading Ford headlong into the future, he hasn't devoted enough time to the basics of running a $170 billion auto company. How else can you explain the embarrassing quality gaffes that have marred the launches of some of Ford's highest-profile vehicles, including the 2002 Explorer? Or the morale problems that have scarred the organization, and prompted class actions from disgruntled employees? "I think Ford management is really stretched," says one source close to Ford's senior management. "There are just too many initiatives going on. Now, they're paying the price for taking their eye off the ball."

No one is more overextended than Nasser himself. He has 16 executives reporting directly to him. General Motors Corp.'s CEO has nine. And Ford has not had a head of worldwide automotive operations since Nasser held the job under his predecessor, Alexander J Trotman, back in 1998. The hard-charging Aussie has also kept the auto job for himself; he has also never named a chief operating officer.[1]

Note: Jacques Nasser left Ford later in 2001 amid controversy about Ford's strategic direction.

How would you evaluate Jacques Nasser as a leader? For an interpretation on this case and additional comments, visit our website:

www.mhhe.com/kinickiob

FOR DISCUSSION

DISAGREEMENT ABOUT THE DEFINITION OF LEADERSHIP stems from the fact that it involves a complex interaction among the leader, the followers, and the situation. For example, some researchers define leadership in terms of personality and physical traits, while others believe leadership is represented by a set of prescribed behaviors. In contrast, other researchers believe that leadership is a temporary role that can be filled by anyone. There is a common thread, however, among the different definitions of leadership. The common thread is social influence.

As the term is used in this chapter, **leadership** is defined as "a social influence process in which the leader seeks the voluntary participation of subordinates in an effort to reach organizational goals."[2] This definition implies that leadership involves more than wielding power and exercising authority and is exhibited on different levels. At the individual level, for example, leadership involves mentoring, coaching, inspiring, and motivating. Leaders build teams, create cohesion, and resolve conflict at the group level. Finally, leaders build culture and create change at the organizational level.[3]

OB researchers have discovered that leaders can make a difference. One study, for instance, revealed that leadership was positively associated with net profits from 167 companies over a time span of 20 years.[4] Research also showed that a coach's leadership skills affected the success of his or her team. Specifically, teams in both Major League Baseball and college basketball won more games when players perceived the coach to be an effective leader.[5] Rest assured, leadership make a difference!

This chapter attempts to enhance your understanding about leadership by focusing on the following areas: (1) trait and behavioral approaches to leadership, (2) alternative situational theories of leadership, (3) charismatic leadership, and (4) additional perspectives on leadership.

Trait and Behavioral Theories of Leadership

This section examines the two earliest approaches used to explain leadership. Trait theories focused on identifying the personal traits that differentiated leaders from followers. Behavioral theorists examined leadership from a different perspective. They tried to uncover the different kinds of leader behaviors that resulted in higher work group performance. Both approaches to leadership can teach current and future managers valuable lessons about leading.

Trait Theory

Leadership

Influencing employees to voluntarily pursue organizational goals.

Leader trait

Personal characteristics that differentiate leaders from followers.

At the turn of the 20th century, the prevailing belief was that leaders were born, not made. Selected people were thought to possess inborn traits that made them successful leaders. A **leader trait** is a physical or personality characteristic that can be used to differentiate leaders from followers.

Before World War II, hundreds of studies were conducted to pinpoint the traits of successful leaders. Dozens of leadership traits were identified. During the postwar period, however, enthusiasm was replaced by widespread criticism. Researchers simply were unable to uncover a consistent set of traits that accurately predicted which individuals became leaders in organizations.

Contemporary Trait Research Two OB researchers concluded in 1983 that past trait data may have been incorrectly analyzed. By applying modern statistical techniques to an old database, they demonstrated that the majority of a leader's behavior could be attributed to stable underlying traits.[6] Unfortunately, their methodology did not single out specific traits.

A 1986 meta-analysis by Robert Lord and his associates remedied this shortcoming. Based on a reanalysis of past studies, Lord concluded that people have leadership *prototypes* that affect our perceptions of who is and who is not an effective leader. Your **leadership prototype** is a mental representation of the traits and behaviors that you believe are possessed by leaders. We thus tend to perceive that someone is a leader when he or she exhibits traits or behaviors that are consistent with our prototypes.[7] Lord's research demonstrated that people are perceived as being leaders when they exhibit the traits associated with intelligence, masculinity, and dominance. More recently, a study of 6,052 middle-level managers from 22 European countries revealed that leadership prototypes are culturally based. In other words, leadership prototypes are influenced by national cultural values.[8] Researchers have not yet identified a set of global leadership prototypes.

> **Leadership prototype**
>
> Mental representation of the traits and behaviors possessed by leaders.

Gender and Leadership The increase of women in the workforce has generated much interest in understanding the similarities and differences in female and male leaders. Research uncovered the following differences: (1) Men and women were seen as displaying more task and social leadership, respectively;[9] (2) women used a more democratic or participative style than men, and men used a more autocratic and directive style than women;[10] (3) men and women were equally assertive,[11] and (4) women executives, when rated by their peers, managers, and direct reports, scored higher than their male counterparts on a variety of effectiveness criteria.[12]

In spite of these positive results, the same behavior by a male and female can be interpreted differently and lead to opposite consequences. Consider the case of Deborah Hopkins, former chief financial officer at Lucent Technologies:

> Ms Hopkins, 46 years old and widely viewed as one of America's hottest female executives, had been at the maker of phone-industry equipment just over a year. . . . Ms Hopkins's management technique, which earned her the nickname "Hurricane Debby," fell flat at Lucent. There, she was known for unforgiving candor, in which she typically cut off colleagues in midsentence. . . . Being a women didn't help, say people close to Ms Hopkins. Indeed, she was the fourth high-ranking female executive to leave Lucent, starting with Ms Fiorina [Carly Fiorina is CEO of Hewlett-Packard] in 1999. And while traits such as candor and abrasiveness can be considered good qualities in male chief executives in a tough turnaround situation, Ms Hopkins was criticized for her personality.[13]

Behavioral Styles Theory

This phase of leadership research began during World War II as part of an effort to develop better military leaders. It was an outgrowth of two events: the seeming inability of trait theory to explain leadership effectiveness and the human relations movement, an outgrowth of the Hawthorne Studies. The thrust of early behavioral leadership theory was to focus on leader behavior, instead of on personality traits. It was believed that leader behavior directly affected work group effectiveness. This led researchers to identify patterns of behavior (called leadership styles) that enabled leaders to effectively influence others.

The Ohio State Studies   Researchers at Ohio State University began by generating a list of behaviors exhibited by leaders. Ultimately, the Ohio State researchers concluded there were only two independent dimensions of leader behavior: consideration and initiating structure. **Consideration** involves leader behavior associated with creating mutual respect or trust and focuses on a concern for group members' needs and desires. **Initiating structure** is leader behavior that organizes and defines what group members should be doing to maximize output. These two dimensions of leader behavior were oriented at right angles to yield four behavioral styles of leadership: low structure-high consideration, high structure-high consideration, low structure-low consideration, and high structure-low consideration.

Consideration

Creating mutual respect and trust with followers.

Initiating structure

Organizing and defining what group members should be doing.

It initially was hypothesized that a high-structure, high-consideration style would be the one best style of leadership. Through the years, the effectiveness of the high-high style has been tested many times. Overall, results have been mixed. Researchers thus concluded that there is not one best style of leadership.[14] Rather, it is argued that effectiveness of a given leadership style depends on situational factors.

University of Michigan Studies   As in the Ohio State studies, this research sought to identify behavioral differences between effective and ineffective leaders. Researchers identified two different styles of leadership: one was employee centered, the other was job centered. These behavioral styles parallel the consideration and initiating-structure styles identified by the Ohio State group.

The Leadership Grid®   Developed by Robert Blake and Jane Srygley Mouton, the Leadership Grid® is based on the idea that there is one best style of leadership. The Grid is formed by the intersection of two dimensions of leader behavior. On the horizontal axis is "concern for production" and "concern for people" is on the vertical axes. By scaling each axis of the grid from 1 (Low) to 9 (High), Blake and Mouton were able to plot five leadership styles. The styles are impoverished management (1, 1) country club management (1, 9), authority-compliance (9, 1), middle-of-the-road management (5, 5), and team management (9, 9). The team management style is considered to be the best style regardless of the situation.

Behavioral Styles Theory in Perspective

By emphasizing leader *behavior,* something that is learned, the behavioral style approach makes it clear that leaders are made, not born. This is the opposite of the trait theorists' traditional assumption. Given what we know about behavior shaping and model-based training, leader *behaviors* can be systematically improved and developed.[15]

Behavioral styles research also revealed that there is no one best style of leadership. The effectiveness of a particular leadership style depends on the situation at hand. For instance, employees prefer structure over consideration when faced with role ambiguity.[16] Finally, research also reveals that it is important to consider the difference between how frequently and how effectively managers exhibit various leader behaviors. For example, a manager might ineffectively display a lot of considerate leader behaviors. Such a style is likely to frustrate employees and possibly result in lowered job satisfaction and performance. Because the frequency of exhibiting leadership behaviors is secondary in importance to effectiveness, managers are encouraged to concentrate on improving the effective execution of their leader behaviors.[17] The Executive Communications Group recommends a set of behaviors (see Skills & Best Practices) managers can focus on to improve their leadership effectiveness.

Tips for Improving Leadership Effectiveness

Behavior	Recommended Behaviors
• Listen	Intensely listen to what others have to say. Determine the true cause of performance problems.
• Examine	Think through problems from all perspectives. Do not play favorites and find solutions that benefit everyone involved.
• Assist	Help others to learn from mistakes and errors.
• Develop	Explain the rationale for decisions, and implement fair policies and procedures.
• Encourage	Provide employees with the resources needed to do a job. Gently push people to advance into more demanding roles.
• Recognize	Praise people for their good work. Focus on the positive whenever possible.

SOURCE: "CEO's Need to Listen, Examine, Assist," *The Arizona Republic,* April 22, 2001, p D2.

Situational Theories

Situational leadership theories grew out of an attempt to explain the inconsistent findings about traits and styles. **Situational theories** propose that the effectiveness of a particular style of leader behavior depends on the situation. As situations change, different styles become appropriate. This directly challenges the idea of one best style of leadership. Let us closely examine three alternative situational theories of leadership that reject the notion of one best leadership style.

> **Situational theories**
>
> Propose that leader styles should match the situation at hand.

Fiedler's Contingency Model

Fred Fiedler, an OB scholar, developed a situational model of leadership. It is the oldest and one of the most widely known models of leadership. Fiedler's model is based on the following assumption:

The performance of a leader depends on two interrelated factors: (1) the degree to which the situation gives the leader control and influence—that is, the likelihood that [the leader] can successfully accomplish the job; and (2) the leader's basic motivation—that is, whether [the leader's] self-esteem depends primarily on accomplishing the task or on having close supportive relations with others.[18]

With respect to a leader's basic motivation, Fiedler believes that leaders are either task motivated or relationship motivated. These basic motivations are similar to initiating structure/concern for production and consideration/concern for people.

Fiedler's theory also is based on the premise that leaders have one dominant leadership style that is resistant to change. He suggests that leaders must learn to manipulate or influence the leadership situation in order to create a "match" between their leadership style and the amount of control within the situation at hand. After discussing the components of situational control and the leadership matching process, we review relevant research and managerial implications.[19]

Situational Control   Situational control refers to the amount of control and influence the leader has in her or his immediate work environment. Situational control ranges from high to low. High control implies that the leader's decisions will produce predictable results because the leader has the ability to influence work outcomes. Low control implies that the leader's decisions may not influence work outcomes because the leader has very little influence. There are three dimensions of situational control: leader–member relations, task structure, and position power. These dimensions vary independently, forming eight combinations of situational control (see Figure 14–1).

FIGURE 14–1   Representation of Fiedler's Contingency Model

Situational Control	High Control Situations			Moderate Control Situations			Low Control Situations	
Leader–member relations	Good	Good	Good	Good	Poor	Poor	Poor	Poor
Task structure	High	High	Low	Low	High	High	Low	Low
Position power	Strong	Weak	Strong	Weak	Strong	Weak	Strong	Weak
Situation	I	II	III	IV	V	VI	VII	VIII
Optimal Leadership Style	Task-Motivated Leadership			Relationship-Motivated Leadership			Task-Motivated Leadership	

SOURCE: Adapted from F E Fiedler, "Situational Control and a Dynamic Theory of Leadership," in *Managerial Control and Organizational Democracy*, eds B King, S Streufert, and F E Fiedler (New York: John Wiley & Sons, 1978), p 114.

The three dimensions of situational control are defined as follows:

- *Leader-member relations* reflect the extent to which the leader has the support, loyalty, and trust of the work group.
- *Task structure* is concerned with the amount of structure contained within tasks performed by the work group.
- *Position power* refers to the degree to which the leader has formal power to reward, punish, or otherwise obtain compliance from employees.[20]

Linking Leadership Motivation and Situational Control   Fiedler's complete contingency model is presented in Figure 14–1. The last row under the Situational Control column shows that there are eight different leadership situations. Each situation represents a unique combination of leader–member relations, task structure, and position power. Situations I, II, and III represent high control situations. Figure 14–1 shows that task-motivated leaders are hypothesized to be most effective in situations of high control. Under conditions of moderate control (situations IV, V, and VI), relationship-motivated leaders are expected to be more effective. Finally, the results orientation of task-motivated leaders is predicted to be more effective under conditions of low control (situations VII and VIII).

Research and Managerial Implications   Research has provided mixed support for Fiedler's model, suggesting that the model needs theoretical refinement.[21] That said, the major contribution of Fiedler's model is that it prompted others to examine the contingency nature of leadership. This research, in turn, reinforced the notion that there is no one best style of leadership. Leaders are advised to alter their task and relationship orientation to fit the demands of the situation at hand.

Path–Goal Theory

Robert House originated the path–goal theory of leadership. He proposed a model that describes how expectancy perceptions are influenced by the contingent relationships among four leadership styles and various employee attitudes and behaviors (see Figure 14–2).[22] According to the path–goal model, leader behavior is acceptable when employees view it as a source of satisfaction or as paving the way to future satisfaction. In addition, leader behavior is motivational to the extent it (1) reduces roadblocks that interfere with goal accomplishment, (2) provides the guidance and support needed by employees, and (3) ties meaningful rewards to goal accomplishment. Because the model deals with pathways to goals and rewards, it is called the path–goal theory of leadership. House sees the leader's main job as helping employees stay on the right paths to challenging goals and valued rewards.

Leadership Styles   House believes leaders can exhibit more than one leadership style. This contrasts with Fiedler, who proposes that leaders have one dominant style. The four leadership styles identified by House are as follows:

- *Directive leadership.* Providing guidance to employees about what should be done and how to do it, scheduling work, and maintaining standards of performance.
- *Supportive leadership.* Showing concern for the well-being and needs of employees, being friendly and approachable, and treating workers as equals.

FIGURE 14–2   A General Representation of House's Path–Goal Theory

- *Participative leadership.* Consulting with employees and seriously considering their ideas when making decisions.
- *Achievement-oriented leadership.* Encouraging employees to perform at their highest level by setting challenging goals, emphasizing excellence, and demonstrating confidence in employee abilities.[23]

Descriptions of business leaders reinforce House's belief that leaders exhibit more than one leadership styles. For example, Michael Capellas, CEO of Compaq Computer Corp., uses multiple leadership styles to influence others:

> His guiding principles: make leaders personally accountable for business-unit performance and insist that they play well together. . . . Now, Capellas has hard wired accountability into the way his management team operates. Starting in January [2000], he made customer-satisfaction goals an essential part of each executive's pay package. . . . The move already is delivering results: In the past year, the company's on-time delivery record has improved by 60%. . . . He can dispel a dark mood at a moment's notice too. On June 17, just before his first telephone conference with Wall Street analysts, Capellas noticed that people gathered in a conference room seemed nervous—and he worried that the analysts would sense it. A fan of 70s rock and roll, he had a Three Dog Night CD in his notebook PC. He turned it on, pumped up the volume, and danced with Alice McGuire, head of investor relations, to the tune "Joy to the World." By the time the conference call started, people were grinning like a bunch of kids watching an Austin Powers movie.[24]

Contingency factors

Variables that influence the appropriateness of a leadership style.

Contingency Factors   **Contingency factors** are situational variables that cause one style of leadership to be more effective than another. In this context, these variables affect expectancy or path–goal perceptions. This model has two groups of contingency variables (see Figure 14–2): employee characteristics and environmental factors.

Research and Managerial Implications   Although research supports the idea that leaders exhibit more than one leadership style, there is limited support for most of the moderating relationships predicted within path–goal theory.[25] This leaves us with two important managerial implications. First, leaders possess and use more than one style of leadership. Managers thus should not be hesitant to try new behaviors when the situation calls for them. Second, a small set of task and employee characteristics are relevant contingency factors. Managers are encouraged to modify their leadership style to fit these various task and employee characteristics. For example, supportive and achievement leadership are more likely to be satisfying when employees have a lot of ability and experience.

Hersey and Blanchard's Situational Leadership Theory

Situational leadership theory (SLT) was developed by management writers Paul Hersey and Kenneth Blanchard.[26] According to the theory, effective leader behavior depends on the readiness level of a leader's followers. **Readiness** is defined as the extent to which a follower possesses the ability and willingness to complete a task. Willingness is a combination of confidence, commitment, and motivation.

> **Readiness**
>
> Follower's ability and willingness to complete a task.

The SLT model is summarized in Figure 14–3. The appropriate leadership style is found by cross-referencing follower readiness, which varies from low to high, with one of four leadership styles. The four leadership styles represent combinations of task and relationship-oriented leader behaviors (S_1 to S_4). Leaders are encouraged to use a "telling style" for followers with low readiness. This style combines high task-oriented leader behaviors, such as providing instructions, with low relationship-oriented behaviors, such as close supervision (see Figure 14–3). As follower readiness increases, leaders are advised to gradually move from a telling, to a selling, to a participating, and, ultimately, to a delegating style. In the most recent description of this model, the four leadership styles depicted in Figure 14–3 are referred to as telling or directing (S_1), persuading or coaching (S_2), participating or supporting (S_3), and delegating (S_4).[27]

Although SLT is widely used as a training tool, it is not strongly supported by scientific research. Finally, researchers have concluded that the self-assessment instrument used to measure leadership style and follower readiness is inaccurate and should be used with caution.[28] In summary, managers should exercise discretion when using prescriptions from SLT.

From Transactional to Charismatic Leadership

Most of the models and theories previously discussed in this chapter represent transactional leadership. **Transactional leadership** focuses on the interpersonal transactions between managers and employees. Leaders are seen as engaging in behaviors that maintain a quality interaction between themselves and followers. The two underlying characteristics of transactional leadership are that (1) leaders use contingent rewards to motivate employees and (2) leaders exert corrective action only when subordinates fail to obtain

> **Transactional leadership**
>
> Focuses on interpersonal interactions between managers and employees.

FIGURE 14–3 | Situational Leadership Model

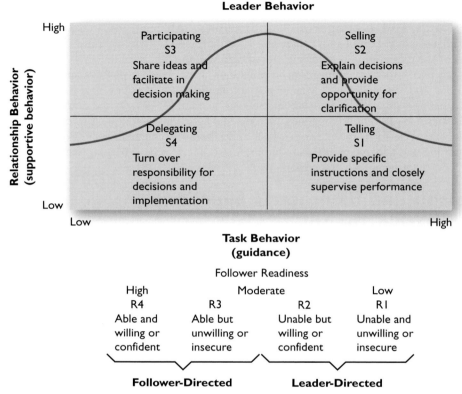

Leader Behavior

SOURCE: Reprinted with permission from Dr Paul Hersey (1984), *The Management of Organizational Behavior: Utilizing Human Resources*, the Center for Leadership Studies, Escondido, CA. All rights reserved.

performance goals. Consider how Samuel Palmisano, the president of IBM, effectively uses transactional leadership to improve organizational performance:

> After several operations missed sales targets in the third quarter last year, Mr Palmisano, newly minted as president, started what he called "morning operations calls" to review performance as often as three days a week. Division general managers, sales managers, manufacturing and distribution heads participated by phone in the 7 AM meetings, which were particularly tough for managers on the West Coast, one executive says.[29]

Charismatic leadership

Transforms employees to pursue organizational goals over self-interests.

In contrast, **charismatic leadership** emphasizes "symbolic leader behavior, visionary and inspirational messages, nonverbal communication, appeal to ideological values, intellectual stimulation of followers by the leader, display of confidence in self and followers, and leader expectations for follower self-sacrifice and for performance beyond the call of duty."[30] Charismatic leadership can produce significant organizational change and results because it "transforms" employees to pursue organizational goals in lieu of self-interests. Let us now examine how charismatic leadership transforms followers.

How Does Charismatic Leadership Transform Followers?

Charismatic leaders transform followers by creating changes in their goals, values, needs, beliefs, and aspirations. They accomplish this transformation by appealing to followers' self-concepts—namely, their values and personal identity. Figure 14–4 presents a model of how charismatic leadership accomplishes this transformation process.

To some, **Colin Powell is an example of a powerful and charismatic leader.**

Figure 14–4 shows that charismatic leader behavior is first influenced by various individual and organizational characteristics. For example, research reveals that charismatic leaders tend to have personalities that are more extraverted, agreeable, and proactive than noncharismatic leaders.[31] Organizational culture also influences the extent to which leaders are charismatic. Cultures that are adaptive and flexible rather than rigid and bureaucratic are more likely to create environments that foster the opportunity for charismatic leadership to be exhibited.

Charismatic leaders tend to engage in three key sets of leader behavior (see Figure 14–4). The first set of charismatic leader behaviors involves establishing a common vision of the future. A vision is "a realistic, credible, attractive future for your

A Charismatic Model of Leadership   FIGURE 14–4

Individual and organizational characteristics	Leader behavior	Effects on followers and work groups	Outcomes
• Traits • Organizational culture	• Leader establishes a vision	• Increased intrinsic motivation, achievement orientation, and goal pursuit	• Personal commitment to leader and vision
	• Leader establishes high performance expectations and displays confidence in him/herself and the collective ability to realize the vision	• Increased identification with the leader and the collective interests of organizational members • Increased cohesion among workgroup members	• Self-sacrificial behavior • Organizational commitment
	• Leader models the desired values, traits, beliefs, and behaviors needed to realize the vision	• Increased self-esteem, self-efficacy, and intrinsic interests in goal accomplishment • Increased role modeling of charismatic leadership	• Task meaningfulness and satisfaction • Increased individual, group, and organizational performance

SOURCE: Based in part on D A Waldman and F J Yammarino, "CEO Charismatic Leadership: Levels-of-Management and Levels-of-Analysis Effects," *Academy of Management Review,* April 1999, pp 266–85; and B Shamir, R J House, and M B Arthur, "The Motivational Effects of Charismatic Leadership: A Self-Concept Based Theory," *Organization Science,* November 1993, pp 577–94.

organization."[32] According to Burt Nanus, a leadership expert, the "right" vision unleashes human potential because it serves as a beacon of hope and common purpose. It does this by attracting commitment, energizing workers, creating meaning in employees' lives, establishing a standard of excellence, promoting high ideals, and bridging the gap between an organization's present problems and its future goals and aspirations.[33]

The second set of leader behaviors involves two key components:

1. Charismatic leaders set high performance expectations and standards because they know challenging, attainable goals lead to greater productivity.

2. Charismatic leaders need to publicly express confidence in the followers' ability to meet high performance expectations. This is essential because employees are more likely to pursue difficult goals when they believe they can accomplish what is being asked of them.

The third and final set of leader behaviors involves being a role model. Through their actions, charismatic leaders model the desired values, traits, beliefs, and behaviors needed to realize the vision.

Returning to Figure 14–4, you can see that charismatic leadership transforms followers by increasing their motivation, identification with the leader, cohesion among workgroup members, and self-esteem and self-efficacy. In turn, these positive effects are expected to produce a host of favorable work outcomes.

Research and Managerial Implications

The charismatic model of leadership presented in Figure 14–4 was partially supported by previous research. For example, a meta-analysis of 54 studies indicated that charismatic leaders were viewed as more effective leaders by both supervisors and followers and had followers who exerted more effort and reported higher levels of job satisfaction than noncharismatic leaders.[34] Other studies showed that charismatic leadership was positively associated with followers' individual performance and their trust and satisfaction with their leaders.[35] At the organizational level, a second meta-analysis demonstrated that charismatic leadership was positively correlated with organizational measures of effectiveness.[36]

These results underscore four important managerial implications. First, the best leaders are not just charismatic, they are both transactional and charismatic. Leaders should attempt these two types of leadership while avoiding a "laissez-faire" or "wait-and-see" style. Laissez-faire leadership is the most ineffective leadership style.

Second, charismatic leadership is not applicable in all organizational situations. According to a team of experts, charismatic leadership is most likely to be effective when

1. The situation offers opportunities for "moral" involvement.
2. Performance goals cannot be easily established and measured.
3. Extrinsic rewards cannot be clearly linked to individual performance.
4. There are few situational cues or constraints to guide behavior.
5. Exceptional effort, behavior, sacrifices, and performance are required of both leaders and followers.[37]

Third, employees at any level in an organization can be trained to be more transactional and charismatic.[38] This reinforces the organizational value of developing and rolling out a combination of transactional and charismatic leadership training for all employees. These programs, however, should be based on an overall corporate philosophy that constitutes the foundation of leadership development. Johnson & Johnson Company, for example, implemented an extensive process of leadership development that was based on seven principles of leadership development (see Skills & Best Practices).[39] Fourth, charismatic leaders can be ethical or unethical. Whereas ethical charismatic leaders enable employees to enhance their self-concepts, unethical ones select or produce obedient, dependent, and compliant followers. Top management can create and maintain ethical charismatic leadership by

1. Creating and enforcing a clearly stated code of ethics.
2. Recruiting, selecting, and promoting people with high morals and standards.
3. Developing performance expectations around the treatment of employees—these expectations can then be assessed in the performance appraisal process.
4. Training employees to value diversity.
5. Identifying, rewarding, and publicly praising employees who exemplify high moral conduct.[40]

SKILLS & BEST PRACTICES

Johnson & Johnson Company Bases Its Leadership Development around Seven Guiding Principles

1. Leadership development is a key business strategy.
2. Leadership excellence is a definable set of standards.
3. People are responsible for their own development.
4. Johnson & Johnson executives are accountable for developing leaders.
5. Leaders are developed primarily on the job.
6. People are an asset of the corporation; leadership development is a collaborative, corporation-wide process.
7. Human resources is vital to the success of leadership development.

SOURCE: Excerpted from R M Fulmer, "Johnson & Johnson: Framework for Leadership," *Organizational Dynamics*, Winter 2001, p 214.

Additional Perspectives on Leadership

This section examines four additional approaches to leadership; leader–member exchange theory, substitutes for leadership, servant leadership, and superleadership. We spend more time discussing leader–member exchange theory and substitutes for leadership because they have been more thoroughly investigated.

The Leader–Member Exchange (LMX) Model of Leadership

The leader–member exchange model of leadership revolves around the development of dyadic relationships between managers and their direct reports. This model is quite different from those previously discussed in that it focuses on the quality of relationships between managers and subordinates as opposed to the behaviors or traits of either leaders or followers. It also is different in that it does not assume that leader behavior is characterized by a stable or average leadership style as does the Leadership Grid® and Fiedler's contingency theory. In other words, these models assume a leader treats all employees in about the same way. In contrast, the LMX model is based on the assumption that leaders develop unique one-to-one relationships with each of the people reporting to them. Behavioral scientists call this sort of relationship a *vertical dyad*. The forming of vertical dyads is said to be a naturally occurring process, resulting from the leader's attempt to delegate and assign work roles. As a result of this process, two distinct types of leader–member exchange relationships are expected to evolve.[41]

In-group exchange

A partnership characterized by mutual trust, respect, and liking.

Out-group exchange

A partnership characterized by a lack of mutual trust, respect, and liking.

One type of leader–member exchange is called the **in-group exchange.** In this relationship, leaders and followers develop a partnership characterized by reciprocal influence, mutual trust, respect and liking, and a sense of common fates. In the second type of exchange, referred to as an **out-group exchange,** leaders are characterized as overseers who fail to create a sense of mutual trust, respect, or common fate.[42]

Research Findings   If the leader–member exchange model is correct, there should be a significant relationship between the type of leader–member exchange and job-related, outcomes. Research supports this prediction. For example, a positive leader–member exchange was positively associated with job satisfaction, job performance, goal commitment, trust between managers and employees, work climate, and satisfaction with leadership.[43] The type of leader–member exchange also was found to predict not only turnover among nurses and computer analysts, but also career outcomes, such as promotability, salary level, and receipt of bonuses over a seven-year period.[44] Finally, studies also have identified a variety of variables that influence the quality of an LMX. For example, LMX was related to personality similarity and demographic similarity.[45] Further, the quality of an LMX was positively related with the extent to which leaders and followers like each other, the leaders' positive expectations of their subordinates, and employees' impression management techniques.[46]

Managerial Implications   There are three important implications associated with the LMX model of leadership. First, leaders are encouraged to establish high-performance expectations for all of their direct reports because setting high-performance standards fosters high-quality LMXs. Second, because personality and demographic similarity between leaders and followers is associated with higher LMXs, managers need to be careful that they don't create a homogeneous work environment in the spirit of having positive relationships with their direct reports. Our discussion of diversity in Chapter 4 clearly documented that there are many positive benefits of having a diverse workforce. The third implication pertains to those of us who find ourselves in a poor LMX. Before providing advice about what to do in this situation, we would like you to assess the quality of your current leader–member exchange. The Hands-On Exercise contains a measure of leader–member exchange that segments an LMX into four subdimensions: mutual affection, loyalty, contribution to work activities, and professional respect.[47]

What is the overall quality of your LMX? Do you agree with this assessment? Which subdimensions are high and low? If your overall LMX and associated subdimensions are all high, you should be in a very good situation with respect to the relationship between you and your manager. Having a low LMX overall score or a low dimensional score, however, reveals that part of the relationship with your manager may need improvement. OB researcher Robert Vecchio offers the following tips to both followers and leaders for improving the quality of leader–member exchanges:

1. New employees should offer their loyalty, support, and cooperativeness to their manager.

2. If you are an out-group member, either accept the situation, try to become an ingroup member by being cooperative and loyal, or quit.

Assessing Your Leader–Member Exchange

INSTRUCTIONS For each of the items shown below, use the following scale to circle the answer that best represents how you feel about the relationship between you and your current manager/supervisor. If you are not currently working, complete the survey by thinking about a previous manager. Remember, there are no right or wrong answers. After circling a response for each of the 12 items, use the scoring key to compute scores for the subdimensions within your leader–member exchange.

1 = Strongly disagree
2 = Disagree
3 = Neither agree nor disagree
4 = Agree
5 = Strongly agree

1. I like my supervisor very much as a person. 1 2 3 4 5

2. My supervisor is the kind of person one would like to have as a friend. 1 2 3 4 5

3. My supervisor is a lot of fun to work with. 1 2 3 4 5

4. My supervisor defends my work actions to a superior, even without complete knowledge of the issue in question. 1 2 3 4 5

5. My supervisor would come to my defense if I were "attacked" by others. 1 2 3 4 5

6. My supervisor would defend me to others in the organization if I made an honest mistake. 1 2 3 4 5

7. I do work for my supervisor that goes beyond what is specified in my job description. 1 2 3 4 5

8. I am willing to apply extra efforts, beyond those normally required, to meet my supervisor's work goals. 1 2 3 4 5

9. I do not mind working my hardest for my supervisor. 1 2 3 4 5

10. I am impressed with my supervisor's knowledge of his/her job. 1 2 3 4 5

11. I respect my supervisor's knowledge of and competence on the job. 1 2 3 4 5

12. I admire my supervisor's professional skills. 1 2 3 4 5

SCORING KEY
Mutual affection (add items 1–3) _____

Loyalty (add items 4–6) _____

Contribution to work activities (add items 7–9) _____

Professional respect (add items 10–12) _____

Overall score (add all 12 items) _____

ARBITRARY NORMS
Low mutual affection = 3–9
High mutual affection = 10–15
Low loyalty = 3–9
High loyalty = 10–15
Low contribution to work activities = 3–9
High contribution to work activities = 10–15
Low professional respect = 3–9
High professional respect = 10–15
Low overall leader–member exchange = 12–38
High overall leader–member exchange = 39–60

SOURCE: Survey items were taken from R C Liden and J M Maslyn, "Multidimensionality of Leader–Member Exchange: An Empirical Assessment through Scale Development," *Journal of Management*, 1998, p 56.

3. Managers should consciously try to expand their in-groups.

4. Managers need to give employees ample opportunity to prove themselves.[48]

Finally, you may want to try using some of the impression management techniques discussed in Chapter 13 in order to improve your LMX.

Substitutes for Leadership

Virtually all leadership theories assume that some sort of formal leadership is necessary, whatever the circumstances. But this basic assumption is questioned by this model of leadership. Specifically, some OB scholars propose that there are a variety of situational variables that can substitute for, neutralize, or enhance the effects of leadership. These situational variables are referred to as **substitutes for leadership.**[49] Substitutes for leadership can thus increase or diminish a leader's ability to influence the work group. For example, leader behavior that initiates structure would tend to be resisted by independent-minded employees with high ability and vast experience. Consequently, such employees would be guided more by their own initiative than by managerial directives.

> **Substitutes for leadership**
>
> Situational variables that can substitute for, neutralize, or enhance the effects of leadership.

Kerr and Jermier's Substitutes for Leadership Model   According to Steven Kerr and John Jermier, the OB researchers who developed this model, the key to improving leadership effectiveness is to identify the situational characteristics that can either substitute for, neutralize, or improve the impact of a leader's behavior. Table 14–1 lists the various substitutes for leadership. Characteristics of the subordinate, the task, and the organization can act as substitutes for traditional hierarchical leadership. Further, different characteristics are predicted to negate different types of leader behavior. For example, tasks that provide feedback concerning accomplishment, such as taking a test, tend to negate task-oriented but not relationship-oriented leader behavior (see Table 14–1). Although the list in Table 14–1 is not all-inclusive, it shows that there are more substitutes for task-oriented leadership than for relationship-oriented leadership.

Research and Managerial Implications   Two different approaches have been used to test this model. The first is based on the idea that substitutes for leadership are contingency variables that moderate the relationship between leader behavior and employee attitudes and behavior.[50] A recent summary of this research revealed that only 318 of 3,741 (9%) contingency relationships tested supported the model.[51] This demonstrates that substitutes for leadership do not moderate the effect of a leader's behavior as suggested by Steve Kerr and John Jermier. The second approach to test the substitutes model examined whether substitutes for leadership have a direct effect on employee attitudes and behaviors. A recent meta-analysis of 36 different samples revealed that the combination of substitute variables and leader behaviors significantly explained a variety of employee attitudes and behaviors. Interestingly, the substitutes for leadership were more important than leader behaviors in accounting for employee attitudes and behaviors.[52]

The key implication is that managers should be attentive to the substitutes listed in Table 14–1 because they directly influence employee attitudes and performance. Managers can positively influence the substitutes through employee selection, job design, work group assignments, and the design of organizational processes and systems.

Substitutes for Leadership **TABLE 14–1**

Characteristic	Relationship-Oriented or Considerate Leader Behavior Is Unnecessary	Task-Oriented or Initiating Structure Leader Behavior Is Unnecessary
Of the Subordinate		
1. Ability, experience, training, knowledge		X
2. Need for independence	X	X
3. "Professional" orientation	X	X
4. Indifference toward organizational rewards	X	X
Of the Task		
5. Unambiguous and routine		X
6. Methodologically invariant		X
7. Provides its own feedback concerning accomplishment		X
8. Intrinsically satisfying	X	
Of the Organization		
9. Formalization (explicit plans, goals, and areas of responsibility)		X
10. Inflexibility (rigid, unbending rules and procedures)		X
11. Highly specified and active advisory and staff functions		X
12. Closely knit, cohesive work groups	X	X
13. Organizational rewards not within the leader's control	X	X
14. Spatial distance between superior and subordinates	X	X

SOURCE: Adapted from S Kerr and J M Jermier, "Substitutes for Leadership: Their Meaning and Measurement," *Organizational Behavior and Human Performance*, December 1978, pp 375–403.

Servant-Leadership

Servant-leadership is more a philosophy of managing than a testable theory. The term *servant-leadership* was coined by Robert Greenleaf in 1970. Greenleaf believes that great leaders act as servants, putting the needs of others, including employees, customers, and community, as their first priority. **Servant-leadership** focuses on increased service to others rather than to oneself.[53] According to Jim Stuart, co-founder of the leadership circle in Tampa, Florida, "Leadership derives naturally from a commitment to service. You know that you're practicing servant-leadership if your followers become wiser, healthier, more autonomous—and more likely to become servant-leaders themselves."[54] Servant-leadership is not a quick-fix approach to leadership. Rather, it is a long-term, transformational approach to life and work. Table 14–2 presents 10 characteristics possessed by servant-leaders. One can hardly go wrong by trying to adopt these characteristics.

> **Servant-leadership**
> Focuses on increased service to others rather than to oneself.

Nelson Mandela was a true servant-leader.

TABLE 14–2   Characteristics of the Servant-Leader

Servant-Leadership Characteristics	Description
1. Listening	Servant-leaders focus on listening to identify and clarify the needs and desires of a group.
2. Empathy	Servant-leaders try to empathize with others' feelings and emotions. An individual's good intentions are assumed even when he or she performs poorly.
3. Healing	Servant-leaders strive to make themselves and others whole in the face of failure or suffering.
4. Awareness	Servant-leaders are very self-aware of their strengths and limitations.
5. Persuasion	Servant-leaders rely more on persuasion than positional authority when making decisions and trying to influence others.
6. Conceptualization	Servant leaders take the time and effort to develop broader based conceptual thinking. Servant-leaders seek an appropriate balance between a short-term, day-to-day focus and a long-term, conceptual orientation.
7. Foresight	Servant-leaders have the ability to foresee future outcomes associated with a current course of action or situation.
8. Stewardship	Servant-leaders assume that they are stewards of the people and resources they manage.
9. Commitment to the growth of people	Servant-leaders are committed to people beyond their immediate work role. They commit to fostering an environment that encourages personal, professional, and spiritual growth.
10. Building community	Servant-leaders strive to create a sense of community both within and outside the work organization.

SOURCE: These characteristics and descriptions were derived from L C Spears, "Introduction: Servant-Leadership and the Greenleaf Legacy," in *Reflections on Leadership: How Robert K Greenleaf's Theory of Servant-Leadership Influenced Today's Top Management Thinkers*, ed L C Spears (New York: John Wiley & Sons, 1995), pp 1–14.

Superleadership

A **superleader** is someone who leads others to lead themselves. Super-leaders empower followers by acting as a teacher and coach rather than as a dictator and autocrat. The need for this form of leadership is under-scored by a survey of 1,046 Americans. Results demonstrated that only 38% of the respondents ever had an effective coach or mentor.[55]

> **Superleader**
>
> Someone who leads others to lead themselves.

Productive thinking is the cornerstone of superleadership. Specifically, managers are encouraged to teach followers how to engage in productive thinking.[56] This is expected to increase employees' feelings of personal control and intrinsic motivation. Superleadership has the potential to free up a manager's time because employees are encouraged to manage themselves. Future research is needed to test the validity of recommendations derived from this new approach to leadership.

chapter summary

- *Review trait theory research, and discuss the idea of one best style of leadership, using the Ohio State studies and the Leadership Grid® as points of reference.* Historical leadership research did not support the notion that effective leaders possessed unique traits from followers. However, teams of researchers reanalyzed this historical data with modern-day statistical procedures. Results revealed that individuals tend to be perceived as leaders when they possess one or more of the following traits: intelligence, dominance, and masculinity. Research also examined the relationship between gender and leadership. Results demonstrated that (a) leadership styles varied by gender, (b) men and women were equally assertive, and (c) women scored higher than their male counterparts on a variety of effectiveness criteria. The Ohio State studies revealed that there were two key independent dimensions of leadership behavior: consideration and initiating structure. Authors of the Leadership Grid® proposed that leaders should adopt a style that demonstrates high concern for production and people. Research did not support the premise that there is one best style of leadership.

- *Explain, according to Fiedler's contingency model, how leadership style interacts with situational control.* Fiedler believes leader effectiveness depends on an appropriate match between leadership style and situational control. Leaders are either task motivated or relationship motivated. Situation control is composed of leader–member relations, task structure, and position power. Task-motivated leaders are effective under situations of both high and low control. Relationship-motivated leaders are more effective when they have moderate situational control.

- *Discuss House's path–goal theory and Hersey and Blanchard's situational leadership theory.* According to path–goal theory, leaders alternately can exhibit directive, supportive, participative, or achievement-oriented styles of leadership. The effectiveness of these styles depends on various employee characteristics and environmental factors. Path–goal theory has received limited support from research. There are two important managerial implications: (a) leaders possess and use more than one style of leadership, and (b) managers are advised to modify their leadership style to fit a small subset of task and employee characteristics. According to situational leadership theory (SLT), effective leader behavior depends on the readiness level of a leader's followers. As follower readiness increases, leaders are advised to gradually move from a telling to a selling to a participating and, finally, to a delegating style. Research does not support SLT.

- *Describe how charismatic leadership transforms followers and work groups.* Individual and organizational characteristics influence whether or not managers exhibit charismatic leadership, which is composed of three sets of leader behavior. These leader behaviors, in turn, positively affect followers' and work groups' goals, values, beliefs, aspirations, and motivation. These positive effects are then associated with a host of preferred outcomes.

- *Explain the leader–member exchange model (LMX) of leadership and the substitutes for leadership.* The LMX model revolves around the development of dyadic relationships between managers and their direct reports. These leader–member exchanges qualify as either in-group or out-group relationships. Substitutes for leadership represent a variety of situational variables that can substitute for, neutralize, or enhance the effects of leadership. These substitutes contain characteristics of the subordinates, the task, and the organization.

- *Review the principles of servant-leadership and superleadership.* Servant-leadership is more a philosophy than a testable theory. It is based on the premise that

great leaders act as servants, putting the needs of others, including employees, customers, and community, as their first priority. A superleader is someone who leads others to lead themselves. Superleaders empower followers by acting as a teacher and coach rather than as a dictator and autocrat.

internet exercise

www.leader-values.com

The topic of leadership has been important since the dawn of time. History is filled with examples of great leaders such as Mohandas Gandhi, Martin Luther King, and Bill Gates. These leaders likely possessed some of the leadership traits discussed in this chapter, and they probably used a situational approach to lead their followers. The purpose of this exercise is for you to evaluate the leadership styles of a historical figure.

Go to the Internet home page for Leadership Values (**www.leader-values.com**), and select the subheading "4 E's" on the left side of the screen. This section provides an overview of leadership and suggests four essential traits/ behaviors that are exhibited by leaders to envision, enable, empower, and energize. After reading this material, go back to the home page, and select the subheading "Historical Lead-

ers" from the list on the left-hand side of the page. Next, choose one of the leaders from the list of historical figures, and read the description about his or her leadership style. You may want to print all of the material you read thus far from this Web page to help you answer the following questions.

QUESTIONS
1. Describe the 4 E's of leadership.
2. Using any of the theories or models discussed in this chapter, how would you describe the leadership style of the historical figure you investigated?
3. Was this leader successful in using the 4 E's of leadership? Describe how he/she used the 4 E's.

Managing Evolving Organizations

SOURCE: © PhotoDisc

five

part

Designing Effective Organizations

Fifteen chapter

LEARNING OBJECTIVES

After reading the material in this chapter, you should be able to:

- Describe the four characteristics common to all organizations.

- Explain the difference between closed and open systems, and contrast the biological and cognitive systems metaphors for organizations.

- Describe the four generic organizational effectiveness criteria.

- Explain what the contingency approach to organization design involves.

- Discuss Burns and Stalker's findings regarding mechanistic and organic organizations.

- List at least five characteristics each for new-style and old-style organizations.

MAKING ORGANIZATIONAL MUSIC

"You!" says the orchestra conductor, waving his baton at a couple of stocky fellows in the percussion section. "You are *so* right for this!"

It's the last session of Bank of America's Florida sales convention, and 200 or so managers and executives are sitting amid an orchestra of classical musicians. Conductor Roger Nierenberg is striding toward the two executives he has singled out, his tuxedo coattails flapping.

"I'm now radically shifting

"But I want to conduct!" protests one of the men. A woman seated in the audience calls out: "See what I have to deal with every day?" Everyone laughs.

Taking a team of talented, independent players and turning them into a well-tuned symphony is routine for musical conductors. Now Nierenberg, 54, whose day job is leading Connecticut's Stamford Symphony Orchestra, has created a program called "The Music Para-

showing them where the music needs to go and why. If you get scared on the podium, you start following the orchestra. Musicians hate it when you do that.

A leader defines for the team what kind of moment they're in. Is this a moment of transition? Is this a dangerous moment? Your job as conductor is to get the orchestra to act together—powerfully. So what do you do? You can't be calling out to people, "Act now! Act now!" That creates disorder. Instead, you say, "Here's where we're headed."

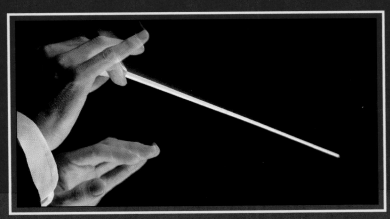

your relationship with this organization," says Nierenberg, leading the men up to the podium. "The orchestra is going to play. Your job up here is to listen."

digm." He teaches managers at companies such as Georgia-Pacific and Lucent Technologies how to be better leaders by giving them a musician's-eye view of a conductor at work. Here are a few lessons and observations from the maestro.

A leader is someone who commits to what hasn't happened yet. I'm always a step ahead of the musicians—I'm

Don't blame the orchestra. I had one experience where I had only one rehearsal with a major orchestra before a concert, and it went absolutely horribly. So when I stepped out in front of the audience the next day, I was sure that the performance was going to be an embarrassment. To my astonishment, the orchestra played perfectly. What I hadn't realized was that during the practice, the musicians were reading from illegible photocopies, so all of their energy was going into deciphering what was on the page. By concert time, they knew the music well enough to get the job done. What did I learn? Never assume. Be sure you know the cause before you decide that you have to fix the problem.

Give people permission to be their best. When teams don't execute as well as you'd like them to, your tendency is to think you have to adjust your connection with the team. But a lot of times, people are unconsciously waiting for permission to do what they're capable of doing. That may seem blatantly obvious to the leader, of course, but the team members need to be told. They're trying to gauge the right level of participation. People often are completely capable of a much higher level of performance, but they haven't gotten the green light from the podium.[1]

FOR DISCUSSION

What is the most important management lesson you have learned from this orchestra metaphor? For an interpretation of this case and additional comments, visit our website:

www.mhhe.com/kinickiob

VIRTUALLY EVERY ASPECT OF LIFE is affected at least indirectly by some type of organization.[2] We look to organizations to feed, clothe, house, educate, and employ us. Organizations attend to our needs for entertainment, police and fire protection, insurance, recreation, national security, transportation, news and information, legal assistance, and health care. Many of these organizations seek a profit, others do not. Some are extremely large, others are tiny mom-and-pop operations. Despite this mind-boggling diversity, modern organizations have one basic thing in common. They are the primary context for *organizational* behavior. In a manner of speaking, organizations are the chessboard upon which the game of organizational behavior is played. Therefore, present and future managers need a working knowledge of modern organizations to improve their chances of making the right moves when managing people at work.

This chapter explores the effectiveness, design, and future of today's organizations. We begin by defining the term *organization,* discussing important dimensions of organization charts, and examining modern organizational metaphors. Our attention then turns to criteria for assessing organizational effectiveness. Next, we discuss the contingency approach to designing organizations. We conclude with a profile of new-style organizations, with special attention to Internet-age *virtual* organizations.

Organizations: Definition and Dimensions

As a necessary springboard for this chapter, we need to formally define the term *organization* and clarify the meaning of organization charts.

What Is an Organization?

Organization

System of consciously coordinated activities of two or more people.

According to Chester I Barnard's classic definition, an **organization** is "a system of consciously coordinated activities or forces of two or more persons."[3] Embodied in the *conscious coordination* aspect of this definition are four common denominators of all organizations: coordination of effort, a common goal, division of labor, and a hierarchy of authority.[4] Organization theorists refer to these factors as the organization's *structure.*

Coordination of effort is achieved through formulation and enforcement of policies, rules, and regulations. Division of labor occurs when the common goal is pursued by individuals performing separate but related tasks. The hierarchy of authority, also called the chain of command, is a control mechanism dedicated to making sure the right people do the right things at the right time. Historically, managers have maintained the integrity of the hierarchy of authority by adhering to the unity of command principle. The **unity of command principle** specifies that each employee should report to only one manager. Otherwise, the argument goes, inefficiency would prevail because of conflicting orders and lack of personal accountability. (Indeed, these are problems in today's more fluid and flexible organizations based on innovations such as cross-functional and self-managed teams.) Managers in the hierarchy of authority also administer rewards and punishments. When operating in concert, the four definitional factors—coordination of effort, a common goal, division of labor, and a hierarchy of authority—enable an *organization* to exist.

Unity of command principle

Each employee should report to a single manager.

Organization chart

Boxes-and-lines illustration showing chain of formal authority and division of labor.

Organization Charts

An **organization chart** is a graphic representation of formal authority and division of labor relationships. To the casual observer, the term *organization chart* means the family tree–like pattern of boxes and lines posted on workplace walls. Within each box one usually finds the names and titles of current position holders. To organization theorists, however, organization charts reveal much more. The partial organization chart in Figure 15–1 reveals four basic dimensions of organizational structure: (1) hierarchy of authority (who reports to whom), (2) division of labor, (3) spans of control, and (4) line and staff positions.

Hierarchy of Authority   As Figure 15–1 illustrates, there is an unmistakable hierarchy of authority.[5] Working from bottom to top, the 10 directors report to the two executive directors who report to the president who reports to the chief executive officer. Ultimately, the chief executive officer answers to the hospital's board of directors. The chart in Figure 15–1 shows strict unity of command up and down the line. A formal hierarchy of authority also delineates the official communication network.

Division of Labor   In addition to showing the chain of command, the sample organization chart indicates extensive division of labor. Immediately below the hospital's president, one executive director is responsible for general administration while

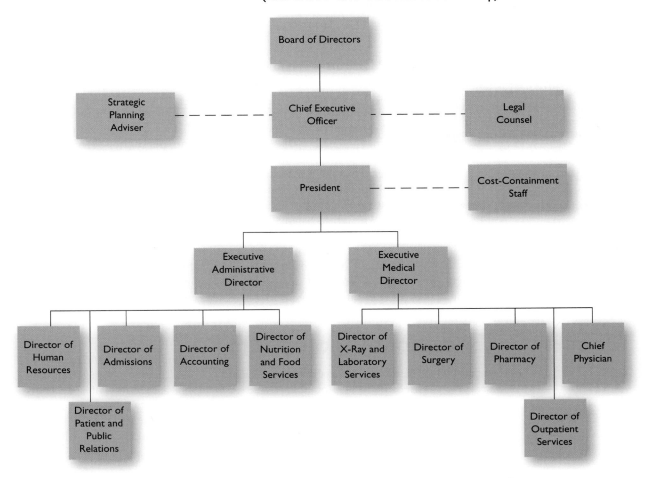

Sample Organization Chart for a Hospital   **FIGURE 15–1**
(executive and director levels only)

Organizations are human inventions to accomplish what individuals cannot do alone. Here, Jeff Bezos, founder and CEO of Amazon.com, gives a pep talk to his employees before the holiday season.

another is responsible for medical affairs. Each of these two specialties is further subdivided as indicated by the next layer of positions. At each successively lower level in the organization, jobs become more specialized.

Spans of Control   The **span of control** refers to the number of people reporting directly to a given manager.[6] Spans of control can range from narrow to wide. For example, the president in Figure 15–1 has a narrow span of control of two. (Staff assistants usually are not included in a manager's span of control.) The executive administrative director in Figure 15–1 has a wider span of control of five. Spans of control exceeding 30 can be found in assembly-line operations where machine-paced and repetitive work substitutes for close supervision. Historically, spans of five to six were considered best. Despite years of debate, organization theorists have not arrived at a consensus regarding the ideal span of control.

Generally, the narrower the span of control, the closer the supervision and the higher the administrative costs as a result of a higher manager-to-worker ratio. Recent emphasis on leanness and administrative efficiency dictates spans of control as wide as possible but guarding against inadequate supervision and lack of coordination. Wider spans also complement the trend toward greater worker autonomy and empowerment.

Span of control

The number of people reporting directly to a given manager.

Staff personnel

Provide research, advice, and recommendations to line managers.

Line managers

Have authority to make organizational decisions.

Line and Staff Positions   The organization chart in Figure 15–1 also distinguishes between line and staff positions. Line managers such as the president, the two executive directors, and the various directors occupy formal decision-making positions within the chain of command. Line positions generally are connected by solid lines on organization charts. Dotted lines indicate staff relationships. **Staff personnel** do background research and provide technical advice and recommendations to their **line managers,** who have the authority to make decisions. For example, the cost-containment specialists in the sample organization chart merely advise the president on relevant matters. Apart from supervising the work of their own staff assistants, they have no line authority over other organizational members. Modern trends such as cross-functional teams and reengineering are blurring the distinction between line and staff.

According to a study of 207 police officers in Israel, line personnel exhibited greater job commitment than did their staff counterparts.[7] This result was anticipated because the line managers' decision-making authority empowered them and gave them comparatively more control over their work situations.

Modern Organizational Metaphors

The complexity of modern organizations makes them somewhat difficult to describe. Consequently, organization theorists have resorted to the use of metaphors.[8] A *metaphor* is a figure of speech that characterizes one object in terms of another object. Good metaphors help us comprehend complicated things by describing them in everyday terms. In the opening case, for example, the organization is likened to an orchestra. OB scholar Kim

Cameron sums up the value of organizational metaphors as follows: "Each time a new metaphor is used, certain aspects of organizational phenomena are uncovered that were not evident with other metaphors. In fact, the usefulness of metaphors lies in their possession of some degree of falsehood so that new images and associations emerge."[9] With the orchestra metaphor, for instance, one could come away with an exaggerated picture of harmony in large and complex organizations. On the other hand, it realistically encourages us to view managers as facilitators rather than absolute dictators.

Early managers and management theorists used military units and machines as metaphors for organizations. These rigid closed-system models have given way to more dynamic and realistic metaphors. Modern organizational metaphors require *open-system* thinking.

Needed: Open-System Thinking

A **closed system** is said to be a self-sufficient entity. It is "closed" to the surrounding environment. In contrast, an **open system** depends on constant interaction with the environment for survival. The distinction between closed and open systems is a matter of degree. Because every worldly system is partly closed and partly open, the key question is: How great a role does the environment play in the functioning of the system? For instance, a battery-powered clock is a relatively closed system. Once the battery is inserted, the clock performs its time-keeping function hour

| **Closed system** |
| A relatively self-sufficient entity. |
| **Open system** |
| Organism that must constantly interact with its environment to survive. |

after hour until the battery goes dead. The human body, on the other hand, is a highly open system because it requires a constant supply of life-sustaining oxygen from the environment. Nutrients also are imported from the environment. Open systems are capable of self-correction, adaptation, and growth, thanks to characteristics such as homeostasis and feedback control.

The traditional military/mechanical metaphor is a closed system model because it largely ignores environmental influences. It gives the impression that organizations are self-sufficient entities. Conversely, the biological and cognitive metaphors discussed next emphasize interaction between organizations and their environments. These newer models are based on open-system assumptions. They reveal instructive insights about organizations and how they work. Each perspective offers something useful.

Organizations as Biological Systems

Drawing upon the field of general systems theory that emerged during the 1950s,[10] organization theorists suggested a more dynamic model for modern organizations. This metaphor likens organizations to the human body. Hence, it has been labeled the *biological model*. In his often-cited organization theory text, *Organizations in Action*, James D Thompson explained the biological model of organizations in the following terms:

> Approached as a natural system, the complex organization is a set of interdependent parts which together make up a whole because each contributes something and receives something from the whole, which in turn is interdependent with some larger environment. Survival of the system is taken to be the goal, and the parts and their relationships presumably are determined through evolutionary processes. . . .
>
> Central to the natural-system approach is the concept of homeostasis, or self-stabilization, which spontaneously, or naturally, governs the necessary relationships

FIGURE 15–2 | The Organization as an Open System: The Biological Model

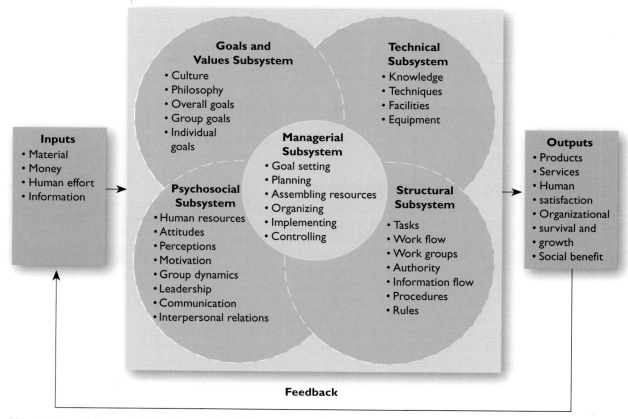

Inputs
- Material
- Money
- Human effort
- Information

Goals and Values Subsystem
- Culture
- Philosophy
- Overall goals
- Group goals
- Individual goals

Technical Subsystem
- Knowledge
- Techniques
- Facilities
- Equipment

Managerial Subsystem
- Goal setting
- Planning
- Assembling resources
- Organizing
- Implementing
- Controlling

Psychosocial Subsystem
- Human resources
- Attitudes
- Perceptions
- Motivation
- Group dynamics
- Leadership
- Communication
- Interpersonal relations

Structural Subsystem
- Tasks
- Work flow
- Work groups
- Authority
- Information flow
- Procedures
- Rules

Outputs
- Products
- Services
- Human
- satisfaction
- Organizational
- survival and
- growth
- Social benefit

Feedback

SOURCE: This model is a combination of Figures 5–2 and 5–3 in F E Kast and J E Rosenzweig, *Organization and Management: A Systems and Contingency Approach*, 4th ed (New York: McGraw-Hill, 1986), pp 112, 114. Copyright © 1986. Reproduced with permission of the McGraw-Hill Companies.

among parts and activities and thereby keeps the system viable in the face of disturbances stemming from the environment.[11]

Unlike the traditional military/mechanical theorists who downplayed the environment, advocates of the biological model stress organization–environment interaction. As Figure 15–2 illustrates, the biological model characterizes the organization as an open system that transforms inputs into various outputs. The outer boundary of the organization is permeable. People, information, capital, and goods and services move back and forth across this boundary. Moreover, each of the five organizational subsystems—goals and values, technical, psychosocial, structural, and managerial—is dependent on the others. Feedback about such things as sales and customer satisfaction or dissatisfaction enables the organization to self-adjust and survive despite uncertainty and change.[12] In effect, the organization is alive.

Organizations as Cognitive Systems

A more recent metaphor characterizes organizations in terms of mental functions. According to respected organization theorists Richard Daft and Karl Weick,

This perspective represents a move away from mechanical and biological metaphors of organizations. Organizations are more than transformation processes or control systems. To survive, organizations must have mechanisms to interpret ambiguous events and to provide meaning and direction for participants. Organizations are meaning systems, and this distinguishes them from lower-level systems. . . .

Almost all outcomes in terms of organization structure and design, whether caused by the environment, technology, or size, depend on the interpretation of problems or opportunities by key decision makers. Once interpretation occurs, the organization can formulate a response.[13]

This interpretation process, as it migrates throughout the organization, leads to organizational *learning* and adaptation.

In fact, the concept of the *learning organization,*[14] discussed in detail in Chapter 16, is very popular in management circles these days. Great Harvest Bread Co., based in Dillon, Montana, is an inspiring case in point (annual revenue for the company's 137 retail franchises, where grains are fresh-ground daily, exceeds $60 million):

> While most franchisors dictate everything about their franchisees' operations in order to ensure a predictable experience for customers everywhere, Great Harvest doesn't even require that its franchisees use the same bread recipes. . . . Instead, Great Harvest sets its franchisees free after a one-year apprenticeship to run their stores in the time-honored mom-and-pop way. Be unique, the company tells them; be yourselves, and experiment. . . .
>
> In other words, Great Harvest says to its bakery owners, *Do whatever you want.* Except in one respect, which makes all the difference: Every owner in the chain is encouraged to be part of Great Harvest's "learning community." Those who join (and most have) must share information, financial results, observations, and ideas. If asked questions, they must give answers. They must keep no secrets.[15]

Thus, it takes a cooperative culture, mutual trust, and lots of internal cross communication to fully exploit the organization as a cognitive system (or learning organization).

Striving for Organizational Effectiveness

Assessing organizational effectiveness is an important topic for an array of people, including managers, stockholders, government agencies, and OB specialists. The purpose of this section is to introduce a widely applicable and useful model of organizational effectiveness.

Generic Effectiveness Criteria

A good way to better understand this complex subject is to consider four generic approaches to assessing an organization's effectiveness (see Figure 15–3). These effectiveness criteria apply equally well to large or small and profit or not-for-profit organizations. Moreover, as denoted by the overlapping circles in Figure 15–3, the four effectiveness criteria can be used in various combinations. The key thing to remember is "no single approach to the evaluation of effectiveness is appropriate in all circumstances or for all organization types."[16] What do Coca-Cola and France Télécom, for example, have in common, other than being large profit-seeking corporations? Because a multidimensional approach is required, we need to look more closely at each of the four generic effectiveness criteria.

Goal Accomplishment   Goal accomplishment is the most widely used effectiveness criterion for organizations. Key organizational results or outputs are compared with previously stated goals or objectives. Deviations, either plus or minus,

FIGURE 15–3   Four Dimensions of Organizational Effectiveness

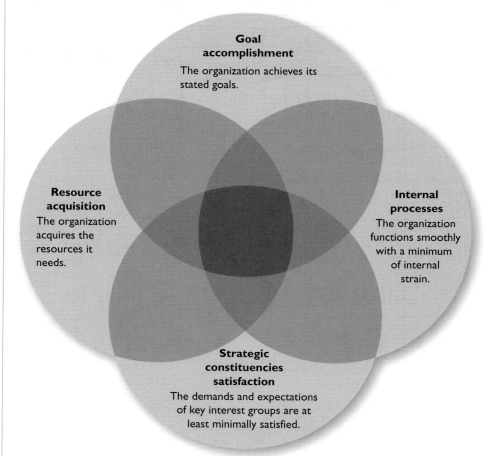

Goal accomplishment

The organization achieves its stated goals.

Resource acquisition

The organization acquires the resources it needs.

Internal processes

The organization functions smoothly with a minimum of internal strain.

Strategic constituencies satisfaction

The demands and expectations of key interest groups are at least minimally satisfied.

SOURCES: Adapted from discussion in K Cameron, "Critical Questions in Assessing Organizational Effectiveness," *Organizational Dynamics,* Autumn 1980, pp 66–80; and K S Cameron, "Effectiveness as Paradox: Consensus and Conflict in Conceptions of Organizational Effectiveness," *Management Science,* May 1986. pp 539–53.

require corrective action. This is simply an organizational variation of the personal goal-setting process discussed in Chapter 7. Effectiveness, relative to the criterion of goal accomplishment, is gauged by how well the organization meets or exceeds its goals.[17]

Productivity improvement, involving the relationship between inputs and outputs, is a common organization-level goal.[18] Goals also may be set for organizational efforts such as minority recruiting, pollution prevention, and quality improvement. Given today's competitive pressures and E-commerce revolution, *innovation* and *speed* are very important organizational goals worthy of measurement and monitoring.[19] Toyota gave a powerful indicator of where things are going in this regard. The Japanese auto maker announced it could custom-build a car in just five days! A customer's new Toyota would roll off the Ontario, Canada, assembly line just five days after the order was placed. A 30-day lag was the industry standard at the time.[20]

Resource Acquisition This second criterion relates to inputs rather than outputs. An organization is deemed effective in this regard if it acquires necessary factors of production such as raw materials, labor, capital, and managerial and technical expertise. Charitable organizations such as the Salvation Army judge their effectiveness in terms of how much money they raise from private and corporate donations.

Internal Processes Some refer to this third effectiveness criterion as the "healthy systems" approach. An organization is said to be a healthy system if information flows smoothly and if employee loyalty, commitment, job satisfaction, and trust prevail. Goals may be set for any of these internal processes. Healthy systems, from a behavioral standpoint, tend to have a minimum of dysfunctional conflict and destructive political maneuvering. M Scott Peck, the physician who wrote the highly regarded book, *The Road Less Traveled,* characterizes healthy organizations in ethical terms:

> A healthy organization, Peck says, is one that has a genuine sense of community: It's a place where people are emotionally present with one another, and aren't afraid to talk about fears and disappointments—because that's what allows us to care for one another. It's a place where there is authentic communication, a willingness to be vulnerable, a commitment to speaking frankly and respectfully—and a commitment not to walk away when the going gets tough.[21]

Strategic Constituencies Satisfaction Organizations both depend on people and affect the lives of people. Consequently, many consider the satisfaction of key interested parties to be an important criterion of organizational effectiveness.

> A **strategic constituency** is any group of individuals who have some stake in the organization—for example, resource providers, users of the organization's products or services, producers of the organization's output, groups whose cooperation is essential for the organization's survival, or those whose lives are significantly affected by the organization.[22]

Southwest Airlines is the envy of the beleaguered commercial airline industry because it is consistently effective at turning a profit by satisfying its customers and employees with a low-cost, on-time strategy and a no-layoff policy.

Strategic constituency

Any group of people with a stake in the organization's operation or success.

Strategic constituencies (or *stakeholders*) generally have competing or conflicting interests.[23] For instance, when pilots and other unionized employees were winning generous wage increases at major US airlines in 2001, profit-conscious investors and cost-conscious ticket buyers weren't cheering.[24]

Mixing Effectiveness Criteria: Practical Guidelines

Experts on the subject recommend a multidimensional approach to assessing the effectiveness of modern organizations. This means no single criterion is appropriate for all stages of the organization's life cycle. Nor will a single criterion satisfy competing stakeholders. Well-managed organizations mix and match effectiveness criteria to fit the unique requirements of the situation.[25] Managers need to identify and seek input from strategic constituencies. This information, when merged with the organization's stated mission and philosophy, enables management to derive an appropriate *combination* of effectiveness criteria. The following guidelines are helpful in this regard:

- *The goal accomplishment approach* is appropriate when "goals are clear, consensual, time-bounded, measurable."[26]
- *The resource acquisition approach* is appropriate when inputs have a traceable effect on results or output. For example, the amount of money the American Red Cross receives through donations dictates the level of services provided.
- *The internal processes approach* is appropriate when organizational performance is strongly influenced by specific processes (e.g., cross-functional teamwork).
- *The strategic constituencies approach* is appropriate when powerful stakeholders can significantly benefit or harm the oranization.[27]

As profiled in Skills & Best Practices, Medtronic, the 22,000-employee medical devices company with $5 billion in annual sales, satisfies an optimum mix of effectiveness criteria.[28]

The Contingency Approach to Designing Organizations

Contingency approach to organization design

Creating an effective organization–environment fit.

Mechanistic organizations

Rigid, command-and-control bureaucracies.

Organic organizations

Fluid and flexible network of multitalented people.

Centralized decision making

Top managers make all key decisions.

Decentralized decision making

Lower-level managers are empowered to make important decisions.

According to the **contingency approach to organization design,** organizations tend to be more effective when they are structured to fit the demands of the situation.[29] The purpose of this section is to introduce you to the contingency approach to organization design by reviewing a landmark study, drawing a distinction between centralized and decentralized decision making, contrasting new-style and old-style organizations, and discussing today's virtual organizations.

Mechanistic versus Organic Organizations

A landmark contingency design study was reported by a pair of British behavioral scientists, Tom Burns and G M Stalker. In the course of their research, they drew a very instructive distinction between what they called mechanistic and organic organizations. **Mechanistic organizations** are rigid bureaucracies with strict rules, narrowly defined tasks, and top-down communication. Ironically, it is at the cutting edge of technology that this seemingly out-of-date approach has found a home. In the highly competitive business of Web hosting—running clients' websites in high-security facilities humming with Internet servers—speed and reliability are everything. Enter military-style managers who require strict discipline, faithful adherence to thick rule books, and flawless execution. But, as *Business Week* observed, "The regimented atmosphere and military themes . . . may be tough to stomach for skilled workers used to a more free-spirited atmosphere."[30]

Oppositely, **organic organizations** are flexible networks of multitalented individuals who perform a variety of tasks.[31] W L Gore & Associates, the Newark, Delaware, maker of waterproof Gore-Tex fabric, is a highly organic organization because it lacks job descriptions and a formalized hierarchy and deemphasizes titles and status.[32]

A Matter of Degree

Importantly, as illustrated in the Hands-On Exercise, each of the mechanistic-organic characteristics is a matter of degree. Organizations tend to be *relatively* mechanistic or *relatively* organic. Pure types are rare because divisions, departments, or units in the same organization may be more or less mechanistic or organic. From an employee's standpoint, which organization structure would you prefer?

Different Approaches to Decision Making

Decision making tends to be centralized in mechanistic organizations and decentralized in organic organizations. **Centralized decision making** occurs when key decisions are made by top management. **Decentralized decision making** occurs when important decisions are made by middle- and lower-level managers. Generally, centralized organizations are more tightly controlled while decentralized organizations are more adaptive to changing situations.[33] Each has its appropriate use. For example, both Delta Air Lines and General Electric are very respected and successful companies, yet the former prefers centralization while the latter pushes decentralization.

Experts on the subject warn against extremes of centralization or decentralization. The challenge is to achieve a workable balance between the two extremes. A management consultant put it this way:

> The modern organization in transition will recognize the pull of two polarities: a need for greater centralization to create low-cost shared resources; and, a need to improve market responsiveness with greater decentralization. Today's winning organizations are the ones that can handle the paradox and tensions of both pulls. These are the firms that analyze the optimum organizational solution in each particular circumstance, without prejudice for one type of organization over another. The result is, almost invariably, a messy mixture of decentralized units sharing cost-effective centralized resources.[34]

Centralization and decentralization are not an either-or proposition; they are an *and-also* balancing act (see Skills & Best Practices).

Practical Research Insights

When they classified a sample of actual companies as either mechanistic or organic, Burns and Stalker discovered one type was not superior to the other. Each type had its appropriate place, depending on the environment. When the environment was relatively *stable and certain,* the

Medtronic Is Effective in Many Ways

Visitors to corporate headquarters in Fridley, Minn., a pastel-bungalow suburb of Minneapolis, are met by a statue of Earl Bakken, the engineer who co-founded Medtronic in 1949 with his brother-in-law, Palmer Hermundslie. Bakken is depicted in late middle age, wearing a baggy suit, squinting through a pair of aviator-frame glasses, and clutching in one hand a spookily banal box with a screwed-on faceplate, an on-off switch, and a dial for revving up the pulse rate—the primitive pacemaker that made Medtronic famous. The box looks like something straight out of Dr Frankenstein's laboratory, which is appropriate, for according to company legend, proudly recounted on the timeline in the lobby, it was the film version of *Frankenstein,* released in 1931, that awakened in young Earl Bakken a lifelong fascination with the role of electricity in medicine.

Bakken, 76, lives in Hawaii now but returns to Fridley often. He shows up at ceremonies to present new hires with their Medtronic medallions—keepsakes inscribed with an excerpt from the mission statement (ALLEVIATE PAIN, RESTORE HEALTH AND EXTEND LIFE). And he never misses the holiday party, Medtronic's annual rite of corporate renewal, where people whose bodies function thanks to Medtronic devices come to give testimonials. It's a teary, communal reminder that what goes on here day after day is not the same as making VCRs. "We have patients who come in who would be dead if it wasn't for us," says Karen McFadzen, a production supervisor. "I mean, they sit right up there and they tell us what their lives are like. You don't walk away from them not feeling anything."

If ever a company had a built-in advantage in the motivating-the-worker department, Medtronic is it. And its leaders know the power of playing to that advantage. But even making lifesaving medical devices is, ultimately, just a job. It takes constant care and feeding of corporate legend (remember *Frankenstein*) and mission (those medallions) to imbue Medtronic employees with a sense of satisfaction in their jobs day after day. In the employee surveys that help determine *Fortune*'s 100 Best Companies to Work For, 86% of Medtronic employees said their work had special meaning; 94% felt pride in what they accomplished.

SOURCE: Excerpted from D Whitford, "A Human Place to Work," *Fortune,* January 8, 2001, pp 110–111.

NOTE: Medtronic emphasizes innovation by having a strategic goal of earning 70% of its annual sales from products less than two years old.

Mechanistic or Organic?

INSTRUCTIONS Think of your present (or a past) place of employment and rate it on the following eight factors. Calculate a total score and compare it to the scale.

Characteristics

1. Task definition and knowledge required	Narrow, technical	1	2	3	4	5	6	7	Broad; general
2. Linkage between individual's contribution and organization's purpose	Vague or indirect	1	2	3	4	5	6	7	Clear or direct
3. Task flexibility	Rigid; routine	1	2	3	4	5	6	7	Flexible; varied
4. Specification of techniques, obligations, and rights	Specific	1	2	3	4	5	6	7	General
5. Degree of hierarchical control	High	1	2	3	4	5	6	7	Low (self-control emphasized)
6. Primary communication pattern	Top-down	1	2	3	4	5	6	7	Lateral (between peers)
7. Primary decision-making style	Authoritarian	1	2	3	4	5	6	7	Democratic; participative
8. Emphasis on obedience and loyalty	High	1	2	3	4	5	6	7	Low

Total score = _____

Scale

 8–24 = Relatively mechanistic

25–39 = Mixed

40–56 = Relatively organic

SOURCE: Adapted from discussion in T Burns and G M Stalker, *The Management of Innovation* (London: Tavistock, 1961), pp. 119–25.

successful organizations tended to be *mechanistic. Organic* organizations tended to be the successful ones when the environment was *unstable and uncertain.*[35]

In a more recent study of 103 department managers from eight manufacturing firms and two aerospace organizations, managerial skill was found to have a greater impact on a global measure of department effectiveness in organic departments than in mechanistic departments. This led the researchers to recommend the following contingencies for management staffing and training:

> If we have two units, one organic and one mechanistic, and two potential applicants differing in overall managerial ability, we might want to assign the more competent to the organic unit since in that situation there are few structural aids available to the manager in performing required responsibilities. It is also possible that managerial training is especially needed by managers being groomed to take over units that are more organic in structure.[36]

Another interesting finding comes from a study of 42 voluntary church organizations. As the organizations became more mechanistic (more bureaucratic) the intrinsic motivation of their members decreased. Mechanistic organizations apparently undermined the volunteers' sense of freedom and self-determination. Additionally, the researchers believe their findings help explain why bureaucracy tends to feed on itself: "A mechanistic organizational structure may breed the need for a more extremely mechanistic system because of the reduction in intrinsically motivated behavior."[37] Thus, bureaucracy begets greater bureaucracy.

Most recently, field research in two factories, one mechanistic and the other organic, found expected communication patterns. Command-and-control (downward) communication characterized the mechanistic factory. Consultative or participative (two-way) communication prevailed in the organic factory.[38]

Both Mechanistic and Organic Structures Have Their Places Although achievement-oriented students of OB typically express a distaste for mechanistic organizations, not all organizations or subunits can or should be organic. For example, McDonald's could not achieve its admired quality and service standards without extremely mechanistic restaurant operations. Imagine the food and service you would get if McDonald's employees used their own favorite ways of doing things and worked at their own pace! On the other hand, mechanistic structure alienates some employees because it erodes their sense of self-control.

New-Style versus Old-Style Organizations

Organization theorists Jay R Galbraith and Edward E Lawler III have called for a "new logic of organizing."[39] They recommend a whole new set of adjectives to describe organizations (see Table 15–1). Traditional pyramid-shaped organizations, conforming to the old-style pattern, tend to be too slow and inflexible today. Leaner, more organic organizations increasingly are needed to accommodate today's strategic balancing act between cost, quality, and speed. These new-style organizations embrace the total quality management (TQM) principles discussed in Chapter 1. This means they are customer focused, dedicated to continuous improvement and learning, and structured around teams. These qualities, along with computerized information technology, hopefully enable big organizations to mimic the speed and flexibility of small organizations.

Virtual Organizations

Like virtual teams, discussed in Chapter 10, modern information technology allows people in virtual organizations to get something accomplished despite being geographically dispersed.[40] Instead of relying heavily on face-to-face meetings, members of virtual organizations send E-mail and voice-mail messages, exchange project

---

SKILLS & BEST PRACTICES

Decentralization Works for Beck Group

Most construction firms wouldn't trust a single individual to control every aspect of a project as big as a $50 million, 1.2-million-square-foot JCPenney Distribution Center; they'd divvy up the purchasing, scheduling, and building. Not Beck Group. "I'm basically the president of my own little company," says senior project manager Jeff Forbes, who oversaw 750 employees for 19 months while running the Penney project in Fort Worth. "There's no micromanaging. I get to make whatever call I want. It gives me a lot more personal pride than in a situation being dictated by some corporate office."

Beck doesn't just throw its employees into the fire; they get lots of training to help them handle their autonomy. The company mandates a minimum of 40 hours of training a year, but most people opt for even more: The average is 66 hours. Employees like Forbes appreciate the opportunity to constantly add to their skills and knowledge; he recently spent a week studying business strategy at Dartmouth's Tuck School of Business Administration.

Beck also rewards those who work hard and do well: Employee recognition lunches are a frequent occurrence, and the company offers bonuses tied to customer satisfaction. Happy employees also make for happy customers: More than 80% of Beck's customers are repeat clients.

SOURCE: T Spencer, "Brainy Builders," *Fortune*, January 8, 2001, p 154.

TABLE 15–1   New-Style versus Old-Style Organizations

New	Old
Dynamic, learning	Stable
Information rich	Information is scarce
Global	Local
Small and large	Large
Product/customer oriented	Functional
Skills oriented	Job oriented
Team oriented	Individual oriented
Involvement oriented	Command/control oriented
Lateral/networked	Hierarchical
Customer oriented	Job requirements oriented

SOURCE: J R Galbraith and E E Lawler III, "Effective Organizations: Using the New Logic of Organizing," p 298 in *Organizing for the Future: The New Logic for Managing Complex Organizations*, eds J R Galbraith, E E Lawler III, and Associates. Copyright 1993 Jossey-Bass Inc. Publishers. Reprinted by permission of Jossey-Bass, Inc., a subsidiary of John Wiley & Sons, Inc.

Both figuratively and literally, people do not march in formation in today's organic organizations.

information over the Internet, and convene video-conferences among far-flung participants. In addition, cellular phones and the wireless Internet have made the dream of doing business from the beach a reality! This disconnection between work and location is causing managers to question traditional assumptions about centralized offices and factories. Why have offices for people who are never there because they are out finding and helping customers? Why have a factory when it is less expensive to contract out the work? Indeed, many so-called virtual organizations are really a *network* of several organizations hooked together contractually and electronically. A prime example is Monorail Inc., the Atlanta-based firm that began selling low-cost multimedia personal computers in late 1996. As *Business Week* reported at the time:

> [Monorail is] a company with just 40 employees that does no manufacturing and owns no inventory. The PCs are made by Phelps Technologies Inc. Finished PCs go from Phelps to Federal Express Corp. vans and direct to dealers. FedEx also handles dealer orders, delivers machines, and accepts and sends electronic payment.
> [Founder Doug] Johns hopes to eliminate retail inventories altogether. Consumers will get machines delivered to their homes in two days. For repairs or upgrades, customers call FedEx and schedule a pickup. The machines will be returned to Phelps and then sent back again by FedEx.[41]

Perhaps because of the inherent flexibility of its structure and business model, Monorail survived the dot-com crash and was still a going concern in 2001.

Gazing into the Crystal Ball   Here is how we envision life in the emerging virtual organizations and organizational networks. Things will be very interesting and profitable for the elite core of entrepreneurs and engineers who hit on the right business formula. Turnover among the financial and information "have nots"—data entry, customer service, and production employees—will be high because of glaring inequities and limited opportunities for personal fulfillment and growth. Telecommuters who work from home will feel liberated and empowered (and sometimes lonely). Commitment, trust, and loyalty could erode badly if managers do not heed this caution by Charles Handy, a British management expert. According to Handy: "A shared commitment still requires personal contact to make the commitment feel real. *Paradoxically, the more virtual an organization becomes the more its people need to meet in person.*"[42] Independent contractors, both individuals and organizations, will participate in many different organizational networks and thus have diluted loyalty to any single one. Substandard working conditions and low pay at some smaller contractors will make them little more than Internet-age sweat shops.[43] Companies living from one contract to another will offer little in the way of job security and benefits. Opportunities to start new businesses will be numerous, but prolonged success could prove elusive at Internet speed.[44]

Needed: Self-Starting Team Players   The only certainty about tomorrow's organizations is they will produce a lot of surprises. Only flexible, adaptable people who see problems as opportunities, are self-starters capable of teamwork, and are committed to life-long learning will be able to handle whatever comes their way.

chapter summary

- *Describe the four characteristics common to all organizations.* They are coordination of effort (achieved through policies and rules), a common goal (a collective purpose), division of labor (people performing separate but related tasks), and a hierarchy of authority (the chain of command).

- *Explain the difference between closed and open systems, and contrast the biological and cognitive systems metaphors for organizations.* Closed systems, such as a battery-powered clock, are relatively self-sufficient. Open systems, such as the human body, are highly dependent on the environment for survival. Organizations are said to be open systems. The biological metaphor views the organization as a living organism striving to survive in an uncertain environment. In terms of the cognitive metaphor, an organization is like the human mind, capable of interpreting and learning from uncertain and ambiguous situations.

- *Describe the four generic organizational effectiveness criteria.* They are goal accomplishment (satisfying stated objectives), resource acquisition (gathering the necessary productive inputs), internal processes (building and maintaining healthy organizational systems), and strategic constituencies satisfaction (achieving at least minimal satisfaction for all key stakeholders).

- *Explain what the contingency approach to organization design involves.* The contingency approach to organization design calls for fitting the organization to the demands of the situation.

- *Discuss Burns and Stalker's findings regarding mechanistic and organic organizations.* British researchers Burns and Stalker found that mechanistic (bureaucratic, centralized) organizations tended to be effective in stable situations. In unstable situations, organic (flexible, decentralized) organizations were more effective. These findings underscored the need for a contingency approach to organization design.

- *List at least five characteristics each for new-style and old-style organizations.* New-style organizations are characterized as dynamic and learning, information rich, global, small and large, product/customer oriented, skills oriented, team oriented, involvement oriented, lateral/networked, and customer oriented. Old-style organizations are characterized as stable, information is scarce, local, large, functional, job oriented, individual oriented, command/control oriented, hierarchical, and job requirements oriented.

internet exercise

There is no single way to measure organizational effectiveness, as discussed in this chapter. Different stakeholders want organizations to do different and often conflicting things. The purpose of this exercise is to introduce alternative effectiveness criteria and to assess real companies with them.

Each year, *Fortune* magazine publishes a ranking of America's Most Admired Companies. Some might pass this off as simply a corporate image popularity contest. But we view it as much more. *Fortune* applies a set of eight attributes that arguably could be called effectiveness criteria. You can judge for yourself by going to *Fortune*'s Internet site (**www.fortune.com**) and clicking on "View all Fortune Lists." Then, select "America's Most Admired Companies." Click on the heading "Custom Ranking," and follow the instructions for both the "Basic" and "Advanced" searches of the Most Admired Companies database. For the advanced search, we recommend you begin with the category "All Industries." You may want to do subsequent rankings for your employer's industry or for one or more industries of particular interest.

QUESTIONS

1. Do you agree that the eight attributes are really organizational effectiveness criteria? Explain. What others would you add to the list? Which would you remove from the list?
2. How did you rank each of the eight attributes?
3. Are you surprised by the top-ranked company (or companies) in the All Industries ranking? Explain.
4. Do you admire the top-ranked company? Why or why not?

Managing Change and Organizational Learning

Sixteen

chapter

After reading the material in this chapter, you should be able to:

- Discuss the external and internal forces that create the need for organizational change.

- Describe Lewin's change model and the systems model of change.

- Explain Kotter's eight steps for leading organizational change.

- Review the 10 reasons employees resist change.

- Identify alternative strategies for overcoming resistance to change.

- Discuss the process organizations use to build their learning capabilities.

BOEING EFFECTIVELY IMPLEMENTS ORGANIZATIONAL CHANGE

When aircraft manufacturers Boeing and McDonnell Douglas merged four years ago, everyone expected the 717 program to crash. Like three other airplane programs housed at McDonnell Douglas' Long Beach, CA facility, the 717 was losing money like jettisoning fuel—millions of dollars, in fact, on each 100-seat commercial jet built. But unlike those other programs, Boeing executives didn't clip the wings of the down-trodden 717. Instead, they decided to fix it. Today, the program that was expected to sell fewer than 200 planes in its lifetime is flying high with orders for more than 300 planes. And unlike the 717s of four years ago—these planes earn Boeing a profit. . . .

In the beginning, the strategic transformation of Boeing's ailing 717 airplane was viewed as just another "flavor of the month," says Ariene Rios, a union representative for employee involvement at Boeing. Employees were skeptical, having seen many "improvement programs" come and go, and were consequently hesitant to jump on board.

Convincing them required a change process that involved leadership training

and mentoring for managers, which taught them the importance of modeling the behaviors and attitudes they expected on the factory floor. "We had to turn managers into team leaders," says Rios.

For managers who admittedly spent more time "fighting fires" than worrying about the future, Rios knew this would be a challenge. In the new environment, dealing with the problems of the day would only be a small part of a manager's job. As leaders of the 717 program, their new roles would include helping teams become aligned with the company's "value goals" and providing them with the tools to achieve those goals.

Before the rest of 717's employees even began training, managers participated in seven, four-hour leadership skills workshops. Over the course of three and a half weeks, they learned how to coach employees and generate commitment and enthusiasm. They also spent time at the Open Leadership Center in St. Louis where they practiced envisioning value goals and looking at the big picture from a profit standpoint. In short, says Rios, "they were shown the difference between managing and leading."[1]

FOR DISCUSSION

What is your reaction to the process of change used by Boeing? For an interpretation on this case and additional comments, visit our website:

www.mhhe.com/kinickiob

THE RATE OF ORGANIZATIONAL AND SOCIETAL CHANGE is clearly accelerating, and companies must change to survive. As exemplified by Boeing in the opening case, people resist change even when the change is occurring for good reason. The Boeing case also illustrates that successful organizational change requires managerial commitment, an implementation plan, and buy-in from all employees. Peter Senge, a well-known expert on the topic of organizational change, made the following comment about organizational change during an interview with *Fast Company* magazine:

> When I look at efforts to create change in big companies over the past 10 years, I have to say that there's enough evidence of success to say that change is possible—and enough evidence of failure to say that it isn't likely.[2]

If Senge is correct, then it is all the more important for current and future managers to learn how they can successfully implement organizational change. This final chapter was written to help managers navigate the journey of change.

Specifically, we discuss the forces that create the need for organization change, models of planned change, resistance to change, and creating a learning organization.

Forces of Change

How do organizations know when they should change? What cues should an organization look for? Although there are no clear-cut answers to these questions, the "cues" that signal the need for change are found by monitoring the forces for change.

Organizations encounter many different forces for change. These forces come from external sources outside the organization and from internal sources. This section examines the forces that create the need for change. Awareness of the forces of change can help managers determine when they should consider implementing an organizational change.

External Forces

External forces for change
Originate outside the organization.

External forces for change originate outside the organization. Because these forces have global effects, they may cause an organization to question the essence of what business it is in and the process by which products and services are produced. There are four key external forces for change: demographic characteristics, technological advancements, market changes, and social and political pressures. Each is now discussed.

Demographic Characteristics Chapter 4 provided a detailed discussion of the demographic changes occurring in the US workforce. We concluded that organizations need to effectively manage diversity if they are to receive maximum contribution and commitment from employees. Consider the implications associated with hiring the 80 million people dubbed the Net or Echo-Boom Generation—people born between 1977 and 1997.

> Employers will have to face the new realities of the Net Generation's culture and values, and what it wants from work if they expect to attract and retain those talents and align them with corporate goals. . . . The new wave of 80 million young people entering the workforce during the next 20 years are technologically equipped and, therefore, armed with the most powerful tools for business. That makes their place in history unique: No previous generation has grown up understanding, using, and expanding on such a pervasive instrument as the PC[3].

The organizational challenge will be to motivate and utilize this talented pool of employees to its maximum potential.

Technological Advancements   Both manufacturing and service organizations are increasingly using technology as a means to improve productivity and market competitiveness. Development and use of information technologies is probably one of the biggest forces for change. Organizations, large and small, private and public, for profit and not for profit, all must adapt to using a host of information technologies. Experts also predict that E-business will continue to create evolutionary change in organizations around the world.

Market Changes   The emergence of a global economy is forcing companies to change the way they do business. For example, many Japanese companies are having to discontinue their jobs-for-life philosophy because of increased international competition. US companies are also forging new partnerships and alliances with their suppliers and potential competitors. For example, AOL has created alliances with drkoop.com, GTE, US West, Sun, and Nintendo, while Oracle has between 15,000 and 16,000 business alliances.[4]

Social and Political Pressures   These forces are created by social and political events. For example, tobacco companies are experiencing a lot of pressure to alter the way they market their products within the United States. This pressure is being exerted through legislative bodies that represent the American populace. Political events can create substantial change. For instance, the collapse of the Berlin Wall and communism in Russia created many new business opportunities.

Internal Forces

Internal forces for change come from inside the organization. These forces can be subtle, such as low job satisfaction, or can manifest in outward signs, such as low productivity or high turnover and conflict. Internal forces for change come from both human resource problems and managerial behavior/decisions. Jacques Nasser, former CEO of Ford Motor Company, for example, instituted a host of internal changes aimed at improving Ford's financial position, productivity, quality, and customer satisfaction:

> **Internal forces for change**
>
> Originate inside the organization.

> Almost as soon as he ascended to the corner office, Nasser began overhauling Ford, unveiling one initiative after another. He signed agreements to partner with Microsoft Corp. and Yahoo! Inc. on the Web. He pushed out Ford's Old Guard and brought in talented young stars from the auto industry and beyond. He flattened Ford's bureaucracy, giving more autonomy to regional executives, and shook up senior managers by tying their bonuses to gains in customer service. Gone were the days of automatic promotions and seniority. "You've got to earn a promotion" he thundered at young execs shortly after becoming CEO. "The days of entitlement at Ford Motor Co. are gone forever."[5]

Models of Planned Change

American managers are criticized for emphasizing short-term, quick-fix solutions to organizational problems. When applied to organizational change, this approach is doomed from the start. Quick-fix solutions do not really solve underlying causes of problems and they have little staying power. Researchers and managers alike have thus tried to identify effective ways to manage the change process. This section reviews three models of planned change—Lewin's change model, a systems model of change, and Kotter's eight steps for leading organizational change—and organizational development.

Lewin's Change Model

Most theories of organizational change originated from the landmark work of social psychologist Kurt Lewin. Lewin developed a three-stage model of planned change which explained how to initiate, manage, and stabilize the change process.[6] The three stages are unfreezing, changing, and refreezing.

Unfreezing   The focus of this stage is to create the motivation to change. In so doing, individuals are encouraged to replace old behaviors and attitudes with those desired by management. Managers can begin the unfreezing process by disconfirming the usefulness or appropriateness of employees' present behaviors or attitudes. In other words, employees need to become dissatisfied with the old way of doing things. Benchmarking is a technique that can be used to help unfreeze an organization.

Benchmarking "describes the overall process by which a company compares its performance with that of other companies, then learns how the strongest-performing companies achieve their results."[7] For example, one company for which we consulted discovered through benchmarking that their costs to develop a computer system were twice as high as the best companies in the industry, and the time it took to get a new product to market was four times longer than the benchmarked organizations. These data were ultimately used to unfreeze employees' attitudes and motivate people to change the organization's internal processes in order to remain competitive.[8] Managers also need to devise ways to reduce the barriers to change during this stage.

> **Benchmarking**
>
> Process by which a company compares its performance with that of high-performing organizations.

Change is constant and unavoidable today. "Unfreezing" prepares employees for change.

Changing   Because change involves learning, this stage entails providing employees with new information, new behavioral models, or new ways of looking at things. The purpose is to help employees learn new concepts or points of view. Consider, for example, the organizational changes implemented by KPMG Consulting as it transforms itself from an organization run by a partnership to one that is publicly held and focuses on meeting financial goals:

> The massive mahogany desks and expansive offices once occupied by KPMG's venerated partners have given way to cookie-cutter work spaces, pint-size offices, and managing directors. . . . KPMG Consulting has already laid off 800 of its 10,000 employees in the past 16 months, for which it will take a $15 million to $20 million charge. . . . Those who are left have had to adapt to an environment in which the focus is firmly on the numbers. Instead of measuring profitability once a year—standard operating procedure in the partnership—the company now monitors financials constantly. Every Friday, Senior Vice President Kenneth C Taormina grills his sales force on every would-be client: "I go through every single deal [asking] 'What do we need to get it done?' " Even the office kitty that partners dipped into freely for moral-building activities such as staff dinners is now under scrutiny.[9]

Directors at KPMG are clearly trying to get employees to become more customer focused and cost conscious. During the change process like that at KPMG, organizations use role models, mentors, consultants, benchmarking results, and training to facilitate change. Experts recommend that it is best to convey the idea that change is a continuous learning process rather than a one-time event.

Refreezing   Change is stabilized during refreezing by helping employees integrate the changed behavior or attitude into their normal way of doing things. This is accomplished by first giving employees the chance to exhibit the new behaviors or attitudes. Once exhibited, positive reinforcement is used to reinforce the desired change. Additional coaching and modeling also are used at this point to reinforce the stability of the change.

A Systems Model of Change

A systems approach takes a "big picture" perspective of organizational change. It is based on the notion that any change, no matter how large or small, has a cascading effect throughout an organization. For example, promoting an individual to a new work group affects the group dynamics in both the old and new groups. Similarly, creating project or work teams may necessitate the need to revamp compensation practices. These examples illustrate that change creates additional change. Today's solutions are tomorrow's problems. A systems model of change offers managers a framework to understand the broad complexities of organizational change.[10] The three main components of a systems model are inputs, target elements of change, and outputs (see Figure 16–1).

Inputs   All organizational changes should be consistent with an organization's mission, vision, and resulting strategic plan. A **mission statement** represents the "reason" an organization exists, and an organization's *vision* is a long-term goal that describes "what" an organization wants to become. Consider how the difference between mission and vision affects organizational change. Your university probably has a mission to educate people. This mission does not necessarily imply anything about change. It simply defines the

Mission statement

Summarizes "why" an organization exists.

FIGURE 16–1   A Systems Model of Change

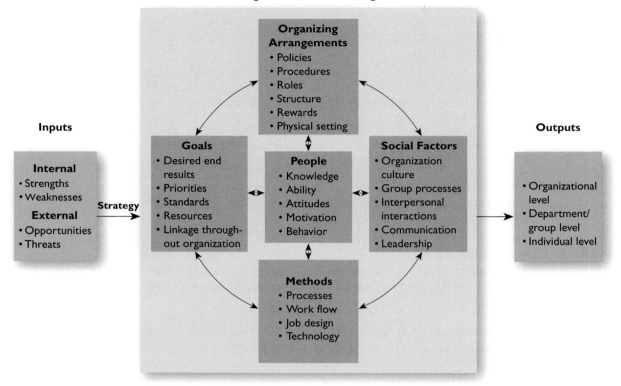

Target Elements of Change

Inputs

Internal
• Strengths
• Weaknesses

External
• Opportunities
• Threats

Strategy

Organizing Arrangements
• Policies
• Procedures
• Roles
• Structure
• Rewards
• Physical setting

Goals
• Desired end results
• Priorities
• Standards
• Resources
• Linkage throughout organization

People
• Knowledge
• Ability
• Attitudes
• Motivation
• Behavior

Social Factors
• Organization culture
• Group processes
• Interpersonal interactions
• Communication
• Leadership

Methods
• Processes
• Work flow
• Job design
• Technology

Outputs

• Organizational level
• Department/ group level
• Individual level

SOURCES: Adapted from D R Fuqua and D J Kurpius, "Conceptual Models in Organizational Consultation," *Journal of Counseling & Development*, July/August 1993, pp 602–18; and D A Nadler and M L Tushman, "Organizational Frame Bending: Principles for Managing Reorientation," *Academy of Management Executive*, August 1989, pp 194–203.

university's overall purpose. In contrast, the university may have a vision to be recognized as the "best" university in the country. This vision requires the organization to benchmark itself against other world-class universities and to create plans for achieving the vision. While vision statements point the way, strategic plans contain the detail needed to create organizational change.

Strategic plan

A long-term plan outlining actions needed to achieve planned results.

A **strategic plan** outlines an organization's long-term direction and actions necessary to achieve planned results. Strategic plans are based on considering an organization's strengths and weaknesses relative to its environmental opportunities and threats. This comparison results in developing an organizational strategy to attain desired outputs such as profits, customer satisfaction, quality, adequate return on investment, and acceptable levels of turnover and employee commitment (see Figure 16–1). In summary, organizations tend to commit resources to counterproductive or conflicting activities when organizational changes are not consistent with its strategic plan.

Target elements of change

Components of an organization that may be changed.

Target Elements of Change   Target elements of change represent the components of an organization that may be changed. As shown in Figure 16–1, change can be directed at realigning organizing arrangements, social factors, methods, goals, and people.[11] The choice is based on the strategy being pursued or the organizational problem at hand. For example, Hershey Foods Corporation targeted a technological change in order to improve the distribution and sales of its products. Unfortunately, the organization struggled with the technological intervention, and competitors benefited from Hershey's problems:

> For the nation's largest candy maker, with revenue of $4.44 billion last year, this could turn out to be a very scary Halloween. New technology that came on line in July has gummed up its ordering-and-distribution system, leaving many stores nationwide reporting spot shortages of Kisses, Kit Kats, Twizzlers, and other stalwarts of the trick-or-treating season. In mid-July, Hershey flipped the switch on a $112 million computer system that was supposed to automate and modernize everything from taking candy orders to putting pallets on trucks. Two months later, the company announced that something was wrong. Now, an additional six weeks later—and with Halloween looming—it's still working out the kinks and says it hopes to have everything running smoothly by early December. . . . Already, rivals are benefiting without making much effort.[12]

This example also highlights that change begets change. Specifically, a change in methods—a new computer system—led to additional changes in organizing arrangements and goals.

Outputs   Outputs represent the desired end results of a change. Once again, these end results should be consistent with an organization's strategic plan. Figure 16–1 indicates that change may be directed at the organizational level, department/group level, or individual level. Change efforts are more complicated and difficult to manage when they are targeted at the organizational level. This occurs because organizational-level changes are more likely to affect multiple target elements of change shown in the model.

Kotter's Eight Steps for Leading Organizational Change

John Kotter, an expert in leadership and change management, believes that organizational change typically fails because senior management makes a host of implementation errors. Kotter recommends that organizations should follow eight sequential steps to overcome these implementation problems (see Table 16–1).[13]

These steps also subsume Lewin's model of change. The first four steps represent Lewin's "unfreezing" stage. Steps 5, 6, and 7 represent "changing," and step 8 corresponds to "refreezing." The value of Kotter's steps is that it provides specific recommendations about behaviors that managers need to exhibit to successfully lead organizational change. It is important to remember that Kotter's research reveals that it is ineffective to skip steps and that successful organizational change is 70% to 90% leadership and only 10% to 30% management. Senior managers are thus advised to focus on leading rather than managing change.[14]

Organization Development

Organization development (OD) is an applied field of study and practice. A pair of OD experts defined **organization development** as follows:

> Organization development is concerned with helping managers plan change in organizing and managing people that will develop requisite commitment, coordination, and competence. Its purpose is to enhance both the effectiveness of organizations and the well-being of their

Organization development

A set of techniques or tools that are used to implement organizational change.

TABLE 16–1   Steps to Leading Organizational Change

Step	Description
1. Establish a sense of urgency	Unfreeze the organization by creating a compelling reason for why change is needed.
2. Create the guiding coalition	Create a cross-functional, cross-level group of people with enough power to lead the change.
3. Develop a vision and strategy	Create a vision and strategic plan to guide the change process.
4. Communicate the change vision	Create and implement a communication strategy that consistently communicates the new vision and strategic plan.
5. Empower broad-based action	Eliminate barriers to change, and use target elements of change to transform the organization. Encourage risk taking and creative problem solving.
6. Generate short-term wins	Plan for and create short-term "wins" or improvements. Recognize and reward people who contribute to the wins.
7. Consolidate gains and produce more change	The guiding coalition uses credibility from short-term wins to create more change. Additional people are brought into the change process as change cascades throughout the organization. Attempts are made to reinvigorate the change process.
8. Anchor new approaches in the culture	Reinforce the changes by highlighting connections between new behaviors and processes and organizational success. Develop methods to ensure leadership development and succession.

SOURCE: The steps were developed by J P Kotter, *Leading Change* (Boston: Harvard Business School Press, 1996).

members through planned interventions in the organization's human processes, structures, and systems, using knowledge of behavioral science and its intervention methods.[15]

As you can see from this definition, OD constitutes a set of techniques or interventions that are used to implement organizational change. These techniques or interventions apply to each of the change models discussed in this section. For example, OD is used during Lewin's "changing" stage. It also is used to identify and implement targeted elements of change within the systems model of change. Finally, OD might be used during Kotter's steps 1, 3, 5, 6, and 7. In this section, we briefly review the four identifying characteristics of OD and its research and practical implications.[16]

OD Involves Profound Change   Change agents using OD generally desire deep and long-lasting improvement. OD consultant Warner Burke, for example, who strives for fundamental *cultural* change, wrote: "By fundamental change, as opposed to fixing a problem or improving a procedure, I mean that some significant aspect of an organization's culture will never be the same."[17]

OD Is Value Loaded   Owing to the fact that OD is rooted partially in humanistic psychology, many OD consultants carry certain values or biases into the client organization. They prefer cooperation over conflict, self-control over institutional control, and democratic and participative management over autocratic management. In addition to OD being driven by a consultant's values, some OD practitioners now believe that there is a broader "value perspective" that should underlie any organizational change. Specifically, OD should always be customer focused. This approach implies that organizational interventions should be aimed at helping to satisfy customers' needs and thereby provide enhanced value of an organization's products and services.

OD Is a Diagnosis/Prescription Cycle　OD theorists and practitioners have long adhered to a medical model of organization. Like medical doctors, internal and external OD consultants approach the "sick" organization, "diagnose" its ills, "prescribe" and implement an intervention, and "monitor" progress.

OD Is Process Oriented　Ideally, OD consultants focus on the form and not the content of behavioral and administrative dealings. For example, product design engineers and market researchers might be coached on how to communicate more effectively with one another without the consultant knowing the technical details of their conversations. In addition to communication, OD specialists focus on other processes, including problem solving, decision making, conflict handling, trust, power sharing, and career development.

OD Research and Practical Implications　Before discussing OD research, it is important to note that many of the topics contained in this book are used during OD interventions. Team building, for example, is commonly used as an OD intervention. It is used to improve the functioning of work groups. The point is that OD research has practical implications for a variety of OB applications previously discussed. OD-related interventions produced the following insights:

- A meta-analysis of 18 studies indicated that employee satisfaction with change was higher when top management was highly committed to the change effort.[18]

- A meta-analysis of 52 studies provided support for the systems model of organizational change. Specifically, varying one target element of change created changes in other target elements. Also, there was a positive relationship between individual behavior change and organizational-level change.[19]

- A meta-analysis of 126 studies demonstrated that multifaceted interventions using more than one OD technique were more effective in changing job attitudes and work attitudes than interventions that relied on only one human-process or technostructural approach.[20]

There are three practical implications derived from this research. First, planned organization change works. However, management and change agents are advised to rely on multifaceted interventions. As indicated elsewhere in this book, goal setting, feedback, recognition and rewards, training, participation, and challenging job design have good track records relative to improving performance and satisfaction. Second, change programs are more successful when they are geared toward meeting both short-term and long-term results. Managers should not engage in organizational change for the sake of change. Change efforts should produce positive results.[21] Finally, organizational change is more likely to succeed when top management is truly committed to the change process and the desired goals of the change program. This is particularly true when organizations pursue large-scale transformation.

Understanding and Managing Resistance to Change

We are all creatures of habit. It generally is difficult for people to try new ways of doing things. It is precisely because of this basic human characteristic that most employees do not have enthusiasm for change in the workplace. Rare is the manager who does not have several stories about carefully cultivated changes that died on the vine because of resistance to change. It is important for managers to learn to manage resistance because failed change efforts are costly. Costs include decreased employee loyalty, lowered probability of achieving corporate goals, waste of money and resources, and difficulty in fixing the failed change effort. This section examines employee resistance to change and practical ways of dealing with the problem.

Why People Resist Change in the Workplace

No matter how technically or administratively perfect a proposed change may be, people make or break it. Individual and group behavior following an organizational change can take many forms. The extremes range from acceptance to active resistance. **Resistance to change** is an emotional/behavioral response to real or imagined threats to an established work routine. Resistance can be as subtle as passive resignation and as overt as deliberate sabotage. Let us now consider the reasons employees resist change in the first place. Ten of the leading reasons are listed here:[22]

Resistance to change

Emotional/behavioral response to real or imagined work changes.

1. *An individual's predisposition toward change.* This predisposition is highly personal and deeply ingrained. It is an outgrowth of how one learns to handle change and ambiguity as a child. While some people are distrustful and suspicious of change, others see change as a situation requiring flexibility, patience, and understanding.[23]

Fear of the unknown and mistrust can prompt resistance to change.

2. *Surprise and fear of the unknown.* When innovative or radically different changes are introduced without warning, affected employees become fearful of the implications. Grapevine rumors fill the void created by a lack of official announcements. Harvard's Rosabeth Moss Kanter recommends appointing a transition manager charged with keeping all relevant parties adequately informed.[24]

3. *Climate of mistrust.* Trust, as discussed in Chapter 10, involves reciprocal faith in others' intentions and behavior. Mutual mistrust can doom to failure an otherwise well-conceived change. Mistrust encourages secrecy, which begets deeper mistrust. Managers who trust their employees make the change process an open, honest, and participative affair. Employees who, in turn, trust management are more willing to expend extra effort and take chances with something different. Robert Shapiro, CEO of Monsanto, believes that trust plays a key role in building employee morale and leading organizational change. He made the following comments during an interview for *USA Today* about this issue:

> You can't get to good morale by lying. You can get to illusion that way. If I was faced with a decision that might hurt morale at a crucial time, I might delay the decision. In companies there is reciprocity. If you manipulate workers, they're going to manipulate you. The old Marxist class model was the people on top tried to manipulate the people on the bottom and the people on the bottom tried to manipulate the people on the top. You can't get innovation that way. You find an enormous amount of time and effort is dealing with the lack of trust of others. Look at all the inefficiencies of lack of trust. It tells you that an honest organization is going to be much more efficient. It just makes good business sense.[25]

4. *Fear of failure.* Intimidating changes on the job can cause employees to doubt their capabilities. Self-doubt erodes self-confidence and cripples personal growth and development.

5. *Loss of status and/or job security.* Administrative and technological changes that threaten to alter power bases or eliminate jobs generally trigger strong resistance. For example, most corporate restructuring involves the elimination of managerial jobs. One should not be surprised when middle managers resist restructuring and participative management programs that reduce their authority and status.

6. *Peer pressure.* Someone who is not directly affected by a change may actively resist it to protect the interest of his or her friends and co-workers.

7. *Disruption of cultural traditions and/or group relationships.* Whenever individuals are transferred, promoted, or reassigned, cultural and group dynamics are thrown into disequilibrium.

8. *Personality conflicts.* Just as a friend can get away with telling us something we would resent hearing from an adversary, the personalities of change agents can breed resistance.

9. *Lack of tact and/or poor timing.* Undue resistance can occur because changes are introduced in an insensitive manner or at an awkward time.

10. *Nonreinforcing reward systems.* Individuals resist when they do not foresee positive rewards for changing. For example, an employee is unlikely to

Assessing an Organization's Readiness for Change

INSTRUCTIONS   Circle the number that best represents your opinions about the company being evaluated.

3 = Yes   2 = Somewhat   1 = No

1. Is the change effort being sponsored by a senior-level executive (CEO, COO)?   3 2 1

2. Are all levels of management committed to the change?   3 2 1

3. Does the organization culture encourage risk taking?   3 2 1

4. Does the organization culture encourage and reward continuous improvement?   3 2 1

5. Has senior management clearly articulated the need for change?   3 2 1

6. Has senior management presented a clear vision of a positive future?   3 2 1

7. Does the organization use specific measures to assess business performance?   3 2 1

8. Does the change effort support other major activities going on in the organization?   3 2 1

9. Has the organization benchmarked itself against world-class companies?   3 2 1

10. Do all employees understand the customers' needs?   3 2 1

11. Does the organization reward individuals and/or teams for being innovative and for looking for root causes of organizational problems?   3 2 1

12. Is the organization flexible and cooperative?   3 2 1

13. Does management effectively communicate with all levels of the organization?   3 2 1

14. Has the organization successfully implemented other change programs?   3 2 1

15. Do employees take personal responsibility for their behavior?   3 2 1

16. Does the organization make decisions quickly?   3 2 1

Total score: _____

ARBITRARY NORMS
40–48 = High readiness for change
 4–39 = Moderate readiness for change
16–23 = Low readiness for change

SOURCE: Based on the discussion contained in T A Stewart, "Rate Your Readiness to Change," *Fortune*, February 7, 1994, pp 106–10.

support a change effort that is perceived as requiring him or her to work longer with more pressure.

Alternative Strategies for Overcoming Resistance to Change

Before recommending specific approaches to overcome resistance, there are four key conclusions that should be kept in mind. First, an organization must be ready for change. Just as a table must be set before you can eat, so must an organization be ready for change before it can be effective.[26] The Hands-On Exercise contains a survey that assesses an organization's readiness for change. Use the survey to evaluate a company that you worked for or are familiar with that undertook a change effort. What was the company's readiness for change, and how did this evaluation relate to the success of the change effort?

Second, organizational change is less successful when top management fails to keep employees informed about the process of change. Third, do not assume that people are consciously resisting change. Managers are encouraged to use a systems model of change to identify the obstacles that are affecting the implementation process. Fourth, employees' perceptions or interpretations of a change significantly affect resistance. Employees are less likely to resist when they perceive that the benefits of a change overshadow the personal costs. At a minimum then, managers are advised to (1) provide as much information as possible to employees about the change, (2) inform employees about the reasons/rationale for the change, (3) conduct meetings to address employees' questions regarding the change, and (4) provide employees the opportunity to discuss how the proposed change might affect them.[27] These recommendations underscore the importance of communicating with employees throughout the process of change.

In addition to communication, employee participation in the change process is another generic approach for reducing resistance. That said, however, organizational change experts have criticized the tendency to treat participation as a cure-all for resistance to change. They prefer a contingency approach because resistance can take many forms and, furthermore, because situational factors vary (see Table 16–2). As

Six Strategies for Overcoming Resistance to Change TABLE 16–2

Approach	Commonly Used in Situations	Advantages	Drawbacks
Education + Communication	Where there is a lack of information or inaccurate information and analysis.	Once persuaded, people will often help with the implementation of the change.	Can be very time consuming if lots of people are involved.
Participation + Involvement	Where the initiators do not have all the information they need to design the change and where others have considerable power to resist.	People who participate will be committed to implementing change, and any relevant information they have will be integrated into the change plan.	Can be very time consuming if participators design an inappropriate change.
Facilitation + Support	Where people are resisting because of adjustment problems.	No other approach works as well with adjustment problems.	Can be time consuming, expensive, and still fail.
Negotiation + Agreement	Where someone or some group will clearly lose out in a change and where that group has considerable power to resist.	Sometimes it is a relatively easy way to avoid major resistance.	Can be too expensive in many cases if it alerts others to negotiate for compliance.
Manipulation + Co-optation	Where other tactics will not work or are too expensive.	It can be a relatively quick and inexpensive solution to resistance problems.	Can lead to future problems if people feel manipulated.
Explicit + Implicit coercion	Where speed is essential and where the change initiators possess considerable power.	It is speedy and can overcome any kind of resistance.	Can be risky if it leaves people mad at the initiators.

SOURCE: Reprinted by permission of the *Harvard Business Review*. An exhibit from "Choosing Strategies for Change" by J P Kotter and L A Schlesinger (March/April 1979). Copyright © 1979 by the President and Fellows of Harvard College; all rights reserved.

seen in Table 16–2, Participation + Involvement does have its place, but it takes time that is not always available. Also as indicated in Table 16–2, each of the other five methods has its situational niche, advantages, and drawbacks. In short, there is no universal strategy for overcoming resistance to change. Managers need a complete repertoire of change strategies.

Creating a Learning Organization

Organizations are finding that yesterday's competitive advantage is becoming the minimum entrance requirement for staying in business. This puts tremendous pressure on organizations to learn how best to improve and stay ahead of competitors. In fact, both researchers and practicing managers agree that an organization's capability to learn is a key strategic weapon. It thus is important for organizations to enhance and nurture their capability to learn.

So what is organizational learning and how do organizations become a learning organization? To help clarify what this process entails, this section begins by defining organizational learning and a learning organization. We then present a model of organizational learning and conclude by reviewing new roles and skills required of leaders to create a learning organization.

Defining Organizational Learning and a Learning Organization

Organizational learning (OL) and a learning organization (LO) are not the same thing. Susan Fisher and Margaret White, experts on organizational change and learning, define organizational learning as follows:

> Organizational learning is a reflective process, played out by members at all levels of the organization, that involves the collection of information from both the external and internal environments. This information is filtered through a collective sensemaking process, which results in shared interpretations that can be used to instigate actions resulting in enduring changes to the organization's behavior and theories in use.[28]

This definition highlights that organizational learning represents a process by which information is gathered and then interpreted through a cognitive, social process. The accumulated information from this interpretative process represents an organization's knowledge base. This knowledge in turn is stored in organizational "memory," which consists of files, records, procedures, policies, and organizational culture.[29] In contrast, learning organizations use organizational knowledge to foster innovation and organizational effectiveness.

Peter Senge, a professor at the Massachusetts Institute of Technology, popularized the term *learning organization* in his best-selling book entitled *The Fifth Discipline*. He described a learning organization as "a group of people working together to collectively enhance their capacities to create results that they truly care about."[30] A practical interpretation of these ideas results in the following definition. A **learning organization** is one that proactively creates, acquires, and transfers knowledge and that changes its behavior on the basis of new knowledge and insights.[31]

Learning organization

Proactively creates, acquires, and transfers knowledge throughout the organization.

By breaking this definition into its three component parts, we can clearly see the characteristics of a learning organization. First, new ideas are a prerequisite for learning. Learning organizations actively try to infuse their organizations with new ideas and information. They do this by constantly scanning their external environments, hiring new talent and expertise when needed, and by devoting significant resources to train and develop their employees. Second, new knowledge must be transferred throughout the organization. Learning organizations strive to reduce structural, process, and interpersonal barriers to the sharing of information, ideas, and knowledge among organizational members. Finally, behavior must change as a result of new knowledge. Learning organizations are results oriented. They foster an environment in which employees are encouraged to use new behaviors and operational processes to achieve corporate goals.[32]

Building an Organization's Learning Capability

Figure 16–2 presents a model of how organizations build and enhance their learning capability. **Learning capabilities** represent the set of core competencies, which are defined as the special knowledge, skills, and technological know-how that differentiate an organization from its competitors, and processes that enable an organization to adapt to its environment.[33] The general idea underlying Figure 16–2 is that learning capabilities are the fuel for organizational success. Just like gasoline enables a car's engine to perform, learning capabilities equip an organization to foresee and respond to internal and external changes. This capability, in turn, increases the chances of satisfying customers and boosting sales and profitability.[34] Let us now consider the two major contributors to an organization's learning capability: facilitating factors and learning mode.

> **Learning capabilities**
>
> The set of core competencies and internal processes that enable an organization to adapt to its environment.

Building an Organization's Learning Capability   FIGURE 16–2

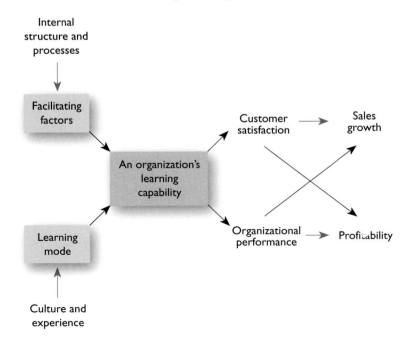

Facilitating Factors *Facilitating factors* represent "the internal structure and processes that affect how easy or hard it is for learning to occur and the amount of effective learning that takes place."[35] Table 16–3 contains a list of 10 key facilitating factors. Keep in mind as you read them that these factors can either enable or impede an organization's ability to respond to its environment. Consider, for example, the "concern for measurement" factor. A national survey of 203 executives compared companies that did and did not focus on measurement-management. Results revealed that those companies who focused on measurement-management were identified as industry leaders, had financial performance that put them in the top third of their industry, and were more successful at implementing and managing major change initiatives.[36] This study suggests that concern for measurement enhanced these organizations' learning capabilities.

TABLE 16–3 Factors That Facilitate Organizational Learning Capabilities

1. Scanning imperative	Interest in external happenings and in the nature of one's environment. Valuing the processes of awareness and data generation. Curious about what is "out there" as opposed to "in here."
2. Performance gap	Shared perception of a gap between actual and desired state of performance. Disconfirming feedback interrupts a string of successes. Performance shortfalls are seen as opportunities for learning.
3. Concern for measurement	Spend considerable effort in defining and measuring key factors when venturing into new areas; strive for specific, quantifiable measures; discourse over metrics is seen as a learning activity.
4. Experimental mind-set	Support for trying new things; curiosity about how things work; ability to "play" with things. Small failures are encouraged, not punished. See changes in work processes, policies, and structures as a continuous series of graded tryouts.
5. Climate of openness	Accessibility of information; relatively open boundaries. Opportunities to observe others; problems/errors are shared, not hidden; debate and conflict are acceptable.
6. Continuous education	Ongoing commitment to education at all levels; support for growth and development of members.
7. Operational variety	Variety exists in response modes, procedures, systems; significant diversity in personnel. Pluralistic rather than monolithic definition of valued internal capabilities.
8. Multiple advocates	Top-down and bottom-up initiatives are possible; multiple advocates and gatekeepers exist.
9. Involved leadership	Leadership at significant levels articulates vision and is very actively engaged in its actualization; takes ongoing steps to implement vision; "hands-on" involvement in educational and other implementation steps.
10. Systems perspective	Strong focus on how parts of the organization are interdependent; seek optimization of organizational goals at the highest levels; see problems and solutions in terms of systemic relationships.

SOURCE: Reprinted by permission of Sage Publications Ltd. from B Moingeon and A Edmondson, in *Organizational Learning and Competitive Advantage* (Thousand Oaks, CA: Sage, © 1996), p 43.

Learning Mode   **Learning modes** represent the various ways in which organizations attempt to create and maximize their learning. Figure 16–2 shows that learning modes are directly influenced by an organization's culture and experience or past history. The Men's Wearhouse, for example, is highly committed to organizational learning. The company sends all employees on average to 40 hours of training a year. Consider how the organizational culture affects this commitment to training:

> "We know that the only constant is change," says Eric Anderson, Men's Wearhouse's director of training. "We have said for a long time that we are in the people business, not the men's clothing business. We happen to sell men's clothing, but by recognizing what is really important—the people—we have a different paradigm than many other businesses. In order of priority, our employees, our customers, our vendors, our communities in which we do business, and our stockholders are our key stakeholders."
>
> Anderson says his challenge has been to create an environment where employees want to bring the best of themselves to work so that the business achieves positive results. "How do you nurture creativity, empowerment, responsibility, trust, and excitement?" he asks. "We try to recognize and nurture the potential in people. Because we are in the people business, training permeates our company culture."[37]

OB researcher Danny Miller reviewed the literature on organizational learning and identified six dominant modes of learning:[38]

1. *Analytic learning.* Learning occurs through systematic gathering of internal and external information. Information tends to be quantitative and analyzed via formal systems. The emphasis is on using deductive logic to numerically analyze objective data.

2. *Synthetic learning.* Synthetic learning is more intuitive and generic than the analytic mode. It emphasizes the synthesis of large amounts of complex information by using systems thinking. That is, employees try to identify interrelationships between issues, problems, and opportunities.

3. *Experimental learning.* This mode is a rational methodological approach that is based on conducting small experiments and monitoring the results.

Individual learning contributes to enhanced organizational learning capability—a never-ending process!

4. *Interactive learning.* This mode involves learning-by-doing. Rather than using systematic methodological procedures, learning occurs primarily through the exchange of information. Learning is more intuitive and inductive.

5. *Structural learning.* This mode is a methodological approach that is based on the use of organizational routines. Organizational routines represent standardized processes and procedures that specify how to carry out tasks and roles. People learn from routines because they direct attention, institutionalize standards, and create consistent vocabularies.

6. *Institutional learning.* This mode represents an inductive process by which organizations share and model values, beliefs, and practices either from their external environments or from senior executives. Employees learn by observing environmental examples or senior executives. Socialization and mentoring play a significant role in institutional learning.

Leadership Is the Foundation of a Learning Organization

Leadership is the key to fostering organizational learning and the creation of a learning organization. To make this happen, however, leaders must adopt new roles and associated activities. Specifically, leaders perform three key functions in building a learning organization: (1) building a commitment to learning, (2) working to generate ideas with impact, and (3) working to generalize ideas with impact.[39]

Building a Commitment to Learning Leaders need to instill an intellectual and emotional commitment to learning. Thomas Tierney, CEO of Bain & Company, proposes that leaders foster this commitment by building a culture that promotes the concept of "teacher-learners." His concept is based on the idea that organizational learning and innovation are enhanced when employees behave like both teachers and learners (see Skills & Best Practices). Of course, leaders also need to invest the financial resources needed to create a learning infrastructure.

Working to Generate Ideas with Impact Ideas with impact are those that add value to one or more of an organization's three key stakeholders: employees, customers, and shareholders. Experts suggest the following ways to generate ideas with impact:

- Implement continuous improvement programs.
- Increase employee competence through training, or buy talent from outside the organization.
- Experiment with new ideas, processes, and structural arrangements.

Characteristics of Teacher-Learners

1. Being actively engaged in teaching, probing, and learning simultaneously.

2. Demonstrating care for their colleagues and making intellectual and emotional connections in and beyond their circle of peers.

3. Relating to as many people from different backgrounds, experience, maturity levels, and positions as possible.

4. Reflecting on what they learn as well as how they learn. After learning or teaching, teacher-learners ask themselves, "What have I learned about learning? What should I explore to enrich my own learning as a result of that interaction?"

5. Keeping their receiver-transmitters on at all times. Teacher-learners possess a child's mind: They don't presuppose; they listen.

SOURCE: Excerpted from J C Meister, "The CEO-Driven Learning Culture," *Training & Development*, June 2000, p 54.

- Go outside the organization to identify world-class ideas and processes.
- Instill systems thinking throughout the organization.

Working to Generalize Ideas with Impact Leaders must make a concerted effort to reduce interpersonal, group, and organizational barriers to learning. This can be done by creating a learning infrastructure. This is a large-scale effort that includes the following activities:

- Measuring and rewarding learning.
- Increasing open and honest dialogue among organizational members.
- Reducing conflict.
- Increasing horizontal and vertical communication.
- Promoting teamwork.
- Rewarding risk taking and innovation.
- Reducing the fear of failure.
- Increasing the sharing of successes, failures, and best practices across organizational members.
- Reducing stressors and frustration.
- Reducing internal competition.
- Increasing cooperation and collaboration.
- Creating a psychologically safe and comforting environment.[40]

Unlearning the Organization

In addition to implementing the ideas discussed earlier, organizations must concurrently unlearn organizational practices and paradigms that made them successful. Quite simply, traditional organizations and the associated organizational behaviors they created have outlived their usefulness. Management must seriously question and challenge the ways of thinking that worked in the past if they want to create a learning organization.[41] For example, the old management paradigm of planning, organizing, and control might be replaced with one of vision, values, and empowerment. The time has come for management and employees to think as owners, not as "us" and "them" adversaries.

chapter summary

- *Discuss the external and internal forces that create the need for organizational change.* Organizations encounter both external and internal forces for change. There are four key external forces for change: demographic characteristics, technological advancements, market changes, and social and political pressures. Internal forces for change come from both human resource problems and managerial behavior/decisions.

- *Describe Lewin's change model and the systems model of change.* Lewin developed a three-stage model of planned change that explained how to initiate, manage, and stabilize the change process. The three stages were *unfreezing*, which entails creating the motivation to change, *changing*, and stabilizing change through *refreezing*. A systems model of change takes a big picture perspective of change. It focuses on the interaction among the key components of change. The three main components of change are inputs, target elements of change, and outputs. The target elements of change represent the components of an organization that may be changed. They include organizing arrangements, social factors, methods, goals, and people.

- *Discuss Kotter's eight steps for leading organizational change.* John Kotter believes that organizational change fails for one or more of eight common errors. He proposed eight steps that organizations should follow to overcome these errors. The eight steps are as follows: (a) establish a sense of urgency, (b) create the guiding coalition, (c) develop a vision and strategy, (d) communicate the change vision, (e) empower broad-based action, (f) generate short-term wins, (g) consolidate gains and produce more change, and (h) anchor new approaches in the culture.

- *Discuss the 10 reasons employees resist change.* Resistance to change is an emotional/behavioral response to real or imagined threats to an established work routine. Ten reasons employees resist change are (a) an individual's predisposition toward change, (b) surprise and fear of the unknown, (c) climate of mistrust, (d) fear of failure, (e) loss of status and/or job security, (f) peer pressure, (g) disruption of cultural traditions and/or group relationships, (h) personality conflicts, (i) lack of tact and/or poor timing, and (j) nonreinforcing reward systems.

- *Identify alternative strategies for overcoming resistance to change.* Organizations must be ready for change. Assuming an organization is ready for change, the alternative strategies for overcoming resistance to change are education + communication, participation + involvement, facilitation + support, negotiation + agreement, manipulation + co-operation, and explicit + implict coercion. Each has its situational appropriateness and advantages and drawbacks.

- *Discuss the process organizations use to build their learning capabilities.* Learning capabilities represent the set of core competencies and processes that enable an organization to adapt to its environment. Learning capabilities are directly affected by organizational facilitating factors and learning modes. Facilitating factors constitute the internal structure and processes that either encourage or impede learning within an organization, Learning modes represent the various ways by which organizations attempt to create and maximize their learning. Researchers believe that there is some type of optimal matching between the facilitating factors and learning modes that affects learning capability.

internet exercise

In this chapter we reviewed several models of organizational change. Because these models are based on different sets of assumptions, each one offers managers a unique set of recommendations for how organizational change should be implemented. We also discussed a variety of recommendations for how managers might better implement organizational change. The purpose of this exercise is for you to expand your knowledge about how organizations should implement organizational change by considering recommendations provided by the Software Engineering Institute (SEI). The SEI is a federally funded research and development center operated by Carnegie Mellon University and sponsored by the US Department of Defense. This organization focuses on assisting organizations to improve the process of software engineering. In so doing, the SEI has learned much about how to implement organizational change. Go to the Internet home page for the SEI (**www.sei.cmu.edu**), and use the quick search option to conduct a search on the keyword "organizational change." Use the sources identified through this search to answer the following questions.

QUESTIONS

1. What are the key elements of organizational change? How do these compare to the components contained in the systems model of organizational change presented in Figure 16–1?
2. What roles do change agents, sponsors, champions, and participants play in the process of implementing organizational change?

Chapter I

[1] Excerpted from J R Healey and D Kiley, "Surprise: Chrysler Loves Its German Boss," *USA Today,* May 3, 2001, pp 1B–2B. Also see A Taylor III, "Can the Germans Rescue Chrysler?" *Fortune,* April 30, 2001, pp 106–112.

[2] Data from "Fortune 5 Hundred Largest U.S. Corporations," *Fortune,* April 16, 2001, pp F-1, F-50.

[3] As quoted in *Nightly Business Report* transcript, March 29, 2001 (www.nbr.com/trnscrpt.htm).

[4] J Pfeffer and J F Veiga, "Putting People First for Organizational Success," *Academy of Management Executive,* May 1999, p 37.

[5] Adapted from ibid.

[6] For alternatives to layoffs, see S Armour, "Workers Take Pay Cuts Over Pink Slips," *USA Today,* April 13, 2001, p 1B.

[7] Data from Pfeffer and Veiga, "Putting People First for Organizational Success," p 47.

[8] H Mintzberg, "The Manager's Job: Folklore and Fact," *Harvard Business Review,* July–August 1975, p 61. For an alternative perspective, see R J Samuelson, "Why I Am Not a Manager," *Newsweek,* March 22, 1999, p 47.

[9] See, for example, H Mintzberg, "Managerial Work: Analysis from Observation," *Management Science,* October 1971, pp B97–B110; and F Luthans, "Successful vs. Effective Real Managers," *Academy of Management Executive,* May 1988, pp 127–32. For an instructive critique of the structured observation method, see M J Martinko and W L Gardner, "Beyond Structured Observation: Methodological Issues and New Directions," *Academy of Management Review,* October 1985, pp 676–95. Also see N Fondas, "A Behavioral Job Description for Managers," *Organizational Dynamics,* Summer 1992, pp 47–58.

[10] See L B Kurke and H E Aldrich, "Mintzberg Was Right! A Replication and Extension of *The Nature of Managerial Work,*" *Management Science,* August 1983, pp 975–84.

[11] For example, see J C McCune, "Brave New World," *Management Review,* October 1997, pp 11–14; and N H Woodward, "The Coming of the X Managers," *HRMagazine,* March 1999, pp 74–80.

[12] Validation studies can be found in E Van Velsor and J B Leslie, *Feedback to Managers, Volume II: A Review and Comparison of Sixteen Multi-Rater Feedback Instruments* (Greensboro, NC: Center for Creative Leadership, 1991); and F Shipper, "A Study of the Psychometric Properties of the Managerial Skill Scales of the Survey of Management Practices," *Educational and Psychological Measurement,* June 1995, pp 468–79.

[13] For example, see S B Parry, "Just What Is a Competency? (And Why Should You Care?)" *Training,* June 1998, pp 58–64; and J Sandberg, "Understanding Competence at Work," *Harvard Business Review,* March 2001, pp 24–28.

[14] See F Shipper, "Mastery and Frequency of Managerial Behaviors Relative to Sub-Unit Effectiveness," *Human Relations,* April 1991, pp 371–88.

[15] Ibid.

[16] Data from F Shipper, "A Study of Managerial Skills of Women and Men and Their Impact on Employees' Attitudes and Career Success in a Nontraditional Organization," paper presented at the Academy of Management Meeting, August 1994, Dallas, Texas. The same outcome for on-the-job studies is reported in A H Eagly and B T Johnson, "Gender and Leadership Style: A Meta-Analysis," *Psychological Bulletin,* September 1990, pp 233–56.

[17] For instance, see J B Rosener, "Ways Women Lead," *Harvard Business Review,* November–December 1990, pp 119–25; and C Lee, "The Feminization of Management," *Training,* November 1994, pp 25–31.

[18] See T J Tetenbaum, "Shifting Paradigms: From Newton to Chaos," *Organizational Dynamics,* Spring 1998, pp 21–32; and R W Oliver, *The Shape of Things to Come* (New York: McGraw-Hill, 1999).

[19] Essential sources on reengineering are M Hammer and J Champy, *Reengineering the Corporation: A Manifesto for Business Revolution* (New York: HarperCollins, 1993); and J Champy, *Reengineering Management: The Mandate for New Leadership* (New York: HarperCollins, 1995). Also see "Anything Worth Doing Is Worth Doing from Scratch," *Inc.,* May 18, 1999 (20th Anniversary Issue), pp 51–52.

[20] For thoughtful discussion, see G G Dess, A M A Rasheed, K J McLaughlin, and R L Priem, "The New Corporate Architecture," *Academy of Management Executive,* August 1995, pp 7–20.

[21] See, for example, "The Dreaded 'E Word,'" *Training,* September 1998, p 19; K Dover, "Avoiding Empowerment Traps," *Management Review,* January 1999, pp 51–55; and G B Weathersby, "Management May Never Be the Same," *Management Review,* February 1999, p 5. A brief case study of empowerment in action can be found in C Dahle, "Big Learning, Fast Futures," *Fast Company,* June 1999, pp 46, 48.

[22] See J B Miner, "The Validity and Usefulness of Theories in an Emerging Organizational Science," *Academy of Management Review,* April 1984, pp 296–306.

[23] B S Lawrence, "Historical Perspective: Using the Past to Study the Present," *Academy of Management Review,* April 1984, p 307. Also see H Rubin, "Past Track to the Future," *Fast Company,* May 2001, pp 166–73.

[24] Evidence indicating that the original conclusions of the famous Hawthorne studies were unjustified may be found in R G Greenwood, A A Bolton, and R A Greenwood, "Hawthorne a Half Century Later: Relay Assembly Participants Remember," *Journal of Management,* Fall–Winter 1983, pp 217–31; and R H Franke and J D Kaul, "The Hawthorne Experiments: First Statistical Interpretation," *American Sociological Review,* October 1978, pp 623–43. For a positive interpretation of the Hawthorne studies, see J A Sonnenfeld, "Shedding Light on the Hawthorne Studies," *Journal of Occupational Behaviour,* April 1985, pp 111–30.

[25] See M Parker Follett, *Freedom and Coordination* (London: Management Publications Trust, 1949).

[26] See D McGregor, *The Human Side of Enterprise* (New York: McGraw-Hill, 1960).

[27] J Hall, "Americans Know How to Be Productive if Managers Will Let Them," *Organizational Dynamics,* Winter 1994, p 38.

[28] See, for example, R Zemke, "TQM: Fatally Flawed or Simply Unfocused?" *Training,* October 1992, p 8.

[29] See A J Slywotzky and D J Morrison, *How Digital Is Your Business?* (New York: Crown Business, 2000); and G Hamel, "Is This All You Can Build with The Net? Think Bigger," *Fortune,* April 30, 2001, pp 134–38.

[30] L Wah, "The Almighty Customer," *Management Review,* February 1999, p 17.

[31] Data from "AMA Global Survey on Key Business Issues," *Management Review,* December 1998, p 30. Also see "1999 Annual Survey: Corporate Concerns," *Management Review,* March 1999, pp 55–56.

[32] Instructive background articles on TQM are R Zemke, "A Bluffer's Guide to TQM," *Training,* April 1993, pp 48–55; R R Gehani, "Quality Value-Chain: A Meta-Synthesis of Frontiers of Quality Movement," *Academy of Management Executive,* May 1993, pp 29–42; P Mears, "How to Stop Talking About, and Begin Progress Toward, Total Quality Management," *Business Horizons,* May–June 1993, pp 11–14; and the Total Quality Special Issue of *Academy of Management Review,* July 1994.

[33] M Sashkin and K J Kiser, *Putting Total Quality Management to Work* (San Francisco: Berrett-Koehler, 1993), p 39.

[34] R J Schonberger, "Total Quality Management Cuts a Broad Swath—Through Manufacturing and Beyond," *Organizational Dynamics,* Spring 1992, p 18. Also see K Y Kim, J G Miller, and J Heineke, "Mastering the Quality Staircase, Step by Step," *Business Horizons,* January–February 1997, pp 17–21; R Bell and B Keys, "A Conversation with Curt W Reimann on the Background and Future of the Baldrige Award," *Organizational Dynamics,* Spring 1998, pp 51–61; and B Kasanoff, "Are You Ready for Mass Customization?" *Training,* May 1998, pp 70–78.

35 See R K Reger, L T Gustafson, S M Demarie, and J V Mullane, "Reframing the Organization: Why Implementing Total Quality Is Easier Said than Done," *Academy of Management Review,* July 1994, pp 565–84.

36 Deming's landmark work is W E Deming, *Out of the Crisis* (Cambridge, MA: MIT, 1986).

37 See M Trumbull, "What Is Total Quality Management?" *The Christian Science Monitor,* May 3, 1993, p 12; and J Hillkirk, "World-Famous Quality Expert Dead at 93," *USA Today,* December 21, 1993, pp 1B–2B.

38 Based on discussion in M Walton, *Deming Management at Work* (New York: Putnam/Perigee, 1990).

39 Ibid., p 20.

40 Adapted from D E Bowen and E E Lawler III, "Total Quality-Oriented Human Resources Management," *Organizational Dynamics,* Spring 1992, pp 29–41. Also see P B Seybold, "Get Inside the Lives of Your Customers," *Harvard Business Review,* May 2001, pp 80–89.

41 See T F Rienzo, "Planning Deming Management for Service Organizations," *Business Horizons,* May–June 1993, pp 19–29. Also see M R Yilmaz and S Chatterjee, "Deming and the Quality of Software Development," *Business Horizons,* November–December 1997, pp 51–58.

42 For example, see J Shea and D Gobeli, "TQM: The Experiences of Ten Small Businesses," *Business Horizons,* January–February 1995, pp 71–77; T L Zeller and D M Gillis, "Achieving Market Excellence through Quality: The Case of Ford Motor Company," *Business Horizons,* May–June 1995, pp 23–31; and P McLagan and C Nel, "A New Leadership Style for Genuine Total Quality," *Journal for Quality and Participation,* June 1996, pp 14–16.

43 See J O'C Hamilton, "The Harder They Fall," *Business Week* **E.BIZ,** May 14, 2001, pp. EB14, EB16.

44 Data from G Colvin, "Shaking Hands on the Web," *Fortune,* May 14, 2001, p 54.

45 See S E Ante, "In Search of the Net's Next Big Thing," *Business Week,* March 26, 2001, pp 140–41.

46 Data from D Temple-Raston, "Net Economy Hale and Hearty," *USA Today,* January 12, 2001, p 6B.

47 See Hamel, "Is This All You Can Build with the Net? Think Bigger."

48 M J Mandel and R D Hof, "Rethinking the Internet," *Business Week,* March 26, 2001, pp 116–22; and B Powell, "The New World Order," *Fortune,* May 14, 2001, pp 134, 136.

49 A Bernasek, "Buried in Tech," *Fortune,* April 16, 2001, p 52.

50 W Echikson, "Nestlé: An Elephant Dances," *Business Week* **E.BIZ,** December 11, 2000, pp EB47–EB48. Also see B Sosnin, "Digital Newsletters 'E-volutionize' Employee Communications," *HRMagazine,* May 2001, pp 99–107.

51 For more, see G Meyer, "eWorkbench: Real-Time Tracking of Synchronized Goals," *HRMagazine,* April 2001, pp 115–18.

52 S Hamm, "E-Biz: Down But Hardly Out," *Business Week,* March 26, 2001, p 130.

53 R Moss Kanter, *Evolve! Succeeding in the Digital Culture of Tomorrow* (Boston: Harvard Business School Press, 2001), p 206. Also see R Moss Kanter, "You Are Here," *Inc.,* February 2001, pp 84–90.

54 Data from "Hurry Up and Decide!" *Business Week,* May 14, 2001, p 16.

55 K Tyler, "E-Learning: Not Just for E-Normous Companies Anymore," *HRMagazine,* May 2001, p 84.

56 F Vogelstein, "Flying on the Web in a Turbulent Economy," *Fortune,* April 30, 2001, p 143.

57 See B Lessard and S Baldwin, *Net Slaves: True Tales of Working the Web* (New York: McGraw-Hill, 2000); and C Wilder and J Soat, "A Question of Ethics," *Information Week.com,* February 19, 2001, pp 38–50.

58 For instance, see M R Buckley, G R Ferris, H J Bernardin, and M G Harvey, "The Disconnect between the Science and Practice of Management," *Business Horizons,* March–April 1998, pp 31–38; and D Cohen, "Research: Food for Future Thought," *HRMagazine,* May 2001, p 184.

59 Complete discussion of this technique can be found in J E Hunter, F L Schmidt, and G B Jackson, *Meta-Analysis. Cumulating Research Findings across Studies* (Beverly Hills, CA: Sage Publications, 1982); and J E Hunter and F L Schmidt, *Methods of Meta-Analysis: Correcting Error and Bias in Research Findings* (Newbury Park, CA: Sage Publications,

1990). Also see R Hutter Epstein, "The Number-Crunchers Drugmakers Fear and Love," *Business Week,* August 22, 1994, pp 70–71.

60 Limitations of meta-analysis technique are discussed in P Bobko and E F Stone-Romero, "Meta-Analysis May Be Another Useful Tool, But It Is Not a Panacea," in *Research in Personnel and Human Resources Management,* vol. 16, ed G R Ferris (Stamford, CT: JAI Press, 1998), pp 359–97.

61 For an interesting debate about the use of students as subjects, see J Greenberg, "The College Sophomore as Guinea Pig: Setting the Record Straight," *Academy of Management Review,* January 1987, pp 157–59; and M E Gordon, L A Slade, and N Schmitt, "Student Guinea Pigs: Porcine Predictors and Particularistic Phenomena," *Academy of Management Review,* January 1987, pp 160–63.

62 Good discussions of case studies can be found in A S Lee, "Case Studies as Natural Experiments," *Human Relations,* February 1989, pp 117–37; and K M Eisenhardt, "Building Theories from Case Study Research," *Academy of Management Review,* October 1989, pp 532–50. The case survey technique is discussed in R Larsson, "Case Survey Methodology: Analysis of Patterns across Case Studies," *Academy of Management Journal,* December 1993, pp 1515–46.

63 Based on discussion found in J M Beyer and H M Trice, "The Utilization Process: A Conceptual Framework and Synthesis of Empirical Findings," *Administrative Science Quarterly,* December 1982, pp 591–622.

64 See J J Martocchio, "Age-Related Differences in Employee Absenteeism: A Meta-Analysis," *Psychology & Aging,* December 1989, pp 409–14.

65 The importance of "people management" skills are discussed in H Mintzberg and J Lampel, "Do MBAs Make Better CEOs? Sorry, Dubya, It Ain't Necessarily So," *Fortune,* February 19, 2001, p 244.

Chapter 2

1 Excerpted from M Mangalindan and S Hwang, "Gang of Six: Coterie of Early Hires Made Yahoo! a Hit but an Insular Plane," *The Wall Street Journal,* March 9, 2001, p A1.

2 E H Schein, "Culture: The Missing Concept in Organization Studies," *Administrative Science Quarterly,* June 1996, p 236.

3 This discussion is based on E H Schein, *Organizational Culture and Leadership,* 2nd ed (San Francisco: Jossey-Bass, 1992), pp 16–48.

4 S H Schwartz, "Universals in the Content and Structure of Values: Theoretical Advances and Empirical Tests in 20 Countries," in *Advances in Experimental Social Psychology,* ed M P Zanna (New York: Academic Press, 1992), p 4.

5 See E Shapiro, "Time Warner Defines, Defends System of Values," *The Wall Street Journal,* March 9, 1999, pp B1, B4.

6 Excerpted from C Terhune, "Home Depot's Home Improvement," *The Wall Street Journal,* March 8, 2001, pp B1, B4.

7 Results can be found in S Clarke, "Perceptions of Organizational Safety: Implications for the Development of Safety Culture," *Journal of Organizational Behavior,* March 1999, pp 185–98.

8 See Terhune, "Home Depot's Home Improvement."

9 A detailed discussion of the culture within Southwest Airlines is provided by K Freiberg and J Freiberg, *Nuts! Southwest Airlines' Crazy Recipe for Business and Personal Success* (Austin, TX: Bard Press, 1996).

10 Adapted from L Smircich, "Concepts of Culture and Organizational Analysis," *Administrative Science Quarterly,* September 1983, pp 339–58.

11 The 3M example was based on material contained in S Branch, "The 100 Best Companies to Work for in America," *Fortune,* January 11, 1999, pp 118–44; and D Anfuso, "3M's Staffing Strategy Promotes Productivity and Pride," *Personnel Journal,* February 1995, pp 28–34.

12 J M Higgins, "Innovate or Evaporate: Seven Secrets of Innovative Corporations," *The Futurist,* September–October 1995, p 45.

13 Anfuso, "3M's Staffing Strategy Promotes Productivity and Pride," p 28.

14 Branch, "The 100 Best Companies to Work for in America," p 144.

15 A review of cultural typologies is provided by N Ashkanasy, L Broadfoot, and S Falkus, "Questionnaire Measures of Organizational Culture," in *Handbook of Organizational Culture & Climate,* ed N Ashkanasy, C Wilderom, and M Peterson (Thousand Oaks, CA: Sage, 2000), pp 131–46.

[16] The validity of these cultural types was investigated and supported by R Cooke and J Szumal, "Using the Organizational Culture Inventory to Understand the Operating Cultures of Organizations," in *Handbook of Organizational Culture & Climate,* ed N Ashkanasy, C Wilderom, and M Peterson (Thousand Oaks, CA: Sage, 2000), pp 147–62.

[17] See V González-Romá, J M Peiró, S Lloret, and A Zornoza, "The Validity of Collective Climates," *Journal of Organizational Behavior,* March 1999, pp 25–40; and Schein, *Organizational Culture and Leadership.*

[18] Results can be found in R Cooke and J Szumal, "Measuring Normative Beliefs and Shared Behavioral Expectations in Organizations: The Reliability and Validity of the Organizational Culture Inventory," *Psychological Reports,* June 1993, pp 1299–1330.

[19] Supportive results can be found in A Van Vianen, "Person-Organization Fit: The Match between Newcomers' and Recruiters' Preferences for Organizational Cultures," *Personnel Psychology,* Spring 2000, pp 113–50; and C Vandenberghe, "Organizational Culture, Person-Culture Fit, and Turnover: A Replication in the Health Care Industry," *Journal of Organizational Behavior,* March 1999, pp 175–84.

[20] See C Wilderom, U Glunk, and R Maslowski, "Organizational Culture as a Predictor of Organizational Performance," in *Handbook of Organizational Culture & Climate,* ed N Ashkanasy, C Wilderom, and M Peterson (Thousand Oaks, CA: Sage, 2000), pp 193–210.

[21] Results can be found in J P Kotter and J L Heskett, *Corporate Culture and Performance* (New York: The Free Press, 1992).

[22] The success rate of mergers is discussed in R J Grossman, "Irreconcilable Differences," *HRMagazine,* April 1999, pp 42–48.

[23] The mechanisms were based on material contained in E H Schein, "The Role of the Founder in Creating Organizational Culture," *Organizational Dynamics,* Summer 1983, pp 13–28.

[24] See the description in T Begley and D Boyd, "Articulating Corporate Values through Human Resource Policies," *Business Horizons,* July–August 2000, pp 8–12.

[25] The program is described in C Cole, "Eight Values Bring Unity to a Worldwide Company," *Workforce,* March 2001, pp 44–45.

[26] Excerpted from D Jones, "Welch: Nurture Best Workers, Lose Bottom 10%," *USA Today,* February 27, 2001, p 2B.

[27] See N M Tichy and C DeRose, "The Pepsi Challenge: Building a Leader-Driven Organization," *Training & Development,* May 1996, pp 58–66.

[28] J Van Maanen, "Breaking In: Socialization to Work," in *Handbook of Work, Organization, and Society,* ed R Dubin (Chicago: Rand-McNally, 1976), p 67.

[29] This definition is based on the network perspective of mentoring proposed by M Higgins and K Kram, "Reconceptualizing Mentoring at Work: A Developmental Network Perspective," *Academy of Management Review,* April 2001, pp 264–88.

[30] For an instructive capsule summary of the five different organizational socialization models, see J P Wanous, A E Reichers, and S D Malik, "Organizational Socialization and Group Development: Toward an Integrative Perspective," *Academy of Management Review,* October 1984, pp 670–83, Table 1. Also see D C Feldman, *Managing Careers in Organizations* (Glenview, IL: Scott, Foresman, 1988), Ch. 5.

[31] Excerpted from N Tichy, "No Ordinary Boot Camp," *Harvard Business Review,* April 2001, pp 65–67.

[32] Results can be found in H Klein and N Weaver, "The Effectiveness of an Organizational-Level Orientation Training Program in the Socialization of New Hires," *Personnel Psychology,* Spring 2000, pp 47–66.

[33] Results from two related studies can be found in D Cable and C Parsons, "Socialization Tactics and Person-Organization Fit," *Personnel Psychology,* Spring 2001, pp 1–23; and E W Morrison, "Longitudinal Study of the Effects of Information Seeking," *Journal of Applied Psychology,* April 1993, pp 173–83.

[34] See A M Saks and B E Ashforth, "Proactive Socialization and Behavioral Self-Management," *Journal of Vocational Behavior,* June 1996, pp 301–23.

[35] For a thorough review of research on the socialization of diverse employees with disabilities see A Colella, "Organizational Socialization of Newcomers with Disabilities: A Framework for Future Research," in *Research in Personnel and Human Resources Management,* ed G R Ferris (Greenwich, CT: JAI Press, 1996), pp 351–417.

[36] See L Eby, S McManus, S Simon, and J Russell, "The Protégé's Perspective Regarding Negative Mentoring Experiences: The Development of a Taxonomy," *Journal of Vocational Behavior,* August 2000, pp 1–21; and D Thomas, "The Truth about Mentoring Minorities: Race Matters," *Harvard Business Review,* April 2001, pp 99–107.

[37] Career functions are discussed in detail in K Kram, *Mentoring of Work: Developmental Relationships in Organizational Life* (Glenview, IL: Scott, Foresman, 1985).

[38] This discussion is based on Higgins and Kram, "Reconceptualizing Mentoring at Work: A Developmental Network Perspective."

[39] Ibid.

[40] Supportive results can be found in T Allen, M Poteet, and J Russell, "Protégé Selection by Mentors: What Makes the Difference?" *Journal of Organizational Behavior,* May 2000, pp 271–82; and A Young and P Perrewé, "What Did You Expect: An Examination of Career-Related Support and Social Support among Mentors and Protégés," *Journal of Management,* 2000, pp 611–32.

[41] Details of these examples can be found in L Wah, "Lip-Service Ethics Programs Prove Ineffective," *Management Review,* June 1999, p 9; and "Workplace Ethics Dilemma," *USA Today,* February 15, 1999, p 1B.

[42] Associated Press, "PG&E Gave Bonuses before Bankruptcy Filing," *The Arizona Republic,* April 9, 2001, p A7.

[43] See C Gilligan, "In a Different Voice: Women's Conceptions of Self and Morality," *Harvard Educational Review,* November 1977, pp 481–517; and C Gilligan, *In a Different Voice: Psychological Theory and Women's Development* (Cambridge, MA: Harvard University Press, 1982).

[44] Branch, "The 100 Best Companies to Work for in America."

[45] The role of incentives and ethical behavior was investigated by A E Tenbrunsel, "Misrepresentation and Expectations of Misrepresentation in an Ethical Dilemma: The Role of Incentives and Temptation," *Academy of Management Journal,* June 1998, pp 330–39.

[46] C Gilligan and J Attanucci, "Two Moral Orientations: Gender Differences and Similarities," *Merril-Palmer Quarterly,* July 1988, pp 224–25.

[47] Results can be found in S Jaffee and J Hyde, "Gender Differences in Moral Orientation: A Meta-Analysis," *Psychological Bulletin,* September 2000, pp 703–26.

[48] Ibid., p 719.

[49] Adapted from W E Stead, D L Worrell, and J Garner Stead, "An Integrative Model for Understanding and Managing Ethical Behavior in Business Organizations," *Journal of Business Ethics,* March 1990, pp 233–42.

[50] For an excellent review of integrity testing, see D S Ones and C Viswesvaran, "Integrity Testing in Organizations," in *Dysfunctional Behavior in Organizations: Violent and Deviant Behavior,* eds R W Griffin et al. (Stamford, CT: JAI Press, 1998), pp 243–76.

[51] The ethics test is discussed in D Fandray, "The Ethical Company," *Workforce,* December 2000, pp 75–77.

Chapter 3

[1] Excerpted from E T Pound, "Saudi Rule Looser than Pentagon's," *USA Today,* April 25, 2001, p 3A. For more background, see E T Pound, "Saudi Rules Anger Top Air Force Pilot," *USA Today,* April 18, 2001, pp 1A, 10A.

[2] G Smith, "Betting on Free Trade," *Business Week,* April 23, 2001, p 60. For more, see M Memmott, "Summit Leaders Vow to Break Trade Barriers," *USA Today,* April 23, 2001, p 8A.

[3] J Shinal, "Can Mike Volpi Make Cisco Sizzle Again?" *Business Week,* February 26, 2001, p 104.

[4] See Y Kashima, "Conceptions of Culture and Person for Psychology," *Journal of Cross-Cultural Psychology,* January 2000, pp 14–32.

[5] "How Cultures Collide," *Psychology Today,* July 1976, p 69. Also see E T Hall, *The Hidden Dimension* (Garden City, NY: Doubleday, 1966).

[6] F Trompenaars and C Hampden-Turner, *Riding the Waves of Culture: Understanding Cultural Diversity in Global Business,* 2nd ed (New York: McGraw-Hill, 1998), pp 6–7.

[7] See M Mendenhall, "A Painless Approach to Integrating 'International' into OB, HRM, and Management Courses," *Organizational Behavior Teaching Review,* no. 3 (1988–89), pp 23–27.

[8] See C L Sharma, "Ethnicity, National Integration, and Education in the Union of Soviet Socialist Republics," *The Journal of East and West Studies,* October 1989, pp 75–93; and R Brady and P Galuszka, "Shattered Dreams," *Business Week,* February 11, 1991, pp 38–42.

[9] J Main, "How to Go Global—And Why," *Fortune,* August 28, 1989, p 73.

[10] An excellent contrast between French and American values can be found in C Gouttefarde, "American Values in the French Workplace," *Business Horizons,* March–April 1996, pp 60–69.

[11] W D Marbach, "Quality: What Motivates American Workers?" *Business Week,* April 12, 1993, p 93.

[12] T Donaldson, "Values in Tension: Ethics Away from Home," *Harvard Business Review,* September–October 1996, p 48.

[13] S R Covey, *Principle-Centered Leadership* (New York: Simon & Schuster, 1991), p 95.

[14] See G A Sumner, *Folkways* (New York: Ginn, 1906). Also see J G Weber, "The Nature of Ethnocentric Attribution Bias: Ingroup Protection or Enhancement?" *Journal of Experimental Social Psychology,* September 1994, pp 482–504.

[15] "US Commander Apologizes to Okinawans," *USA Today,* February 7, 2001, p 9A.

[16] D A Heenan and H V Perlmutter, *Multinational Organization Development* (Reading, MA: Addison-Wesley, 1979), p 17.

[17] Data from R Kopp, "International Human Resource Policies and Practices in Japanese, European, and United States Multinationals," *Human Resource Management,* Winter 1994, pp 581–99.

[18] Data from B Hagerty, "Trainers Help Expatriate Employees Build Bridges to Different Cultures," *The Wall Street Journal,* June 14, 1993, pp B1, B3. Also see A Weiss, "Global Doesn't Mean 'Foreign' Anymore," *Training,* July 1998, pp 50–55; and G Dutton, "Do You Think Globally?" *Management Review,* February 1999, p 6.

[19] C M Farkas and P De Backer, "There Are Only Five Ways to Lead," *Fortune,* January 15, 1996, p 111. The shortage of global managers is discussed in L K Stroh and P M Caligiuri, "Increasing Global Competitiveness through Effective People Management," *Journal of World Business,* Spring 1998, pp 1–16.

[20] For complete details, see G Hofstede, *Culture's Consequences: International Differences in Work-Related Values,* abridged ed (Newbury Park, CA: Sage Publications, 1984); G Hofstede, "The Interaction between National and Organizational Value Systems," *Journal of Management Studies,* July 1985, pp 347–57; and G Hofstede, "Management Scientists Are Human," *Management Science,* January 1994, pp 4–13. Also see V J Shackleton and A H Ali, "Work-Related Values of Managers: A Test of the Hofstede Model," *Journal of Cross-Cultural Psychology,* March 1990, pp 109–18; R Hodgetts, "A Conversation with Geert Hofstede," *Organizational Dynamics,* Spring 1993, pp 53–61; P B Smith, S Dugan, and F Trompenaars, "National Culture and the Values of Organizational Employees: A Dimensional Analysis Across 43 Nations," *Journal of Cross-Cultural Psychology,* March 1996, pp 231–64; and G Hofstede, "Problems Remain, but Theories Will Change: The Universal and the Specific in 21st-Century Global Management," *Organizational Dynamics,* Summer 1999, pp 34–44.

[21] A similar conclusion is presented in the following replication of Hofstede's work: A Merritt, "Culture in the Cockpit: Do Hofstede's Dimensions Replicate?" *Journal of Cross-Cultural Psychology,* May 2000, pp 283–301. Another extension of Hofstede's work can be found in S M Lee and S J Peterson, "Culture, Entrepreneurial Orientation, and Global Competitiveness," *Journal of World Business,* Winter 2000, pp 401–16.

[22] A discussion of Japanese stereotypes in America can be found in L Smith, "Fear and Loathing of Japan," *Fortune,* February 26, 1990, pp 50–57. Diversity in so-called Eastern bloc countries in Central and Eastern Europe is discussed in F Luthans, R R Patrick, and B C Luthans, "Doing Business in Central and Eastern Europe: Political, Economic, and Cultural Diversity," *Business Horizons,* September–October 1995, pp 9–16.

[23] Based on discussion in P R Harris and R T Moran, *Managing Cultural Differences,* 3rd ed (Houston: Gulf Publishing, 1991) p 12. Also see "Workers' Attitudes Similar Worldwide," *HRMagazine,* December 1998,

pp 28–30; and C Comeau-Kirschner, "It's a Small World," *Management Review,* March 1999, p 8.

[24] Data from Trompenaars and Hampden-Turner, *Riding the Waves of Culture: Understanding Cultural Diversity in Global Business,* Ch 5. For relevant research evidence, see K Phalet and U Schonpflug, "Intergenerational Transmission of Collectivism and Achievement Values in Two Acculturation Contexts: The Case of Turkish Families in Germany and Turkish and Moroccan Families in the Netherlands," *Journal of Cross-Cultural Psychology,* March 2001, pp 186–201; and C Gomez, B L Kirkman, and D L Shapiro, "The Impact of Collectivism and In-Group/Out-Group Membership on the Evaluation Generosity of Team Members," *Academy of Management Journal,* December 2000, pp 1097–1106.

[25] See J A Vandello and D Cohen, "Patterns of Individualism and Collectivism Across the United States," *Journal of Personality and Social Psychology,* August 1999, pp 279–92.

[26] As quoted in E E Schultz, "Scudder Brings Lessons to Navajo, Gets Some of Its Own," *The Wall Street Journal,* April 29, 1999, p C12.

[27] Trompenaars and Hampden-Turner, *Riding the Waves of Culture: Understanding Cultural Diversity in Global Business,* p 56. The importance of "relationships" in Eastern and Western cultures is explored in S H Ang, "The Power of Money: A Cross-Cultural Analysis of Business-Related Beliefs," *Journal of World Business,* Spring 2000, pp 43–60.

[28] See M Munter, "Cross-Cultural Communication for Managers," *Business Horizons,* May–June 1993, pp 69–78.

[29] I Adler, "Between the Lines," *Business Mexico,* October 2000, p 24.

[30] See, for example, N R Mack, "Taking Apart the Ticking of Time," *The Christian Science Monitor,* August 29, 1991, p 17.

[31] For a comprehensive treatment of time, see J E McGrath and J R Kelly, *Time and Human Interaction: Toward a Social Psychology of Time* (New York: Guilford Press, 1986). Also see L A Manrai and A K Manrai, "Effects of Cultural-Context, Gender, and Acculturation on Perceptions of Work versus Social/Leisure Time Usage," *Journal of Business Research,* February 1995, pp 115–28.

[32] A good discussion of doing business in Mexico is G K Stephens and C R Greer, "Doing Business in Mexico: Understanding Cultural Differences," *Organizational Dynamics,* Summer 1995, pp 39–55.

[33] R W Moore, "Time, Culture, and Comparative Management: A Review and Future Direction," in *Advances in International Comparative Management,* vol. 5, ed S B Prasad (Greenwich, CT: JAI Press, 1990), pp 7–8.

[34] See A C Bluedorn, C F Kaufman, and P M Lane, "How Many Things Do You Like to Do at Once? An Introduction to Monochronic and Polychronic Time," *Academy of Management Executive,* November 1992, pp 17–26.

[35] "Multitasking" term drawn from S McCartney, "The Breaking Point: Multitasking Technology Can Raise Stress and Cripple Productivity," *The Arizona Republic,* May 21, 1995, p D10.

[36] O Port, "You May Have To Reset This Watch—In a Million Years," *Business Week,* August 30, 1993, p 65.

[37] See C A Rodrigues, "The Situation and National Culture as Contingencies for Leadership Behavior: Two Conceptual Models," in *Advances in International Comparative Management,* vol. 5, ed S B Prasad (Greenwich, CT: JAI Press, 1990), pp 51–68. For a study that found consistent perception of six leadership styles across four countries (Norway, United States, Sweden, and Australia), see C B Gibson and G A Marcoulides, "The Invariance of Leadership Styles across Four Countries," *Journal of Managerial Issues,* Summer 1995, pp 176–93.

[38] For details, see D H B Welsh, F Luthans, and S M Sommer, "Managing Russian Factory Workers: The Impact of US-Based Behavioral and Participative Techniques," *Academy of Management Journal,* February 1993, pp 58–79. Also see F Luthans, S J Peterson, and E Ibrayeva, "The Potential for the 'Dark Side' of Leadership in Post-Communist Countries," *Journal of World Business,* Summer 1998, pp 185–201.

[39] Data from J Kahn, "The World's Most Admired Companies," *Fortune,* October 26, 1998, pp 206–26.

[40] Data from "5 Hundred Largest U.S. Corporations," *Fortune,* April 16, 2001, pp F1–F20.

[41] J S Black and H B Gregersen, "The Right Way to Manage Expats," *Harvard Business Review,* March–April 1999, p 53. A more optimistic picture is presented in R L Tung, "American Expatriates Abroad: From

Neophytes to Cosmopolitans," *Journal of World Business,* Summer 1998, pp 125–44.

42 Adapted from R L Tung, "Expatriate Assignments: Enhancing Success and Minimizing Failure," *Academy of Management Executive,* May 1987, pp 117–26.

43 S Dallas, "Rule No. 1: Don't Diss the Locals," *Business Week,* May 15, 1995, p 8.

44 See B A Anderson, "Expatriate Management: An Australian Tri-Sector Comparative Study," *Thunderbird International Business Review,* January–February 2001, pp 33–51.

45 These insights come from Tung, "American Expatriates Abroad: From Neophytes to Cosmopolitans"; P M Caligiuri and W F Cascio, "*Can We Send Her There?* Maximizing the Success of Western Women on Global Assignments," *Journal of World Business,* Winter 1998, pp 394–416; T L Speer, "Gender Barriers Crumbling, Traveling Business Women Report," *USA Today,* March 16, 1999, p 5E; G Koretz, "A Woman's Place Is . . . ," *Business Week,* September 13, 1999, p 28; and L K Stroh, A Varma, and S J Valy-Durbin, "Why Are Women Left at Home: Are They Unwilling to Go on International Assignments?" *Journal of World Business,* Fall 2000, pp 241–55.

46 An excellent reference book on this topic is J S Black, H B Gregersen, and M E Mendenhall, *Global Assignments: Successfully Expatriating and Repatriating International Managers* (San Francisco: Jossey-Bass, 1992). Also see M Harvey and M M Novicevic, "Staffing Global Marketing Positions: What We Don't Know Can Make a Difference," *Journal of World Business,* Spring 2000, pp 80–94.

47 See K Roberts, E E Kossek, and C Ozeki, "Managing the Global Workforce: Challenges and Strategies," *Academy of Management Executive,* November 1998, pp 93–106.

48 J S Lublin, "Younger Managers Learn Global Skills," *The Wall Street Journal,* March 31, 1992, p B1.

49 See P C Earley, "Intercultural Training for Managers: A Comparison of Documentary and Interpersonal Methods," *Academy of Management Journal,* December 1987, pp 685–98; and J S Black and M Mendenhall, "Cross-Cultural Training Effectiveness: A Review and a Theoretical Framework for Future Research," *Academy of Management Review,* January 1990, pp 113–36. Also see M R Hammer and J N Martin, "The Effects of Cross-Cultural Training on American Managers in a Japanese-American Joint Venture," *Journal of Applied Communication Research,* May 1992, pp 161–81; and J K Harrison, "Individual and Combined Effects of Behavior Modeling and the Cultural Assimilator in Cross-Cultural Management Training," *Journal of Applied Psychology,* December 1992, pp 952–62.

50 See G P Ferraro, "The Need for Linguistic Proficiency in Global Business," *Business Horizons,* May–June 1996, pp 39–46. For a study demonstrating that employees tend to prefer foreign assignments in culturally similar locations, see S Aryee, Y W Chay, and J Chew, "An Investigation of the Willingness of Managerial Employees to Accept an Expatriate Assignment," *Journal of Organizational Behavior,* May 1996, pp 267–83.

51 See Harris and Moran, *Managing Cultural Differences,* pp 223–28; M Shilling, "Avoid Expatriate Culture Shock," *HRMagazine,* July 1993, pp 58–63; D Stamps, "Welcome to America: Watch Out for Culture Shock," *Training,* November 1996, pp 22–30; and L Glanz, R Williams, and L Hoeksema, "Sensemaking in Expatriation—A Theoretical Basis," *Thunderbird International Business Review,* January–February 2001, pp 101–19.

52 S Tully, "The Modular Corporation," *Fortune,* February 8, 1993, pp 108, 112.

53 Additional instructive resources on the expatriate cycle are C M Solomon, "One Assignment, Two Lives," *Personnel Journal,* May 1996, pp 36–47; L A Collins Allard, "Managing Globe-Trotting Expats," *Management Review,* May 1996, pp 39–43; J S Lublin, "Is Transfer to Native Land a Passport to Trouble?" *The Wall Street Journal,* June 3, 1996, pp B1, B4; and M Richey, "Global Families: Surviving an Overseas Move," *Management Review,* June 1996, pp 57–61.

54 See H H Nguyen, L A Messe, and G E Stollak, "Toward a More Complex Understanding of Acculturation and Adjustment," *Journal of Cross-Cultural Psychology,* January 1999, pp 5–31.

55 K L Miller, "How a Team of Buckeyes Helped Honda Save a Bundle," *Business Week,* September 13, 1993, p 68.

56 B Newman, "For Ira Caplan, Re-Entry Has Been Strange," *The Wall Street Journal,* December 12, 1995, p A12.

57 See Black, Gregersen, and Mendenhall, *Global Assignments: Successfully Expatriating and Repatriating International Managers,* p 227. Also see H B Gregersen, "Commitments to a Parent Company and a Local Work Unit During Repatriation," *Personnel Psychology,* Spring 1992, pp 29–54; and H B Gregersen and J S Black, "Multiple Commitments upon Repatriation: The Japanese Experience," *Journal of Management,* no. 2, 1996, pp 209–29.

58 Ibid., pp 226–27.

59 See J R Engen, "Coming Home," *Training,* March 1995, pp 37–40; and L K Stroh, H B Gregersen, and J S Black, "Closing the Gap: Expectations versus Reality among Repatriates," *Journal of World Business,* Summer 1998, pp 111–24.

Chapter 4

1 Excerpted from S Armour, "Welcome Mat Rolls Out for Hispanic Workers: Corporate America Cultivates Talent as Ethnic Population Booms," *USA Today,* April 12, 2001, pp 1B, 2B.

2 Excerpted from D A Blackmon, "Racial Bind: Black Utility Workers in Georgia See Nooses as Sign of Harassment," *The Wall Street Journal,* April 2, 2001, p A1.

3 Ibid., pp A1, A8.

4 The negativity bias was examined and supported by O Ybarra and W G Stephan, "Misanthropic Person Memory," *Journal of Personality and Social Psychology,* April 1996, pp 691–700; and Y Ganzach, "Negativity (and Positivity) in Performance Evaluation: Three Field Studies," *Journal of Applied Psychology,* August 1995, pp 491–99.

5 E Rosch, C B Mervis, W D Gray, D M Johnson, and P Boyes-Braem, "Basic Objects in Natural Categories," *Cognitive Psychology,* July 1976, p 383.

6 For a thorough discussion of the role of schema during encoding, see S T Fiske and S E Taylor, *Social Cognition,* 2nd ed (Reading, MA: Addison-Wesley, 1991).

7 C M Judd and B Park, "Definition and Assessment of Accuracy in Social Stereotypes," *Psychological Review,* January 1993, p 110.

8 For a thorough discussion of stereotype accuracy, see M C Ashton and V M Esses, "Stereotype Accuracy: Estimating the Academic Performance of Ethnic Groups," *Personality and Social Psychology Bulletin,* February 1999, pp 225–36.

9 Results can be found in E H James, "Race-Related Differences in Promotions and Support: Underlying Effects of Human and Social Capital," *Organization Science,* September–October 2000, pp 493–508.

10 This study was conducted by K S Lyness and D E Thompson, "Climbing the Corporate Ladder: Do Female and Male Executives Follow the Same Route?" *Journal of Applied Psychology,* February 2000, pp 86–101.

11 For a thorough discussion about the structure and organization of memory, see L R Squire, B Knowlton, and G Musen, "The Structure and Organization of Memory," in *Annual Review of Psychology,* eds L W Porter and M R Rosenzweig (Palo Alto, CA: Annual Reviews Inc., 1993), vol. 44, pp 453–95.

12 The structure of event memory is thoroughly discussed by J M Zacks and B Tversky, "Event Structure in Perception and Conception," *Psychological Bulletin,* January 2001, pp 3–21.

13 A thorough discussion of the reasoning process used to make judgments and decisions is provided by S A Sloman, "The Empirical Case for Two Systems of Reasoning," *Psychological Bulletin,* January 1996, pp 3–22.

14 Results can be found in C M Marlowe, S L Schneider, and C E Nelson, "Gender and Attractiveness Biases in Hiring Decisions: Are More Experienced Managers Less Biased?" *Journal of Applied Psychology,* February 1996, pp 11–21.

15 Details of this study can be found in C K Stevens, "Antecedents of Interview Interactions, Interviewers' Ratings, and Applicants' Reactions," *Personnel Psychology,* Spring 1998, pp 55–85.

16 See R C Mayer and J H Davis, "The Effect of the Performance Appraisal System on Trust for Management: A Field Quasi-Experiment," *Journal of Applied Psychology,* February 1999, pp 123–36.

[17] Results can be found in W H Bommer, J L Johnson, G A Rich, P M Podsakoff, and S B Mackenzie, "On the Interchangeability of Objective and Subjective Measures of Employee Performance: A Meta-Analysis," *Personnel Psychology,* Autumn 1995, pp 587–605.

[18] The effectiveness of rater training was supported by D V Day and L M Sulsky, "Effects of Frame-of-Reference Training and Information Configuration on Memory Organization and Rating Accuracy," *Journal of Applied Psychology,* February 1995, pp 158–67.

[19] Results can be found in J S Phillips and R G Lord, "Schematic Information Processing and Perceptions of Leadership in Problem-Solving Groups," *Journal of Applied Psychology,* August 1982, pp 486–92.

[20] Kelley's model is discussed in detail in H H Kelley, "The Processes of Causal Attribution," *American Psychologist,* February 1973, pp 107–28.

[21] For examples, see J Susskind, K Maurer, V Thakkar, D L Hamilton, and J W Sherman, "Perceiving Individuals and Groups: Expectancies, Dispositional Inferences, and Causal Attributions," *Journal of Personality and Social Psychology,* February 1999, pp 181–91; and J McClure, "Discounting Causes of Behavior: Are Two Reasons Better than One?" *Journal of Personality and Social Psychology,* January 1998, pp 7–20.

[22] Results can be found in D A Hofmann and A Stetzer, "The Role of Safety Climate and Communication in Accident Interpretation: Implications for Learning from Negative Events," *Academy of Management Journal,* December 1998, pp 644–57.

[23] The effect of the self-serving bias was tested and supported by P E De Michele, B Gansneder, G B Solomon, "Success and Failure Attributions of Wrestlers: Further Evidence of the Self-Serving Bias," *Journal of Sport Behavior,* August 1998, pp 242–55; and C Sedikides, W K Campbell, G D Reeder, and A J Elliot, "The Self-Serving Bias in Relational Context," *Journal of Personality and Social Psychology,* February 1998, pp 378–86.

[24] Details may be found in S E Moss and M J Martinko, "The Effects of Performance Attributions and Outcome Dependence on Leader Feedback Behavior Following Poor Subordinate Performance," *Journal of Organizational Behavior,* May 1998, pp 259–74; and E C Pence, W C Pendelton, G H Dobbins, and J A Sgro, "Effects of Causal Explanations and Sex Variables on Recommendations for Corrective Actions Following Employee Failure," *Organizational Behavior and Human Performance,* April 1982, pp 227–40.

[25] See D Konst, R Vonk, and R V D Vlist, "Inferences about Causes and Consequences of Behavior of Leaders and Subordinates," *Journal of Organizational Behavior,* March 1999, pp 261–71.

[26] See M Miserandino, "Attributional Retraining as a Method of Improving Athletic Performance," *Journal of Sport Behavior,* August 1998, pp 286–97; and F Forsterling, "Attributional Retraining: A Review," *Psychological Bulletin,* November 1985, pp 496–512.

[27] Definitions of diversity are discussed by A Wellner, "How Do You Spell Diversity?" *Training,* April 2000, pp 34–38; and R R Thomas, Jr, *Redefining Diversity* (New York: AMACOM, 1996), pp 4–9.

[28] The following discussion is based on L Gardenswartz and A Rowe, *Diverse Teams at Work* (New York: McGraw-Hill, 1994), pp 31–57.

[29] This distinction is made by M Loden, *Implementing Diversity* (Chicago: Irwin, 1996).

[30] H Collingwood, "Who Handles a Diverse Work Force Best?" *Working Women,* February 1996, p 25.

[31] See A Karr, "Work Week: A Special News Report about Life on the Job—and Trends Taking Shape There," *The Wall Street Journal,* June 1, 1999, p A1.

[32] See M Minehan, "Islam's Growth Affects Workplace Policies," *HRMagazine,* November 1998, p 216.

[33] J K Laabs, "Thinking Outside the Box at the Container Store," *Workforce,* March 2001, p 35.

[34] See R J Grossman, "Is Diversity Working?" *HRMagazine,* March 2000, pp 47–50; and R R Thomas, Jr, "From Affirmative Action to Affirming Diversity," *Harvard Business Review,* March–April 1990, pp 107–17.

[35] See D A Kravitz and S L Klinberg, "Reactions to Two Version of Affirmative Action Among Whites, Blacks, and Hispanics," *Journal of Applied Psychology,* August 2000, pp 597–611.

[36] For a thorough review of relevant research, see M E Heilman, "Affirmative Action: Some Unintended Consequences for Working Women," in *Research in Organizational Behavior,* vol 16, eds B M Staw and L L Cummings (Greenwich, CT: JAI Press, 1994), pp 125–69.

[37] A M Morrison, *The New Leaders: Guidelines on Leadership Diversity in America* (San Francisco: Jossey-Bass, 1992), p 78.

[38] Data were obtained from H N Fullerton, Jr, "Employment Projections: Entrants to the Labor Force by Sex, Race, and Hispanic Origin," *Bureau of Labor Statistics Online,* Table 6, January 1998 (http://stats.bls.gov/emptab3.htm).

[39] The pay gap is discussed in "Compensation: Is There Really Still a Gender Pay Gap?" *HRFOCUS,* June 2000, pp 3–4.

[40] Results can be found in K S Lyness and D E Thompson, "Above the Glass Ceiling: A Comparison of Matched Samples of Female and Male Executives," *Journal of Applied Psychology,* June 1997, pp 359–75.

[41] See R Sharpe, "As Leaders Women Rule," *Business Week,* November 20, 2000, pp 75–84.

[42] Details of this study can be found in B R Ragins, B Townsend, and M Mattis, "Gender Gap in the Executive Suite: CEOs and Female Executives Report on Breaking the Glass Ceiling," *Academy of Management Executive,* February 1998, pp 28–42.

[43] Here are the ranks for each career strategy: Strategy 1 = 12; Strategy 2 = 6; Strategy 3 = 5; Strategy 4 = 11; Strategy 5 = 9; Strategy 6 = 3; Strategy 7 = 10; Strategy 8 = 1; Strategy 9 = 7; Strategy 10 = 8; Strategy 11 = 4; Strategy 12 = 2; and Strategy 13 = 13.

[44] "Employed White, Black, and Hispanic-Origin Workers by Sex, Occupation, Class of Worker, and Full- or Part-Time Status," *Bureau of Labor Statistics,* February 13, 1997 (http://ferret.bls.census.gov/macro/171996/empearn/aa12.txt).

[45] See R J Grossman, "Race in the Workplace," *HRMagazine,* March 2000, pp 41–45.

[46] See "Median Household Income by Race and Hispanic Origin: 1967 to 1999," *U.S. Census Bureau,* September 29, 2000 (http://www.census.gov/hhes/income/income99/incxrace.html).

[47] See "USA Statistics in Brief—Law, Education, Communications, Transportation, Housing," *U.S. Census Bureau,* April 12, 2001 (http://www.census.gov/statab/www/part2.html).

[48] These statistics were drawn from E S Rubenstein, "The College Payoff Illusion," *American Outlook,* Fall 1999, pp 14–18.

[49] See D Dooley and J Prause, "Underemployment and Alcohol Misuse in the National Longitudinal Survey of Youth," *Journal of Studies on Alcohol,* November 1998, pp 669–80; and D C Feldman, "The Nature, Antecedents and Consequences of Underemployment," *Journal of Management,* 1966, pp 385–407.

[50] See E C Newburger and A E Curry, "Educational Attainment in the United States (Update)," *U.S. Census Bureau,* March 2000; J C Day and A E Curry, "School Enrollment—Social and Economic Characteristics of Students: October 1996 (Update)," *Current Population Reports,* October 1996 (http://www.census.gov); and "Facts on Literacy," *National Literacy Facts,* August 27, 1998 (http://www.svs.net/wpci/Litfacts.htm).

[51] "Facts on Literacy."

[52] See H London, "The Workforce, Education, and the Nation's Future," Summer 1998 (http://www.hudson.org/american_outlook/articles_sm98/london.htm).

[53] Excerpted from Armour, "Welcome Mat Rolls Out for Hispanic Workers: Corporate America Cultivates Talent as Ethnic Population Booms," p 2B.

[54] Employee training is discussed by C D'Amico, "Got Skills?" *American Outlook,* Fall 1998, pp 36–38.

[55] Managerial issues and solutions for an aging workforce are discussed by D G Albrecht, "Getting Ready for Older Workers," *Workforce,* February 2001, pp 56–62; and S J Wells, "The Elder Care Gap," *HRMagazine,* May 2000, pp 39–46.

[56] K Greene, "Firms Try Again to Help Workers with Elder Care," *The Wall Street Journal,* March 29, 2001, p. B1.

[57] These barriers were taken from discussions in Loden, *Implementing Diversity;* E E Spragins, "Benchmark: The Diverse Work Force," *Inc.,* January 1993, p 33; and Morrison, *The New Leaders: Guidelines on Leadership Diversity in America.*

[58] See the related discussion in A C Logue, "Girl Gangs," *Training & Development Journal,* January 2001, pp 24–28; and S Davis, "Minority Execs Want an Even Break," *Workforce,* April 2000, pp 50–55.

[59] For complete details and results from this study, see A M Morrison, *The New Leaders: Guidelines on Leadership Diversity in America* (San Francisco: Jossey-Bass, 1992).

[60] Results are presented in P Digh, "The Next Challenge: Holding People Accountable," *HRMagazine,* October 1998, pp 63–69.

[61] Development differences across racial groups is discussed by D A Thomas, "The Truth about Mentoring Minorities: Race Matters," *The Harvard Business Review,* April 2001, pp 99–107.

[62] Excerpted from R Kazel, "Hotel Speaks Employees' Languages," *Business Insurance,* November 24, 1997, p 14.

Chapter 5

[1] P Gogoi, "Teaching Men the Right Stuff," *Business Week,* November 20, 2000, p 84.

[2] D Seligman, "The Trouble with Buyouts," *Fortune,* November 30, 1992, p 125.

[3] See P Dass and B Parker, "Strategies for Managing Human Resource Diversity: From Resistance to Learning," *Academy of Management Executive,* May 1999, pp 68–80; A Etzioni, "Are White Students Hurt by Others Who Look 'Just Like Them'?" *USA Today,* February 6, 2001, p 13A; E Iwata, "Tech World Makes Strides Toward Diversity," *USA Today,* April 16, 2001, p 1B; and B Leonard, "Diverse Workforce Tends to Attract More Female and Minority Job Applicants," *HRMagazine,* April 2001, p 27.

[4] Data from "If We Could Do It Over Again," *USA Today,* February 19, 2001, p 4D.

[5] V Gecas, "The Self-Concept," in *Annual Review of Sociology,* eds R H Turner and J F Short, Jr. (Palo Alto, CA: Annual Reviews Inc., 1982), vol. 8, p 3. Also see A P Brief and R J Aldag, "The 'Self' in Work Organizations: A Conceptual Review," *Academy of Management Review,* January 1981, pp 75–88; J J Sullivan, "Self Theories and Employee Motivation," *Journal of Management,* June 1989, pp 345–63; P Cushman, "Why the Self Is Empty," *American Psychologist,* May 1990, pp 599–611; and L Gaertner, C Sedikides, and K Graetz, "In Search of Self-Definition: Motivational Primacy of the Individual Self, Motivational Primacy of the Collective Self, or Contextual Primacy?" *Journal of Personality and Social Psychology,* January 1999, pp 5–18.

[6] L Festinger, *A Theory of Cognitive Dissonance* (Stanford, CA: Stanford University Press, 1957), p 3.

[7] See J Holt and D M Keats, "Work Cognitions in Multicultural Interaction," *Journal of Cross-Cultural Psychology,* December 1992, pp 421–43.

[8] A Canadian versus Japanese comparison of self-concept can be found in J D Campbell, P D Trapnell, S J Heine, I M Katz, L F Lavallee, and D R Lehman, "Self-Concept Clarity: Measurement, Personality Correlates, and Cultural Boundaries," *Journal of Personality and Social Psychology,* January 1996, pp 141–56.

[9] See D C Barnlund, "Public and Private Self in Communicating with Japan," *Business Horizons,* March–April 1989, pp 32–40; and the section on "Doing Business with Japan" in P R Harris and R T Moran, *Managing Cultural Differences,* 4th ed (Houston: Gulf Publishing, 1996), pp 267–76.

[10] Based in part on a definition found in Gecas, "The Self-Concept." Also see N Branden, *Self-Esteem at Work: How Confident People Make Powerful Companies* (San Francisco: Jossey-Bass, 1998).

[11] H W Marsh, "Positive and Negative Global Self-Esteem: A Substantively Meaningful Distinction or Artifacts?" *Journal of Personality and Social Psychology,* April 1996, p 819.

[12] Ibid.

[13] For related research, see R C Liden, L Martin, and C K Parsons, "Interviewer and Applicant Behaviors in Employment Interviews," *Academy of Management Journal,* April 1993, pp 372–86; M B Setterlund and P M Niedenthal, " 'Who Am I? Why Am I Here?': Self-Esteem, Self-Clarity, and Prototype Matching," *Journal of Personality and Social Psychology,* October 1993, pp 769–80; and G J Pool, W Wood, and K Leck, "The Self-Esteem Motive in Social Influence: Agreement with Valued Majorities and Disagreement with Derogated Minorities," *Journal of Personality and Social Psychology,* October 1998, pp 967–75.

[14] E Diener and M Diener, "Cross-Cultural Correlates of Life Satisfaction and Self-Esteem," *Journal of Personality and Social Psychology,* April 1995, p 662. For cross-cultural evidence of a similar psychological process for self-esteem, see T M Singelis, M H Bond, W F Sharkey, and C S Y Lai, "Unpackaging Culture's Influence on Self-Esteem and Embarrassability," *Journal of Cross-Cultural Psychology,* May 1999, pp 315–41.

[15] J L Pierce, D G Gardner, L L Cummings, and R B Dunham, "Organization-Based Self-Esteem: Construct Definition, Measurement, and Validation," *Academy of Management Journal,* September 1989, p 625. Also see J L Pierce, D G Gardner, R B Dunham, and L L Cummings, "Moderation by Organization-Based Self-Esteem of Role Condition-Employee Response Relationships," *Academy of Management Journal,* April 1993, pp 271–88.

[16] Practical steps are discussed in M Kaeter, "Basic Self-Esteem," *Training,* August 1993, pp 31–35. Also see G Koretz, "The Vital Role of Self-Esteem," *Business Week,* February 2, 1998, p 26. The opposite, excessive ego, is discussed in P Sellers, "Get Over Yourself," *Fortune,* April 30, 2001, pp 76–88.

[17] M E Gist, "Self-Efficacy: Implications for Organizational Behavior and Human Resource Management," *Academy of Management Review,* July 1987, p 472. Also see A Bandura, "Self-Efficacy: Toward a Unifying Theory of Behavioral Change," *Psychological Review,* March 1977, pp 191–215; M E Gist and T R Mitchell, "Self-Efficacy: A Theoretical Analysis of Its Determinants and Malleability," *Academy of Management Review,* April 1992, pp 183–211; and T J Maurer and K D Andrews, "Traditional, Likert, and Simplified Measures of Self-Efficacy," *Educational and Psychological Measurement,* December 2000, pp 965–73.

[18] D Rader, "I Always Believed There Was a Place for Me," *Parade Magazine,* May 21, 2000, p 6.

[19] Based on D H Lindsley, D A Brass, and J B Thomas, "Efficacy-Performance Spirals: A Multilevel Perspective," *Academy of Management Review,* July 1995, pp 645–78.

[20] See, for example, V Gecas, "The Social Psychology of Self-Efficacy," in *Annual Review of Sociology,* eds W R Scott and J Blake (Palo Alto, CA: Annual Reviews, Inc., 1989), vol. 15, pp 291–316; C K Stevens, A G Bavetta, and M E Gist, "Gender Differences in the Acquisition of Salary Negotiation Skills: The Role of Goals, Self-Efficacy, and Perceived Control," *Journal of Applied Psychology,* October 1993, pp 723–35; and D Eden and Y Zuk, "Seasickness as a Self-Fulfilling Prophecy: Raising Self-Efficacy to Boost Performance at Sea," *Journal of Applied Psychology,* October 1995, pp 628–35.

[21] For more on learned helplessness, see Gecas, "The Social Psychology of Self-Efficacy"; M J Martinko and W L Gardner, "Learned Helplessness: An Alternative Explanation for Performance Deficits," *Academy of Management Review,* April 1982, pp 195–204; and C R Campbell and M J Martinko, "An Integrative Attributional Perspective of Empowerment and Learned Helplessness: A Multimethod Field Study," *Journal of Management,* no. 2, 1998, pp 173–200. Also see A Dickerson and M A Taylor, "Self-Limiting Behavior in Women: Self-Esteem and Self-Efficacy as Predictors," *Group & Organization Management,* June 2000, pp 191–210.

[22] Research on this connection is reported in R B Rubin, M M Martin, S S Bruning, and D E Powers, "Test of a Self-Efficacy Model of Interpersonal Communication Competence," *Communication Quarterly,* Spring 1993, pp 210–20.

[23] Excerpted from T Petzinger Jr, "Bob Schmonsees Has a Tool for Better Sales, and It Ignores Excuses," *The Wall Street Journal,* March 26, 1999, p B1.

[24] Data from A D Stajkovic and F Luthans, "Self-Efficacy and Work-Related Performance: A Meta-Analysis," *Psychological Bulletin,* September 1998, pp 240–61.

[25] Based in part on discussion in Gecas, "The Social Psychology of Self-Efficacy."

[26] See S K Parker, "Enhancing Role Breadth Self-Efficacy: The Roles of Job Enrichment and Other Organizational Interventions," *Journal of Applied Psychology,* December 1998, pp 835–52.

[27] The positive relationship between self-efficacy and readiness for retraining is documented in L A Hill and J Elias, "Retraining Midcareer Managers: Career History and Self-Efficacy Beliefs," *Human Resource Management,* Summer 1990, pp 197–217. Also see A M Saks, "Longitudinal Field Investigation of the Moderating and Mediating Effects of Self-Efficacy on the Relationship between Training and Newcomer Adjustment," *Journal of Applied Psychology,* April 1995, pp 211–25.

28 See A D Stajkovic and Fred Luthans, "Social Cognitive Theory and Self-Efficacy: Going Beyond Traditional Motivational and Behavioral Approaches," *Organizational Dynamics,* Spring 1998, pp 62–74.

29 See P C Earley and T R Lituchy, "Delineating Goal and Efficacy Effects: A Test of Three Models," *Journal of Applied Psychology,* February 1991, pp 81–98.

30 See W S Silver, T R Mitchell, and M E Gist, "Response to Successful and Unsuccessful Performance: The Moderating Effect of Self-Efficacy on the Relationship between Performance and Attributions," *Organizational Behavior and Human Decision Processes,* June 1995, pp 286–99; R Zemke, "The Corporate Coach," *Training,* December 1996, pp 24–28; and J P Masciarelli, "Less Lonely at the Top," *Management Review,* April 1999, pp 58–61.

31 For a comprehensive update, see S W Gangestad and M Snyder, "Self-Monitoring: Appraisal and Reappraisal," *Psychological Bulletin,* July 2000, pp 530–55.

32 M Snyder and S Gangestad, "On the Nature of Self-Monitoring: Matters of Assessment, Matters of Validity," *Journal of Personality and Social Psychology,* July 1986, p 125.

33 Data from M Kilduff and D V Day, "Do Chameleons Get Ahead? The Effects of Self-Monitoring on Managerial Careers," *Academy of Management Journal,* August 1994, pp 1047–60.

34 Data from D B Turban and T W Dougherty, "Role of Protege Personality in Receipt of Mentoring and Career Success," *Academy of Management Journal,* June 1994, pp 688–702.

35 See F Luthans, "Successful vs. Effective Managers," *Academy of Management Executive,* May 1988, pp 127–32.

36 See A Bandura, *Social Learning Theory* (Englewood Cliffs, NJ: Prentice Hall, 1977). A further refinement is reported in A D Stajkovic and F Luthans, "Social Cognitive Theory and Self-Efficacy: Going Beyond Traditional Motivational and Behavioral Approaches," *Organizational Dynamics,* Spring 1998, pp 62–74. Also see M Uhl-Bien and G B Graen, "Individual Self-Management: Analysis of Professionals' Self-Managing Activities in Functional and Cross-Functional Work Teams," *Academy of Management Journal,* June 1998, pp 340–50.

37 Bandura, *Social Learning Theory,* p 13.

38 For related research, see M Castaneda, T A Kolenko, and R J Aldag, "Self-Management Perceptions and Practices: A Structural Equations Analysis," *Journal of Organizational Behavior,* January 1999, pp 101–20.

39 "Career Self-Management," *Industry Week,* September 5, 1994, p 36.

40 For more, see M O'Brien, "Personal Mastery: The New Executive Curriculum," *Training,* July 1996, p 82; B Moses, "The Busyness Trap," *Training,* November 1998, pp 38–42; and D J Abernathy, "A Get-Real Guide to Time Management," *Training & Development,* June 1999, pp 22–26.

41 S R Covey, *The 7 Habits of Highly Effective People* (New York: Simon & Schuster, 1989), p 42. Also see J Hillkirk, "Golden Rules Promoted for Work Success," *USA Today,* August 20, 1993, pp 1B–2B; L Bongiorno, "Corporate America, Dr. Feelgood Will See You Now," *Business Week,* December 6, 1993, p 52; T K Smith, "What's So Effective About Stephen Covey?" *Fortune,* December 12, 1994, pp 116–26; E Brown, "Stephen Covey's New One-Day Seminar," *Fortune,* February 1, 1999, pp 138–40; and "Put More Passion in Your Life," *Nonprofit World,* May–June 2000, p 39.

42 "Labor Letter: A Special News Report on People and their Jobs in Offices, Fields, and Factories," *The Wall Street Journal,* October 15, 1985, p 1.

43 R McGarvey, "Rehearsing for Success," *Executive Female,* January/February 1990, p 36.

44 See W P Anthony, R H Bennett, III, E N Maddox, and W J Wheatley, "Picturing the Future: Using Mental Imagery to Enrich Strategic Environmental Assessment," *Academy of Management Executive,* May 1993, pp 43–56.

45 D S Looney, "Mental Toughness Wins Out," *The Christian Science Monitor,* July 31, 1998, p B4.

46 For excellent tips on self-management, see C P Neck, "Managing Your Mind," *Internal Auditor,* June 1996, pp 60–63.

47 C Zastrow, *Talk to Yourself: Using the Power of Self-Talk* (Englewood Cliffs, NJ: Prentice Hall, 1979), p 60. Also see C C Manz and C P Neck, "Inner Leadership: Creating Productive Thought Patterns," *Academy of Management Executive,* August 1991, pp 87–95; and C P Neck and R F Ashcraft, "Inner Leadership: Mental Strategies for Nonprofit Staff Members," *Nonprofit World,* May–June 2000, pp 27–30.

48 E Franz, "Private Pep Talk," *Selling Power,* May 1996, p 81.

49 Drawn from discussion in A Bandura, "Self-Reinforcement: Theoretical and Methodological Considerations," *Behaviorism,* Fall 1976, pp 135–55.

50 R Kreitner and F Luthans, "A Social Learning Approach to Behavioral Management: Radical Behaviorists 'Mellowing Out,' " *Organizational Dynamics,* Autumn 1984, p 63.

51 Adult personality changes are documented in L Kaufman Cartwright and P Wink, "Personality Change in Women Physicians from Medical Student to Mid-40s," *Psychology of Women Quarterly,* June 1994, pp 291–308. Also see L Pulkkinen, M Ohranen, and A Tolvanen, "Personality Antecedents of Career Orientation and Stability among Women Compared to Men," *Journal of Vocational Behavior,* February 1999, pp 37–58.

52 The landmark report is J M Digman, "Personality Structure: Emergence of the Five-Factor Model," *Annual Review of Psychology,* vol. 41, 1990, pp 417–40. Also see C Viswesvaran and D S Ones, "Measurement Error in 'Big Five Factors' Personality Assessment: Reliability Generalization across Studies and Measures," *Educational and Psychological Measurement,* April 2000, pp 224–35.

53 See K M DeNeve and H Cooper, "The Happy Personality: A Meta-Analysis of 137 Personality Traits and Subjective Well-Being," *Psychological Bulletin,* September 1998, pp 197–229; and D P Skarlicki, R Folger, and P Tesluk, "Personality as a Moderator in the Relationship between Fairness and Retaliation," *Academy of Management Journal,* February 1999, pp 100–108.

54 Data from S V Paunonen et al., "The Structure of Personality in Six Cultures," *Journal of Cross-Cultural Psychology,* May 1996, pp 339–53. Also see M Dalton and M Wilson, "The Relationship of the Five-Factor Model of Personality to Job Performance for a Group of Middle Eastern Expatriate Managers," *Journal of Cross-Cultural Psychology,* March 2000, pp 250–58.

55 See M R Barrick and M K Mount, "The Big Five Personality Dimensions and Job Performance: A Meta-Analysis," *Personnel Psychology,* Spring 1991, pp 1–26. Also see R P Tett, D N Jackson, and M Rothstein, "Personality Measures as Predictors of Job Performance: A Meta-Analytic Review," *Personnel Psychology,* Winter 1991, pp 703–42; and S E Seibert and M L Kraimer, "The Five-Factor Model of Personality and Career Success," *Journal of Vocational Behavior,* February 2001, pp 1–21.

56 Barrick and Mount, "The Big Five Personality Dimensions and Job Performance: A Meta-Analysis," p 18. See O Behling, "Employee Selection: Will Intelligence and Conscientiousness Do the Job?" *Academy of Management Executive,* February 1998, pp 77–86; and J A Lepine and L Van Dyne, "Peer Responses to Low Performers: An Attributional Model of Helping in the Context of Groups," *Academy of Management Review,* January 2001, pp 67–84.

57 Barrick and Mount, "The Big Five Personality Dimensions and Job Performance: A Meta-Analysis," p 21. Also see D M Tokar, A R Fischer, and L M Subich, "Personality and Vocational Behavior: A Selective Review of the Literature, 1993–1997," *Journal of Vocational Behavior,* October 1998, pp 115–53; and K C Wooten, T A Timmerman, and R Folger, "The Use of Personality and the Five-Factor Model to Predict New Business Ventures: From Outplacement to Start-up," *Journal of Vocational Behavior,* February 1999, pp 82–101.

58 See S B Gustafson and M D Mumford, "Personal Style and Person-Environment Fit: A Pattern Approach," *Journal of Vocational Behavior,* April 1995, pp 163–88.

59 For an instructive update, see J B Rotter, "Internal versus External Control of Reinforcement: A Case History of a Variable," *American Psychologist,* April 1990, pp 489–93. A critical review of locus of control and a call for a meta-analysis can be found in R W Renn and R J Vandenberg, "Differences in Employee Attitudes and Behaviors Based on Rotter's (1966) Internal-External Locus of Control: Are They All Valid?" *Human Relations,* November 1991, pp 1161–77.

60 See the entire issue of "State of Small Business 2001," *Inc.,* May 29, 2001.

61 For an overall review of research on locus of control, see P E Spector, "Behavior in Organizations as a Function of Employee's Locus of Control," *Psychological Bulletin,* May 1982, pp 482–97; the relationship between locus of control and performance and satisfaction is examined in D R Norris and R E Niebuhr, "Attributional Influences on the Job Performance–Job Satisfaction Relationship," *Academy of Management Journal,* June 1984, pp 424–31; salary differences between internals and externals were examined by P C Nystrom, "Managers' Salaries and Their Beliefs about Reinforcement Control," *Journal of Social Psychology,* August 1983, pp 291–92. Also see S S K Lam and J Schaubroeck, "The Role of Locus of Control in Reactions to Being Promoted and to Being Passed Over: A Quasi Experiment," *Academy of Management Journal,* February 2000, pp 66–78.

62 See S R Hawk, "Locus of Control and Computer Attitude: The Effect of User Involvement," *Computers in Human Behavior,* no. 3, 1989, pp 199–206. Also see A S Phillips and A G Bedeian, "Leader-Follower Exchange Quality: The Role of Personal and Interpersonal Attributes," *Academy of Management Journal,* August 1994, pp 990–1001.

63 These recommendations are from Spector, "Behavior in Organizations as a Function of Employee's Locus of Control."

64 See "What Men Think About," *Training,* March 1995, p 14; and P Cappelli, "Is the 'Skills Gap' Really about Attitudes?" *California Management Review,* Summer 1995, pp 108–24.

65 M Fishbein and I Ajzen, *Belief, Attitude, Intention and Behavior: An Introduction to Theory and Research* (Reading, MA: Addison-Wesley Publishing, 1975), p 6. For more, see D Andrich and I M Styles, "The Structural Relationship between Attitude and Behavior Statements from the Unfolding Perspective," *Psychological Methods,* December 1998, pp 454–69; A P Brief, *Attitudes In and Around Organizations* (Thousand Oaks, CA: Sage Publications, 1998); and "Tips to Pick the Best Employee," *Business Week,* March 1, 1999, p 24.

66 For a discussion of the difference between values and attitudes, see B W Becker and P E Connor, "Changing American Values—Debunking the Myth," *Business,* January–March 1985, pp 56–59.

67 See B M Staw and J Ross, "Stability in the Midst of Change: A Dispositional Approach to Job Attitudes," *Journal of Applied Psychology,* August 1985, pp 469–80. Also see J Schaubroeck, D C Ganster, and B Kemmerer, "Does Trait Affect Promote Job Attitude Stability?" *Journal of Organizational Behavior,* March 1996, pp 191–96.

68 Data from P S Visser and J A Krosnick, "Development of Attitude Strength Over the Life Cycle: Surge and Decline," *Journal of Personality and Social Psychology,* December 1998, pp 1389–1410.

69 For interesting reading on intelligence, see E Cose, "Teaching Kids to Be Smart," *Newsweek,* August 21, 1995, pp 58–60; A Farnham, "Are You Smart Enough to Keep Your Job?" *Fortune,* January 15, 1996, pp 34–48; D Stamps, "Are We Smart Enough for Our Jobs?" *Training,* April 1996, pp 44–50; K S Peterson, "Do New Definitions of Smart Dilute Meaning?" *USA Today,* February 18, 1997, pp 1D–2D; and J R Flynn, "Searching for Justice: The Discovery of IQ Gains Over Time," *American Psychologist,* January 1999, pp 5–20.

70 For an excellent update on intelligence, including definitional distinctions and a historical perspective of the IQ controversy, see R A Weinberg, "Intelligence and IQ," *American Psychologist,* February 1989, pp 98–104.

71 Ibid. Also see M Elias, "Mom's IQ, Not Family Size, Key to Kids' Smarts," *USA Today,* June 12, 2000, p 1D; and R Sapolsky, "Score One for Nature—or Is It Nurture?" *USA Today,* June 21, 2000, p 17A.

72 S L Wilk, L Burris Desmarais, and P R Sackett, "Gravitation to Jobs Commensurate with Ability: Longitudinal and Cross-Sectional Tests," *Journal of Applied Psychology,* February 1995, p 79.

73 B Azar, "People Are Becoming Smarter—Why?" *APA Monitor,* June 1996, p 20. Also see " 'Average' Intelligence Higher than It Used to Be," *USA Today,* February 18, 1997, p 6D.

74 See F L Schmidt and J E Hunter, "Employment Testing: Old Theories and New Research Findings," *American Psychologist,* October 1981, p 1128. Also see Y Ganzach, "Intelligence and Job Satisfaction," *Academy of Management Journal,* October 1998, pp 526–39.

75 A Reinhardt, "I've Left a Few Dead Bodies," *Business Week,* January 31, 2000, p 69. Also see D Jones, "Explosive CEOs Passé, But Are Nice Ones Here to Stay?" *USA Today,* May 22, 2000, p 6B; K S Peterson, "Why Everyone Is So Short-Tempered," *USA Today,* July 18, 2000,

pp 1A–2A; and K Fackelmann, "A Different Take On Anger," *USA Today,* March 15, 2001, p 8D.

76 Quoted in B Schlender, "Why Andy Grove Can't Stop," *Fortune,* July 10, 1995, p 91.

77 D Lieberman, "Fear of Failing Drives Diller," *USA Today,* February 10, 1999, p 3B. Also see L Wah, "The Emotional Tightrope," *Management Review,* January 2000, pp 38–43.

78 R S Lazarus, *Emotion and Adaptation* (New York: Oxford University Press, 1991), p 6. Also see, Goleman, *Emotional Intelligence,* pp 289–90; and J A Russell and L F Barrett, "Core Affect, Prototypical Emotional Episodes, and Other Things Called *Emotion:* Dissecting the Elephant," *Journal of Personality and Social Psychology,* May 1999, pp 805–19.

79 Based on discussion in R D Arvey, G L Renz, and T W Watson, "Emotionality and Job Performance: Implications for Personnel Selection," in *Research in Personnel and Human Resources Management,* vol. 16, ed G R Ferris (Stamford, CT: JAI Press, 1998), pp 103–47. Also see L A King, "Ambivalence Over Emotional Expression and Reading Emotions," *Journal of Personality and Social Psychology,* March 1998, pp 753–62.

80 Based on J M Kidd, "Emotion: An Absent Presence in Career Theory," *Journal of Vocational Behavior,* June 1998, pp 275–88.

81 Data from A M Kring and A H Gordon, "Sex Differences in Emotions: Expression, Experience, and Physiology," *Journal of Personality and Social Psychology,* March 1998, pp 686–703.

82 Drawn from P Totterdell, S Kellett, K Teuchmann, and R B Briner, "Evidence of Mood Linkage in Work Groups," *Journal of Personality and Social Psychology,* June 1998, pp 1504–15.

83 D Goleman, *Emotional Intelligence* (New York: Bantam Books, 1995), p 34. For more, see Q N Huy, "Emotional Capability, Emotional Intelligence, and Radical Change," *Academy of Management Review,* April 1999, pp 325–45; and V U Druskat and S B Wolff, "Building the Emotional Intelligence of Groups," *Harvard Business Review,* March 2001, pp 80–90.

84 M N Martinez, "The Smarts That Count," *HRMagazine,* November 1997, pp 72–78.

85 "What's Your EQ at Work?" *Fortune,* October 26, 1998, p 298.

86 Based on M Davies, L Stankov, and R D Roberts, "Emotional Intelligence: In Search of an Elusive Construct," *Journal of Personality and Social Psychology,* October 1998, pp 989–1015.

87 A Fisher, "Success Secret: A High Emotional IQ," *Fortune,* October 26, 1998, p 294.

Chapter 6

1 Excerpted from J K Logan, "Retention Tangibles and Intangibles," *Training & Development,* April 2000, pp 48–49.

2 T R Mitchell, "Motivation: New Direction for Theory, Research, and Practice," *Academy of Management Review,* January 1982, p 81.

3 This discussion is based on T R Mitchell, "Matching Motivational Strategies with Organizational Contexts," in *Research in Organizational Behavior* (vol 19), eds L L Cummings and B M Staw (Greenwich, CT: JAI Press, 1997), pp 57–149.

4 Excerpted from S Boehle, "From Humble Roots," *Training,* October 2000, p 108.

5 Ibid., pp. 106–13.

6 For a complete description of Maslow's theory, see A H Maslow, "A Theory of Human Motivation," *Psychological Review,* July 1943, pp 370–96.

7 Excerpted from M Murray, "An Added Benefit for Workers: Flexibility," *The Wall Street Journal,* April 29, 2001, p D7.

8 Excerpted from K Tyler, "A Roof Over Their Heads," *HRMagazine,* February 2001, p 41.

9 H A Murray, *Explorations in Personality* (New York: John Wiley & Sons, 1938), p 164.

10 See K G Shaver, "The Entrepreneurial Personality Myth," *Business and Economic Review,* April/June 1995, pp 20–23.

11 See the following series of research reports: D K McNeese-Smith, "The Relationship between Managerial Motivation, Leadership, Nurse Outcomes and Patient Satisfaction," *Journal of Organizational Behavior,* March 1999, pp 243–59; A M Harrell and M J Stahl, "A Behavioral Decision Theory Approach for Measuring McClelland's Trichotomy of

Needs," *Journal of Applied Psychology,* April 1981, pp 242–47; and M J Stahl, "Achievement, Power and Managerial Motivation: Selecting Managerial Talent with the Job Choice Exercise," *Personnel Psychology,* Winter 1983, pp 775–89.

[12] Evidence for the validity of motivation training can be found in H Heckhausen and S Krug, "Motive Modification," in *Motivation and Society,* ed A J Stewart (San Francisco: Jossey-Bass, 1982). Also see S D Bluen, J Barling, and W Burns, "Predicting Sales Performance, Job Satisfaction, and Depression by Using the Achievement Strivings and Impatience–Irritability Dimensions of Type A Behavior," *Journal of Applied Psychology,* April 1990, pp 212–16.

[13] Results can be found in D B Turban and T L Keon, "Organizational Attractiveness: An Interactionist Perspective," *Journal of Applied Psychology,* April 1993, pp 184–93.

[14] See D Steele Johnson and R Perlow, "The Impact of Need for Achievement Components on Goal Commitment and Performance," *Journal of Applied Social Psychology,* November 1992, pp 1711–20.

[15] J L Bowditch and A F Buono, *A Primer on Organizational Behavior* (New York: John Wiley & Sons, 1985), p 210.

[16] This framework was proposed by M A Campion and P W Thayer, "Development and Field Evaluation of an Interdisciplinary Measure of Job Design," *Journal of Applied Psychology,* February 1985, pp 29–43.

[17] These outcomes are discussed by J R Edwards, J A Scully, and M D Brtek, "The Nature and Outcomes of Work: A Replication and Extension of Interdisciplinary Work-Design Research," *Journal of Applied Psychology,* December 2000, pp 860–68.

[18] Supporting results can be found in B Melin, U Lundberg, J Söderlund, and M Granqvist, "Psychological and Physiological Stress Reactions of Male and Female Assembly Workers: A Comparison between Two Different Forms of Work Organization," *Journal of Organizational Behavior,* January 1999, pp 47–61; and S Melamed, I Ben-Avi, J Luz, and M S Green, "Objective and Subjective Work Monotony: Effects on Job Satisfaction, Psychological Distress, and Absenteeism in Blue-Collar Workers," *Journal of Applied Psychology,* February 1995, pp 29–42.

[19] See Edwards, Scully, and Brtek, "The Nature and Outcomes of Work: A Replication and Extension of Interdisciplinary Work-Design Research."

[20] This type of program was developed and tested by M A Campion and C L McClelland, "Follow-Up and Extension of the Interdisciplinary Costs and Benefits of Enlarged Jobs," *Journal of Applied Psychology,* June 1993, pp 339–51.

[21] See F Herzberg, B Mausner, and B B Snyderman, *The Motivation to Work* (New York: John Wiley & Sons, 1959).

[22] F Herzberg, "One More Time: How Do You Motivate Employees?" *Harvard Business Review,* January/February 1968, p 56.

[23] For a thorough review of research on Herzberg's theory, see C C Pinder, *Work Motivation: Theory, Issues, and Applications* (Glenview, IL: Scott, Foresman, 1984).

[24] J R Hackman, G R Oldham, R Janson, and K Purdy, "A New Strategy for Job Enrichment," *California Management Review,* Summer 1975, p 58.

[25] Results can be found in J Barbian, "In the Battle to Attract and Retain Talent, Companies Are Finding New Ways to Keep Employees Smiling," *Training,* January 2001, pp 93–96.

[26] K W Thomas, "Intrinsic Motivation and How It Works," *Training,* October 2000, pp 130–35.

[27] Definitions of the job characteristics were adapted from J R Hackman and G R Oldham, "Motivation through the Design of Work: Test of a Theory," *Organizational Behavior and Human Performance,* August 1976, pp 250–79.

[28] A review of this research can be found in M L Ambrose and C T Kulik, "Old Friends, New Faces: Motivation Research in the 1990s," *Journal of Management,* 1999, pp 231–92.

[29] Excerpted from C L Cole, "Sun Microsystems' Solution to Traffic That Doesn't Move? Satellite Work Centers," *Workforce,* January 2001, pp 108, 110.

[30] Results can be found in M R Kelley, "New Process Technology, Job Design, and Work Organization: A Contingency Model," *American Sociological Review,* April 1990, pp 191–208.

[31] Productivity studies are reviewed in R E Kopelman, *Managing Productivity in Organizations* (New York: McGraw-Hill, 1986).

[32] The turnover meta-analysis was conducted by R W Griffeth, P W Hom, and S Gaertner, "A Meta-Analysis of Antecedents and Correlates of Employee Turnover: Update, Moderator Tests, and Research Implications for the Next Millennium," *Journal of Management,* 2000, pp 463–488. Absenteeism results are discussed in Y Fried and G R Ferris, "The Validity of the Job Characteristics Model: A Review and Meta-Analysis," *Personnel Psychology,* Summer 1987, pp 287–322.

[33] See K Dobbs, "Knowing How to Keep Your Best and Brightest," *Workforce,* April 2001, pp 557–60.

[34] A thorough discussion of reengineering and associated outcomes can be found in J Champy, *Reengineering Management: The Mandate for New Leadership* (New York: Harper Business, 1995).

[35] See J D Jonge and W B Schaufeli, "Job Characteristics and Employee Well-Being: A Test of Warr's Vitamin Model in Health Care Workers Using Structural Equation Modelling," *Journal of Organizational Behavior,* July 1998, pp 387–407; and D C Ganster and D J Dwyer, "The Effects of Understaffing on Individual and Group Performance in Professional and Trade Occupations," *Journal of Management,* 1995, pp 175–90.

[36] This description was taken from Edwards, Scully, and Brtek, "The Nature and Outcomes of Work: A Replication and Extension of Interdisciplinary Work-Design Research."

[37] Ibid.

[38] Injury statistics are presented in R J Grossman, "Makes Ergonomics," *HRMagazine,* April 2000, pp 37–42.

[39] Ibid., pp 39–40.

[40] Excerpted from S Nearman, "The Simple Billionaire," *Selling Power,* June 1999, p 48.

[41] For norms on this survey, see D J Weiss, R V Dawis, G W England, and L H Lofquist, *Manual for the Minnesota Satisfaction Questionnaire* (Minneapolis: Industrial Relations Center, University of Minnesota, 1967).

[42] Results are reported in M Boyle, "Happiness Index: Nothing Is Rotten in Denmark," *Fortune,* February 19, 2001, p 242.

[43] For a review of these models, see A P Brief, *Attitudes In and Around Organizations* (Thousand Oaks, CA: Sage Publications, 1998).

[44] See A R Karr, "Work Week: A Special News Report about Life on the Job—And Trends Taking Shape There," *The Wall Street Journal,* June 29, 1999, p A1.

[45] For a review of need satisfaction models, see E F Stone, "A Critical Analysis of Social Information Processing Models of Job Perceptions and Job Attitudes," in *Job Satisfaction: How People Feel about Their Jobs and How It Affects Their Performance,* eds C J Cranny, P Cain Smith, and E F Stone (New York: Lexington Books, 1992), pp 21–52.

[46] See J P Wanous, T D Poland, S L Premack, and K S Davis, "The Effects of Met Expectations on Newcomer Attitudes and Behaviors: A Review and Meta-Analysis," *Journal of Applied Psychology,* June 1992, pp 288–97.

[47] A complete description of this model is provided by E A Locke, "Job Satisfaction," in *Social Psychology and Organizational Behavior,* eds M Gruneberg and T Wall (New York: John Wiley & Sons, 1984).

[48] For a test of the value fulfillment value, see W A Hochwarter, P L Perrewe, G R Ferris, and R A Brymer, "Job Satisfaction and Performance: The Moderating Effects of Value Attainment and Affective Disposition," *Journal of Vocational Behavior,* April 1999, pp 296–313.

[49] Results from the meta-analysis can be found in L A Witt and L G Nye, "Gender and the Relationship between Perceived Fairness of Pay or Promotion and Job Satisfaction," *Journal of Applied Psychology,* December 1992, pp 910–17.

[50] A thorough discussion of this model is provided by T A Judge, E A Locke, and C C Durham, "The Dispositional Causes of Job Satisfaction: A Core Evaluations Approach," in *Research in Organizational Behavior* (vol 19), eds L L Cummings and B M Staw (Greenwich, CT: JAI Press, 1997), pp 151–88.

[51] Results can be found in T A Judge and J E Bono, "Relationship of Core Self-Evaluations Traits—Self-Esteem, Generalized Self-Efficacy, Locus of Control, and Emotional Stability—with Job Satisfaction and Job Performance: A Meta-Analysis," *Journal of Applied Psychology,* February 2001, pp 80–92.

[52] Supportive results can be found in H M Weiss, J P Nicholas, and C S Daus, "An Examination of the Joint Effects of Affective Experiences and

Job Beliefs on Job Satisfaction and Variances in Affective Experiences Over Time," *Organizational Behavior and Human Decision Processes,* April 1999, pp 1–24; R P Steel and J R Rentsch, "The Dispositional Model of Job Attitudes Revisited: Findings of a 10-Year Study," *Journal of Applied Psychology,* December 1997, pp 873–79; and B M Staw and J Ross, "Stability in the Midst of Change: A Dispositional Approach to Job Attitudes," *Journal of Applied Psychology,* August 1985, pp 469–80.

[53] See E Diener and C Diener, "Most People Are Happy," *Psychological Science,* May 1996, pp 181–85; D Lykken and A Tellegen, "Happiness Is a Stochastic Phenomenon," *Psychological Science,* May 1996, pp 186–89; and R D Arvey, T J Bouchard, Jr, N L Segal, and L M Abraham, "Job Satisfaction: Environmental and Genetic Components," *Journal of Applied Psychology,* April 1989, pp 187–92.

[54] Results can be found in A J Kinicki, F M McKee-Ryan, C A Schriesheim, and K P Carson, "Assessing the Construct Validity of the Job Descriptive Index (JDI): A Review and Analysis," *Journal of Applied Psychology,* in press.

[55] See S P Brown, "A Meta-Analysis and Review of Organizational Research on Job Involvement," *Psychological Bulletin,* September 1996, pp 235–55.

[56] D W Organ, "The Motivational Basis of Organizational Citizenship Behavior," in *Research in Organizational Behavior,* eds B M Staw and L L Cummings (Greenwich, CT: JAI Press, 1990), p 46.

[57] See D W Organ and K Ryan, "A Meta-Analytic Review of Attitudinal and Dispositional Predictors of Organizational Citizenship Behavior," *Personnel Psychology,* Winter 1995, pp 775–802.

[58] Supportive results can be found in P M Podsakoff, S B MacKenzie, J B Paine, and D G Bachrach, "Organizational Citizenship Behaviors: A Critical Review of the Theoretical and Empirical Literature and Suggestions for Future Research," *Journal of Management,* 2000, pp 513–63.

[59] Ibid.

[60] See R P Tett and J P Meyer, "Job Satisfaction, Organizational Commitment, Turnover Intention, and Turnover: Path Analysis Based on Meta-Analytic Findings," *Personnel Psychology,* Summer 1993, pp 259–93.

[61] See R D Hackett, "Work Attitudes and Employee Absenteeism: A Synthesis of the Literature," *Journal of Occupational Psychology,* 1989, pp 235–48.

[62] The results can be found in R W Griffeth, P W Hom, and S Gaertner, "A Meta-Analysis of Antecedents and Correlates of Employee Turnover: Update, Moderator Tests, and Research Implications for the Next Millennium," *Journal of Management,* 2000, pp 463–88.

[63] See P W Hom and R W Griffeth, *Employee Turnover* (Cincinnati, OH: SouthWestern, 1995), pp 35–50; and C Kalb and A Rogers, "Stress," *Newsweek,* June 14, 1999, pp 56–63.

[64] Results can be found in M A Blegen, "Nurses' Job Satisfaction: A Meta-Analysis of Related Variables," *Nursing Research,* January/February 1993, pp 36–41.

[65] The relationship between performance and satisfaction was reviewed by M T Iaffaldano and P M Muchinsky, "Job Satisfaction and Job Performance: A Meta-Analysis," *Psychological Bulletin,* March 1985, pp 251–73.

[66] For a thorough discussion, see J R Edwards and N P Rothbard, "Mechanisms Linking Work and Family: Clarifying the Relationship between Work and Family Constructs," *Academy of Management Review,* January 2000, pp 178–99; and S C Clark, "Work/Family Border Theory: A New Theory of Work/Family Balance," *Human Relations,* 2000, pp 747–70.

[67] The meta-analysis was conducted by M Tait, M Y Padgett, and T T Baldwin, "Job and Life Satisfaction: A Reevaluation of the Strength of the Relationship and Gender Effects as a Function of the Date of the Study," *Journal of Applied Psychology,* June 1989, pp 502–7.

[68] Excerpted from S Shellenbarger, "Work & Family: Finding Ways to Keep a Partner's Job Stress from Hitting Home," *The Wall Street Journal,* October 29, 2000, p B1.

[69] Illustrative examples can be found in M R Frone, "Work-Family Conflict and Employee Psychiatric Disorders: The National Comorbidity Survey," *Journal of Applied Psychology,* December 2000, pp 888–95; and R D Iverson and C Maguire, "The Relationship between Job and Life Satisfaction: Evidence from a Remote Mining Community," *Human Relations,* 2000, pp 807–39.

[70] Examples of family friendly initiatives are provided by K Taylor, "Concierge Services Come in Almost as Many Varieties as the Chores and Errands They Help Get Done," *HRMagazine,* August 2000, pp 90–96; and "What Benefits Are Companies Offering Now?" *HRFOCUS,* June 2000, pp 5–7.

[71] Excerpted from "How to Nurture and Retain Baby Boomer Employees," *HRFOCUS,* November 2000, p 6.

[72] For examples, see F J Milliken, L L Martins, and H Morgan, "Explaining Organizational Responsiveness to Work-Family Issues: The Role of Human Resource Executives as Issue Interpreters," *Academy of Management Journal,* October 1998, pp 580–92; E J Hill, "Influences of the Virtual Office on Aspects of Work and Work/Life Balance," *Personnel Psychology,* Autumn 1998, pp 667–83; and T J Rothausen, J A Gonzalez, N E Clarke, and L L O'Dell, "Family-Friendly Backlash—Fact or Fiction? The Case of Organizations' On-Site Child Care Centers," *Personnel Psychology,* Autumn 1998, pp 685–706.

Chapter 7

[1] Excerpted from P L Moore, "The Most Aggressive CEO," *Business Week,* May 28, 2001, pp 70, 77,

[2] See L Festinger, A *Theory of Cognitive Dissonance* (Stanford, CA: Stanford University Press, 1957).

[3] See B P Niehoff and R J Paul, "Causes of Employee Theft and Strategies That HR Managers Can Use for Prevention," *Human Resource Management,* Spring 2000, pp 51–64.

[4] Inputs and outputs are discussed by J S Adams, "Toward and Understanding of Inequity," *Journal of Abnormal and Social Psychology,* November 1963, pp 422–36.

[5] The generalizability of the equity norm was examined by J K Giacobbe-Miller, D J Miller, and V I Victorov, "A Comparison of Russian and U.S. Pay Allocation Decisions, Distributive Justice Judgments, and Productivity Under Different Payment Conditions," *Personnel Psychology,* Spring 1998, pp 137–63.

[6] The choice of a comparison person is discussed by P P Shah, "Who Are Employees' Social Referents? Using a Network Perspective to Determine Referent Others," *Academy of Management Journal,* June 1998, pp 249–68; and J Greenberg and C L McCarty, "Comparable Worth: A Matter of Justice," in *Research in Personnel and Human Resources Management,* eds G R Ferris and K M Rowland (Greenwich, CT: JAI Press, 1990), vol. 8, pp 265–303.

[7] M N Bing and S M Burroughs, "The Predictive and Interactive Effects of Equity Sensitivity in Teamwork-Oriented Organizations," *Journal of Organizational Behavior,* May 2001, p 271.

[8] Types of equity sensitivity are discussed by ibid., pp 271–90; and K S Sauley and A G Bedeian, "Equity Sensitivity: Construction of a Measure and Examination of Its Psychometric Properties," *Journal of Management,* 2000, pp 885–910.

[9] See the discussion by M A Konovsky, "Understanding Procedural Justice and Its Impact on Business Organizations," *Journal of Management,* 2000, pp 489–511.

[10] M A Korsgaard, L Roberson, and R D Rymph, "What Motivates Fairness? The Role of Subordinate Assertive Behavior on Manager's Interactional Fairness," *Journal of Applied Psychology,* October 1998, p 731.

[11] Supportive results can be found in S Aryee and Y W Chay, "Workplace Justice, Citizenship Behavior, and Turnover Intentions in a Union Context: Examining the Mediating Role of Perceived Union Support and Union Instrumentality," *Journal of Applied Psychology,* February 2001, pp 154–60; B J Tepper, "Consequences of Abusive Supervision," *Academy of Management Journal,* April 2000, pp 178–90; and T L Robbins, T P Summers, J L Miller, and W H Hendrix, "Using the Group-Value Model to Explain the Role of Noninstrumental Justice in Distinguishing the Effects of Distributive and Procedural Justice," *Journal of Occupational and Organizational Psychology,* December 2000, pp 511–18.

[12] See C R Wanberg, L W Bunce, and M B Gavin, "Perceived Fairness of Layoffs among Individuals Who Have Been Laid Off: A Longitudinal Study," *Personnel Psychology,* Spring 1999, pp 59–84.

[13] See Korsgaard, Roberson, and Rymph, "What Motivates Fairness? The Role of Subordinate Assertive Behavior on Managers' Interactional Fairness."

[14] The role of equity in organizational change is thoroughly discussed by A T Cobb, R Folger, and K Wooten, "The Role Justice Plays in Organizational Change," *Public Administration Quarterly,* Summer 1995, pp 135–51.

[15] Group level effects of justice were examined by S E Naumann and N Bennett, "A Case for Procedureal Justice Climate: Development and Test of a Multilevel Model," *Academy of Management Journal,* October 2000, pp 881–89.

[16] The legal issues of pay equity and employment at-will are discussed by M Adams, "Fair and Square," *HRMagazine,* May 1999, pp 38–44.

[17] Results can be found in K W Mossholder, N Bennett, and C L Martin, "A Multilevel Analysis of Procedural Justice Context," *Journal of Organizational Behavior,* March 1998, pp 131–41.

[18] The relationship between organizational justice and customer service is discussed by D E Bowen, S W Gilliland, and R Folger, "HRM Service Fairness: How Being Fair with Employees Spills Over to Customers," *Organizational Dynamics,* Winter 1999, pp 7–23.

[19] For a complete discussion of Vroom's theory, see V H Vroom, *Work and Motivation* (New York: John Wiley & Sons, 1964).

[20] See J Chowdhury, "The Motivational Impact of Sales Quotas on Effort," *Journal of Marketing Research,* February 1993, pp 28–41; and C C Pinder, *Work Motivation* (Glenview, IL: Scott, Foresman, 1984), ch 7.

[21] M Frase-Blunt, "Driving Home Your Awards Program," *HRMagazine,* February 2001, p 109.

[22] The measurement and importance of valence was investigated by N T Feather, "Values, Valences, and Choice: The Influence of Values on the Perceived Attractiveness and Choice of Alternatives," *Journal of Personality and Social Psychology,* June 1995, pp 1135–51.

[23] Excerpted from "Federal Express's Fred Smith," *Inc.,* October 1986, p 38.

[24] Results can be found in W van Eerde and H Thierry, "Vroom's Expectancy Models and Work-Related Criteria: A Meta-Analysis," *Journal of Applied Psychology,* October 1996, pp 575–86.

[25] See J P Wanous, T L Keon, and J C Latack, "Expectancy Theory and Occupational/Organizational Choices: A Review and Test," *Organizational Behavior and Human Performance,* August 1983, pp 66–86.

[26] For a review of the criticisms of expectancy theory, see F J Landy and W S Becker, "Motivation Theory Reconsidered," in *Research in Organizational Behavior,* vol. 9, eds L L Cummings and B M Staw (Greenwich, CT: JAI Press, 1987), pp 1–38.

[27] Supportive results are presented in L Morris, "Employees Not Encouraged to Go Extra Mile," *Training & Development,* April 1996, pp 59–60.

[28] See D R Spitzer, "Power Rewards: Rewards That Really Motivate," *Management Review,* May 1996, pp 45–50; and A Kohn, *Punished by Rewards: The Trouble with Gold Stars, Incentive Plans, A's, Praise, and Other Bribes* (Boston: Houghton Mifflin, 1993).

[29] Result can be found in G D Jenkins, Jr, A Mitra, N Gupta, and J D Shaw, "Are Financial Incentives Related to Performance? A Meta-Analytic Review of Empirical Research," *Journal of Applied Psychology,* October 1998, pp 777–87.

[30] See S Kerr, "Organizational Rewards: Practical, Cost-Neutral Alternatives That You May Know, But Don't Practice," *Organizational Dynamics,* Summer 1999, pp 61–70.

[31] Details regarding the incentive system can be found in E Zehnder, "A Simpler Way to Pay," *Harvard Business* Review, April 2001, pp 53–61.

[32] R Charan, "Conquering a Culture of Indecision," *Harvard Business Review,* April 2001, pp 75–82.

[33] E A Locke, K N Shaw, L M Saari, and G P Latham, "Goal Setting and Task Performance: 1969–1980," *Psychological Bulletin,* July 1981, p 126.

[34] A through discussion of MBO is provided by P F Drucker, *The Practice of Management* (New York: Harper, 1954).

[35] Results from both studies can be found in R Rodgers and J E Hunter, "Impact of Management by Objectives on Organizational Productivity," *Journal of Applied Psychology,* April 1991, pp 322–36; and R Rodgers, J E Hunter, and D L Rogers, "Influence of Top Management Commitment on Management Program Success," *Journal of Applied Psychology,* February 1993, pp 151–55.

[36] Excerpted from M Campbell, "Dream Work: How Steven Spielberg, the Most Successful Film Director of All Time, Turned His Dreams into Reality," *Selling Power,* April 1999, pp 92–93.

[37] See E Weldon and S Yun, "The Effects of Proximal and Distal Goals on Goal Level, Strategy Development, and Group Performance," *Journal of Applied Behavioral Science,* September 2000, pp 336–44.

[38] Excerpted from "Empire Builders," *Business Week,* May 14, 2001, p EB 28.

[39] Results can be found in P M Wright, "Operationalization of Goal Difficulty as a Moderator of the Goal Difficulty–Performance Relationship," *Journal of Applied Psychology,* June 1990, pp 227–34.

[40] This linear relationship was not supported by P M Wright, J R Hollenbeck, S Wolf, and G C McMahan, "The Effects of Varying Goal Difficulty Operationalizations on Goal Setting Outcomes and Processes," *Organizational Behavior and Human Decision Processes,* January 1995, pp 28–43.

[41] See Locke, Shaw, Saari, and Latham, "Goal Setting and Task Performance: 1969–1980"; and A J Mento, R P Steel, and R J Karren, "A Meta-Analytic Study of the Effects of Goal Setting on Task Performance: 1966–1984," *Organizational Behavior and Human Decision Processes,* February 1987, pp 52–83.

[42] Results from the meta-analysis can be found in R E Wood, A J Mento, and E A Locke, "Task Complexity as a Moderator of Goal Effects: A Meta-Analysis," *Journal of Applied Psychology,* August 1987, pp 416–25.

[43] See the related discussion in L A King, "Personal Goals and Personal Agency: Linking Everyday Goals to Future Images of the Self," in *Personal Control in Action: Cognitive and Motivational Mechanisms,* eds M Kofta, G Weary, and G Sedek (New York: Plenum Press, 1998), pp 109–28.

[44] See R P DeShon and R A Alexander, "Goal Setting Effects on Implicit and Explicit Learning of Complex Tasks," *Organizational Behavior and Human Decision Processes,* January 1996, pp 18–36.

[45] Supportive results can be found in K L Langeland, C M Johnson, and T C Mawhinney, "Improving Staff Performance in a Community Mental Health Setting: Job Analysis, Training, Goal Setting, Feedback, and Years of Data," *Journal of Organizational Behavior Management,* 1998, pp 21–43; and L A Wilk, "The Effects of Feedback and Goal Setting on the Productivity and Satisfaction of University Admissions Staff," *Journal of Organizational Behavior Management,* 1998, pp 45–68.

[46] See E A Locke and G P Latham, *A Theory of Goal Setting & Task Performance* (Englewood Cliffs, NJ: Prentice Hall, 1990).

[47] See J J Donovan and D J Radosevich, "The Moderating Role of Goal Commitment on the Goal Difficulty-Performance Relationship: A Meta-Analytic Review and Critical Reanalysis," *Journal of Applied Psychology,* April 1998, pp 308–15.

[48] Results can be found in G H Seijts and G P Latham, "The Effect of Distal Learning, Outcome, and Proximal Goals on a Moderately Complex Task," *Journal of Organizational Behavior,* May 2001, pp 291–307.

[49] See the related discussion in T P Flannery, D A Hofrichter, and P E Platten, *People, Performance, & Pay* (New York: The Free Press, 1996).

[50] See F M Moussa, "Determinants, Process, and Consequences of Personal Goals and Performance," *Journal of Management,* 2000, pp 1259–85; and P M Wright, J M George, S R Farnsworth, and G C McMahan, "Productivity and Extra-Role Behavior: The Effects of Goals and Incentives on Spontaneous Helping," *Journal of Applied Psychology,* June 1993, pp 374–81.

[51] See J A Colquitt and M J Simmering, "Conscientiousness, Goal Orientation, and Motivation to Learn During the Learning Process: A Longitudinal Study," *Journal of Applied Psychology,* August 1998, pp 654–65.

[52] D VandeWalle, S P Brown, W L Cron, and J W Slocum, Jr, "The Influence of Goal Orientation and Self-Regulated Tactics on Sales Performance: A Longitudinal Field Test," *Journal of Applied Psychology,* April 1999, p 250.

[53] See ibid., pp 249–59; and H Grant and C S Dweck, "A Goal Analysis of Personality and Personality Choice," in *The Coherence of Personality: Social-Cognitive Bases of Consistency, Variability, and Organization,* eds D Cervone and Y Shoda (New York: Guilford Press, 1999), pp 345–71.

[54] Results can be found in D Steele-Johnson, R S Beauregard, P B Hoover, and A M Schmidt, "Goal Orientation and Task Demand Effects on Motivation, Affect, and Performance," *Journal of Applied Psychology,* October 2000, pp 724–38.

[55] E A Locke and G P Latham, *Goal Setting: A Motivational Technique That Works!* (Englewood Cliffs, NJ: Prentice Hall, 1984), p 79.

56 T R Mitchell, "Motivation: New Directions for Theory, Research, and Practice," *Academy of Management Review,* January 1982, p 81.

57 Excerpted from C Hymowitz, "Ranking Systems Gain Popularity but Have Many Staffers Riled," *The Wall Street Journal,* May 15, 2001, p B1.

58 See D J Burrough, "More Firms Rank Employees," *The Arizona Republic,* May 20, 2001, p EC1.

59 This conclusion is consistent with research summarized in F Luthans and A D Stajkovic, "Reinforce for Performance: The Need to Go Beyond Pay and Even Rewards," *The Academy of Management Executive,* May 1999, pp 49–57.

60 Excerpted from "Work Week: A Special News Report about Life on the Job—And Trends Taking Shape There," *The Wall Street Journal,* April 6, 1999, p A1.

61 For a thorough discussion about the use of team rewards, see L N McClurg, "Team Rewards: How Far Have We Come?" *Human Resource Management,* Spring 2001, pp 73–86.

Chapter 8

1 A Diba, "If Pat Sajak Were Your CEO . . . ," *Fortune,* December 18, 2000, p 330.

2 "Workplace Changes Employees Want to See," *Management Review,* January 1999, p 6.

3 For instance, see "Worker Retention Presents Challenge to U.S. Employers," *HRMagazine,* September 1998, p 22; L Wah, "An Ounce of Prevention," *Management Review,* October 1998, p 9; and S Armour, "Cash or Critiques: Which Is Best?" *USA Today,* December 16, 1998, p 6B.

4 As quoted in C Fishman, "Fred Smith," *Fast Company,* June 2001, pp 64, 66.

5 Data from M Hequet, "Giving Feedback," *Training,* September 1994, pp 72–77.

6 C Bell and R Zemke, "On-Target Feedback," *Training,* June 1992, p 36.

7 Both the definition of feedback and the functions of feedback are based on discussion in D R Ilgen, C D Fisher, and M S Taylor, "Consequences of Individual Feedback on Behavior in Organizations," *Journal of Applied Psychology,* August 1979, pp 349–71; and R E Kopelman, *Managing Productivity in Organizations: A Practical People-Oriented Perspective* (New York: McGraw-Hill, 1986), p 175.

8 See P C Earley, G B Northcraft, C Lee, and T R Lituchy, "Impact of Process and Outcome Feedback on the Relation of Goal Setting to Task Performance," *Academy of Management Journal,* March 1990, pp 87–105.

9 For relevant research, see J S Goodman, "The Interactive Effects of Task and External Feedback on Practice Performance and Learning," *Organizational Behavior and Human Decision Processes,* December 1998, pp 223–52.

10 See B D Bannister, "Performance Outcome Feedback and Attributional Feedback: Interactive Effects on Recipient Responses," *Journal of Applied Psychology,* May 1986, pp 203–10.

11 For complete details, see P M Podsakoff and J-L Farh, "Effects of Feedback Sign and Credibility on Goal Setting and Task Performance," *Organizational Behavior and Human Decision Processes,* August 1989, pp 45–67. Also see S J Ashford and A S Tsui, "Self-Regulation for Managerial Effectiveness: The Role of Active Feedback Seeking," *Academy of Management Journal,* June 1991, pp 251–80.

12 See "How to Take the Venom Out of Vitriol," *Training,* June 2000, p 28.

13 W S Silver, T R Mitchell, and M E Gist, "Responses to Successful and Unsuccessful Performance: The Moderating Effect of Self-Efficacy on the Relationship between Performance and Attributions," *Organizational Behavior and Human Decision Processes,* June 1995, p 297. Also see T A Louie, "Decision Makers' Hindsight Bias after Receiving Favorable and Unfavorable Feedback," *Journal of Applied Psychology,* February 1999, pp 29–41.

14 See S H Barr and E J Conlon, "Effects of Distribution of Feedback in Work Groups," *Academy of Management Journal,* June 1994, pp 641–55.

15 See M R Edwards, A J Ewen, and W A Verdini, "Fair Performance Management and Pay Practices for Diverse Work Forces: The Promise of Multisource Assessment," *ACA Journal,* Spring 1995, pp 50–63.

16 See G D Huet-Cox, T M Nielsen, and E Sundstrom, "Get the Most from 360-Degree Feedback: Put It on the Internet," *HRMagazine,* May 1999, pp 92–103.

17 This list is based in part on discussion in H J Bernardin, "Subordinate Appraisal: A Valuable Source of Information about Managers," *Human Resource Management,* Fall 1986, pp 421–39.

18 For a complete list, see "Companies Where Employees Rate Executives," *Fortune,* December 27, 1993, p 128. Also see S Gruner, "Turning the Tables," *Inc.,* May 1996, pp 87–89.

19 Data from D Antonioni, "The Effects of Feedback Accountability on Upward Appraisal Ratings," *Personnel Psychology,* Summer 1994, pp 349–56.

20 See L Atwater, P Roush, and A Fischthal, "The Influence of Upward Feedback on Self- and Follower Ratings of Leadership," *Personnel Psychology,* Spring 1995, pp 35–59.

21 Data from J W Smither, M London, N L Vasilopoulos, R R Reilly, R E Millsap, and N Salvemini, "An Examination of the Effects of an Upward Feedback Program Over Time," *Personnel Psychology,* Spring 1995, pp 1–34.

22 Data from J L Seglin, "Reviewing Your Boss," *Fortune,* June 11, 2001, p 248. For a comprehensive overview of 360-degree feedback, see W W Tornow and M London, *Maximizing the Value of 360-Degree Feedback* (San Francisco: Jossey-Bass, 1998). Also see R Hoffman, "Ten Reasons You Should Be Using 360-Degree Feedback," *HRMagazine,* April 1995, pp 82–85; "360-Degree Feedback: Will The Circle Be Broken?" *Training,* October 1996, pp 24–25; R Lepsinger and A D Lucia, "360° Feedback and Performance Appraisal," *Training,* September 1997, pp 62–70; and K M Nowack, J Hartley, and W Bradley, "How to Evaluate Your 360 Feedback Efforts," *Training & Development,* April 1999, pp 48–53.

23 See S Haworth, "The Dark Side of Multi-Rater Assessments," *HRMagazine,* May 1998, pp 106–14; and D A Waldman, L E Atwater, and D Antonioni, "Has 360 Degree Feedback Gone Amok?" *Academy of Management Executive,* May 1998, pp 86–94.

24 See K E Morical, "A Product Review: 360 Assessments," *Training & Development,* April 1999, pp 43–47. Also see N E Fried, "360° Software Shootout: Comparing Features with Needs," *HRMagazine* (Focus), December 1998, pp 8–13.

25 See M M Harris and J Schaubroeck, "A Meta-Analysis of Self-Supervisor, Self-Peer, and Peer-Supervisor Ratings," *Personnel Psychology,* Spring 1988, pp 43–62; and J Lane and P Herriot, "Self-Ratings, Supervisor Ratings, Positions and Performance," *Journal of Occupational Psychology,* March 1990, pp 77–88.

26 Fisher Hazucha, S A Hezlett, and R J Schneider, "The Impact of 360-Degree Feedback on Managerial Skills Development," *Human Resource Management,* Summer/Fall 1993, p 42. Also see M K Mount, T A Judge, S E Scullen, M R Sytsma, and S A Hezlett, "Trait, Rater and Level Effects in 360-Degree Performance Ratings," *Personnel Psychology,* Autumn 1998, pp 557–76.

27 See D E Coates, "Don't Tie 360 Feedback to Pay," *Training,* September 1998, pp 68–78.

28 Adapted from C Bell and R Zemke, "On-Target Feedback," *Training,* June 1992, pp 36–44.

29 See B Filipczak, "Can't Buy Me Love," *Training,* January 1996, pp 29–34; and S Kerr, "Risky Business: The New Pay Game," *Fortune,* July 22, 1996, pp 94–95.

30 See M Schrage, "Actually, I'd Rather Have That Favor Than a Raise," *Fortune,* April 16, 2001, p 412.

31 For example, see B Nelson, *1001 Ways to Reward Employees* (New York: Workman Publishing, 1994); and "Emerging Optional Benefits," *Management Review,* December 1998, p 8. For more on stock options, see B McLean, "The Bad News about Options," *Fortune,* November 13, 2000, pp 429–30; and "Employee Stock Options Are Still Hot," *Business Week,* May 28, 2001, p 16.

32 W J Wiatrowski, "Family-Related Benefits in the Workplace," *Monthly Labor Review,* March 1990, p 28. Also see R Kuttner, "Pensions: How Much Risk Should Workers Have to Bear?" *Business Week,* April 16, 2001, p 23.

33 For complete discussions, see A P Brief and R J Aldag, "The Intrinsic-Extrinsic Dichotomy: Toward Conceptual Clarity," *Academy of Management Review,* July 1977, pp 496–500; E L Deci, *Intrinsic Motivation*

(New York: Plenum Press, 1975), ch 2; and E L Deci, R Koestner, and R M Ryan, "A Meta-Analytic Review of Experiments Examining the Effects of Extrinsic Rewards on Intrinsic Motivation," *Psychological Bulletin,* November 1999, pp 627–68.

34 See K I Kim, H-J Park, and N Suzuki, "Reward Allocations in the United States, Japan, and Korea: A Comparison of Individualistic and Collectivistic Cultures," *Academy of Management Journal,* March 1990, pp 188–98. Also see C C Chen, J R Meindl, and H Hui, "Deciding on Equity or Parity: A Test of Situational, Cultural, and Individual Factors," *Journal of Organizational Behavior,* March 1998, pp 115–29.

35 See "The Business World Is Still a Man's World," *USA Today,* April 11, 2001, p 1B; L Lavelle, "For Female CEOs, It's Still Stingy at the Top," *Business Week,* April 23, 2001, pp 70–71; and G Koretz, "She's a Woman, Offer Her Less," *Business Week,* May 7, 2001, p 34.

36 Based on M Bloom, "The Performance Effects of Pay Dispersion on Individuals and Organizations," *Academy of Management Journal,* February 1999, pp 25–40.

37 For recent data, see L Lavelle, "Executive Pay," *Business Week,* April 16, 2001, pp 76–80.

38 List adapted from J L Pearce and R H Peters, "A Contradictory Norms View of Employer–Employee Exchange," *Journal of Management,* Spring 1985, pp 19–30.

39 Ibid., p 25.

40 M Von Glinow, "Reward Strategies for Attracting, Evaluating, and Retaining Professionals," *Human Resource Management,* Summer 1985, p 193.

41 A Markels and J S Lublin, "Longevity-Reward Programs Get Short Shrift," *The Wall Street Journal,* April 27, 1995, p B1.

42 Six reward system objectives are discussed in E E Lawler III, "The New Pay: A Strategic Approach," *Compensation & Benefits Review,* July–August 1995, pp 14–22.

43 See K Labich, "Hot Company, Warm Culture," *Fortune,* February 27, 1989, pp 74–78. For enjoyable reading about the Herman Miller philosophy of managing people, see M De Pree, *Leadership Jazz* (New York: Dell, 1992).

44 D R Spitzer, "Power Rewards: Rewards That Really Motivate," *Management Review,* May 1996, p 47. Also see S Kerr, "An Academy Classic: On the Folly of Rewarding A, while Hoping for B," *Academy of Management Executive,* February 1995, pp 7–14.

45 List adapted from discussion in Spitzer, "Power Rewards: Rewards That Really Motivate," pp 45–50. Also see R Eisenberger and J Cameron, "Detrimental Effects of Reward: Reality or Myth?" *American Psychologist,* November 1996, pp 1153–66.

46 See, for example, T P Flannery, D A Hofrichter, and P E Platten, *People, Performance, and Pay: Dynamic Compensation for Changing Organizations* (New York: The Free Press, 1996). Also see R S Allen and R H Kilmann, "Aligning Reward Practices in Support of Total Quality Management," *Business Horizons,* May–June 2001, pp 77–84.

47 For a recent unconventional perspective, see R J DeGrandpre, "A Science of Meaning? Can Behaviorism Bring Meaning to Psychological Science?" *American Psychologist,* July 2000, pp 721–38.

48 See E L Thorndike, *Educational Psychology: The Psychology of Learning, Vol. II* (New York: Columbia University Teachers College, 1913).

49 Discussion of an early behaviorist who influenced Skinner's work can be found in P J Kreshel, "John B Watson at J Walter Thompson: The Legitimation of 'Science' in Advertising," *Journal of Advertising,* no. 2, 1990, pp 49–59. Recent discussions involving behaviorism include M R Ruiz, "B F Skinner's Radical Behaviorism: Historical Misconstructions and Grounds for Feminist Reconstructions," *Psychology of Women Quarterly,* June 1995, pp 161–79; J A Nevin, "Behavioral Economics and Behavioral Momentum," *Journal of the Experimental Analysis of Behavior,* November 1995, pp 385–95; and H Rachlin, "Can We Leave Cognition to Cognitive Psychologists? Comments on an Article by George Loewenstein," *Organizational Behavior and Human Decision Processes,* March 1996, pp 296–99.

50 For more recent discussion, see J W Donahoe, "The Unconventional Wisdom of B F Skinner: The Analysis-Interpretation Distinction," *Journal of the Experimental Analysis of Behavior,* September 1993, pp 453–56.

51 See B F Skinner, *The Behavior of Organisms* (New York: Appleton-Century-Crofts, 1938).

52 For modern approaches to respondent behavior, see B Azar, "Classical Conditioning Could Link Disorders and Brain Dysfunction, Researchers Suggest," *APA Monitor,* March 1999, p 17.

53 For interesting discussions of Skinner and one of his students, see M B Gilbert and T F Gilbert, "What Skinner Gave Us," *Training,* September 1991, pp 42–48; and "HRD Pioneer Gilbert Leaves a Pervasive Legacy," *Training,* January 1996, p 14.

54 See F Luthans and R Kreitner, *Organizational Behavior Modification and Beyond: An Operant and Social Learning Approach* (Glenview, IL: Scott, Foresman, 1985), pp 49–56.

55 The effect of praise is explored in C M Mueller and C S Dweck, "Praise for Intelligence Can Undermine Children's Motivation and Performance," *Journal of Personality and Social Psychology,* July 1998, pp 33–52.

56 See D H B Welsh, D J Bernstein, and F Luthans, "Application of the Premack Principle of Reinforcement to the Quality Performance of Service Employees," *Journal of Organizational Behavior Management,* no. 1, 1992, pp 9–32.

57 Research on punishment is reported in B P Niehoff, R J Paul, and J F S Bunch, "The Social Effects of Punishment Events: The Influence of Violator Past Performance Record and Severity of the Punishment on Observers' Justice Perceptions and Attitudes," *Journal of Organizational Behavior,* November 1998, pp 589–602.

58 See C B Ferster and B F Skinner, *Schedules of Reinforcement* (New York: Appleton-Century-Crofts, 1957).

59 See L M Saari and G P Latham, "Employee Reactions to Continuous and Variable Ratio Reinforcement Schedules Involving a Monetary Incentive," *Journal of Applied Psychology,* August 1982, pp 506–8.

60 P Brinkley-Rogers and R Collier, "Along the Colorado, the Money's Flowing," *The Arizona Republic,* March 4, 1990, p A12.

61 The topic of managerial credibility is covered in J M Kouzes and B Z Posner, *Credibility* (San Francisco: Jossey-Bass, 1993).

62 See, for example, J C Bruening, "Shaping Workers' Attitudes toward Safety," *Occupational Hazards,* March 1990, pp 49–51.

63 Data from K L Alexander, "Continental Airlines Soars to New Heights," *USA Today,* January 23, 1996, p 4B. Also see J Huey, "Outlaw Flyboy CEOs," *Fortune,* November 13, 2000, pp 237–50.

Chapter 9

1 Excerpted from N Byrnes, "Avon: The New Calling," *Business Week,* September 18, 2000, pp 137, 139–40, 142.

2 Results are presented in "The Big Picture: 'Hurry Up and Decide!'" *Business Week,* May 14, 2001, p 16.

3 For a review of research on rational decision making, see K E Stanovich, *Who Is Rational?* (Mahwah, NJ: Lawrence Erlbaum, 1999), pp 1–31.

4 Excerpted from G L White, "GM Takes Advice from Disease Sleuths to Debug Cars," *The Wall Street Journal,* April 8, 1999, p B1.

5 H A Simon, "Rational Decision Making in Business Organizations," *American Economic Review,* September 1979, p 510.

6 For a complete discussion of bounded rationality, see H A Simon, *Administrative Behavior,* 2nd ed (New York: Free Press, 1957).

7 Biases associated with using shortcuts in decision making are discussed by A Tversky and D Kahneman, "Judgment under Uncertainty: Heuristics and Biases," *Science,* September 1974, pp 1124–31.

8 For a study of the availability heuristic, see L A Vaughn, "Effects of Uncertainty on Use of the Availability of Heuristic for Self-Efficacy Judgments," *European Journal of Social Psychology,* March–May 1999, pp 407–10.

9 For a complete discussion, see L R Beach and T R Mitchell, "A Contingency Model for the Selection of Decision Strategies," *Academy of Management Review,* July 1978, pp 439–44.

10 See B Azar, "Why Experts Often Disagree," *APA Monitor,* May 1999, p 13.

11 Supportive results can be found in N Harvey, "Why Are Judgments Less Consistent in Less Predictable Task Situations?" *Organizational Behavior and Human Decision Processes,* September 1995, pp 247–63; and

J W Dean, Jr, and M P Sharfman, "Does Decision Process Matter? A Study of Strategic Decision-Making Effectiveness," *Academy of Management Journal,* April 1996, pp 368–96.

[12] Results can be found in W H Stewart and P L Roth, "Risk Propensity Differences between Entrepreneurs and Managers: A Meta-Analytic Review," *Journal of Applied Psychology,* February 2001, pp 145–53.

[13] See P E Johnson, S Graziolo, K Jamal, and I A Zualkernan, "Success and Failure in Expert Reasoning," *Organizational Behavior and Human Decision Processes,* November 1992, pp 173–203.

[14] This definition was derived from A J Rowe and R O Mason, *Managing with Style: A Guide to Understanding, Assessing and Improving Decision Making* (San Francisco: Jossey-Bass, 1987).

[15] The discussion of styles was based on material contained in ibid.

[16] Norms were obtained from Rowe and Mason, *Managing with Style: A Guide to Understanding, Assessing and Improving Decision Making.*

[17] See ibid.; and M J Dollinger and W Danis, "Preferred Decision-Making Styles: A Cross-Cultural Comparison," *Psychological Reports,* 1998, pp 755–61.

[18] A thorough discussion of escalation situations can be found in B M Staw and J Ross, "Behavior in Escalation Situations: Antecedents, Prototypes, and Solutions," in *Research in Organizational Behavior,* vol. 9, eds L L Cummings and B M Staw (Greenwich, CT: JAI Press, 1987), pp 39–78.

[19] The details of this case are discussed in J Ross and B M Staw, "Organizational Escalation and Exit: Lessons from the Shoreham Nuclear Power Plant," *Academy of Management Journal,* August 1993, pp 701–32.

[20] Ibid.

[21] Supportive results can be found in H Moon, "Looking Forward and Looking Back: Integrating Completion and Sunk-Cost Effects within an Escalation-of-Commitment Progress Decision," *Journal of Applied Psychology,* February 2001, pp 104–13.

[22] See D A Hantula and J L D Bragger, "The Effects of Feedback Equivocality on Escalation of Commitment: An Empirical Investigation of Decision Dilemma Theory," *Journal of Applied Social Psychology,* February 1999, pp 424–44.

[23] Results can be found in C R Greer and G K Stephens, "Escalation of Commitment: A Comparison of Differences between Mexican and U.S. Decision Makers," *Journal of Management,* 2001, pp 51–78.

[24] See Ross and Staw, "Organizational Escalation and Exit: Lessons from the Shoreham Nuclear Power Plant."

[25] This definition was based on R J Sternberg, "What Is the Common Thread of Creativity?" *American Psychologist,* April 2001, pp 360–62.

[26] Excerpted from S Stern, "How Companies Can Be More Creative," *HRMagazine,* April 1998, p 59.

[27] Details of this study can be found in M Basadur, "Managing Creativity: A Japanese Model," *Academy of Management Executive,* May 1992, pp 29–42.

[28] Examples are provided in S Thomke, "Enlightened Experimentation: The New Imperative for Innovation," *Harvard Business Review,* February 2001, pp 67–75; and C Bangle, "The Ultimate Creativity Machine: How BMW Turns Art into Profit," *Harvard Business Review,* January 2001, pp 47–55.

[29] "Caring Enough," *Selling Power,* June 1999, p 18.

[30] These guidelines were derived from G P Huber, *Managerial Decision Making* (Glenview, IL: Scott, Foresman, 1980), p 149.

[31] G W Hill, "Group versus Individual Performance: Are N + 1 Heads Better than One?" *Psychological Bulletin,* May 1982, p 535.

[32] See D L Gladstein and N P Reilly, "Group Decision Making under Threat: The Tycoon Game," *Academy of Management Journal,* September 1985, pp 613–27.

[33] Results are presented in J T Delaney, "Workplace Cooperation: Current Problems, New Approaches," *Journal of Labor Research,* Winter 1996, pp 45–61.

[34] This issue is thoroughly discussed by D E Drehmer, J A Belohlav, and R W Coye, "An Exploration of Employee Participation Using a Scaling Approach," *Group & Organization Management,* December 2000, pp 397–418.

[35] For an extended discussion of this model, see M Sashkin, "Participative Management Is an Ethical Imperative," *Organizational Dynamics,* Spring 1984, pp 4–22.

[36] See G Yukl and P P Fu, "Determinants of Delegation and Consultation by Managers," *Journal of Organizational Behavior,* March 1999, pp 219–32.

[37] Supporting results can be found in L A Witt, M C Andrews, and M Kacmar, "The Role of Participation in Decision-Making in the Organizational Politics-Job Satisfaction Relationship," *Human Relations,* March 2000, pp 341–58; J Hunton, T W Hall, and K H Price, "The Value of Voice in Participative Decision Making." *Journal of Applied Psychology.* October 1998, pp 788–97; and C R Leana, R S Ahlbrandt, and A J Murrell, "The Effects of Employee Involvement Programs on Unionized Workers' Attitudes, Perceptions, and Preferences in Decision Making," *Academy of Management Journal,* October 1992, pp 861–73.

[38] Results can be found in B D Cawley, L M Keeping, and P E Levy, "Participation in the Performance Appraisal Process and Employee Reactions: A Meta-Analytic Review of Field Investigations," *Journal of Applied Psychology,* August 1998, pp 615–33.

[39] Results are contained in J A Wagner III, C R Leana, E A Locke, and D M Schweiger, "Cognitive and Motivational Frameworks in US Research on Participation: A Meta-Analysis of Primary Effects," *Journal of Organizational Behavior,* 1997, pp 49–65.

[40] See V H Vroom and P W Yetton, *Leadership and Decision Making* (Pittsburgh, PA: University of Pittsburgh Press, 1973); and V H Vroom and A G Jago, *The New Leadership: Managing Participation in Organizations* (Englewood Cliffs, NJ: Prentice Hall, 1988), p 184.

[41] For a complete discussion of these decision trees, see Vroom and Jago, *The New Leadership: Managing Participation in Organizations.*

[42] G M Parker, *Team Players and Teamwork: The New Competitive Business Strategy* (San Francisco, CA: Jossey-Bass, 1990).

[43] The effect of group dynamics on brainstorming is discussed by P B Paulus and H-C Yang, "Idea Generation in Groups: A Basis for Creativity in Organizations," *Organizational Behavior and Human Decision Processes,* May 2000, pp 76–87.

[44] These recommendations were obtained from Parker, *Team Players and Teamwork: The New Competitive Business Strategy.*

[45] See A F Osborn, *Applied Imagination: Principles and Procedures of Creative Thinking,* 3rd ed (New York: Scribners, 1979).

[46] See W H Cooper, R Brent Gallupe, S Pollard, and J Cadsby, "Some Liberating Effects of Anonymous Electronic Brainstorming," *Small Group Research,* April 1998, pp 147–78.

[47] These recommendations were derived from C Caggiano, "The Right Way to Brainstorm," *Inc,* July 1999, p 94; and G McGartland, "How to Generate More Ideas in Brainstorming Sessions," *Selling Power,* July/August 1999, p 46.

[48] See J G Lloyd, S Fowell, and J G Bligh, "The Use of the Nominal Group Technique as an Evaluative Tool in Medical Undergraduate Education," *Medical Education,* January 1999, pp 8–13; and A L Delbecq, A H Van de Ven, and D H Gustafson, *Group Techniques for Program Planning: A Guide to Nominal Group and Delphi Processes* (Glenview, IL: Scott, Foresman, 1975).

[49] See N C Dalkey, D L Rourke, R Lewis, and D Snyder, *Studies in the Quality of Life: Delphi and Decision Making* (Lexington, MA: Lexington Books: D C Heath and Co., 1972).

[50] Benefits of the Delphi technique are discussed by N I Whitman, "The Committee Meeting Alternative: Using the Delphi Technique," *Journal of Nursing Administration,* July/August 1990, pp 30–36.

[51] A thorough description of computer-aided decision-making systems is provided by M C Er and A C Ng, "The Anonymity and Proximity Factors in Group Decision Support Systems," *Decision Support Systems,* May 1995, pp 75–83.

[52] Excerpted from T E Weber, "How Bringing Doctors Together Online Helps Brothers Build Business," *The Wall Street Journal,* April 2, 2001, p B1.

[53] Supportive results can be found in S S Lam and J Schaubroeck, "Improving Group Decisions by Better Polling Information: A Comparative Advantage of Group Decision Support Systems," *Journal of Applied Psychology,* August 2000, pp 565–73; and I Benbasat and J Lim, "Information Technology Support for Debiasing Group Judgments: An Empirical Evaluation," *Organizational Behavior and Human Decision Processes,* September 2000, pp 167–83.

Chapter 10

[1] Excerpted from J Appleby and R Davis, "Teamwork Used to Be a Money Saver; Now It's a Lifesaver," *USA Today,* March 1, 2001, pp 1B–2B.

[2] E Van Velsor and J Brittain Leslie, "Why Executives Derail: Perspectives across Time and Cultures," *Academy of Management Executive,* November 1995, p 62.

[3] Ibid., p 63.

[4] According to one survey, "getting along with others who work at the company" was the top-ranked skill believed to be most important for organizational success. See "Gets Along Well with Others," *Training,* August 1996, pp 17–18.

[5] This applies to life in general, as well. See M Elias, "Friends May Make Breast Cancer More Survivable," *USA Today,* March 8, 2001, p 2D.

[6] This definition is based in part on one found in D Horton Smith, "A Parsimonious Definition of 'Group': Toward Conceptual Clarity and Scientific Utility," *Sociological Inquiry,* Spring 1967, pp 141–67.

[7] E H Schein, *Organizational Psychology,* 3rd ed (Englewood Cliffs, NJ: Prentice Hall, 1980), p 145. For more, see L R Weingart, "How Did They Do That? The Ways and Means of Studying Group Process," in *Research in Organizational Behavior,* vol. 19, eds L L Cummings and B M Staw (Greenwich, CT: JAI Press, 1997), pp 189–239.

[8] For related research, see P P Shah, "Who Are Employees' Social Referents? Using a Network Perspective to Determine Referent Others," *Academy of Management Journal,* June 1998, pp 249–68; and A Mehra, M Kilduff, and D J Brass, "At the Margins: A Distinctiveness Approach to the Social Identity and Social Networks of Underrepresented Groups," *Academy of Management Journal,* August 1998, pp 441–52.

[9] See Schein, *Organizational Psychology,* pp 149–53.

[10] J Castro, "Mazda U.," *Time,* October 20, 1986, p 65.

[11] For an instructive overview of five different theories of group development, see J P Wanous, A E Reichers, and S D Malik, "Organizational Socialization and Group Development: Toward an Integrative Perspective," *Academy of Management Review,* October 1984, pp 670–83. Also see L R Offermann and R K Spiros, "The Science and Practice of Team Development: Improving the Link," *Academy of Management Journal,* April 2001, pp 376–92.

[12] See B W Tuckman, "Developmental Sequence in Small Groups," *Psychological Bulletin,* June 1965, pp 384–99; and B W Tuckman and M A C Jensen, "Stages of Small-Group Development Revisited," *Group & Organization Studies,* December 1977, pp 419–27. An instructive adaptation of the Tuckman model can be found in L Holpp, "If Empowerment Is So Good, Why Does It Hurt?" *Training,* March 1995, p 56.

[13] Practical advice on handling a dominating group member can be found in M Finley, "Belling the Bully," *HRMagazine,* March 1992, pp 82–86.

[14] For related research, see K Aquino and A Reed II, "A Social Dilemma Perspective on Cooperative Behavior in Organizations: The Effects of Scarcity, Communication, and Unequal Access on the Use of a Shared Resource," *Group & Organization Management,* December 1998, pp 390–413; B Fehr, "Laypeople's Conceptions of Commitment," *Journal of Personality and Social Psychology,* January 1999, pp 90–103; and G L Stewart, C C Manz, and H P Sims, Jr, *Team Work and Group Dynamics* (New York: Wiley, 1999).

[15] G Graen, "Role-Making Processes within Complex Organizations," in *Handbook of Industrial and Organizational Psychology,* ed M D Dunnette (Chicago: Rand McNally, 1976), p 1201. Also see L Van Dyne and J A LePine, "Helping and Voice Extra-Role Behaviors: Evidence of Construct and Predictive Validity," *Academy of Management Journal,* February 1998, pp 108–19; and B E Ashforth, G E Kreiner, and M Fugate, "All in a Day's Work: Boundaries and Micro Role Transitions," *Academy of Management Review,* July 2000, pp 472–91.

[16] See K D Benne and P Sheats, "Functional Roles of Group Members," *Journal of Social Issues,* Spring 1948, pp 41–49.

[17] See H J Klein and P W Mulvey, "Two Investigations of the Relationships among Group Goals, Goal Commitment, Cohesion, and Performance," *Organizational Behavior and Human Decision Processes,* January 1995, pp 44–53; D F Crown and J G Rosse, "Yours, Mine, and Ours: Facilitating Group Productivity through the Integration of Individual and Group Goals," *Organizational Behavior and Human Decision Processes,* November 1995, pp 138–50; and D Knight, C C Durham, and E A Locke, "The Relationship of Team Goals, Incentives, and Efficacy to Strategic Risk, Tactical Implementation, and Performance," *Academy of Management Journal,* April 2001, pp 326–38.

[18] A Zander, "The Value of Belonging to a Group in Japan," *Small Group Behavior,* February 1983, pp 7–8. Also see P R Harris and R T Moran, *Managing Cultural Differences,* 4th ed (Houston: Gulf Publishing, 1996), pp 267–76.

[19] R R Blake and J Srygley Mouton, "Don't Let Group Norms Stifle Creativity," *Personnel,* August 1985, p 28.

[20] See D Kahneman, "Reference Points, Anchors, Norms, and Mixed Feelings," *Organizational Behavior and Human Decision Processes,* March 1992, pp 296–312; and J M Marques, D Abrams, D Paez, and C Martinez-Taboada, "The Role of Categorization and In-Group Norms in Judgments of Groups and Their Members," *Journal of Personality and Social Psychology,* October 1998, pp 976–88.

[21] A Dunkin, "Pepsi's Marketing Magic: Why Nobody Does It Better," *Business Week,* February 10, 1986, p 52.

[22] D C Feldman, "The Development and Enforcement of Group Norms," *Academy of Management Review,* January 1984, pp 50–52.

[23] Ibid.

[24] See P F Drucker, "The Coming of the New Organization," *Harvard Business Review,* January–February 1988, pp 45–53. Also see F Mueller, S Procter, and D Buchanan, "Teamworking in Its Context(s): Antecedents, Nature and Dimensions," *Human Relations,* November 2000, pp 1387–1424.

[25] J Pfeffer and J F Veiga, "Putting People First for Organizational Success," *Academy of Management Executive,* May 1999, p 41.

[26] See N Enbar, "What Do Women Want? Ask 'Em," *Business Week,* March 29, 1999, p 8; and M Hickins, "Duh! Gen Xers Are Cool with Teamwork," *Management Review,* March 1999, p 7.

[27] J R Katzenbach and D K Smith, *The Wisdom of Teams: Creating the High-Performance Organization* (New York: HarperBusiness, 1999), p 45.

[28] Condensed and adapted from ibid., p 214.

[29] See L G Bolman and T E Deal, "What Makes a Team Work?" *Organizational Dynamics,* Autumn 1992, pp 34–44.

[30] J R Katzenbach and D K Smith, "The Discipline of Teams," *Harvard Business Review,* March–April 1993, p 112.

[31] "A Team's-Eye View of Teams," *Training,* November 1995, p 16.

[32] J C McCune, "That Elusive Thing Called TRUST," *Management Review,* July–August 1998, p 11.

[33] L Prusak and D Cohen, "How to Invest in Social Capital," *Harvard Business Review,* June 2001, p 90. Also see V U Druskat and S B Wolff, "Building the Emotional Intelligence of Groups," *Harvard Business Review,* March 2001, pp 80–90.

[34] Also see D M Rousseau, S B Sitkin, R S Burt, and C Camerer, "Not So Different After All: A Cross-Discipline View of Trust," *Academy of Management Review,* July 1998, pp 393–404; and A C Wicks, S L Berman, and T M Jones, "The Structure of Optimal Trust: Moral and Strategic Implications," *Academy of Management Review,* January 1999, pp 99–116.

[35] J D Lewis and A Weigert, "Trust as a Social Reality," *Social Forces,* June 1985, p 971. Trust is examined as an *indirect* factor in K T Dirks, "The Effects of Interpersonal Trust on Work Group Performance," *Journal of Applied Psychology,* June 1999, pp 445–55. Also see J B Cunningham and J MacGregor, "Trust and the Design of Work: Complementary Constructs in Satisfaction and Performance," *Human Relations,* December 2000, pp 1575–88.

[36] Adapted from C Johnson-George and W C Swap, "Measurement of Specific Interpersonal Trust: Construction and Validation of a Scale to Assess Trust in a Specific Other," *Journal of Personality and Social Psychology,* December 1982, pp 1306–17; and D J McAllister, "Affect- and Cognition-Based Trust as Foundations for Interpersonal Cooperation in Organizations," *Academy of Management Journal,* February 1995, pp 24–59.

[37] For interesting new theory and research on telling lies, see B M DePaulo, D A Kashy, S E Kirkendol, M M Wyer, and J A Epstein, "Lying in Everyday Life," *Journal of Personality and Social Psychology,* May 1996, pp 979–95; and D A Kashy and B M DePaulo, "Who Lies?" *Journal of Personality and Social Psychology,* May 1996, pp 1037–51.

[38] For support, see G M Spreitzer and A K Mishra, "Giving Up Control without Losing Control: Trust and Its Substitutes' Effects on Managers' Involving Employees in Decision Making," *Group & Organization Management,* June 1999, pp 155–87.

39 For more on fairness, see K Seiders and L L Berry, "Service Fairness: What It Is and Why It Matters," *Academy of Management Executive,* May 1998, pp 8–20.

40 Adapted from F Bartolomé, "Nobody Trusts the Boss Completely—Now What?" *Harvard Business Review,* March–April 1989, pp 135–42.

41 Data from C Joinson, "Teams at Work," *HRMagazine,* May 1999, pp 30–36.

42 B Dumaine, "Who Needs a Boss?" *Fortune,* May 7, 1990, p 52.

43 For example, see M Selz, "Testing Self-Managed Teams, Entrepreneur Hopes to Lose Job," *The Wall Street Journal,* January 11, 1994, pp B1–B2. Also see "Even in Self-Managed Teams There Has to Be a Leader," *Supervisory Management,* December 1994, pp 7–8.

44 See M Moravec, O J Johannessen, and T A Hjelmas, "The Well-Managed SMT," *Management Review,* June 1998, pp 56–58; and "Case Study in C-Sharp Minor," *Training,* October 1998, p 21.

45 See D R Denison, S L Hart, and J A Kahn, "From Chimneys to Cross-Functional Teams: Developing and Validating a Diagnostic Model," *Academy of Management Journal,* August 1996, pp 1005–23. Cross-functional teams are discussed in D Lei, J W Slocum, and R A Pitts, "Designing Organizations for Competitive Advantage: The Power of Unlearning and Learning," *Organizational Dynamics,* Winter 1999, pp 24–38.

46 A Erdman, "How to Keep that Family Feeling," *Fortune,* April 6, 1992, p 95.

47 See "1996 Industry Report: What Self-Managing Teams Manage," *Training,* October 1996, p 69.

48 See L L Thompson, *Making the Team: A Guide for Managers* (Upper Saddle River, NJ: Prentice Hall, 2000).

49 See P S Goodman, R Devadas, and T L Griffith Hughson, "Groups and Productivity: Analyzing the Effectiveness of Self-Managing Teams," in *Productivity in Organizations,* eds J P Campbell, R J Campbell and Associates (San Francisco: Jossey-Bass, 1988), pp 295–327. Also see E F Rogers, W Metlay, I T Kaplan, and T Shapiro, "Self-Managing Work Teams: Do They Really Work?" *Human Resource Planning,* no. 2, 1995, pp 53–57; V U Druskat and S B Wolff, "Effects and Timing of Developmental Peer Appraisals in Self-Managing Work Groups," *Journal of Applied Psychology,* February 1999, pp 58–74; and R C Liden, S J Wayne, and M L Kraimer, "Managing Individual Performance in Work Groups," *Human Resource Management,* Spring 2001, pp 63–72.

50 For more, see W F Cascio, "Managing a Virtual Workplace," *Academy of Management Executive,* August 2000, pp 81–90.

51 See A M Townsend, S M DeMarie, and A R Hendrickson, "Virtual Teams: Technology and the Workplace of the Future," *Academy of Management Executive,* August 1998, pp 17–29.

52 Based on P Bordia, N DiFonzo, and A Chang, "Rumor as Group Problem Solving: Development Patterns in Informal Computer-Mediated Groups," *Small Group Research,* February 1999, pp 8–28.

53 See K A Graetz, E S Boyle, C E Kimble, P Thompson, and J L Garloch, "Information Sharing in Face-to-Face, Teleconferencing, and Electronic Chat Groups," *Small Group Research,* December 1998, pp 714–43.

54 Based on F Niederman and R J Volkema, "The Effects of Facilitator Characteristics on Meeting Preparation, Set Up, and Implementation," *Small Group Research,* June 1999, pp 330–60.

55 Based on J J Sosik, B J Avolio, and S S Kahai, "Inspiring Group Creativity: Comparing Anonymous and Identified Electronic Brainstorming," *Small Group Research,* February 1998, pp 3–31. For practical advice on brainstorming, see C Caggiano, "The Right Way to Brainstorm," *Inc.,* July 1999, p 94.

56 See E Kelley, "Keys to Effective Virtual Global Teams," *Academy of Management Executive,* May 2001, pp 132–33.

57 For practical tips, see K Kiser, "Building a Virtual Team," *Training,* March 1999, p 34.

58 For a comprehensive update on groupthink, see the entire February–March 1998 issue of *Organizational Behavior and Human Decision Processes* (12 articles).

59 I L Janis, *Groupthink,* 2nd ed (Boston: Houghton Mifflin, 1982), p 9. Alternative models are discussed in K Granstrom and D Stiwne, "A Bipolar Model of Groupthink: An Expansion of Janis's Concept," *Small Group Research,* February 1998, pp 32–56; and A R Flippen, "Under-standing Groupthink From a Self-Regulatory Perspective," *Small Group Research,* April 1999, pp 139–65.

60 Ibid. For an alternative model, see R J Aldag and S Riggs Fuller, "Beyond Fiasco: A Reappraisal of the Groupthink Phenomenon and a New Model of Group Decision Processes," *Psychological Bulletin,* May 1993, pp 533–52. Also see A A Mohamed and F A Wiebe, "Toward a Process Theory of Groupthink," *Small Group Research,* August 1996, pp 416–30.

61 Adapted from Janis, *Groupthink,* pp 174–75.

62 L Baum, "The Job Nobody Wants," *Business Week,* September 8, 1986, p 60. Also see A Bianco and J A Byrne, "The Rush to Quality on Corporate Boards," *Business Week,* March 3, 1997, pp 34–35; B Leonard, "Workplace Diversity Should Include Board Room," *HRMagazine,* February 1999, p 12; J D Westphal, "Collaboration in the Boardroom: Behavioral and Performance Consequences of CEO-Board Social Ties," *Academy of Management Journal,* February 1999, pp 7–24; and G Koretz, "Friendly Boards Are Not All Bad," *Business Week,* June 14, 1999, p 34.

63 For an ethical perspective, see R R Sims, "Linking Groupthink to Unethical Behavior in Organizations," *Journal of Business Ethics,* September 1992, pp 651–62.

64 Based on discussion in B Latane, K Williams, and S Harkins, "Many Hands Make Light the Work: The Causes and Consequences of Social Loafing," *Journal of Personality and Social Psychology,* June 1979, pp 822–32; and D A Kravitz and B Martin, "Ringelmann Rediscovered: The Original Article," *Journal of Personality and Social Psychology,* May 1986, pp 936–41.

65 See J A Shepperd, "Productivity Loss in Performance Groups: A Motivation Analysis," *Psychological Bulletin,* no. 1, 1993, pp 67–81; R E Kidwell, Jr, and N Bennett, "Employee Propensity to Withhold Effort: A Conceptual Model to Intersect Three Avenues of Research," *Academy of Management Review,* July 1993, pp 429–56; and S J Karau and K D Williams, "Social Loafing: Meta-Analytic Review and Theoretical Integration," *Journal of Personality and Social Psychology,* October 1993, pp 681–706.

66 See S J Zaccaro, "Social Loafing: The Role of Task Attractiveness," *Personality and Social Psychology Bulletin,* March 1984, pp 99–106; J M Jackson and K D Williams, "Social Loafing on Difficult Tasks: Working Collectively Can Improve Performance," *Journal of Personality and Social Psychology,* October 1985, pp 937–42; and J M George, "Extrinsic and Intrinsic Origins of Perceived Social Loafing in Organizations," *Academy of Management Journal,* March 1992, pp 191–202.

67 For complete details, see K Williams, S Harkins, and B Latane, "Identifiability as a Deterrent to Social Loafing: Two Cheering Experiments," *Journal of Personality and Social Psychology,* February 1981, pp 303–11.

68 See J M Jackson and S G Harkins, "Equity in Effort: An Explanation of the Social Loafing Effect," *Journal of Personality and Social Psychology,* November 1985, pp 1199–1206.

69 Both studies are reported in S G Harkins and K Szymanski, "Social Loafing and Group Evaluation," *Journal of Personality and Social Psychology,* June 1989, pp 934–41.

70 Data from J A Wagner III, "Studies of Individualism-Collectivism: Effects on Cooperation in Groups," *Academy of Management Journal,* February 1995, pp 152–72. Also see P W Mulvey and H J Klein, "The Impact of Perceived Loafing and Collective Efficacy on Group Goal Processes and Group Performance," *Organizational Behavior and Human Decision Processes,* April 1998, pp 62–87; and P W Mulvey, L Bowes-Sperry, and H J Klein, "The Effects of Perceived Loafing and Defensive Impression Management on Group Effectiveness," *Small Group Research,* June 1998, pp 394–415.

71 See S G Scott and W O Einstein, "Strategic Performance Appraisal in Team-Based Organizations: One Size Does Not Fit All," *Academy of Management Executive,* May 2001, pp 107–16.

Chapter II

1 Excerpted from M Boitano, "You Got a Problem with That?" *Fortune,* June 11, 2001, pp 196[C]–196[F].

2 D Tjosvold, *Learning to Manage Conflict: Getting People to Work Together Productively* (New York: Lexington Books, 1993), p xi.

3 Ibid., pp xi–xii.

4 J A Wall, Jr, and R Robert Callister, "Conflict and Its Management," *Journal of Management,* no. 3, 1995, p 517.

5 Ibid., p 544.

6 See O Jones, "Scientific Management, Culture and Control: A First-Hand Account of Taylorism in Practice," *Human Relations,* May 2000, pp 631–53.

7 See A M O'Leary-Kelly, R W Griffin, and D J Glew, "Organization-Motivated Aggression: A Research Framework," *Academy of Management Review,* January 1996, pp 225–53; and D Bencivenga, "Dealing with the Dark Side," *HRMagazine,* January 1999, pp 50–58.

8 See S Alper, D Tjosvold, and K S Law, "Interdependence and Controversy in Group Decision Making: Antecedents to Effective Self-Managing Teams," *Organizational Behavior and Human Decision Processes,* April 1998, pp 33–52.

9 S P Robbins, " 'Conflict Management' and 'Conflict Resolution' Are Not Synonymous Terms," *California Management Review,* Winter 1978, p 70.

10 Cooperative conflict is discussed in Tjosvold, *Learning to Manage Conflict: Getting People to Work Together Productively.* Also see A C Amason, "Distinguishing the Effects of Functional and Dysfunctional Conflict on Strategic Decision Making: Resolving a Paradox for Top Management Teams," *Academy of Management Journal,* February 1996, pp 123–48.

11 K Brooker, "Can Anyone Replace Herb?" *Fortune,* April 17, 2000, p 190.

12 K Brooker, "I Built This Company, I Can Save It," *Fortune,* April 30, 2001, p 102.

13 Adapted in part from discussion in A C Filley, *Interpersonal Conflict Resolution* (Glenview, IL: Scott, Foresman, 1975), pp 9–12; and B Fortado, "The Accumulation of Grievance Conflict," *Journal of Management Inquiry,* December 1992, pp 288–303. Also see D Tjosvold and M Poon, "Dealing with Scarce Resources: Open-Minded Interaction for Resolving Budget Conflicts," *Group & Organization Management,* September 1998, pp 237–55.

14 Adapted from discussion in Tjosvold, *Learning to Manage Conflict: Getting People to Work Together Productively,* pp 12–13.

15 L Gardenswartz and A Rowe, *Diverse Teams at Work: Capitalizing on the Power of Diversity* (New York: McGraw-Hill, 1994), p 32.

16 See L M Andersson and C M Pearson, "Tit for Tat? The Spiraling Effect of Incivility in the Workplace," *Academy of Management Review,* July 1999, pp 452–71; and C Lee, "The Death of Civility," *Training,* July 1999, pp 24–30.

17 M Elias, "Study: Rudeness Is Poisoning US Workplace," *USA Today,* June 14, 2001, p 1D; and S Anderson, "Courtesy Becomes Uncommon on Job," *The Arizona Republic,* January 15, 2001, pp E1–E4.

18 Data from D Stamps, "Yes, Your Boss Is Crazy," *Training,* July 1998, pp 35–39. Also see L Huggler, "Companies on the Couch," *HRMagazine,* November 1997, pp 80–84; and J C Connor, "The Paranoid Personality at Work," *HRMagazine,* March 1999, pp 120–26.

19 See S H Milne and T C Blum, "Organizational Characteristics and Employer Responses to Employee Substance Abuse," *Journal of Management,* no. 6, 1998, pp 693–715; P J Petesch, "Are the Newest ADA Guidelines 'Reasonable?' " *HRMagazine,* June 1999, pp 54–58; T Mauro, "Court Narrows Disability Act, But Expands Rights of the Mentally Ill," *USA Today,* June 23, 1999, p 1A; and K Holland, "Who's Disabled? The Court Rules," *Business Week,* July 5, 1999, p 36.

20 See J Muller, "Keeping an Investigation on the Right Track," *Business Week,* July 5, 1999, p 84.

21 See Bencivenga, "Dealing with the Dark Side"; and C Lee, "Tips for Surviving Rude Encounters," *Training,* July 1999, p 29.

22 Drawn from J C McCune, "The Change Makers," *Management Review,* May 1999, pp 16–22.

23 Based on discussion in G Labianca, D J Brass, and B Gray, "Social Networks and Perceptions of Intergroup Conflict: The Role of Negative Relationships and Third Parties," *Academy of Management Journal,* February 1998, pp 55–67. Also see C Gómez, B L Kirkman, and D L Shapiro, "The Impact of Collectivism and In-Group/Out-Group Membership on the Evaluation Generosity of Team Members," *Academy of Management Journal,* December 2000, pp 1097–1106; and K A Jehn and E A Mannix, "The Dynamic Nature of Conflict: A Longitudinal Study of Intragroup Conflict and Group Performance," *Academy of Management Journal,* April 2001, pp 238–51.

24 Labianca, Brass, and Gray, "Social Networks and Perceptions of Intergroup Conflict: The Role of Negative Relationships and Third Parties," p 63 (emphasis added).

25 For example, see S C Wright, A Aron, T McLaughlin-Volpe, and S A Ropp, "The Extended Contact Effect: Knowledge of Cross-Group Friendships and Prejudice," *Journal of Personality and Social Psychology,* July 1997, pp 73–90.

26 See C D Batson, M P Polycarpou, E Harmon-Jones, H J Imhoff, E C Mitchener, L L Bednar, T R Klein, and L Highberger, "Empathy and Attitudes: Can Feeling for a Member of a Stigmatized Group Improve Feelings toward the Group?" *Journal of Personality and Social Psychology,* January 1997, pp 105–18.

27 For more, see A K Gupta and V Govindarajan, "Converting Global Presence into Global Competitive Advantage," *Academy of Management Executive,* May 2001, pp 45–56.

28 For an interesting case study, see W Kuemmerle, "Go Global—or No?" *Harvard Business Review,* June 2001, pp 37–49.

29 "Negotiating South of the Border," *Harvard Management Communication Letter,* August 1999, p 12.

30 Reprinted from A Rosenbaum, "Testing Cultural Waters," *Management Review,* July–August 1999, p 43 © 1999 American Management Association International. Reprinted by permission of American Management Association International, New York, NY. All rights reserved. http://www.amanet. org.

31 See R L Tung, "American Expatriates Abroad: From Neophytes to Cosmopolitans," *Journal of World Business,* Summer 1998, pp 125–44.

32 R A Cosier and C R Schwenk, "Agreement and Thinking Alike: Ingredients for Poor Decisions," *Academy of Management Executive,* February 1990, p 71. Also see J P Kotter, "Kill Complacency," *Fortune,* August 5, 1996, pp 168–70; and S Caudron, "Keeping Team Conflict Alive," *Training & Development,* September 1998, pp 48–52.

33 D Jones, "CEOs Need X-Ray Vision in Transition," *USA Today,* April 23, 2001, p 4B.

34 A statistical validation for this model can be found in M A Rahim and N R Magner, "Confirmatory Factor Analysis of the Styles of Handling Interpersonal Conflict: First-Order Factor Model and Its Invariance Across Groups," *Journal of Applied Psychology,* February 1995, pp 122–32.

35 M A Rahim, "A Strategy for Managing Conflict in Complex Organizations," *Human Relations,* January 1985, p 84.

36 For background, see D L Jacobs, "First, Fire All the Lawyers," *Inc.,* January 1999, pp 84–85; and S Higginbotham, "Next, Online Bids Over Jail Time?" *Business Week,* July 19, 1999, p 8.

37 See M Bordwin, "Do-It-Yourself Justice," *Management Review,* January 1999, pp 56–58.

38 B Morrow and L M Bernardi, "Resolving Workplace Disputes," *Canadian Manager,* Spring 1999, p 17.

39 Adapted from discussion in K O Wilburn, "Employment Disputes: Solving Them Out of Court," *Management Review,* March 1998, pp 17–21; and Morrow and Bernardi, "Resolving Workplace Disputes," pp 17–19, 27. Also see L Ioannou, "Can't We Get Along?" *Fortune,* December 7, 1998, p 244[E]; and D Weimer and S A Forest, "Forced into Arbitration? Not Any More," *Business Week,* March 16, 1998, pp 66–68.

40 Wilburn, "Employment Disputes: Solving Them Out of Court," p 19.

41 For more, see S Armour, "Arbitration's Rise Raises Fairness Issue," *USA Today,* June 12, 2001, pp 1B–2B.

42 Based on a definition in M A Neale and M H Bazerman, "Negotiating Rationally: The Power and Impact of the Negotiator's Frame," *Academy of Management Executive,* August 1992, pp 42–51.

43 See, for example, J K Sebenius, "Six Habits of Merely Effective Negotiators," *Harvard Business Review,* April 2001, pp 87–95; A Fisher, "Ask Annie: Being Lowballed on Salary? How to Eke Out More Bucks," *Fortune,* April 30, 2001, p 192; G Koretz, "She's a Woman, Offer Her Less," *Business Week,* May 7, 2001, p 34; and K Hannon, "Want a Family Life? Negotiate," *USA Today,* June 11, 2001, p 7B.

44 M H Bazerman and M A Neale, *Negotiating Rationally* (New York: The Free Press, 1992), p 16. Also See J F Brett, G B Northcraft, and R L Pinkley, "Stairways to Heaven: An Interlocking Self-Regulation Model of Negotiation," *Academy of Management Review,* July 1999, pp 435–51.

45 Good win-win negotiation strategies can be found in R R Reck and B G Long, *The Win-Win Negotiator: How to Negotiate Favorable Agreements That Last* (New York: Pocket Books, 1987); R Fisher and W Ury, *Getting to YES: Negotiating Agreement without Giving In* (Boston: Houghton Mifflin, 1981); and R Fisher and D Ertel, *Getting Ready to Negotiate: The Getting to YES Workbook* (New York: Penguin Books, 1995).

46 Adapted from K Albrecht and S Albrecht, "Added Value Negotiating," *Training,* April 1993, pp 26–29.

Chapter 12

1 Excerpted from T Terez, "Can We Talk?" *Workforce,* July 2000, pp 47–48.

2 Excerpted from L Grensing-Pophal, "Follow Me," *HRMagazine,* February 2000, pp 36–37.

3 See M A Jaasma and R J Koper, "The Relationship of Student-Faculty Out-of-Class Communication to Instructor Immediacy and Trust and to Student Motivation," *Communication Education,* January 1999, pp 41–47; and P G Clampitt and C W Downs, "Employee Perceptions of the Relationship between Communication and Productivity: A Field Study," *Journal of Business Communication,* 1993, pp 5–28.

4 J L Bowditch and A F Buono, *A Primer on Organizational Behavior,* 4th ed (New York: John Wiley & Sons, 1997), p 120.

5 L Labich, "How to Fire People and Still Sleep at Night," *Fortune,* June 10, 1996, p 65.

6 For a detailed discussion about a contingency approach for selecting medium, see R H Lengel and R L Daft, "The Selection of Communication Media as an Executive Skill," *Academy of Management Executive,* August 1988, pp 225–32.

7 See B Coates, "This Financial Consultant Really Listens to His Clients," *The Arizona Republic/The Phoenix Gazette,* May 4, 1996, p 8.

8 For a thorough discussion of communication distortion, see E W Larson and J B King, "The Systematic Distortion of Information: An Ongoing Challenge to Management," *Organizational Dynamics,* Winter 1996, pp 49–61.

9 J Fulk and S Mani, "Distortion of Communication in Hierarchical Relationships," in *Communication Yearbook 9,* ed M L McLaughlin (Beverly Hills, CA: Sage Publications, 1986), p 483.

10 For a review of this research, see ibid., pp 483–510.

11 Results can be found in B Davenport Sypher and T E Zorn, Jr., "Communication-Related Abilities and Upward Mobility: A Longitudinal Investigation," *Human Communication Research,* Spring 1986, pp 420–31.

12 See E Raudsepp, "Are You Properly Assertive?" *Supervision,* June 1992, pp 17–18; and D A Infante and W I Gorden, "Superiors' Argumentativeness and Verbal Aggressiveness as Predictors of Subordinates' Satisfaction," *Human Communication Research,* Fall 1985, pp 117–25.

13 J A Waters, "Managerial Assertiveness," *Business Horizons,* September–October 1982, p 25.

14 Ibid., p 27.

15 This statistic was provided by A Warfield, "Do You Speak Body Language?" *Training & Development,* April 2001, pp 60–61.

16 See N Morgan, "The Kinesthetic Speaker: Putting Action into Words," *Harvard Business Review,* April 2001, pp 113–20; and G E Wright and K D Multon, "Employer's Perceptions of Nonverbal Communication in Job Interviews for Persons with Physical Disabilities," *Journal of Vocational Behavior,* October 1995, pp 214–27.

17 A thorough discussion of cross-cultural differences is provided by R E Axtell, *Gestures: The Do's and Taboos of Body Language Around the World* (New York: John Wiley & Sons, 1991). Problems with body language analysis also are discussed by C L Karrass, "Body Language: Beware the Hype," *Traffic Management,* January 1992, p 27.

18 Related research is summarized by J A Hall, "Male and Female Nonverbal Behavior," in *Multichannel Integrations of Nonverbal Behavior,* eds A W Siegman and S Feldstein (Hillsdale, NJ: Lawrence Erlbaum, 1985), pp 195–226.

19 See R E Axtell, *Gestures: The Do's and Taboos of Body Language Around the World* (New York: John Wiley & Sons, 1991).

20 See J A Russell, "Facial Expressions of Emotion: What Lies Beyond Minimal Universality?" *Psychological Bulletin,* November 1995, pp 379–91.

21 Norms for cross-cultural eye contact are discussed by C Engholm, *When Business East Meets Business West: The Guide to Practice and Protocol in the Pacific Rim* (New York: John Wiley & Sons, 1991).

22 Excerpted from Warfield, "Do You Speak Body Language?" p 60.

23 See D Ray, "Are You Listening?" *Selling Power,* June 1999, pp 28–30; and P Meyer, "So You Want the President's Job," *Business Horizons,* January–February 1998, pp 2–6.

24 For a thorough discussion of the different listening styles, see R T Bennett and R V Wood, "Effective Communication via Listening Styles," *Business,* April–June 1989, pp 45–48.

25 D Tannen, "The Power of Talk: Who Gets Heard and Why," *Harvard Business Review,* September–October 1995, p 139.

26 For a thorough review of the evolutionary explanation of sex differences in communication, see A H Eagly and W Wood, "The Origins of Sex Differences in Human Behavior," *American Psychologist,* June 1999, pp 408–23.

27 See D Tannen, "The Power of Talk: Who Gets Heard and Why," in *Negotiation: Readings, Exercises, and Cases,* 3rd ed, eds R J Lewicki and D M Saunders (Boston, MA: Irwin/McGraw-Hill, 1999), pp 160–73; and D Tannen, *You Just Don't Understand: Women and Men in Conversation* (New York: Ballantine Books, 1990).

28 Research on gender differences in communication can be found in A Mulac, J J Bradac, and P Gibbons, "Empirical Support for the Gender-as-Culture Hypothesis: An Intercultural Analysis of Male/Female Language Differences," *Human Communication Research,* January 2001, pp 121–52; and K Hawkins and C B Power, "Gender Differences in Questions Asked During Small Decision-Making Group Discussions," *Small Group Research,* April 1999, pp 235–56.

29 Tannen, "The Power of Talk: Who Gets Heard and Why," pp 147–48.

30 Excerpted from W H Bulkeley, "The View from the Top," *The Wall Street Journal,* June 21, 1999, p R6.

31 The Harris Poll was reported in "USA Snapshots: Computer Age," *USA Today,* June 7, 1999, p 1A.

32 Results can be found in D Smith, "One-Tenth of College Students Are Dependent on the Internet, Research Finds," *Monitor on Psychology,* May 2001, p 10.

33 Results were reported in A Petersen, "A Fine Line: Companies Face a Delicate Task When It Comes to Deciding What to Put on Their Intranets: How Much Is Too Much?" *The Wall Street Journal,* June 21, 1999, p R8.

34 This conclusion is discussed by O Edwards, "Inflammation Highway," *Forbes,* February 26, 1996, p 120.

35 Excerpted from Petersen, "A Fine Line: Companies Face a Delicate Task When It Comes to Deciding What to Put on Their Intranets: How Much Is Too Much?"

36 See J Useem, "For Sale Online: You," *Fortune,* July 5, 1999, pp 67–78.

37 See S J Wells, "Communicating Benefits Information Online," *HRMagazine,* February 2001, pp 69–76.

38 Excerpted from "Websmart," *Business Week* **E.BIZ,** May 14, 2001, p EB 56.

39 Statistics are reported in C Tejada, "Work Week: A Special News Report About Life on the Job—and Trends Taking Shape There," *The Wall Street Journal,* May 8, 2001, p A1; and J Wallace, "The (E-Mail) Postman Rings More Than Twice," *HRMagazine,* March 2001, p 176.

40 Results are summarized in S Armour, "Boss: It's in the E-mail," *USA Today,* August 10, 1999, p 3B.

41 The benefits of using E-mail were derived from discussion in R F Federico and J M Bowley, "The Great E-Mail Debate," *HRMagazine,* January 1996, pp 67–72.

42 S Schafer, "Operations: 'E-Mail, or Else!' " *Inc.,* January 1996, p 94.

43 Results can be found in M L Markus, "Electronic Mail as the Medium of Managerial Choice," *Organization Science,* November 1994, pp 502–27.

44 Results can be found in J Yaukey, "E-Mail Out of Control for Many: Take Steps to Ease Load," *The Wall Street Journal,* May 8, 2001, p F1.

45 R Blumenstein, "For Your Eyes Only," *The Wall Street Journal,* June 21, 1999, p R10.

46 M Fleschner, "Bold Goals: How Pinacor Wraps Itself Around the Customer," *Selling Power,* June 1999, p 57.

[47] Results can be found in M S Thompson and M S Feldman, "Electronic Mail and Organizational Communication: Does Saying 'Hi' Really Matter?" *Organization Science,* November–December 1998, pp 685–98.

[48] See the discussion in S Prasso, "Workers, Surf at Your Own Risk," *Business Week,* June 11, 2001, p 14; and S Miller and J Weckert, "Privacy, the Workplace and the Internet," *Journal of Business Ethics,* 2000, pp 255–65.

[49] The types of information technology used by virtual teams is discussed by A M Townsend, S M DeMarie, and A R Hendrickson, "Virtual Teams: Technology and the Workplace of the Future," *Academy of Management Executive,* August 1998, pp 17–29.

[50] Challenges associated with virtual operations are discussed by S O'Mahony and S R Barley, "Do Digital Telecommunications Affect Work and Organization? The State of Our Knowledge," in *Research in Organizational Behavior,* vol. 21, eds R I Sutton and B M Staw (Stamford, CT: JAI Press, 1999), pp 125–61.

[51] Telecommuting statistics were presented in "Work Life: What is the Future of Telework?" *HRFOCUS,* March 2001, pp 5–6.

[52] Supporting evidence is presented in S Fister, "A Lure for Labor," *Training,* February 1999, pp 56–62; M Apgar IV, "The Alternative Workplace: Changing Where and How People Work," *Harvard Business Review,* May–June 1998, pp 121–36; and C Hymowitz, "Remote Managers Find Ways to Narrow the Distance Gap," *The Wall Street Journal,* April 6, 1999, p B1.

[53] The legal considerations of telecommuting are discussed by B A Hartstein and M L Schulman, "Telecommuting: The New Workplace of the 90s," *Employee Relations L J,* Spring 1996, pp 179–88.

[54] The preceding barriers are discussed by J P Scully, "People: The Imperfect Communicators," *Quality Progress,* April 1995, pp 37–39.

[55] For a thorough discussion of these barriers, see C R Rogers and F J Roethlisberger, "Barriers and Gateways to Communication," *Harvard Business Review,* July–August 1952, pp 46–52.

[56] Ibid., p 47.

Chapter 13

[1] Excerpted from A Bianco and P L Moore, "Downfall," *Business Week,* March 5, 2001, pp 82–92.

[2] See D Kipnis, S M Schmidt, and J Wilkinson, "Intraorganizational Influence Tactics: Explorations in Getting One's Way," *Journal of Applied Psychology,* August 1980, pp 440–52. Also see C A Schriesheim and T R Hinkin, "Influence Tactics Used by Subordinates: A Theoretical and Empirical Analysis and Refinement of the Kipnis, Schmidt, and Wilkinson Subscales," *Journal of Applied Psychology,* June 1990, pp 246–57; and G Yukl and C M Falbe, "Influence Tactics and Objectives in Upward, Downward, and Lateral Influence Attempts," *Journal of Applied Psychology,* April 1990, pp 132–40.

[3] Based on Table 1 in G Yukl, C M Falbe, and J Y Youn, "Patterns of Influence Behavior for Managers," *Group & Organization Management,* March 1993, pp 5–28. An additional influence tactic is presented in B P Davis and E S Knowles, "A Disrupt-then-Reframe Technique of Social Influence," *Journal of Personality and Social Psychology,* February 1999, pp 192–99.

[4] For related reading, see M Lippitt, "How to Influence Leaders," *Training & Development,* March 1999, pp 18–22; L Schlesinger, "I've Got Three Words for You: Suck It Up," *Fast Company,* April 1999, p 104; and S M Farmer and J M Maslyn, "Why Are Styles of Upward Influence Neglected? Making the Case for a Configurational Approach to Influences," *Journal of Management,* no. 5, 1999, pp 653–682.

[5] Based on discussion in G Yukl, H Kim, and C M Falbe, "Antecedents of Influence Outcomes," *Journal of Applied Psychology,* June 1996, pp 309–17.

[6] Data from Ibid.

[7] Data from G Yukl and J B Tracey, "Consequences of Influence Tactics Used with Subordinates, Peers, and the Boss," *Journal of Applied Psychology,* August 1992, pp 525–35. Also see C M Falbe and G Yukl, "Consequences for Managers of Using Single Influence Tactics and Combinations of Tactics," *Academy of Management Journal,* August 1992, pp 638–52.

[8] Data from R A Gordon, "Impact of Ingratiation on Judgments and Evaluations: A Meta-Analytic Investigation," *Journal of Personality and Social Psychology,* July 1996, pp 54–70. Also see S J Wayne, R C Liden,

and R T Sparrowe, "Developing Leader-Member Exchanges," *American Behavioral Scientist,* March 1994, pp 697–714; A Oldenburg, "These Days, Hostile Is Fitting for Takeovers Only," *USA Today,* July 22, 1996, pp 8B, 10B; and J H Dulebohn and G R Ferris, "The Role of Influence Tactics in Perceptions of Performance Evaluations' Fairness," *Academy of Management Journal,* June 1999, pp 288–303.

[9] Data from Yukl, Kim, and Falbe, "Antecedents of Influence Outcomes."

[10] Data from B J Tepper, R J Eisenbach, S L Kirby, and P W Potter, "Test of a Justice-Based Model of Subordinates' Resistance to Downward Influence Attempts," *Group & Organization Management,* June 1998, pp 144–60.

[11] See A R Cohen and D L Bradford, *Influence without Authority* (New York: John Wiley & Sons, 1990), pp 23–24.

[12] Ibid., p 28. Another excellent source on this subject is R B Cialdini, *Influence* (New York: William Morrow, 1984).

[13] D Tjosvold, "The Dynamics of Positive Power," *Training and Development Journal,* June 1984, p 72. Also see T A Stewart, "Get with the New Power Game," *Fortune,* January 13, 1997, pp 58–62.

[14] See G Koretz, "The Last Step Up Is a Big One," *Business Week,* May 14, 2001, p 38.

[15] M W McCall, Jr, *Power, Influence, and Authority: The Hazards of Carrying a Sword,* Technical Report No. 10 (Greensboro, NC: Center for Creative Leadership, 1978), p 5. For an excellent update on power, see E P Hollander and L R Offermann, "Power and Leadership in Organizations," *American Psychologist,* February 1990, pp 179–89. Also see E Lesly, "Manager See, Manager Do," *Business Week,* April 3, 1995, pp 90–91. Also see R Greene, *The 48 Laws of Power* (New York: Viking, 1998).

[16] D Weimer, "Daughter Knows Best," *Business Week,* April 19, 1999, pp 132, 134.

[17] See J R P French and B Raven, "The Bases of Social Power," in *Studies in Social Power,* ed D Cartwright (Ann Arbor: University of Michigan Press, 1959), pp 150–67. Also see C M Fiol, E J O'Connor, and H Aguinis, "All for One and One for All? The Development and Transfer of Power across Organizational Levels," *Academy of Management Review,* April 2001, pp 224–42.

[18] Data from J R Larson, Jr, C Christensen, A S Abbott, and T M Franz, "Diagnosing Groups: Charting the Flow of Information in Medical Decision-Making Teams," *Journal of Personality and Social Psychology,* August 1996, pp 315–30.

[19] See D A Morand, "Forms of Address and Status Leveling in Organizations," *Business Horizons,* November–December 1995, pp 34–39; and H Lancaster, "A Father's Character, Not His Success, Shapes Kids' Careers," *The Wall Street Journal,* February 27, 1996, p B1.

[20] P M Podsakoff and C A Schriesheim, "Field Studies of French and Raven's Bases of Power: Critique, Reanalysis, and Suggestions for Future Research," *Psychological Bulletin,* May 1985, p 388. Also see M A Rahim and G F Buntzman, "Supervisory Power Bases, Styles of Handling Conflict with Subordinates, and Subordinate Compliance and Satisfaction," *Journal of Psychology,* March 1989, pp 195–210; D Tjosvold, "Power and Social Context in Superior-Subordinate Interaction," *Organizational Behavior and Human Decision Processes,* June 1985, pp 281–93; and C A Schriesheim, T R Hinkin, and P M Podsakoff, "Can Ipsative and Single-Item Measures Produce Erroneous Results in Field Studies of French and Raven's (1950) Five Bases of Power? An Empirical Investigation," *Journal of Applied Psychology,* February 1991, pp 106–14.

[21] See T R Hinkin and C A Schriesheim, "Relationships between Subordinate Perceptions and Supervisor Influence Tactics and Attributed Bases of Supervisory Power," *Human Relations,* March 1990, pp 221–37. Also see D J Brass and M E Burkhardt, "Potential Power and Power Use: An Investigation of Structure and Behavior," *Academy of Management Journal,* June 1993, pp 441–70; and K W Mossholder, N Bennett, E R Kemery, and M A Wesolowski, "Relationships between Bases of Power and Work Reactions: The Mediational Role of Procedural Justice," *Journal of Management,* no. 4, 1998, pp 533–52.

[22] See H E Baker III, " 'Wax On—Wax Off:' French and Raven at the Movies," *Journal of Management Education,* November 1993, pp 517–19.

[23] See R Forrester, "Empowerment: Rejuvenating a Potent Idea," *Academy of Management Executive,* August 2000, pp 67–80; M Kaminski,

J S Kaufman, R Graubarth, and T G Robins, "How Do People Become Empowered? A Case Study of Union Activists," *Human Relations*, October 2000, pp 1357–83; and P Haspeslagh, T Noda, and F Boulos, "It's Not Just about the Numbers," *Harvard Business Review*, July–August 2001, pp 65–73.

24 J Macdonald, "The Dreaded 'E Word,'" *Training*, September 1998, p 19. Also see R C Liden and S Arad, "A Power Perspective of Empowerment and Work Groups: Implications for Human Resources Management Research," in *Research in Personnel and Human Resources Management*, vol. 14, ed G R Ferris (Greenwich, CT: JAI Press, 1996), pp 205–51.

25 R M Hodgetts, "A Conversation with Steve Kerr," *Organizational Dynamics*, Spring 1996, p 71. See L Holpp, "If Empowerment Is So Good, Why Does It Hurt?" *Training*, March 1995, pp 52–57; Liden and Arad, "A Power Perspective of Empowerment and Work Groups: Implications for Human Resources Management Research"; and G M Spreitzer, "Social Structural Characteristics of Psychological Empowerment," *Academy of Management Journal*, April 1996, pp 483–504.

26 L Shaper Walters, "A Leader Redefines Management," *The Christian Science Monitor*, September 22, 1992, p 14.

27 For related discussion, see M M Broadwell, "Why Command & Control Won't Go Away," *Training*, September 1995, pp 62–68; R E Quinn and G M Spreitzer, "The Road to Empowerment: Seven Questions Every Leader Should Consider," *Organizational Dynamics*, Autumn 1997, pp 37–49; and I Cunningham and L Honold, "Everyone Can Be a Coach," *HRMagazine*, June 1998, pp 63–66.

28 W A Randolph, "Navigating the Journey to Empowerment," *Organizational Dynamics*, Spring 1995, p 31.

29 C Pasternak, "Corporate Politics May Not Be a Waste of Time," *HRMagazine*, September 1994, p 18. Also see D J Burrough, "Office Politics Mirror Popular TV Program," *The Arizona Republic*, February 4, 2001, p EC1.

30 See P L Perrewé, G R Ferris, D D Frink, and W P Anthony, "Political Skill: An Antidote for Workplace Stressors," *Academy of Management Executive*, August 2000, pp. 115–23; and B Rosenstein, "Author: Don't Avoid Office Politics; Become a Master," *USA Today*, February 12, 2001, p 6B.

31 R W Allen, D L Madison, L W Porter, P A Renwick, and B T Mayes, "Organizational Politics: Tactics and Characteristics of Its Actors," *California Management Review*, Fall 1979, p 77. Also see K M Kacmar and G R Ferris, "Politics at Work: Sharpening the Focus of Political Behavior in Organizations," *Business Horizons*, July–August 1993, pp 70–74. A comprehensive update can be found in K M Kacmar and R A Baron, "Organizational Politics: The State of the Field, Links to Related Processes, and an Agenda for Future Research," in *Research in Personnel and Human Resources Management*, vol. 17, ed G R Ferris (Stamford, CT: JAI Press, 1999), pp 1–39.

32 See P M Fandt and G R Ferris, "The Management of Information and Impressions: When Employees Behave Opportunistically," *Organizational Behavior and Human Decision Processes*, February 1990, pp 140–58.

33 First four based on discussion in D R Beeman and T W Sharkey, "The Use and Abuse of Corporate Politics," *Business Horizons*, March–April 1987, pp 26–30.

34 A Raia, "Power, Politics, and the Human Resource Professional," *Human Resource Planning*, no. 4, 1985, p 203.

35 A J DuBrin, "Career Maturity, Organizational Rank, and Political Behavioral Tendencies: A Correlational Analysis of Organizational Politics and Career Experience," *Psychological Reports*, October 1988, p 535.

36 This three-level distinction comes from A T Cobb, "Political Diagnosis: Applications in Organizational Development," *Academy of Management Review*, July 1986, pp 482–96.

37 An excellent historical and theoretical perspective of coalitions can be found in W B Stevenson, J L Pearce, and L W Porter, "The Concept of 'Coalition' in Organization Theory and Research," *Academy of Management Review*, April 1985, pp 256–68.

38 See K G Provan and J G Sebastian, "Networks within Networks: Service Link Overlap, Organizational Cliques, and Network Effectiveness," *Academy of Management Journal*, August 1998, pp 453–63.

39 Allen, Madison, Porter, Renwick, and Mayes, "Organizational Politics: Tactics and Characteristics of Its Actors," p 77.

40 See W L Gardner III, "Lessons in Organizational Dramaturgy: The Art of Impression Management," *Organizational Dynamics*, Summer 1992, pp 33–46.

41 A Rao, S M Schmidt, and L H Murray, "Upward Impression Management: Goals, Influence Strategies, and Consequences," *Human Relations*, February 1995, p 147. Also see M C Andrews and K M Kacmar, "Impression Management by Association: Construction and Validation of a Scale," *Journal of Vocational Behavior*, February 2001, pp 142–61.

42 For related research, see M G Pratt and A Rafaeli, "Organizational Dress as a Symbol of Multilayered Social Identities," *Academy of Management Journal*, August 1997, pp 862–98. Also see B Leonard, "Casual Dress Policies Can Trip Up Job Applicants," *HRMagazine*, June 2001, pp 33, 35.

43 S Friedman, "What Do You Really Care About? What Are You Most Interested In?" *Fast Company*, March 1999, p 90. Also see B M DePaulo and D A Kashy, "Everyday Lies in Close and Casual Relationships," *Journal of Personality and Social Psychology*, January 1998, pp 63–79.

44 See S J Wayne and G R Ferris, "Influence Tactics, Affect, and Exchange Quality in Supervisor-Subordinate Interactions: A Laboratory Experiment and Field Study," *Journal of Applied Psychology*, October 1990, pp 487–99. For another version, see Table 1 (p 246) in S J Wayne and R C Liden, "Effects of Impression Management on Performance Ratings: A Longitudinal Study," *Academy of Management Journal*, February 1995, pp 232–60.

45 See R Vonk, "The Slime Effect: Suspicion and Dislike of Likeable Behavior toward Superiors," *Journal of Personality and Social Psychology*, April 1998, pp 849–64; and M Wells, "How to Schmooze Like the Best of Them," *USA Today*, May 18, 1999, p 14E.

46 See P Rosenfeld, R A Giacalone, and C A Riordan, "Impression Management Theory and Diversity: Lessons for Organizational Behavior," *American Behavioral Scientist*, March 1994, pp 601–04; R A Giacalone and J W Beard, "Impression Management, Diversity, and International Management," *American Behavioral Scientist*, March 1994, pp 621–36; and A Montagliani and R A Giacalone, "Impression Management and Cross-Cultural Adaptation," *Journal of Social Psychology*, October 1998, pp 598–608.

47 M E Mendenhall and C Wiley, "Strangers in a Strange Land: The Relationship between Expatriate Adjustment and Impression Management," *American Behavioral Scientist*, March 1994, pp 605–20.

48 For a humorous discussion of making a bad impression, see P Hellman, "Looking BAD," *Management Review*, January 2000, p 64.

49 T E Becker and S L Martin, "Trying to Look Bad at Work: Methods and Motives for Managing Poor Impressions in Organizations," *Academy of Management Journal*, February 1995, p 191.

50 Ibid., p 181.

51 Adapted from ibid., pp 180–81.

52 Based on discussion in ibid., pp 192–93.

53 A Zaleznik, "Real Work," *Harvard Business Review*, January–February 1989, p 60.

54 C M Koen, Jr, and S M Crow, "Human Relations and Political Skills," *HR Focus*, December 1995, p 11.

55 See L A Witt, "Enhancing Organizational Goal Congruence: A Solution to Organizational Politics," *Journal of Applied Psychology*, August 1998, pp 666–74; and F F Reichheld, "Lead for Loyalty," *Harvard Business Review*, July–August 2001, pp 76–84.

Chapter 14

1 Excerpted from J Muller, "Ford: Jacques Nasser Can't Do It All," *Business Week*, June 18, 2001, p 36.

2 C A Schriesheim, J M Tolliver, and O C Behling, "Leadership Theory: Some Implications for Managers," *MSU Business Topics*, Summer 1978, p 35.

3 The different levels of leadership are thoroughly discussed by F J Yammarino, F Dansereau, and C J Kennedy, "A Multiple-Level Multidimensional Approach to Leadership: Viewing Leadership through an Elephant's Eye," *Organizational Dynamics*, 2001, pp 149–62.

4 See S Lieberson and J F O'Connor, "Leadership and Organizational Performance: A Study of Large Corporations," *American Sociological Review*, April 1972, pp 117–30.

[5] Results can be found in K T Dirks, "Trust in Leadership and Team Performance: Evidence from NCAA Basketball," *Journal of Applied Psychology,* December 2000, pp 1004–12; and D Jacobs and L Singell, "Leadership and Organizational Performance: Isolating Links between Managers and Collective Success," *Social Science Research,* June 1993, pp 165–89.

[6] See D A Kenny and S J Zaccaro, "An Estimate of Variance Due to Traits in Leadership," *Journal of Applied Psychology,* November 1983, pp 678–85.

[7] See J S Phillips and R G Lord, "Schematic Information Processing and Perceptions of Leadership in Problem-Solving Groups," *Journal of Applied Psychology,* August 1982, pp 486–92.

[8] Results from this study can be found in F C Brodbeck et al., "Cultural Variation of Leadership Prototypes across 22 European Countries," *Journal of Occupational and Organizational Psychology,* March 2000, pp 1–29.

[9] Gender and the emergence of leaders was examined by A H Eagly and S J Karau, "Gender and the Emergence of Leaders: A Meta-Analysis," *Journal of Personality and Social Psychology,* May 1991, pp 685–710; and R K Shelly and P T Munroe, "Do Women Engage in Less Task Behavior Than Men?" *Sociological Perspectives,* Spring 1999, pp 49–67.

[10] See A H Eagly, S J Karau, and B T Johnson, "Gender and Leadership Style among School Principals: A Meta-Analysis," *Educational Administration Quarterly,* February 1992, pp 76–102.

[11] Supportive findings are contained in J M Twenge, "Changes in Women's Assertiveness in Response to Status and Roles: A Cross-Temporal Meta-Analysis, 1931–1993," *Journal of Personality and Social Psychology,* July 2001, pp 133–45.

[12] For a summary of this research, see R Sharpe, "As Leaders, Women Rule," *Business Week,* November 20, 2000, pp 74–84.

[13] Excerpted from D K Berman and J S Lublin, "Restructuring, Personality Clashes Led to Lucent Executive's Exit," *The Wall Street Journal,* May 16, 2001, p B1.

[14] This research is summarized and critiqued by E A Fleishman, "Consideration and Structure: Another Look at Their Role in Leadership Research," in *Leadership: The Multiple-Level Approaches,* eds F Dansereau and F J Yammarino (Stamford, CT: JAI Press, 1998), pp 51–60.

[15] For a corporate example of how leadership can be developed, see D Goldwasser, "Reinventing the Wheel: How American Home Products Transforms Senior Managers into Leaders," *Training,* February 2001, pp 54–65.

[16] See See B M Bass, *Bass & Stogdill's Handbook of Leadership: Theory, Research, and Managerial Applications,* 3rd ed (New York: The Free Press, 1990), chs 20–25.

[17] The relationships between the frequency and mastery of leader behavior and various outcomes were investigated by F Shipper and C S White, "Mastery, Frequency, and Interaction of Managerial Behaviors Relative to Subunit Effectiveness," *Human Relations,* January 1999, pp 49–66.

[18] F E Fiedler, "Job Engineering for Effective Leadership: A New Approach," *Management Review,* September 1977, p 29.

[19] For more on this theory, see F E Fiedler, "A Contingency Model of Leadership Effectiveness," in *Advances in Experimental Social Psychology,* vol. 1, ed L Berkowitz (New York: Academic Press, 1964); F E Fiedler, *A Theory of Leadership Effectiveness* (New York: McGraw-Hill, 1967).

[20] Additional information on situational control is contained in F E Fiedler, "The Leadership Situation and the Black Box in Contingency Theories," in *Leadership Theory and Research: Perspectives and Directions,* eds M M Chemers and R Ayman (New York: Academic Press, 1993), pp 2–28.

[21] See L H Peters, D D Hartke, and J T Pohlmann, "Fiedler's Contingency Theory of Leadership: An Application of the Meta-Analyses Procedures of Schmidt and Hunter," *Psychological Bulletin,* March 1985, pp 274–85; and C A Schriesheim, B J Tepper, and L A Tetrault, "Least Preferred Co-Worker Score, Situational Control, and Leadership Effectiveness: A Meta-Analysis of Contingency Model Performance Predictions," *Journal of Applied Psychology,* August 1994, pp 561–73.

[22] For more detail on this theory, see R J House, "A Path–Goal Theory of Leader Effectiveness," *Administrative Science Quarterly,* September 1971, pp 321–38.

[23] Adapted from R J House and T R Mitchell, "Path–Goal Theory of Leadership," *Journal of Contemporary Business,* Autumn 1974, p 83.

[24] Excerpted from S Hamm, "Compaq's Rockin Boss," *Business Week,* September 4, 2000, pp 92, 95.

[25] Results can be found in P M Podsakoff, S B MacKenzie, M Ahearne, and W H Bommer, "Searching for a Needle in a Haystack: Trying to Identify the Illusive Moderators of Leadership Behaviors," *Journal of Management,* 1995, pp 422–70.

[26] A thorough discussion of this theory is provided by P Hersey and K H Blanchard, *Management of Organizational Behavior: Utilizing Human Resources,* 5th ed (Englewood Cliffs, NJ: Prentice Hall, 1988).

[27] A comparison of the original theory and its latent version is provided by P Hersey and K Blanchard, "Great Ideas Revisited," *Training & Development,* January 1996, pp 42–47.

[28] See D C Lueder, "Don't Be Misled by LEAD," *Journal of Applied Behavioral Science,* May 1985, pp 143–54; and C L Graeff, "The Situational Leadership Theory: A Critical View," *Academy of Management Review,* April 1983, pp 285–91.

[29] Excerpted from W M Bulkeley, "IBM's Next CEO May be the One to Bring Change," *The Wall Street Journal,* May 21, 2001, p. B1.

[30] B Shamir, R J House, and M B Arthur, "The Motivational Effects of Charismatic Leadership: A Self-Concept Based Theory," *Organization Science,* November 1993, p 578.

[31] Supportive results can be found in T A Judge and J E Bono, "Five-Factor Model of Personality and Transformational Leadership," *Journal of Applied Psychology,* October 2000, pp 751–65; and J M Crant and T Bateman, "Charismatic Leadership Viewed from Above: The Impact of Proactive Personality," *Journal of Organizational Behavior,* February 2000, pp 63–75.

[32] B Nanus, *Visionary Leadership* (San Francisco: Jossey-Bass, 1992), p 8.

[33] See ibid; and S Yearout, G Miles, and R H Koonce, "Multi-Level Visioning," *Training & Development,* March 2001, pp 31–39.

[34] Results can be obtained from T G DeGroot, D S Kiker, and T C Cross, "A Meta-Analysis to Review the Consequences of Charismatic Leadership," paper presented at the annual meeting of the Academy of Management, Cincinnati, Ohio, 1996.

[35] Results can be found in J A Conger, R N Kanungo, and S T Menon, "Charismatic Leadership and Follower Effects," *Journal of Organizational Behavior,* November 2000, pp 747–68; and R Pillai and J R Meindl, "Context and Charisma: A 'Meso' Level Examination of the Relationship of Organic Structure, Collectivism, and Crisis to Charismatic Leadership," *Journal of Management,* 1998, 643–71.

[36] See K B Lowe, K G Kroeck, and N Sivasubramaniam, "Effectiveness Correlates of Transformational and Transactional Leadership: A Meta-Analytic Review of the MLQ Literature," *Leadership Quarterly,* 1996, pp 385–425.

[37] See B Shankar Pawar and K K Eastman, "The Nature and Implications of Contextual Influences on Transformational Leadership: A Conceptual Examination," *Academy of Management Review,* January 1997, pp 80–109.

[38] Supporting research is summarized by Bass and Avolio, "Transformation Leadership: A Response to Critiques," pp 49–80. The effectiveness of leadership training is discussed by J Huey, "The Leadership Industry," *Fortune,* February 21, 1994, pp 54–56.

[39] Johnson & Johnson's leadership development program is thoroughly discussed by R M Fulmer, "Johnson & Johnson: Frameworks for Leadership," *Organizational Dynamics,* Winter 2001, pp 211–20.

[40] These recommendations were derived from J M Howell and B J Avolio, "The Ethics of Charismatic Leadership: Submission or Liberation," *The Executive,* May 1992, pp 43–54.

[41] See F Dansereau, Jr, G Graen, and W Haga, "A Vertical Dyad Linkage Approach to Leadership within Formal Organizations," *Organizational Behavior and Human Performance,* February 1975, pp 46–78; and R M Dienesch and R C Liden, "Leader–Member Exchange Model of Leadership: A Critique and Further Development," *Academy of Management Review,* July 1986, pp 618–34.

[42] These descriptions were taken from D Duchon, S G Green, and T D Taber, "Vertical Dyad Linkage: A Longitudinal Assessment of

Antecedents, Measures, and Consequences," *Journal of Applied Psychology,* February 1986, pp 56–60.

[43] Supportive results can be found in C Gomez and B Rosen, "The Leader–Member Exchange as a Link between Managerial Trust and Employee Empowerment," *Group & Organization Management,* March 2001, pp 53–69; C A Schriesheim, S L Castro, and F J Yammarino, "Investigating Contingencies: An Examination of the Impact of Span of Supervision and Upward Controllingness on Leader–Member Exchange Using Traditional and Multivariate Within- and Between-Entities Analysis," *Journal of Applied Psychology,* October 2000, pp 659–77; and C Cogliser and C A Schriesheim, "Exploring Work Unit Context and Leader–Member Exchange: A Multi-Level Perspective," *Journal of Organizational Behavior,* August 2000, pp 487–511.

[44] A turnover study was conducted by G B Graen, R C Liden, and W Hoel, "Role of Leadership in the Employee Withdrawal Process," *Journal of Applied Psychology,* December 1982, pp 868–72. The career progress study was conducted by M Wakabayashi and G B Graen, "The Japanese Career Progress Study: A 7-Year Follow-Up," *Journal of Applied Psychology,* November 1984, pp 603–14.

[45] A review of this research can be found in R T Sparrowe and R C Liden, "Process and Structure in Leader–Member Exchange," *Academy of Management Review,* April 1997, pp 522–52.

[46] Supporting evidence can be found in S J Wayne, L M Shore, and R C Liden, "Perceived Organizational Support and Leader–Member Exchange: A Social Exchange Perspective," *Academy of Management Journal,* February 1997, pp 82–11.

[47] The reliability and validity of this measure is provided by R C Liden and J M Maslyn, "Multidimensionality of Leader–Member Exchange: An Empirical Assessment through Scale Development," *Journal of Management,* 1998, pp 43–72.

[48] These recommendations are from R P Vecchio, "Are You In or Out with Your Boss?" *Business Horizons,* November–December 1986, pp 76–78.

[49] For an expanded discussion of this model, see S Kerr and J Jermier, "Substitutes for Leadership: Their Meaning and Measurement," *Organizational Behavior and Human Performance,* December 1978, pp 375–403.

[50] See J P Howell, P W Dorfman, and S Kerr, "Moderator Variables in Leadership Research," *Academy of Management Review,* January 1986, pp 88–102.

[51] Results can be found in Podsakoff, MacKenzie, Ahearne, and Bommer, "Searching for a Needle in a Haystack: Trying to Identify the Illusive Moderators of Leadership Behaviors."

[52] For details of this study, see P M Podsakoff, S B MacKenzie, and W H Bommer, "Meta-Analysis of the Relationship between Kerr and Jermier's Substitutes for Leadership and Employee Job Attitudes, Role Perceptions, and Performance," *Journal of Applied Psychology,* August 1996, pp 380–99.

[53] An overall summary of servant leadership is provided by L C Spears, *Reflections on Leadership: How Robert K Greenleaf's Theory of Servant-Leadership Influenced Today's Top Management Thinkers* (New York: John Wiley & Sons, 1995).

[54] J Stuart, *Fast Company,* September 1999, p 114.

[55] See E McShulskis, "HRM Update: Coaching Helps, But Is Not Often Used," *HRMagazine,* March 1966, pp 15–16.

[56] For a discussion of superleadership, see C C Manz and H P Sims, Jr, "SuperLeadership: Beyond the Myth of Heroic Leadership," in *Leadership: Understanding the Dynamics of Power and Influence in Organizations,* ed Vecchio, pp 411–28; and C C Manz and H P Sims, Jr, *Superleadership: Leading Others to Lead Themselves* (New York: Berkley Books, 1989).

Chapter 15

[1] J Rosenfeld, "Lead Softly, But Carry a Big Baton," *Fast Company,* July 2001, pp 46, 48.

[2] See R W Oliver, *The Shape of Things to Come: Seven Imperatives for Winning in the New World of Business* (New York: McGraw-Hill, 1999).

[3] C I Barnard, *The Functions of the Executive* (Cambridge, MA: Harvard University Press, 1938), p 73. Also see M C Suchman, "Managing Legiti-

macy: Strategic and Institutional Approaches," *Academy of Management Review,* July 1995, pp 571–610.

[4] Drawn from E H Schein, *Organizational Psychology,* 3rd ed (Englewood Cliffs, NJ: Prentice Hall, 1980), pp 12–15.

[5] For an interesting historical perspective of hierarchy, see P Miller and T O'Leary, "Hierarchies and American Ideals, 1900–1940," *Academy of Management Review,* April 1989, pp 250–65.

[6] For an excellent overview of the span of control concept, see D D Van Fleet and A G Bedeian, "A History of the Span of Management," *Academy of Management Review,* July 1977, pp 356–72. Also see E E Lawler III and J R Galbraith, "New Roles for the Staff: Strategic Support and Service," in *Organizing for the Future: The New Logic for Managing Complex Organizations,* eds J R Galbraith, E E Lawler III, and Associates (San Francisco: Jossey-Bass, 1993), pp 65–83.

[7] M Koslowsky, "Staff/Line Distinctions in Job and Organizational Commitment," *Journal of Occupational Psychology,* June 1990, pp 167–73.

[8] See, for example, R J Marshak, "Managing the Metaphors of Change," *Organizational Dynamics,* Summer 1993, pp 44–56; R Garud and S Kotha, "Using the Brain as a Metaphor to Model Flexible Production Systems," *Academy of Management Review,* October 1994, pp 671–98; and R W Keidel, "Rethinking Organizational Design," *Academy of Management Executive,* November 1994, pp 12–30.

[9] K S Cameron, "Effectiveness as Paradox: Consensus and Conflict in Conceptions of Organizational Effectiveness," *Management Science,* May 1986, pp 540–41. Also see S Sackmann, "The Role of Metaphors in Organization Transformation," *Human Relations,* June 1989, pp 463–84; and H Tsoukas, "The Missing Link: A Transformational View of Metaphors in Organizational Science," *Academy of Management Review,* July 1991, pp 566–85.

[10] A management-oriented discussion of general systems theory—an interdisciplinary attempt to integrate the various fragmented sciences—may be found in K E Boulding, "General Systems Theory—The Skeleton of Science," *Management Science,* April 1956, pp 197–208.

[11] J D Thompson, *Organizations in Action* (New York: McGraw-Hill, 1967), pp 6–7. Also see A C Bluedorn, "The Thompson Interdependence Demonstration," *Journal of Management Education,* November 1993, pp 505–09.

[12] For interesting updates on the biological systems metaphor, see A M Webber, "How Business Is a Lot Like Life," *Fast Company,* April 2001, pp 130–36; and E Bonabeau and C Meyer, "Swarm Intelligence: A Whole New Way to Think about Business," *Harvard Business Review,* May 2001, pp 106–14.

[13] R L Daft and K E Weick, "Toward a Model of Organizations as Interpretation Systems," *Academy of Management Review,* April 1984, p 293.

[14] For good background reading, see the entire Autumn 1998 issue of *Organizational Dynamics;* D Lei, J W Slocum, and R A Pitts, "Designing Organizations for Competitive Advantage: The Power of Unlearning and Learning," *Organizational Dynamics,* Winter 1999, pp 24–38; L Baird, P Holland, and S Deacon, "Learning from Action: Imbedding More Learning into the Performance Fast Enough to Make a Difference," *Organizational Dynamics,* Spring 1999, pp 19–32; "Leading-Edge Learning: Two Views," *Training & Development,* March 1999, pp 40–42; and A M Webber, "Learning for a Change," *Fast Company,* May 1999, pp 178–88.

[15] Excerpted from M Hopkins, "Zen and the Art of the Self-Managing Company," *Inc.,* November 2000, pp 56, 58.

[16] K Cameron, "Critical Questions in Assessing Organizational Effectiveness," *Organizational Dynamics,* Autumn 1980, p 70. Also see J Pfeffer, "When It Comes to 'Best Practices'—Why Do Smart Organizations Occasionally Do Dumb Things?" *Organizational Dynamics,* Summer 1996, pp 33–44.

[17] See B Wysocki, Jr, "Rethinking a Quaint Idea: Profits," *The Wall Street Journal,* May 19, 1999, pp B1, B6; and J Collins, "Turning Goals into Results: The Power of Catalytic Mechanisms," *Harvard Business Review,* July–August 1999, pp 71–82.

[18] See, for example, R O Brinkerhoff and D E Dressler, *Productivity Measurement: A Guide for Managers and Evaluators* (Newbury Park, CA: Sage Publications, 1990); J McCune, "The Productivity Paradox," *Management Review,* March 1998, pp 38–40; and R J Samuelson, "Cheerleaders vs. The Grumps," *Newsweek,* July 26, 1999, p 78.

[19] For example, see B Breen, "Change Is Sweet," *Fast Company,* June 2001, pp 168–77; and C Dahle, "Is the Internet Second Nature?" *Fast Company,* July 2001, pp 145–51.

[20] Data from M Maynard, "Toyota Promises Custom Order in 5 Days," *USA Today,* August 6, 1999, p 1B.

[21] "Interview: M Scott Peck," *Business Ethics,* March–April 1994, p 17.

[22] Cameron, "Critical Questions in Assessing Organizational Effectiveness," p 67. Also see W Buxton, "Growth from Top to Bottom," *Management Review,* July–August 1999, p 11.

[23] See R K Mitchell, B R Agle, and D J Wood, "Toward a Theory of Stakeholder Identification and Salience: Defining the Principle of Who and What Really Counts," *Academy of Management Review,* October 1997, pp 853–96; W Beaver, "Is the Stakeholder Model Dead?" *Business Horizons,* March–April 1999, pp 8–12; J Frooman, "Stakeholder Influence Strategies," *Academy of Management Review,* April 1999, pp 191–205; and T M Jones and A C Wicks, "Convergent Stakeholder Theory," *Academy of Management Review,* April 1999, pp 206–21.

[24] See M Adams, "Big Raises Pound Airlines at Bad Time," *USA Today,* July 5, 2001, p 1B.

[25] See C Ostroff and N Schmitt, "Configurations of Organizational Effectiveness and Efficiency," *Academy of Management Journal,* December 1993, pp 1345–61.

[26] K S Cameron, "Effectiveness as Paradox: Consensus and Conflict in Conceptions of Organizational Effectiveness," *Management Science,* May 1986, p 542.

[27] Alternative effectiveness criteria are discussed in ibid.; A G Bedeian, "Organization Theory: Current Controversies, Issues, and Directions," in *International Review of Industrial and Organizational Psychology,* eds C L Cooper and I T Robertson (New York: John Wiley & Sons, 1987), pp 1–33; and M Keeley, "Impartiality and Participant-Interest Theories of Organizational Effectiveness," *Administrative Science Quarterly,* March 1984, pp 1–25.

[28] Data from D Whitford, "A Human Place to Work," *Fortune,* January 8, 2001, pp 108–22.

[29] For updates, see J M Pennings, "Structural Contingency Theory: A Reappraisal," *Research in Organizational Behavior* (Greenwich, CT: JAI Press, 1992), vol. 14, pp 267–309; A D Meyer, A S Tsui, and C R Hinings, "Configurational Approaches to Organizational Analysis," *Academy of Management Journal,* December 1993, pp 1175–95; and D H Doty, W H Glick, and G P Huber, "Fit, Equifinality, and Organizational Effectiveness: A Test of Two Configurational Theories," *Academy of Management Journal,* December 1993, pp 1196–1250.

[30] B Elgin, "Running the Tightest Ships on the Net," *Business Week,* January 29, 2001, p 126.

[31] See D A Morand, "The Role of Behavioral Formality and Informality in the Enactment of Bureaucratic versus Organic Organizations," *Academy of Management Review,* October 1995, pp 831–72.

[32] See J Huey, "The New Post-Heroic Leadership," *Fortune,* February 21, 1994, pp 42–50; and F Shipper and C C Manz, "Employee Self-Management without Formally Designated Teams: An Alternative Road to Empowerment," *Organizational Dynamics,* Winter 1992, pp 48–61.

[33] See G P Huber, C C Miller, and W H Glick, "Developing More Encompassing Theories about Organizations: The Centralization-Effectiveness Relationship as an Example," *Organization Science,* no. 1, 1990, pp 11–40; and C Handy, "Balancing Corporate Power: A New Federalist Paper," *Harvard Business Review,* November–December 1992, pp 59–72. Also see W R Pape, "Divide and Conquer," *Inc. Technology,* no. 2, 1996, pp 25–27; and J Schmidt, "Breaking Down Fiefdoms," *Management Review,* January 1997, pp 45–49.

[34] P Kaestle, "A New Rationale for Organizational Structure," *Planning Review,* July–August 1990, p 22.

[35] Details of this study can be found in T Burns and G M Stalker, *The Management of Innovation* (London: Tavistock, 1961).

[36] D J Gillen and S J Carroll, "Relationship of Managerial Ability to Unit Effectiveness in More Organic versus More Mechanistic Departments," *Journal of Management Studies,* November 1985, pp 674–75.

[37] J D Sherman and H L Smith, "The Influence of Organizational Structure on Intrinsic versus Extrinsic Motivation," *Academy of Management Journal,* December 1984, p 883.

[38] See J A Courtright, G T Fairhurst, and L E Rogers, "Interaction Patterns in Organic and Mechanistic Systems," *Academy of Management Journal,* December 1989, pp 773–802.

[39] See J R Galbraith and E E Lawler III, "Effective Organizations: Using the New Logic of Organizing," in J R Galbraith, E E Lawler III, and Associates, eds, *Organizing for the Future: The New Logic for Managing Complex Organizations* (San Francisco: Jossey-Bass, 1993), pp 285–99.

[40] See W F Cascio, "Managing a Virtual Workplace," *Academy of Management Executive,* August 2000, pp 81–90; C M Christensen, "Limits of the New Corporation," *Business Week,* August 28, 2000, pp 180–81; and S. Hamm, "E-Biz: Down but Hardly Out," *Business Week,* March 26, 2001, pp 126–30.

[41] G McWilliams, "Got a Grand? Get a Pentium PC," *Business Week,* November 4, 1996, p 52. For an update, see www.monorail.com.

[42] C Handy, *The Hungry Spirit: Beyond Capitalism—A Quest for Purpose in the Modern World* (New York: Broadway Books, 1998), p 186. (Emphasis added.)

[43] See B Lessard and S Baldwin, *NetSlaves: True Tales of Working the Web* (New York: McGraw-Hill, 2000).

[44] See R M Kanter, "You Are Here," *Inc.,* February 2001, pp. 84–90; M J Mandel and R D Hof, "Rethinking the Internet," *Business Week,* March 26, 2001, pp 116–22; and M Beer, "How to Develop an Organization Capable of Sustained High Performance: Embrace the Drive for Results-Capability Development Paradox," *Organizational Dynamics,* Spring 2001, pp 233–47.

Chapter 16

[1] Excerpted from S F Gale, "The Little Airplane That Could," *Training,* December 2000, pp 61–62, and 67.

[2] A M Webber, "Learning for a Change," *Fast Company,* May 1999, p 180.

[3] Excerpted from M L Alch, "Get Ready for the Net Generation," *Training & Development,* February 2000, pp 32, 34.

[4] A discussion of strategic alliances and partnerships is contained in D Sparks, "Special Report: Partners," *Business Week,* October 25, 1999, pp 106–12.

[5] Excerpted from J Muller, "Ford: Why It's Worse Than You Think," *Business Week,* June 25, 2001, p 81.

[6] For a thorough discussion of the model, see K Lewin, *Field Theory in Social Science* (New York: Harper & Row, 1951).

[7] C Goldwasser, "Benchmarking: People Make the Process," *Management Review,* June 1995, p 40.

[8] Benchmark data for "America's Best Plants" can be found in J H Sheridan, "Lessons from the Best," *Industry Week,* February 1996, pp 13–20.

[9] Excerpted from L Lavelle, "KPMG's Brave Leap into the Cold," *Business Week,* May 21, 2001, pp 72, 73.

[10] Systems models of change are discussed by D W Haines, "Letting 'The System' Do the Work," *Journal of Applied Behavioral Science,* September 1999, pp 306–24.

[11] A thorough discussion of the target elements of change can be found in M Beer and B Spector, "Organizational Diagnosis: Its Role in Organizational Learning," *Journal of Counseling & Development,* July/August 1993, pp 642–50.

[12] Excerpted from E Nelson and E Ramstad, "Trick or Treat: Hershey's Biggest Dud Has Turned Out to Be New Computer System," *The Wall Street Journal,* October 29, 1999, p A1.

[13] These errors are discussed by J P Kotter, "Leading Change: The Eight Steps to Transformation," in *The Leader's Change Handbook,* eds J A Conger, G M Spreitzer, and E E Lawler III (San Francisco: 1999), pp 87–99.

[14] The type of leadership needed during organizational change is discussed by J P Kotter, *Leading Change* (Boston: Harvard Business School Press, 1996); and B Ettorre, "Making Change," *Management Review,* January 1996, pp 13–18.

[15] M Beer and E Walton, "Developing the Competitive Organization: Interventions and Strategies," *American Psychologist,* February 1990, p 154.

[16] A historical overview of the field of OD can be found in G Farias and H Johnson, "Organizational Development and Change Management," *Journal of Applied Behavioral Science,* September 2000, pp 376–79.

[17] W W Burke, *Organization Development: A Normative View* (Reading, MA: Addison-Wesley, 1987), p 9.

[18] See R Rodgers, J E Hunter, and D L Rogers, "Influence of Top Management Commitment on Management Program Success," *Journal of Applied Psychology,* February 1993, pp 151–55.

[19] Results can be found in P J Robertson, D R Roberts, and J I Porras, "Dynamics of Planned Organizational Change: Assessing Empirical Support for a Theoretical Model," *Academy of Management Journal,* June 1993, pp 619–34.

[20] Results from the meta-analysis can be found in G A Neuman, J E Edwards, and N S Raju, "Organizational Development Interventions: A Meta-Analysis of Their Effects on Satisfaction and Other Attitudes," *Personnel Psychology,* Autumn 1989, pp 461–90.

[21] The importance of results-oriented change efforts is discussed by R J Schaffer and H A Thomson, "Successful Change Programs Begin with Results," *Harvard Business Review,* January–February 1992, pp 80–89.

[22] Adapted in part from B W Armentrout, "Have Your Plans for Change Had a Change of Plan?" *HRFOCUS,* January 1996, p 19; and A S Judson, *Changing Behavior in Organizations: Minimizing Resistance to Change* (Cambridge, MA: Blackwell, 1991).

[23] An individual's predisposition to change was investigated by C R Wanberg and J T Banas, "Predictors and Outcomes of Openness to Changes in a Reorganizing Workplace," *Journal of Applied Psychology,* February 2000, pp 132–42.

[24] See R Moss Kanter, "Managing Traumatic Change: Avoiding the 'Unlucky 13,'" *Management Review,* May 1987, pp 23–24.

[25] Excerpted from D Jones, "Driving Change—Too Fast?" *USA Today,* August 11, 1999, p 6B.

[26] Readiness for change is discussed and investigated by L T Eby, D M Adams, J E A Russell, and S H Gaby, "Perceptions of Organizational Readiness for Change: Factors Related to Employee's Reactions to the Implementation of Team-Based Selling," *Human Relations,* March 2000, pp 419–42.

[27] For a discussion of how managers can reduce resistance to change by providing different explanations for an organizational change, see D M Rousseau and S A Tijoriwala, "What's a Good Reason to Change? Motivated Reasoning and Social Accounts in Promoting Organizational Change," *Journal of Applied Psychology,* August 1999, pp 514–28.

[28] S Reynolds Fisher and M A White, "Downsizing in a Learning Organization: Are There Hidden Costs?" *Academy of Management Review,* January 2000, p 245.

[29] See ibid., pp 244–51.

[30] R M Fulmer and J B Keys, "A Conversation with Peter Senger: New Development in Organizational Learning," *Organizational Dynamics,* Autumn 1998, p 35.

[31] This definition was based on D A Garvin, "Building a Learning Organization," *Harvard Business Review,* July/August 1993, pp 78–91.

[32] Learning organizations are discussed by R Stanley Snell, "Moral Foundations of the Learning Organization," *Human Relations,* March 2001, pp 319–42.

[33] A discussion of learning capabilities and core competencies is provided by R Lubit, "Tacit Knowledge and Knowledge Management," *Organizational Dynamics,* 2001, pp 164–78.

[34] The relationship between organizational learning and various effectiveness criteria is discussed by S F Slater and J C Narver, "Market Orientation and the Learning Organization," *Journal of Marketing,* July 1995, pp 63–74.

[35] A J DiBella, E C Nevis, and J M Gould, "Organizational Learning Style as a Core Capability," in *Organizational Learning and Competitive Advantage,* eds B Moingeon and A Edmondson (Thousand Oaks, CA: Sage, 1996), pp 41–42.

[36] Details of this study can be found in J H Lingle and W A Schiemann, "From Balanced Scorecard to Strategic Gauges: Is Measurement Worth It?" *American Management Association,* March 1996, pp 56–61.

[37] Excerpted from V D Infante, "Men's Wearhouse: Tailored for Any Change That Retail Brings," *Workforce,* March 2001, p 48.

[38] This discussion and definitions are based on D Miller, "A Preliminary Typology of Organizational Learning: Synthesizing the Literature," *Journal of Management,* 1996, pp 485–505.

[39] This discussion is based in part on D Ulrich, T Jick, and M Von Glinow, "High-Impact Learning: Building and Diffusing Learning Capability," *Organizational Dynamics,* Autumn 1993, pp 52–66.

[40] See N A Wishart, J J Elam, D Robey, "Redrawing the Portrait of a Learning Organization: Inside Knight-Ridder, Inc.," *Academy of Management Executive,* February 1996, pp 7–20; and C Argyris, "Good Communication That Blocks Learning," *Harvard Business Review,* July–August 1994, pp 77–85.

[41] See the related discussion in D Lei, J W Slocum, and R A Pitts, "Designing Organizations for Competitive Advantage: The Power of Unlearning and Learning," *Organizational Dynamics,* Winter 1999, pp 24–38.

PHOTO CREDITS

ability Stability characteristic responsible for a person's maximum physical or mental performance.

Accountability practices Focus on treating diverse employees fairly.

Added-value negotiation Cooperatively developing multiple-deal packages while building a long-term relationship.

Affirmative action Focuses on achieving equality of opportunity in an organization.

Aggressive style Expressive and self-enhancing, but takes unfair advantage of others.

Aided-analytic Using tools to make decisions.

Alternative dispute resolution Avoiding costly lawsuits by resolving conflicts informally or through mediation or arbitration.

Assertive style Expressive and self-enhancing, but does not take advantage of others.

Attention Being consciously aware of something or someone.

Attitude Learned predisposition toward a given object.

Availability heuristic Tendency to base decisions on information readily available in memory.

Benchmarking Process by which a company compares its performance with that of high-performing organizations.

Bounded rationality Constraints that restrict decision making.

Brainstorming Process to generate a quantity of ideas.

Care perspective Involves compassion and an ideal of attention and response to need.

Case study In-depth study of a single person, group, or organization.

Causal attributions Suspected or inferred causes of behavior.

Centralized decision making Top managers make all key decisions.

Charismatic leadership Transforms employees to pursue organizational goals over self-interests.

Closed system A relatively self-sufficient entity.

Coalition Temporary groupings of people who actively pursue a single issue.

Coercive power Obtaining compliance through threatened or actual punishment.

Cognitions A person's knowledge, opinions, or beliefs.

Cognitive categories Mental depositories for storing information.

Collaborative computing Using computer software and hardware to help people work better together.

Collectivist culture Personal goals less important than community goals and interests.

Communication Interpersonal exchange of information and understanding.

Communication distortion Purposely modifying the content of a message.

Conflict One party perceives its interests are being opposed or set back by another party.

Consensus Presenting opinions and gaining agreement to support a decision.

Consideration Creating mutual respect and trust with followers.

Contingency approach Using management tools and techniques in a situationally appropriate manner; avoiding the one-best-way mentality.

Contingency approach to organization design Creating an effective organization–environment fit.

Contingency factors Variables that influence the appropriateness of a leadership style.

Continuous reinforcement Reinforcing every instance of a behavior.

Core job dimensions Job characteristics found to various degrees in all jobs.

Creativity Process of developing something new or unique.

Cross-cultural training Structured experiences to help people adjust to a new culture/country.

Cross-functionalism Team made up of technical specialists from different areas.

Culture shock Anxiety and doubt caused by an overload of new expectations and cues.

Decentralized decision making Lower-level managers are empowered to make important decisions.

Decision making Identifying and choosing solutions that lead to a desired end result.

Decision-making style A combination of how individuals perceive and respond to information.

Delphi technique Process to generate ideas from physically dispersed experts.

Development practices Focus on preparing diverse employees for greater responsibility and advancement.

Distributive justice The perceived fairness of how resources and rewards are distributed.

Diversity The host of individual differences that make people different from and similar to each other.

Dysfunctional conflict Threatens organization's interests.

E-business Running the *entire* business via the Internet.

Electronic mail Uses the Internet/Intranet to send computer-generated text and documents.

Emotions Complex human reactions to personal achievements and setbacks that may be felt and displayed.

Empowerment Sharing varying degrees of power with lower-level employees to better serve the customer.

Enacted values The values and norms that are exhibited by employees.

Equity sensitivity An individual's tolerance for negative and positive equity.

Equity theory Holds that motivation is a function of fairness in social exchanges.

Escalation of commitment Sticking to an ineffective course of action too long.

Espoused values The stated values and norms that are preferred by an organization.

Ethics Study of moral issues and choices.

Ethnocentrism Belief that one's native country, culture, language, and behavior are superior.

Expatriate Anyone living or working in a foreign country.

Expectancy Belief that effort leads to a specific level of performance.

Expectancy theory Holds that people are motivated to behave in ways that produce valued outcomes.

Expert power Obtaining compliance through one's knowledge or information.

External factors Environmental characteristics that cause behavior.

External forces for change Originate outside the organization.

External locus of control Attributing outcomes to circumstances beyond one's control.

Extinction Making behavior occur less often by ignoring or not reinforcing it.

Extranet Connects internal employees with selected customers, suppliers, and strategic partners.

Extrinsic rewards Financial, material, or social rewards from the environment.

Feedback Objective information about performance.

Field study Examination of variables in real-life settings.

Formal group Formed by the organization.

Functional conflict Serves organization's interests.

Fundamental attribution bias Ignoring environmental factors that affect behavior.

Glass ceiling Invisible barrier blocking women and minorities from top management positions.

Goal What an individual is trying to accomplish.

Goal commitment Amount of commitment to achieving a goal.

Goal difficulty The amount of effort required to meet a goal.

Goal specificity Quantifiability of a goal.

Group Two or more freely interacting people with shared norms and goals and a common identity.

Group cohesiveness A "we feeling" binding group members together.

Groupthink Janis's term for a cohesive in-group's unwillingness to realistically view alternatives.

High-context cultures Primary meaning derived from nonverbal situational cues.

Hygiene factors Job characteristics associated with job dissatisfaction.

Impression management Getting others to see us in a certain manner.

Individualistic culture Primary emphasis on personal freedom and choice.

Informal group Formed by friends.

In-group exchange A partnership characterized by mutual trust, respect, and liking.

Initiating structure Organizing and defining what group members should be doing.

Instrumentality A performance → outcome perception.

Intelligence Capacity for constructive thinking, reasoning, problem solving.

Interactional justice The perceived fairness of the decision maker's behavior in the process of decision making.

Intermittent reinforcement Reinforcing some but not all instances of behavior.

Internal factors Personal characteristics that cause behavior.

Internal forces for change Originate inside the organization.

Internal locus of control Attributing outcomes to one's own actions.

Internal motivation Motivation caused by positive internal feelings.

Internet The global system of networked computers.

Intranet An organization's private internet.

Intrinsic rewards Self-granted, psychic rewards.

Job design Changing the content and/or process of a specific job to increase job satisfaction and performance.

Job enlargement Putting more variety into a job.

Job enrichment Building achievement, recognition, stimulating work, responsibility, and advancement into a job.

Job rotation Moving employees from one specialized job to another.

Job satisfaction An affective or emotional response to one's job.

Judgmental heuristics Rules of thumb or shortcuts that people use to reduce information-processing demands.

Justice perspective Based on the ideal of reciprocal rights and driven by rules and regulations.

Laboratory study Manipulation and measurement of variables in contrived situations.

Law of effect Behavior with favorable consequences is repeated; behavior with unfavorable consequences disappears.

Leadership Influencing employees to voluntarily pursue organizational goals.

Leadership prototype Mental representation of the traits and behaviors possessed by leaders.

Leader trait Personal characteristics that differentiate leaders from followers.

Learned helplessness Debilitating lack of faith in one's ability to control the situation.

Learning capabilities The set of core competencies and internal processes that enable an organization to adapt to its environment.

Learning modes The various ways in which organizations attempt to create and maximize their learning.

Learning organization Proactively creates, acquires, and transfers knowledge throughout the organization.

Legitimate power Obtaining compliance through formal authority.

Line managers Have authority to make organizational decisions.

Linguistic style A person's typical speaking pattern.

Listening Actively decoding and interpreting verbal messages.

Low-context cultures Primary meaning derived from written and spoken words.

Maintenance roles Relationship-building group behavior.

Management Process of working with and through others to achieve organizational objectives efficiently and ethically.

Management by objectives Management system incorporating participation in decision making, goal setting, and feedback.

Managing diversity Creating organizational changes that enable all people to perform up to their maximum potential.

Mechanistic organizations Rigid, command-and-control bureaucracies.

Mentoring Process of forming and maintaining developmental relationships between a mentor and a junior person.

Meta-analysis Pools the results of many studies through statistical procedure.

Met expectations The extent to which one receives what he or she expects from a job.

Mission statement Summarizes "why" an organization exists.

Monochronic time Preference for doing one thing at a time because time is limited, precisely segmented, and schedule driven.

Motivation Psychological processes that arouse and direct goal-directed behavior.

Motivators Job characteristics associated with job satisfaction.

Need for achievement Desire to accomplish something difficult.

Need for affiliation Desire to spend time in social relationships and activities.

Need for power Desire to influence, coach, teach, or encourage others to achieve.

Needs Physiological or psychological deficiencies that arouse behavior.

Negative inequity Comparison in which another person receives greater outcomes for similar inputs.

Negative reinforcement Making behavior occur more often by contingently withdrawing something negative.

Negotiation Give-and-take process between conflicting interdependent parties.

Noise Interference with the transmission and understanding of a message.

Nominal group technique Process to generate ideas and evaluate solutions.

Nonanalytic Using preformulated rules to make decisions.

Nonassertive style Timid and self-denying behaviour.

Nonverbal communication Messages sent outside of the written or spoken word.

Norm Shared attitudes, opinions, feelings, or actions that guide social behavior.

Normative beliefs Thoughts and beliefs about expected behavior and modes of conduct.

Open system Organism that must constantly interact with its environment to survive.

Operant behavior Skinner's term for learned, consequence-shaped behavior.

Optimizing Choosing the best possible solution.

Organic organizations Fluid and flexible network of multitalented people.

Organization System of consciously coordinated activities of two or more people.

Organizational behavior Interdisciplinary field dedicated to better understanding and managing people at work.

Organizational culture Shared values and beliefs that underlie a company's identity.

Organizational politics Intentional enhancement of self-interest.

Organizational socialization Process by which employees learn an organization's values, norms, and required behaviors.

Organization-based self-esteem An organization member's self-perceived value.

Organization chart Boxes-and-lines illustration showing chain of formal authority and division of labor.

Organization development A set of techniques or tools that are used to implement organizational change.

Ostracism Rejection by other group members.

Out-group exchange A partnership characterized by a lack of mutual trust, respect, and liking.

Participative management Involving employees in various forms of decision making.

Perception Process of interpreting one's environment.

Personality Stable physical and mental characteristics responsible for a person's identity.

Personality conflict Interpersonal opposition driven by personal dislike or disagreement.

Polychronic time Preference for doing more than one thing at a time because time is flexible and multidimensional.

Positive inequity Comparison in which another person receives lesser outcomes for similar inputs.

Positive reinforcement Making behavior occur more often by contingently presenting something positive.

Problem Gap between an actual and desired situation.

Procedural justice The perceived fairness of the process and procedures used to make allocation decisions.

Process-style listeners Likes to discuss issues in detail.

Programmed conflict Encourages different opinions without protecting management's personal feelings.

Punishment Making behavior occur less often by contingently presenting something negative or withdrawing something positive.

Rational model Logical four-step approach to decision making.

Readiness Follower's ability and willingness to complete a task.

Reasons-style listeners Interested in hearing the rationale behind a message.

Reciprocity Widespread belief that people should be paid back for their positive and negative acts.

Recruitment practices Attempts to attract qualified, diverse employees at all levels.

Representativeness heuristic Tendency to assess the likelihood of an event occurring based on impressions about similar occurrences.

Resistance to change Emotional/behavioral response to real or imagined work changes.

Respondent behavior Skinner's term for unlearned stimulus–response reflexes.

Results-style listeners Interested in hearing the bottom line or result of a message.

Reward equality norm Everyone should get the same rewards.

Reward equity norm Rewards should be tied to contributions.

Reward power Obtaining compliance with promised or actual rewards.

Roles Expected behaviors for a given position.

Sample survey Questionnaire responses from a sample of people.

Satisficing Choosing a solution that meets a minimum standard of acceptance.

Schema Mental picture of an event or object.

Self-concept Person's self-perception as a physical, social, spiritual being.

Self-efficacy Belief in one's ability to do a task.

Self-esteem One's overall self-evaluation.

Self-managed teams Groups of employees granted administrative oversight for their work.

Self-monitoring Observing one's own behavior and adapting it to the situation.

Self-serving bias Taking more personal responsibility for success than failure.

Self-talk Evaluating thoughts about oneself.

Servant-leadership Focuses on increased service to others rather than to oneself.

Shaping Reinforcing closer and closer approximations to a target behavior.

Situational theories Propose that leader styles should match the situation at hand.

Social loafing Decrease in individual effort as group size increases.

Social power Ability to get things done with human, informational, and material resources.

Societal culture Socially derived, taken-for-granted assumptions about how to think and act.

Span of control The number of people reporting directly to a given manager.

Spillover model Describes the reciprocal relationship between job and life satisfaction.

Staff personnel Provide research, advice, and recommendations to line managers.

Stereotype Beliefs about the characteristics of a group.

Strategic constituency Any group of people with a stake in the organization's operation or success.

Strategic plan A long-term plan outlining actions needed to achieve planned results.

Substitutes for leadership Situational variables that can substitute for, neutralize, or enhance the effects of leadership.

Superleader Someone who leads others to lead themselves.

Target elements of change Components of an organization that may be changed.

Task roles Task-oriented group behavior.

Team Small group with complementary skills who hold themselves mutually accountable for common purpose, goals, and approach.

Telecommuting Doing work that is generally performed in the office away from the office using different information technologies.

Theory Y McGregor's modern and positive assumptions about employees being responsible and creative.

360-degree feedback Comparison of anonymous feedback from one's superior, subordinates, and peers with self-perceptions.

Total quality management An organizational culture dedicated to training, continuous improvement, and customer satisfaction.

Transactional leadership Focuses on interpersonal interactions between managers and employees.

Trust Reciprocal faith in others' intentions and behavior.

Unaided-analytic Analysis is limited to processing information in one's mind.

Underemployment The result of taking a job that requires less education, training, or skills than possessed by a worker.

Unity of command principle Each employee should report to a single manager.

Upward feedback Employees evaluate their boss.

Valence The value of a reward or outcome.

Value attainment The extent to which a job allows fulfillment of one's work values.

Values Enduring belief in a mode of conduct or end-state.

Virtual team Information technology allows group members in different locations to conduct business.

INDEX

Name

3M, 25–27

Subject